ARTIFICIAL INTELLIGENCE IN THE 21ST CENTURY

SECOND EDITION

ARTIFICIAL INTELLIGENCE IN THE 21ST CENTURY

A Living Introduction

SECOND EDITION

Stephen Lucci
The City College of New York, CUNY

Danny Kopec
Brooklyn College, CUNY

MERCURY LEARNING AND INFORMATION
Dulles, Virginia
Boston, Massachusetts
New Delhi

Publisher: David Pallai

Mercury Learning and Information
22841 Quicksilver Drive
Dulles, VA 20166
info@merclearning.com
www.merclearning.com
(800) 232-0223

Stephen Lucci and Danny Kopec. Artificial Intelligence in the 21st Century: A Living Introduction 2/E
ISBN: 978-1-942270-00-3

Library of Congress Control Number: 2015934535

151617321   Printed in the United States of America
This book is printed on acid-free paper.

Our titles are available for adoption, license, or bulk purchase by institutions, corporations, etc.
For additional information, please contact the Customer Service Dept. at 800-232-0223 (toll free). Digital versions of our titles are available at: www.authorcloudware.com and other e-vendors. All companion files are available by writing to the publisher at info@merclearning.com.

Contents

Preface

In 2006 Professor James Moor of the Philosophy Department at Dartmouth College asked me to organize a computer games exhibit and competition at *AI @ 50*, a conference that celebrated the 50th Anniversary of the Dartmouth Summer Conference where John McCarthy coined the term "Artificial Intelligence." A number of the original attendees of that Dartmouth Conference were able to attend *AI @ 50* including the late John McCarthy, Marvin Minsky, the late Oliver Selfridge, and Ray Solomonoff. Professor Lucci also attended *AI @ 50* and shortly thereafter we agreed to collaborate on an AI text.

Perspective and Needs

Our view is that AI is comprised of PEOPLE, IDEAS, METHODS, MACHINES, and OUTCOMES. First, it is *people* who make up AI. People have ideas and these ideas become *methods*. Those ideas can be represented by algorithms, heuristics, procedures or systems that are the backbone of computation; and finally we have the production of those *machines* (programs) which we can call "*outcomes.*" Every outcome can be measured for its value, effectiveness, efficiency, etc.

We have found that existing AI books are often lacking in one or more of these areas. Without people there is no AI. Hence we have decided that it is important to "showcase" the people who have made AI successful through the *human interest boxes* which are sprinkled throughout the text. From people come the ideas and the development of the *methods* that we present over the seventeen chapters of this book. AI and computer science are relatively young fields, compared to other sciences such as mathematics, physics, chemistry and biology. Yet, AI is a discipline that is truly interdisciplinary, combining elements of many other fields. *Machines/computers* are the tools of AI researchers allowing them to experiment, learn, and improve methods for problem-solving that can be applied in many interesting domains that can be beneficial to humankind. And finally, not in the least, there are the *outcomes*, measurable as the results of applying AI to various problems and disciplines that remind us that AI must also be accountable. In a number of places in our text you will find discussions of the distinction between "performance" and "competence." Both are needed, as the field of AI matures and advances.

To date, as faculty members who have taught from and observed the development of AI texts, we have found that most of the available texts sometimes fall short in one or more of the areas described above. The names and vast contributions of Turing, McCarthy, Minsky, Michie,

McLelland, Feigenbaum, Shortliffe, Lenat, Newell and Simon, Brooks, and many others should be familiar to students. Yet, this is not a history book! We believe, however, that the discipline, as interesting and widespread as it is, with its infinite potential, should justifiably be colored with the fascinating ideas and work of the people who comprise it.

Furthermore, students need hands on experience with problem solving, i.e., students need to get their hands "dirty" with the fundamentals of search techniques fully explained in Chapters 2 through 4, the methods of logic in Chapter 5, and the role of knowledge representation in AI (Chapter 6). Chapter 7 sets the stage for learning about fuzzy logic (Chapter 8) and expert systems (Chapter 9).

Advanced methods such as neural networks and genetic algorithms are thoroughly presented in Chapters 11 and 12. And finally, advanced topics such as natural language processing, planning, robotics and advanced computer games are covered in Chapters 13, 14, 15 and 16 respectively. Chapter 17, Reprise, summarizes where you've been on your journey with us through AI, with a view to the future.

The presentation is enhanced with several hundred fully worked examples, as well as over 300 figures and images, many in color. Students will also benefit from the significant number of solutions to exercises that have been provided.

How to Use This Book

This text contains more material than can comfortably be covered in a one semester (45 contact hours) course. The authors have taught the following courses using material that has led to the development of *AI in the 21st Century*. Note that at CUNY, graduate courses often meet for three hours per week for 15 weeks.

As a first course in AI (graduate or undergraduate):

I   **A Brief History of AI:** Uses and limitations of the subject. Application areas.
     Chapter 1   6 contact hours

II   **Search Methodologies:** State Space. Graphs. Generate and Test. Backtracking, Greedy Search. Blind Search Methods – depth first search breadth first search and depth-first iterative deepening.
     Chapter 2   3 hours

III **Informed Search:** Heuristics, Hill Climbing, Beam Search, Best First Search, Branch and Bound based Search and A* Search; And/Or Trees.
     Chapter 3 (Section 3.7.3 – Bidirectional Search is optional)   **3 hours**

IV   **Search Using Games:** Game Trees and Minimax Evaluation. Elementary two-person games: tic-tac-toe and nim. Minimax with Alpha-Beta Pruning.
     Chapter 4 (Section 4.5 – Game Theory and The Iterated Prisoner's Dilemma is optional).
     3 hours.

V   **Logic in AI:** Propositional Logic and Predicate Logic (FOPL); Unification and Resolution in FOPL. Converting a Predicate Expression to Clause Form.
     Chapter 5 (Section 5.4 – Other Logics is optional)   **6 hours**

VI   **Knowledge Representation:** Choices of representation; Semantic Nets, Frames, and Scripts. Inheritance and Object-Oriented Programming.Production Systems; Agent Methods.
     Chapter 6 (Sections 6.10, 6.11 – Association and More Recent Approaches are optional)
     3 hours.

VII Production Systems: Architecture and Examples, Resolution Strategies. Conflict Resolution Strategies. State Space Search – Data Driven and Goal Driven Approaches, Cellular Automata (CA). One-dimensional CA (Wolfram) and Two-Dimensional CA and The Game of Life (Conway).
  Chapter 7 (Section 7.6 Stochastic Processes and Markov Chains are optional) **3 hours**

VIII Expert Systems (ES): An Introduction: Why ES? Characteristics and Architectures for ES; Knowledge Engineering, Knowledge Acquisition and Classic Expert Systems; Newer Systems Case-based Approaches. Chapter 9 (Sections 9.6, 9.7 and 9.8 are optional). **3 hours**

IX Introduction to Neural Computing: Rudiments of Artificial Neural Networks and and The Perceptron Learning Rule.
  Chapter 11 Sections 1.0, 11.1 and 11.3 only **3 hours**

X Introduction to Evolutionary Computing - Genetic Algorithms:
  Chapter 12 Sections 12.0 and 12.2 (only) **2 hours**

XI Automated Planning: The Problem, Planning as Search; Means Ends Analysis (GPS)STRIPS; Various planning algorithms and methods. More Modern Systems: Nonlin, Graphplan, etc.
  Chapter 14 Sections 14.0, 14.1, 14.3.1, 14.3.12, 14.4.1 **2 hours**

XII Epilog: Accomplishments of the First 50 years of AI. Prospects for the Future -Where are we going?
  Chapter 17 **2 hours**
  Midterm Exam **3 hours**
  Final Exam **3 hours**
  Two-Three Programming Assignments (one in Prolog)
  One Term Paper

As a second course in AI

(AI-2, usually at the graduate level). Originally it was taught as a course in Neural Computing. Artificial neural networks (ANN) are often used for learning—e.g., in the distinction between pattern classes; it therefore seemed natural to incorporate genetic algorithms (GA) into the curriculum. AI systems are often required to justify their reasoning, especially characteristic of expert systems. ANN's are not especially proficient in this capacity. Fuzzy logic was added to ANN's and fuzzy ANN's are often used in conjunction to remedy this deficiency.

Emergence, ant colony optimization, fractals, artificial life and evolutionary computation (beyond GA) found their way into this course as all of these perspectives are useful in solving difficult problems. Many refer to such a rubric as "natural computing" because Mother Nature provides inspiration for these approaches. A proposed syllabus for AI-2:

I Preliminaries: Elementary Concepts: Natural Computing, AI, A-Life, emergence, feedback, agent top-down vs. bottom-up development. Supplementary material may be used here.
  3 hours

II Search inspired by Mother Nature: Search and State Space Graphs. Hill Climbing and its drawbacks. Simulated Annealing, Genetic Algorithms and Genetic Programming. Tabu Search. Ant Colony Optimization.

Chapter 2 Sections 2.0, 2.1, and 2.1.1.

Chapter 3 Sections 3.0, 3.1, and 3.2

Chapter 12   **(10 – 15 hours)**

III   **Neural Networks:** Artificial neurons vs. their biological counterparts. McCulloch-Pitts Neurons. The Perceptron Learning Rule and its limitations. The Delta Rule. Backpropagation, Analyzing patterns and some guidelines for training. Discrete Hopfield Networks. Application Areas. Introduction to Machine Learning Chapter 10
Chapter 11   **18 Hours**

IV   **Fuzzy Sets and Fuzzy Logic:** Crisp Sets vs. Fuzzy Sets. Membership functions. Fuzzy logic and fuzzy inference systems.
Chapter 8 Sections 8.0 – 8.3   **3 Hours**

V   **Optional Topics:** Selected from:
   • Unsupervised Learning in ANN.
   • Artificial Life including Cellular Automata
   • Fractals and Complexity
   • Immunocomputing
   • Quantum Computing   **2+ Hours**

A 3-hour midterm and a 3-hour final are given. There are 5–6 programming assignments and a term paper.

Some alternative courses could easily be designed from the 17 Chapters we've developed.

A first course could, for example include: **Chapter 1** (Introduction/Overview) **Chapter 2** (Uninformed Search), **Chapter 3** (Intelligent Search), **Chapter 4** (Search Using Games), **Chapter 5** (Logic), **Chapter 6** (Knowledge Representation) **Chapter 7** (Production Systems), and **Chapter 9** (Expert Systems).

A second course could consist of: **Chapter 8** (Fuzzy Logic) **Chapter 10** (Machine Learning: Part 1) **Chapter 11** (Neural Networks), **Chapter 12** (Search Inspired by Mother Nature) and then one or two of the special topics chapters from **Chapter 13** (Natural Language Processing), **Chapter 14** (Planning), **Chapter 15** (Robotics), and **Chapter 16** (Advanced Computer Games).

A **Special Topics Course on Expert Systems** might run: **Chapter 1** (Introduction), **Chapter 7** (Production Systems), **Chapter 9** (Expert Systems) "spiced-up" with **Chapter 12** (Search Inspired by Mother Nature) and some supplemental papers / readings.

Stephen Lucci's vast classroom experience teaching AI courses at City College, Brooklyn College, and other CUNY schools, has often been lauded by students. Danny Kopec has considerable research experience in Computer Chess (University of Edinburgh, Machine Intelligence Research Unit), Intelligent Tutoring Systems (University of Maine, 1988–1992) and Computer Science Education / Software Engineering / Medical Errors, Technological Mishaps and Problem Solving (Brooklyn College from 1991 – present). The text represents a strong collaboration of our efforts. You will occasionally hear two voices sharing their ideas and experience. The writing process itself has often been joint, listening and adjusting to each other for knowledge, opinion, and style.

A Shared Vision

Writing this book has not been an overnight process. We also believe that our approaches, to writing and development of material, while different in many respects are complementary.

We believe that the composite work should provide a strong foundation for anyone interested in AI with sufficient opportunity to accrue knowledge, experience, and competence in the methods that define the field. We are fortunate that both the authors and the publisher, David Pallai, president and founder of Mercury Learning and Information, have shared the same goals and vision for this book. Fundamental to this effort has been the agreement that the book should be balanced with theory and applications, accurate, pedagogically sound, and reasonably priced. The process has required several years, but we are particularly appreciative to Mr. Pallai for seeing the potential in our book and bringing it to fruition.

We hope that you will enjoy and learn from our efforts.

Preface to the Second Edition

Much time has passed since the publication of our first edition. Artificial Intelligence concepts, methods, and systems are becoming more integrated into everyday activities. For example, at the time when our first edition was being developed, many automobiles were built with the capability to parallel park themselves; it has now become commonplace to build cars with collision avoidance systems. Technologies that were the fantasies of sci-fi enthusiasts, e.g. drones and robots, are now a reality; increasingly, they are becoming a part of our everyday existence. Phone apps, GPS systems, and social networks, which were just surfacing in the first decade of 21st Century, are now pervasive. They include, optimal traffic routing, health advising, and personal attendants for diverse aspects of our lives, each typically using some form of AI. Advances in Natural Language Processing and Speech have dramatically changed how we interact with machines.

The Second Edition has a new Chapter 10 (Machine Learning: Part I) with presentation and discussion of Decision Trees for machine learning. Hence Chapter 10, combined with Chapters 11 (Neural Approaches) and Chapter 12 (an introduction to genetic approaches) together provide a foundation for further study. Chapter 13 (Natural Understanding) has a new Section (13.10) which presents the theory, methods, and applications of speech understanding. A new section on Metaphor in NLP is also included. Chapter 15 offers an overview of the field of Robotics, including recent applications. The end of this chapter, in conjunction with Chapter 17 (Reprise) provides a glimpse of what the future may hold for us. New exercises have been added to many of the original chapters.

Instructor Resource Files (Available Upon Adoption)

The instructor files contain the complete set of PowerPoint slides, solutions, sample exams, high resolution color figures, and an instructor's guide with teaching suggestions.

Online Resources

Digital versions of the text and all of the instructor and student materials are available at *www.authorcloudware.com*, *Vital Source*, and many other e-vendors. Electronic review and desk copies are also available.

Stephen Lucci
The City College of New York
NY, NY
November, 2015

Danny Kopec
Brooklyn College (The City University of New York)

Acknowledgments

Development of a book like this is not just a job. It is in some sense representative of AI itself. In some sense it is like putting together the pieces of a large complex puzzle.

During the spring and summer of 2010, Ms. Debra Luca was particularly helpful, adding some much needed energy for preparation and completion of our manuscript. In 2011 Ms. Sharon Vanek, helped us with obtaining the rights for images and also provided the requisite energy for manuscript completion. Two graduate students in the computer science department at Brooklyn College, Shawn Hall and Sajida Noreen, were particularly helpful to us in the summer of 2011.

David Kopec was especially helpful in a number of critical junctures where he successfully and efficiently solved software problems.

We would like to mention students who contributed to this project in various capacities, roughly in the order in which we perceive their contributions: Dennis Kozobov, Daniil Agashiyev, Julio Heredia, Olesya Yefimzhanova, Oleg Yefimzhanov, Pjotr Vasilyev, Paul Wong, Georgina Oniha, Marc King, Uladzimir Aksionchykau, and Maxim Titley.

We would like to thank the administrative staff at the Brooklyn College Computer Science Department, including Camille Martin, Natasha Dutton, Audrey Williams, Lividea Jones, and Mr. Lawrence Goetz, our computer systems administrator for being particularly helpful. We are also grateful to Professor Graciela Elizalde-Utnick for allowing us to continue to work at the Center for Teaching. Mark Gold, VP of Information Technology, was particularly helpful in providing computer equipment.

We would also like to thank all the AI researchers who co-operated with us by giving us the right to use their images for this book. We apologize in advance if anyone has been left out of our acknowledgment.

Danny Kopec also wishes to acknowledge his wife Sylvia and son David for enduring this lengthy project and its demands. I also wish to thank Professor Larry Harris, at Dartmouth College, who introduced me to Artificial Intelligence (AI) as a discipline in computer science in 1973. This led to my meeting Professor Donald Michie, who provided me with six unforgettable years (1976–1982) as a PhD student and researcher, and many lessons for life.

Professor Dragomir Radev, at the Department of Electrical Engineering and Computer Science at the University of Michigan, was particularly helpful in suggesting topics that should be included in Chapter 12, Natural Language Processing.

Noteworthy assistance came from the following individuals: Harun Iftikhar, by developing a few sections of Chapter 12; Dr. Christina Schweikert, St. John's University, with the preparation and editing of Chapter 13, Automated Planning; Erdal Kose of Brooklyn College, for Section 3.7.3. on the Bidirectional Search; and Edgar Troudt for material in Chapter 6 on Baecker's work (Section 6.11.3).

Other colleagues at Brooklyn College who have been supportive include Professors Keith Harrow, James Cox, Neng-Fa Zhou, Gavriel Yarmish, Noson Yanofsky, David Arnow, Ronald Eckhardt, and Myra Kogen. Professor Jill Cirasella, of the Brooklyn College Library has always been very helpful with research assistance and development of a history of computer games. *Danny Kopec* also thanks Professor Aaron Tenenbaum, chairman of the Department of Computer Science at Brooklyn College for many years, for hiring him, encouraging this book, and for providing some crucial advice. Professor Yedidyah Langsam, chairman of the Department of Computer Science at Brooklyn College, is acknowledged for enabling the teaching and working conditions whereby this book could be completed. Likewise, Professors James Davis and Paula Whitlock are thanked for encouraging him to be the director of the Center for Teaching at Brooklyn College between 2008 and 2010, facilitating completion of the text.

Old friends from the world of computer chess have always been helpful, including David Levy, Jonathan Schaeffer, Monty Newborn, Hans Berliner, and Ken Thompson. During the past year and a half I would like to mention a new friend, Dr. Ira Cohen, who has been particularly supportive.

Stephen Lucci would like to acknowledge the excellent education I received from The City College of New York and later from The CUNY Graduate School and University Center. Many years ago my academic mentor, Prof. Michael Anshel, displayed almost infinite patience in guiding my dissertation research. He taught me the importance of "thinking outside the box" – i.e., there is often a relationship between seemingly unrelated topics in computer science. Prof. Gideon Lidor was a teacher who taught me, early in my career, the value of excellence in the classroom. Prof. Valentin Turchin always respected my competence. I think of Prof. George Ross as my administrative mentor. He helped to provide my first employment in *academe* as an instructor before having obtained my PhD. I served as deputy chair of the CCNY Computer Science Department for many years under his auspices, work experience that prepared me later for my six year stint as department chairperson. He was always supportive in my career advancement. I would also like to thank Prof. Izidor Gertner who always had respect for the quality of my writing. I would also like to acknowledge Dr. Gordon Bassen and Dr. Dipak Basu who have been close friends and colleagues ever since our doctoral student days. And a heartfelt "Thank You" is extended to the many students in my classrooms who have inspired and educated *me* during these past years.

Writing a textbook is both a challenging and (at times) an exasperating enterprise. Along the way numerous individuals have provided much-appreciated assistance. It is my pleasure at this juncture to thank those individuals.

Tayfun Pay supplied technical expertise early in our work. The chessboards in Chapter 2 along with the many search trees in Chapters 2 and 4 were drawn by him and the Three Wise Men figure in Chapter 5 benefitted from his artistic flair.

Later in the text Jordan Tadeusz provided a much-needed infusion of talent and hard work. He is responsible for many of the excellent figures in Chapters 10 and 11. He also "worked magic" with the scores of vector equations in Chapter 10.

Junjie Yao, Rajesh Kamalanathan, and Young Joo Lee helped us meet an early deadline. Nadine Bennett was instrumental in putting the finishing touches on Chapters 4 and 5. Ashwini Harikrishnan (Ashu) lent technical assistance later in this project. Ashu also helped "finesse" some of the figures during the editing process. The following students also contributed their time and talent to this text: Anuthida Intamon, Shilpi Pandey, Moni Aryal, Ning Xu, and Ahmet Yuksel. And finally I wish to thank my sister Rosemary for her friendship.

Acknowledgments for the Second Edition

We are very pleased that David Pallai, founder and president of Mercury Learning, Inc. encouraged and supported our efforts to produce a second edition of this text. We are also fortunate to be surrounded by a number of fine students at each of our respective institutions, who assisted in identifying errors in our first edition and in the development of new content.

Danny Kopec acknowledges Daniil Agashiyev for his contributions to sections in Chapters 13 and 14 on *metaphor* and *SCIBox*, respectively. Sona Brambhatt permitted use of segments of her Master's thesis on speech understanding that were revised and condensed by Mimi-Lin Gao. She also contributed sections on robotic applications (ASIMO) and the Lovelace Project. Peter Tan helped develop sections on robotic applications including Big Dog, Cog, and Google Car. He also obtained rights for many images which appear in the new edition. Oleg Tosic prepared the applications box on the CISCO Voice System. Chris Pileggi indirectly helped with a number of new exercises.

Stephen Lucci wishes to thank the following students: Alejandro Morejon, Juan Emmanuel Sanchez, Ebenezer Reyes, and Feiyu Chen for typing Chapter 10 on Machine Learning under great time constraints. Additionally, Alan Mendez drew the figures for *A Robotic Classroom and Umbrella Balancing* in that chapter.

Credits for the 2nd Edition

Chapter 1

Turing Statue © Guy Erwood/ Shutterstock.com
Fig. 1.0 Genetic Code © Bruce Riff/Shutterstock.com
Fig. 1.8 Human brain by X-rays © Dim Dimich/ Shutterstock
Fig. 1.23 Analytical Engine © Mirko Tobias, Utrecht University
Fig. 1.25 Robot Car Assembly © Boykov/ Shutterstock.com
John McCarthy (Stanford University, CIS Department)
John Conway (Courtesy Thane Plambeck)
Sherry Turkle (Courtesy Sherry Turkle, Director MIT Initiative on Technology and Self)

Chapter 2

Edsgar Dijkstra (Courtesy Hamilton Richards, CIS Department, University of Texas at Austin)
Donald Knuth (Case Alumni Association and Foundation 2010, Flicker and
http://www.casealum.org/view.image?Id=1818)

Chapter 3

Fig. 3.0 The Climber © Nubephoto
Fig. 3.1 Brooklyn College to Yankee Stadium (Mapquest.com)
Fig. 3.2 Brooklyn College to Yankee Stadium (Yahoo Maps)
Fig. 3.6 (a,b,c) Hill Climbing: (a)Foothills Problem (b) Plateau Problem (c) Ridge Problem
    Designed by Oleg Yefimzhanov, Brooklyn College
Figs. 3.28 and 3.29 Bidirectional Search (Designed by Erdal Kose, Brooklyn College)
Judea Pearl (Courtesy Judea Pearl, UCLA, Computer Science Department)

Chapter 4

Two Game Figurines © Melanie Kintz
Fig. 4.0 Prisoner's Dilemma © Vladmir V. Georgievskiy
Fig. 4.1 Chinatown Chicken © DenisNata and Tham Ying Kit
Richard Korf (Courtesy Richard E. Korf, UCLA, Computer Science Department)
Dana Nau (Courtesy Dana S. Nau, University of Maryland, Computer Science Department)

Chapter 5

Fig. 5.0 Puzzle © aroas
Nils Nilsson (Courtesy Nils Nilsson, Stanford University, Computer Science Department)

Chapter 6

Figs. 6.0, 6.20(a,b,c,d) (Courtesy IROBOT Corporation)
Figs 6.12a and 6.12b (Courtesy Roger Schank, CEO/Founder Socratic Arts)
Figs 6.5 (Repeated as Fig. 15.2) 6.6 Based on *http://mathworld.wolfram.com/KönigsbergBridgeProblem.html*; Kåhre, J. "Königsberg) January 15, 2008.
Fig. 6.13 Ross Quillian's Semantic Networks (in Minsky, Marvin, ed., Semantic Information Processing, Fig.: "The semantic networks for the word plant", © 1969 Massachusetts Institute of Technology, by permission of The MIT Press.)
Donald Michie (Courtesy Jack Walas, from The University of Maine 1988 Spring Symposium on Artificial Intelligence and Intelligent Tutoring Systems)
Hubert Dreyfus (Courtesy Genevieve Dreyfus)
Marvin Minsky (Ntávkav, Flicker, July 11,2009)
Rodney Brooks (Courtesy Rodney Brooks, MIT)
Text Passage on Agents: (*http://www.cs.ubc.ca/labs/lci.home.html*) 3/1/2011(Permission Jim Little, Laboratory for Computational Intelligence, University of British Columbia)

Chapter 7

Fig. 7.0 What If Problem Solving © marekuliasz
Table 7.1 The CarBuyer Database (Designed by Oleg Yefimzhanov
Herbert Simon (Courtesy James L. McClelland, Stanford University, Department of Psychology)
John Conway (Courtesy John H. Conway, Princeton University)

Chapter 8

Fig. 8.0 Car with Automatic Traction Control © Matthew Jacques/ Shutterstock.com
Lofti Zadeh (Courtesy Lofti Zadeh, Berkeley University)
Fig. 8.1 Lofti Zadeh (Flicker by Tingandgang)

Chapter 9

Fig. 9.1 Brain on Integrated Circuit © takito
Figs. 9.5a and 9.5b Pseudo-examples from MYCIN (Courtesy H Edward Shortliffe, President and CEO, AMIA)
Fig. 9.8 Satellite Image of an Oil Slick (NASA Satellite Image)
Edward Feigenbaum (Courtesy Edward Feigenbaum, Kumagai Professor of Computer Science Emeritus, Stanford University)
Douglas Lenat (Courtesy Douglas Lenat, President and CEO, Cycorp, Inc.)
Edward H. Shortliffe (Courtesy Edward H. Shortliffe, President and CEO, AMIA)
Janet L. Kolodner (Courtesy Janet L. Kolodner, Georgia Tech University)

Chapter 10

Fig 10.0 Classroom (Alan Mendez)
Fig 10.2 Balancing an Umbrella (Alan Mendez)

Chapter 11

Fig. 11.1 Colored Ticker Board on Black © AshDesign
Figs 11.60, 11.61 (Courtesy James A. Ackles, President, LBS Capital Management, Inc.)
John Hopfield (Courtesy John Hopfield, Professor Emeritus, Carl Icahn Laboratory, Princeton University)
Donald Michie (Courtesy University of Edinburgh, School of Informatics)

Chapter 12

Fig. 12.0 Business Team holding different currency symbols © Ioannis Pantzi
Fig. 12.1a Simulated Annealing © sima
Fig. 12.1b Molecular Structure © Master3D
Tabu Image 1 Giant Tiki http://flickr.com/photos/hibiscus/131769533/ © Mariko Matsumura
Tabu Image 2 kapu_ki'i at National Historic Park Hawaii *http://flickr.com/photos/15104132@N08/1570594321* © Guy A. Hebert
Painting of HMS Beagle at Tierra del Fuego by Conrad Maartens (1831–1836), from The Illustrated Origin of Species by Charles Darwin, abridged and illustrated by Richard Leakey ISBN 0-571-14586-8.
John H. Holland (Courtesy of John H. Holland, University of Michigan, Computer Science and Psychology Departments)

Chapter 13

Fig. 13.0 Communication Icons © artizarus
Fig. 13.1 The Chomsky Hierarchy Based on Jurafsky and Martin (2008, p.530) Speech and Language Processing 2nd, edition, Prentice Hall Publishers.
Fig. 13.3 From Charniak, E. 2006. Why natural-language processing is now statistical natural language processing. In Proceedings of AI at 50, Dartmouth College, July 13–15.
MARGIE and SAM Examples (with permission Roger Schank, Founder / CEO Socratic Arts)
Figs. 13.4 a,b,c Interactions with EasyAsk (Courtesy Larry Harris, Founder/CEO EasyAsk Corp.)
Section 13.7.3 Models of Metaphor in NLP (Daniil Agashiyev)
Section 13.10 Speech Understanding (Sona Brahmbhatt and Mimi-Lin Gao)
Section 13.11.2 Dragon Systems and Windows Speech Recognition System (Sona Brahmbhatt and Mimi-Lin Gao)
Section 13.11.3 CISCO Voice System (Oleg Tosic)
Eugene Charniak (Courtesy Eugene Charniak, Brown University, Computer Science Department)
Roger Schank (Courtesy Roger Schank, Founder / CEO Socratic Arts)
James Maisel (Courtesy James Maisel, Retina Group of New York, Director, ZYDOC)
Larry Harris (Courtesy Jack Walas, from The University of Maine 1988 Spring Symposium on Artificial Intelligence and Intelligent Tutoring Systems)

Chapter 14

Fig. 14.1 Futuristic space station © Andreas Meyer

Fig. 14.3 Smith, S. J., Nau, D., and Throop, T. Computer bridge: A big win for AI planning. AI Magazine 19-2. 1988. Fig. 5, Page 99. American Association for Artificial Intelligence, Menlo Park, CA. with Permission to Reprint.

Fig. 14.5 Designed by Kendel Campbell (Brooklyn College)

Section 14.5.5 SCIBox Automated Planner (Oleg Tosic)

Fig. 14.6 Maintainability of a Pipe Motion (permission Liangjun Zhang, Stanford University)

From Zhang, L., Huang, X., Kim, Y. J., and Manocha, D. 2008. D-plan: Efficient collision-free path computation for part removal and disassembly. Computer-Aided Design & Applications 5(1–4).

Fig. 14.7 Robot Car Assembly Line © Rainer Plendl

Fig. 14.8 Negotiating a dynamic environment (permission M. Lau)

From Lau, M. and Kuffner, J. J. 2005. Behavior planning for character animation. In Proceedings of the 2005 ACM Siggraph/Eurographics symposium on computer animation, 271–280. Los Angeles, California, July 29–31. New York, NY: ACM.

Fig. 14.9 Snapshot of the Blocks World (Redrawn by Christina Schweikert, St. John's University)

Fig. 14.14 Practical Applications for O-Plan (Designed by Christina Schweikert)

Austin Tate (Courtesy Austin Tate, Director, AIAI, University of Edinburgh)

Frederick Hayes-Roth (Courtesy Frederick Hayes-Roth, Naval Postgraduate School)

Chapter 15

Fig 15.0 Urban Robot (Courtesy JPL, NASA)

Fig 15.11 Spiderbot (Courtesy JPL, NASA)

Fig 15.14 ASIMO (Courtesy Honda)

Fig 15.15 Jaemi The Humanoid Robot with Kids (Lisa-Joy Zgorski, National Science Foundation)

Fig. 15.17 New England Scene (Watercolor by Magdalena Kopec)

Table 15.1 Summary of Robotics from 1960–2010 Avinash Jairam, Parker Rappaport, Yusif Alomeri, Mohammed Amin, Brian Ramdin

Application Boxes Big Dog and Cog (Peter Tan)

Aplication Box ASIMO (Mimi-Lin Gao)

Sebastian Thrun (Courtesy Sebastian Thrun)

Chapter 16

Fig. 16.0 The Card Player (Oil Painting by Magdalena Kopec)

Fig. 16.3 Alpha-Beta Tree for Checkers Position (Erdal Kose, Brooklyn College)

Fig. 16.4 Second Series of Generalization Tests. (Fig.4, from Samuel, A. (1967). Some studies in machine learning using the game of checkers: Recent progress. IBM Journal of Research and Development 11, 601–617).

Figs. 16.5 and 15.6 Checkers is Solved (Permission Jonathan Schaeffer, Vice-Provost and Associate Vice-President , Information Technology, University of Alberta)

Fig. 16.19 Chess Rating vs. Depth of Search (Adapted from Hsu, F. H, Anantharaman, T., Campbell, M., & Nowatzyk, A. (1990). A Grandmaster Chess Machine, Scientific American, Vol. 263, No. 4, October, 1990, 44–50).

Table 16.2 Olyesa Yefimzhanova, Brooklyn College

Gary Kasparov vs. Deeper Blue (Courtesy Murray Campbell, IBM)

Jonathan Schaeffer (Courtesy Jonathan Schaeffer, University of Alberta)

Chinook vs. Marion Tinsley, Checkers World Championship Match, 1992 (Courtesy Jonathan Schaeffer)

Hans Berliner (Courtesy Hans Berliner, Carnegie Mellon University)

Monty Newborn (Courtesy Monty Newborn, McGill University)

David Levy and Jaap van den Herik (Courtesy Frederic Friedel, www.chessbase.com)

Chapter 17

Fig. 17.0 Wlodek Zadrozny at CCNY addressing faculty (Courtesy Jerry Moy, IBM)

Fig. 17.1 The Wright Brothers © Brad Whitsitt

Fig 17.5 Google Car (Steve Jurvetson via Wikimedia)

Fig. 17.6 The IBM WATSON Team at CCNY (Courtesy Jerry Moy, IBM)

Fig. 17.7 Wlodek Zadrozny at CCNY (Courtesy Jerry Moy, IBM)

Fig. 17.8 Jerry Moy (Courtesy IBM)

Fig 17.9 Singularity from KurzweilAI.net homepage / Source: Shutterstock

Fig 17.10 Ray Kurzweil (Courtesy of Kurzweil Technologies, Inc.)

Fig 17.11 Moore's Law (Courtesy Kurzweil.net)

David Ferucci (Courtesy IBM)

Application Box Google Car (Peter Tan)

Part Openers

Part I

Cyber Love © photobank.kiev.ua

Part II

Technology head © Bruce Riff

Part III

Militarya Robot from *http://militarya.wikispaces.com/file/view/artificial-intelligence-45. jpg/149410871/artificial-intelligence*

Part IV

Orange Automatic Robot © Maksim Dubinsky

Part V

Humans Dream Abstract © IR Stone

Appendix A

Clips Example (Olyesa Yefimzhanova, Brooklyn College)

Appendix B

Hidden Markov Chain Code in Java (Harun Iftikhar, Columbia University)

Appendix C

Walter Browne (Courtesy United States Chess Federation)

Solutions to Exercises

Chapter 12 Exercises 1,3, 7, 9, 13 Daniil Agashiyev
Chapter 13 Exercises 3, 7 Pjotr Vasiljev

This Chapter sets the stage for all that follows.   It presents the history and early motivations behind Artificial Intelligence (AI) stemming from the 1956 Dartmouth Conference.

Notions of thinking and intelligence lead to discussion of the Turing Test and the various controversies and criticisms surrounding it. This sets the stage for distinguishing Strong AI from Weak AI. Integral to any classical view is interest in how humans solve problems and the heuristics they use. From this background and perspective it becomes feasible to identify problems suitable for AI. Various recognized disciplines and approaches to AI such as search, neural computation, fuzzy logic, automated reasoning, and knowledge representation, are then presented. This discussion transitions to a review of the early history of AI and to more recent domains, problems as well as considerations of what lies ahead of us.

OVERVIEW OF ARTIFICIAL INTELLIGENCE

Alan Turing (photo ©Guy Erwood/Shutterstock.com)

Early man had to contend with nature through such tools and weapons as the wheel and fire. In the 15th century, Gutenberg's invention of the printing press made widespread changes in peoples' lives. In the 19th century, the Industrial Revolution exploited natural resources to develop power, which facilitated manufacturing, transportation, and communication. The 20th century has evidenced man's continuing advancement through air and space exploration, the invention of the computer, and microminiaturization leading to personal computers, the Internet, World Wide Web, and smart phones. The last 60 years have witnessed the nascence of a world which has emerged with an abundance of data, facts, and information that must be converted to knowledge (an instance being the data contained in the genetic code for humans – see Figure 1.0). This chapter provides the conceptual framework for the discipline of Artificial Intelligence, its successful application areas and methods, recent history, and future prospects.

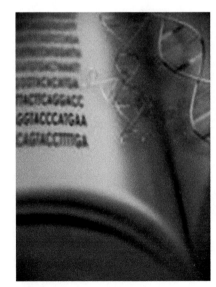

Figure 1.0
Genetic Code. (Photo ©Bruce Rolff/Shutterstock.com)

▐1.0▌ INTRODUCTION

Artificial Intelligence (AI) means different things to different people. Some believe that AI is synonymous with any form of **intelligence** achieved by nonliving systems; they maintain that it is not important if this intelligent behavior is not arrived at via the same mechanisms on which humans rely. For others, AI systems must be able to mimic human intelligence. No one would argue with the premise that to study AI or to implement AI systems, it is helpful if we first understand how humans accomplish intelligent behavior; that is, we must understand activities that are deemed intelligent in an intellectual, scientific, psychological, and technical sense. For example, if we want to build a robot capable of walking like a human, then we must first understand the process of walking from each of those perspectives; people, however, do not accomplish locomotion by constantly stating and following a prescribed set of formal rules that explain how to take steps. In fact, the more human experts are asked to explain how they achieve their level of performance in any discipline or endeavor, the more they are likely to fail. For example, when Israeli fighter pilots were asked to explain their prowess for flying, their performance actually declined.[1] Expert performance stems not from constant, conscious analysis but from the subconscious levels of the mind. Imagine trying to drive on an expressway during rush hour and needing to consciously weigh each vehicle-control decision.

Consider the story of the professor of mechanics and the unicyclist.[2] If the professor is asked to cite principles of mechanics as he attempts to ride the unicycle and bases his success on the unicycle on knowing those principles, he is doomed to failure. Likewise, if the unicyclist attempts to learn the laws of mechanics and apply them while he performs his craft, he, too, is destined for failure and perhaps a tragic accident. The point is, human skill and expertise in many disciplines seems to be developed and stored in the subconscious, rather than being available upon explicit request from memory or first principles.

▐1.0.1▌ What Is Artificial Intelligence?

In everyday parlance, the term artificial means synthetic (i.e., man-made) and generally has a negative connotation as being a lesser form of a real thing. Artificial objects are often superior to real or natural objects, however. Consider, for example, an artificial flower, an object made of silk and wire and arranged to resemble a bud or blossom. This artifact has the advantage of not requiring sunshine or water for its sustenance, so it provides practical decoration for a home or business. Its feel and fragrance are arguably inferior to those of a natural flower; however, an artificial flower can look very much like the real thing.

Another example is artificial light produced by candles, kerosene lanterns, or electric light bulbs. Artificial light is superior to natural light because it is always accessible. Sunlight, obviously, is available only when the sun appears in the sky.

Finally, consider the advantages provided by artificial motion devices—such as automobiles, trains, planes, and bicycles—in terms of speed and durability when compared with running, walking, and other natural forms of transportation, such as horseback riding. The advantages of artificial forms of transportation are tempered by stark drawbacks—our planet is paved with ubiquitous highways, our atmosphere is laden with vehicle exhaust, and our peace of mind (and often our sleep) is interrupted by the din of aircraft.[3]

Like artificial light, flowers, and transportation, AI is not natural but is man-made. To identify the advantages and drawbacks of AI, you must first understand and define intelligence.

1.0.2 What Is Thinking? What Is Intelligence?

A definition for intelligence is perhaps more elusive than a definition for the term artificial. R. Sternberg, in a text on human consciousness, provides the following useful definition:

> Intelligence is the cognitive ability of an individual to learn from experience, to reason well, to remember important information, and to cope with the demands of daily living.[4]

We are all familiar with questions on standardized tests asking us to provide the next number in a given sequence, as in: **1, 3, 6, 10, 15, 21 ?**

You probably noticed that the gap between successive numbers increases by one; for example from 1 to 3, the increase is two, whereas from 3 to 6, it is three, and so on. The correct response is 28. Such questions are designed to measure our proficiency at identifying salient features in patterns. We can detect patterns by learning from experience.

Try your luck with the following:

a.	1,	2,	2,	3,	3,	3,	4,	4,	4,	4	?
b.	2,	3,	3,	5,	5,	5,	7,	7,	7,	7	?

Now that we have settled on a definition for intelligence, you might ask the following questions:

1. How do you decide if someone (something?) is intelligent?
2. Are animals intelligent?
3. If animals are intelligent, how do you measure their intelligence?

Most of us can answer the first question easily. We gauge the intelligence of other people many times each day by interacting with them — by making comments or posing questions, and then observing their responses. Although we have no direct access to someone else's mind, we feel confident that this indirect view provided by questions and answers gives us an accurate assessment of internal cerebral activity.

If we adhere to this conversational approach to measuring intelligence, how do we address the question of animal intelligence? If you have a pet, you have probably answered this question for yourself. Dogs seem to remember people they haven't seen for a month or two, and can find their way home after getting lost. Cats often show excitement during the opening of cans at dinner time. Is this simply a matter of a Pavlovian reflex or do cats consciously associate the sound of cans opening with the impending pleasure of dinner?

An intriguing anecdote regarding animal intelligence is that of Clever Hans, a horse in Berlin, Germany, circa 1900, which was purportedly proficient in mathematics (see Figure 1.1).

Audiences were transfixed as Hans added numbers or calculated square roots. Later people observed that Hans did not perform as well without an audience. In fact, Hans was talented in identifying human emotions,

Figure 1.1
Clever Hans—A horse doing calculus?

not mathematics. Horses generally have astute hearing. As Hans came closer to a correct answer, audience members became more excited and their heart rates accelerated. Perhaps it was Hans' uncanny ability to detect these changes that enabled him to obtain correct answers.[5] You might be reluctant to attribute Clever Han's actions to intelligence; however, you should consult Sternberg's earlier definition before reaching a conclusion.

Some creatures are intelligent only in groups. For example, ants are simple insects and their isolated behavior would hardly warrant inclusion in a text on AI. Ant colonies, on the other hand, exhibit extraordinary solutions to complex problems, such as finding the optimal route from a nest to a food source, carrying heavy objects, and forming bridges. A collective intelligence arises from effective communication among individual insects. More will be said about emergent intelligence and swarm intelligence in our discussion of advanced search methods in Chapter 12, "Search Inspired by Mother Nature."

Brain mass and brain-to-body mass ratios are often regarded as indications of animal intelligence. Dolphins compare favorably with humans in both metrics. Breathing in dolphins is under voluntary control, which could account for excess brain mass and for the interesting fact that alternate halves of the dolphin brain take turns sleeping. Dolphins score well on animal self-awareness tests such as the mirror test, in which they recognize that the image in the mirror is actually their image. They can also perform complex tricks, as visitors to Sea World can testify. This illustrates the ability of dolphins to remember and perform complex sequences of physical motions. The use of tools is another litmus test for intelligence and is often used to separate homo erectus from earlier ancestors of human beings. Dolphins share this trait with humans. For example, dolphins use deep-sea sponges to protect their spouts while foraging for food. It becomes clear that intelligence is not an attribute possessed by humans alone. Many living forms possess intelligence to some extent. You should ask yourself the following question: "Do you believe that being alive is a necessary precondition for possessing intelligence?" or, "Is it possible for inanimate objects, for example, computers, to be intelligent?" The declared goal of **Artificial Intelligence** is to create computer software and/or hardware systems that exhibit thinking comparable to that of humans, in other words, to display characteristics usually associated with human intelligence. A pivotal question is, "Can machines think?" More generally, you might ask, "Does a person, animal, or machine possess intelligence?"

At this juncture it is wise to underscore the distinction between thinking and intelligence. Thinking is the facility to reason, analyze, evaluate, and formulate ideas and concepts. Not every being capable of thinking is intelligent. Intelligence is perhaps akin to efficient and effective thinking. Many people approach this issue with biases, saying, "Computers are made of silicon and power supplies, and therefore are not capable of thinking," or, at the other extreme, "Computers perform much faster than humans and therefore must be more intelligent than humans." The truth is most likely somewhere between these two extremes.

As we have discussed, different animal species possess intelligence to varying degrees. We will expound on software and hardware systems that have been developed by the Artificial Intelligence community that also possess intelligence to varying degrees. We are not sufficiently concerned with measuring animal intelligence in order to develop standardized IQ tests for animals; however, we *are* interested in a test to ascertain the existence of machine intelligence.

Perhaps Raphael [6] put it best:

> Artificial Intelligence is the science of making machines do things that would require intelligence if done by man.

▐▄▌ THE TURING TEST

The first two questions posed in the last section have already been addressed: How do you determine intelligence, and are animals intelligent? The answer to the second question is not necessarily "yes" or "no" — some people are smarter than others and some animals are smarter than others. The question of machine intelligence is equally problematic.

Alan Turing sought to answer the question of intelligence in operational terms. He wanted to separate functionality (what something does) from implementation (how something is built).

▐▄▌ Definition of the Turing Test

Alan Turing[7] proposed two imitation games. In an imitation game, one person or entity behaves as if he were another. In the first, a person (called an interrogator) is in a room with a curtain that runs across the center of the room. On the other side of the curtain is a person, and the interrogator must determine whether it is a man or a woman. The interrogator (whose gender is irrelevant) accomplishes this task by asking a series of questions. The game assumes that the man will perhaps lie in his responses, but the woman is always truthful. In order that the interrogator cannot determine gender from voice, communication is via computer rather than through spoken words. See Figure 1.3. If it is a man on the other side of the curtain, and he is successful in deceiving the interrogator, then he wins the imitation game. In Turing's original format for this test, both a man and a woman were seated behind a curtain and the interrogator had to identify both correctly (Turing might have based this test on a game that was popular during this period. This same game could also have been the impetus behind his machine intelligence test).

As Erich Fromm wrote [8], men and women are equal but not necessarily the same. For instance, the genders might differ in their knowledge of colors, flowers, or the amount of time spent shopping.

What does distinguishing a man from a woman have to do with the question of intelligence? Turing understood that there might be different types of thinking, and it is important to both understand these differences and to be tolerant of them. Figure 1.4 shows the second version of the **Turing test.**

This second game is more appropriate to the study of AI. Once again, an interrogator is in a room with a curtain. This time, a computer or a person is behind the curtain. Here, the machine plays the role of the male and could find it convenient on occasion to lie. The person, on the other hand, is consistently truthful. The interrogator asks questions, and then evaluates the responses to determine whether she is

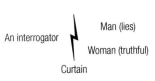

Figure 1.3
The first Turing imitation game.

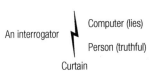

Figure 1.4
The second Turing imitation game.

communicating with a person or a machine. If the computer is successful in deceiving the interrogator, it **passes the Turing test,** and is thereby considered intelligent. As we all know, machines are many times faster than humans in performing arithmetic calculations. A human would have little trouble in discerning that a computer, rather than a person, is behind the curtain, if the result of a Taylor Series approximation to a trigonometric function is provided within microseconds. Naturally, by mere chance, the computer could successfully deceive the interrogators during any Turing test; to be a valid barometer for intelligence, this test should be executed many times. Again, in Turing's original version of this test, both a person and a computer were behind the curtain, and the interrogator had to identify each correctly.

What questions would you propose for the Turing test? Consider the following examples:

- **What is $(1,000,017)^{1/2}$?** Calculations such as this one are probably not a good idea. Recall that the computer attempts to deceive the interrogator. Rather than responding in fractions of a microsecond with the correct answer, it would intentionally take longer and perhaps make a mistake, "knowing" that people are not adept at these sorts of calculations.

- **What are the current weather conditions?** You might be tempted to ask about the weather, assuming that a computer cannot peek outside the window. Computers are usually connected to the Web, however, and can connect to weather Web sites before responding.

- **Are you afraid of dying?** Because it is difficult for a computer to feign human emotions, you might propose this question and others such as: How does the dark make you feel? or What does it feel like to be in love? Recall, however, that you are trying to determine intelligence, and human emotions might not be a valid barometer for intelligence.

Turing anticipated many objections to the idea of machine intelligence in his original paper.[7] One is the so-called "head-in-the-sand objection." It was believed that mankind's ability to think placed humans at the apex of creation. Admitting the possibility of computer thought would challenge this lofty perch enjoyed by humans. Turing believed that this concern was more cause for consolation than for refutation. Another objection he anticipated is the theological objection. Many believed that it is a person's soul that enables thinking, and we would be usurping God's authority by creating machines with this capability. Turing rebutted this argument by proposing that we would merely be carrying out God's will by preparing vessels awaiting endowment of souls. Finally we mention Lady Lovelace's (often referred to in the literature as the first computer programmer) objection. Commenting on the analytical engine, she exults that it would be impossible for this mere machine to surprise us. She was reiterating the belief held by many that a computer is not capable of performing any activity for which it is not preprogrammed. Turing counters that machines surprise him all the time. He maintains that proponents of this objection subscribe to the belief that human minds can instantaneously deduce all consequences of a given fact or action. The reader is referred to Turing's original paper [7] for a collection of these aforementioned objections, as well as several others. The next section covers additional noteworthy criticisms of the Turing test for intelligence.

1.1.2 Controversies and Criticisms of the Turing Test
Block's Criticism of the Turing Test

Ned Block argues that English text is encoded in ASCII, in other words, as a series of 0s and 1s inside a computer.[9] Hence, a particular Turing test, which is a series of questions and answers, can be stored as a very large number. For instance, assuming an upper bound on the length of a Turing test, the first three characters in tests that begin "Are you afraid of dying?" are stored as binary numbers, as shown in Figure 1.5.

A	R	E
01000001	01110010	01100101

Figure 1.5
Storing the beginning of a Turing test in ASCII code.

Suppose that a typical Turing test lasts an hour, and that about 50 questions are asked and 50 responses given during this time. The binary number corresponding to a test would be very long. Now suppose that a large database stores all Turing tests consisting of 50 questions or fewer and the reasonable responses. Passing the test could then be accomplished by table lookup. Granted, a computer system that can handle such a huge collection of data does not yet exist. But if it did, Block asks, "Would you feel comfortable ascribing intelligence to such a machine?" In other words, Block's criticism is that a computer could pass the Turing test by the mechanical means of a lookup table, not through intelligence.

Searle's Criticism: The Chinese Room

John Searle's criticism of the Turing test is more fundamental.[10] Imagine an interrogator who asks questions as expected—this time, however, in Chinese. In a separate room is someone who does not know Chinese, but does have a detailed rulebook. Although the Chinese questions appear as a series of squiggles, the person in the room consults the rulebook, processes the Chinese characters according to the rules, and responds with answers written using Chinese characters. See Figure 1.6.

"How do i get to carnegie hall?"

去? 內畢篤麼走 ?

Questions in Chinese

Interrogator

Answers in Chinese

Person

Rule book

... The rule book is at the squiggle level

練習, 練習, 練習

"Practice, practice, practice"

Figure 1.6
The Chinese Room argument.

The interrogator is obtaining syntactically correct and semantically reasonable responses to the questions. Does this mean that the person inside the room knows Chinese? If you answer "No," does the combination of the person and the Chinese rule book know Chinese? No—the person is not learning or understanding Chinese, but is only processing symbols. In the same way, a computer running a program receives, processes, and responds with symbols without learning or understanding what the symbols themselves mean.

Instead of a single person with a rulebook, Searle also asks us to envision a gymnasium of people with notes that are passed to one another. When a person receives such a note, the rulebook will determine that they should either produce an output or merely pass a message on to another individual in the gymnasium. See Figure 1.7

Now, where does the knowledge of Chinese reside? With the ensemble of people? Or, with the gymnasium?

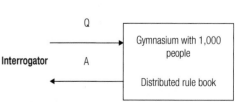

Interrogator

Q

A

Gymnasium with 1,000 people

Distributed rule book

Figure 1.7
Variation of the Chinese Room argument.

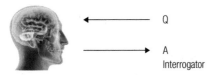

Figure 1.8
Chinese speaker receiving and responding to questions in Chinese.

Consider a final example. Picture the brain of a person who does indeed know Chinese, as shown in Figure 1.8. This person can receive questions asked in Chinese, interpret them accurately, and then respond in Chinese.

Again, where does the knowledge of Chinese reside? With an individual neuron? Or, does it reside with a collection of these neurons? (It must reside somewhere!)

The crux of both Block's and Searle's criticisms of the Turing test is that it is not possible to gain insight into the internal state of some entity from external observations alone. That is, we should not expect to learn anything new about intelligence by treating an agent possessing intelligence (man or machine) as a black box. This is not always true, however. In the Nineteenth Century, the physicist Ernest Rutherford correctly deduced the internal state of matter: that it consists mostly of empty space, by bombarding gold foil with alpha particles. He predicted that these high-energy particles would either pass through the foil or be somewhat deflected. The outcome is consistent with his orbital theory of atoms: that they consist of a dense core surrounded by orbiting electrons. This is our current model of the atom, with which many of us became acquainted in high school chemistry. Rutherford successfully gained insight into the internal state of the atom through external observations alone.

In summary, it is difficult to define intelligence. It is precisely because of this difficulty in both defining intelligence and determining whether an agent possesses this attribute that Turing developed the Turing test. Implicit in his treatise is that any agent capable of passing the Turing test would invariably possess the "cerebral wherewithal" to cope with any reasonable intellectual challenge on a level commensurate with that of a person widely accepted to be intelligent.[11]

1.2 STRONG AI VERSUS WEAK AI

ALAN TURING

Alan Turing (1912–1954) was a British mathematician and a rather remarkable figure in the history of computer science. Students taking courses in AI, computer science, and cryptology should become familiar with his contributions. His contribution to AI is his famous Turing test for intelligence. This test was his attempt to address controversial questions in AI such as, "Are computers intelligent?" In theoretical computer science, one studies the Turing machine model of computation. A Turing machine is a mathematical model that captures the essence of computation. It is designed to answer the question: "What does it mean for a function to be computable?"[12] It should be appreciated

by the reader that Turing was essentially discussing the notion of using algorithms to solve particular problems some seven or eight years before the advent of the first digital computers.

You perhaps have seen movies about World War II that depict the Battle of Britain. German aircraft dropped close to 200,000 tons of bombs on Great Britain between 1940 and 1944. Alan Turing led the group of mathematicians at Bletchley Park, outside of London, whose task it was to break the German code, called the *Enigma Code*. They eventually broke the code by using the Enigma Machine. This device encoded all military commands to German ships and planes. The success of Turing's group might have played a decisive role in the Allied victory over Germany.

ALAN TURING AND AI

Turing is credited with the **stored program concept**, which is the foundation for all modern-day computers. By 1935, he had described an abstract computing machine with an unlimited memory, and a read head (scanner) that moves back and forth through memory, reading and writing symbols dictated by a program that is also stored in memory. His conception is called the **Universal Turing Machine.**

Turing had early insights into how the nervous system is possibly organized to facilitate brain function. Craig Webster (*http://home.clear.net.nz/pages/cw/unorganized.htm*), describing Turing's paper, "Computing Machinery and Intelligence" (eventually published in *Mind* in 1950), presents Turing B-type networks as unorganized machines that would be found in the cortex of human infants. This farsighted observation reminds us of the agent view of the world, which you will read about in Chapter 6, "Knowledge Representation."

Turing discusses two types of unorganized machines, called Type A and Type B. Type A machines are comprised of NAND gates (where every node has two states representing 0 or 1, two inputs and any number of outputs). Each A-Type network is intersected with three further A-type nodes in special ways, generating binary pulses that comprise the B-type nodes. Turing already recognized the possibility of training, and the needs for self-stimulating feedback loops, which you will read about in "Neural Networks," Chapter 11. Turing also considered the need for a "genetic search" to train the B-type networks to discover desirable values (or patterns). This was an insight into genetic algorithms, which are explained in Chapter 12.

At Bletchley Park he often discussed with Donald Michie (one of his colleagues and disciples) notions of how machines could learn from experience and solve new problems. This later became known as heuristic problem solving (See Chapters 3, "Intelligent Search Methods," 6, "Knowledge Representation," and 9, "Expert Systems.") and machine learning (see Chapters 10 and 11).

Turing also achieved early insights into problem-solving methods using the game of chess as a testbed for AI. Although the computing machines of his time were not powerful enough to develop a strong chess program, he realized the challenges that chess—with its estimated 10^{120} possible legal games—posed. His aforementioned 1948 paper, "Computing Machinery and Intelligence," set the stage for what later became the foundation for all chess programs, leading to the development of grandmaster level machines that could compete with the World Champion in the 1990s (see Chapter 16, "Advanced Computer Games").

References

Turing, A. M. 1959. Computing machinery and intelligence. *Mind*, New Series, 59(236): 433–460.

Webster, C. Unorganized machines and the brain – Description of Turing's' ideas. Available at *http://home.clear.net.nz/pages/cw/unorganized.htm* (accessed August 2010).

Hodges, A. (1992). *Alan Turing: The enigma*. London: Vintage, Random House. *http://www.turing.org.uk/book/index.html* (This book was the basis for the award-winning movie "*The Imitation Game*" in 2014).

Over the years, two distinct, pervasive strains of AI research have developed. One school of thought is associated with the Massachusetts Institute of Technology; it views any system that exhibits intelligent behavior as an example of AI. To this school of thought, it does not matter whether the artifact performs its task in the same way humans do. The sole criterion is that the program performs correctly. Results of AI projects in electrical engineering, robotics, and related fields are primarily concerned with satisfactory performance. This approach is called **weak AI.**

Another school of thought is represented by the Carnegie-Mellon University approach to AI, which is primarily concerned with biological plausibility. That is, when an artifact exhibits intelligent behavior, its performance should be based upon the same methodologies used by humans. Consider for example, a system capable of hearing. Weak AI proponents would be concerned merely with the system's performance, whereas proponents of **strong AI** might aim to achieve success by simulating the human hearing system, with the equivalents to cochlea, hearing canal, eardrum, and other parts of the ear, each performing its required tasks in the system. Proponents of weak AI measure the success of the systems that they build based on their performance alone, whereas proponents of strong AI are concerned with the structure of the systems they build. See Chapter 16 for further discussion of this distinction.

Proponents of weak AI maintain that the *raison d'être* of AI research is to solve difficult problems regardless of how they are actually solved. Strong AI proponents, on the other hand, maintain that by sheer dint of possessing heuristics, algorithms, and knowledge of AI programs, computers can possess a sense of consciousness and intelligence. Hollywood falls into this latter camp. Movies that come to mind are "I, Robot," "AI," and "Blade Runner."

■1.3■ HEURISTICS

AI applications often rely on the application of heuristics. A **heuristic** is a rule of thumb for solving a problem. In other words, a heuristic is a set of guidelines that *often* works to solve a problem. Contrast a heuristic with an **algorithm**, which is a prescribed set of rules to solve a problem and whose output is entirely predictable. The reader is undoubtedly familiar with many algorithms used in computer programs, such as those for sorting, including bubblesort and quicksort, and for searching, including sequential search and binary search. With a heuristic, a favorable outcome is likely, but is not guaranteed. Heuristic methods were especially popular in the early days of AI, a period including the 1950s and into the 1960s.

You are likely to employ heuristics in your everyday life. For example, many people hate to ask for directions when driving. When exiting a highway at night, however, they sometimes have difficulty finding their way back to the main thoroughfare. One heuristic that could prove helpful is to proceed in the direction with more streetlights whenever they come to a fork in the road. You might have a favorite ploy for recovering a dropped contact lens or for finding a parking space in a crowded shopping mall. Both are examples of heuristics.

■1.3.1■ The Diagonal of a Rectangular Solid: Solving a Simpler, but Related Problem

An excellent reference on heuristics is George Polya's classic work, *How to Solve It*.[13] One heuristic he describes is that when confronted with a difficult problem, first try to solve a simpler but related problem. This often provides insight, which is useful to the solution of the original problem.

For example, what is the length of the diagonal of a rectangular solid? Those of you who have not recently completed a course in solid geometry probably find that this is a difficult problem. Following Polya's heuristic to solve a simpler but related problem first, you might attempt to find the diagonal of a rectangle. See Figure 1.9.

Using the Pythagorean theorem, you can calculate that $d = Sqrt(h^2 + w^2)$. Armed with this insight, you can then revisit the original problem. See Figure 1.10.

We now observe that the diagonal of the rectangular solid equals:

$$\text{Diagonal} = Sqrt(d^2 + \text{depth}^2) = Sqrt(h^2 + w^2 + \text{depth}^2)$$

Solving the simpler problem of calculating the diagonal of a rectangle helps to solve the more difficult problem of calculating the diagonal of a rectangular solid.

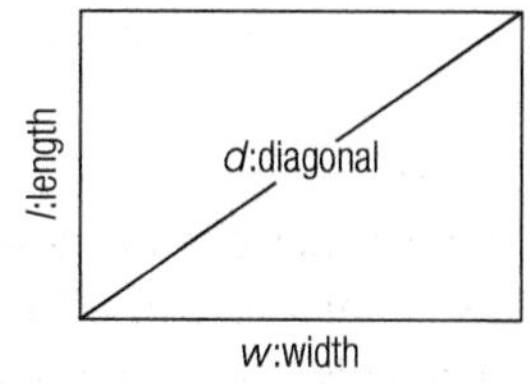

Figure 1.9
Finding the diagonal of a rectangle.

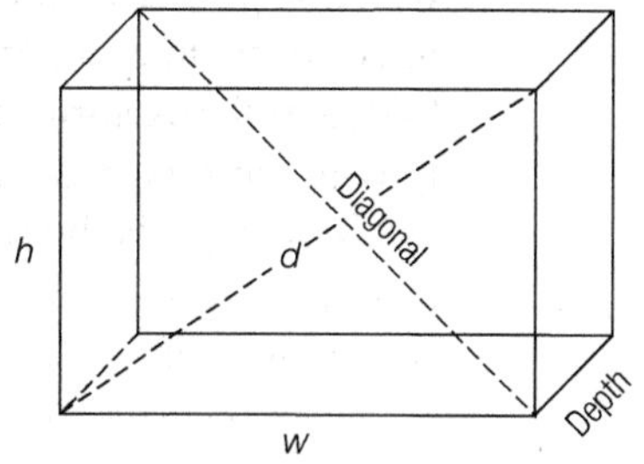

Figure 1.10
Finding the diagonal of a rectangular solid.

1.3.2 The Water Jug Problem: Working Backward

A second example from Polya is the **Water Jug Problem**. You are provided with two jugs of sizes m and n respectively; and you are required to measure r quarts of water where m, n, and r are all different quantities. An instance of this problem is: How can you measure exactly twelve quarts of water from a tap or a well when you have only an eight-quart jug and an eighteen-quart jug? See Figure 1.11.

One way to solve the problem is to use trial and error and hope for the best. Instead, Polya suggests the heuristic of starting with the goal state and working backward. See Figure 1.12.

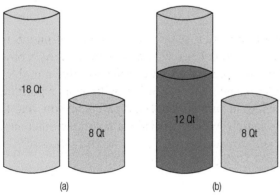

Figure 1.11
Water Jug Problem. (a) Initial state and (b) Final state.

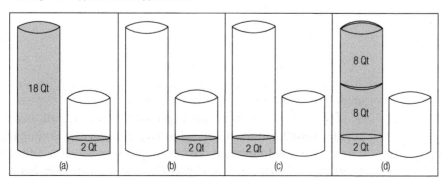

Figure 1.12
Starting with the goal state and working backward. (Drawing by authors.)

Observe in part (a) the eighteen-quart jug has been filled up and there are two quarts of water in the eight-quart jug. This state is just one step away from the goal state, where you pour an additional six quarts of water into the eight-quart jug; where twelve quarts of water remains in the eighteen-quart jug. Parts (b) through (d) of the figure provide the requisite steps to reach this penultimate state in part (a). You should turn your attention to part (d) and work your way back to portion (b) to see all the states that precede the state depicted in part (a).

Working backward to solve the Water Jug Problem and measure 12 quarts of water using only an 18-quart pail and an eight-quart pail, path (a), (b), (c), (d) shows how to go from the desired goal state back to the initial state. To actually solve this problem, you reverse the order of the states. First fill the 18-quart pail (state d). Then fill and empty the eight-quart pail twice by transferring water from the 18-quart pail. This leaves you with two quarts in the 18-quart pail (state c). Pour the last two quarts into the eight-quart pail (state b). Fill the 18-quart pail again from the tap or well, and pour water from the larger container to fill the eight-quart pail, which removes six quarts from the 18, leaving 12 quarts in the larger pail (state a).

As previously mentioned, heuristic methods were especially popular in the early days of AI—in the 1950s and into the 1960s. A landmark research project during this period was **General Problem Solver (GPS)**.[14] GPS solved problems using methods used by human problem solvers. Researchers gleaned the requisite problem solving heuristics by having human problem solvers vocalize their problem-solving methodology as they tackled various problems.

1.4 IDENTIFYING PROBLEMS SUITABLE FOR AI

As we become more familiar with AI and learn how it is distinct from traditional computer science, we must answer the question: "What makes a problem suitable for AI?" There are three characteristics that are common to most AI problems:

1. AI problems tend to be large.
2. They are computationally complex and cannot be solved by straightforward algorithms.
3. AI problems and their domains tend to embody a large amount of human expertise, especially if tackled by strong AI methods.

Some types of problems are better solved using AI, whereas others are more suitable for traditional computer science approaches involving simple decision-making or exact computations to produce solutions. Let us consider a few examples:

- Medical diagnosis
- Shopping using a cash register with barcode scanning
- ATMs
- Two person games such as chess and checkers

Medical diagnosis is a field of science that has for many years employed and welcomed contributions from AI, particularly through the development of **expert systems**. Expert systems are typically built in domains where there is considerable human expertise and where there exist many rules (rules of the form: if condition, then action; for example: if you have a headache, then take two aspirins and call me in the morning.) — more rules than any human can or wishes to hold in his/her head. Expert systems are among the most successful AI techniques for producing results that are comprehensive and effective.

One might ask: "Why is medical diagnosis a good candidate for an expert system?" First, medical diagnosis is a complex process with many possible valid approaches. Diagnosis involves identifying a disease or medical problem based on patient symptoms and history, as well as precedent cases. In most instances, no deterministic algorithm exists that can identify the underlying disease or condition. For example, MYCIN is the best-known, rule-based (expert) system (See Section 1.8.2) for aiding in diagnosis of bacterial infections of blood; MYCIN has over 400 rules[15] and has been used predominantly as a tool for training medical students. MYCIN does not provide a definite diagnosis, but rather a probability for which illness is most likely to be present, together with a degree of certainty that the diagnosis is correct. The process of developing these rules is referred to as knowledge engineering. A **knowledge engineer** will meet with a domain expert, in this case a doctor or other medical professional, and over the course of intensive interviews will glean the expert's knowledge into the form of discrete rules. Another feature of expert systems is that they could reach conclusions, which are unexpected even by the domain specialist who designed them. This is because the number of possible permutations of the expert's rules is more than anyone can hold in their head. A good candidate domain for building an expert system has the following characteristics:

- It contains a large amount of domain-specific knowledge, (knowledge about a particular problem area such as medical diagnosis, or area of human endeavor e.g., control mechanism for a nuclear power plant to ensure its safe operation).
- It allows for some hierarchical ordering of its knowledge.
- It can be developed as a repository for the knowledge of several experts.

An expert system is therefore more than the sum of the knowledge of the experts who built it. Chapter 9 is devoted to the presentation and discussion of expert systems. Shopping at a supermarket where bar codes are used to scan products into a cash register is not typically considered an AI domain. Imagine, however, that the grocery shopping experience extends into an interaction with an intelligent machine. The machine might remind shoppers about what products to purchase: "Don't you need a box of laundry detergent?" (because these products have not been purchased since a date that is known by the machine). The system might prompt the consumer to purchase food that goes well with those already selected. (e.g., "Do you need a quart of milk to go with your cereal purchase?"). This system could serve as a food advisor for a balanced nutritional diet and could be adjusted for a person's age, weight, ailments, and nutritional goals. This would represent an intelligent system because it embodies considerable knowledge about diet, nutrition, health, and diverse products; furthermore it can make intelligent decisions, which are presented as advice to the consumer.

The ATM, as used for the past 30 years, does not represent an AI system. Suppose this machine served as a general financial advisor, however, keeping track of a person's spending, as well as the categories and frequencies of items purchased. The machine could interpret spending for entertainment, necessities, travel, and other categories and offer advice on how spending patterns might be beneficially altered. ("Do you really need to spend so much on fancy restaurants?") An ATM as described here would be considered an intelligent system.

Another example of an intelligent system is one that plays chess. Although the rules of chess are easy to learn, playing this game at an expert level is no easy matter. More books have been written about chess than about all other games combined. It is generally accepted that chess has some 10^{42} possible reasonable games (whereby "reasonable" games are distinguished from the number of "possible" games earlier given as 10^{120}). This is such a large number that, even if the entire world's fastest computers worked together to solve the game of chess (i.e., develop a program to play perfect chess, one which always makes the best move), they wouldn't finish for 50 years. Ironically, despite chess being a zero-sum game (meaning neither player has an edge initially) and a two-person game of perfect information (no chance involved and no unknown factors to anyone's advantage), the following questions still remain:

- What is the outcome of chess with perfect play? Does White win, does Black win, or is it a draw? (Most people believe it is a draw.)
- What is the best first move for White? Most people believe it is 1.e4 or 1.d4, which is chess notation for moving the pawn in front of the White King two squares up (1.e4) or moving the pawn in front of the White Queen two squares up (1.d4). Statistics support this belief, but there is no proof.

Building a strong (Master-plus level) chess program has been based on the supposition that playing master level chess requires and exhibits intelligence.

During the past 20 years, computer chess programs have been built that can beat all but the world's very best players. However, no computer program is the official world chess champion. All matches played to date have been relatively short and have exploited human frailties (humans get tired, anxious, etc.). Many in the field of AI strongly believe that programs do not yet play better than any person. Furthermore, despite the success of recent chess-playing programs, these programs do not necessarily use "strong AI methods," (this is explored further in the next section). A truly intelligent computer chess program would not only play world championship-level chess, but would also be able to explain the reasoning behind its moves. It would have an enormous amount of knowledge about chess (domain-specific knowledge) that it would be able to share and present as part of its decision-making process.

Recently (July 2007) the game of checkers was weakly solved. See Chapter 16 "Advanced Computer Games," Section 16.1.5 for a discussion.

■1.5■ APPLICATIONS AND METHODS

If a system is to exhibit intelligence, it must interact with the real world; to do so it must have a formal framework, such as logic, that can be used to represent external reality. Interaction with the world also entails some degree of uncertainty. A medical diagnosis system, for example, must contend with the possibility that a patient's fever can be due to one of several factors: bacterial infection, a viral attack, or inflammation of some internal organ.

Identifying causes of events, whether they are medical conditions or automotive mishaps, often requires a great deal of knowledge. Reasoning from symptoms to eventual causes also involves sound inference rules. AI research has therefore spent considerable effort in designing both expert systems and automated reasoning systems.

Prowess at game playing is often taken as a sign of intelligence. The first fifty years of AI research witnessed much effort to design better checker and chess playing programs. Expertise in game playing often hinges on search algorithms that can look ahead to the long-term consequences that a move will have on subsequent play. Consequently there has been much research on the discovery and the development of efficient search algorithms.

You might have heard the old joke: "How do I get to Carnegie Hall?" —the answer being "Practice, practice, practice." The serious point is that learning must be an integral part of any viable AI system. Approaches to AI based on animal nervous systems (neural computation) and human evolution (evolutionary computation) have proved to be valuable paradigms for learning.

Building an intelligent system is a daunting enterprise. Some researchers have advocated letting the system "grow" or emerge from some seed, under the control of a few simple rules. Cellular Automata (CA) are theoretical systems that have demonstrated how simple rules can produce complex patterns. CA lend hope that we will perhaps someday have the wherewithal to create human-level AI systems. Applications are presented below from the aforementioned areas of AI research:

- Search algorithms and puzzles
- Two-person games
- Automated reasoning
- Production systems and expert systems
- Cellular automata
- Neural computation
- Evolutionary computation
- Knowledge representation
- Uncertainty reasoning

The following sections introduce each type of application. This discussion is merely meant to serve as an overview. A thorough exposition of these areas is presented in subsequent chapters.

1.5.1 Search Algorithms and Puzzles

The 15-puzzle and related search puzzles, such as the **8-puzzle** and the **3-puzzle**, serve as helpful examples of search algorithms, problem-solving techniques, and the application of heuristics. In the 15-puzzle, the numbers 1 through 15 are written on small plastic squares. These small squares are arranged within a larger plastic square frame. One position is left blank so that smaller tiles can slide in from as many as four directions. See Figure 1.13.

Notice that the 3 is free to move down, while the 12 is free to move to the right. Smaller instances of this puzzle are more convenient to work with, including the 8-puzzle and the 3-puzzle. For example, consider the 3-puzzle, shown in Figure 1.14. In these puzzles, it is naturally the numbered tiles that slide; however, it is more convenient to consider the blank square to be moving.

The blank can move in one of four directions:

- Up (↑)
- Down (↓)
- Right (→)
- Left (←)

Figure 1.13
Setting up a 15-puzzle.

Figure 1.14
Using a 3-puzzle.

When moves are to be attempted in turn, they will adhere to this precedence order. In the 3-puzzle, at most two of these moves are possible at any time.

To solve the puzzle, define a start state and goal state, as you did in the Water Jug Problem. The first, the **start state**, is arbitrary. The second, the **goal state**, is also arbitrary, but often displays the tiles in numeric order. See Figure 1.15.

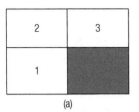 

Figure 1.15
States for solving the 3-puzzle. (a) Initial state and (b) Goal state.

The objective of this puzzle is to get from the start state to the goal state. In some instances, a solution with the minimum number of moves is desired. The structure that corresponds to all possible states of a given problem is called the **state-space graph**. It can be thought of as the **universe of discourse** for a problem because it describes every configuration that the puzzle can assume. The graph consists of all possible states of a problem, denoted by nodes, with arcs representing all legal transitions between states (legal moves in a puzzle). The **space tree**, which is generally a proper subset of the state-space graph, is a tree whose root is the start state, and one or more of its leaves is a goal state.

One search methodology you can use to traverse state-space graphs is called a **blind search**. It presumes no knowledge of the search space for a problem. There are two classic blind search algorithms that are often explored in courses on data structures and algorithms; they are **depth first search (dfs)** and **breadth first search (bfs)**. In dfs, you plunge as deeply into the search tree as possible. That is, when you have a choice of moves, you usually (but not always) move left. With bfs, you first visit all nodes close to the root, level by level, usually moving from left to right.

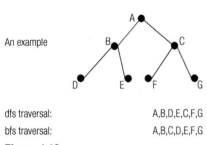

An example

dfs traversal: A,B,D,E,C,F,G
bfs traversal: A,B,C,D,E,F,G

Figure 1.16
Comparing dfs and bfs traversals of a state-space graph.

A dfs traversal of the tree, shown in Figure 1.16, would inspect nodes in the order A, B, D, E, C, F, G. Meanwhile, a bfs traversal of this tree would visit the nodes in the order A, B, C, D, E, F, G. In Chapter 2, "Uninformed Search," we will apply these search algorithms to solve instances of the 3-puzzle.

One theme that is repeated in the study of AI is that of **combinatorial explosion.** This means that the number of possible states of the puzzle is too high to be practical. Solving problems of a reasonable size can involve search spaces that grow too rapidly to allow blind search methods to succeed. (This will remain true regardless of how fast computers become in the future.) For example, the state-space graph for the 15-puzzle might contain more than $16! \leq (2.09228 \times 10^{13})$ states. Because of combinatorial explosion, success with AI problems depends more upon the successful application of heuristics than the design of faster machines.

One class of heuristic search algorithms looks forward into the state-space graph. Whenever two or more alternative paths appear, these algorithms pursue the path or paths closest to the goal. The astute reader will of course ask: "How can these search algorithms possibly know the distance to the goal state along any perceived path, when the sequence of moves that culminates at a goal is not known a priori?" The answer is that they cannot. The algorithms can use heuristic estimates of remaining distance, however.

Three search methods in this "look forward" class are **hill climbing, beam search**, and **best first search**. These searches will be explored thoroughly in Chapter 3. Another class of algorithms progresses toward a goal by continually gauging their distance from the root. These algorithms "look backward," and are referred to as **branch-and-bound** methods; these will also be covered in Chapter 3. For example, the **A* algorithm**, a well-known algorithm that uses overall estimated path cost to determine the order in which solutions are sought, is in this class of algorithms.

A* does some looking forward as well, however, and will be discussed in a later chapter.

1.5.2 ■ Two-Person Games

Two-person games such as **Nim** (This games involves several piles of stones. Two players alternately remove a number of stones from one of the piles. In one version of this game, the last person to remove a stone loses.), tic-tac-toe, and chess differ in one fundamental aspect from puzzles: when you play a two-person game, you cannot concentrate solely on reaching the goal; you must also remain vigilant to monitor and block the progress of your opponent. These **adversarial games** have been the mainstay of AI during its first half-century. Games follow rules that contain many of the attributes of real-world scenarios, albeit in simplified form.

A game that embodies the tension inherent in this class of problems is the **Iterated Prisoner's Dilemma**. Two perpetrators of a crime are arrested by the police and are immediately whisked off to separate cells. Each suspect is promised a reduced jail sentence if they betray their accomplice. The suspect who remains loyal will likely receive a longer sentence. What should each suspect do? Naturally, if a suspect intends to "go straight" after this incident, then betrayal is undoubtedly the best policy. However, if a suspect intends to remain committed to a life of crime, then betrayal comes with a heavy price tag. If arrested again, the accomplice will recall the partner's disloyalty and act accordingly. Game playing is the focus of Chapter 4, "Search Using Games," and Chapter 16, "Advanced Computer Games".

Games, although they often have attributes of real-world scenarios, do not have real-world consequences, and hence are an excellent testbed for AI methods.

1.5.3 ■ Automated Reasoning

With an **automated reasoning** system, the software is presented with a collection of facts. Deduction is a type of reasoning in which given information is used to derive new and hopefully useful facts. Suppose you are presented with the following puzzle:

> Two people are named Michael and Louis. Between them they hold two jobs. Each has one job. These jobs are post office clerk and French professor. Michael speaks only English, whereas Louis holds a PhD in French. Who holds which job?

First, one must have an appropriate representation language in order to present this information to an automated reasoning program. Statements such as the following are helpful in representing this problem:

Works_As (Clerk, Michael) | Works_ As (Clerk, Louis)

Such a logical statement is referred to as a clause. The initial slash is interpreted as "or." This clause means either Michael works as a clerk or Louis works as a clerk.

If you translate the puzzle into a language of clauses suitable for input to a program, you would still not have sufficient information to solve this puzzle. Much **common sense** or **world knowledge** would be missing. Common sense, for example, would suggest that if you own a car, then you also own its steering wheel. On the other hand, world knowledge could be used to deduce that precipitation will be in the form of snow when the temperature is 32°F or lower. In this puzzle, common sense tells us that a French professor must be able to speak that language. However: Why would a reasoning program have this knowledge unless you supply it?

Consider additional knowledge that you might use to solve this puzzle, such as the fact that Michael speaks only English; he cannot be the French professor. Although you can probably solve this problem without assistance, having an automated reasoning program as a problem-solving aide would be helpful when problems become larger and more involved.

1.5.4 Production Rules and Expert Systems

Production rules are used in AI as a method of knowledge representation. A production rule has the general forms:

IF (Condition), THEN Action

or

IF (Condition), THEN Fact

HUMAN INTEREST NOTES

JOHN MCCARTHY

John McCarthy (1927 – 2011) No textbook on Artificial Intelligence can be complete without paying proper tribute to the late John McCarthy, who coined the term at the 1956 Dartmouth Conference.

Professor McCarthy had stints at MIT, Dartmouth College, Princeton University, and Stanford University. He spent most of his career at Stanford, where he was Professor Emeritus.

He is credited with the invention of the LISP programming language which had been the standard language for developing AI programs for many years, particularly in this country. With a strong aptitude for Mathematics, McCarthy received a B.S. in Mathematics from Caltech in 1948 and then a PhD in Mathematics from Princeton University in 1951, under Solomon Lefschetz.

Professor McCarthy's interests and contributions were profound and wide ranging, covering many areas of AI, including, for example, publications on diverse areas of logic, natural language processing, computer chess, cognition, counterfactuals, common sense, and a number of philosophical problems from the standpoint of AI. His home page (*http://www-formal.stanford.edu/jmc/*) is a great treat in itself where most of his publications in these areas are available. There you can also find more recent pages on "The Sustainability of Human Progress" which he is quite optimistic about. Some other well-known titles include: "Circumscription – a form of Nonmonotonic Reasoning," "Artificial Intelligence, Logic and Formalizing Common Sense," and "The Little Thoughts of Thinking Machines" which is a popular article that appeared in *Psychology Today* in 1983.

As a founding father of AI, McCarthy had often used his papers, such as "Some Expert Systems Need Common Sense (1984) and "Free Will – Even for Robots," as a means of commentary on what AI systems need in order to be practically useful and effective.

He was the recipient of the Turing Award for his contributions to AI in 1971. Other awards he received include The National Medal of Science in Mathematical, Statistical, and Computational Sciences (1971), and the Benjamin Franklin Medal in Computer and Cognitive Science (2003).

Common examples are included below:

IF (headache), THEN take two aspirins and call me in the morning.

IF ((A > B) and (B > C)), THEN A > C

One application area for production systems is in the design of expert systems that were introduced in Section 1.4. An expert system is software that possesses detailed knowledge in a limited problem domain. A portion of an expert system for automobile diagnosis might contain the following rules:

IF (car won't start), THEN check headlights.

IF (headlights work), THEN check gas gauge.

IF (gas tank empty), THEN add gasoline to fuel tank.

IF (headlights don't work), THEN check battery.

Supplied with an extensive set of production rules, someone with little mechanical acumen could properly diagnose their vehicle. Expert systems were first developed in the early 1970s (MYCIN, DENDRAL, PROSPECTOR) and the field reached its maturity in the late 1980s. The architecture of production systems and expert systems is explored in Chapters 6, 7, and 9.

1.5.5 Cellular Automata

A **cellular automaton** (CA) can be viewed as a collection of cells in n-dimensional space. Each cell can be in any one of a small number of states, with two being a typical number. For example, a cell can be black or white. Each cell in the system has a neighborhood of adjacent cells. A CA is also characterized by two additional properties:

1. *Physical topology*, which refers to the shape of the CA, such as rectangular or hexagonal.

2. The *update rule*, which is used to determine the next state of a cell in terms of its present state, as well as the states of cells in its neighborhood. Cellular automata are synchronous systems in which updating occurs at fixed intervals.

Figure 1.17 shows a CA with rectangular topology. The CA is generally assumed to be unbounded in each dimension. Each cell can be in one of two states, shown as "0" and "1."

Figure 1.17
Part of a one-dimensional CA.

A cell in state 1 is sometimes characterized as being "alive," whereas a cell in state 0 is sometimes said to be "dead." Cells that are alive are often shaded, as in Figure 1.18; dead cells often appear without shading. In many examples, a cell's neighborhood includes the eight cells directly above, below, to the left, to the right, and diagonally above and below a cell. In Figure 1.18, the cells in the neighborhood of the central cell are indicated by shading.

Cellular automata are remarkable in that complex patterns can be created by the application of a few simple rules.

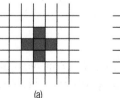 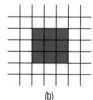

(a)   (b)

Figure 1.18
Neighborhoods in a two-dimensional rectangular cellular automaton. (a) The Von Neumann neighborhood and (b) the Moore neighborhood.

1.5.6 Neural Computation

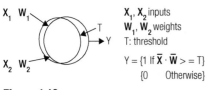

X_1, X_2 inputs
W_1, W_2 weights
T: threshold

$Y = \{1$ If $\overline{X} \cdot \overline{W} >= T\}$
$\{0 \quad$ Otherwise$\}$

Figure 1.19
Threshold Logic Unit.

In the quest for Artificial Intelligence, researchers often design systems based on the architecture of the best exemplar for intelligence on this planet. **Neural networks** attempt to capture the parallel and distributed structure of the human nervous system. Early work in **neural computing** began in the 1940s with the research of McCulloch and Pitts.[17] The basic building block for such systems is the artificial neuron, which can be modeled as a **threshold logic unit** (TLU). See Figure 1.19.

The inputs to this neuron, X_1 and X_2, are assumed to be binary in this example. These inputs are mitigated by the real-valued weights, W_1 and W_2. The output of this TLU is also assumed to be either 0 or 1. The output of a TLU equals 1 whenever the dot product of an input vector multiplied by this set of weights exceeds or equals the unit's threshold, which is also a real-valued quantity.

The dot product of two vectors $\overline{X}$ and $\overline{W}$, denoted by $\overline{X} \cdot \overline{W}$, is the component-wise product of these vectors.

For example, the TLU illustrated in Figure 1.20 implements the two-input Boolean AND function.

The dot product of the two inputs and the two weights will be greater than or equal to the threshold, only when both inputs are equal to 1.

As Figure 1.21 shows, $\overline{X} \cdot \overline{W}$ is greater than or equal to the threshold of 1.5 only when both inputs are equal to 1. Where did these weights come from? As discussed later in Chapter 11, they are the result of an **iterative learning algorithm** known as the **Perceptron Learning Rule**. In this rule, weights are changed as long as the system continues to respond incorrectly. The algorithm is iterative in the sense that, in each pass through the inputs, the response of the system converges towards the desired weights. Once the system produces only correct outputs, the learning is complete.

When the dot product of X and W is greater than or equal to the threshold T, then the output of the TLU should equal one; when this product is less than T the output should equal zero. Setting the dot product of X with W equal to T and substituting 1 for each of the weights, W_1 and W_2, one can obtain, with the help of some algebra, that $X_2 = -X_1 + 1.5$. This is the equation of a straight line; one whose slope is -1 and X_2 intercept is 1.5. This straight line, known as a **discriminant**, is drawn in Figure 1.21; it separates those inputs that yield an output of 0 ((0, 0), (0,1), (1,0)) from the input (1,1), which produces 1 as output. Useful pattern recognition tasks will naturally require more than a single threshold unit. Neural networks composed of hundreds or even thousands of simple units as described above can be used to perform valuable data processing tasks such as reading handwritten text or predicting the future price of a stock based upon its recent historical activity. **Learning rules** that are appropriate for these more complicated networks will be described in Chapter 11.It is believed that the brain itself is composed of a huge interconnected network of such simple processing elements.

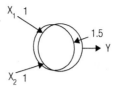

1.5.7 Genetic Algorithms

Neural networks—software systems that attempt to model the human nervous system—provide a fruitful arena for AI research. Another promising paradigm is Darwin's theory of evolution. Natural selection occurs in nature at a rate of thousands or millions of years. Inside a computer, evolution (or the iterative process whereby a proposed solution to a problem improves through the application of small incremental changes) proceeds somewhat faster. This is to be compared and contrasted with the process of evolution in the plant and animal world in which species adapt to their environments through the genetic operators of natural selection, reproduction, mutation, and recombination. **Genetic algorithms (GA)** are a specific methodology from the general field known as **evolutionary computation**, which is that branch of AI wherein proposed solutions to a problem adapt much as animal creatures adapt to their environments in the real world. In a GA, a problem is encoded as a string. Recall that in the 3-puzzle, a series of moves of the blank could be encoded as a sequence of 0s and 1s. The GA begins with a population of such binary strings that are randomly chosen. Genetic operators are then systematically applied to these strings and a **fitness function** is used to glean more optimal strings. A fitness function is designed to assign higher values to those strings corresponding to sequences of moves that bring the puzzle state closer to a goal state. Refer to Figure 1.14, which describes the 3-puzzle, and let us represent an upward motion (of the blank) by the string 00. Similarly, let 01 denote a downward motion, 10 a move right and finally 11 a move left. Next, refer to the instance of this puzzle depicted in Figure 1.15. Each of the following binary strings of length eight can be interpreted as four moves in this puzzle. 11100010, 00110110. Why should the latter string be assigned a higher fitness value? Detailed examples of this methodology will be provided in Chapter 12.

$$(X_1 * W_1) + (X_2 * W_2) = T$$
$$X_2 * W_2 = -W_1 . X_1 + T$$
$$X_2 = -((W_1/W_2) * X_1) + (T/W_2)$$
$$X_2 = -X_1 + 1.5$$

(a)

X_1	X_2	$\bar{X} \cdot \bar{W}$	Y
0	0	0	0
0	1	1	0
1	0	1	0
1	1	2	1

(b)

Figure 1.20
TLU simulating the AND function.

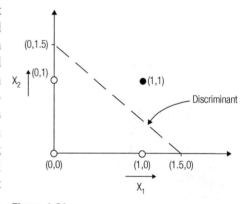

Figure 1.21
Discriminant for a TLU that simulates the two-input AND function.

1.5.8 Knowledge Representation

As soon as one considers the problems of AI, the issue of representation comes to the fore. If AI systems acquire and store knowledge in order to process it and produce intelligent results, they need to be able to identify and represent that knowledge. The choice of a representation is intrinsic to the nature of problem solving and understanding. As Polya [13] commented, a good representation choice is almost as important as the algorithm or solution plan devised for a particular problem. Good and natural representations facilitate fast and comprehensible solutions. Poor representational choices can be equally stifling. For example, consider the familiar **Missionaries and Cannibals Problem**. The problem is to get three missionaries and three cannibals from the west bank to the east bank of a river with a boat. At any point during the transitions from west to east, you can quickly see and comprehend the solution path by selecting an appropriate representation. Constraints can also be efficiently represented; such as that the boat can hold no more than two people at any time and that the cannibals on any bank can never outnumber the number of missionaries. One representation would be to list the start state by W:3M3CB (three missionaries and three cannibals with the boat on the West Bank). The goal state is E:3M3CB. A transition of one missionary and one cannibal with the boat could be represented by ➔ E: 1M1CB. Leaving W:2M2C ~~~~~~~ E:1M1CB. Another representation would be to pictorially represent the boat, Missionaries, and Cannibals with stick figures and a sketch for the boat on each bank as each transition occurs.

Logic has been used as a knowledge representation and problem-solving technique by AI researchers since the field's inception, starting with Newell and Simon's **Logic Theorist,** [18] and **GPS,** [14] which was based on Russell and Whitehead's *Principia Mathematica.*[19] Both the Logic Theorist and GPS programs use the rules of logic to solve problems. A seminal example of the use of logic for knowledge representation and language understanding was Winograd's **Blocks World** (1972),[20] in which a robot arm interacts with blocks on a tabletop. This program encompassed issues of language understanding and scene analysis as well as other aspects of AI. Many AI researchers have based their research on a logic-based approach, including Nils Nilsson in his *Principles of Artificial Intelligence text,*[21] Genesereth and Nilsson, [22] and Alan Bundy in *The Computer Modeling of Mathematical Reasoning.*[23]

Recall from Section 1.5.4, that production rules and production systems are used to construct many successful expert systems. The appeal of production rules and expert systems is based on the feasibility of representing heuristics clearly and concisely. Thousands of expert systems have been built incorporating this methodology.

On the other hand, considering the possible alternatives for knowledge representation, graphical approaches offer greater appeal to the senses, such as vision, space, and motion. Possibly the earliest graphical approaches were state-space representations, which display all the possible states of a system. (Recall the discussion of the 15-puzzle in Section 1.5.1.) **Semantic networks** are another graphical, though complex, representation of knowledge, dating back to the work of Quillian.[24] Semantic networks are a predecessor of object-oriented languages. Object orientation uses inheritance (wherein an object from a particular class inherits many of the properties of a superclass). Much of the work employing semantic networks has focused on representing the knowledge and structure of language. Examples include Stuart Shapiro's [25] SNePS (Semantic Net Processing System) and the work of Roger Schank in natural language processing.[26]

Marvin Minsky, [27] a founding AI researcher and thinker, introduced **frames**, another primary graphical approach to knowledge representation. Frames enable a compact description of objects in a systematic and hierarchical way. They are typically organized by **slots and fillers** in tables (which can be related in a similar plane) or three-dimensionality for concepts that exploit the prototypical nature of structures in our world. They also employ inheritance to facilitate repetition, predictability, and the variety of forms that define real-world objects, such as a university with its buildings, faculty, administration, and students. Although the particulars of these elements vary from university to university, this variety can be easily captured by frames.

Frames will be fully described, with examples, in Chapter 6.

Scripts [28] are an extension of frames that further exploit the expectancy inherent in human interactions. Through their work, Schank and Abelson have been able to build a number of systems that seem to comprehend descriptions of well-defined settings. **Conceptual graphs** by Sowa [29] and Novak and Gowin [30] are a simplified but pervasive heuristic technology that has often been used to represent the knowledge in a discipline.

In 1985, Marvin Minsky published *Society of Mind*.[31] Minsky proposes theories to explain the organization of the human mind. He suggests that the intelligent world could be run by agents. These agents are themselves unintelligent, but could be combined in sophisticated ways to form a society, which seems to exhibit intelligent behavior. Concepts such as multiple hierarchies, scales, learning, remembering, sensing similarities, emotion, and frames are presented by Minsky through the agent model.

There are a number of examples of early research contributions in AI that have been "absorbed" by mainstream computer science; for example, the programming language Smalltalk, hierarchical methods, and frames led to advances in the object-oriented paradigm.

1.5.9 Uncertainty Reasoning

Traditional mathematics often deals with certitudes. The set A is either a subset of the set B, or it is not. AI systems, much like life itself, are plagued with **uncertainty**. Chance is an inimitable component of our existence; for example, you could catch a cold during your morning commute if the passengers next to you on the bus or the train were coughing or sneezing; then again you might not. Consider the following sets: the set of people that are satisfied with their jobs, and the set of people that are not satisfied. It is not at all unusual for some people to belong to both sets. Some people might love their jobs, though they might believe they are underpaid. You can consider the set of people who are satisfied with their jobs as a fuzzy set [32] because it varies depending on the conditions. Often one is satisfied with the work itself. However, one considers the paycheck to be insufficient. That is, one is satisfied with one's job *to a certain extent*. The degree of membership for a particular person in this set could range from 1.0 for someone who thoroughly loves their work to 0.0 for an individual who should seriously consider a career change.

Fuzzy sets arise in many domains. Cameras vary shutter speed based upon the amount of sunlight present. Washing machines control wash cycles that are based, in part, on the dirtiness of the clothes they contain. Thermostats regulate room temperatures by making sure that temperatures actually fall within an accepted range, rather than at a precise value. Modern automobiles adjust brake pressure in accordance with weather conditions. Fuzzy-logic controllers can be found in each of these devices. A more comprehensive discussion on the role that uncertainty plays in AI is found in Chapter 8, "Uncertainty in AI."

1.6 EARLY HISTORY OF AI

Building an intelligent machine has long been a dream of mankind, dating back to the ancient Egyptians who took "short cuts" by building statues that contained hidden priests who attempted to provide sage counsel to citizens. This type of hoax has unfortunately appeared throughout the history of AI; the field has been understandably tainted by such chicanery while trying to achieve the status of an accepted scientific discipline—*artificial intelligentsia*.

The strongest foundations for AI stem from the logical premises established by Aristotle (circa 350 BC). Aristotle established the models for scientific thinking and disciplined thought that have become the standard of the present day scientific method. His distinction between *matter* and *form* was a forerunner to one of the most important concepts in computer science today: data abstraction, which distinguishes methods (forms) from the shells in which they are encapsulated, or in distinguishing the form (shape) of a concept from its actual representation. (Recall the discussion of abstraction in the sidebar in Section 1.1.)

Aristotle also emphasized the ability of people to reason, maintaining that this facility distinguishes us from all other living beings. Any attempt to build an artificially intelligent machine requires this ability to reason. This is why the work of the nineteenth century British logician, George Boole, was so important; his established system for expressing logical relationships later became known as Boolean algebra.

Raymond Llull, the thirteenth century Spanish hermit and scholar, was probably the first person to attempt to mechanize human thought processes. His work predates Boole by more than five centuries. Llull, a devout Christian, set about developing a system based on logic whose aim was to prove that the tenets of Christianity were true. In his *Ars Magna* (Great Art), Llull used geometrical diagrams and primitive logical devices to realize this goal. Llull's corpus of work inspired later pioneers, including Wilhelm Leibniz (1646–1716). Leibniz, a great mathematician and philosopher

HUMAN INTEREST NOTES

GEORGE BOOLE

For a computer program to exhibit any kind of intelligence it was decided early on that it needed to be able to reason. The British mathematician, George Boole (1815–1864) developed a mathematical framework for representing the laws of human logic. His work consisted of some 50 individual papers. His main achievement was the well-known Treatise on *Differential Equations* that appeared in 1859. This was followed, in 1860, by a *Treatise on the Calculus of Finite Differences*. The latter was designed to serve as a sequel to the former work. Boole's *Laws of Thought* provided a general method of symbolic inference, which is perhaps his greatest achievement. If you are given a logical proposition involving any number of terms, Boole showed how, with

purely symbolic treatment of these premises, sound logical inferences could be made.

In the second part of the *Laws of Thought*, Boole attempted to discover a general method for translating antecedent probabilities for a system of events, to determine the consequent probability of any other event that was logically connected with the given events.

The algebraic language (or notation) that he developed allowed for variables to have interactions (or relationships) based on only two states, *true* and *false*. He developed Boolean Algebra, as it is now known, wherein there are three logical operators: and, or, and not. The combination of Boolean Algebra and the rules of logic enables us to prove things "automatically." Hence, a machine that can do this is in some sense capable of reasoning. [33]

An example of Boolean logic is shown here:

IF $A \geq B$ and $B \geq C$, THEN $A \geq C$

That is the law of transitivity—IF A implies B and B implies C, THEN A implies C.

in his own right, took Llull's ideas one step further: he believed that a kind of "logical calculus" or "universal algebra" could be built that could resolve all logical arguments and could reason about almost anything; he states:

> All our reasoning is nothing but the joining and substituting of characters, whether these characters be words or symbols or pictures… (ibid., p.7)

More than two centuries later, Kurt Gödel (1931) [34] demonstrated the over-optimism of Leibniz's goal. He proved that any branch of mathematics would always contain some propositions that could not be proven to be either true or false, using only the rules and axioms of that branch of mathematics which is complete itself. The great French philosopher Rene Descartes,[35] in his *Meditations*, addressed the question of his physical reality through cognitive introspection. He justified his own existence through the reality of thought; culminating in his famous statement, *"Cogito ergo sum,"* or, "I think therefore I am." In this way, Descartes and the philosophers who followed him established the independence of the mind and the physical world. Ultimately, this has led to the preferred contemporary view that the mind and the body are not fundamentally different at all. [36]

1.6.1 Logicians and Logic Machines

The world's first real logic machine was built by Charles Stanhope (1753–1816), the third Earl of Stanhope. The Stanhope Demonstrator, as it was known, was built circa 1775 and consisted of two colored slides made of transparent glass, one red and one gray, which the user pushed into slots on the sides of a box. See Figure 1.22.

Manipulating the demonstrator, the user could verify the validity of simple deductive arguments involving two assumptions and a single conclusion.[33] Despite its limitations, the Stanhope Demonstrator was the first step toward the mechanization of thought processes. In 1800, Stanhope printed the early chapters of a book explaining his machine, but it wasn't until 60 years after his death (1879) that Reverend Robert Harley published the first article on the Stanhope Demonstrator.

The best-known and first prototype for modern-day computers was Charles Babbage's Difference Engine. Babbage was a prolific and talented inventor; he built the first general-purpose programmable computer but did not secure enough funding (1500 pounds from the British

Figure 1.22
The Stanhope Demonstrator.

Chancellor of the Exchequer) to complete the project. Babbage continued to fund the project from his own resources until granted a further 3000 pounds. His plans became more ambitious, however (e.g., calculating to 20 decimal places instead of his original 6), and he never completed the Difference Engine once his funding stopped.

Babbage also never realized his plans to build the Analytical Engine, which was the successor to his Difference Engine. See Figure 1.23. He intended that the Analytical Engine would perform various tasks that require human thought, such as playing games of skill, akin to checkers, tic-tac-toe, and chess. Babbage, with his collaborator, Lady Ada Lovelace, envisioned that their Analytical Engine would reason with abstract concepts as well as with numbers. Lady Lovelace is

Figure 1.23
Image of Babbage's Analytical Engine.

considered the world's first programmer. She was the daughter of Lord Byron, and was the person after whom the programming language ADA is named.[33]

Babbage was at least 100 years ahead of the time that the first chess programs were written. He certainly realized the level of complexity in terms of logic and calculation entailed in building a mechanical device to play chess.

The work of George Boole, who was introduced earlier, was extremely important to the foundations of AI and the mathematical formalization of the laws of logic that provide a foundation for computer science. Boolean algebra significantly informs the design of logic circuitry. Boole's goals in developing his system are also close to those of contemporary AI researchers. In *An Investigation of Logic and Probabilities*, Chapter 1, he states:

> to investigate the fundamental laws of those operations of the mind by which reasoning is performed; to give expression to them in the symbolical language of a Calculus, and upon this foundation to establish the science of logic and to instruct its method; … and finally to collect from these various elements of truth brought to view in the course of these inquiries some probable intimations concerning the nature and constitution of the human mind.[38]

Boole's system was extremely simple and formal, captured the full power of logic, and was the basis for all systems that followed it.

Claude Shannon (1916–2001) is widely recognized as the father of information science. His seminal paper on the application of symbolic logic to relay circuits [39] was based on his Master's thesis at MIT. His pioneering work was important to the operation of both telephones and computers. Shannon also contributed to AI via his research on computer learning and game-playing. His groundbreaking paper on computer chess had a great influence on the field and lingers to this day.[40]

The Nimotron, developed in 1938, was the first machine built that could play a complete game of skill. It was designed and patented by Edward Condon, Gerald Twoney, and Willard Derr and played the game of Nim. An algorithm was developed to play the best move in any position of this game. (See Chapter 4 for a thorough discussion of Nim and other games.) This was a prelude to robotics (Chapter 15).

The best-known attempt at developing thinking machines was *The Turk*, which was developed in 1790 by Baron von Kempelen, Counselor on Mechanics to the Royal Chamber in Vienna. This machine, which toured Europe for many years, fooled people into thinking they were playing chess against a machine. In fact, a small, master-level human chess player was hidden inside the box.

Torres y Quevedo was a prolific Spanish inventor (1852–1936) who built what might be the first expert system. He created a rule-based system for playing the endgame King and Rook vs. King. Rules were based on the relative positions of these three pieces. See Figure 1.24.

SIDEBAR

The Mythical Man-Month

The story of Babbage trying to fund his Difference Engine is a good forerunner to the saga that is the basis of the landmark work by Frederick Brooks, *The Mythical Man-Month*,[37] which demonstrated that programmers have been very poor at estimating the costs required to complete a project, where the costs are measured in terms of time, effort, and money. This led to the discipline of software engineering, which certainly benefits from instances when AI techniques can be applied to obtain more realistic project requirements and costs.

To this day, the field of AI is plagued by the suspicion that advances in AI are based more on hype than on substance.

Konrad Zuse (1910–1995) was a German who invented the first digital computer powered by electricity. Zuse worked independently, and initially his work was dedicated to pure number crunching. Zuse recognized the connection between engineering and mathematical logic, and he learned that calculations in Boolean algebra are identical to the propositional calculus of mathematics. He developed a system corresponding to the Boolean algebra of conditional propositions for relays, and because much work in AI is based on the importance of being able to manipulate conditional propositions (that is, IF – THEN propositions), we can see the importance of Zuse's work. His work on logic circuits predates Shannon's thesis by several years. Zuse recognized the need for an efficient and vast memory and developed computers based on vacuum tubes and electromechanical memory, which he called the Z1, Z2, and Z3. It is universally accepted that the Z3 (May 12, 1941) was the

Figure 1.24
Torres y Quevedo's Machine from "Les Automates" by H. Vigneron, La Natura, 1914.

world's first reliable, freely programmable working computer based on floating-point numbers. It was destroyed by bombings in World War II, but a replica is on display in the Deutsches Museum in Munich.

■1.7■ RECENT HISTORY OF AI TO THE PRESENT

Since World War II and the advent of computers, much progress in computer science and proficiency in programming techniques has been acquired through the challenges of trying to get computers to play and master complex board games. Some examples of games whose play by computer have benefitted from the application of AI insights and methodologies have included chess, checkers, GO, and Othello.

■1.7.1■ Games

Games have spurred the development and interest in AI. Early efforts were highlighted by the efforts of Arthur Samuel in 1959 on the game of checkers.[41] His program was based on tables of 50 heuristics and was used to play against different versions of itself. The losing program in a series of matches would adopt the heuristics of the winning program. It played strong checkers, but never mastered the game. A detailed discussion of Samuel's contributions to checker-playing programs will be found in Chapter 16.

People have been trying to get machines to play strong chess for several centuries. The infatuation with chess machines probably stems from the generally accepted view that it requires intelligence to play chess well. The first real chess program, following the Shannon-Turing Paradigm,[40, 42] was developed in 1959 by Newell, Simon, and Shaw. Richard Greenblatt's[43] program was the first to play club-level chess. Computer chess programs improved steadily in the 1970s until, by the end of that decade, they reached the Expert level (equivalent to the top 1% of chess tournament players). In 1983, Ken Thompson's Belle was the first program to officially achieve the Master level. This was followed by the success of Hitech, from Carnegie-Mellon University,[44] which successfully accomplished a major milestone as the first Senior Master (over 2400-rated) program. Shortly thereafter the program Deep Thought (also from Carnegie-Mellon) was developed and became the first program capable of beating Grandmasters on a regular basis.[45] Deep Thought evolved into Deep Blue when IBM took over the project in the 1990s, and Deep Blue played a six-game match with World Champion Garry Kasparov who "saved mankind" by winning 4–2 in a match in Philadelphia in 1996.[46] In 1997, however, against Deeper Blue, the successor of Deep Blue, Kasparov lost 3.5–2.5 and the chess world was shaken. In subsequent six-game matches against Kasparov, Kramnik, and other World Championship-level players, programs have fared well, but these were not World Championship Matches. Although it is generally agreed that these programs might still be slightly inferior to the best human players, most would be willing to concede that top programs play chess indistinguishably from the most accomplished humans (if one is thinking of the Turing Test), and there is little doubt that sometime in the next 10–15 years, a program will likely claim the World Chess Championship.

In 1989, Jonathan Schaeffer, at the University of Alberta in Edmonton,[47] began his long-term goal of conquering the game of checkers with his program Chinook. In a 40-game match in 1992 against longtime Checkers World Champion Marion Tinsley, Chinook lost 4–2 with 34 draws. In 1994 their match was tied after six games, when Tinsley had to forfeit because of health reasons. Since that time, Schaeffer and his team have been working to solve checkers from both the end of the game (all eight-pieces and fewer endings) as well as from the beginning.

Other games (addressed in Chapter 16) for their use of AI techniques include backgammon, poker, bridge, Othello, and GO (often called the new drosophila).

1.7.2 Expert Systems

Expert systems are one of the areas that have been investigated for almost as long as AI itself. It is one discipline that AI can claim as a great success. Expert systems have many characteristics that make them desirable for AI research and development. These include separation of the knowledge base from the inference engine, being more than the sum of any or all of their experts, relationship of knowledge to search techniques, reasoning, and uncertainty.

One of the earliest and most often referenced systems was heuristic DENDRAL. Its purpose was to identify unknown chemical compounds on the basis of their mass spectrographs.[48] DENDRAL was developed at Stanford University with the goal of performing a chemical analysis of the Martian soil. It was one of the first systems to illustrate the feasibility of encoding domain-expert knowledge in a particular discipline.

Perhaps the most famous expert system is MYCIN, also from Stanford University (1984). Mycin was developed to facilitate the investigation of infectious blood diseases. Even more important than its domain, however, was the example that Mycin established for the design of all future knowledge-based systems. It had over 400 rules, which were eventually used to provide a training dialogue for residents at the Stanford hospital. In the 1970s, PROSPECTOR (also at Stanford University) was developed for mineral exploration.[49] PROSPECTOR was also an early and valuable example of the use of inference networks.

Other famous and successful systems that followed in the 1970s were XCON (with some 10,000 rules), which was developed to help configure electrical circuit boards on VAX computers; [50]

GUIDON, [51] a tutoring system that was an offshoot of Mycin; TEIRESIAS, a knowledge acquisition tool for Mycin; [52] and HEARSAY I and II, the premier examples of speech understanding using the Blackboard Architecture.[53] The AM (Artificial Mathematician) system of Doug Lenat [54] was another important result of research and development efforts in the 1970s, as well as the

Dempster-Schafer Theory for reasoning under uncertainty, together with Zadeh's aforementioned work in fuzzy logic. [32]

Since the 1980s, thousands of expert systems have been developed in such areas as configuration, diagnosis, instruction, monitoring, planning, prognosis, remedy, and control. Today, in addition to stand-alone expert systems, many expert systems have been embedded into other software systems for control purposes, including those in medical equipment and automobiles (for example, when should traction control engage in an automobile).

In addition, a number of expert systems shells, such as Emycin [55], OPS [56], EXSYS, and CLIPS, [57] have become industry standards. A number of knowledge representation languages have also been developed. Today, many expert systems work behind the scenes to enhance day-to-day experiences, such as the online shopping cart. We will discuss many of the major expert systems— including their methodologies, designs, purposes, and main features— in Chapter 9.

1.7.3 Neural Computing

Section 1.5.6 mentions that McCulloch and Pitts conducted early research in neural computing. [17] They were trying to understand the behavior of animal nervous systems. Their model of artificial neural networks (ANN) had one serious drawback: it did not include a mechanism for learning.

Frank Rosenblatt [58] developed an iterative algorithm known as the Perceptron Learning Rule for finding the appropriate weights in a single-layered network (a network in which all neurons are directly connected to inputs). Research in this burgeoning discipline might have been severely hindered by the pronouncement by Minsky and Papert [59] that certain problems could not be solved by single-layer perceptrons, such as the exclusive OR (XOR) function. Federal funding for neural network research was severely curtailed immediately after this proclamation.

The field witnessed a second flurry of activity in the early 1980s with the work of Hopfield.[60] His asynchronous network model (Hopfield networks) used an energy function to find approximate solutions to NP-complete problems.[61] The mid-eighties also witnessed the discovery of **backpropagation**, a learning algorithm appropriate for multilayered networks. Backpropagation-based networks are routinely employed to predict Dow Jones' averages and to read printed material in optical character recognition systems. Consult Chapter 11 for details. Neural networks are also used in control systems. ALVINN was a project at Carnegie Mellon University [62,63] in which a backpropagation network senses the highway and assists in the steering of a Navlab vehicle. One immediate application of this work was to warn a driver impaired by lack of sleep, excess of alcohol, or other condition whenever the vehicle strayed from its highway lane. Looking toward the future, it is hoped that, someday, similar systems will drive vehicles so that we are free to read newspapers and talk on our cell phones with impunity.

1.7.4 Evolutionary Computation

In Section 1.5.7, we discussed genetic algorithms. These algorithms are more generally classified as evolutionary computation. Recall that genetic algorithms use probability and parallelism to solve combinatorial problems, also called optimization problems. This approach to search was developed by John Holland.[65]

Evolutionary computation, however, is not solely concerned with optimization problems. Rodney Brooks was formerly the director of the MIT Computer Science and AI Laboratory. His

SIDEBAR

NETtalk[64] was a backpropagation application that learned the correct pronunciation for English text. It was claimed to pronounce English sounds with 95% accuracy. Obviously, problems arose because of inconsistencies inherent in the pronunciation of English words, such as *rough* and *through*, and the pronunciation of words with different foreign sources such as *pizza* and *fizzy*. Chapter 11 will more fully explore the contributions of neural computing to the design of intelligent systems

approach to the successful creation of a human-level Artificial Intelligence, which he aptly cites as the holy grail of AI research,[66] renounces reliance on the symbol-based approach. This latter approach relies upon the use of heuristics (see Section 1.3) and representational paradigms (see Sections 1.5.3 and 1.5.4). In his subsumption (Intelligent systems can be designed in multiple layers in which higher leveled layers rely upon those layers beneath them. For example, if you wanted to build a robot capable of avoiding obstacles, the obstacle avoidance routine would be built upon a lower layer, which would merely be responsible for robotic locomotion.) architectural approach, he advocates that the world itself should serve as our representation. Brooks maintains that intelligence emerges through the interaction of an agent with its environment. He is perhaps most well-known for the insect-like robots built in his lab that embody this philosophy of intelligence, wherein a community of autonomous robots interact with their environment and with each other. Chapter 12 explores the field of evolutionary computation.

1.7.5 Natural Language Processing

If we wish to build intelligent systems, it seems natural to ask that our systems possess a language understanding facility. This is an axiom that was well understood by many early practitioners. Two well-known early application programs were Weizenbaum's Eliza and Winograd's SHRDLU.[20]

Eliza was a program written by Joseph Weizenbaum, an MIT computer scientist working with Kenneth Colby, a Stanford University psychiatrist.[67] Eliza was intended to imitate the role played by a psychiatrist of the Carl Rogers School. For instance, if the user typed in "I feel tired," Eliza might respond, "You say you feel tired. Tell me more." The "conversation" would go on in this manner, with the machine contributing little or nothing in terms of originality to the dialogue. A live psychoanalyst might behave in this fashion in the hope that the patient would discover their true (perhaps hidden) feelings and frustrations. Meanwhile, Eliza is merely using pattern matching to feign human-like interaction.

The most frequently used letters in the English language are ETAOIN SHRDLU on linotype machines. Winograd's program was named after the second set of these letters.

Curiously, Weizenbaum was disturbed by the avid interest that his students (and the public in general) took in interacting with Eliza, even though they were fully aware that Eliza was only a program. Meanwhile, Colby, the psychiatrist, remained dedicated to the project and went on to author a successful program called DOCTOR. Although Eliza has contributed little to natural language processing (NLP), it is software that pretends to possess what is perhaps our last vestige of "specialness"—our ability to feel emotions.

What will happen when the line between a human and machine (example: android) becomes less clear—perhaps in some 50 years—and these androids will be less mortal and more like immortals?

There will be no controversy surrounding the next milestone in NLP. Terry Winograd [20] wrote SHRDLU as his doctoral dissertation at MIT. SHRDLU used meaning, syntax, and deductive reasoning to both understand and respond to English commands. Its universe of discourse was a tabletop upon which blocks of various shapes, sizes, and colors resided.

HUMAN-INTEREST NOTES

SHERRY TURKLE

Sherry Turkle. (Reprinted with permission. Photo source: http://web.mit.edu/sturkle/www/)

To many it seems sad that some people become addicted to Eliza-like programs, because they believe it to be a sign of the frustration some people feel with their lives. Such concern about Eliza was expressed in a casual conversation among attendees at the AI @ 50 Conference ("Dartmouth **Artificial Intelligence Conference:** The Next Fifty Years") on the Dartmouth College campus in the summer of 2006. One of the participants in that discussion was Sherry Turkle, a psychologist with analytic training who works at the MIT Program in Science, Technology, and Society. Naturally, Turkle was sympathetic.

Turkle [68] has done much research with what she calls "relational artifacts." These are devices—both toys and robots—whose defining attribute is not their intelligence, but their ability to evoke caring behavior in those with whom they interact. The first relational artifacts in America were Tamagotchis in 1997, virtual creatures that lived on an LCD screen. These creatures often made veritable slaves of many children (and their parents), requiring constant feeding, cleaning, and nurturing if they were to "grow" to become healthy adults. More recently, several MIT robots, including Cog, Kismet, and Paro, have been developed with the uncanny ability to feign human emotions and evoke emotional responses from those with whom they interact. Turkle has studied the relationships that children and older persons in nursing homes have formed with these robots; relationships that involve genuine emotion and caring. Turkle speaks of the need to perhaps redefine the word "relationship" to include the encounters that people have with these so-called "relational artifacts." She remains confident, however, that such relationships will never replace the bonds that can only occur between human beings who must confront their mortality on a daily basis.

(Winograd's blocks world was introduced in Section 1.5.8.)

A robot arm could interact with this tabletop to achieve various goals. For example, if SHRDLU was asked to lift a red block upon which there was a small green block, it knew that it must remove the green block before it could lift the red one. Unlike Eliza, SHRDLU was able to understand English commands and respond to them appropriately.

HEARSAY,[69] an ambitious program in speech recognition (mentioned in Section 1.7.2), employed a **blackboard architecture** wherein independent knowledge sources (agents) for various components of language, such as phonetics and phrases, could freely communicate. Both syntax and semantics were used to prune improbable word combinations.

The HWIM (pronounced "Whim" and short for *Hear What I Mean*) Project [70] used augmented transition networks to understand spoken language. It had a vocabulary of 1000 words dealing with travel budget management. Perhaps this project was too ambitious in scope because it did not perform as well as HEARSAY II.

Parsing played an integral part in the success of these natural language programs. SHRDLU employed a **context-free grammar** to help parse English commands. Context-free grammars provide a syntactic structure for dealing with strings of symbols. However, to effectively process natural languages, semantics must be considered as well.

Each of the aforementioned early language processing systems employed world knowledge to some extent. However, in the late 1980s the greatest stumbling block for progress in NLP was the problem of common sense knowledge. For example, although many successful programs were built in particular areas of NLP and AI, these were often criticized as **microworlds**, meaning that the programs did not have general, real-world knowledge or common sense. For example, a program might know a lot about a particular scenario, such as ordering food in a restaurant, but it would have no knowledge of whether the waiter or waitress was alive or whether they would ordinarily be wearing any clothing. During the past 25 years, Douglas Lenat [71] of MCC in Austin, Texas, has been building the largest repository of common sense knowledge to address this issue.

Recently, a major paradigm shift has occurred in the field of NLP. Statistics, rather than world knowledge, govern the parse trees for sentences in this relatively new approach.

Charniak [72] describes how context-free grammars can be augmented such that each rule has an associated probability. These associated probabilities could be taken, for instance, from the Penn Treebank.[73] The Penn Treebank contains more than one million words of English text that have been parsed manually, mostly from the *Wall Street Journal*. Charniak demonstrated how this statistical approach successfully obtained a parse for a sentence from the front page of *The New York Times* (no trivial feat, even for most humans).

Recent successes achieved by this statistical approach to NLP and machine translation will be described further in Chapter 13.

1.7.6 Bioinformatics

Bioinformatics is the nascent discipline that concerns the application of the algorithms and techniques of computer science to molecular biology. It is mainly concerned with the management and analysis of biological data. In structural genomics, one attempts to specify a structure for each observed protein. Automated discovery and data mining could help in this pursuit.[74] Juristica and Glasgow demonstrate how case-based reasoning could assist in the discovery of the representative structure for each protein. In their 2004 survey article in the AAAI special issue on AI and Bioinformatics, Glasgow, Jurisica, and Rost note: "Possibly the most rapidly growing area of recent activity in bioinformatics is the analysis of microarray data." [74]

Microbiologists are overwhelmed with both the variety and quantity of data available to them. They are being asked to comprehend molecular sequence, structure, and data based solely on huge databases. Many researchers believe that AI techniques from knowledge representation and machine learning will prove beneficial as well.

1.8 AI IN THE NEW MILLENNIUM

AI is a unique academic discipline because it allows us to explore the possibilities of what future life might be like. In the short history of AI, its methodologies have already been absorbed into standard technologies for computer science. Examples of this include search techniques and expert systems that, spawned from AI research, are now embedded in many control systems, financial systems, and Web-based applications:

- ALVINN, a neural network-based system to control a vehicle; it used to drive around the Carnegie Mellon campus.

- Many AI systems are currently in use to control financial decisions—such as the purchase and sale of stocks. These systems use various AI technologies, such as neural networks, genetic algorithms, and expert systems.

- Web-based agents search the World Wide Web in pursuit of news articles that will interest their users.

This trend will no doubt continue as technological advances dramatically affect our lives. Ultimately, in the next millennium, the question of what it means to be a human being could well become a point of discussion.

Today it is not uncommon for people to live into their 80s and 90s. Life will continue to be extended. Medicine, coupled with advances in drugs, nutrition, and knowledge about human health, will continue to make remarkable advances that will combat the major causes of illness and death. In addition, advanced prosthetic devices will help handicapped individuals to lead lives with fewer physical restrictions. Eventually, intelligent systems that are small, unobtrusive, and embedded will be able to preserve and enhance peoples' mental capabilities. At some point, we will be confronted with the question, "Where does the person end and the machine begin, and vice versa?"

Initially, such systems will be very expensive, and therefore not available to the general population. In the early years there will arise major political issues to address and decisions concerning who should be privy to these advanced technologies. In time, standards of normalization will arise. But what will be the societal consequences of people living more than a hundred years? Who would not subject themselves to embedded hybrid materials (such as silicon circuitry) that could extend their lives to more than 100 years? How would life on this planet be different if it were to become overpopulated by seniors? Who will address where everyone lives, what will be the definition of life, and perhaps more importantly, when it ends? These will indeed be difficult moral and ethical issues.

The science fiction classic film, Soylent Green, delivers an interesting perspective on the future of AI.

Which AI methodology will be the champion of the future—the technique that will pave the way for the most progress in our lives? Will it be advances in logic, search, or knowledge representation? Or will we learn from the way that simple-looking systems organize to become complex systems with remarkable possibilities (e.g., from cellular automata, genetic algorithms, and agents)? What will expert systems do for us? Will fuzzy logic become the heretofore unheralded showcase for AI? What will be the progress in natural language processing, in vision, in robotics? And what of the possibilities provided by neural networks and machine learning? The answers to these questions will be difficult to obtain, but certainly as AI continues to emerge and affect our lives, a plethora of techniques will be employed to facilitate our lives.

With any technological advances come wonderful possibilities, but also new dangers. Dangers can be related to unexpected interactions of components and environments that can lead to accidents, and even catastrophes. Equally dangerous are the possibilities that technological advances combined with AI could fall into the hands of the wrong people. Consider, for example, the havoc and mayhem that would be caused if combat-enabled robots were snared by terrorists. It is probable that progress will not be stymied. People will probably accept the risks associated with the

Figure 1.25
Robot car assembly in the new millennium.

astounding possibilities accorded by these technologies, as well as their possible detrimental consequences; this will be done either explicitly or tacitly.

The notion of robots had been around even before AI. Currently, robots play an instrumental role in machine assembly. See Figure 1.25. Additionally, it is clear that robots are able to help mankind with mundane physical tasks such as vacuuming and shopping, and have the potential to help in more challenging arenas such as search and rescue, and telemedicine. In time, robots will also display emotion, feelings, and love (consider Paro and Cog),[67] behavior that we have always believed to be unique to mankind. Robots will be able to help people in every aspect of their lives, many of which are unforeseen at present. It is not far-fetched, however, to consider that robots perhaps blur the distinction between our "online lives" and our "real-world" lives. When will we define a person to be an android and what happens if (when?) robot intelligence becomes superior to that of humans? In attempting to predict the future of AI, it is hoped that consideration of these questions will better prepare us for the vagaries that could present themselves.

1.9 ■ CHAPTER SUMMARY

Chapter 1 sets the tone for thinking about AI. It addresses fundamental questions such as: What defines AI? What is thinking and what is intelligence? The reader is poised with considerations of what distinguishes human intelligence and how intelligence in animals would be measured.

Definitions of the Turing Test are provided, as well as controversies and criticisms surrounding it, such as Searle's Chinese Room.

The distinction between strong and weak AI methods is made and invites discussion of typical AI problems as well as solutions to them. The importance of heuristic methods in strong AI approaches and solutions is emphasized.

It is advisable to consider what kinds of problems are suitable for AI solutions and which kinds of problems are not. For example, medical challenges and similar domains where there exists much accrued human expertise (i.e., the game of chess) are particularly suitable for AI. Other domains, where simple and pure computation can be used to attain a solution or answer, are not considered suitable.

This chapter has introduced an exploration of AI applications and methods, including search algorithms, puzzles, and two person games. We have shown that closely related, often, as part of the underpinnings of many AI solutions, is the subject of automated reasoning. Considerable history and practical applications in the areas of production systems and expert systems have been presented with a distinctly historical perspective on the players and machines of early AI; and the more recent history with respect to games, expert systems, neural computing, evolutionary computation and natural language processing has also been reviewed. It has been shown that cellular automata and neural computation are sophisticated areas, which are less knowledge-based, but produce good results. We have discussed evolutionary computation as a newer area of AI that has great promise, and knowledge representation, which addresses the diverse representational choices open to AI researchers for solution design. It has also been made evident that uncertainty reasoning employing statistical, probabilistic decision-making has become a popular and rewarding approach to many AI challenges. This chapter has answered the significant questions: "Who did the work that brought us to where we are?" and "How was this accomplished?"

Questions for Discussion

1. How would you define Artificial Intelligence?

2. Distinguish between strong and weak AI.

3. ALICE is the software that has won the Loebner Prize several times in the recent past. Go online to find a version of this software. What can you tell us about ALICE?

4. What was Alan Turing's significant contribution to Artificial Intelligence?

5. What did John McCarthy contribute to Artificial Intelligence?

6. Why would an ATM and its programming not be a good example of AI programming?

7. Why is medical diagnosis a very typical and suitable domain for AI research?

8. Why have two-person games been a very suitable domain of study for AI?

9. Explain the role of computer chess with regard to AI.

10. What is an expert system?

11. Name three forms of knowledge representation.

Exercises

1. A variation of the Turing test is the so-called Inverted Turing test; in this test, a computer must determine whether it is dealing with a person or another computer. Can you envision any practical applications for this version of the Turing test? (*Hint*: In recent years, have you tried purchasing tickets for a popular sports or entertainment event online?)

2. A second variation of the Turing test is the Personal Turing test. Imagine you are trying to determine if you are communicating with your friend or with a computer pretending to be your friend. If a computer passes this test, what legal or ethical questions do you envision will arise?

3. Many people consider the use of language as a necessary attribute of intelligence. Koko is a gorilla trained by Dr. Francine Patterson of Stanford University in the use of American Sign Language. Koko was able to form word combinations for words unknown to her; for example, she represented the word ring by the words bracelet and finger, which she already knew. Does this gorilla's possession of knowledge modify your thinking on the subject of animal intelligence? If so, then in what ways? Could you envision an intelligence test for Koko?

4. Consider the following tests for a city to be considered a great city:

    - It should be possible to obtain a steak dinner at 3:00 a.m.
    - A classical music concert should be scheduled somewhere within the city bounds each evening.
    - A major sporting event should be scheduled each evening.

    Further, suppose a small town somewhere in America determines that they want to pass this test. To do so, they open a 24-hour steak joint and purchase a symphony orchestra and major sports franchise. Do you feel that this small town passes our litmus test for being a great city? Relate this discussion to the criteria for passing the original Turing test and the possession of intelligence (Dennett, 2004).

5. Suppose you want to design a threshold logic unit to emulate a two-input OR function. Can you determine a threshold and the weights to accomplish this task?

6. Suggest a strategy for the Iterated Prisoner's Dilemma, wherein the game is repeated n times for some unknown value n. How might you measure its success in the long run?

7. A genetic algorithm is to be employed to solve the instance of the 3-puzzle provided in the text. Suggest a string representation for a potential solution. What fitness function would you suggest?

8. Suggest a heuristic that would help to hail a taxi on a visit to New York City (or any other major city) during rush hour when taxis are scarce.

9. What heuristic do lions employ as they pursue their prey?

10. Suggest possible rules for an expert system designed to help select a suitable dog for your household.

11. Before Copernicus, the earth was considered to be the center of the heavens. After Copernicus, the earth was merely one of many planets circling the sun. Before Darwin, humans were considered to be a species apart (and above?) the rest of the living organisms on this planet. After Darwin, we were just another species of animals that had evolved from one-celled organisms. Suppose that in fifty years we have achieved human-level AI, and further suppose that successors to the robots Cog, Paro, and Kismet actually experience emotions rather than just pretending to do so. At such a point in our history, what claims will humans cling to as forming the core of their "specialness"? Are such claims essential or even desirable?

12. Suppose that at some time in the future, NASA plans an unmanned mission to Europa, a moon of the planet Jupiter. Suppose that at the time of launch our understanding of this moon's surface is scant. Suggest advantages to sending an "army" of Rodney Brooks-insect-type robots rather than one or two more substantial machines.

13. Should Eliza be considered a relational artifact? Defend your answer.

14. Listen to the song "Are We Human or Are We Dancer?" by Killers. What do you believe the lyrics of this song mean, and how do they relate to our course of study? You might wish to consult the lively online discussion (the song can be accessed on YouTube).

15. How would you define AI problems to be different from other types of problems? Name five problem solving techniques typically used in AI?

16. Develop a new Turing Test for AI that would be applicable today.

17. Research the Lovelace 2 Robot (*http://www.bbc.com/news/technology-30144069*) . Do you feel that the criteria for this new Turing Test for Robots is acceptable? How would you compare it to your answer in Question 2?

Keywords

15-puzzle	discriminant	neural computing
3-puzzle	domain-specific knowledge	neural networks
8-puzzle	evolutionary computation	Nim
A* algorithm	expert system	parse trees
abstraction	fitness function	passing the Turing test
adversarial games	frames	perceptron learning rule
agent	functionality	perfect information
algorithm	Game of Life	production rules
artificial	General Problem Solver	script
Artificial Intelligence (AI)	(GPS)	semantic network
automated reasoning	genetic algorithm (GA)	slots and fillers
backpropagation	goal state	space tree
beam search	heuristic	start state
best first search	hill climbing	state-space graph
black box	imitation game	stored program concept
blackboard architecture	implementation	strong AI
blind search	intelligence	Turing test
blocks world	Iterated Prisoner's Dilemma	threshold logic unit (TLU)
branch and bound	iterative learning algorithm	Universal Turing machine
breadth first search	knowledge engineer	uncertainty
cellular automaton (CA)	learning rules	universe of discourse
combinatorial explosion	logic	Water Jug Problem
common sense	Logic Theorist	weak AI
conceptual graph	microworld	world knowledge
context-free grammar	Missionaries and Cannibals	zero sum game
depth first search	Problem	

References

1. Dreyfus, H. L., and Dreyfus, S. E. 1986. *Mind over machine*. New York, NY: The Free Press.

2. Michie, D. L. 1986. *On Machine Intelligence,* 2nd edition. Chichester, England: Ellis Horwood.

3. Sokolowksi, R. 1989. Natural and Artificial Intelligence. In *The Artificial Intelligence debate*, ed. S. R. Graubard. Cambridge, MA: The MIT Press.

4. Sternberg, R. J. 1994. *In search of the human mind*. 395–396. New York, NY: Harcourt-Brace.

5. Reader's Digest 1994. *Intelligence in animals*. London, England: Toucan Books Limited.

6. Raphael, B. 1976. *The thinking computer*. San Francisco, CA: W.H. Freeman.

7. Turing, A. M. 1950. Computing machinery and intelligence. *Mind* L I X 236:433–460.

8. Fromm, E. 1956. *The art of loving*. (Paperback ed). Harper Perennial.

9. Block, N. 2004. Psychoanalysis and behaviorism. Reprinted in *The Turing Test*. Ed. S. Shieber. Cambridge, MA: The MIT Press.

10. Searle, J. R. 2004 Minds, brains, and programs. Reprinted in *The Turing Test*. Ed. S. Shieber. Cambridge, MA: The MIT Press.

11. Dennett, D.C. 2004. Can machines think? Reprinted in *The Turing Test*. Ed. by S. Shieber. Cambridge, MA: The MIT Press.

12. Turing, A.M. 1936. On computable numbers, with an application to the entscheidongs problem. In *Proceedings of the London Mathematical Society* 2:230–265.

13. Polya, G. 1957. *How to solve it*, 2nd ed., Princeton, NJ: Princeton University Press.

14. Newell, A. and Simon, H. A. 1963. GPS: a program that simulates human thought. In *Computers and thought*, ed. Feigenbaum and Feldman. New York, NY: McGraw Hill.

15. Shortliffe, E. H. 1976. *Computer-based medical consultation: MYCIN*. Amsterdam, London, New York, NY: Elsevier-North-Holland.

16. Gardner, M. 1970. Mathematical games: The fantastic combinations of John Conway's new solitaire game "life." *Scientific American* 223 (October):120–123.

17. McCulloch, W. S. and Pitts, W. 1943. A logical calculus of the ideas imminent in nervous activity. *Bulletin of Mathematical Biophysics* 5:115–133.

18. Newell, A. and Simon, H. A. 1963. Empirical explorations with the logic theory machine: A case study in heuristics. In *Computers and thought*, ed. Feigenbaum and Feldman., New York, NY: McGraw Hill.

19. Whitehead, A. N. and Russell, B. 1950. *Principia Mathematica*, 2nd ed. London, England: Cambridge University Press.

20. Winograd, T. 1972. *Understanding natural language*. New York, NY: Academic Press.

21. Nilsson, N. 1980. *Principles of Artificial Intelligence*. Palo Alto, CA: Tioga.

22. Genesereth, M. and Nilsson, N. 1987. *Logical foundations of Artificial Intelligence*. Los Altos, CA: Morgan Kaufmann.

23. Bundy, A. 1983. *The computer modeling of mathematical reasoning*. Academic Press, San Diego, CA.

24. Quillian, M. R. 1967. World concepts: A theory and simulation of some basic semantic capabilities. In *Readings in Knowledge Representation*, ed. R. Brachman and H. Levesque. Los Altos, CA: Morgan Kaufmann, 1985.

25. Shapiro, S. C. 1979. The SNePS semantic network processing system. In *Associative networks: Representation and use of knowledge by computers*, ed. N.V. Findler, 179–203. New York, NY: Academic Press.

26. Schank, R. C. and Rieger, C. J. 1974. Inference and the computer understanding of natural language. *Artificial Intelligence*, 5(4):373–412.

27. Minsky, M. 1975. A framework for representing knowledge. In *Readings in Knowledge Representation*, ed. R. Brachman and H. Levesque. Los Altos, CA: Morgan Kaufmann, 1985.

28. Schank, R. C. and Abelson, R. 1977. *Scripts, plans, goals, and understanding*. Hillsdale, NJ: Erlbaum.

29. Sowa, J. F. 1984. *Conceptual structures: Information processing in mind and machine*. Reading, MA: Addison-Wesley.

30. Nowak, J. D. and Gowin, R. B. 1985. *Learning how to learn*. Cambridge, England: Cambridge University Press.

31. Minsky, M. 1985. *A society of mind*. New York, NY: Simon and Schuster.

32. Zadeh, L. 1983. Commonsense knowledge representation based on fuzzy logic. *Computer*, 16:61–64.

33. Levy, D. N. L. 2006. *Robots unlimited: Life in the virtual age*. Wellesley, MA: AK Peters, LTD.

34. Godel, K. 1931. On formally undecideable propositions of 'principia mathematica' and related systems (Paperback). New York, NY: Dover Publications.

35. Descartes, R. 1680. *Six metaphysical meditations. Wherein it is proved that there is a God and the man's mind is really distinct from his body*. Translated by W. Moltneux. London: Printed for B. Tooke.

36. Luger, G. F. 2002. *Artificial Intelligence: Structures and strategies for complex problem solving*. Reading, MA: Addison-Wesley.

37. Brooks, F. P. 1975/1995 2nd ed. *The mythical man-month: Essays on software engineering* paperback. Reading, MA: Addison-Wesley.

38. Boole, G. 1854. *An investigation of the laws of thought*. London, England: Walton & Maberly.

39. Shannon, C. E. 1938. A symbolic analysis of relay and switching circuits. *Transactions American Institute of Electrical Engineers* 57:713–723.

40. Shannon, C. E. 1950. Programming a computer for playing chess. *Philosophical Magazine* 7th Ser., 41: 256–275.

41. Samuel, A. L. 1959. Some studies in machine learning using the game of checkers. *IBM Journal of Research and Development* 3(3).

42. Turing, A. M. 1953. Digital computers applied to games. In *Faster than thought*, ed. B. V. Bowden, 286–310. London, England: Pitman.

43. Greenblatt, R. D., Eastlake III, D. E., and Crocker S. D. 1976. The Greenblatt chess program. In *Proceedings of the Fall Joint Computing Conference* 31:801–810. San Francisco, New York, NY: ACM.

44. Berliner, H. J. and Ebeling, C. 1989. Pattern knowledge and search: The SUPREM architecture. *Artificial Intelligence* 38:161–196.

45. Hsu, F-H., Anantharaman, T., Campbell, M., and Nowatzyk, A.1990. A grandmaster chess machine. *Scientific American* 2634.

46. Kopec, D. 1996. Kasparov vs. Deep Blue: Mankind is safe – for now. *Chess Life* May:42–51.

47. Schaeffer, J. 1997. *One jump ahead*. New York, NY: Springer-Verlag.

48. Buchanan, B. G. and Feigenbaum, E. A. 1978. Dendral and meta-dendral: Their applications dimensions. *Intelligence Artificial* 11.

49. Duda, R. O., Gaschnig, J., and Hart, P. E. 1979. Model design in the PROSPECTOR consultant for mineral exploration. In *Expert systems in the microelectronic age*, ed. D. Michie. Edinburgh, Scotland: Edinburgh University Press.

50. McDermott, J. 1982. R1: A rule-based configurer of computer systems. *Artificial Intelligence* 19(1).

51. Clancey, W. J. and Shortliffe, E. H., eds. 1984. *Readings in medical Artificial Intelligence: The first decade*. Reading, MA: Addison-Wesley.

52. Davis, R. and Lenat, D. B. 1982. Knowledge-based systems in artificial intelligence. New York, NY: McGraw-Hill.

53. Erman, L. D., Hayes-Roth, F., Lesser, V., and Reddy, R. D. 1980. The HEARSAY II speech understanding system: Integrating knowledge to resolve uncertainty. *Computing Surveys* 12(2):213–253.

54. Lenat, D. B. 1977. On automated scientific theory formation: A case study using the AM program. *Machine Intelligence* 9:251–256.

55. Van Melle,W., Shortliffe, E. H., and Buchanan, B. G. 1981. EMYCIN: A domain-independent system that aids in constructing knowledge-based consultation programs. *Machine Intelligence. Infotech State of the Art Report 9*, no. 3.

56. Forgy, C. L. 1979. On the efficient implementation of production systems. *PhD thesis*, Carnegie-Mellon University.

57. Giarratano, J. 1993. *CLIPS user's guide*. NASA, Version 6.2 of CLIPS.

58. Rosenblatt, F. 1958. The perceptron: A probabilistic model for information storage and organization in the brain. *Psychological Review* 65: 386–408.

59. Minsky, M. and Papert, S. 1969. *Perceptrons: An introduction to computational geometry*. Cambridge, MA: The MIT Press.

60. Hopfield, J. J. 1982. Neural networks and physical systems with emergent collective computational abilities. In Proceedings of the National Academy of Sciences 79: 2554–2558.

61. Hopfield, J. J. and Tank, D. 1985. Neural computation of decisions in optimization problems. *Biological Cybernetics* 52:141–152.

62. Sejnowski, T. J. and Rosenberg, C. R. 1987. Parallel networks that learn to pronounce English text. *Complex Systems* 1:145–168.

63. Pomerleau, D. A. 1989. ALVINN: An autonomous land vehicle in a neural network. In *Advances in neural information processing systems 1*. Palo Alto, CA: Morgan Kaufman.

64. Holland, J. H. 1975. *Adaptation in natural and artificial systems*. Ann Arbor, Michigan: University of Michigan Press.

65. Brooks, R. A. 1996. The cog project. *Journal of the Robotics Society of Japan*, Special Issue (Mini) on Humanoid, ed. T. Matsui. 15(7).

66. Weizenbaum, J. 1966. Eliza – A computer program for the study of natural language communication between man and machine. *Communications of the ACM* 9:36–45.

67. Turkle, S. 2006. Artificial Intelligence at 50: From building intelligence to nurturing sociabilities.

In *Proceedings of AI @ 50*, Dartmouth College, Hanover, New Hampshire.

68. Fennell, R. D. and Lesser, V. R. 1986. Parallelism in Artificial Intelligence problem-solving: A case study of Hearsay-II. *Tutorial on parallel processing* 185–198. New York, NY: IEEE Computer Society.

69. Wolf, J. J. and Woods, W. A. 1976. The Journal of the *Acoustical Society of America* 60(S1):811.

70. Lenat, D. B. 1995. Cyc: A large-scale investment in knowledge infrastructure. *Communications of the ACM* 38(11).

71. Charniak, E. 2006. Why natural language processing is now statistical natural language processing.

In *Proceedings of AI @ 50*, Dartmouth College, Hanover, New Hampshire.

72. Marcus, M. P. Santorini, B., and Marcinkiewicz, M. A. 1993. Building a large annotated corpus of English: The Penn Treebank. *Computational Linguistics* 19(2):313–330.

73. Livingston, G. R., Rosenberg, J. M., and Buchanan, B. J. 2001. Closing the loop: Heuristics for autonomous discovery. In *Proceedings of the 2001 IEEE International Conference on Data Mining* 393–400. San Jose, CA: IEEE Computer Society Press.

74. Glasgow, J., Jurisica, I., and Rost, B. 2004. AI and bioinformatics (Editorial). *AI Magazine* Spring: 7–8.

Bibliography

Boole, G. *The Mathematical Analysis of Logic: Being an Essay Towards a Calculus of Deductive Reasoning.* Cambridge: Macmillan, Barclay, and MacMillan, 1847.

Brachman, R. J. and Levesque, J. *Readings in Knowledge Representation.* Los Altos, CA: Morgan Kaufmann, 1985.

Brooks, R. A. "Elephants Don't Play Chess." *Robotics and Autonomous Systems* 6(1990):3–15.

Buchanan, B. G. and Feigenbaum, E. A. *Rule-Based Expert Programs: The MYCIN Experiments of the Stanford University Heuristic Programming Project.* Reading, Massachusetts: Addison-Wesley, 1984.

Glasgow, J., Jurisica, I., and Burkhard, R. "AI and Bioinformatics." *AAAI Magazine* 25, 1 (Spring 2004): 7–8.

Kopec, D. Advances in Man-Machine Play. In *Computers, Chess and Cognition*, Edited by T.A. Marsland and J. Schaeffer, 9–33. New York: Springer-Verlag, 1990.

Kopec, D., Shamkovich, L., and Schwartzman, G. Kasparov – Deep Blue. *Chess Life* Special Summer Issue (July 1997): 45–55.

Levy, David N. L. *Chess and Computers.* Rockville, Maryland: Computer Science Press, 1976.

Michie, D. "King and Rook against King: Historical Background and a Problem for the Infinite Board." In

Advances in Computer Chess I. Edited by M. R. B. Clarke. Edinburgh, Scotland: Edinburgh University Press, 1977.

Michie, D. "Chess with Computers." *Interdisciplinary Science Reviews* 5, 3(1980): 215–227.

Michie, D. (with R. Johnston). *The Creative Computer.* Harmondsworth, England: Viking, 1984.

Molla, M.,Waddell, M., Page, D., Shavlik, J. "Using Machine Learning to Design and Interpret Gene-Expression Microarrays." *AI Magazine* 25 (2004): 23–44.

Nair, R. and Rost, B. "Annotating Protein Function Through Lexical Analysis." *AAA Magazine* 25, 1 (Spring 2004): 44–56.

Newborn, M. Deep Blue: *An Artificial Intelligence Milestone.* New York: Springer-Verlag, 2002.

Rich, E. *Artificial Intelligence.* New York: McGraw-Hill, 1983.

SAT – Aptitude and subject exams administered several times annually by the College Board. For information go to *www.collegeboard.com.*

Standage, T. *The Turk.* New York: Walker Publishing Company, 2002.

Many **AI researchers** would argue that *search* and the methods by which it is performed are fundamental to AI. Chapter 2 concentrates on uninformed search and how it is performed.

Chapter 3 introduces the notion of heuristics and diverse search techniques that have been developed to exploit them. The concept of optimality in search including the branch and bound techniques and the relatively neglected bidirectional search are presented. Search in games is the focus of Chapter 4. The well-defined rules and objectives of games, particularly two-person games, allow for development of methods such as minimax, alpha-beta, and expectimax to effectively guide computer play.

Some researchers view logic as the basis for AI. Logic for representation, propositional logic, predicate logic, and several other logics, are presented in Chapter 5. Others would argue that the choice of representation is integral to human and machine problem solving. Notions of graphs, frames, concept maps, semantic networks, and the agent view of the world are presented in Chapter 6. Discussion of "*Strong*" and "*Weak*" approaches to AI provides the background for production systems as a powerful and well-recognized method for knowledge representation and problem-solving in AI (Chapter 7). Cellular automata and Markov Chains are also introduced.

UNINFORMED SEARCH

Missionaries and Cannibals

In this chapter, we begin our study with one of the most important problems frequently encountered in Artificial Intelligence—search. Our goal in this text is to present the most prevalent methods used to solve problems in AI: search, knowledge representation, and learning. We begin our study of rudimentary search algorithms—so-called "uninformed" or "blind search" methods. These algorithms do not rely on any special knowledge about a problem domain. As we shall see, these algorithms often require inordinate amounts of space and time.

▪2.0▪ INTRODUCTION: SEARCH IN INTELLIGENT SYSTEMS

Search is a natural part of most peoples' lives. Who among us has not misplaced house keys or the TV's remote control, and then retraced our footsteps around our home, overturning cushions and checking pockets? At times a search might be more cerebral. You have probably had occasions when you simply cannot recall the name of a place you have visited, the name of an actor in a movie you had really enjoyed, or the words to a song you once knew so well. It could be seconds (or longer, as one grows older) before the memory ceases to elude you.

Many algorithms are devoted to searching and sorting through a list. Certainly, one would agree that searching is facilitated if the data is organized in logical order. Imagine how cumbersome it would be to search through a phone book of a relatively large city if the names and phone numbers were arranged randomly. It should therefore come as no surprise that search and organization play important roles in the design of intelligent systems. Perhaps it is the search for the name of a locale once visited, or the next number in a sequence (Chapter 1, "Overview of Artificial Intelligence"), the next best move in a game of tic-tac-toe or checkers (Chapters 4, "Search Using Games," and 16, "Advanced Computer Games") or perhaps the shortest route through some number of cities (later in this chapter). People who can solve such problems very quickly are often deemed to be more intelligent than others. The same term is often applied to software systems, where, for example, a better chess-playing program could also be considered to be more intelligent than its counterparts.

This chapter provides an introduction to several basic search algorithms. Section 2.1 begins with an explanation of state-space graphs, a mathematical structure that helps to formalize the search process. This structure is shown for the well-known False Coin Problem in which a counterfeit coin must be identified by weighing two or more coins. Next, the chapter introduces and explains the generate-and-test search paradigm. A generator module systematically proposes possible solutions for a problem, and the tester module verifies their correctness.

Two classic approaches to search are also introduced: the *greedy algorithm* and *backtracking*. Each of these approaches begins by dividing a problem into stages. For example, if you want to place eight Queens on a chessboard so that no two Queens are attacking each other —that is, so that no two Queens occupy the same row, column, or diagonal—then Stage 1 might consist of placing the first Queen on the board, Stage 2 in placing the second Queen on a safe square, and so on. As you will see in Section 2.2, these methods differ from one another with regard to the criteria used for making a particular choice.

Blind search algorithms are explained in Section 2.3. A blind, or uninformed, search algorithm is one that makes no use of problem domain knowledge. Suppose, for example, that you are finding your way through a maze. In a blind search you might always choose the far left route regardless of any other alternatives. Two quintessential blind search algorithms are **breadth first search (bfs)** and **depth first search (dfs)**, which were introduced briefly in Chapter 1. Recall that bfs explores all alternatives at a prescribed distance from the start position before proceeding any further. A bfs has the advantage that if a solution exists for a problem, then bfs will find it. However, if the number of alternatives at each juncture is large, then bfs could require too much memory, and it becomes infeasible. Dfs, on the other hand, pursues a different strategy to reach the goal: it pursues a single path to its conclusion before pursuing alternate paths. Dfs has reasonable memory requirements; however, it could stray arbitrarily far from the start position and might thereby miss a solution that lies closer to the beginning of the search. Dfs with iterative deepening is a compromise between bfs and dfs; it combines the moderate space requirements of dfs with the certainty of finding a solution, which bfs provides.

2.1 ■ STATE-SPACE GRAPHS

State-space graphs display a representation of a problem whereby possible alternative paths leading to a solution can be explored and analyzed. A solution to a particular problem will correspond to a path through a state-space graph. Sometimes we search for any solution to a problem; at other times we desire a shortest (or optimal) solution. This chapter will focus primarily on so-called blind search methods that seek to discover any solution. Chapter 3, "Informed Search," will concentrate on informed search algorithms, which often discover optimal solutions to a problem.

2.1.1 ■ The False Coin Problem

A well-known problem in computer science is the **False Coin Problem**. There are 12 coins, one of which is known to be false, or counterfeit. It is not known, however, whether the false coin is lighter or heavier than the others. An ordinary balance scale can be used to determine if any two sets of coins weigh the same or if one set is heavier or lighter than the other. To solve the problem, you should be able to create a procedure to identify the false coin by weighing only three combinations of coins.

In this chapter, we will solve a simpler instance of this problem involving only six coins; it also requires comparing three sets of coins as in the original problem above, but in this case the sets are smaller. We call this the Mini False Coin Problem. We use the notation $C_{i1} C_{i2}...C_{ir} : C_{j1} C_{j2}...C_{jr}$ to indicate that the r coins $C_{i1} C_{i2}...C_{ir}$ are being weighed against the r coins $C_{j1} C_{j2}...C_{jr}$. The result will be that the two sets of coins weigh the same or that they do not. We will not require further knowledge about whether the coins on the left weigh more or less than the coins on the right. (That additional knowledge is required to solve the 12-coin version of this problem.) Finally, we employ the notation $[C_{k1} C_{k2}...C_{km}]$ to indicate that a subset of m coins is the smallest set known to contain the false coin. One solution to this Mini False Coin Problem is provided in Figure 2.1.

Figure 2.1 is an example of a state-space tree. A state-space tree consists of nodes and branches. An oval is a node and represents a state of the problem. Arcs between nodes represent operators (or results of operators) that take the state-space tree to new nodes. Consult the node in Figure 2.1 labeled with (*). This node $[C_1 C_2 C_3 C_4]$ indicates that the false coin might be any one of C_1, C_2, C_3, or C_4. We have decided to weigh C_1 and C_2 versus C_5 and C_6 (operator applied). If the result is that these sets of two coins each are equal in weight, then we know that the false coin must be one of C_3 or C_4; if they are unequal then we are sure that one of C_1 or C_2 is the false coin. *Why?* There are two special types of nodes. The first is a **start node** that represents the **start state** of a problem. In Figure 2.1, the start node is $[C_1 C_2 C_3 C_4 C_5 C_6]$, which indicates that when we begin, the false coin could be any one of the six coins. Another special type of node corresponds to a final or terminal state of the

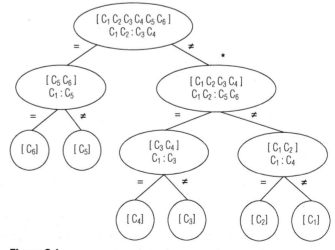

Figure 2.1
A solution for the Mini False Coin Problem.

problem. The state-space tree in Figure 2.1 has six terminal nodes; each labeled $[C_i]$, where $i = 1,...,6$ and where the value of i specifies which coin is false.

The state-space tree for a problem contains all states that a problem could be in, as well as all possible transitions between these states. In fact, because loops often occur, such a structure is more generally called a state-space graph. The solution for a problem often entails a search through this structure (whether it is a tree or graph) that begins at a start state and culminates at a final or **goal state**. Sometimes we are concerned with finding a solution (whatever its cost); at other times we might desire a solution of minimum cost.

> By the *cost* of a solution, we are referring to the number of operators required to reach a goal state and *not* to the amount of work required to actually find this solution. An analogy to computer science might be that we are equating a solution's cost with *running time* rather than *software development time*.

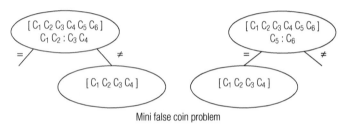

Mini false coin problem

Figure 2.2
Distinct nodes in a state-space graph can represent the same state.

A solution to the Mini False Coin Problem is shown in Figure 2.1. It might be true that the person solving this problem is wearing a blue shirt, or that someone else needed a tall cup of coffee before tackling the 12-coin version of the problem. Such details, however, are, and should remain, extraneous to a solution. Abstraction allows you to exorcise such minutiae.

Heretofore we have used the terms node and state interchangeably. However, these are distinct concepts. In general, a state-space graph can contain many nodes that represent the same problem state, as shown in Figure 2.2. Revisiting the Mini False Coin Problem, we observe that by weighing two different sets of coins, we can arrive at distinct nodes that represent the same state.

Abstraction was defined in Chapter 1 as the process whereby certain details of a system can be advantageously ignored in order to allow interaction at an appropriate level. For example, if you want to play baseball, it would serve you better to practice learning how to hit a curveball than to spend six years earning a PhD in the mechanics of moving objects.

2.2 GENERATE-AND-TEST PARADIGM

A straightforward way to solve a problem is to propose possible solutions and then to check whether each proposal constitutes a solution. This is referred to as the **generate-and-test paradigm**; the approach is illustrated with the *n*-Queens Problem, shown in Figure 2.3.

The *n*-**Queens Problem** involves placing *n* Queens on an $n \times n$ chessboard so that no two Queens are attacking. That is, no two Queens should occupy the same row, column, or diagonal on the board. These conditions are referred to as the constraints of the problem. The proposed solutions in Figure 2.4(a) – (c) violate various constraints of the problem. A solution to the 4-Queens problem appears in Figure 2.4(d).

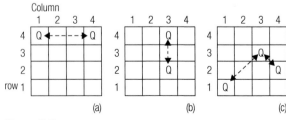

Figure 2.3
The n-Queens problem. No two Queens should occupy (a) the same row, (b) the same column, or (c) the same diagonal.

In this problem four queens need to be placed on a 4 × 4 chessboard. There are a total of $_{16}C_4$, or 1820, ways to accomplish this. As Figure 2.4 illustrates, many of these proposed solutions violate one or more of the problem constraints. However, if a solution is not to be missed, then a reliable generator must propose every subset of size four that satisfies the problem constraints. More generally, a reliable generator is complete if it proposes every possible solution. Furthermore, if a proposed solution is rejected, it should not be proposed again (in fact, even successful proposals should be made only once). In other words, a good generator should be **nonredundant**. Finally, recall that there are 1820 ways to place four Queens on a 4 × 4 chessboard. The generator would be more efficient if it did not propose solutions that would obviously fail. Figure 2.4(a) shows an example in which all problem constraints are violated. We say that a generator is **informed** if it possesses some information that allows it to limit its proposals.

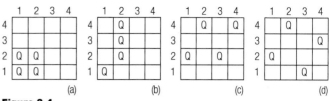

Figure 2.4
Several proposed solutions for the 4-Queens problem: (a) every constraint is violated; (b) two Queens appear on the same diagonal and three in the same column; (c) Queens appear in the same row; (d) a solution has been found.

A procedure for the generate-and-test paradigm would look like the following:

```
{While no solution is found and more candidates remain
     [Generate a possible solution
      Test if all problem constraints are satisfied]
End While}
If a solution has been found, announce success and output it.
Else announce no solution found.
```

EXAMPLE 2.1: GENERATE AND TEST FOR PRIME NUMBERS

Suppose you must determine whether a given number between 3 and 100, inclusive, is a prime. Recall that an integer $N \geq 2$ is prime if its only factors are 1 and itself. So 17 and 23 are prime whereas 33 is not, because it is the product of 3 and 11. Assume that you must solve this problem without benefit of a computer or pocket calculator. Your first attempt at a solution, using the generate-and-test approach, might look like the following pseudocode:

```
{While the problem is not yet solved and more
     possible factors for Number
remain:
     [Generate a possible factor for Number
     /*possible factors will be generated in the
     order 2, 3, 4, 5, ..
Number*/
     Test: If (Number) / (possible factor) is an integer >= 2
     Then return not prime]
End While}
```

If possible factor equals Number,
Then return Number is prime

If Number is equal to 85, then the Test fails for possible factors of 2, 3, and 4. However, 85/5 yields 17, so we can declare that 85 is not prime. If number is equal to 37, then we exit the While Loop with possible factors equal to 37 as well and return that 37 is prime.

A more informed generator checks only possible factors up to floor (square root (Number)). Recall that floor of a number is the largest integer ≤ that number; for example floor (3.14) = 3, floor (2) = 2, and floor (−5.17) = −6. For Number equal to 37 in the previous example, the informed generator returns that 37 is prime after only checking 2, 3, 4, 5, and 6 as possible factors. More informed generators lead to vast savings in time and complexity.

2.2.1 Backtracking

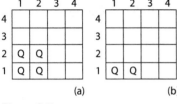

Our first approach to solving the 4-Queens problem employed a generator that, in the worst case, checks each of the 1820 ways of placing four Queens on a 4 × 4 chessboard.

Note that the placement depicted in part (a) of Figure 2.5 is not a solution to the 4-Queens problem. In fact, this proposed solution violates every constraint of that problem. It is safe to assume that the solution in Figure 2.5(a) was generated one Queen at a time.

Figure 2.5
(a) Four Queens on a 4 x 4 Chessboard. (b) Two Queens on a 4 x 4 chessboard. Is it prudent to continue with this proposed solution?

Suppose that the first two Queens proposed are as shown in Figure 2.5(b). This is called a **partial solution.**

Exhaustive enumeration is a search methodology that looks everywhere for a solution to a problem. A partial solution is developed further even after it has been discovered that this set of steps cannot possibly lead to a successful problem solution.

Exhaustive enumeration, having started with the partial solution depicted in Figure 2.5(b), would continue to place two additional Queens on the chessboard, even though any way of placing these Queens is doomed to failure. It is required that the tester check that no problem constraints are violated after each portion of a proposed solution is provided.

Backtracking is an improvement to exhaustive enumeration. A proposed solution to a problem is divided into stages. In our 4-Queens problem, we naturally equate each stage with the placement of one Queen on the chessboard. Consider the possible squares on which a Queen is placed in some prescribed order. In Stage i, Queens have been successfully placed in Stages $1,...,$ i-1. If no square remains on which the ith Queen may be placed without violating any of the constraints, then we must return to Stage i-1. That is, we must backtrack to the stage concerned with placement of the $(i$-1)st Queen. We undo the placement of this Queen at Stage i-1, make the next choice for the Queen, and return to Stage i. If it is not possible to successfully place the $(i$-1)st Queen, then backtracking continues to Stage i-2.

We can use backtracking with the generate-and-test paradigm. The test module is permitted to view a possible solution as it is being developed. We will use a generator that attempts to place one Queen in each column of the chessboard as opposed to the less informed generator that considered all $_{16}C_4$, or 1820, placements. Our algorithm contains four stages, as shown in Figure 2.6.

In Stage 1, we attempt to place the first Queen in column one. Figure 2.6 illustrates the beginning of a backtracking solution to the 4-Queens problem. Board positions may be represented by a vector with four row components: (1,3,-,-) represents the partial solution shown in Figure 2.6(c).

The Queen in column 1 is in row 1, the Queen in column 2 is in row 3, and the two dashes in positions 3 and 4 of the vector indicate that the third and fourth Queens have not yet been placed in the two remaining rows. This vector (1,3,-,-) is shown in (column 3) Figure 2.6(d) to represent a partial solution that cannot possibly lead to a total solution; this insight is reached in Stage 3 as the algorithm attempts to place a Queen in the third column. Backtracking to Stage 2 and then eventually to Stage 1 will be required before it is possible to successfully place the third and fourth Queens on this chessboard. These steps are shown in Figure 2.7.

The algorithm will eventually backtrack all the way to Stage 1; Queen 1 is now placed in row 2 as shown in Figure 2.7(e). The algorithm is poised to move forward once again. Subsequent proposed steps on the way to finding a solution are shown in Figure 2.8.

This solution can be represented in a vector as (2,4,1,3). Are other solutions possible? If so, how would we find them?

It turns out that the 4-Queens problem has one additional solution. To find it, print out the solution shown in Figure 2.8, and then invoke your backtracking routine. Figure 2.9 shows the steps in discovering the second solution, which is (3,1,4,2).

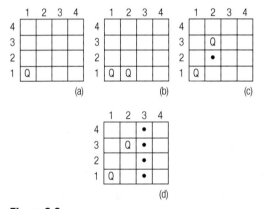

Figure 2.6
Backtracking-based solution to the 4-Queens problem. (a) Stage 1: Queen 1 is placed in row 1, column 1. (b) Stage 2: Queen 2 is placed in row 1, column 2. (c) The test module returns "invalid" to the placement in (b). Queen 2 is next placed in row 2 and then in row 3 of column 2. (d) Stage 3: We attempt to place a Queen in column 3; this is not possible; it is necessary to backtrack to Stage 2.

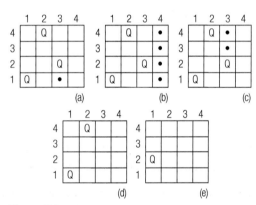

Figure 2.7
Backtracking-based solution to the 4-Queens problem, continued.(a) Backtracking to Stage 2 has occurred; Queen 2 is placed on row 4. Return to Stage 3. Queen 3 may not be placed on row 1. (Why not?) It is then placed on row 2. This figure is represented by vector (1,4,2,-). (b) Stage 4: The algorithm is unable to place Queen 4; a return to Stage 3 is required. (c) Stage 3: Queen 3 cannot be successfully placed in column 3. Backtracking to Stage 2 is required. (d) In Stage 2 there is no place to put Queen 2; we must backtrack once again. (e) Stage 1: Queen 1 is placed in row 2, column 1.

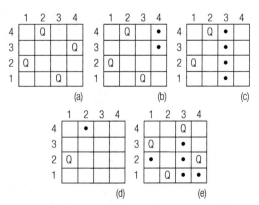

Figure 2.8
Backtracking-based solution to the 4-Queens problem,concluded. In Stage 2, Queen 2 is finally positioned in row 4. In Stage 3, the Queen rests in row 1, and in Stage 4 Queen 4 is placed in row 3.

Figure 2.9
The 4-Queens Problem—finding a second solution. (a) The first solution. (b) Previous placement (2,4,1,3) declared void and backtracking begins. (c) Nowhere for Queen 3 to reside. (d) Bactrack to Stage 2.; Queen has nowhere to rest. Backtrack to Stage 1. (e) Second solution is found.

The 4-Queens problem has two solutions: (2,4,1,3) and (3,1,4,2). These solutions have a symmetric relationship. In fact you can obtain one solution from the other by vertically flipping the chessboard. (The issue of **symmetry** and the role that it plays will be pursued further in the Chapter 4 exercises.)

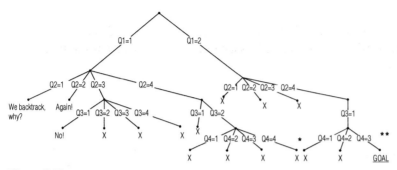

Figure 2.10
Search tree representing the previous backtracking-based solution to the 4-Queens problem. The four levels in this tree correspond to the four stages in the problem. The left branch from the root corresponds to all partial solutions that begin with the first Queen in row 1.

The information for the search conducted by backtracking to find the first solution to the 4-Queens problem, as illustrated in Figures 2.6 through 2.8, can also be represented by the search tree in Figure 2.10.

The node in the left subtree at level 4, marked with *, corresponds to proposed solution (1,4,2,4). The tester will obviously reject this proposal. Backtracking in this tree is reflected by a return to a level closer to the root, and (1,4,2,4) will cause the search to return to the root. The search will continue in the right subtree, which corresponds to partial solutions that begin with Queen 1 in row 2. A solution is finally discovered at the leaf node marked **.

EXAMPLE 2.2: BACKTRACKING TO SOLVE THE 4-QUEENS PROBLEM

Recall that a good generator should be informed. Suppose we employ a generator based on the insight that any solution for the 4-Queens problem will place only one Queen in each column and row; solutions to the problem will come only from vectors that correspond to permutations of the integers 1, 2, 3, and 4. Figure 2.11 illustrates a backtracking search based upon this generator.

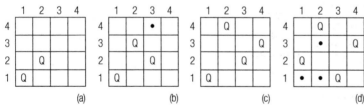

Figure 2.11
Backtracking solution to the 4-Queens problem that employs a generator that proposes only permutations of {1,2,3,4} as solutions. (a) (1,2,-,-) is rejected. (b) (1,3,2,-) and (1,3,4,-) are rejected. (c) (1,4,2,3) is proposed but the tester says no. (d) (2,1,-,-) fails. However, (2,4,1,3) will eventually solve this problem.

The generator in Example 2.2 is more informed than the one in our previous approach. A total of $4! = 24$ possibilities are proposed (in the worst case) as opposed to $4^4 = 256$ in the earlier generator. Naturally, both of these generators compare favorably with exhaustive enumeration, which proposed up to $^{16}C_4$,

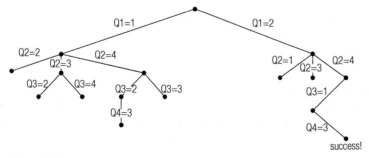

Figure 2.12
Solving the 4-Queens problem using a more informed generator.

or 1820, solutions. The search tree corresponding to the search in Example 2.2 is shown in Figure 2.12.

Observe that a smaller portion of the state space was explored before a solution was found.

In the exercises at the end of this chapter, you will be asked if even more informed generators can be found for the 4-Queens problem. We will return to this issue in Chapter 3, with a discussion of constraint satisfaction search.

2.2.2 The Greedy Algorithm

The previous section described back-tracking, a search procedure that divides a search into stages. At each stage, choices are made in a prescribed manner. If the problem constraints can be satisfied, then the search proceeds to the next stage; if no choice yields a feasible partial solution, then the search continues to backtrack to each previous stage, where the last choice is undone and the next possibility is pursued.

The **greedy algorithm** is another classic search method, which also operates by first dividing a problem into stages. A greedy algorithm always contains an **objective function** that must be optimized (i.e., either maximized or minimized). Typical objective functions might be distance traveled, cost expended, or time elapsed.

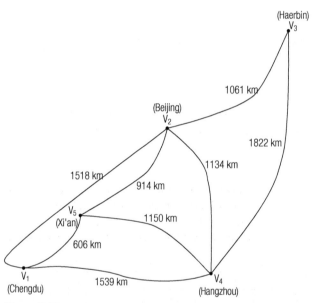

Figure 2.13
Five cities in China with supposed airline distances between cities that are directly linked to one another.

Figure 2.13 (a) represents a map of northeastern China. Suppose that a salesperson is starting from Chengdu and wants to find the shortest path to Haerbin that passes only through the cities that are circled: Chengdu (V_1), Beijing (V_2), Haerbin (V_3), Hangzhou (V_4), and Xi'an (V_5). Distances between these five cities are shown in kilometers. In Stage 1, a greedy approach to this problem proceeds from Chengdu to Xi'an because, at a distance of only 606 km, Xi'an is the closest city. Subsequent steps in the algorithm are explained in Figure 2.14.

1. In Stage 1, the path from V_1 to V_5 is taken because Xi'an is the closest city to Chengdu.

2. We may consider paths that go through vertices only if they have been visited previously. In Stage 2, the next path generated goes directly from V_1 to V_2; its cost (distance) is 1518 km. This direct route is less expensive than the path going through V_5, which would cost 606 + 914 = 1520 km.

3. The least expensive path from V_1 to V_3 is constructed from the least expensive path from V_1 to an intermediate node (V_i) plus the least costly path from V_i to V_3. Here I equals V_2; the least costly path from V_1 to V_3 passes through V_2 and has a cost of $1518 + 1061 = 2579$ km. The direct path from V_1 to V_4, however, is less costly (1539). We are going to V_4 (Hangzhou).

4. Stage 4: We are searching for the next least expensive path from V_1 to anywhere. We already have the least expensive path from V_1 to V_5, at a cost of 606 km. The second least expensive path is the direct one from V_1 to V_2, with a cost of 1518 km. The direct path from V_1 to V_4 (1539 km) is less costly than either the one that first passes through V_5 ($606 + 1150 = 1756$ km) or V_2 ($1518 + 1134 = 2652$ km). Hence, the next least costly path is the one to V_3 (2579). There are several possibilities:

- V_1 to V_5: cost = 606; then V_5 to V_2: cost = 914; the cost of going from V_1 to V_2 through V_5 is 1520. You then need to get from V_2 to V_3; this distance is 1061. The path from V_1 to V_3 that passes through V_5 and V_2 has a total cost of $1520 + 1061 = 2581$.
- V_1 to V_2: cost = 1518; then V_2 to V_3: cost = 1061; total cost = 2579 km.
- V_1 to V_4: cost = 1539; then V_4 to V_3: cost = 1822; this total cost is 3361 km.

We are taking the path from V_1 to V_3, which first passes through V_2. Its total cost is 2579 km.

Figures 2.14 (a–d) show the various stages in a greedy approach to finding a shortest path from Chengdu to Haerbin (V_1 to V_3).

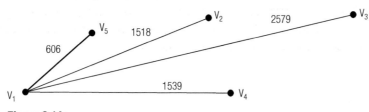

Figure 2.14a
Stage 1.

We may consider paths that go through vertices only if they have been visited previously. In Stage 2, the next path generated goes directly from V_1 to V_2.

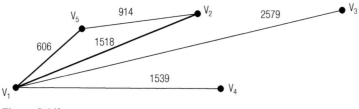

Figure 2.14b
Stage 2.

The least costly path from V_1 to V_3 passes through V_2 and has a cost of $1518 + 1061$. The direct path from V_1 to V_4 is less costly.

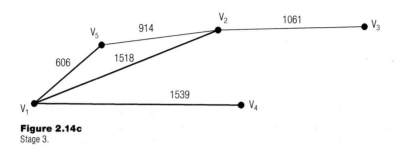

Figure 2.14c
Stage 3.

The least expensive path is from V_1 to V_5. The second least expensive path is the direct one from V_1 to V_2. The next least costly path is the one to V_3, via V_2.

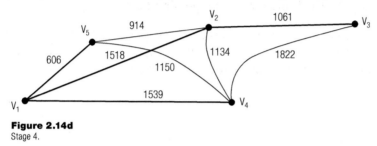

Figure 2.14d
Stage 4.

The specific algorithm employed in the last example is Dijkstra's shortest path algorithm;[1] Dijkstra's algorithm is an example of a greedy algorithm. A greedy algorithm can solve a problem in an efficient amount of running time; unfortunately, however, some problems in computer science cannot be solved using this paradigm. The Traveling Salesperson Problem, described next, is one such problem.

The mathematical discipline of matroid theory is useful in identifying those problems for which use of a greedy algorithm would not be successful.

2.2.3 The Traveling Salesperson Problem

In the **Traveling Salesperson Problem (TSP)**, you are given *n* vertices in a **weighted graph** (i.e., a graph with costs on the edges). You must find the shortest circuit that starts at some vertex V_i, passes through each vertex in the graph once and only once, and then returns to V_i. The previous example concerning five cities from China is employed. Suppose that our salesperson resides in Xi'an, and must therefore visit each of Chengdu, Beijing, Hangzhou, and Haerbin, in some order, and then return home to Xi'an. The least expensive such circuit is sought. A greedy-based solution to the TSP always visits the closest city next, as shown in Figure 2.15.

The greedy algorithm visits Chengdu, Beijing, Haerbin, Hangzhou, and then finally returns to Xi'an. The cost of this circuit is $606 + 1518 + 1061 + 1822 + 1050 = 6057$

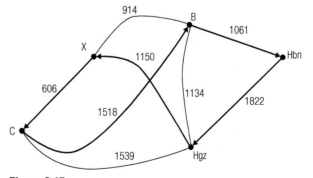

Figure 2.15
A greedy-based solution to the TSP. Our salesperson begins in Xi'an and first visits Chengdu because its distance is only 606 km. Beijing, Haerbin, and Hangzhou are visited in that order with a final return to Xi'an.

HUMAN INTEREST NOTES

EDSGAR DIJKSTRA

Edsgar Dijkstra (1930 – 2002), a Dutch computer scientist whose early training was in theoretical physics, is best known for his writing about good programming style (e.g., structured programming) and good educational techniques, as well as the algorithm—known by his name—for finding the shortest path to a goal, through a graph.

He received the 1972 Turing Award for fundamental contributions to developing programming languages and was the Schlumberger Centennial Chair of Computer Sciences at The University of Texas at Austin from 1984 until 2000.

He favored structured languages such as Algol-60 (which he helped develop) and disliked the teaching of BASIC. He gained considerable notoriety with his writing, such as his 1968 letter titled "Go To Statement Considered Harmful," written to the editor of the Communications of the Association for Computing Machinery (ACM).

Much of his work since the 1970s has been on developing formal verification of program correctness proofs, which he hoped to do with elegant mathematics rather than through the complexities of such correctness proofs, which often become quite convoluted. Dijkstra produced over 1300 "EWDs" (his initials), which were his handwritten personal notes to himself that later were corresponded to others and then published. These have been archived at *http://userweb.cs.utexas.edu/users/EWD/advancedSearch.html*.

Shortly before his death, Dijkstra received the ACM Principles of Distributed Computing (PODC) Influential Paper Award in Distributed Computing for his work on self-stabilization of program computation, which, in his honor, was renamed the Dijkstra Prize.

References

Dijkstra, E. W. 1968. Letters to the editor: Go to statement considered harmful. *Communications of the ACM* 11(3):147–148.

Dahl, O-J., Dijkstra, E. W., and Hoare, C. A. R. 1972. *Structured programming*, London: Academic Press.

Dijkstra, E. W. 1974. Self-stabilizing systems in spite of distributed control. *Communications of the ACM* 17(11):643–644.

Dijkstra, E. W. 1976. *A discipline of programming*. Prentice-Hall Series in Automatic Computation. Prentice-Hall.

km. If the salesperson visits Beijing, Haerbin, Hangzhou, Chengdu, and then returns to Xi'an, the total accrued cost is $914 + 1061 + 1822 + 1539 + 606 = 5942$ km. Clearly, the greedy algorithm has failed to find an optimal route.

A variation on breadth first search, in which nodes are explored in terms of nondecreasing cost, is *branch and bound*. Branch and bound is also referred to as **uniform cost search**. Branch and bound algorithms will be explored in Chapter 3 (Informed Search), where we will discover that this search strategy is successful at solving instances of the TSP.

2.3 ■ BLIND SEARCH ALGORITHMS

Blind search algorithms, as mentioned earlier, are uninformed search algorithms that do not use problem domain knowledge. With these approaches, nothing is presumed to be known about the state space. Three principal algorithms that fall under this heading are: **depth first search (dfs),**

breadth first search (bfs), and **depth first search with iterative deepening (dfs-id).** These algorithms share two properties:

1. They do not use heuristic measures in which the search would proceed along the most promising path.

2. Their aim is to find *some* solution to the given problem.

Chapter 3 will describe search algorithms that rely on the judicious application of heuristics to reduce search time. Some of these algorithms attempt to find an optimal solution, which means increased search time; however, if you intend to use the optimal solutions many times, then the extra effort is likely to be worthwhile.

2.3.1 Depth First Search

Depth first search (dfs), as the name suggests, attempts to plunge as deeply into a tree as quickly as possible. Whenever the search can make a choice, it selects the far left (or far right) branch (though it usually selects the far left branch). As an example of dfs, consider the tree in Figure 2.16.

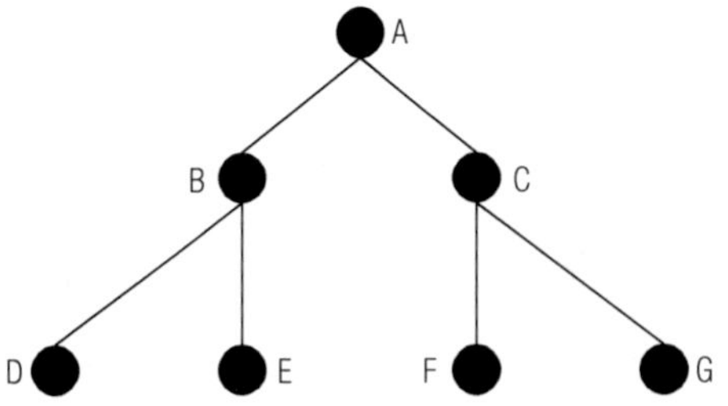

You are reminded that tree traversal algorithms will often "visit" a node several times, for example, in Figure 2.16 a dfs encounters nodes in the order: A,B,D,B,E,B,A,C,F,C,G. It is traditional to announce only the first visit as shown in the caption.

The 15-puzzle shown in Figure 2.17 was a popular children's puzzle before the advent of computer and video games. Fifteen numbered square tiles are encased within a plastic frame. One space is left vacant so that tiles can slide in one of four directions.

As shown in Figure 2.17(a), the 1 tile can slide south, the 7 can move north one square, the 2 can travel east, and the 15 tile can move one position west. The aim of this puzzle is to rearrange the numbered tiles from an arbitrary start state to another goal state. In Figure 2.17(b), the goal state consists of the tiles in order; however, any arbitrary arrangement can be chosen as the goal. From a given start state, exactly half of the possible puzzle arrangements are not reachable. Number the frame positions 1 to 16 as they appear in the **goal state** shown in Figure 2.17(b). The blank square occupies position 16. Location (*i*) represents the location number in the start state of the tile numbered *i*. Less (*i*) is the number of tiles *j* with $j < i$ and Location (*j*) > Location (*i*).

In the start state in Figure 2.17(a), Less (4) equals 1 because numbered tile 2 is the only tile that appears in a higher location.

Refer to Horowitz et al. [2] for more information on the 15-puzzle, and Rotman [3] for insights on the group theory behind this theorem.

Figure 2.16
Depth-first search traversal of a tree. The nodes will be visited in the order A, B, D, E, C, F, G.

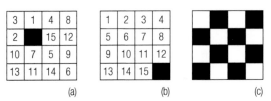

Figure 2.17
The Fifteen-Puzzle: (a) start state, (b) goal state, and (c) useful in calculating reachable states.

THEOREM 2.1
The goal state of Figure 2.17(b) is reachable from the start state only if the Sum of $j = 1$ to $j = 16$ of Less (*i*) + *x* is even. The value of *x* is 1 if in the start state, the blank is in one of the shaded regions in Figure 2.17(c), otherwise, its value is 0.

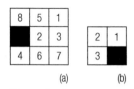

Figure 2.18
The (a) 8-puzzle and the (b) 3-puzzle.

Recall that state spaces can be incredibly large; in fact the 15-puzzle has 16! $= 2.9 \times 10^{13}$ different arrangements. As a consequence of the theorem involving Figure 2.17, any search for a goal state from some specified start position will perhaps have to navigate through a space consisting of half this number of states. Other popular versions of this numbered-tile puzzle are the 8-puzzle and 3-puzzle. See Figure 2.18.

For clarity in presentation, several search algorithms are illustrated using the 3-puzzle.

EXAMPLE 2.3: SOLVING A 3-PUZZLE USING DFS

To find a dfs solution for the 3-puzzle, start by defining the start state and goal state, as shown in Figure 2.19.

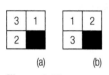

Figure 2.19
An instance of the 3-puzzle: (a) start state; (b) goal state.

In Figure 2.19(a) the 1 tile is free to move south one square and the 2 tile can move east. Instead, assume that the blank moves. In Figure 2.19(a), the blank can move north or west. Four operators can change the state of the puzzle—the blank can move north, south, east, or west. Because possible moves must be tried in this order, we will represent moves by an arrow pointing in the appropriate direction: N, S, E, and W. This order is arbitrary, though some order must be specified. A dfs is employed to solve this instance of the 3-puzzle. The results of this search are shown in Figure 2.20.

Each step in the search applies the first operator from the set {N, S, E, W}. No effort is expended trying to determine which move arrives at a solution fastest—in this sense, the search is blind. However, the search avoids repeated states. Starting at the root and applying N and then S, you arrive at the state marked with a * in Figure 2.20. As we shall see in Section 2.4, avoiding repeated states is an essential feature of many efficient search algorithms.

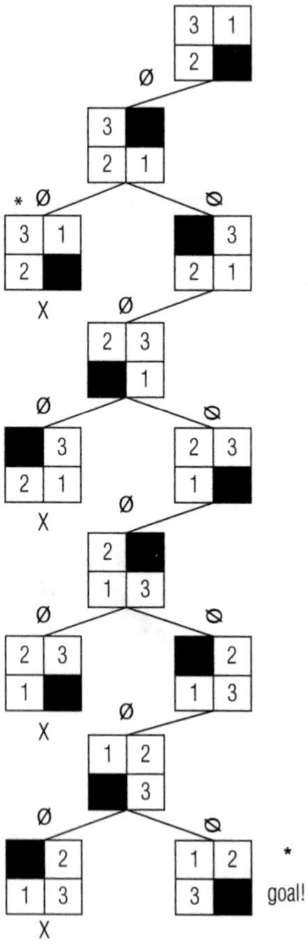

2.3.2 Breadth First Search

A second blind search approach is provided by *breadth first search* (bfs). In bfs, nodes are visited level by level from the top of the tree to the bottom, in left to right fashion (or right to left, though left to right is more traditional). All nodes at level i are visited before any nodes at level $i+1$ are encountered. Figure 2.21 shows a bfs.

Figure 2.20
Depth first search to solve an instance of the 3-puzzle. Operators are tried in this order: ↑↓→← Repeated states are abandoned and are marked with an X.

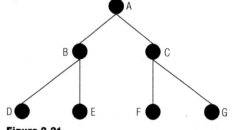

Figure 2.21
Breadth-first traversal of a tree. The nodes will be visited in the order: A, B, C, D, E, F, G.

EXAMPLE 2.4: SOLVING A 3-PUZZLE USING BFS

To find a bfs solution for the 3-puzzle we will once again solve the instance of the puzzle shown in Figure 2.19. This time bfs will be employed. See Figure 2.22. Note that a solution is found at depth 4 (where, as is usual, the root is considered to be at depth 0), which means that four moves of the blank are required to reach the goal.

The implementations of dfs and bfs and the relative merits of these two searches are discussed in the next section. First, consider one additional problem that is well known in AI lore—the **Missionaries and Cannibals** Problem—which is an example of a search problem with constraints.

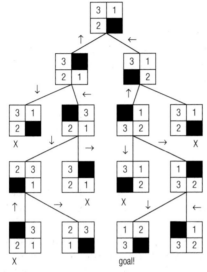

Figure 2.22
Breadth-first search to solve an instance of the 3-puzzle. Operators are tried in order: ↑↓→← Repeated states are abandoned and are marked with an X.

EXAMPLE 2.5: MISSIONARIES AND CANNIBALS PROBLEM

Three missionaries and three cannibals stand on the west bank of a river. Nearby is a row boat that can accommodate either one or two persons. How can everyone cross to the east bank in such a manner that cannibals never outnumber mis-

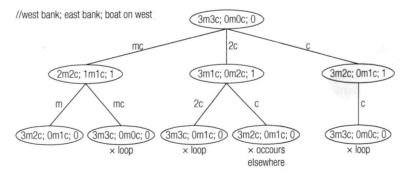

Figure 2.23
Breadth first search for the Missionaries and Cannibals Problem, extended two levels. Note that no move was pursued that would lead to an unsafe state on either bank. Note also that repeated states are to be pruned. Moves are tried in the order m, mc, 2c, c.

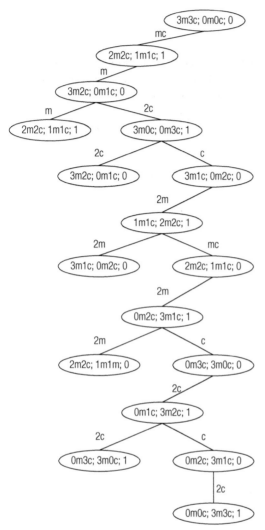

Figure 2.24
A dfs solution for the Missionaries and Cannibals Problem. No move was pursued that would lead to an unsafe state on either river bank. Loop states were also not pursued.

sionaries on either side of the river? If the cannibals ever outnumber the missionaries on either shore or on the boat, then those missionaries will be eaten.

Before beginning a search, we must decide on a representation for the problem. We can use 3m3c; 0m0c; 0 to represent the start state. This denotes that three missionaries (3m) and three cannibals (3c) are on the West bank, no missionaries (0m) nor cannibals (0c) are on the East bank. The final 0 indicates that the boat is on the West bank, whereas 1 in this position specifies that the boat is on the East bank. (A computer program written to solve this problem might represent the start state as 33000; the representation as given in this text [3m3c; 0m0c; 0] adds clarity for readers.) The goal state is accordingly represented by the string 0m0c; 3m3c; 1. Moves will be tried in the order m, mc, 2c, and c, which represent that a single missionary, a missionary and cannibal, two cannibals, and a lone cannibal are to cross the river (note 2m was not considered for use here). The direction of travel is made obvious by the boat's position. To ensure that our notation is clear, we provide a bfs solution in Figure 2.23, which has been extended to two levels.

A dfs solution for the Missionaries and Cannibals Problem is provided in Figure 2.24.

2.4 IMPLEMENTING AND COMPARING BLIND SEARCH ALGORITHMS

We have discussed in general terms two blind approaches to searching through state-space graphs: depth first search and breadth first search. Dfs plunges deeply into a state-space graph as quickly as possible, whereas bfs explores all nodes at a prescribed distance from the root before progressing one level deeper. In this section we provide pseudocode for implementing these search methodologies and also discuss their relative prowess at finding problem solutions, as well as their time-and-space requirements.

2.4.1 ■ Implementing a Depth First Search Solution

The various search algorithms in this chapter and the next vary greatly in the way a tree is inspected. Each algorithm, however, shares one attribute in that two lists are maintained: an open list and a closed list. An open list contains all nodes in the tree that are still being explored (or expanded); the closed list contains those nodes that have already been explored and are no longer under consideration. Recall that a dfs moves deeply into a search tree as quickly as possible. As the code for dfs in Figure 2.25 illustrates, this is accomplished by maintaining the open list as a stack. A stack is a last in, first out (LIFO) data structure.

```
Begin
Open? [Start state] // The open list is
// maintained as a stack. i.e., a list in which the last
// item inserted is the first item deleted. This is often referred
// to as a LIFO list.
Closed   ?   [   ] // The closed list contains nodes that have
// already been inspected; it is initially empty.


While Open not empty
      Begin
              Remove first item from open, call it X
              If X equals goal then return Success
              Else
               Generate immediate descendants of X
              Put X on Closed List.
              If children of X already encountered then discard
// loop check


              Else place children not yet encountered on Open
              // end else
        // end While
        Return Goal not Found
```

Figure 2.25
Code for depth first search.

As soon as a node is visited, it moves to the front of the open list, ensuring that its children will be generated next. This algorithm is applied to the search tree in Figure 2.26.

The tree in Figure 2.26 will be used to illustrate the blind search algorithms in this chapter as well as the heuristic searches in Chapter 3. This tree is redrawn in Figure 2.27 without heuristic estimates and node to node distances because dfs does not use these metrics. Depth first search is applied to the tree in Figure 2.27.

The results of this search (Figures 2.26 and 2.27) are given in Figure 2.28.

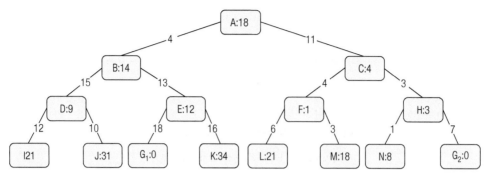

Figure 2.26

Numbers on the arcs represent the actual distance between a node and its immediate descendant. For example, the 4 that labels the left branch below the root indicates that the distance from node A to node B is 4. Numbers next to the node letters represent the heuristic estimate from that node to a goal node; for example, 12 in node E indicates that the estimate of remaining distance from node E to some goal is 12.

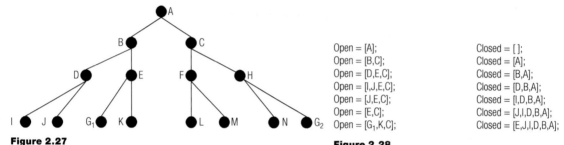

```
Open = [A];              Closed = [ ];
Open = [B,C];            Closed = [A];
Open = [D,E,C];          Closed = [B,A];
Open = [I,J,E,C];        Closed = [D,B,A];
Open = [J,E,C];          Closed = [I,D,B,A];
Open = [E,C];            Closed = [J,I,D,B,A];
Open = [G1,K,C];         Closed = [E,J,I,D,B,A];
```

Figure 2.27

Search tree to illustrate depth first search. Because dfs is a blind search, all heuristic estimates and node-to-node distances have been omitted.

Figure 2.28

Depth first search applied to the search tree in Figure 2.27. Algorithm returns success, G1 is a goal.

Breadth first search explores all nodes close to the root before plunging deeper into the search tree. The code for bfs is shown in Figure 2.29.

2.4.2 Implementing a Breadth First Search Solution

Breadth first search maintains the open list as a queue. A **queue** is a FIFO (first in, first out) data structure. Once a node is expanded, its children move to the rear of the open list: hence these children are explored only after every other node at its parent's level has been visited. Figure 2.30 traces the steps of bfs on the tree in Figure 2.27.

2.4.3 Measuring Problem-Solving Performance

To determine which solution works best for a particular problem, we can compare dfs and bfs. Before doing so, it is helpful to provide metrics to measure these and other search algorithms. Four measures are described in the following sections. (In Chapter 3, additional metrics will be provided.)

Completeness

A search algorithm is said to be complete when it is guaranteed to find a solution when there is one. Using the generate-and-test paradigm introduced earlier in this chapter, suppose we are trying to identify all integers x between 100 and 1000, inclusive, that are perfect cubes. In other words, we want to know all x with $100 \leq x \leq 1000$ such that $x = y^3$ with y an integer. If our generator checks ev-

Begin

 Open ? [Start state] // The open list is

 // maintained as a queue, i.e., a list in which the

 // first item inserted is the first item deleted. This is

 // often referred to as a FIFO list.

 Closed ? [ ] // The closed list contains nodes

 // that have already been inspected; it is initially empty.

 While Open not empty

 Begin

   Remove first item from Open, call it X.

   If X equals goal then return Success

   Else

    Generate immediate descendants of X

    Put X on Closed List..

    If children of X already encountered

     then discard. // loop check

    Else place children not yet encountered on Open

    // end else

    // end while

    Return, Goal not found

End Algorithm breadth first search

Figure 2.29
Code for breadth first search.

ery integer between 100 and 1000, inclusive, then this search would be complete. In fact, the results would be such that 125, 216, 343, 512, 729, and 1000 are perfect cubes.

Optimality

A search algorithm is said to be **optimal** if it provides the lowest-cost path among all solutions. Figure 2.20 depicts a dfs solution for an instance of the 3-puzzle. A solution is found whose path length is eight. Figure 2.22 illustrates a bfs solution for this same instance, with a path length of four. Therefore, dfs is not an optimal search strategy.

Open = [A];   Closed = [ ];
Open = [B,C];   Closed = [A];
Open = [C,D,E];   Closed = [B,A];
Open = [D,E,F,H];   Closed = [C,B,A];
Open = [E,F,H,I,J];   Closed = [D,C,B,A];
Open = [F,H,I,J,G$_1$,K];   Closed = [E,D,C,B,A];
Open = [H,I,J,G$_1$,K,L,M];   Closed = [F,E,D,C,B,A];
... Until G$_1$ is at left end of Open list.

Figure 2.30
Breadth first search applied to the search tree in Figure 2.27. The algorithm returns success, the goal G1 is found.

Time Complexity

The **time complexity** of a search algorithm concerns how long it takes to find a solution. Time is measured in terms of the number of nodes generated (or expanded) during the search.

Space Complexity

The **space complexity** of a search algorithm measures how much memory is required to perform the search. We must determine the maximum number of nodes stored in memory. Complexity in AI is expressed in terms of three parameters:

1. The **branching factor** (b) of a node is the number of branches emanating from it (see Figure 2.31).

2. The parameter (d) measures depth of the shallowest goal node.

3. The parameter (m) measures the maximum length of any path in the state space.

If every node in a search tree has a branching factor of b, then the **branching factor of the tree** equals b.

Figure 2.31
The branching factor of a node is the number of branches emanating from it. Node A has a branching factor equal to three.

2.4.4 Comparing dfs and bfs

We have encountered two blind search algorithms — dfs and bfs. Which is preferable?

First, let's clarify the criteria. By preferable, do we mean which algorithm requires less work to find a path? Or do we mean which algorithm will find a shorter path? In both cases, as expected, the answer is: It depends.

Depth first search is preferred if

- the tree is deep
- the branching factor is not excessive and
- solutions occur relatively deep in the tree.

Breadth first is preferred if

- the branching factor of the search tree is not excessive (reasonable b)
- a solution occurs at a reasonable level in the tree (d is reasonable), and
- no path is excessively deep.

Depth first search has modest memory requirements. For a state space with branching factor m and maximum depth m, dfs requires only $b * m + 1$ nodes, which is $O(b*m)$. Backtracking is actually a variant of dfs in which only one successor of a node is generated at a time (for example: in which row should the third Queen be placed?). Backtracking requires only $O(m)$ memory.

Is dfs complete? Consider the search space in Figure 2.32. As this figure shows, dfs is not complete. The search might get lost in relatively long or even infinite paths in the left portion of the search space, while a goal node remains unexplored in the upper-right portion of the tree. Recall also that dfs is also not optimal. (Review Figures 2.20 and 2.22.)

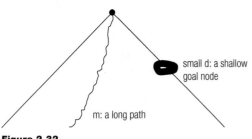

small d: a shallow goal node

m: a long path

Figure 2.32
A search space in which depth first search would not fare well. Dfs "gets lost" deep in the left portion of the search space. A goal node in the upper right side might never be searched.

If you are assured that the branching factor of a search space is finite, then bfs is complete. In bfs, you first search all b children of the root, then all b^2 grandchildren, and finally all b^d nodes at level d. This latter argument should also convince the reader that bfs will find the "shallowest" goal node first; however, this does not necessarily mean that bfs is optimal. If the path cost is a nonincreasing function of the depth of the node, then bfs is optimal.

The time complexity $(t(n))$ for bfs grows exponentially. If the branching factor of a search tree equals b, then the root node will have b children. Each of these b descendants will have b children of their own. In fact, one will need to expand all but the last node at level d for a total of

$$T(n) = b + b^2 + b^3 + \dots + (b^{d-1} - b) = O(b^{d+1})$$

Because every node that is generated must remain in memory, the space complexity $(S(n))$ for bfs is also $O(b^{d+1})$. Actually: $S(n) = t(n)+1$ because the root of the search tree must also be stored.

The harshest critique for bfs is that it requires exponential space complexity. For even modest problem sizes, bfs quickly becomes infeasible. To combine the modest space requirements of dfs without its propensity to pursue lengthy paths, we can use **dfs with iterative deepening (dfs-id)**.

Dfs-id performs a dfs of the state space with a depth bound of zero; see Figure 2.33, where we apply dfs-id to our example in Figure 2.27. If it fails to find a goal, it performs another dfs with a depth bound of one. The search continues in this fashion, increasing the depth bound by one, at each iteration. A complete dfs to the current depth is performed at each iteration. The search begins anew at each iteration.

It must be emphasized that each tree in this figure is drawn from scratch; no tree is built from a tree resulting from a depth bound, which is one lower.

Figure 2.33 (a – d)
The stages in dfs with iterative deepening applied to one example. (a) Dfs search with depth bound = 0; (b) dfs search with depth bound = 1; (c) dfs search with depth bound = 2; (d) dfs search with depth bound = 3.

In the search space at depth one, b nodes are generated d times. The b^2 nodes at depth two are generated $d-1$ times, and so on. Finally the b^d nodes at level d are generated just once. Hence, the total number of nodes generated is:

$$((d+ 1) * 1) + (d*b) + (d-1) * b^{2 + \dots + 1} * b^d$$

The time complexity for dfs-id is $O(bd)$, which is somewhat better than bfs. In the worst case, all uninformed searches – dfs, bfs, and dfs-id—display exponential time complexity. Only one path needs to be stored in memory at a time, so its space complexity is $O(b*d)$, the same as for dfs.

Consider a dfs-id solution for the 3-puzzle depicted in Figure 2.20. In that figure, dfs finds a solution at depth $d = 8$ after having both generated and visited a total of 13 nodes. Dfs-id will find a solution at depth $d = 4$ after having generated complete binary trees of depth i, where $i = 0, \dots, 4$. (Consulting Figure 2.22 where a bfs solution is provided will perhaps help you to see this.)

As with bfs, dfs-id is complete when the branching factor is finite, and optimal when path costs are a nondecreasing function of a node's depth.

HUMAN INTEREST NOTES

DONALD KNUTH

Donald Knuth, Professor Emeritus, Stanford University, is one of the greatest computer scientists of all time. He made his reputation by publishing three monumental volumes in a series titled The Art of Computer Programming (TAOCP). The series became known as the "Bible of Computer Science" and the volumes were available in the 1970s:

Fundamental Algorithms
Seminumerical Algorithms
Sorting and Searching

The international esteem in which these volumes are held is substantiated by the fact that they have been translated into many languages.

In 1978, dismayed with the typography in the galley proofs for the second edition of his second volume, Knuth journeyed into the world of typesetting for many years, until he developed a stable version of the language TeX. During the past 30 years it has become a marvelous tool and a standard to assist scientists in developing their technical papers.

Volume 4, *Combinatorial Algorithms*, has been long-awaited. Instead Knuth has written what he calls "Fascicles" of 128 pages, listed below. Ever modest, Knuth states:

These fascicles will represent my best attempt to write a comprehensive account, but computer science has grown to the point where I cannot hope to be an authority on all the material covered in these books. Therefore I'll need feedback from readers in order to prepare the official volumes later.

Volume 4 Fascicle 0, Introduction to Combinatorial Algorithms and Boolean Functions

Volume 4 Fascicle 1, Bitwise Tricks & Techniques; Binary Decision Diagrams

Volume 4 Fascicle 2, Generating All Tuples and Permutations

Volume 4 Fascicle 3, Generating All Combinations and Partitions

Volume 4 Fascicle 4, Generating All Trees; History of Combinatorial Generation

An insight into Donald Knuth comes from his own home page:

I have been a happy man ever since January 1, 1990, when I no longer had an email address. I'd used email since about 1975, and it seems to me that 15 years of email is plenty for one lifetime. Email is a wonderful thing for people whose role in life is to be on top of things. But not for me; my role is to be on the bottom of things. What I do takes long hours of studying and uninterruptible concentration. I try to learn certain areas of computer science exhaustively; then I try to digest that knowledge into a form that is accessible to people who don't have time for such study.

He has plans to write Volume 5, on the topic of syntactic algorithms (for 2015), and then to revise Volumes 1–3, and write a "Readers Digest" version of Volumes 1–5. He plans to publish Volume 6 (on the theory of context-free languages) and Volume 7 (about compiler techniques), "but only if the things I want to say about those topics are still relevant and still haven't been said."

Reference: ————————————

http://www-cs-faculty.stanford.edu/~uno/taocp.html

2.5 CHAPTER SUMMARY

This chapter presented an overview of blind, or uninformed, search algorithms: algorithms that do not use problem domain knowledge. Searches take place within state-space graphs (or state-space trees). Nodes in this structure correspond to problem states. For example, when solving the Mini False Coins Problem, nodes correspond to subsets of coins known to contain the false coin. The generate-and-test paradigm can be a straightforward way to solve a problem. A generator proposes solutions to a problem and the tester determines their validity. Good generators should be complete, non-redundant, and informed. A generator used in the 4-Queens problem that possessed these qualities reduced search time dramatically.

Exhaustive enumeration is a search procedure that looks everywhere for a solution. Backtracking, on the other hand, improves search time by abandoning partial solutions once it is discovered that they violate problem constraints.

The greedy algorithm is a search paradigm that is often useful in solving problems, such as finding the shortest path between a pair of cities. However, the greedy algorithm is not suitable for all problems. For example, it does not successfully solve the Traveling Salesperson Problem.

Three blind search algorithms are breadth first search (bfs), depth first search (dfs), and depth first search with iterative deepening (dfs-id). Bfs traverses a tree level by level in its search for a problem solution. Bfs is complete and optimal (under various constraints). It is however, hindered by its inordinate space demands. Dfs has more reasonable space requirements, though it has a tendency to get lost on very long or infinite paths. Hence, dfs is neither complete nor optimal. Dfs-id can serve as a compromise between bfs and dfs; it performs a complete dfs on a search tree on bounded trees of depth 0, 1, 2, and so on. It has the favorable properties of both dfs and bfs, in other words, the space requirements of dfs with the completeness and optimality properties of bfs. All blind search algorithms exhibit exponential time complexity. To solve problems of reasonable size, we will need better algorithms. Chapter 3 presents informed searches that fare better with regard to some of the aforementioned benchmarks.

Questions for Discussion

1. Why is search an important component of an AI system?

2. What is a state-space graph?

3. Describe the generate-and-test paradigm.

4. What properties should a generator possess?

5. How does backtracking improve on exhaustive enumeration?

6. Describe the greedy algorithm in a sentence or two.

7. State the Traveling Salesperson Problem.

8. Name three blind search algorithms.

9. In what sense are blind search algorithms blind?

10. Compare the three blind search algorithms described in this chapter with respect to: completeness, optimality, and time-and-space complexity.

11. When is dfs preferable to bfs?

12. When is bfs preferable to dfs?

13. In what sense is dfs-id a compromise between bfs and dfs?

Exercises

1. Solve the False Coin Problem for 12 coins. Only three combinations of coins are permitted to be weighed. Recall that a balance scale returns one of three results: equal, left side is lighter, or left side is heavier.

2. Solve the Mini False Coin Problem weighing only twice, or prove that this is not possible.

3. A blind search not discussed in this chapter is a **nondeterministic search**. It is a form of blind search in which the children of nodes that have just been expanded are placed on the open list in random order. Is a nondeterministic search complete? Optimal?

4. Another generator for the n-Queens Problem is: Place a Queen in row 1. Do not place the second Queen in any square that is attacked by the first Queen. In state i, place a Queen in column i in a square that is not under attack from any of the previous i-1 Queens. See Figure 2.34.

Figure 2.34
2.34 Generator for the 4-Queens problem.

   a. Solve the 4-Queens problem using this generator.
   b. Argue that this generator is more informed than either of the two generators used in the text.
   c. Draw the portion of the search tree expanded in the search for a first solution.

5. Consider the following generator for the 4-Queens problem: *for $i = 1$ to 4, randomly assign Queen i to a row.*
Is this generator complete? Is it nonredundant? Explain your answer.

6. A number is said to be perfect if it equals the sum of its divisors (excluding itself). For example, 6 is perfect because $6 = 1 + 2 + 3$, where each of the integers 1, 2, and 3 are divisors of 6. Give the most informed generator that you can think of to find all perfect numbers between 1 and 100, inclusive.

7. Use Dijkstra's Algorithm to find the shortest path from the source vertex V_o to all other vertices in Figure 2.35.

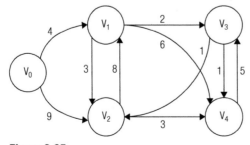

Figure 2.35
A labeled graph for use with Dijkstra's Algorithm.

8. Create a representation for a puzzle such as the 15-puzzle that is appropriate for checking repeated states.

9. Solve the Missionaries and Cannibals Problem using breadth first search.

10. A farmer with a wolf, a goat, and a container of cabbage are on the west bank of the river. On the river is a boat in which the farmer and one of the other three (wolf, goat, or cabbage) can fit. If the wolf is left alone with the goat, the wolf will eat the goat. If the goat is left alone with the container of cabbage, the goat will eat the cabbage. Your goal is to transfer everyone to the other side of the river safely. Solve this problem using:

    a. Depth first search   b. Breadth first search

11. Use bfs and then dfs to get from start node (S) to goal node (G) in parts (a) and (b) of Figure 2.36. At each step, explore nodes in alphabetical order.

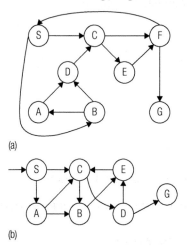

(a)

(b)

Figure 2.36
Getting to the goal node using bfs and dfs.

12. Label the maze in Figure 2.37.

Figure 2.37
A maze.

13. Use bfs and then dfs to get from the start to the goal, for the maze in Figure 2.37.

14. Having determined that the Twelve Coins Problem requires us to weigh three combinations of coins to identify the false coin: How many weighings would be needed to determine a false coin amongst 15 coins? What about 20 coins? Can you develop an algorithm to prove your conclusions?

    Hint: Consider the underlying minimum number of weighings needed for 2,3,4, and 5 coins to develop a knowledge base of facts for a bottom up solution to this problem.[++] (Reference AIP&TS Ch. 4)

15. We discussed The Missionaries and Cannibals Problem. Develop a solution to this problem given that the "moves" or "transitions" are forced.
    Identify "subgoal states" to the problem solution state which must be achieved in order to solve the problem. [++]

Programming Exercises

1. Write a program to solve an instance of the 15-puzzle that first checks if a goal state is reachable. Your program should employ:
   a. Depth first search
   b. Breadth first search
   c. Depth first search with iterative deepening.

2. Write a program that employs the greedy algorithm to find the minimum spanning tree for a graph. A spanning tree T for a graph G is a tree whose vertex set is the same as the vertex set for the graph. Consider the graph in 2.38(a). A spanning tree is provided in Figure 2.38(b). Observe that the Spanning tree in Figure 2.38(c) has minimal cost. The latter tree is referred to as a minimum spanning tree. Your program should find a minimum spanning tree for the graph in 2.38(d).

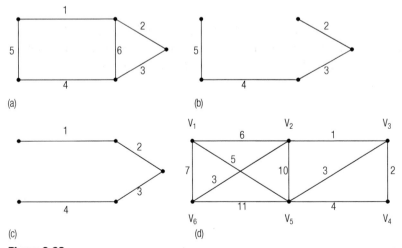

Figure 2.38
Finding the minimum spanning tree for a graph. (a) A graph G. (b) A spanning tree for G. (c) A minimum spanning tree for G. (d) A graph for which the minimum spanning tree must be found.

3. Write a program that employs backtracking to solve the 8–Queens problem and then answer the following questions:
   a. How many solutions are there?
   b. How many of these solutions are distinct? (You can look ahead to Exercise 5 in Chapter 4 for hints.)
   c. Which generator did your program employ?

4. Write a program to solve the 8-Queens problem that employs the generator suggested in Exercise 5.

5. In Chess, a Knight may move in eight different ways:

   1. Up one square, right two squares

   2. Up one, left two

   3. Up two, right one

   4. Up two, left one

   5. Down one right two

   6. Down one, left two

   7. Down two, right one

   8. Down to left one

   A Knight's tour of an $n \times n$ chess board is a sequence of $n^2 - 1$ moves so that a Knight visits each square on the board only once when started from an arbitrary square.

   Write a program to perform a Knight's tour when $n = 3$, 4, and 5. Employ a random number generator to select the start square randomly.

   Report on your results.

6. When you color a graph, you assign colors to the nodes of a graph so that no two adjacent nodes have the same color. For example, in Figure 2.39, if node V_1 is colored red, then none of the vertices V_2, V_3, nor V_4 could be colored red. Vertex V_5, however, might be colored with red as V_1 and V_5 are not adjacent.

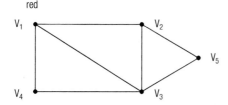

Figure 2.39
Graph to color.

The chromatic number of graph is the minimum number of colors required to color a graph. The chromatic number for various graphs is shown in Figure 2.40.

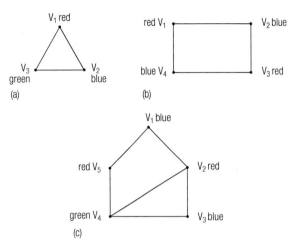

Figure 2.40 (a – c)
Chromatic numbers for various graphs.

Write a backtracking program to color the graph in Figure 2.41. Employ the most informed generator that you can think of.

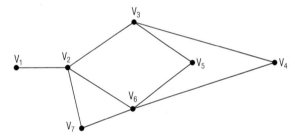

Figure 2.41
A graph whose chromatic number is to be determined.

Keywords

backtracking
blind search algorithms
branching factor of a node
branching factor of a tree
breadth first search (bfs)
closed list
complete
constraints
depth first search (dfs)
dfs with iterative deepening
   (dfs-id)
exhaustive enumeration
False Coin Problem
generate and test

goal state
greedy algorithm
informed
Mini False Coin Problem
minimum spanning tree
Missionaries and Cannibals
   Problem
nondeterministic search
   nonredundant search
n-Queens Problem
objective function
open list
optimal
partial solution

queue
space complexity
start node
start state
state-space graph
state-space tree
symmetry
time complexity
Traveling Salesperson Problem
   (TSP)
uniform cost search
weighted graph

References

1. Cormen, T. H, Anderson, C. E., Rivest, R. L, and Stein, C. 2009. *Introduction to algorithms*, 3rd ed. Cambridge, MA: MIT Press.

2. Horowitz, E., and Sahni, S. 1984. *Fundamentals of computer algorithms,* New York, NY: Computer Science Press.

3. Rotman, J. J. 1973. *The Theory of Groups,* 2nd ed. Boston, MA: Allyn and Bacon.

Bibliography

Gersting, J. L. *Mathematical Structures for Computer Science,* 4th ed. New York, NY: W.H. Freeman, 1999.

Knuth, D. *Fundamental Algorithms, 3rd* ed. Reading, MA: Addison-Wesley, 1997.

Knuth, D. *Seminumerical Algorithms, 3rd* ed. Reading, MA: Addison-Wesley, 1997.

Knuth, D. *Sorting and Searching,* 2nd ed. Reading, MA: Addison-Wesley, 1998.

Knuth, D. *Introduction to Combinatorial Algorithms and Boolean Functions.* Vol. 4 Fascicle 0, The Art of Computer Programming. Boston, MA: Addison-Wesley, 2008.

Knuth, D. *Bitwise Tricks & Techniques; Binary Decision Diagrams.* Vol. 4 Fascicle 1, The Art of Computer Programming. Boston, MA: Addison-Wesley, 2009.

Knuth, D. *Generating All Tuples and Permutations.* Vol. 4 Fascicle 2, The Art of Computer Programming. Boston, MA: Addison-Wesley, 2005.

Knuth, D. *Generating All Combinations and Partitions.* Vol. 4 Fascicle 3, The Art of Computer Programming. Boston, MA: Addison-Wesley, 2005.

Knuth, D. *Generating All Trees – History of Combinatorial Generation.* Vol. 4 Fascicle 4, The Art of Computer Programming. Boston, MA: Addison-Wesley, 2006.

Luger, G. F. *Artificial Intelligence – Structures and Strategies for Complex Problem Solving,* 6th ed. Boston, MA: Addison -Wesley, 2008.

Reingold, E. M. *Combinatorial Algorithms–Theory and Practice*, Upper Saddle River, NJ: Prentice-Hall, 1977.

Winston, P. H. *Artificial Intelligence,* 3rd ed. Reading, MA: Addison-Wesley, 1992.

INFORMED SEARCH

Mountain Climber.

The large problems tackled by AI are often not amenable to solution by uninformed search algorithms. This chapter introduces informed search methods that utilize heuristics to reduce a problem space, either by limiting the depth or the breadth of the search. Henceforth, domain knowledge is used to avoid search paths that are likely to be fruitless.

3.0 INTRODUCTION

In this chapter, we continue our study of search techniques. Chapter 2, "Uninformed Search," introduced blind search algorithms wherein exploration through a **search space** proceeded in a fixed manner. *Depth first search* (dfs) probed deeply into a tree, whereas *breadth first search* (bfs) examined nodes close to the root before venturing farther. Dfs is not *complete* because it can resolutely follow long paths and consequently miss a goal node closer to the root; bfs, on the other hand, has exorbitant **space requirements** and can be easily overwhelmed by even moderate **branching factors.**

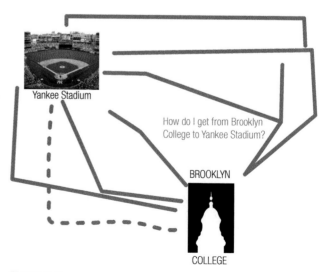

Yankee Stadium

How do I get from Brooklyn College to Yankee Stadium?

BROOKLYN

COLLEGE

Figure 3.0
From Brooklyn College to Yankee Stadium.

Both of these algorithms exhibit worst-case time complexity, which is exponential. *Dfs-iterative deepening* was shown to possess the advantageous features of both algorithms—the moderate space requirements of dfs combined with the prospect of completeness displayed by bfs. Even dfs iterative deepening, however, is doomed to exponential time complexity in the worst case.

In Chapters 4, "Search Using Games," and 16, "Advanced Computer Games," we will demonstrate how search algorithms are employed to enable computers to compete against humans in games such as nim, tic-tac-toe, checkers, and chess. Our triad of blind search algorithms would fare adequately with the first two games on our list—however, the huge search spaces lurking behind games such as checkers and chess would easily overwhelm this ensemble of search algorithms.

In Chapter 1, we presented *heuristics* as rules of thumb that are often useful tools in problem solving. In this chapter we present search algorithms that employ heuristics that help guide progress through a search space. Sections 3.2–3.4 describe three algorithms—**hill climbing**, the **best-first search**, and **beam search**—that "never look back." Their journey through a state space is steered solely by heuristic measure (approximation) of their remaining distance to the goal. Suppose that one was hitchhiking from New York City to Madison, Wisconsin. Along the way, there are many choices about which highway should next be chosen. This class of searches might employ the heuristic of choosing the road that minimizes one's straight-line distance to the goal (i.e., Madison).

Section 3.5 provides four metrics that are useful in evaluating heuristics and/or search algorithms. A heuristic—if it is to be useful—should provide an **underestimate** of remaining distance. In the previous paragraph, it is evident that the straight-line distance is always less than or equal to the actual distance (highways often need to circle around mountains, large forests, and urban areas). This property of a search heuristic is referred to as **admissibility**.

Monotonicity asks more of a search heuristic than admissibility; this property requires that, as the search forges ahead, the heuristic estimate of remaining distance should continually decrease. As any traveler knows, highways are continually being repaired and detours are often unavoidable. It is certainly possible that at some juncture in a journey to Madison, all of the available roads take one farther away from one's goal (albeit temporarily).

Heuristics can also be graded based on their ability to avoid unnecessary search effort. A search algorithm that evaluates a small portion of a search tree in its quest for the goal will undoubtedly run faster than one that must examine a larger fraction of the tree. The former search algorithm would be deemed to be **more informed** than the latter.

Some search algorithms examine only a single path. Usually such algorithms produce results that are suboptimal. As this chapter will illustrate, hill climbing will continue its progress until a node is reached from which no successor node can get one any closer to the goal. The goal might have been reached, or one could merely be stuck in a **local optimum**. Alternately, if backtracking is permitted, then the exploration of alternative paths is enabled; in these cases, the search algorithm is categorized as **tentative**.

The ensemble of search algorithms described in Section 3.6 all have one characteristic in common—they include the distance traveled from the root as part (or all) of their heuristic measure of goodness. These methods, which in a sense always look backward, are referred to as **branch and bound algorithms**. "Plain vanilla" branch and bound can be augmented by heuristic estimates of remaining distance or provisions to retain only the best path to any intermediate node. When both of these strategies are incorporated into the search we have the well-known **A* algorithm**.

Section 3.7 includes a discussion of two additional searches: **constraint satisfaction search (CSP)** and **bidirectional search** (or *wave search*). We have already seen that many searches incorporate constraints that must be satisfied. For example, in the *n*-Queens Problem discussed

in Chapter 2, the constraints were that no two Queens could occupy the same row, column, or diagonal. CSP attempts to employ these restrictions in order to facilitate tree pruning and thereby increase efficiency.

Solving a problem often involves solving subproblems. In some cases, all of the subproblems must be solved; at other times, solving one subproblem could suffice. For example, if one is doing one's laundry, it is required to both wash *and* dry the clothing. Drying, however, can be accomplished by either putting the wet clothes into a machine or hanging them on a clothesline. This section also includes a discussion of AND/OR trees, which are helpful in modeling this problem-solving process.

The chapter concludes with a discussion of bidirectional search, and, as the name alludes, it develops two breadth first trees in parallel, one from each of the start and goal nodes. This method is found to be especially useful in cases where the location of the goal node is not known a priori.

■3.1■ HEURISTICS

One of the topics most central to this text is the subject of heuristics, which was first introduced in Section 1.6 of Chapter 1. With his landmark book, *How to Solve It* [1] George Polya could perhaps be called the "Father of Heuristics." As mentioned in Chapter 1, Polya's efforts focused on problem solving, thinking, and learning. He developed a "heuristic dictionary" of heuristic primitives. Polya's approach was both practical and experimental. By formalizing the observation and experimental processes, he sought to develop and gain insight into human problem-solving processes.[2]

Bolc and Cytowski [3] note that recent approaches to the study of heuristics seek more formal and rigid algorithmic-like solutions to specific problem domains, rather than the development of more general approaches that could be appropriately selected from and applied to specific problems.

The goal of heuristic search methods is to greatly reduce the number of nodes considered in order to reach a goal state. They are ideally suited for problems whose **combinatorial complexity** grows very quickly. Through knowledge, information, rules, insights, analogies, and simplification—in addition to a host of other techniques—heuristic search methods aim to reduce the number of objects that must be examined. Good heuristics do not guarantee the achievement of a solution, but they are often helpful in guiding one to a solution path.

In 1984 Judea Pearl published a book titled *Heuristics,* [4] dedicated to the subject from a formal mathematical perspective. One must make the distinction between having (or executing) an algorithm and using heuristics. Algorithms are definite methods—a well-defined sequence of steps to solve a problem. Heuristics are more intuitive, human-like approaches; they are based on insight, experience, and know-how. They are probably the best way of describing human problem-solving methods and approaches as distinct from machine-like approaches.

Pearl notes that, with heuristics, strategies are being modified in order to arrive at a quasi-optimal (instead of optimal) solution—with a significant cost reduction. Games, especially two-person, zero-sum games of perfect information, such as chess and checkers, have proven to be a very promising domain for the study and testing of heuristics (see Chapters 4 and 16).

As an adjective, heuristic (pronounced hyu-RIS-tik and from the Greek "heuriskein" meaning "to discover") pertains to the process of gaining knowledge or some desired result by intelligent

The Web site whatis.techtarget.com

HUMAN INTEREST NOTES

JUDEA PEARL

Judea Pearl (1936–) is perhaps best known for his book, *Heuristics,*[4] published in 1984; however, he has also done significant work on knowledge representation, probabilistic and causal reasoning, nonstandard logics, and learning strategies. Some of his many honors include the following:

–The David E. Rumelhart Prize, for Contributions to the Theoretical Foundations of Human Cognition, in 2010

–The Festschrift and Symposium in honor of Judea Pearl, 2010

–An Honorary Doctorate of Humane Letters degree from Chapman University, Orange, CA, in 2008

–The Benjamin Franklin Medal in Computers and Cognitive Science, "For creating the first general algorithms for computing and reasoning with uncertain evidence" in 2008

–An Honorary Doctorate of Science degree from the University of Toronto, in recognition of "groundbreaking contributions to the field of computer science . . ."

Judea Pearl received a B.S. degree in Electrical Engineering from the Technion, Haifa, Israel, in 1960, a Master's degree in Physics from Rutgers University, New Brunswick, New Jersey, in 1965, and a PhD in Electrical Engineering from the Polytechnic Institute of Brooklyn, Brooklyn, New York, in 1965. He then worked at RCA Research Laboratories, Princeton, New Jersey, on superconductive parametric and storage devices and at Electronic Memories, Inc., Hawthorne, California, on advanced memory systems. He joined UCLA in 1970 where he is now in the Cognitive Systems Laboratory of the Computer Science Department.

guesswork rather than by following some pre-established formula. (Heuristic can be contrasted with algorithmic.) The term seems to have two usages:

1. Describing an approach to learning by trying without necessarily having an organized hypothesis or way of proving that the results proved or disproved the hypothesis. That is, "seat-of-the-pants" or "trial-and-error" learning.

2. Pertaining to the use of the general knowledge gained by experience, sometimes expressed as "using a rule-of-thumb." (However, heuristic knowledge can be applied to complex as well as simple everyday problems. Human chess players use a heuristic approach.)

Here are a few definitions of heuristic search:

As a noun, a heuristic is a specific rule-of-thumb or argument derived from experience. The application of heuristic knowledge to a problem is sometimes known as heuristics. *http://whatis.techtarget.com/definition/0,,sid9_gci212246_top1,00.html*

• It is a practical strategy for increasing the effectiveness of complex problem solving.

• It leads to a solution along the most probable path, omitting the least promising ones.

- It should enable one to avoid the examination of dead ends, and to use only gathered data.[15]

Heuristic information can be added to a search:

- To decide which node to expand next, instead of doing expansions in a strictly breadth first or depth first style
- To decide which successor or successors to generate when generating nodes, rather than blindly generating all possible successors at once
- To decide that certain nodes should be discarded (or pruned) from the search tree [2]

Bolc and Cytowski [3] add:

> . . . use of heuristics in the solution construction process increases the uncertainty of arriving at a result . . . due to the use of informal knowledge (rules, laws, intuition, etc.) whose usefulness have never been fully proven. Because of this, heuristic methods are employed in cases where algorithms give unsatisfactory results or do not guarantee to give any results. They are particularly important in solving very complex problems (where an accurate algorithm fails), especially in speech and image recognition, robotics, and game strategy construction.

Let us consider a few more examples of heuristics. One might, for example, choose the motor oil for a vehicle depending on the season. In winter, with cold temperatures, liquids tend to freeze, so we would want to use engine oils with lower viscosity (thickness); whereas in summer, with hotter temperatures, we would be wise to choose oils with greater viscosity. Analogously, one adds more air to automobile tires in winter (when gases compress), versus less air in summer when gases expand.

HUMAN INTEREST NOTES

GEORGE POLYA

George Polya (1887 – 1985) is most famous today for his ground-breaking work, *How to Solve It* (1945). This book has been translated into 17 languages, and nearly a million copies have been sold.

Polya was born in Budapest, Hungary and, like many young, intelligent people, was uncertain which discipline to choose for his future work. He tried a term at law school and dreaded it. He became interested in Darwin and biology but feared there was little income to be had from it. He also received a certificate to teach Latin and Hungarian (which he never used). He then tried philosophy, whereby his professor advised him to try physics and mathematics. Eventually he concluded: "I thought I am not good enough for physics and I am too good for philosophy. Mathematics is in between" (G. L. Alexanderson, George Polya Interviewed on His 90th Birthday, *The Two-Year College Mathematics Journal*. 1979).

Polya obtained a PhD in mathematics from Eötvös Loránd University in Budapest, taught at Swiss Technical University of Zurich from 1914 to 1940, and, like many others, fled the war and persecution in Europe for the United States. He taught at Stanford University from

1940–1953, where he became Professor Emeritus for the remainder of his career and life.

His interests spanned a number of areas of mathematics, including number theory, series analysis, geometry, combinatorics, and probability. The main focus of his later career, however, was to try to characterize the methods that people use to solve problems—and this is precisely why he is so important in the field of AI—the notion of *heuristics*—a word which has its roots in Greek, meaning "discovery."

Heuristics are the foundation of *strong AI*, which you will hear more about in Chapter 6 (Knowledge Representation), and it is heuristics that distinguish AI methods from traditional computer science methods. Heuristics distinguish pure algorithms from human problem-solving methods, which are inexact, intuitive, creative, sometimes powerful, and hard to define. A point of some controversy was Polya's belief that effective problem-solving is a skill that can be taught and learned.

The Knight's Tour Problem (see Exercise 10a.) demonstrates the power of heuristics: it is an example of one heuristic making the problem much easier to solve.

Polya did develop a general method for problem solving that has been accepted as a standard in mathematics, computer science, and other disciplines:

1. Understand the problem.

2. Develop a plan.

3. Implement the plan.

4. Evaluate the outcome.

These four steps have been a universal standard, although there have been some variations, themes, and refinements on them, across disciplines.

Polya authored four other highly influential books: *Mathematics and Plausible Reasoning,* Volumes I and II, and *Mathematical Discovery*: *On Understanding, Learning, And Teaching Problem Solving* Volumes I & II.

References

Alexanderson, G. L. January 1979. George Pólya interviewed on his ninetieth birthday. *The Two-Year College Mathematics Journal* 10(1):13–19.

Mayer, R. E. 2003. *Learning and instruction.* Upper Saddle River, NJ: Pearson Education.

Pólya, G. 1954. *Mathematics and plausible reasoning: Induction and analogy in mathematics,* Volume I. Princeton, NJ: Princeton University Press.

Pólya, G. 1954. *Mathematics and plausible reasoning: Patterns of plausible inference,* Volume II. Princeton, NJ: Princeton University Press.

Pólya, G. 1966. *Mathematical discovery: On understanding, learning, and teaching problem solving* Volumes I & II. USA: John Wiley & Sons.

Pólya, G. 1978. Guessing and proving. *The Two-Year College Mathematics Journal* 9(1):21–27.

Pólya, G. 1979. More on guessing and proving. *The Two-Year College Mathematics Journal* 10(4):255–258.

Pólya, G. 1988. *How to Solve It*: *A New Aspect of Mathematical Method*, First Princeton Science Library Edition, with Foreword by John H. Conway. United States: Princeton University Press.

Pólya, George. 2001. The goals of mathematical education. Videotaped lecture transcribed by T. C. O'Brien for the *ComMuniCator* September (2001). Mathematically Sane Web site: *http://mathematicallysane.com/analysis/polya.asp* (retrieved January 18, 2008).

A common example of the application of heuristics versus pure calculation and algorithmic problem-solving would be transportation in a large city. Many students use as a heuristic, never travel by car to their colleges between 7:00 and 9:00 am and never go home between 4:00 and 6:00 pm, because this is the rush hour in most major cities; a 45-minute trip can easily require one to two hours. If, travel *is* necessary during those times, then an exception is made.

It is now quite common to use programs such as MapQuest®, Google® Maps, or Yahoo!® Maps to obtain the suggested driving directions between two locations. Do you ever wonder if these programs have built-in AI, employing heuristics to enable them to perform intelligently? If they employ heuristics, then what are they? For example, do the programs take into account whether the road is an interstate highway, a local highway, an expressway, or a boulevard? Are driving conditions considered? How would this affect the average speed and difficulty of driving on a particular road and its choice as a means to a particular destination?

It is important to remember that heuristics are only "rules of thumb." How else could you explain the fact that a student drove his friend home to lower Manhattan at 2:00 am and was heading back to the Brooklyn Battery Tunnel, when he suddenly found himself frozen in place for more than 15 minutes, surrounded by taxis and a garbage truck near the Holland Tunnel entrance? Mention of the Holland Tunnel often is a sour note for any New York metropolitan area driver who is intent on getting anywhere quickly. Perhaps one should add a sub-heuristic: "stay away from any route that takes you past the entrance to the Holland Tunnel — even if you must go out of your way."

Figure 3.1

The MapQuest solution for driving from Brooklyn College to Yankee Stadium.

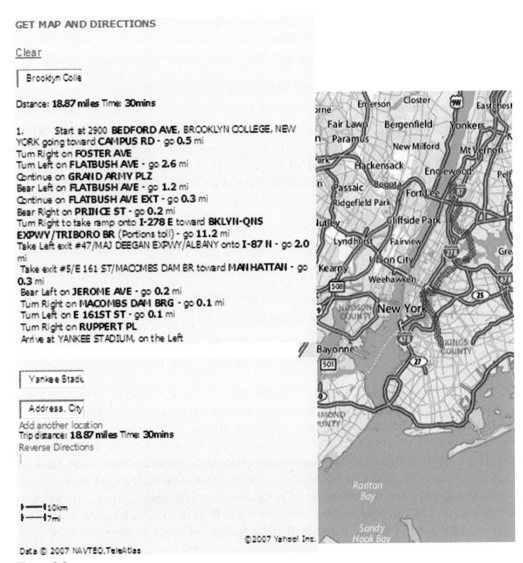

GET MAP AND DIRECTIONS

Clear

Brooklyn Colle

Distance: 18.87 miles Time: 30mins

1.   Start at 2900 **BEDFORD AVE**, BROOKLYN COLLEGE, NEW YORK going toward **CAMPUS RD** - go **0.5** mi
Turn Right on **FOSTER AVE**
Turn Left on **FLATBUSH AVE** - go **2.6** mi
Continue on **GRAND ARMY PLZ**
Bear Left on **FLATBUSH AVE** - go **1.2** mi
Continue on **FLATBUSH AVE EXT** - go **0.3** mi
Bear Right on **PRINCE ST** - go **0.2** mi
Turn Right to take ramp onto **I-278 E** toward **BKLYN-QNS EXPWY/TRIBORO BR** (Portions toll) - go **11.2** mi
Take Left exit #47/MAJ DEEGAN EXPWY/ALBANY onto **I-87 N** - go **2.0** mi
Take exit #5/E 161 ST/MACOMBS DAM BR toward **MANHATTAN** - go **0.3** mi
Bear Left on **JEROME AVE** - go **0.2** mi
Turn Right on **MACOMBS DAM BRG** - go **0.1** mi
Turn Left on **E 161ST ST** - go **0.1** mi
Turn Right on **RUPPERT PL**
Arrive at YANKEE STADIUM, on the Left

Yankee Stadi

Address, City

Add another location
Trip distance: **18.87** miles Time: **30mins**
Reverse Directions

├──┤ 10km
├──┤ 7mi

©2007 Yahoo! Inc.

Data © 2007 NAVTEQ,TeleAtlas

Figure 3.2
The Yahoo! Maps Solution for driving from Brooklyn College to Yankee Stadium.

When using any driving directions or map, it's a good idea to check and make sure the road still exists, watch out for construction, and follow all traffic safety precautions. These maps and directions are to be used only as aids in planning.

As can be seen from comparing the two programs' solutions in Figure 3.1 (MapQuest) and Figure 3.2 (Yahoo! Maps), the MapQuest solution is about 2 miles, and 6 minutes, longer. That is mainly because the solutions are started differently. What is important about this example, however, is the general concept of the use of heuristics: a person familiar with driving in New York City during rush hour would use experience-based techniques to decide how to get to Yankee Stadium for a 7:05 pm baseball game. No seasoned New York driver would take the Brooklyn - Queens Expressway (Route 278) during these times; it is usually a logjam to be avoided at all costs. In this case, it would be much wiser to take an alternate route, which might be longer in miles but shorter in time.

Programs such as Google Maps, Yahoo! Maps, and MapQuest are continually becoming "smarter" in order to suit our needs, and they can include such features as shortest time (used in the

examples in Figures 3.1 and 3.2), shortest distance, avoid highways (there might be circumstances in which a driver would wish to avoid highways), tolls, seasonal closings, and so forth.

3.2 ▪ INFORMED SEARCH ALGORITHMS (PART I) – FINDING ANY SOLUTION

Now that we have discussed heuristics and have seen the importance of their role in AI, we are ready to address three specific search algorithms that use heuristics to help guide the intelligent search process. Most fundamental is the *hill climbing* algorithm. A bit smarter is *steepest-ascent hill climbing*, and then an algorithm, which, at times, can match an optimal algorithm in efficiency—the best-first search algorithm.

3.2.1 ▪ Hill Climbing

The concept behind this algorithm is that even though you might be climbing a hill, presumably getting closer to a goal node at the top, your goal/destination will perhaps not be reachable from your current location. In other words, you could be close to a goal state without having access to it. Traditionally, hill climbing is the first **informed** search algorithm that is discussed. In its simplest form, it is a greedy algorithm in the sense that it has no sense of history, nor the ability to recover from mistakes or false paths. It will use one measure to guide it to a goal—whether that measure is minimized or maximized, to direct the next "move" choice. Imagine a climber who is trying to reach the peak of a mountain. The only device she has is an altimeter, to indicate how high up the mountain she is, but that measure cannot guarantee that she will reach the peak of the mountain. The climber, at every point where she must make a choice, will take a step that indicates the highest altitude, but there is no certainty, beyond the given altitude, that she is on the right path. Obviously, the drawback of this simple hill-climbing method is that the decision-making process (heuristic measure) is so naïve and the climber does not really have enough information to be sure that she is on the right track.

Hill climbing will consider only estimates of remaining distance; actual distances traveled are ignored. In Figure 3.3, hill climbing decides between A and B. A is chosen, because the estimate of remaining distance is less than for B. Node B is "forgotten." Then hill climbing looks out on the search space from A. Each of the nodes C and D are considered but C is selected, for obvious reasons, and then H follows.

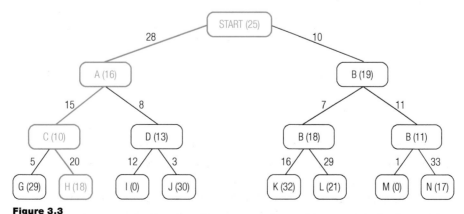

Figure 3.3
Example of hill climbing. Note that in this example, the numbers in the nodes are the estimates of distance to a goal state and the numbers on the vertices are indicators only of distance traveled, adding no important information.

3.2.2 Steepest-Ascent Hill Climbing

It would be desirable to be able to make decisions in a given state knowing that you will be able to get closer to a certain goal state and that your decision is the best from a number of possible choices. In essence, this explains the advantage of **steepest-ascent hill climbing** over simple hill climbing described above. The advantage is that a choice can be made from a number of possible "better nodes" than the current state. Rather than merely choosing a move that is "better" (higher) than the current state, this approach selects the "best" move (in this case the highest number) from a given set of possible nodes.

Figure 3.4 illustrates steepest-ascent hill climbing. If the program chooses nodes in alphabetical order, then starting with node A (-30) it would conclude that the best next state would be node B which has a score of (-15). But it's still worse than the current state (0), so eventually it will move to

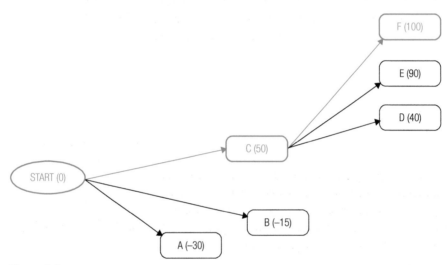

Figure 3.4
Steepest-ascent hill climbing: here we have a climber who is presented with nodes in alphabetical order. From node C (50), hill climbing chooses node E (90), and steepest-ascent hill climbing chooses F(100).

```
// steepest-ascent Hill climbing

Hillclimbing (Root_Node, goal)
{
Create Queue Q
If (Root_Node = goal) return successes
Push all the children of Root_Node in to Q
While (Q_Is_Not_Empty)
    {
    Find the child which has minimum distance to goal
    } // end of while
Best_child = the child which has minimum distance to goal
If (Best_child is not a leaf)
    Hillclimbing(Best_child, goal)
Else
    If (Best_child = goal) return Succees
    retum failure;
}// end of the function
}
```

Figure 3.5
Pseudocode for steepest-ascent hill climbing.

node C (50). From node C it could consider nodes D, E, or F. Because node D takes it to a "worse" state than its current state, however, it won't be chosen. Node E, at 90, is an improvement over its current state (50) and therefore it would be chosen.

Standard hill climbing, if used as described here, would never get to examine node F, which would return a higher score than node E, namely 100. In contrast to standard hill climbing, steepest-ascent hill climbing would evaluate all three nodes D, E, and F, and conclude that F (100) is the best node to choose from node C. Figure 3.5 provides the pseudocode for steepest-ascent hill climbing.

The Foothills Problem

There are some circumstances that can be problematic for hill climbing. One is called the **foothills problem**. Hill climbing is a greedy algorithm and has no sense of the past or future, therefore it can get stuck at a local maximum such that although a solution or goal state seems within reach (it might even be seen) it cannot be reached from our current position even though the top of our current foothill is visible. The actual mountaintop itself (the global maximum) might also be visible, but it cannot be reached from our current lo-cale. (See Figure 3.6a) Imagine the hill climber who thinks he might be reaching the top of the mountain, but instead he

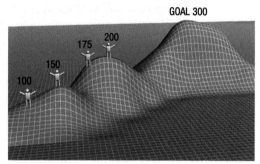

Figure 3.6a
The foothills problem.

is just reaching the top of a hill that he is presently climbing. An analogy for the foothills problem would be a scenario such as the following: imagine we were traveling 400 miles west by car on a highway to reach a particular state park, and all indications on our odometer are that we are indeed getting closer to that state park, and then once we are closer to our destina-tion we discover that the only entrance to this park is 200 miles north of where we had thought it would be.

The Plateau Problem

Another typical problem for hill climbing is known as the **plateau problem**. Suppose there are a number of simi-lar and good local maxima, but to reach the real solution state we must move on to another plateau. Figure 3.6b de-picts the analogy of looking for a certain apartment in a large apartment building; it shows what it would be like to be stuck on the wrong plateau.

Figure 3.6b:
Hill climbing—the plateau problem.

We might think we are getting closer to our goal apart-ment (e.g., Apt. 101) but we are in the wrong building!

The Ridge Problem

Finally there is the familiar **ridge problem**, wherein there might be good heuristic values indicating that we are approaching a goal or solution, but they are on the wrong level of the building. (See Figure 3.6c) This would be akin to visiting a major department store and finding ourselves on the wrong level (e.g., Women's Clothing is on the first floor,

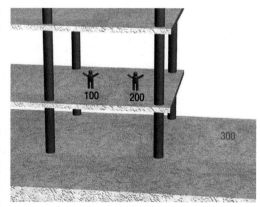

Figure 3.6c
The ridge problem of hill climbing.

but we want to buy something in the Men's Clothing department on the second floor). That we see a wide selection of nice Women's Clothing doesn't change the fact that we are on the wrong floor of the store and will not be finding any appropriate attire anytime soon.

There are a few remedies that can be tried for these hill-climbing problems. One solution to the problem of local maxima is to backtrack (Chapter 2, Section 2) to an earlier node and try a different direction. Consider paths that were almost taken (particularly with steepest-ascent hill climbing), and if a path led to a dead end, consider an alternate path.

The plateau problem arises when many points in a neighboring region have similar values. The best way to deal with this problem is to try to get to a new region of the search space by applying the same rule several times; in this way, new and extreme values will be generated.

Finally, by applying several rules at once, the search will be pushed into several directions. This will help to avoid the kinds of values that will lead to the ridge problem (see Figure 3.6c). Direction will be diversified early and often, thereby preventing the search from getting stuck.

Let us consider Figure 3.4 again: if it turns out that the selected path to node F (100) leads nowhere, we might return to node B and consider the alternate path, which takes us to node E (90)—assuming we have stored that value from the previous search. This would be an example of an attempted remedy to the local maximum problem that we discussed above. Likewise, if we choose to return to and explore node A (-30), which looked bad at first, we might take the search in new directions where our plateau-like problem seemed to exist.

■3.3■ THE BEST-FIRST SEARCH

The problem with hill climbing is that it is a short-sighted greedy algorithm. Steepest-ascent hill climbing has a little more perspective because it compares possible successor nodes before making a choice; it is still, however, subject to the problems identified with hill climbing (the foot-hills problem, the plateau problem, and the ridge problem). If we consider the possible remedies and formalize them somewhat, the result is the *best-first search*. The best-first search is the first intelligent search algorithm in our discussion that can make an impact on which nodes and how many nodes are explored in order to reach a goal node. Best-first search maintains a list of open and closed nodes, as do depth first search and breadth first search. The open nodes are nodes that are on the **fringe** of the search and might later be further explored. The closed nodes are nodes that will no longer be explored and will form the basis of a solution. Nodes on the open list are ordered by a heuristic estimate of their proximity to a goal state. Thus, each iteration of the search considers the most promising node on the open list and thereby brings the *best* state to the front of the open list. Duplicate states (e.g., states that can be reached by more than one path, but with different costs), are not retained. Instead, the least costly, most promising, and heuristically closest state to the goal state of the duplicate nodes is retained.

As we can see from the above discussion and from the pseudocode for the best-first search in Figure 3.7, the most significant advantage of best-first search over hill climbing is that it can recover from mistakes, false leads, and dead ends by backtracking to nodes on the open list. Children of nodes on the open list can be reconsidered, if alternate solutions are sought. The closed-node list, if traced in reverse order, represents the best solution found, by omitting dead-end states.

As described above, the best-first search maintains a priority queue for the open-node list. Recall, a priority queue has the features (1) that an element can be inserted, and (2) the maximum (or minimum node) can be deleted. Figure 3.8 illustrates how best-first search works. Note that the efficiency of best-first search depends on the effectiveness of the heuristic measure(s) that are being used.

```
//Best-First Search

BestFirstSearch(Root_Node, Goal)
{
Create Queue Q
Insert Root_Node to Q
While Q_Is_not_Empty)
{
     G = remove from Q
     If (G = goal ) return path from root_node to G  // successes
     While(G has child nodes){
      If (child is not inside Q)
          Insert child node to Q
                Else
                   insert the child which has minimum value in to the Q,
                   delete all the other nodes.
              } // end of second whlie
 sort Q by the value   // smallest Node at the top
}// end of first while
return failure
}
```

Figure 3.7
Pseudocode for the best-first search.

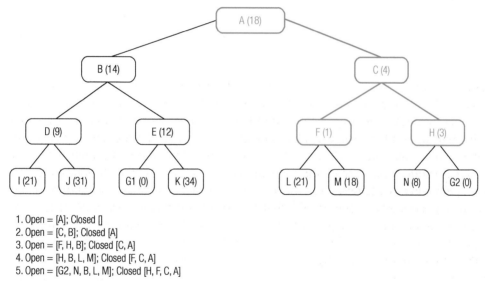

1. Open = [A]; Closed []
2. Open = [C, B]; Closed [A]
3. Open = [F, H, B]; Closed [C, A]
4. Open = [H, B, L, M]; Closed [F, C, A]
5. Open = [G2, N, B, L, M]; Closed [H, F, C, A]

Figure 3.8
The best-first search. At each level, the node with the lowest estimated cost to a goal is kept on the open queue. Earlier nodes kept on the open-node list might later be explored. The "winning" path is A→C→F→H. The search will always find a path if it exists.

Good heuristic measures will quickly find a solution that could even be optimal. Poor heuristic measures will sometimes find a solution, but even when they do so, such solutions are usually far from optimal.

Using Figure 3.9, we return to the problem of driving from Brooklyn College to Yankee Stadium. We will trace the best-first search algorithm and its solution and then consider what this solution means in real-world terms—in other words, does it work?

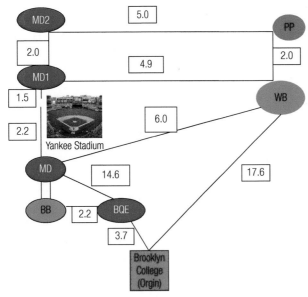

Figure 3.9
Using the best-first search to determine a good route to Yankee Stadium from Brooklyn College at 5:30 pm.

SIDEBAR

The Mythical Man-Month

A good analogy with regard to why best-first search is not optimal, or might be far from optimal, can be taken from the housing industry in the United States at the time of this writing (January 2008). When the housing market was peaking several years ago, many people elected to improve their homes rather than move and buy another home. In such instances, a contractor would usually provide a homeowner (or the parties responsible for a large construction operation such as an apartment building or hotel) with an estimate of the cost and time involved for the project. Often, contractors' projects have been known to overrun the estimated costs (both in terms of dollars and time). So, when the renovated homes were finally completed (long past their scheduled date) it turned out that the housing market had severely deflated, and the homes, despite the renovations, in most cases had lower market value than they'd had before the renovations. As you would expect, many home owners were left very disappointed— some without a home to move back into, because, given unexpected costs that might have arisen, the construction project was never completed! So it is important to have a good heuristic measure and for it to be as accurate as possible.

Abbreviations:

BQE = Brooklyn-Queens Expressway
BB = Brooklyn Bridge
WB = Bronx-Whitestone Bridge
MD = Major Deegan Expressway
PP = Pelham Parkway

Brooklyn College to Yankee Stadium: 36 minutes (20.87 miles)

NOTE: estimated travel times (and distances) from Map-Quest are as follows:

Brooklyn Bridge to Yankee Stadium: 25 minutes (8.5 miles)

Brooklyn-Queens Expressway to Yankee Stadium: 24 minutes (16.8 miles)

Brooklyn College to Bronx-Whitestone Bridge: 35 minutes (17.6 miles)

Abbreviations:

BC = Brooklyn College
BQE = Brooklyn-Queens Expressway
BB = Brooklyn Bridge
WB = White Stone Bridge
MD = Major Deegan Expressway
YS = Yankee Stadium

Table 3.1
The best-first search algorithm finds a solution for driving the shortest distance from Brooklyn College to Yankee Stadium.

Loop Number	Closing Vertex	Open List	Closed List
1	BC	BC (null 0 + 3.7)	WB (17.6)
2	BQE	BB(2.2), MD (14.6), WB(17.6)	BC (null 0), BQE(3.7)
3	BB	MD(8.5), MD (14.6), WB(17.6)	BC (null 0), BQE(3.7), BB(2.2)
4	MD	YS (2.2), MD (14.6), WB(17.6)	BC (null 0), BQE(3.7), BB(2.2), MD(8.5)
5	YS	MD (14.6), WB(17.6)	BC (null 0), BQE(3.7), BB(2.2), MD (8.5), YS (2.2)

As we can see in Table 3.1, the best-first search returns the solution **BC (null 0), BQE (3.7), BB (2.2), MD (8.5), YS (2.2)** which is a total of only 16.6 miles, and is even shorter (in distance) than the MapQuest solution. Little wonder, however, that the MapQuest solution, which was trying to minimize on time (not distance) did not offer this route. Instead it offered a slightly longer route that entailed traveling on the Brooklyn Queens Expressway (BQE) rather than the shorter route, which travels through midtown Manhattan.

3.4 ■ THE BEAM SEARCH

The **beam search** has its name because when the best W nodes (e.g., $W = 2$ as in Figure 3.10) are expanded at each level, they form a kind of thin, focused "beam of light" as illustrated in Figure 3.11.

In beam search, investigation spreads through the search tree level by level, but only the best W nodes are expanded. W is called the beam width.

The beam search is an attempted improvement on a breadth first search by reducing the memory costs from exponential to linear, dependent on the depth of the search tree. A breadth first search is used to build its search tree but then splits each level of the search tree into slices at most W *states where W is the beam width.* [6]

The number of slices (of width W) is limited to one at each level.

When beam search expands a level, it generates all successors of the states' current level, sorts them in order of increasing heuristic values (from left to right), splits

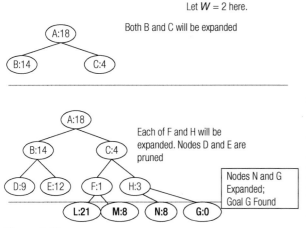

Figure 3.10
The beam search: best W (2 in this case) nodes expanded at each level. Goal (G) found.

Figure 3.11
The beam search—can look like a beam of light.

them into slices of at most W states each, and then extends the beam by storing the first slice only. Beam search terminates when it generates a goal state or runs out of memory (ibid.).

Furcy and Koenig studied variations on the "discrepancy" and learned that using larger beams enabled the discovery of shorter paths, without running out of memory. A discrepancy in this context was the choice of successor nodes that did not return the best heuristic values from left to right. Recall that one of the problems with beam search is that if too thin a beam (of size W) is chosen, there is a good chance that a potential solution will be missed in the heuristic decision-making process. Furcy and Koenig found that use of the beam search with limited discrepancy backtracking could facilitate solution of some difficult problems.

■3.5■ ADDITIONAL METRICS FOR SEARCH ALGORITHMS

In Chapter 2, we introduced several metrics to evaluate search algorithms. Recall that a search algorithm is *complete* if it always finds a solution when one exists. Breadth first search (bfs) is complete when the branching factor of a search space is finite. A search algorithm is *optimal* if it returns the lowest-cost path from among all possible solutions. When one is assured that the path cost is a nonincreasing function of tree depth, then bfs is also optimal. Space and time complexity were also defined; each of the blind search algorithms presented in the previous chapter were shown to exhibit exponential time complexity in the worst case. Furthermore, bfs was plagued by exponential space requirements. Consult Table 3.2.

Branching factor is denoted by b; the depth of a solution by d, the maximum depth of the search tree by m; and the depth limit is denoted by l. All search algorithms described in this chapter employ heuristics. These rules of thumb are intended to guide a search toward promising portions of the search space and thereby reduce search time. Suppose that, at some point in a search, our algorithm is situated at an intermediate node n. The search began at start node "S" and will hopefully culminate at a goal node "G." At this point in the search, one might wish to calculate $f(n)$—the exact cost of an S to G path that passes through n; $f(n)$ has two components: $g(n)$, the actual distance traveled from S to this node n, and $h^*(n)$, the remaining distance to G via a shortest path. In other words, $f(n) = g(n) + h^*(n)$. We have a problem. We are at node n and are searching for a shortest path to G. How can we possibly know the exact cost—$h^*(n)$—of this path, when the path has not yet been discovered? We cannot! Hence we must settle for $h(n)$, which is an estimate of remaining distance. If this estimate is to be useful, then it must be an underestimate, or, $h(n) \leq h^*(n)$ for all nodes n. When this is so, $h(n)$ is said to be an **admissible heuristic**. Hence, our evaluation function

Table 3.2
Comparing the complexity of various search algorithms.

Criterion	Breadth-First	Uniform-Cost	Depth-First	Iterative Deepening	Depth-Limited	Bidirectional (if applicable)
Time	b^d	b^d	b^m	b^l	b^d	$b^{d/2}$
Space	b^d	b^d	b^m	b^l	b^d	$b^{d/2}$
Optimal?	Yes	Yes	No	No	Yes	Yes
Complete?	Yes	Yes	No	Yes, if $1 \geq d$	Yes	Yes

is $f(n) = g(n) + h(n)$. Recall the 3-puzzle from Chapter 2. There are two examples of admissible heuristics for this puzzle:

1. h_1 – the number of tiles out of place, and
2. h_2 – the sum of the distances that each tile must travel to reach the goal state.

How can one be sure that these heuristics are admissible? Can the reader think of any other admissible heuristics for this puzzle?

A search algorithm is said to be *admissible* if it always results in an *optimal* solution whenever some solution does indeed exist (note that in Chapter 2 we used the term optimal in this context). We will denote the actual cost of an optimal solution by f^* where: $f^*(n) = g^*(n) + h^*(n)$. We have already commented that $h^*(n)$ is an elusive quantity, and instead we must settle for a heuristic estimate $h(n)$, where $h(n) \leq h^*(n)$. Similarly, obtaining the optimal "S to n" path is no easy task, and we must often employ $g(n)$, which is the *actual* cost from S to this node, n. Naturally, it is possible that $g(n) \geq g^*(n)$. If the search algorithm for the previously cited trip to Madison, Wisconsin, were admissible, then we would be certain that the selected path to Madison is optimal. However, an admissible algorithm does *not* guarantee shortest paths to intermediate nodes (in this example, cities such as Cleveland, Detroit, and Chicago). A search algorithm is said to be **monotonic** if it is guaranteed to produce the optimal path to every intermediate node as well. A monotonic algorithm for our NYC to Madison junket *would* provide optimal tours for all intermediate nodes as well. Intuition will perhaps lead the reader to conclude (*correctly*) that a monotonic search algorithm is always admissible. You are asked to consider the converse of this assertion: "Is an admissible search algorithm always monotonic?" (*Justify* your answer!).

We categorize search heuristics based on the amount of effort they are likely to save us. Suppose that one has two heuristics, h_1 and h_2 for some problem. Suppose further that $h_1(n) \leq h_2(n)$, for all nodes n. Then h_2 is said to be *more informed than* h_1; $h_2(n)$ being greater than or equal to $h_1(n)$ means that $h_2(n)$ is closer to (or at least as close to) $h^*(n)$, the *exact cost* to the goal as $h_1(n)$. Consider the two heuristics previously cited for the 3-puzzle. We will demonstrate shortly that h_2, which corresponds to the sum of the distances that each tile must travel, is more informed than h_1, which merely considers the number of tiles out of place.

In Chapter 2 we showed how to solve the 4-Queens Problem by using backtracking. Many tentative solutions were considered and then rejected. Such algorithmic approaches are aptly termed *tentative*. These are to be contrasted with methods that examine only one path, such as "plain vanilla" hill climbing. These latter approaches are referred to as **irrevocable**.

■3.6■ INFORMED SEARCH (PART 2) – FINDING AN OPTIMAL SOLUTION

The family of searches in Section 2 had one attribute in common: they each employed a heuristic measure of remaining distance to the goal in order to guide their progress. We now turn our attention to a collection of search algorithms that *look backward*—backward in the sense that *distance from the start node* (i.e., $g(n)$), is either the entire path estimate or at least a major component. By including $g(n)$ as part of the total estimated path cost, $f(n)$, we are decreasing the likelihood that our search follows a less-than-optimal path to the goal.

3.6.1. Branch and Bound

We refer to our first algorithm as "plain vanilla" branch and bound.

This algorithm is often referred to in the literature as **uniform-cost search**. [7] Paths are developed in terms of increasing cost—more accurately, in terms of nondecreasing cost. The estimated cost of a path is simply: $f(n) = g(n)$. No heuristic estimate of remaining distance is employed; or,

Suppose one visited an ice cream shop while on a diet—one might well forego the chocolate syrup and whipped cream and the "fancier" flavors and instead settle for plain vanilla ice cream.

equivalently, this estimate, $h(n)$, is set to zero everywhere. The similarity to breadth first search is apparent in that nodes closest to the start node are visited first; however, with branch and bound, cost values might assume any positive real values. A major difference between these two searches is that bfs strives to find some path to the goal, whereas branch and bound endeavors to find an *optimal* path. With branch and bound, when a path to the goal is found, it is likely that this path is optimal. To ensure that the path found is indeed optimal, branch and bound continues generating partial paths until each has a cost greater than or equal to the best path to the goal found thus far. Plain vanilla branch and bound is shown in Figure 3.12.

The tree we have been using to illustrate our search algorithms is reproduced in Figure 3.13. Because branch and bound does not employ heuristic estimates, they are not included in this figure.

Figures 3.14(a–f) and 3.14(g) follow branch and bound as it pursues an optimal path to a goal. Observe that nodes are expanded in terms of increasing path length.

The search continues in (f) and (g) until every partial path has a cost greater than or equal to 21, the shortest path to the goal. See continuation of the branch and bound in Figure 3.14(g).

Branch and bound finds that the shortest path to a goal in Figure 3.14(g) is A to C to H to G_2 with a cost of 21.

In Chapter 2, we discussed the Traveling Salesperson Problem (TSP) and demonstrated that a greedy-based algorithm was incapable of solving an instance of this problem. Figure 2.13 is reproduced for convenience as Figure 3.15.

```
//Branch and Bound Search.

Branch_Bound (Root_Node, goal)
{
Create Queue Q
Insert Root Node into Q
While (Q_Is_Not_Empty)
    {
    G = Remove from Q
    If (G= goal) Return the path from Root_Node to G;
    else
    Insert children of G in to the Q
    Sort Q by path length
    } // and while
Return failure
}
```

Figure 3.12
Plain vanilla branch and bound.

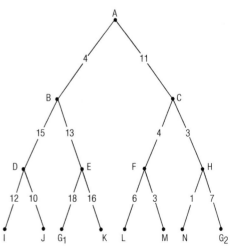

Figure 3.13
Our search tree without heuristic estimates.

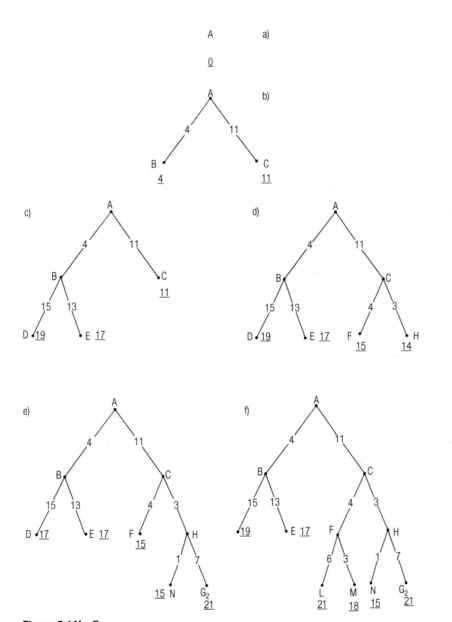

Figure 3.14(a–f)
(a) Start with root node A. Paths from root are generated. (b) Because B has the least cost, it is expanded. (c) Of three choices, C has the least cost, so it is expanded. (d) Node H has least cost, so it is expanded. (e) A path to goal G_2 is discovered, but expanding to other branches is needed in order to see if there is a goal with less distance. (f) Both F and N nodes have a cost of 15; the leftmost node is expanded first.

g)

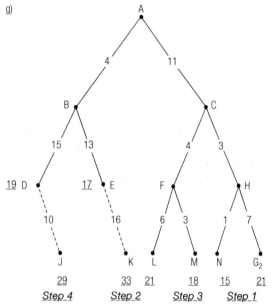

Figure 3.14(g)
The next four steps of the branch and bound algorithm. Step 1: The path to node N cannot be extended. Step 2: the next shortest path, A→B→E is extended; its cost now exceeds 21. Step 3: The paths to nodes M and N cannot be extended. Step 4: The least partial path with a cost of ≤ 21 is extended. Its cost is now 29 and exceeds the start ≥ goal path.

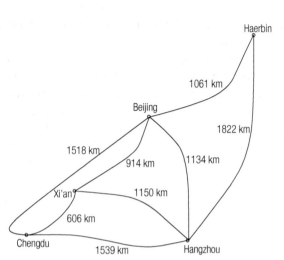

Figure 3.15
An instance of the Traveling Salesperson Problem—revisited.

We had assumed, in Chapter 2, that our salesperson lived in Xi'an and that he or she must visit each of the remaining four cities and then return to Xi'an, and must do so via a shortest tour. Consider the tree depicted in Figure 3.16.

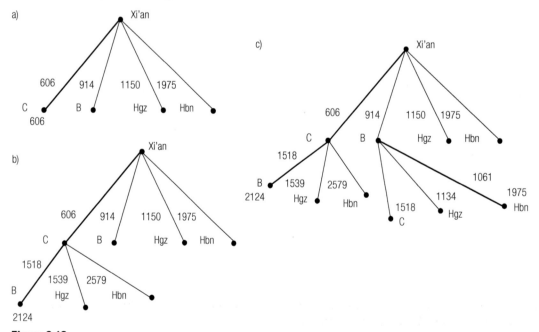

Figure 3.16
The beginning of a branch and bound solution to the TSP. (a) From Xi'an, the first node to be visited is Chengdu at a cost of 606. (b) From Chengdu, the path to Beijing is selected. The path from Xi'an to Chengdu and then to Beijing has a total cost of 2124. (c) Branch and bound expands node B (at level 1) next, because Xi'an to Beijing with a cost of 914 is the shortest path. From Beijing we next go to Hungzhou. The cost of this Xi'an →Beijing →Haerbin partial path is 914+1061 = 1975 km.

Branch and bound would begin by generating paths in terms of increasing (i.e., nondecreasing) length. First, the path from Xi'an to Chengdu is developed, and then on to Beijing. Next, the path expands from Xi'an to Beijing, and then to Chengdu, and so on until an optimal tour has been found.

The TSP is an example of a problem which is **NP-complete**. **NP** is an abbreviation for the class of problems that are solvable in polynomial time *if* guessing is permitted. **P** stands for the class of problems that are solvable in deterministic polynomial time (i.e., polynomial time when *no* guessing is employed). The class P includes many familiar problems in computer science, such as sorting, determining if a graph G is **Eulerian**, in other words, if G possesses a cycle that traverses each edge once and only once (consult Chapter 6, "Knowledge Representation"), or finding a shortest path from vertices i to j in a weighted graph G (Chapter 2). NP-complete problems are the most difficult problems in the class NP. NP-complete problems *seem* to require exponential time (in the worst case) to solve. No one, however, has proven that polynomial time (i.e., deterministic polynomial time) algorithms do not exist for NP-complete problems. We know that $P \subseteq NP$. What is unknown is whether $P = NP$. This remains the most significant open question in theoretical computer science. NP-complete problems are all **polynomial-time reducible** to one another. That is, if a polynomial time algorithm were found for any NP-complete problem, then one would have polynomial time algorithms for all NP-complete problems. The class NP-complete also contains many well-known problems, such as the aforementioned TSP, the **satisfiability problem** in the propositional logic (Chapter 5, "Logic in Artificial Intelligence"), and the **Hamiltonian problem** (this topic is revisited in Chapter 6), in other words, determining if a connected graph G has a circuit that traverses each vertex once and only once. The pseudocode for **branch and bound with underestimates** is shown in Figure 3.17.

```
// Branch and Bound with Underestimates
B_B_Estimate (Root_Node, Goal)
{
Create Queue Q
Insert Root_Node into Q
While (Q_Is_Not_Empty)
      {
      G = Remove from Q
      If (G = Goal) return the path from Root_Node to G.
      else
      Add each child node's estimated distance to current distance.
      Insert children of G into the Q
      Sort Q by path length   // the smallest value at front of Q
      } // end while
Return failure.
}
```

Figure 3.17
Branch and bound with underestimates. Paths are generated in terms of their estimated overall length.

3.6.2 Branch and Bound with Underestimates

In this section, we will augment branch and bound search with underestimates of remaining distance. Consult Figure 3.18 for our search tree.

Branch and bound search with underestimates is shown in Figures 3.19(a–d) and 3.19(e–f).

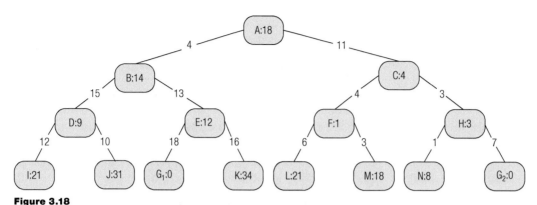

Figure 3.18
Tree with both node-to-node distances (on the branches) and heuristic estimates to the goal (inside the nodes).

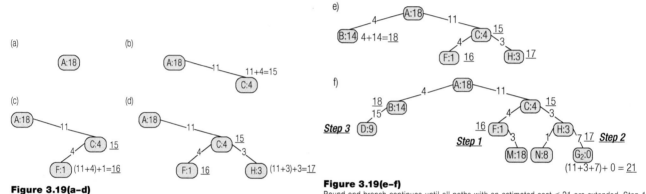

Figure 3.19(a–d)
Branch and bound search with underestimates. (a) A is not a goal; we continue. (b) In this search we went to C first, instead of B, which we had done in plain vanilla branch and bound.

Figure 3.19(e–f)
Bound and branch continues until all paths with an estimated cost ≤ 21 are extended. Step 1: The path A→C→F is extended to M. We are over 21. Step 2: A→C→H is extended to N; over 21. Step 3: A→B is extended to D; over 21.

By consulting Figures 3.18 and 3.19(a–d) and (e–f), one observes that paths are generated in terms of estimated overall length.

After confirming that it is *not* a goal, node A is expanded. From A, there is a choice of going to either of nodes B or C. The distance to B is 4, whereas the cost of C is 11. The estimated costs of paths from either B or C to some goal are 14 and 4 respectively. Therefore, the overall estimate of a path from the start node A, to some goal, passing through B is 4 + 14 = 18, whereas one that passes through C has an estimated cost of 11 + 4 = 15. As Figure 3.19(b) illustrates, branch and bound with underestimates first proceeds to node C. Continuing in this fashion, the search algorithm reaches the goal node G_2 via a path of cost 21 (Figure 3.19(f)). As indicated in the figure, the search is not completed until partial paths with an estimated cost less than or equal to 21 have been extended.

EXAMPLE 3.1 THE 3-PUZZLE REVISITED

We revisit the instance of the 3-puzzle provided in Chapter 2. This puzzle is solved by the two versions of branch and bound just discussed. Figure 3.20 illustrates plain vanilla branch and bound, whereas branch and bound with underestimates is employed in the solution shown in Figure 3.21. Observe that plain vanilla branch and bound requires a search tree with four levels, in which 15 nodes are expanded.

Several observations are apparent:

1. The estimated cost of a solution is set to the distance from the start node, i.e., $f(n) = g(n)$. As stated, the estimate of remaining distance to some goal, $h(n)$, is merely set to zero everywhere.

2. Because the cost of each operator (i.e., moving the blank in one of four directions) equals one, plain vanilla branch and bound appears similar to breadth first search.

3. In this initial version of the branch and bound algorithm, no effort has been made to suppress repeated nodes.

4. The leaf nodes on the bottom right portion of the search tree would ordinarily be expanded, unless the algorithm is modified for this application.

On the other hand, Figure 3.21 demonstrates that branch and bound with underestimates requires a search tree wherein only five nodes have been expanded. It should be apparent that in general, branch and bound *with underestimates is a more informed search algorithm* than plain vanilla branch and bound. It should also be apparent that *both of the branch and bound approaches are admissible.*

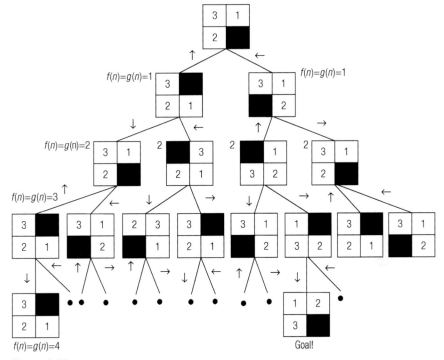

Figure 3.20
Plain vanilla branch and bound on an instance of the 3-puzzle.

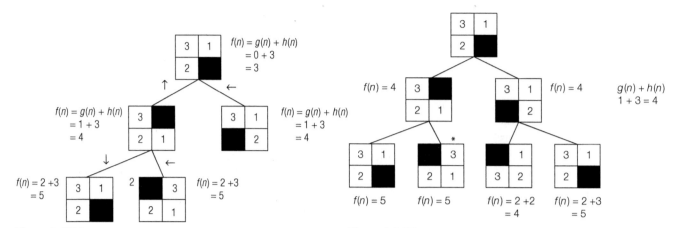

Figure 3.21(a)

Figure 3.21(b)

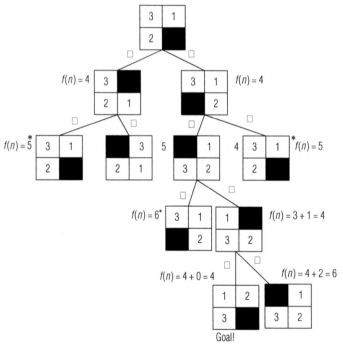

Figure 3.21(a–c)
Branch and bound with underestimates. The heuristic estimate of distance to the goal that is employed is the *number of tiles out of place*. We had commented earlier that this heuristic is admissible. Observe in (b) and (c) that by including $g(n)$ in the estimated cost of a solution $f(n)$, we penalize nodes that correspond to loops: the three nodes marked with * that represent loops are *not* expanded.

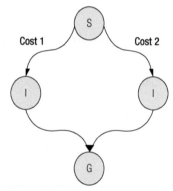

Figure 3.22
The Principle of Optimality. Optimal paths are constructed from optimal subpaths. Suppose that there are two paths from S to some intermediate node I. Path 1 has a cost equal to cost 1 and Path 2 has a cost equal to cost 2. Suppose that cost 1 is less than cost 2. An optimal S to G path that passes through node I cannot possibly begin by taking the more costly path (path 2 with cost 2) to I.

3.6.3 Branch and Bound with Dynamic Programming

Suppose that, at some time in the future, interplanetary travel were to become common place, and suppose that one wanted a minimal cost trip (in terms of total distance traveled) from Earth to Mars. One would not begin the journey by first going from Earth to the moon and then from the moon to Mars. The wisdom in this small example is formalized by the **Principle of Optimality**: optimal paths are constructed from optimal subpaths. In Figure 3.22, an optimal subpath from S to

```
// Branch and Bound with Dynamic Programing
B_B_W_Dynamic_Programming (Root_Node, goal)
{
Create Queue Q
Insert Root_Node into Q
While (Q_Is_Not_Empty)
        {
        G = Remove from Q
        Mark G visited
                If this mode has been visited previously, retain only the shortest
path to G
        If (G= goal) Return the path from Root Node to G;
        Insert the children of G which have not been previously visited into the Q
        } // end while
Return failure
}// end of the branch and bound with dynamic programming function.
```

Figure 3.23
Pseudocode for the branch and bound algorithm with dynamic programming.

G that passes through some intermediate node I is composed of an optimal S to I path, followed by an optimal I to G path.

The branch and bound algorithm that employs dynamic programming (i.e., that makes use of the Principle of Optimality) is shown in Figure 3.23.

This algorithm advises us as follows: If two or more paths reach a common node, only the path that reaches this common node with the minimum cost should be stored. (Delete the others!) Implementing this search procedure on the instance of the 3-puzzle, we have been considering results in a search tree that resembles breadth first search (consult Figure 2.22 in Chapter 2). Retaining only the shortest path to each puzzle state will serve to suppress looping.

3.6.4 The A* Search

The last incantation of branch and bound search is the A* search. This approach employs branch and bound with both estimates of remaining distance and dynamic programming. The A* algorithm is shown in Figure 3.24.

```
//A* Search
A* Search (Root_Node, Goal)
{
Create Queue Q
Insert Root_Node into Q
While (Q_Is_Not_Empty)
        {
        G = Remove from Q
        Mark G visited
        If (G= goal) Return the path from Root_Node to G;
        Else
        Add each child node's estimated distance to current distance.
        Insert the children of G which have not been previously visited into the Q
        Sort Q by path length
        } // end while
Return failure
}// end of A* function.
```

Figure 3.24
The A* search algorithm employs both heuristic estimates of remaining distance and dynamic programming.

EXAMPLE 3.2: THE 3-PUZZLE EMPLOYED ONE LAST TIME TO
ILLUSTRATE A* SEARCH

The solution to this puzzle via the A* search is shown in Figure 3.25.

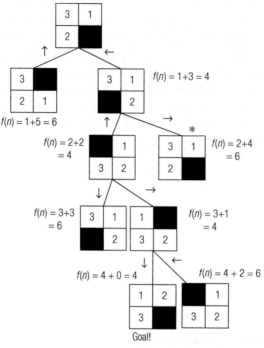

Figure 3.25
A* search that employs total Manhattan distance as the heuristic estimate. Refer to
the node marked with a * in level 3 of this tree. Tile 1 must travel one square left;
tile 2 must move one square east and one square north (or equivalently one square
north and then one square east) and tile 3 needs to travel one square south. Hence
the sum of the Manhattan distances, h(n) = 1 + 2 + 1 = 4 for this node.

The term Manhattan distance is employed because a tile must travel north, south, east, and west similar to how a taxi cab would maneuver through the streets of Manhattan.

Observe that the A* search in Figure 3.25 that employs Manhattan distance as
a heuristic is *more informed* than the branch and bound search in Figure 3.21
that used a number of tiles out of place as a heuristic estimate of remaining
distance.

3.7 ■ INFORMED SEARCH (PART 3) – ADVANCED SEARCH ALGORITHMS

3.7.1 ■ Constraint Satisfaction Search

The technique of **problem reduction** is another important approach in AI. That is, to solve a
complex or larger problem by identifying smaller manageable problems (or subgoals), which you
know can be solved in fewer steps.

For example, Figure 3.26 shows the "Donkey Sliding Block" Puzzle. It has been known for
over 100 years and is presented in the wonderful book *Winning Ways for Your Mathematical Plays*. [8]

Subject to the constraints on the movement of "pieces" in the sliding block puzzle, the task is to slide the Blob around the Vertical Bar with the goal of moving it to the other side. The Blob occupies four spaces and needs two adjacent vertical or horizontal spaces in order to be able to move, whereas the Vertical Bar needs two adjacent empty vertical spaces to move left or right, or one empty space above or below it to move up or down. The Horizontal Bars' movements are comple-mentary to the Vertical Bar. Likewise, the circles can move to any emp-ty space around them in a horizontal or vertical line. For this problem to

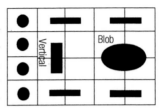

Figure 3.26
Constraint satisfaction, problem reduction, and the Donkey Sliding Block Puzzle.

be solved, a relatively uninformed state-space search can result in over 800 moves, with plenty of backtracking necessary.[2] By employing problem reduction, resulting in the recognition of the sub-goal that needs to be solved before the overall puzzle can be solved: *you must get the Blob on the two rows above or below the vertical bar* (so that they can pass each other); it is possible to solve this puzzle in just 82 moves!

Only 82 moves is quite a reduction, and it is based on understanding the constraints of the problem solution. The message here is that it is usually better to spend extra time trying to understand a problem and its constraints before you begin the problem-solving process.

3.7.2 AND/OR Trees

Another well-known technique for problem reduction is called **AND/OR** trees. Here the goal is to find a solution path in a given tree by applying the following rules:

A node is solvable if

1. It is a terminal node (a primitive problem),
2. It is a nonterminal node whose successors are AND nodes that are all solvable, or
3. It is a nonterminal node whose successors are OR nodes and at least one of them is solvable.

Similarly, a node is unsolvable if

1. it is a nonterminal node that has no successors (a nonprimitive problem to which no operator applies),
2. it is a nonterminal node whose successors are AND nodes and at least one of them is unsolvable, or
3. it is a nonterminal node whose successors are OR nodes and all of them are unsolvable.

In Figure 3.27, nodes B and C serve as exclusive parents to subproblems EF and GH, respectively. One way of viewing the tree is with nodes B, C, and D

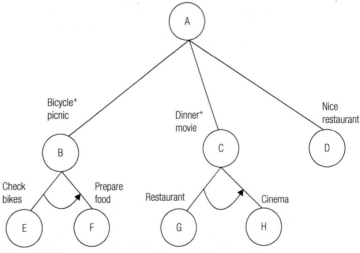

Figure 3.27
AND/OR tree representing the choice of a "date" with Bicycle and a Picnic, Dinner and a Movie, or a Nice Restaurant.

serving as individual, alternative subproblems representing OR nodes. Node pairs E & F and G & H, respectively, with curved arrowheads connecting them, represent AND nodes. That is, to solve problem B you must solve both subproblems E and F. Likewise, to solve subproblem C, you must solve subproblems G and H. Solution paths would therefore be: {A→B→E→F}, {A→C→G→H}, and {A→D}. In this case, we are representing three distinct activity scenarios. In one, if you are going bicycling {A→B} and on a picnic, you must check the bikes {E} and get the food ready {F}. Or, if you are going out to dinner and a movie {A→C}, you must pick a restaurant {G} and a cinema {H}. Or, you could just go out to a nice restaurant {A→D}.

In the special case where no AND nodes occur, we have the ordinary graph occurring in a state-space search. However, the presence of AND nodes distinguishes AND/OR trees (or graphs) from ordinary state structures, which call for their own specialized search techniques. Typical problems tackled by AND/OR trees include games or puzzles, and other well-defined state-space goal oriented problems, such as robot planning, movement through an obstacle course, or setting a robot the task of reorganizing blocks on a flat surface.[2]

3.7.3 The Bidirectional Search

Forward search as described heretofore is known to be a costly process, which can grow exponentially. The idea of bidirectional search is to find a solution path by searching forward for a goal state and searching backward from a known goal state toward a start state. Figure 3.28 illustrates the essence of bidirectional search. The search terminates when the two subpaths intersect. The technique, combining forward and backward reasoning approaches, was developed by Pohl[9] and is known to expand only about ¼ as many nodes as a unidirectional search.

Pohl's original idea regarding the bidirectional search was brilliant, barring that he incorrectly thought that his algorithm (known as BHPA, or traditional front to end bidirectional search) would typically have the search frontiers pass each other. He described this possibility in terms of what came to be called the Missile Metaphor: a missile and an anti-missile targeted toward each other that then pass each other.

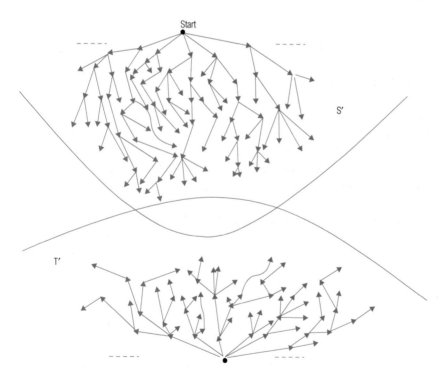

S' ∩ T' is a Potential Solution Space. - - - - - indicates More Search Branches

Figure 3.28
Bidirectional search involves both a forward search from a start node (S) and backward from a goal node (T), hoping that the paths will meet at S' ∩ T'.

de Champeaux and Saint [10] demonstrated that the long-held belief that the algorithm is afflicted by the **Missile Metaphor Problem**, is unfounded. They developed a new generic approach uniquely applicable to the bidirectional search that can be used to dynamically improve heuristic values. Their empirical findings also suggested that the bidirectional search can be performed very efficiently, with limited memory demands, a known deficiency of the standard approach. [2]

Consequently, **wave-shaping algorithms** were developed by de Champeaux and Saint [11] and de Champeaux, [12] and Politowski and Pohl [13] with the idea of steering the two search "wave fronts" towards each other. In contrast the BHPA and bidirectional search (BS*; developed by Kwa [14] to combat the inefficiencies of BHPA) methods, the main idea behind the work of Kaindl and Kainz was that it was unnecessary (and inefficient) to do heuristic *front-to-end* evaluations. Their idea was to improve the efficiency of the BS* by

1. minimizing the number of switches of search direction (a version of the perimeter search), and

2. adding a dynamic feature to the heuristic function of search in the opposite search direction of the front-to-end evaluation, an idea originally presented by Pohl.

The wave front approaches introduced above use *front-to-front* evaluations, or, evaluations that estimate the minimal cost of some path from the evaluated node on one search front to the nodes on the opposing front.[9] "In fact, these algorithms achieve large reductions in the number of nodes searched compared with algorithms that perform front to end evaluations. However, they are either excessively computationally demanding, or they have restrictions on the solution quality" [11] (p. 284–85).

Kaindl and Kainz demonstrated, both theoretically and experimentally, that their improvements to the bidirectional search were valid and that the bidirectional search itself is more efficient and risk-free than previously thought. The "traditional" bidirectional search, as Kaindl and Kainz called it, attempted to develop solutions by storing nodes from both frontiers as the result of forward and backward searches. The traditional approach would use a best-first search and run into the problems of exponential storage requirements as the two frontiers tried to "find each other." This is known as the **frontiers problem**.

The frontiers problem of the bidirectional search was thought to occur as a result of the costs of maintaining in memory the possible solution paths from two directions.

Instead, the "nontraditional approach to bidirectional search" developed by Kaindl and Kainz would store nodes of only one frontier, using a hashing scheme, because "it is possible to search in only one direction first storing nodes, and then to search in the other direction." This comprises a **perimeter search**.[15, 16]

> In perimeter search, a breadth first search generates and stores all the nodes around *t* up to a predetermined (and fixed) *perimeter-depth*. The final frontier of this breadth first search is called the *perimeter*. After this search is finished and the nodes are stored, a forward search starts from *s*, targeting all of the perimeter nodes [11 (p. 291).]

The forward search, depending on the problem and available storage, can be performed by a number of search algorithms including A* and a variant of the iterative deepening dfs (See Section 2.4.4), among others. (See Figure 3.29)

In a nutshell, the improvement of the nontraditional bidirectional search developed by Kaindl and Kainz is that search is mainly in one forward direction to a frontier using a

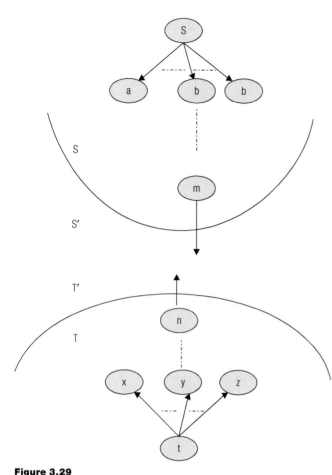

perimeter search. Key information is stored, and then backward search is performed from the goal to see if the stored forward path can be met. Front-to-end methods (as opposed to front-to-front methods) are more efficient for this approach.

In more recent work Kose tested the effectiveness of the bidirectional search by applying it to the Donkey puzzle and other problems.[17] He compared its CPU time and memory usage with those of conventional forward direction searches. The bidirectional search was implemented as a frontier search, with a breadth first search storing all nodes to a specified depth, followed by a heuristic search in the reverse direction—from the goal state to nodes—in this frontier.

One search from a start node *s* toward a goal node *t*, while the other search starts from a goal node *t*, towards a start node, *s*. The two frontiers begin to search while S′∩T′=Ø. After the frontiers meet, S′∩T′ is no longer empty (S′∩T′ ≠ Ø), a path is found. The second level of bidirectional search is to find an optimal path in the set S′∩T′. This second level of search adds more complexity to bidirectional search.

Figure 3.29
The bidirectional search employs two A* searches in order to achieve a task.

s = the start node.
t = the goal node.
S = the collection of nodes reached from s.
T = the same with respect to t.
S′ = the collection of nodes that are neither in S nor in T but are direct successors of nodes in S.
T′ = the same as S′ with respect to T.

In CPU time and memory usage, the bidirectional search was more efficient than other search algorithms with regard to finding an optimal solution to the Donkey sliding block puzzle with the fewest nodes generated and explored in the search space. We also varied the depth of the frontier, expecting the search algorithm to become less efficient when the breadth first search was allowed to continue for too many levels. The best results were achieved with a frontier of 30, mainly because in the solution, the 2 × 2 square makes little progress for the first 30 moves, leading us to conclude that the heuristic search is a better option in the reverse direction from the goal state to a frontier of nodes at move 30. Further work intends to compare different programming paradigms with the bidirectional search for the solution to the Donkey puzzle.[17]

▓3.8▓ CHAPTER SUMMARY

This Chapter introduces a number of intelligent search methods that have been the standards distinguishing AI methods from conventional computer science methods. *Hill climbing* is greedy and primitive, but sometimes can be "lucky" enough to concur with optimal approaches in *steepest-ascent hill climbing*. More usually, hill climbing can be afflicted by three familiar problems—the *foothills problem*, the *plateau problem*, and the *ridge problem*. The more intelligent, preferred approach to searching is the *best-first search*, whereby the open-node queue is maintained for feedback with regard to how close to the solution a given path may be. The *beam search* offers a more focused view whereby a narrow path can be pursued toward a solution.

Section 3.5 introduces four very important metrics for assessing the effectiveness of heuristics, including *admissibility*, which occurs when $h(n)$ is an effective and consistent underestimate of the distance to a solution. A search is monotonic if all the intermediate stages (nodes), are consistently minimal compared with other nodes for the "smaller" trips. A heuristic, $h(2)$ is said to be more informed than a heuristic $h(1)$, when it is consistently closer to the exact cost to a goal, $h*(n)$. Tentative approaches offer a number of alternatives for evaluation, whereas irrevocable approaches offer no alternatives.

Section (3.6) focuses on the discovery of optimal solutions. The *branch and bound search* explores partial paths until every partial path has cost greater than or equal to the shortest path to a goal. Notions of *NP-completeness, polynomial time reducibility*, and the *satisfiability problem* are also introduced. *Branch and bound search with underestimates* is a more informed way to achieve optimality. Finally, the *branch and bound search with dynamic programming*, employing memory of shortest paths found so far—another way of attaining optimality—is explored. The A* algorithm (Section 3.6.4) achieves optimality by employing both underestimates and dynamic programming.

Section 3.7.1 introduces the notion of *problem reduction* by employing constraint satisfaction search. It is considered with respect to the Donkey Sliding Block Puzzle. In Section 3.7.2, we explain how *AND/OR trees* are another way that knowledge can be used to effectively split up and reduce a problem space.

The *bidirectional search* offers an entirely new perspective by employing both forward and backward search to and from a goal state. Its efficiency is considered, and possible problems and remedies, such as the *frontiers problem*, the *Missiles Metaphor*, and *wave-shaping algorithms* are also presented. Improvements to the bidirectional search via the research of Kaindl and Kainz are also presented.[11] Erdal Kose contributed material related to his thesis work for Section 3.7.3. [17]

In the next chapter, we will use the heuristics developed above to play simple two-person games such as Nim and tic-tac-toe.

Questions for Discussion

1. What distinguishes heuristic search methods from those discussed in Chapter 2?

   a. Give three definitions of heuristic search.

   b. Give three ways heuristic information can be added to a search.

2. Explain why hill climbing would be classified as a greedy algorithm.

3. Explain how steepest-ascent hill climbing can also provide an optimal solution.

4. Why is the best-first search more effective than hill climbing?

5. Explain how beam search works.

6. What does it mean for a heuristic to be admissible?

    a. How does admissibility relate to monotonicity?

    b. Can there be monotonicity without admissibility? Explain.

7. What does it mean for a heuristic to be more informed than another heuristic?

8. What is the idea behind the branch and bound search?

9. Explain why underestimates are likely to result in better solutions.

10. a. What is the notion of dynamic programming?

    b. Describe the Principle of Optimality.

11. Why should the A* algorithm be better than branch and bound with underestimates or branch and bound with dynamic programming?

12. Explain the ideas behind the constraint satisfaction search and how it might apply to the Donkey Puzzle.

13. Explain how AND/OR trees can be used to divide a search problem.

14. Describe how the bidirectional search works.

    a. How is it different from the other techniques discussed in the chapter?

    b. Describe the frontiers problem and the Missiles Metaphor.

    c. What are wave-shaping algorithms?

Exercises

1. Give three examples of heuristics and explain how they play a significant role in

    a. your day-to-day life, and

    b. the problem-solving process for some challenge that faces you.

2. Explain why hill climbing is called a "greedy algorithm."

    a. Describe some other algorithms that you know that are "greedy."

    b. Explain how steepest-ascent hill climbing is an improvement over simple hill climbing. How does the best first search improve over hill climbing?

3. Suggest an admissible heuristic, not mentioned in the text, for solving the 3-puzzle.

    a. Employ your heuristic to conduct an A* search to solve the instance of the puzzle presented in this chapter.

    b. Is your heuristic more or less informed than the two heuristics that are presented?

4. **a.** Suggest an admissible heuristic for the Missionaries and Cannibals Problem that is robust enough to avoid unsafe states.

   b. Is your heuristic informed enough to appreciably reduce the search-base explored by an A* search?

5. **a.** Provide a heuristic that is appropriate for graph coloring.

   b. Employ your heuristic to find the chromatic number of the graph in Figure 2.41 in Chapter 2.

6. Consider the following variation of the *n*-Queens Problem:

   If some of the squares that would be attacked by the placement are obstructed by the placement of pawns on an n x n chessboard, can more than *n*-Queens be placed on the partial board that remains? For example, if five pawns are added to a 3 × 3 chessboard, then four non-attacking Queens may be placed on the board (Figure 3.30).

Q	P	Q
P	P	p
Q	P	Q

Figure 3.30
Four Queens on 3 × 3 Chessboard with five Pawns strategically placed. How many non-attacking Queens may be placed on a 5 × 5 chessboard if one has 3 Pawns at one's disposal? [18]

7. Use both the "plain vanilla" branch and bound, and branch and bound with dynamic programming, to get from the start node (S) to the goal node (G) in parts (a) and (b) of Figure 3.31. When all else is equal, explore nodes in alphabetical order.

8. **a.** Develop an admissible heuristic to solve the Maze Problem from Chapter 2 (Exercise 13).

   b. Employ your heuristic to conduct an A* search to solve this problem.

9. **a.** Suggest an admissible heuristic for the Water Jug Problem.

   b. Employ your heuristic to conduct an A* search to solve the instance of this problem presented in Chapter 1.

10. Recall that in Chapter 2 we posed the Knight's Tour problem, in which a chess Knight is to visit each of the *n* × *n* squares on a chessboard. The challenge is to start on a given source square on a full 8 × 8 chess board (say (1,1)), and to find a sequence of moves that visits every square on the board once and only once, returning to the source square on that last move.

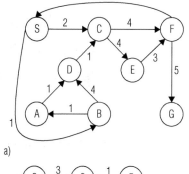
a)

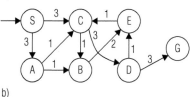
b)

Figure 3.31
Getting to the goal using branch and bound.

   a. Starting on the (1,1) square try to solve the Knight's Tour Problem (hint: you will perhaps find that this version of the problem requires excessive memory and so you might find it useful to identify a heuristic that will help guide the search. (See b. below.)

   b. Try to identify a heuristic that will help guide the first-time Knight's Tour Solver to a correct solution.

11. Write a program to apply the primary heuristic search algorithms, described in this chapter, to Figure 3.17. That is, hill climbing, beam search, best first search, branch and bound with and without underestimates, and the A* algorithm.

12. In Chapter 2, we presented the *n*-Queens Problem. Write a program to solve the Eight-Queens Problem by applying constraints that remove any row or column from consideration once a queen has been placed.

13. In the 64 move solution to the Knight's Tour Problem at some point it becomes necessary to abandon the heuristic you were asked to find in Problem 10.b. Try to identify that point. [++]

14. Develop a solution to the Donkey Sliding Block Puzzle (Figure 3.26 in this Chapter). It requires 81 moves at minimum. Consider a subgoal that may apply to developing this solutions.[++]

Keywords

A* algorithm
admissible heuristic
admissibility
AND/OR trees
beam search
best-first search
bidirectional search (or wave search)
branch and bound algorithm
branch and bound with underestimates
branching factor
combinatorial complexity
constraint satisfaction search

Eulerian
finite
foothills problem
fringe
Hamiltonian problem
hill climbing
informed
irrevocable
monotonic
monotonicity
more informed
NP-complete
perimeter search
plateau problem

polynomial-time reducible
problem reduction
ridge problem
search space
space requirements
steepest-ascent hill climbing
tentative
the frontiers problem
the Missile Metaphor
the satisfiability problem
underestimate
uniform-cost search
wave-shaping algorithms

References

1. Polya, G. 1945. *How to solve it*. Princeton, NJ: Princeton University Press.

2. Kopec, D., Cox, J. and Lucci,. 2014. SEARCH. In *The computer science and engineering handbook*, 2nd ed., edited by A. Tucker, Chapter 38. Boca Raton, FL: CRC Press

3. Bolc, L. and Cytowski, J. 1992. *Search methods for Artificial Intelligence*. San Diego, CA: Academic Press.

4. Pearl, J. 1984. *Heuristics: Intelligent search strategies for computer problem solving*. Reading, MA: Addison-Wesley.

5. Feigenbaum, E. and Feldman, J., eds. 1963. *Computers and thought*. New York, NY: McGraw-Hill.

6. Furcy, D. and Koenig, S. 1996. Limited discrepancy beam search. Available at *http://www.ijcai.org/papers/0596.pdf*

7. Russell, S. and P. Norvig. 2009. *Artificial Intelligence: A modern approach*, 3rd ed. Upper Saddle River, NJ: Prentice-Hall.

8. Berlekamp, H. and Conway, J. 2001. *Winning ways for your mathematical plays*. Natick, MA: A. K. Peters.

[++]*Both problems are addressed in separate Chapters in Artificial Intelligence Problems and Their Solutions, Mercury Learning Inc. 2014.*

9. Pohl, I. 1971. Bi-directional search. In *Machine intelligence 6,* ed., B. Meltzer and D. Michie, 127–140 New York, NY: American Elsevier .

10. de Champeaux, D. and Saint, L. 1977. An improved bidirectional heuristic search algorithm. *Journal of the ACM* 24(2):177– 91.

11. Kaindl, H. and Kainz, G. 1997 Bidirectional heuristic search reconsidered. *Journal of AI Research* 7: 283–317.

12. de Champeaux, D. 1983. Bidirectional heuristic search again. *Journal of the ACM* 30(1): 22–32.

13. Politowski, G., and Pohl, I. 1984. D-node retargeting in bidirectional heuristic search. In *Proceedings of the fourth national conference on Artificial Intelligence* (AAAI-84), 274 – 277. Menlo Park, CA: AAAI Press / The MIT Press.

14. Kwa, J. 1989. BS*: An admissible bidirectional staged heuristic search algorithm. *Artificial Intelligence* 38(2):95–109.

15. Dillenburg, J. and Nelson, P. 1994. Perimeter search. *Artificial Intelligence* 65(1):165 – 178.

16. Manzini, G. 1995. BIDA*, an improved perimeter search algorithm. *Artificial Intelligence* 75(2): 347–360.

17. Kose, E. 2012. Comparing AI Search Algorithms and Their Efficiency When Applied to Path Finding Problems. (*Ph.D Thesis*). The Graduate Center, City University of New York: New York.

18. Zhao, K. 1998. The combinatorics of chessboards. *Ph.D Thesis*, City University of New York.

SEARCH USING GAMES

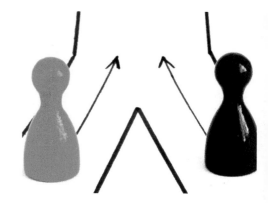

Strategy Boardgames

The previous two chapters discussed search algorithms. This chapter introduces the rudiments of two-person games in which an adversary who attempts to hinder your progress is present. Algorithms for identifying optimal game strategies are provided. The chapter concludes with a discussion of the Iterated Prisoner's Dilemma, a game that is useful for modeling societal conflicts.

DENY EVERYTHING

The Prisoner's Dilemma

4.0 ■ INTRODUCTION

Chapter 4 continues the discussion of search methodologies, with an important variation. In Chapter 2, "Uninformed Searches," and Chapter 3, "Informed Search," you examined problems or puzzles that had a specified start state and goal state; you used operators to transform problem states and to help you eventually reach the goal. The only obstacle to your progress was the immensity of the associated state space.

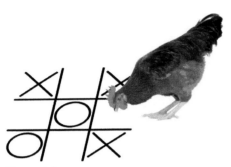

Figure 4.1
Chinatown Chicken.

Some chickens have indeed been trained to play tic-tac-toe without electronic help. For training details, search the Web using Boger Chicken University in your favorite search engine. You can also search for or visit the Tropicana in Atlantic City or the Trump 29 Casino in Palm Springs, which both feature chickens playing tic-tac-toe. (Although you should first finish reading this chapter).

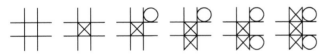

Figure 4.2
Sample game of tic-tac-toe in which X wins. One new move is made in each figure, from left to right.

Game playing introduces an additional challenge: an **adversary** who is trying to impede your advancement. Nearly all games include one or more opponents who are actively trying to defeat you. In fact, much of the excitement in game playing—whether in a friendly card game or a tension-filled night of poker— is derived from the risk of losing.

Many people experienced game-playing sessions at the Chinatown Fair, a small amusement park on Mott Street in Manhattan's Chinatown. In a small booth poised next to a huge electronic tic-tac-toe board, stood the two-foot tall opponent: the Chinatown Chicken. See Figure 4.1. The chicken always moved first, indicating its move by tapping its beak against the board. On a good night, many people would settle for a draw in the game; most of the time the chicken would walk away victorious.

You might realize that it was a computer program and not a chicken that was matching wits with the game players.

In this chapter we will explore the algorithms that enable a computer to play two-person games such as tic-tac-toe and Nim.

Tic-tac-toe, also known as naughts and crosses, is a game played by two individuals on a 3×3 grid. The players, usually identified as X and O, alternate moves as they attempt to align three of their symbols on the same row, column, or diagonal. A sample game is shown in Figure 4.2.

4.1 ■ GAME TREES AND MINIMAX EVALUATION

To evaluate the effectiveness, or "goodness," of a move in a game, you can pursue that move and see where it leads. In other words, you can play "what if " to ask, "If I make this move, how will my opponent respond, and then how will I counter?" After charting the consequences of a move, you can evaluate the effectiveness of the original move. You are doing this to determine whether a move improves your chances of winning the game. You can use a structure called a **game tree** for this evaluation process. In a game tree, nodes represent game states and branches represent moves between these states. A game tree for tic-tac-toe is shown in Figure 4.3.

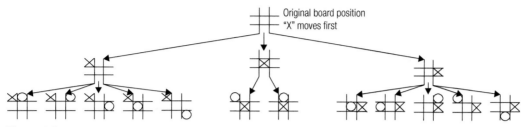

Figure 4.3
Game tree for tic-tac-toe.

As you examine this game tree, keep a few points in mind: First, the tree in Figure 4.3 shows only the first two moves and is not complete. A game of tic-tac-toe can last anywhere from five to nine moves, depending on the relative skill of the players. In fact, there are 3^9 possible games of tic-tac-toe. This is another example of **combinatorial explosion**, which you first encountered in Chapter 2, when enumerating puzzle states. Recall that the total number of ways in which some event can occur, or the number of possible states for a puzzle or game, can grow exponentially.

Even if you accounted for increases in computer speeds over the next 5 billion years, it is still unclear whether complete enumeration for the game of chess could be accomplished before the earth's inevitable demise, when the sun enters the red-giant category and expands perilously close to Earth's present orbit.

With present-day computer speeds, which are about several hundred million instructions per second, you can completely enumerate all possible games of tic-tac-toe and, hence, it is always possible to accurately determine the goodness of a move in this game. On the other hand, it has been estimated that the total number of distinct (good and bad) chess games is about 10^{120}. In comparison, experts say there are 10^{63} molecules in the universe.

With games of greater complexity, the main challenge in evaluating moves is the ability to look ahead as far as possible and then apply a **heuristic evaluation** of game positions, which involves estimating the goodness of the current state based on factors you believe will contribute to a win, such as the number of opponent's pieces captured, or center control. More complex games have more possible moves at each juncture, which makes charting and evaluating moves more costly in terms of computing time and space, because the game tree explored will be larger.

Referring again to Figure 4.3, notice that symmetry has been employed to greatly reduce the number of possibilities. In this context, **symmetry** means solutions that are equivalent. For example, follow the path where the first move of X is to the center square. This node in the game tree could have any one of eight descendants, one for each position where an O could be placed. However, the two nodes that do appear, where O is in the upper-left or upper-center position, represent two distinct **equivalence classes.** An equivalence class is a set of elements that are viewed as the same. For example, $\frac{2}{4}$ and $\frac{4}{8}$ are equivalent to $\frac{1}{2}$ and, hence, are in the same equivalence class. If you are familiar with discrete math or abstract algebra, you know that two game positions are equivalent if an element of a **symmetry group** maps one position into the other. A symmetry group is the set of physical motions that leave an object unchanged. For example, an equilateral triangle can be rotated 0°, 120°, or 240° (clockwise), or flipped about each perpendicular bisector.

Refer to the end-of-chapter exercises for the role of symmetry in game-tree enumeration. For now, note that an O in the upper-left corner, as shown in Figure 4.4a, is equivalent to an O in any of the other three corners. This is so because each game state on the right can be obtained by either rotating or flipping the one shown on the left.

Similarly, the game position shown in Figure 4.4b is equivalent to the three other positions illustrated.

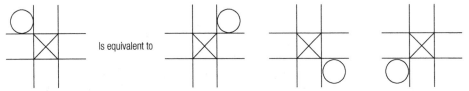

Figure 4.4a
Equivalent positions with O in corner in tic-tac-toe.

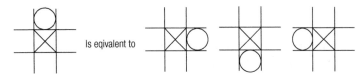

Figure 4.4b
Equivalent positions in tic-tac-toe.

4.1.1 Heuristic Evaluation

When a game tree has been expanded to the end of a game, measuring the goodness of a move is trivial. If the move resulted in a win, then it was good; if a loss ensued, it was not as good. Combinatorial explosion, however, prevents a complete evaluation for all but the most basic games. For more complicated games, you need to use heuristic evaluation. Recall that a heuristic is a set of guidelines that usually works to solve a problem. Heuristic evaluation is the process whereby a single number is attached to the state of a game; those states more likely to lead to a win are accorded larger numbers. You can use a heuristic evaluation to reduce the number of computations required to solve a problem complicated by combinatorial explosion.

You can use heuristic evaluation to solve the game of tic-tac-toe. Let N(X) equal the number of rows, columns, and diagonals that X could possibly complete, as shown in Figure 4.5(a). N(O) is similarly defined for moves the O player can complete (see Figure 4.5(b)).

When X is in the upper-left corner (with O in the adjacent space to the right), it can complete three possible moves: the leftmost column, and both diagonals. The heuristic evaluation of a game position E(X) is defined as N(X) – N(O). Hence, E(X) for the upper-left position illustrated in Figure 4.5 is 3 – 1 = 2. The exact number that a heuristic attaches to a game position is not that important. What *does* matter, however, is that more advantageous positions (*better positions*) are accorded higher heuristic values. Heuristics evaluation provides a strategy for dealing with combinational explosion.

Heuristic evaluation provides a tool to assign values to leaf nodes in the game tree shown in Figure 4.3. Figure 4.6 shows the game tree again where the **heuristic evaluation function** has been added.

The X player would pursue those moves with the highest evaluation (that is 2 in this game) and avoid those game states that evaluate to 0 (or worse). Heuristic evaluation has permitted the X player to identify advantageous moves without exploring the entire game tree.

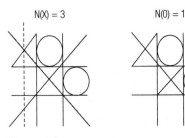

Figure 4.5
Heuristic evaluation in tic-tac-toe.

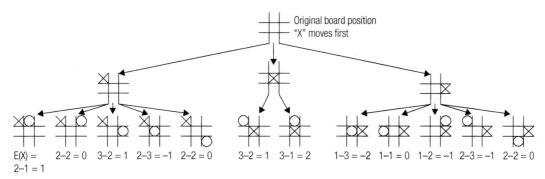

E(X) = 2–2 = 0   3–2 = 1   2–3 = –1   2–2 = 0   3–2 = 1   3–1 = 2   1–3 = –2   1–1 = 0   1–2 = –1   2–3 = –1   2–2 = 0
2–1 = 1

Figure 4.6
Heuristic evaluation applied to a game tree E(X) = N(X) − N(O).

We now require a technique so that these heuristic values can "percolate" upward so that all of this information can be used by the X player before she makes her first move. **Minimax evaluation** will provide just such a technique.

4.1.2 ■ Minimax Evaluation of Game Trees

In tic-tac-toe, the X player can use heuristic evaluation to find the most promising path to victory, the O player, however, can block that path in any move. A game between two experienced players will always end in a draw (unless one player makes a mistake). Instead of following the quickest path to victory, X needs to find the path that leads to victory even if O blocks it. Minimax evaluation is a technique that identifies such a path (when it exists), and is helpful in most two-person games.

The two players in a two-person game are traditionally referred to as **Max** and **Min**, with Max representing the player who attempts to maximize the heuristic evaluation and Min representing the player seeking to minimize it. Players alternate moves, with Max generally moving first. Assume that heuristic values have been assigned to each of the moves possible for any player in a given position. Also assume that for any game (not necessarily tic-tac-toe), each position has only two possible moves. See Figure 4.7.

The value of the Max node is the maximum of the values in either of its immediate successor nodes; hence, the value of the Max node shown in Figure 4.7(a) is 5. Keep in mind that Max and Min are opponents. A move that is good for Max is bad for Min. Additionally, all values in a game tree are considered from Max's vantage point. The Min player always makes the move with the minimum value attached to

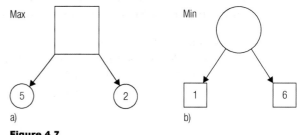

Figure 4.7
Evaluation of Max and Min nodes in a game tree. (a) The Max node is represented by a square, and (b) the Min node by a circle.

it, because the Min player is trying to minimize the value that accrues to Max. So the value of the Min node shown in Figure 4.7(b) is 1, because this is the minimum of the two values present for the successor nodes. This minimax procedure is illustrated in Figure 4.8 on a small game tree.

In this figure, an arbitrary game has been pursued for two levels, in other words, Max and Min have each had the opportunity to make a move. However, *no moves* have been made yet. This evaluation is taking place in Max's head, in an effort to evaluate the best opening move. The value

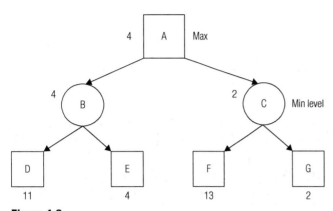

Figure 4.8
Example of minimax evaluation.

of nodes D, E, F, and G are then determined by employing a heuristic. For each of nodes B and C, it is Min's turn to move. The value of each of these two nodes is the minimum of the values in immediate successor nodes. The value of B is therefore 4 and C is 2. Node A is assumed to correspond to the first move of the game. The value of node A, or the **value of the game** (from Max's vantage point), equals 4. Max therefore decides that the best move is to go to node B, which returns the value of 4.

Now, you can evaluate the sample game of tic-tac-toe shown in Figure 4.6. For convenience, Figure 4.6 has been redrawn as Figure 4.9. In this figure, minimax evaluation is employed to back up heuristic values to the root, where Max is provided with information about the best first move. After inspecting this tree, Max sees that moving X to the middle square is the best opening strategy because her return is 1, which is maximal. Note, however, that this analysis and placing an X in the center square does not guarantee a win for Max

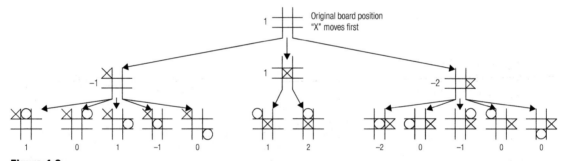

Figure 4.9
Minimax evaluation for a tic-tac-toe game.

For players with equal ability and with a thorough knowledge of strategy, a game of tic-tac-toe invariably ends in a draw. After Max has moved to the center square, Min will repeat this evaluation process, possibly with deeper heuristic values, attempting to minimize the score.

EXAMPLE 4.1: GAME OF NIM

Nim is a two-person game. Initially there are n stones in *r* separate piles. The initial state of the game can be expressed as $(n_1, n_2, \ldots n_r)$ where $n_1 + n_2 + \ldots + n_r = n$. In each move of the game, a player can take any number of stones (> 0) from any one of the r distinct piles. In one version of the game, *the last person to make a move wins*. Assume that the initial state of a game is (3,1): there are two piles of stones, with three stones in the first pile, and one stone in the second. The game tree with this initial state of Nim is shown in Figure 4.10a.

After the game is played to its conclusion, a minimax evaluation is created for this tree, which appears in Figure 4.10b.

A leaf node was given a value of 1 if it corresponded to a win for Max, and a value of zero if it represented a win for Min. The game did not need heuristic estimates. Minimax evaluation was employed to back up values from the game tree. You should trace through this example carefully to ensure that you understand the significance of the 0s and 1s in Figure 4.10b. For example, follow the leftmost path in this tree; the Max box at the leaf level is labeled with a 0. This is because, on the previous step (refer to Figure 4.10a) Min has removed the last stone from the right pile, thereby winning. The 0 in the leftmost leaf node, therefore, signifies that Max has lost.

The value of 1 in Figure 4.10b at the root signifies that Max is *guaranteed* to win, assuming that the opponents in a game are rational and that they always make the best available move.

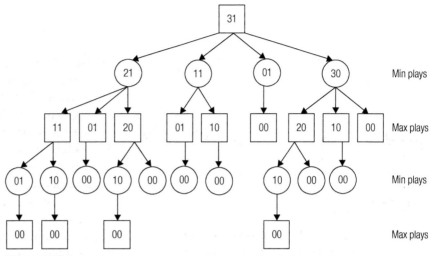

Figure 4.10(a)
Game tree for Nim, in its initial state.

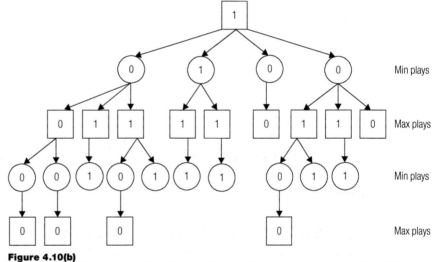

Figure 4.10(b)
Minimax evaluation of the game tree for Nim. In this version of the game, the last player to remove a stone wins. A '1' in a square box indicates that Max has won, whereas a '1' in a circular box indicates that Min has lost.

Finally, note that the minimax algorithm is a two-pass procedure. In the first phase, a depth first search is used to search to a game's conclusion, or to a fixed level, where an evaluation function is applied. In the second phase of minimax, values are backed up to the root, where the Max player is provided with feedback on the desirability of each move. Backing up values refers to the process whereby insights that are discovered when the game is pursued to leaf nodes are made available to the players earlier in the game process.

Dana Nau is a researcher in the field of game theory and automated planning; he is known for the discovery of "pathological" games, in which, looking ahead, counterintuitively leads to worse decision making. See Human Interest Box which follows.

4.2 ■ MINIMAX WITH ALPHA-BETA PRUNING

In Example 4.1, you analyzed a complete game of Nim. Because the game tree is relatively small, the game does not need heuristic evaluation. Instead, nodes that correspond to a win for Max are labeled with a 1, whereas those Min would win are labeled with a 0. Because most game trees are not this small, complete evaluation is not generally feasible. In such cases, the tree is typically developed to a level whose depth is constrained by memory requirements and computer speeds. Alpha-beta pruning (sometimes abbreviated as α-β pruning) can be combined with minimax and returns the same measures as minimax alone, but without needing to inspect every node in the tree. In fact, alpha-beta pruning usually examines only about one-half as many nodes as minimax alone. With the savings in computation that accrue from such pruning, you can go deeper into a game tree, using the same amount of time and space, and the evaluations of possible game continuations are likely to be more trustworthy and accurate.

The basic tenet of alpha-beta pruning is that after a move has been discovered to be bad, it is abandoned, and additional resources are not expended to discover how truly bad it is. This is similar to branch and bound search (Chapter 3), in which partial paths are abandoned when they are found to be suboptimal. Consider the examples in Figure 4.11 (no particular game is intended). The figure includes time stamps in boxes to indicate the order in which values are computed.

Figure 4.11 shows the first five steps in alpha-beta pruning:

1. Min discovers that game position D has a value of 3.
2. The value of position B is ≤ 3. This upper-bound value for B is referred to as a **beta value** for B.
3. The value of E is 5.
4. Consequently, at time 4, Min knows that the value of B equals 3.

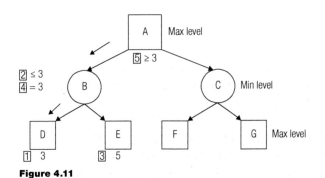

Figure 4.11
Alpha-beta pruning.

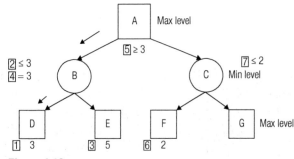

Figure 4.12
Alpha-beta pruning steps 6–8.

5. A is worth at least 3.

   Next, examine Figure 4.12, which shows the next three steps in alpha-beta pruning. Max now knows that making a move to game position B guarantees a return of 3. Therefore, A is worth *at least* 3 (as moving to C might yield an even greater return). This lower-bound for node A is called an **alpha value** for A.

6. At time 6, Min observes that the value of a move to F is worth 2.

7. Therefore, at time 7, Min knows that C's worth is ≤ 2.

8. Max now knows that a move to C will return a value of 2 or less. Max will not be moving to C because a move to B ensures a return of 3. The value at G will not change this appraisal, so why look? Evaluation of this tree can now end.

   Alpha-beta pruning is an essential tool for evaluation of game trees resulting from games more complex than tic-tac-toe and Nim. To explore this approach more thoroughly, consider the more sizable example shown in Figure 4.13. Again, time stamps appear in boxes to highlight the order in which steps take place.

1. We move left at every branch until leaf node L is encountered. Its static value is 4.

2. Max is guaranteed a score of at least 4. Again, this lower bound of 4 is referred to as an alpha value for E.

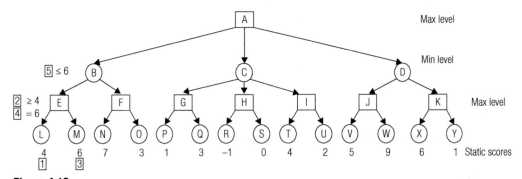

Figure 4.13
Second example of alpha-beta pruning, steps 1–5.

3. Max wants to ensure that no score higher than 4 exists in the subtree at E. At time 3, M's value is equal to 6.

4. At time 4, node E has a value, which is now *equal to 6.*

5. At time 5, Min node B has a beta value of 6. *Why?* Try to answer this question before continuing with the next steps.

   This example of alpha-beta pruning is continued in Figure 4.14.

   Node N is found to have a value of 8.

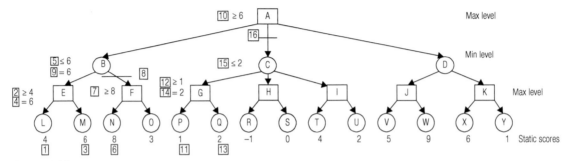

Figure 4.14
Second example of alpha-beta pruning, continued.

6. The entire subtree at F is pruned. The value at F is ≥ 8. Min at position B would never allow Max to get to position F.

7. The value at node B is now *equal* to 6.

8. The lower bound (alpha value) for Max is at the start position A.

9. Max wants to know if a value > 6 is available in the subtree at C. So the search next explores node P to derive its value, which is 1.

10. Now it is known that the value of G is ≥ 1.

11. Is G worth more than 1 to Max? To answer, the value at node Q must be obtained.

12. An exact value at node G is now known to equal 2.

13. Consequently, this value of G serves as an upper bound at position C (i.e., the beta value of C = 2).

14. Max observes that a move to node B is worth 6, but a move to C guarantees a return of *at most* 2. Max will not be moving to C and therefore this entire subtree can be pruned. More generally, whenever a node (here node A) has an alpha value of x, and a grandchild of this node (here node G) has a value y less than x, the entire subtree whose root is the latter's parent (here the subtree with root C) can be pruned. This is referred to as an **alpha cutoff**. Beta cutoffs (i.e., prunes caused by beta values for Min nodes), are defined analogously.

   Completion of this example of alpha-beta pruning is shown in Figure 4.15.

15. Max still wants to know if a return better than 6 is possible. To get an answer, the subtree at node D must be explored. At this time, the search proceeds to node V.

16. The value at node J is ≥ 5.

17. Node W is explored.

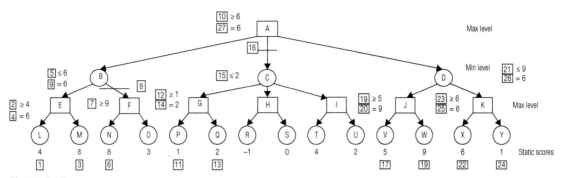

Figure 4.15
Second example of alpha-beta pruning, steps 15–25.

18. The value of node W (9) is backed up to node J.

19. An upper bound at D is established.

20. Min needs to know how much *less than* 9 node D is worth. So far Max has no reason to stop the search. Therefore, at time 22, attention is drawn to node X.

21. A lower bound of 6 at node K is obtained.

22. Y is scanned.

23. An exact value of 6 is obtained for node K.

24. The value for Min at node D is equal to 6.

25. The value of node A, and hence the value of the game itself to the Max player equals 6. Consequently, Max has a choice of moving to node B or node D.

For more practice with minimax evaluation and alpha-beta pruning, see the exercises at the end of this chapter.

Another two-person game is the simple child's Game of Eight. Unlike tic-tac-toe, it is not possible for the game to end in a draw. See Example 4.2.

EXAMPLE 4.2: GAME OF EIGHT

The **Game of Eight** is a simple children's game played by two opponents. The first player (Max) chooses a number n_i from the set $n = \{1, 2, 3\}$. Next the opponent (Min) chooses a number $n_j \varepsilon n$ with $n_j \neq n_i$ (i.e., Min must choose a different number from this set). A running total of the numbers chosen along each path is maintained. The first player to bring this total to eight wins the game. If a player exceeds eight, he loses and the opponent wins. In this game, no draws are possible. Figure 4.16 is a complete game tree for the game of Eight. Numbers chosen are displayed along the branches. The current sum is drawn within the rectangles or circles. Note that scores can exceed eight.

Referring to Figure 4.16, we observe that on the rightmost branch, the first player (Max) has chosen the number 3; this fact is reflected by the 3 that appears in the circle below this branch. Min may now choose the number 1 or 2. If 2 is chosen, we continue on this rightmost branch where you observe 5 in the Max square. If Max next chooses the number 3, the total is 8 and she wins the game. Alternately, if she chooses 1, Min is provided with an opportunity to win.

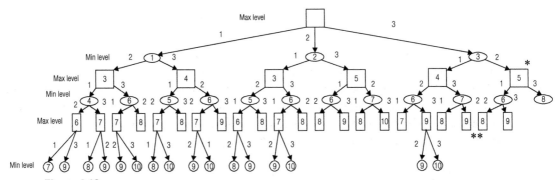

Figure 4.16
Game tree for the game of Eight.

Minimax evaluation for this game tree is shown in Figure 4.17. For clarity, we omitted players' choices for numbers (they are shown earlier in Figure 4.16), but preserved totals within the rectangles and circles. A win by Max is denoted with a 1, and −1 denotes a win for Min (or equivalently, a loss for Max). It is customary to reserve 0 for ties; however, as mentioned earlier, in this game ties do not occur.

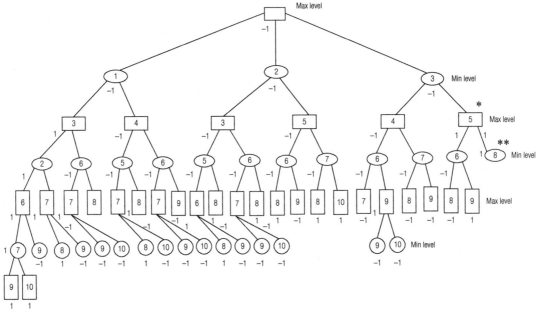

Figure 4.17
Minimax evaluation for the game of Eight.

Let us follow two paths in Figure 4.17 to reinforce our understanding. Once again, we focus on the rightmost path in this tree. As mentioned above, Max has selected the number 3. This is followed by Min choosing 2. These actions are reflected by the 5 inside the box at level two (marked with a *). Next, Max decides on 3; the sum of 8 has been reached. Max has won, as evidenced by the evaluation of 1 outside the rightmost leaf node. Next, consider a path that also begins with Max selecting 3, followed by Min selecting 2. We are once again at the level-two node, marked with a *. Then, suppose Max chooses 1 and Min 2 (two branches are followed), until node ** is reached. Min has won the game; this is reflected by the −1 outside the leaf node.

Again, because even trivial games can require large game trees, you need insightful evaluation functions if you want to design successful computer game-playing programs. Once again we trace through the rightmost portion of this tree. The Max player chose the number 3 and Min chose 2. The Max box along this path therefore contains the total, which is 5. Continuing along the rightmost branch, Max next chooses 3 and hence wins the game. This outcome is reflected by the 1 that appears below the Min leaf (circle node containing an 8).

The exercises provide more practice with evaluation functions. For a good introduction to minimax and α-β pruning, see Discrete Math by Johnsonburg. [1] Additional examples can be found in Firebaugh [2] and Winston. [3]

■ 4.3 ■ VARIATIONS AND IMPROVEMENTS TO MINIMAX

Game playing has received widespread attention throughout the first half-century of AI research. Minimax is the straightforward algorithmic approach to evaluating two-person games. It is natural that improvements to this algorithm have been avidly sought. This section highlights some of the variations to minimax (in addition to alpha-beta pruning) that have improved its performance.

■ 4.3.1 ■ Negamax Algorithm

An improvement to minimax is the **negamax algorithm**, discovered by Knuth and Moore; [4] the negamax algorithm uses the same function as minimax to evaluate nodes, while percolating values up from both the Max and Min levels of the tree.

Assume that you are evaluating the ith leaf node in a game tree, and the following stand for a loss, draw, and win:

$e_i = -1$ for a loss
$e_i = 0$ for a draw
$e_i = 1$ for a win

You can write the negamax evaluation function E(i) as follows:

$E(i) = e_i$ for leaf notes
$E(i) = \text{Max}(-F(j_1), -F(j_2), \ldots -F(j_n))$ for predecessor nodes $j_1, j_2, \ldots j_n$.

Negamax concludes that the optimal move for either Max or Min is the move that maximizes E(i). Figure 4.18 demonstrates this observation, with 1, −1, and 0 indicating a win, loss, and draw, respectively.

In this figure, consider the three nodes labeled as *, **, and *** and described in Table 4.1.

The negamax algorithm is applied to the game of Eight in Figure 4.19. Compare this to Figure 4.17 where straightforward minimax evaluation was employed.

Table 4.1
Description of nodes labeled with *, **, and ***.

Node	Evaluation
*	$E(i) = \text{Max}(-0, -(+1)) = \text{Max}(0, -1) = -1$
**	$E(i) = \text{Max}(-(1), -(-1)) = \text{Max}(-1, +1) = +1$
***	$\text{Max}(-(+1), -(+1)) = \text{Max}(-1, -1) = -1$

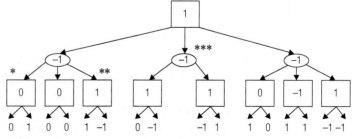

Figure 4.18
Game tree using negamax evaluation to implement a minimax search.

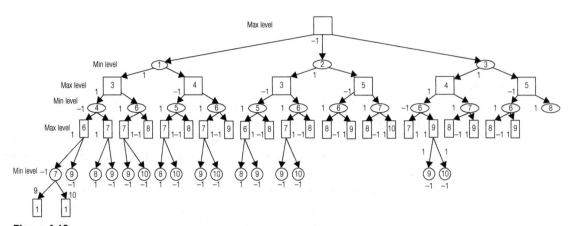

Figure 4.19
Negamax evaluation for the game of Eight.

Negamax is a slight improvement to straightforward minimax in that only the maximization operation needs to be used. The sign of the expressions for negamax evaluation will alternate from level to level of the game tree; reflecting the fact that a large positive return for Max corresponds to a large negative return for Min; these players alternate their moves, and so must the signs of the returned values alternate.

Problem-solving, heuristic search, and planning in Artificial Intelligence have been subjects of research for Richard Korf, who discovered iterative deepening for depth first search—a methodology similar to that of progressive deepening, the topic of out next section. Please see the sidebar to learn more about Dr. Korf.

4.3.2 Progressive Deepening

Although this chapter has thus far examined simple games, you can use similar approaches to evaluate complex games, with some important variations. For example, consider tournament chess, where time is a limiting factor because each player must make a move before the clock runs out. Remember that the goodness of a computer's move in a game depends upon how deep in the game tree a search algorithm proceeds before a heuristic function is applied. When evaluating a chess move, if you focus on the clock and keep the searches short and shallow, your level of play is likely to suffer. Alternately, if you travel deep into a game tree, your moves will be superior but the game clock might expire, forcing you to forfeit the move.

To solve this problem, you could explore the game tree to a depth of one, and then return the best move found. If more time remains, you then proceed to depth two. If still more time remains, you go down to depth three, and so on. This approach is referred to as **progressive deepening**. This methodology is similar to the depth first search with iterative deepening algorithm from Chapter 2. Because the number of leaf nodes in a search tree grows exponentially with respect to the branching factor of the tree, re-inspecting the tree from scratch but delving one level deeper with each iteration does not entail much overhead. When the chess clock does eventually wind down, you are prepared to make the best move, given the allotted time.

4.3.3 Heuristic Continuation and the Horizon Effect

The horizon is that imaginary line on the earth that appears in the distance across your plane of view. If you live away from a big city, perhaps close to an ocean or other large body of water, then you probably have observed the following phenomenon while staring at the water: a ship or a boat appears in the distance, apparently out of nowhere. In fact, it was out there in the distance for some time, though just below the horizon. A similar **horizon effect** can occur in search trees if you search to an a priori bound. A catastrophic move might be lurking in a game tree just out of sight.

Tournament chess will be discussed in a Chapter 16, "Advanced Computer Games" in which you will learn more about progressive deepening and the horizon effect. You will also learn about the famous chess match between Kasparov and Deep Blue.

4.4 GAMES OF CHANCE AND THE EXPECTIMINIMAX ALGORITHM

Recall that at any point in a tic-tac-toe game, a player has complete knowledge of the entire game, including what moves are available to either opponent as the game progresses, as well as the consequences of these moves. In these situations, the player has **perfect information** (or complete information). Additionally, if a player can always make the best move in a game, the player can make **perfect decisions**. Making perfect decisions is not difficult when you know the consequences of every move, including which moves culminate in a win and which lead to a loss. If you can generate the entire game tree for a game, then you can easily have perfect information, as you can with tic-tac-toe. Because generating an entire game tree for tic-tac-toe is not difficult for a computer, the computer player can also make perfect decisions. The same can be said for the game of Nim, as long as the number of stones is reasonable. Checkers, chess, Go, and Othello are additional examples of games with perfect information. However, the game trees for these games are so huge that it is unrealistic to generate them. Instead, you need to rely on heuristics, as discussed earlier in the chapter. Furthermore, computers cannot possibly make perfect decisions for these games. The level of computer play in these board games depends, to a great extent, upon the performance of the heuristics.

Another attribute of some games that must be modeled is *chance*. You roll dice in backgammon to determine how to move your markers. In a game of poker, chance is introduced by the random dealing of cards. You can have perfect information in backgammon because you can know all of your opponent's possible moves. In poker, your opponent's cards are hidden, so you cannot know all of your opponent's moves, meaning you have *imperfect information*.

Games of chance are called **nondeterministic games** because you cannot predict the next state of the game based upon its present state. To analyze nondeterministic games, you use the **expectiminimax** algorithm. A game tree for a game that contains a significant element of chance is composed of three types of nodes: Max, Min, and chance. Max and Min nodes occur in alternate layers as shown in the discussion of minimax in Section 4.1. In addition, these rows are interleaved with a layer of **chance nodes**, which introduce the uncertainty that is a sine qua non of nondeterminism.

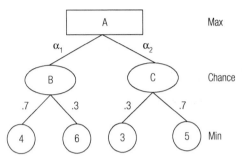

Figure 4.20
Game tree for a game involving chance.

Figure 4.20 includes Max, Min, and chance nodes. A layer of chance nodes (nodes B and C) occurs between the Max and Min nodes. To calculate which move is preferable (α_1 or α_2), Max must calculate the expectiminimax values for each of nodes B and C. Assume that the aspect of chance in this game is provided by an unfair coin wherein P(H) = 0.7 and P(T) = 0.3.

Max needs to calculate the expected value of the random variable X, denoted by E(X), where E(X) is given by the following formula:

$$E(X) = \Sigma\, x_i * P\,(x_i)$$
$$x_i \,\varepsilon\, X,$$

where x_i is a value that X may assume, and P(x_i) is the probability that X assumes this value x_i.

We have the expected return at B, or E(B) = (4 * 0.7) + (6 * 0.3) = 2.8 + 1.8 = 4.6. Meanwhile E(C), the expected return for Max if move α_2 is chosen, equals (3 * 0.3) + (5 * 0.7) = 0.9 + 3.5 = 4.4

Because the expected return to Max is greater if Max moves to B, the Max player should make move α_1.

The expectiminimax algorithm warrants another more extensive example. Recall the version of Nim and the minimax algorithm discussed in Section 4.1.3 and shown in Figure 4.10. To keep the expectiminimax tree at a reasonable size (and to fit on a printed page) the start state can equal (2,1), that is, there are two piles of stones with two in the first pile and one in the second. The complete game tree using minimax evaluation is shown in Figure 4.21.

Now, suppose this game involves chance — the players can specify from which pile to remove stones. However, the

*If you have not been exposed to probability recently, consider the experiment of tossing a coin twice. The set of possible outcomes is {TT, TH, HT, HH} each with a probability of one-fourth. Suppose the random variable X is equal to the number of heads that occur in this experiment. Then E(X) = 0 * ¼ + 1 * 2/4 + 2 * ¼, which equals 0 + ½ + ½ =1.*

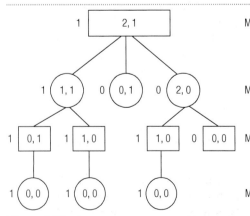

Figure 4.21
Game tree for game of Nim in which the last player to move wins.

actual number of stones removed is obtained as output from a random number generator that returns integer values from 1 to n_p with equal probability, where n_i is the number of stones in pile i. The game tree illustrating expectiminimax for this modified version of Nim is shown in Figure 4.22.

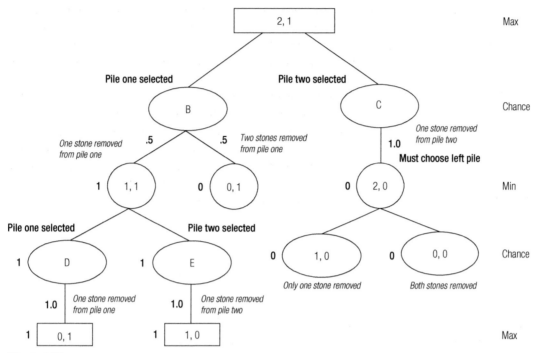

Figure 4.22
Version of Nim with chance introduced.

The expected value of game position B is E(B) equals $(1 * 0.5) + (0 * 0.5) = 0.5$. E(C) is equal to 0, meaning that Min is guaranteed a win. Choosing the right pile of stones takes the game to node C, where Max is guaranteed to lose. Clearly, Max should choose the left pile, because it provides a 50% chance of winning.

4.5 GAME THEORY

In the movie *The Postman Always Rings Twice* the two lead characters fall in love and decide to "eliminate" the husband of the female character. The police have insufficient evidence for convictions. However, after the murder, the lovers are apprehended by the police and held for questioning in separate interrogation rooms where each is offered the same proposition: "Defect on your partner and we'll go easy on you." Both perpetrators know that their accomplice is being offered this same deal. What should each prisoner do? What makes this predicament intriguing is that neither person is privy to their counterpart's thoughts. In an ideal world, both would remain loyal to one another and, without supporting testimony, would probably be convicted of a lesser crime. However, if either accomplice defects, then the other would certainly be better off by defecting as well, rather than serving a certain murder sentence.

This so-called **Prisoner's Dilemma** was first formulated in game-theoretical terms by Merrill Floyd and Melvin Dresher at the RAND Corporation in 1950. [5] At this time, most countries were involved in the Cold War between two nuclear super powers—the Soviet Union and the United

Prisoner B

	Cooperate (remain silent)	Defect (betray partner)
Prisoner A Cooperate (remain silent)	A: 1 year B: 1 year	A: 10 years B: 0 years
Prisoner A Defect (betray partner)	A: 0 years B: 10 years	A: 5 years B: 5 years

Figure 4.23
Payoff matrix for the Prisoner's Dilemma.

States, together with allies aligned on either side—poised against one another. Should these two super powers cooperate with one another and work toward mutual disarmament (aware at all times that the other side might renege) or should each mistrust the other and continue developing new and more lethal armaments? This is the dilemma that confronted our planet for four decades, from the end of World War II until the eventual end of the Cold War in 1989 with the fall of the Berlin Wall. The Prisoner's Dilemma aptly models that era of mistrust. This dilemma can also be modeled by the **payoff matrix**, in Figure 4.23. A payoff matrix specifies the return to each player for every combination of actions by the two game participants.

Assume that the two players (that is, the prisoners) in this game are rational and want to minimize their jail sentences. Each prisoner has two choices: cooperate with their partner in crime and remain silent, or defect by confessing to the police in return for a lesser sentence.

You might notice that this game differs in an important aspect from the games discussed earlier in this chapter. To determine a course of action in other games, you need to know your opponent's course of action. For example, if you are the second person to move in a game of tic-tac-toe, you need to know where the other player has placed the initial X. This is not the case in the Prisoner's Dilemma. Suppose you are the A player and that you choose to defect. However, the B player decides to remain loyal and chooses the cooperate-with-partner strategy. In this case, your decision results in no prison time as opposed to a one-year term you would have received if you had chosen instead to also cooperate. If your partner chooses to defect, your outcome is still superior if you choose to defect. In game-theoretic terms, defecting is a **dominant strategy**. Because you assume that your opponent in this game is rational, he will arrive at the same strategy.

The strategies {Betray, Betray} on the part of the two participants are referred to as a **Nash equilibrium**. This strategy is named after John F. Nash who won the Nobel Prize in Economics for his groundbreaking work in game theory. A change in strategy by either player results in a lesser return to them (i.e., more jail time).

As shown in Figure 4.23, if each player acts more on faith than rationality (faith that their partners would remain loyal) then the total payoff would exceed the total of 10 prison years accorded by the Nash equilibrium of {Defect, Defect}. This strategy of {Cooperate, Cooperate} yields the best possible outcome in terms of total payoff to the two players. This optimal strategy is referred to as a **Pareto Optimal**. This strategy is named after Alfredo Pareto whose late nineteenth Century work in economics laid the foundations for more recent work in game theory. It should be noted that the Prisoner's Dilemma is not a **zero-sum game**. *Why not?* In such games the Nash equilibrium does not necessarily correspond to a Pareto Optimal.

EXAMPLE 4.3: GAME OF MORRA

Morra is a game that can be played by two or more people. (Most of us can probably recall using two-finger Morra to help choose sides in games of baseball or stickball.) One version of this game is played by two people; one is designated as Even, the other as Odd. Simultaneously, the two players each extend one or two fingers. The parity of the total numbers of fingers shown determines which player wins. The payoff matrix for this version of the game is shown in Figure 4.24. Note that this game *is* a zero-sum game.

A game of two-finger Morra does not have a Nash equilibrium. For either {1, 1} or {2, 2} the Odd player is better off deviating. (The numbers inside the curly brackets represent the number of fingers extended by the Even and Odd players, respectively.) Also, the Even player fares better by changing its action for {1, 2} and {2, 1}.

Odd player

		1 Finger extended	2 Fingers extended
Even player	1 Finger extended	(1, −1) Even wins	(−1, 1) Odd wins
	2 Fingers extended	(−1, 1) Odd wins	(1, −1) Even wins

Figure 4.24

Payoff matrix for a version of two-finger Morra. (1, -1) indicates that the first player, i.e., even wins and the second player, i.e., odd loses. For (-1, 1) indicates that odd has won.

4.5.1 The Iterated Prisoner's Dilemma

If you play the Prisoner's Dilemma only once, defecting is a dominating strategy for either player. In another version of this game, you play repeatedly—*n* times—and there is some memory of previous actions. When having more than one turn, each player is not as quick to defect, knowing that revenge from the opponent is forthcoming. One strategy might be to start with a single cooperative move to give your opponent a chance to act compassionately. If your opponent chooses to defect anyway, you can counter by continually defecting. If your opponent eventually chooses to cooperate, you can return to a more magnanimous policy. The exercises at the end of this chapter discuss other two-person games that are similar to the Prisoner's Dilemma. For a more detailed discussion of game theory, see Russell et al. [6]

4.6 CHAPTER SUMMARY

To evaluate the effectiveness of a move in a game, you can use a game tree to chart your possible moves, opponent's responses, and your counter moves. In a *game tree*, nodes represent game states and branches represent moves between these states.

For all but the most basic games, you cannot create a complete game tree because of *combinatorial explosion*. In these cases, you need to use heuristic evaluation to determine the most effective moves.

Minimax evaluation is an algorithm used to evaluate game trees. It examines the state of the game and returns a value indicating whether the state is a win, loss, or draw for the current player. *Alpha-beta pruning* is often used in conjunction with minimax evaluation. It will return the same values as minimax alone, but by examining only about one-half as many nodes in a game tree as minimax. This allows a deeper inspection of a game tree, resulting in more trustworthy and accurate evaluations.

Similar to a minimax evaluation, you can use a *negamax search* in a two-player game to simplify calculations. One variation of minimax is *progressive deepening*, in which you search a game tree in iterations. For example, you can explore the game tree to a depth of one, and then return the best move found. If more time remains, you proceed to depth two. If still more time remains, you go down to depth three, and so on. Because the number of leaf nodes in a search tree grows exponentially with respect to the branching factor of the tree, re-inspecting the tree from scratch but exploring one level deeper at each iteration does not involve much overhead.

In a two-player, *zero-sum game* such as tic-tac-toe, a player can have *perfect information*—knowing what moves are available to either opponent throughout the game and understanding the consequences of these moves. Additionally, if a player can always make the best move in a game, the player can make perfect decisions. In games of chance, however, you cannot have perfect information or make perfect decisions. In the *Prisoner's Dilemma*, two players can cooperate with or betray (defect from) each other. It illustrates game theory, in which players are rational and are concerned only with maximizing their payoff without concern for the other player's payoff. If a change in strategy by either player results in a lesser payoff to them, they are engaged in a *Nash equilibrium*. If a strategy yields the best possible outcome in terms of total payoff to the two players, they are using an optimal strategy, which is called a *Pareto Optimal*.

Questions for Discussion

1. How does a game tree help to evaluate moves in a game?

2. What is combinational explosion?

3. What is heuristic evaluation and why is it helpful in games with large game trees?

4. Briefly explain the principle behind minimax evaluation.

5. What do we mean by *symmetry* in a game move? How does it help in game tree evaluation?

6. What is the principle behind alpha-beta pruning? Why is it helpful in minimax evaluation?

7. What is progressive deepening? When is it useful?

8. What is the *expectiminimax algorithm*? For what types of games is it useful?

9. What is the Prisoner's Dilemma? Why has it received so much attention?

10. Define the following terms.

    a. Nash equilibrium   b. Pareto Optimal

11. Does a Nash equilibrium always correspond to an optimal strategy? Explain.

Exercises

1. Perform a minimax evaluation for the game tree in Figure 4.25.

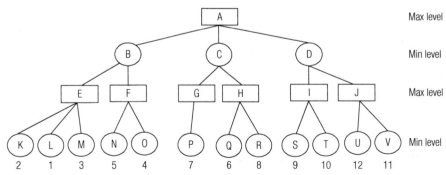

Figure 4.25
Game tree 1.

2. Perform a minimax evaluation for the game tree in Figure 4.26.

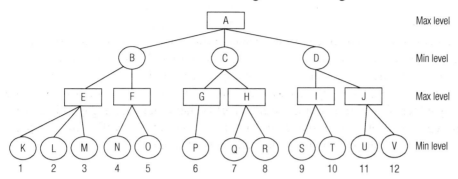

Figure 4.26
Game tree 2.

3. Perform a minimax evaluation for the game tree in Figure 4.27.

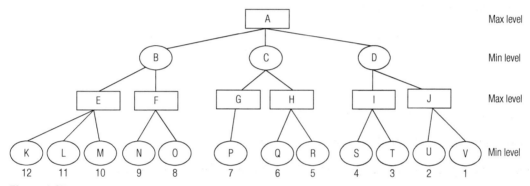

Figure 4.27
Game tree 3.

4. One variation on the game of nim is described in Luger. [7] The game begins with a single pile of stones. The move by a player consists of dividing a pile into two piles that contain an unequal number of stones. For example, if one pile contains six stones, it could be subdivided into piles of five and one, or four and two, *but not* three and three. *The first player who cannot make a move loses the game.*

a. Draw the complete game tree for this version of Nim if the start state consists of six stones.

b. Perform a minimax evaluation for this game. Let 1 denote a win and 0 a loss.

5. A group < G, **o** > is a set G together with a binary operation o such that:

- the operation o has *closure*—for all x, y in G, x **o** y is in G

- *associativity* (x **o** y) **o** z = x **o** (y **o** z)—for all x, y, z in G

- *identity exists* $\exists\, e \in G$ *such that*

    $\forall\, x \in$ G x **o** $e = e$ **o** = x

- *inverses exist*—for all x in G there exist x^{-1} such that x **o** x^{-1} = x^{-1} **o** x = e

Subtraction of natural numbers is not closed as $3 - 7 = -4$ and -4 is not in the set of natural numbers. Addition of natural numbers, however, is a binary operation. Addition of integers is associative: $(2 + 3) + 4 = 2 + (3 + 4) = 9$. However, subtraction of integers is not: $(2 - 3) - 4$ does not equal $2 - (3 - 4)$; i.e., -5 does not equal 3; 0 is an identity element for addition of integers $7 + 0 = 0 + 7 = 7$. The inverse for 4 with respect to addition of integers is -4 as $4 + (-4) = 0$.

Examples of groups: $< Z, +>$: The set of integers with respect to addition. $<Q, *>$: The set of non-zero rationals with respect to multiplication.

a. Consider a square (Sq), shown in Figure 4.28, which is free to move in 3-dimensional space labeled as follows: Let Π_0, Π_1, Π_2 and Π_3 be clockwise rotations through $0°$, $90°$, $180°$, and $270°$, respectively. And let o represent composition of these rotations. For example Π_1 o Π_2 is a $90°$ rotation followed by a $180°$ rotation which corresponds to Π_3 which is a $270°$ clockwise rotation. Prove that $<Sq, o>$ is a group.

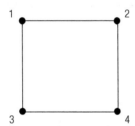

Figure 4.28
Square with labeled vertices.

b. Apply this group to the tic-tac-toe board introduced in section 4.1. Verify that $<Sq, \mathbf{o}>$ gives us justification for the notion of equivalence stated in Figure 4.4. Consult McCoy. [8]

6. Use alpha-beta pruning to evaluate the game trees shown in Figure 4.25. Be sure to indicate all alpha values and all beta values. Specify alpha cutoffs and beta cutoffs, if any.

7. Use alpha-beta pruning to evaluate the game trees shown in Figure 4.26. Be sure to indicate all alpha values and all beta values. Specify alpha cutoffs and beta cutoffs, if any.

8. Use alpha-beta pruning to evaluate the game trees shown in Figure 4.27. Be sure to indicate all alpha values and all beta values. Specify alpha cutoffs and beta cutoffs, if any.

9. Consider the work entailed in evaluating the game trees from exercises 1–3 and 6–8. Minimax evaluation required the same amount of time regardless of the ordering of heuristic evaluations. What impact, if any, did the ordering of heuristic evaluations have on the amount of pruning that resulted when the alpha-beta pruning procedure was employed? In particular, when was the alpha-beta method most efficient? In other words, when did it inspect the fewest number of nodes?

10. Examine the game of Dots and Boxes. Two players take turns drawing lines between adjacent dots on a 3×3 grid. Completing the last line on a box makes that box yours. The player that completes the most boxes wins.

a. Draw the first several levels in the game tree for this game.

b. Compare the complexity of this tree with that for tic-tac-toe.

c. Cite several heuristics for this game that might lead to a good strategy.

11. The game of Sprouts was developed by M. S. Paterson and J. J. Conway. Draw two or more points on a piece of paper. Two players then alternate making moves according to these rules:

- Draw a line (or curve) joining two points, or one point to itself (a self-loop). The line may not pass through another point.

- Draw a new point anywhere on this new line.

- At most, three lines might emerge from any point.

The last player who can still make a move wins. Try to develop a strategy for this game.

12. Consider the game of three-dimensional tic-tac-toe. As usual the X and O players alternate and the object of play is to get three in a row on any row, column, or diagonal.

a. Compare the complexity for 3-D tic-tac-toe with the more traditional 2-D version of the game described in the chapter.

b. Develop a heuristic suitable for evaluation of nonterminal nodes.

13. Use the negamax algorithm to evaluate the game tree in Figure 4.25.

14. Following are several well-known problems. Discuss whether they are instances of essentially the same problem as the Prisoner's Dilemma discussed in Section 4.6.

If you conclude that a problem is equivalent to the Prisoner's Dilemma, then design an appropriate payoff matrix. Comment on the existence of a Nash equilibrium and Pareto Optimal in each case.

a. Linux is a version of Unix that has been developed under the General Public License (GPL). Under this agreement, you are given free software and may study the source code, which is modifiable. You can defect by keeping these improvements to yourself, or cooperate by distributing the improved version of the code. In fact, cooperation is forced by making it illegal to distribute only the source code without your improvements.

b. Cigarette companies were at one time allowed to advertise in the United States. If only one company decided to advertise, an increase in sales invariably followed. However, if two companies launched advertising campaigns, their ads would essentially cancel one another and no increase in revenue resulted.

c. In New Zealand newspaper boxes are left unlocked. One can easily steal a paper (defect). Naturally, if everyone did this, no papers would remain. [9]

d. (Tragedy of the Commons) There is a village with n farmers where grassland is limited. Each of these farmers might decide to keep a sheep. Each farmer obtains some utility from these sheep in the form of wool and milk. However, the common grassland (the Commons) will suffer somewhat from a sheep's grazing there.

15. Give pseudocode for the minimax algorithm.

16. The Nine Tails Problem is depicted in Figure 4.29.

    It is a one-player game where the goal is to flip coins so that they are all showing a Tails face. Once a coin with a Heads face is selected, that coin and the coins perpendicular (not diagonal) to it are flipped. So if the coin on the bottom left (Row 1, Column 1) is selected for the first move, then that coin and the coins directly above it (Row 2, Column 1) and to its right (Row 1, Column 2) become Heads. But the coin in Row 2, Column 2 (Diagonal to the coin in Row 1, Column) is not flipped. The goal of the puzzle is to flip all the coins to Tails in the fewest number of moves.

    The puzzle is played on the same grid as tic-tac-toe is played and is of similar complexity (9! with reduction for symmetry) Develop a heuristic for this puzzle.

Figure 4.29
The Nine Tails Problem

17. Problem 16 is reminiscent of the game known as Othello (or Reversi) which is covered in Chapter 16 (Advanced Computer Games). Othello starts with four stones (two White and two Black) placed in the middle of an 8 × 8 board (as in chess and checkers). When a stone is flipped to the opposite color, the perpendicular adjacent stones are flipped as in the problem above. Consider what might be a strong strategy for playing this game.

Programming Exercises

Use the high-level language of your choice to complete the programming exercises.

1. Write a program to perform minimax evaluation. (refer to Exercise 15).

   Test your program on the game trees of exercises 1, 2, and 3.

2. Write a program to perform alpha-beta pruning.

   Test your program on the game trees of exercises 6, 7, and 8.

3. Write a program to play Dots and Boxes as described in exercise 10. Employ alpha-beta pruning in your work. Test your program in machine vs. man mode (i.e., let people challenge your program in this game). The machine should move first.

4. Write a program to play tic-tac-toe as discussed in the chapter (minimax is sufficient here). Your program should play in machine vs. machine mode (the computer makes both moves). The first player should follow a procedure that goes three levels into the game tree before heuristic evaluation is employed, whereas the second player should go only two levels deep. Comment on the results of play after 50 games.

5. Write a program to play 3D tic-tac-toe (see Exercise 12). Your program should employ the negamax algorithm. Test your program in machine vs. man mode, using a testing procedure similar to programming Exercise 4.

Keywords

adversary	game tree	payoff matrix
alpha cutoff	heuristic evaluation	perfect decision
alpha value	heuristic evaluation function	perfect information
alpha-beta pruning	horizon effect	Prisoner's Dilemma
beta value	Max	progressive deepening
combinatorial explosion	Min	symmetry
chance nodes	minimax evaluation	symmetry group
dominant strategy	Nash equilibrium	value of the game
equivalence classes	negamax algorithm	zero-sum game
expectiminimax	nondeterministic games	
Game of Eight	Pareto Optimal	

References

1. Johnsonbaugh, R. 2005. *Discrete Mathematics*, 6th ed. Upper Saddle River, NJ: Prentice-Hall.

2. Firebaugh, M. W. 1988. *Artificial Intelligence*: *A knowledge-based approach*. Boston, MA: Boyd & Fraser.

3. Winston, P. H. 1993. *Artificial Intelligence*, 3rd ed. Reading, MA: Addison-Wesley.

4. Knuth, D. and Moore, R. W. 1975. An analysis of alpha-beta pruning, *Artificial Intelligence* 6(4):293–326.

5. Merrill, F. and Dresher, M. 1961. *Games of strategy: Theory and applications*, Upper Saddle River, NJ: Prentice-Hall.

6. Russell, S. and Norvig, P. 2009. *Artificial Intelligence: A modern approach*, 3nd ed. Upper Saddle River, NJ: Prentice-Hall.

7. Luger, G. F. 2008. *Artificial Intelligence – Structures and strategies for complex problem solving*, 6th ed. Reading, MA: Addison-Wesley.

8. McCoy N. H. 1975. *Introduction to modern algebra*, 3rd ed. Boston, MA: Allyn and Bacon

9. Poundstone, W. 1992. *Prisoner's dilemma*. New York, NY: Doubleday.

LOGIC IN ARTIFICIAL INTELLIGENCE

Nils Nilsson

Nils Nilsson has been a chief proponent of the logic school of AI and has published numerous articles and, together with Michael Genesereth, a well-received text on the subject titled Logical Foundations of Artificial Intelligence.

In "Overview of Artificial Intelligence" (Chapter 1), we stated that in addition to a search facility, an intelligent system must be able to represent its knowledge. In this chapter, we begin our foray into knowledge representation with a discussion of logic. Propositional logic is presented first, focusing on its theorems and proof strategies. Predicate logic is discussed next and is shown to be a more expressive representation language. Resolution refutation is seen to be powerful for theorem proving. Extensions to predicate logic are then briefly introduced.

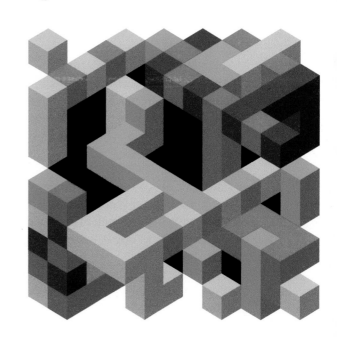

▰5.0▰ ■ INTRODUCTION

This chapter introduces logic as a knowledge representation paradigm in Artificial Intelligence. We begin our discussion in Section 5.1 with a well–known puzzle: The King's Wise Men puzzle, to illustrate the expressive power of logic. Additionally, when a problem is well represented, the task of drawing inferences (i.e., discovering new knowledge), is facilitated.

Propositional Logic is described in Section 5.2. Logical expressions are the basic building blocks; these are expressions or propositions that can be characterized as either true or false. Logic connectives such as AND, OR, and NOT are introduced, and the role of truth tables in analyzing the resulting compound expressions is also discussed. An **argument** is defined as a collection of **premises** that is assumed to be true, and a conclusion that could or could not logically follow from these premises. When a conclusion follows logically from an argument's premises, we characterize the argument as *valid*. Two strategies for determining the **validity** of an argument are explored. The first uses a truth table and the second uses resolution. In the latter approach, you combine the negation of the conclusion with the premises. If you can arrive at a contradiction, then the original argument is valid. Before resolution can be applied, all propositional logic expressions must be converted to a special form known as **clause form**. A procedure for converting propositional logic expressions into clause form is provided.

Section 5.3 introduces predicates; these are seen to have greater expressive power than propositional logic expressions. Two quantifiers: $\exists x$ – **existential quantification** and $\forall x$ – **universal quantification** can be applied to predicate logic variables. $\exists x$ is to be interpreted as "there exists an x" and $\forall x$ as "for all x."

We will see that this greater expressive power of predicate logic comes with a price tag. The procedure for converting predicate logic expressions into clause form, so that resolution can be applied, is more arduous. The nine-step algorithm to accomplish this conversion is explained in Section 5.3.3. Several resolution proofs are also provided to illustrate the techniques.

In Section 5.4, we provide brief introductions to several other logics. In the (first order) predicate logic, quantifiers can be applied only to variables, thus limiting their expressive power. In the second order logic, however, quantifiers can also be applied to predicates themselves. An example from mathematics is provided.

First order predicate logic is said to be monotonic, that is, conclusions derived cannot be retracted once more information is obtained. Real life is often not this irreversible. Trials illustrate this tentative nature of conclusions. At the beginning of a trial in the United States, a defendant is presumed to be innocent. During the course of a trial, however, as damning evidence is introduced and eyewitness testimony is presented, this early presumption of innocence will possibly need to be amended. Non-monotonic logic captures this provisional nature of conclusions.

Throughout this chapter we proclaim that logical expressions can be classified as either true or false. The statement: "It is raining" can be so classified by either looking out the window or consulting a weather report. Real-life situations do not necessarily fit nicely into these two truth compartments. For example: "He is a good man." Suppose the man being discussed is nice to his children and his pet dog but cheats on his taxes. As we mature, we learn that many qualities in life are tempered by degree. We might therefore characterize the previous assertion as being true, to a certain extent. **Fuzzy logic** incorporates this "grayness" that is an integral part of life. Fuzzy logic has found widespread applications in the control of many modern appliances. Several examples are described.

Modal logics are logic models that confront important concerns such as moral imperatives: "You should…" and "One ought to…" The issue of time is also tackled. Proven mathematical theorems were always true and will be so in the future; other premises might be true now but were not so in the past (e.g., the prevalence of cell phones). It is difficult, however, to unequivocally determine truth-values for things that should be so. A widespread use for modal logics is in the analysis of philosophical arguments.

5.1 ■ LOGIC AND REPRESENTATION

Induction puzzles are logic puzzles that are solved via the identification and subsequent elimination of perhaps a series of obvious cases. One such puzzle is the well-known King's Wise Men.

The King's Wise Men puzzle (Figure 5.1) involves a king looking for a new wise man. After prescreening, the three smartest applicants for the position travel to his court. The three men are seated facing one another and are then blindfolded. A blue or white hat is placed on each of their heads. Now the king has their eyes uncovered all at the same time. The king then tells them "You each have either a blue or white hat and at least one of you has a blue hat. Whoever guesses the color of his hat first and raises his hand, will be my next wise man."

Before we can solve this puzzle (by machine) we must have a suitable representation. Predicate logic will be used for this puzzle because it allows each state to be denoted by a distinct expression. For example, we can let the predicate WM_1( ) denote that wise man 1 has a hat of some color (to be specified), then the situation in which wise man one has a blue hat and both wise men two and three are wearing white hats is represented by:

$$\text{WM\_1 (B)} \wedge \text{WM\_2 (W)} \wedge \text{WM\_3 (W)} \tag{1}$$

If a representation for this puzzle is to be useful, then it must be possible to make inferences, in other words, to draw conclusions that help to solve the puzzle. Scanning Expression (1) for example, you should be able to conclude that wise man one will raise his hand and declare that his hat is blue. He can correctly do so because the king promised that at least one of the three hats must be blue, and he observes that both of the other wise men are wearing white hats, hence his hat must be blue. By consulting Table 5.1, you should be able to deduce the outcome for the other two cases in which only one blue hat is present (Expressions 2 and 3).

Recall that the symbol "∧" is the conjunction operator and stands for the AND' ing of terms, and the symbol "∨" stands for disjunction and represents the OR'ing of terms.

The king has promised that at least one of the hats will be blue, so we do not include the expression WM_1(W) ∧ WM_2(W) ∧ WM_3(W), which denotes that all three wise men are wearing white hats.

(a)   (b)

Figure 5.1
The King's Wise Men puzzle. Each must guess the color of his hat.

Table 5.1
The seven distinct cases for The King's Wise Men Problem.

$(WM\_1(B) \wedge WM\_2(W) \wedge WM\_3(W))$	(1)
$(WM\_1(W) \wedge WM\_2(B) \wedge WM\_3(W))$	(2)
$(WM\_1(W) \wedge WM\_2(W) \wedge WM\_3(B))$	(3)
$(WM\_1(B) \wedge WM\_2(B) \wedge WM\_3(W))$	(4)
$(WM\_1(W) \wedge WM\_2(B) \wedge WM\_3(B))$	(5)
$(WM\_1(B) \wedge WM\_2(W) \wedge WM\_3(B))$	(6)
$(WM\_1(B) \wedge WM\_2(B) \wedge WM\_3(B))$	(7)

The cases with two blue hats are more subtle. We consider the situation depicted by Expression (4) in Table 5.1. Put yourself in the shoes of one of the wise men with a blue hat, say wise man one. You reason that if your hat were white, then the second wise man would observe two white hats and therefore declare his own hat to be blue. Wise man two makes no such claim and hence you conclude (correctly) that your hat must be blue. The other cases involving two blue hats are handled similarly.

The most difficult case (and in fact the one that actually occurs) is that all three wise men are wearing blue hats, as depicted by Expression (7). We have already seen that those situations with either one or two blue hats can be resolved without much delay. In this scenario however, we are told that an inordinate amount of time passes. It is therefore reasonable for one of the wise men (the wisest) to conclude that none of the aforementioned cases apply and hence all three hats (and in particular his own hat) are (is) blue. Later in this chapter, we will describe the various inference rules that permit conclusions to be drawn from observed facts. For now, it is sufficient that you appreciate the way that logic can be used to represent knowledge.

■ 5.2 ■ PROPOSITIONAL LOGIC

We begin our more rigorous discussion of logic with the propositional logic, a logic that does not have the same expressive power as predicate logic. For example, with the propositional logic we can represent the situation wherein wise man one has a blue hat, by the variable **p**. If we wish to represent that wise man one has a white hat, then a different variable, say, **q**, must be used. The propositional logic is less expressive than predicate logic; however, as we shall see, it is easier to work with and thereby affords us a convenient place to begin our discussion of logic.

■ 5.2.1 ■ Propositional Logic – Basics

If we were to begin a study of English, a good starting point might be with a sentence. A sentence is a collection of words with proper syntax (or form) that conveys some meaning. Here are several English language sentences:

1. He is taking the bus home tonight.
2. The music was beautiful.
3. Watch out.

Similarly, a good place to begin a discussion of propositional logic is with **statements**. A statement (or logical expression) is a sentence that can be categorized with a truth-value of *true* or *false*. Sentence 1, above, is a statement. To determine its truth-value, you simply observe how the "he" referred to actually goes home. Sentence 2 is also a statement (though truth-value will vary with listener). Sentence 3, however, is not a statement. If a car is approaching dangerously close, then this sentence is certainly appropriate, however, it cannot be classified as either *true* or *false*.

In this text, we use lower case letters from the middle of the English alphabet to denote propositional logic variables: **p**, **q**, **r**. These variables are the primitives, or basic building blocks in this logic. Table 5.2 shows various compound expressions that can be formed by applying **logical connectives** (sometimes called **functions**).

The semantics or meaning of these logical connectives is defined by a truth table, in which the value of the compound expression is given for each value of the variables.

In Table 5.3, **F** denotes false and **T** denotes true. (Some texts use **0** and **1** respectively for these two truth-values.) Observe, as shown in the last row of Table 5.3(a), that the AND of two variables is true only when both of the variables are true. The OR function is true when one or both variables is (are) true. Note in the first row of Table 5.3(b), that **p** ∨ **q** is false only when both **p** and **q** are false. The OR function defined here is referred to as the **inclusive-or** function. Contrast this with the two- variable **exclusive-or** (XOR) function defined in Table 5.4. Finally, in Table 5.3(c), you note that the negation of **p**, written ~**p** is true only when **p** is false.

The **XOR** of two variables is true when either variable is true, but is false when both variables are true (consult the last row of Table 5.4). If you are a parent, then the distinction between these two OR functions is perhaps best made clear by the different interpretations by you and your child to the following proclamation at a restaurant: "You can have the chocolate cake or the ice cream for dessert."

Each of the AND, OR, and exclusive-or functions defined thus far require two variables. The NOT function as defined in Table 5.3 requires only one variable; where NOT false is true and NOT true is false.

Implication (⇒) and the biconditional (⇔) functions are defined in Table 5.5. When we say "**p** implies **q**," or "if **p** then **q**" in everyday parlance we mean that if some condition **p** is present, then **q** will result. For example, "If it rains, then the streets will get wet" is taken to mean that if **p**: "it rains" is true, then **q**: "the streets will get wet" is necessarily true. This interpretation is provided in Table 5.5 by the last row of the truth table for **p** ⇒ **q**. This table defines each of **F** ⇒ **F** and **F** ⇒ **T** as true; there is no rationale from everyday life why this should be so. In propositional logic, however, you can argue that it is impossible to prove that "**p** does not imply **q**" when p is false, and hence, in a vacuous sense, the implication is defined as true. Finally, you should have no trouble accepting as false the third line for **p** ⇒ **q**, the case in which **p** is true and **q** is false.

The rightmost column in Table 5.5 defines the biconditional operator: **p** ⇔ **q**, which can be interpreted as "**p** if and only if **q**"; we can represent this last phrase as "**p iff q**." Observe that **p** ⇔ **q** is true whenever both **p** and **q** have the same truth-value (both are false, or both true); for this reason the biconditional operator is sometimes referred to as the equivalence operator.

Table 5.2
Compound expressions formed by using logical connections.

Symbol	Name	Example	English Equivalent
∧	conjunction	**p** ∧ **q**	p and q
∨	disjunction	**p** ∨ **q**	p or q
~	negation	~**p**	not p
⇒	implication	**p** ⇒ **q**	if p then q *or* p implies q
⇔	biconditional	**p** ⇔ **q**	p if and only if q *or* p is equivalent to q

Table 5.3
Truth table for twovariables (p and q) for AND, OR, and NOT operations.

(a) AND function			(b) OR function			(c) NOT function	
p	**q**	**p** ∧ **q**	**p**	**q**	**p** ∨ **q**		
F	**F**	**F**	**F**	**F**	**F**	**p**	~**p**
F	**T**	**F**	**F**	**T**	**T**	**F**	**T**
T	**F**	**F**	**T**	**F**	**T**	**T**	**F**
T	**T**	**T**	**T**	**T**	**T**		

Table 5.4
Truth table for the two-variable XOR function.

p	**q**	**p** ∨ **q**
F	**F**	**F**
F	**T**	**T**
T	**F**	**T**
T	**T**	**F**

Table 5.5
Truth table for Implication (⇒) and the biconditional (⇔) operators.

p	**q**	**p** ⇒ **q**	**p** ⇔ **q**
F	**F**	**T**	**T**
F	**T**	**T**	**F**
T	**F**	**F**	**F**
T	**T**	**T**	**T**

A professor of mathematics, after proving a theorem in class, might inquire, "Is the converse also true?" Suppose you are given the implication: "If a number is divisible by four, then it is even." In the original implication, let **p** represent: "A number is divisible by four," and let q represent: "It is even." Then the above implication can be represented in propositional logic by the expression: $p \Rightarrow q$. The left side of an implication, **p** in this example, is referred to as the antecedent; the right side, **q**, as the **consequent**. The **converse** of an implication is formed by reversing the roles of antecedent and consequent (consult Table 5.6). The converse of this implication is therefore: $q \Rightarrow p$, or, "If a number is even, then it is divisible by four." Referring to the original implication, if a number n is divisible by four then $n = 4 * k$, where k is an integer. Since $4 = 2 * 2$, we have $n = (2 * 2) * k$, which, by the **associative law** of multiplication equals $2 * (2*k)$; therefore n is indeed even.

The converse to the above implication is false. A useful method to disprove an assertion that is false is to produce a counterexample, in other words, an example for which the assertion is not true.

Imagine you are a student in an advanced calculus course, and you are challenged by the professor to prove that the sqrt(2) is not rational. Perhaps, indeed, this has happened to you. What was—or would be—your response?

A number n is rational if it can be expressed as the ratio of two integers. For example, 4 which equals 4/1, and 2/3 are rationals whereas sqrt(2), pi, and e are not.

Table 5.6
Truth table for an implication (column 3), as well its converse (column 4), inverse (column 5), and contrapositive (column 6), where columns are numbered for ease of reference.

1	2	3	4	5	6
p	q	$p \Rightarrow q$	$q \Rightarrow p$	$\sim p \Rightarrow \sim q$	$\sim q \Rightarrow \sim p$
F	F	T	T	T	T
F	T	T	F	F	T
T	F	F	T	T	F
T	T	T	T	T	T

Augustus De Morgan was an early nineteenth century mathematician of British descent who spent much of his adult life in India after studying at and being chair of mathematics at Cambridge. His laws of logic are universally pervasive across many disciplines.

You can verify that the number 6 is a counterexample for the converse of this implication, as 6 is even; however, it is not divisible by 4.

The **inverse** of an implication is formed by negating both the antecedent and consequent. The inverse of $p \Rightarrow q$ is $\sim p \Rightarrow \sim q$. The inverse for our example is: "If a number is not divisible by four, then it is not even." You are asked to find a counterexample for this assertion.

A useful proof technique in mathematics is a proof by contrapositive. The **contrapositive** for our example is: "If a number is not even, then it is not divisible by four."

We use the symbol $\equiv$ to denote that two logical expressions are equivalent by definition. For example, $(p \Rightarrow q) \equiv \sim p \vee q$. Such a compound expression is referred to as a tautology or a theorem. Observe that parentheses are employed to clarify the interpretation of an expression.

Using a truth table to demonstrate that a logical expression is a tautology and is therefore always true is referred to as a proof by **perfect induction**. The last column in Table 5.7 shows that $(\sim p \vee \sim q)$ and $\sim (p \wedge q)$ are always identical in truth-value. This theorem is one form of **De Morgan's law**. Table 5.8 lists additional theorems in the propositional logic.

Table 5.7
Two tautologies in the propositional logic. Observe that in the last two columns, all the entries are true.

p	q	$(p \Rightarrow q)$	$(\sim p \vee q)$	$(p \Rightarrow q) \equiv (\sim p \vee q)$	$(\sim p \vee \sim q) \equiv \sim (p \wedge q)$
F	F	T	T	T	T
F	T	T	T	T	T
T	F	F	F	T	T
T	T	T	T	T	T

Table 5.8
Theorems in propositional logic.

Theorem	Name
$p \lor q \equiv q \lor p$	Commutative Property 1
$p \land q \equiv q \land p$	Commutative Property 2
$p \lor p \equiv p$	Idempotency Law 1
$p \land p \equiv p$	Idempotency Law 2
$\sim \sim p \equiv p$	Double Negation (or Involution)
$(p \lor q) \lor r \equiv p \lor (q \lor r)$	Associative Law 1
$(p \land q) \land r \equiv p \land (q \land r)$	Associative Law 2
$p \land (q \lor r) \equiv (p \land q) \lor (p \land r)$	Distributive Law 1
$p \lor (q \land r) \equiv (p \lor q) \land (p \lor r)$	Distributive Law 2
$p \lor T \equiv T$	Domination Law 1
$p \land F \equiv F$	Domination Law 2
$(p \equiv q) \equiv (p \Rightarrow q) \land (q \Rightarrow p)$	Law of Elimination 1
$(p \equiv q) \equiv (p \land q) \lor (\sim p \land \sim q)$	Law of Elimination 2
$p \lor \sim p \equiv T$	Law of Excluded Middle
$p \land \sim p \equiv F$	Contradiction

Theorems in the propositional logic can be used to prove additional theorems through a process known as deduction. An example follows:

EXAMPLE 5.1: A PROOF IN THE PROPOSITIONAL LOGIC

Prove that $[(\sim \mathbf{p} \lor \mathbf{q}) \land \sim \mathbf{q}] \Rightarrow \sim \mathbf{p}$ is a tautology

$[(\sim \mathbf{p} \land \sim \mathbf{q}) \lor (\mathbf{q} \land \sim \mathbf{q})] \Rightarrow \sim p$	distributive law 1
$[(\sim \mathbf{p} \land \sim \mathbf{q}) \lor F] \Rightarrow \sim \mathbf{p}$	non-contradiction
$(\sim \mathbf{p} \land \sim \mathbf{q}) \Rightarrow \sim \mathbf{p}$	domination law 2
$\sim (\sim \mathbf{p} \land \sim \mathbf{q}) \lor \sim \mathbf{p}$	alternate definition for implication
$(\sim \sim \mathbf{p} \lor \sim \sim \mathbf{q}) \lor \sim \mathbf{p}$	De Morgan's law
$(\mathbf{p} \lor \mathbf{q}) \lor \sim \mathbf{p}$	involution
$\mathbf{p} \lor (\mathbf{q} \lor \sim \mathbf{p})$	associative law 1
$\mathbf{p} \lor (\sim \mathbf{p} \lor \mathbf{q})$	commutative law1
$(\mathbf{p} \lor \sim \mathbf{p}) \lor \mathbf{q}$	associative law 1
$\mathbf{T} \lor \mathbf{q}$	law of excluded middle
$\mathbf{T}$	domination law 1

We have seen that an expression whose value is always true is referred to as a tautology. An expression whose value is always false is called a **contradiction**. An example of a contradiction is $\mathbf{p} \land \sim \mathbf{p}$. Finally, an expression in the propositional logic is said to be **satisfiable** when there is at least one truth assignment for the variables that makes the expression true. For example, the expression $\mathbf{p} \land \mathbf{q}$ is satisfiable; it evaluates to true precisely when each of $\mathbf{p}$ and $\mathbf{q}$ are true. The

Satisfiability Problem (SAT) in the propositional logic is the problem of determining if there is some assignment of truth-values to the variables in an expression that makes the expression true. SAT in the propositional logic is NP-Complete (NPC). Recall from Chapter 3, "Informed Search," that a problem is NPC if the best algorithm to solve the problem seems to require exponential time (though no one has proven that a polynomial time algorithm does not exist). Perusing Tables 5.3 – 5.7, you can observe that a truth table for two variables has four rows, with each row corresponding to a distinct truth assignment. A truth table for three variables has $2^3 = 8$ rows; generalizing, a truth table for n variables has 2^n rows. There is no known algorithm for solving SAT that performs better than the approach that exhaustively scans each and every one of the 2^n rows.

5.2.2 Arguments in the Propositional Logic

An argument in the propositional logic has the form:

A: P_1
    P_2
    .
    .
    .
    P_r
    _____

C // Conclusion

An argument A is said to be valid if the implication formed by taking the conjunction of the premises as the antecedent and the conclusion as the consequent, i.e.,

$$(P_1 \wedge P_2 \wedge \ldots \wedge P_r) \Rightarrow C \text{ is a tautology.}$$

EXAMPLE 5.2 PROVE THAT THE FOLLOWING ARGUMENT IS VALID

1. $p \Rightarrow q$

2. $q \Rightarrow \sim r$

3. $\sim p \Rightarrow \sim r$
     _____

     $\therefore \sim r$

The symbol "∴" is shorthand for "therefore." Informally, an argument is valid if, whenever the premises are true, then you are certain that the conclusion is true as well. Premises are assumed to be true. Premise 1 states that **p** implies **q**. Premise 2 maintains that **q** implies ~**r**. Premises 1 and 2 taken together, imply that if **p** is true then ~**r** will be true (using transitivity). Premise 3 addresses the case when **p** is false; it states that ~p implies ~**r**. We know that **p** ∨ ~**p** is a tautology, ~**r** will follow, and hence this argument is indeed valid.

More formally, to prove that the previous argument is valid we must show that the implication

$$[(p \Rightarrow q) \wedge (q \Rightarrow \sim r) \wedge (\sim p \Rightarrow \sim r)] \Rightarrow \sim r \text{ is a tautology (consult Table 5.9).}$$

Table 5.9
A proof that the argument in Example 5.2 is valid.

1	2	3	4	5	6	7	8
p	q	r	$p \Rightarrow q$	$q \Rightarrow \sim r$	$\sim p \Rightarrow \sim r$	$4 \wedge 5 \wedge 6$	$7 \Rightarrow \sim r$
F	F	F	T	T	T	T	T
F	F	T	T	T	F	F	T
F	T	F	T	T	T	T	T
F	T	T	T	F	F	F	T
T	F	F	F	T	T	F	T
T	F	T	F	T	T	F	T
T	T	F	T	T	T	T	T
T	T	T	T	F	T	F	T

Column 7 contains the conjunction of the three premises. The rightmost column of Table 5.9 corresponds to the aforementioned implication and it contains all true values, confirming that the implication is indeed a tautology and that the argument is therefore valid. The reader is advised not to confuse an argument's *validity* with the *truth* of an expression. A logical argument is *valid* if its conclusion follows from its premises (informally, that the argument has the right "structure"); arguments are not true or false. An example will help to clarify this distinction. Consider the following argument:

"If the moon is made of green cheese, then I am rich."

Let **g** represent: "the moon is made of green cheese" and r represent: "I am rich." This argument has the form:

g
_____

∴ r

Since **g** is false, the implication **g** $\Rightarrow$ **r** is true and hence the argument is valid. Many additional examples of truth tables, as well as logical arguments and inference rules can be found in *Discrete Mathematic* [1], *Mathematical Structures for Computer Science* [2], and *Discrete and Combinatorial Mathematics*.[3]

5.2.3 Proving Arguments in the Propositional Logic Valid – A Second Approach

A second approach to proving validity of propositional logic arguments is known as resolution. This strategy is also referred to as **resolution-refutation**.[4] This approach assumes that the premises are true and that the conclusion is false. If you can thereby arrive at a contradiction, then the original conclusion must follow logically from the premises and hence the original argument is valid. Resolution proofs require that the premises and conclusion of the argument be in a special form referred to as *clause form*.

An expression in the propositional logic is in clause form if:

There is no:

1. implication
2. conjunction
3. **double negation**

Removing implication can be accomplished by replacing each occurrence of $(\mathbf{p} \Rightarrow \mathbf{q})$ by $(\sim\mathbf{p} \vee \mathbf{q})$. Removing conjunction is more subtle; $\mathbf{p} \wedge \mathbf{q}$ can always be replaced by $\mathbf{p}, \mathbf{q}$ via simplification. And finally, each occurrence of $\sim \sim\mathbf{p}$ can be simplified to $\mathbf{p}$ (involution or double negation).

EXAMPLE 5.2 REVISITED

Use resolution to prove that the following argument is valid:
1. $\mathbf{p} \Rightarrow \mathbf{q}$
2. $\mathbf{q} \Rightarrow \sim\mathbf{r}$
3. $\sim\mathbf{p} \Rightarrow \sim\mathbf{r}$

$\therefore \sim\mathbf{r}$

Step 1: Convert the premises to clause form. To do so, you first remove implication:

    1') $\sim\mathbf{p} \vee \mathbf{q}$
    2') $\sim\mathbf{q} \vee \sim\mathbf{r}$
    3') $\sim \sim\mathbf{p} \vee \sim\mathbf{r}$

There are no conjunction operators, therefore we need only to remove the double negation operation from the third expression yielding 3') $\mathbf{p} \vee \sim\mathbf{r}$.

Step 2: Negate the conclusion
1) $\sim \sim\mathbf{r}$

Step 3: Convert the negation of the conclusion to clause form:

4') $\mathbf{r}$.   // via involution

Finally, in **Step 4:** Search for a contradiction in this list of clauses. If a contradiction is found, then the argument is valid, as the contradiction is due to the presence of the negation of the conclusion in the list of clauses (recall that the premises are true by definition).

Our clause base (list of clauses) is listed once more for ease of presentation:

1') $\sim\mathbf{p} \vee \mathbf{q}$
2') $\sim\mathbf{q} \vee \sim\mathbf{r}$
3') $\mathbf{p} \vee \sim r$
4') $\mathbf{r}$

We combine clauses together to arrive at new clauses.

3'), 4')	$\mathbf{p}$	(5'
1'), 5')	$\mathbf{q}$	(6'
2', 6')	$\sim\mathbf{r}$	(7'
4', 7')	□// contradiction	

Combining 3' with 4': 4' states that $\mathbf{r}$ is true whereas 3' asserts that $\mathbf{p} \vee \sim\mathbf{r}$ is true. However, because $\mathbf{r}$ is true, we know that $\mathbf{p} \vee \sim\mathbf{r}$ is true because $\mathbf{p}$ is true ($\sim\mathbf{r}$ cannot be true). This process of combining clauses to obtain new clauses is called *resolution*. The proof of validity culminates when the empty clause (denoted by □) is derived as a result of combining clauses 4′ with 7′, in other words, **r** with ~**r**.

....

EXAMPLE 5.3: RESOLUTION THEOREM
PROVING – A SECOND EXAMPLE

Use resolution to prove that the following argument is valid:
1. **p** $\Rightarrow$ (**q** $\vee$ **r**)
2. ~**r**

_____

∴ **q**

Step 1: Once again, you first convert the premises to clause form.
    1′) ~**p** $\vee$ (**q** $\vee$ **r**)
    2′) ~**r**

Step 2: Negate the conclusion.
    3′) ~**q**

Step 3: Convert the negation of the conclusion to clause form:
    3′) ~**q**   // it was already in clause form

Step 4: Search for a contradiction in this list of clauses: 1′), 2′), and 3′)
We try combining 1′) with 3′) and we obtain:
    4′) ~**p** $\vee$ **r**
Then combining 4′) with 2′):
    5′) ~**p**

It soon becomes apparent that "we are spinning our wheels", i.e., there is no contradiction present. Once you have searched (everywhere) to find a contradiction and are sure that none is present, then you can safely assume that the argument is **not** valid. If **p** had been given as a premise as well, then this argument would indeed be valid.

....

▐ 5.3 ▌ PREDICATE LOGIC – INTRODUCTION

We have previously observed that predicate logic has greater expressive power than propositional logic. If we wished to express The King's Wise Men problem with propositional logic, distinct variables would be required for each of:

    "wise man one is wearing a blue hat"
    "wise man one is wearing a white hat"

and so on. You cannot directly refer to a part of an expression in the propositional logic.

A predicate logic expression consists of a predicate name followed by a list (possibly empty) of arguments. In this text predicate names will begin with capital letters, for example: WM_1(). The number of elements in a predicate's list of arguments (or variables) is referred to as its **arity**. For example: Win ( ), Favorite Composer (Beethoven), Greater-Than (6,5) are predicates of arity zero, one, and two respectively. (Note, we will allow constants such as Beethoven, me, you, to be capitalized or not). As with the propositional logic, predicate logic expressions can be combined with the

Table 5.10
Predicate logic expressions.

Predicates	English Equivalent
(~ Win (you) ⇒ Lose (you)) ∧	If you don't win, then you lose and
(Lose (you) ⇒ Win (me))	If you lose then I win.
[Play_in_Rosebowl (Wisconsin Badgers) ∨	If either the Wisconsin Badgers or
Play_in_Rosebowl (Oklahoma Sooners)] ⇒	The Oklahoma Sooners play in the Rosebowl, then
Going_to_California (me).	I am going to California. [// to watch the game].
∀(x){[Animal(x) ∧ Has_Hair (x)	If x is a warm-blooded animal with hair
∧ Warm_Blooded (x)] ⇒ Mammal (x)}	then x is a mammal.
(x) [Natural_number (x)	Some natural numbers are even.
∧ Divisible_by_2 (x)]	
{Brother (**x**, Sam) ⇒	If x is Sam's brother then
(∃**y**) [(Parent (**y**, **x**) ∧ Parent (**y**, Sam) ∧	x and Sam must have a common parent,
Male (**x**) ∧	x must be male, and
~ Equal (**x**, Sam)]}	x must be someone other than Sam.

Without the last predicate in Table 5.10, a computer program would incorrectly identify a male person as their own brother.

operators: ~ , ∧ , ∨, ⇒, ⇔. Furthermore, two quantifiers can be applied to predicate variables. The first (∃) is an **existential quantifier**. ∃**x** is read as: "there exists an **x**" this means that one or more values of **x** are guaranteed to exist. The second quantifier, (∀) is a **universal quantifier.** ∀**x** reads as: "for all **x**", this means that the predicate expression is stating something for all values that **x** can assume. Consult Table 5.10 for examples that will clarify this terminology.

5.3.1 Unification in the Predicate Logic

We discussed resolution within the propositional logic in Section 5.2.3. It was easy to determine that two literals cannot both be true at the same time; you just look for L and ~L. This matching process in the predicate logic is more complicated because you must also consider the arguments of the predicates. For example: Setting (sun) and ~Setting (sun) is a contradiction, whereas Beautiful (Day) and ~Beautiful (Night) is not, as the arguments do not match. In order to find contradictions, we require a matching procedure that compares two literals to detect whether there exists a set of substitutions that makes them identical. This procedure is called **unification**.

If two literals are to unify, then first, their predicate symbols must match; if they do not, then these two literals cannot be unified. For example:

Kite_is_flying (X) and
Trying_to_fly_Kite (Y) cannot be unified.

If the predicate symbols match, then you check the arguments one pair at a time. If the first matches, then continue with the second, and so on.

Matching Rules:

• Different constants or predicates cannot match ... only identical ones can.

- A variable can match another variable, any constant, or a predicate expression with the restriction that the predicate expression must not contain any instances of the variable being matched.

There is one caveat: The substitution that is found must be a single consistent one, in other words, you cannot use separate ones for each piece of the expression. To ensure this consistency, a substitution must be applied to the rest of the literals before you continue with unification.

EXAMPLE 5.4: UNIFICATION

Coffees (**x**, **x**)
Coffees (**y**, **z**)

The predicates match, so next check the first arguments, the variables **x** and **y**. Recall that one variable can be substituted for another; we will substitute y for **x**, this is written as **y** | **x**. There is nothing special about this choice; we could have chosen instead to substitute **x** for **y**. The algorithm must make some choice. After substituting **y** for **x**, we have:

Coffees (**y**, **x**)
Coffees (**y**, **z**)

Continuing, we try to match **x** and **z**. Suppose we decide upon the substitution **z** | **x**. There is a problem. The substitution is not consistent. You cannot substitute both y and **z** for **x**. Let us begin again. After making the first substitution **y** | **x**, you should make this substitution throughout the literals, yielding:

Coffees (**y**, **y**)
Coffees (**y**, **z**)

Next, you try to unify the variables **y** and **z**. You settle on the substitution **z** | **y** yielding:

Coffees (**y**, **z**)
Coffees (**y**, **z**)

Success! The two literals are identical. This substitution is the composition of two substitutions:

(**z** | **y**) (**y** | **x**)

You should read this the same way that you read the composition of functions, in other words, from right to left. First, **y** is substituted for **x** and then **z** for **y**.

When there is one substitution, there are usually many.

EXAMPLE 5.5: ADDITIONAL UNIFICATION EXAMPLES

a. Wines (**x**, **y**)
    Wines (Chianti, **z**)

These predicates can be unified with any of the following substitutions:

1. (Chianti | **x**, **z** | **y**)
2. (Chianti | **x**, **y** | **z**)

Observe that substitutions 1 and 2 are equivalent. The following substitutions are also possible:

3.   (Chianti | **x**, Pinot_Noir | **y**, Pinot_Noir | **z**)
4.   (Chianti | **x**, Amarone | **y**, Amarone | **z**)

Note that substitutions 3 and 4 are more restrictive than is necessary. We desire the **most general unifier** (**mgu**) possible. Each of substitutions 1 or 2 qualifies as an mgu.

b.   Coffees (**x**, **y**)
     Coffees (Espresso, **z**)

     {Espresso | **x**, **y** | **z** } is one possible set of substitutions.

c.   Coffees (**x**, **x**)
Coffees (Brazilian, Colombian)

The substitution Brazilian | **x**, Colombian | **x** is not legal, because you cannot substitute two distinct constants for the same variable **x**. Therefore, unification is not possible.

d.   Descendant (**x**, **y**)
     Descendant (bob, son (bob))

> NOTE: Son () is a *function* that takes a person as input, and yields their father as output.

A legal substitution is:
     {bob | **x** , son (bob) | **y**}

5.3.2 Resolution in the Predicate Logic

Resolution provides a method for finding contradictions in a database of clauses. Resolution refutation proves a theorem by negating the statement that needs to be proved and then adding this negation to the set of axioms that are known (have been assumed) to be true.

Resolution refutation proofs involve the following steps:

1.   Put the premises (these are sometimes called axioms or hypotheses) into clause form.
2.   Add the negation of what is to be proved (i.e., the negation of either the conclusion or goal), in clause form, to the set of premises.
3.   Resolve these clauses together, producing new clauses that logically follow from them.
4.   Produce a contradiction by generating what is referred to as the empty clause.
5.   The substitutions used to produce the empty clause are precisely those under which the opposite of the negated goal is true.

Resolution is refutation complete. This means that a contradiction can always be generated *whenever* one exists. Resolution refutation proofs require that the premises and the negation of the conclusion be placed in a **normal form** called clause form (as was required in the propositional logic). Clause form represents both the premises and the negation of the conclusion as a set of disjunction of literals.

We use the following well-known argument to illustrate resolution proofs.

Premise 1) Socrates is a mortal.

Premise 2) All mortals will die.

Conclusion: Socrates will die.

First we represent this argument in the predicate logic. We use the predicates Mortal(x) and Will Die (x).

Premise 1) Mortal (Socrates)

Premise 2) ($\forall$**x**) (Mortal (**x**) $\Rightarrow$ Will _ Die (**x**))

Conclusion) $\therefore$ Will _ Die (Socrates).

The parentheses around Mortal(x) Will _ Die (x) are not necessary; but they aid clarity.

Next, the premises are converted into clause form:

Premise 1) Mortal (Socrates)

Premise 2) ~ Mortal (**x**) $\vee$ Will _ Die (**x**)

Negate the conclusion: ~ Will _ Die (Socrates)

Observe this last predicate is already in clause form.

Our clause base consists of:

1) Mortal (Socrates)

2) ~ Mortal (**x**) $\vee$ Will Die (**x**)

3) ~Will _ Die (Socrates)

Combining 2) with 3) under the substitution Socrates | **x** yields:

4) ~Mortal (Socrates).

Note that we have assumed that both clauses 2) and 3) are true. If clause 3) is true, then the only reason clause 2) can be true is if ~Mortal(Socrates) is true. Finally, by combining 1) with 4) we derive □, in other words, the empty clause, and so we have a contradiction. Therefore, the negation of what was assumed true, in other words, not (~ Will _ Die (Socrates)), which is equivalent to Will_Die (Socrates), must be true. The original conclusion *does* logically follow from the argument's premises, and therefore the argument is valid.

EXAMPLE 5.6: RESOLUTION EXAMPLE

1. All great chefs are Italian.
2. All Italians enjoy good food.
3. Either Michael or Louis is a great chef.
4. Michael is not a great chef.
5. Therefore, Louis enjoys good food.

We use the following predicates:

GC (**x**) : **x** is a great chef

I (**x**) : **x** is Italian

EF (**x**) : **x** enjoys good food

The argument can be represented in the predicate logic as :

1. ($\forall$**x**) (GC (**x**) $\Rightarrow$ I (**x**))
2. ($\forall$**x**) (I (**x**) $\Rightarrow$ EF (**x**))
3. GC (Michael) $\vee$ GC (Louis)
4. ~ GC (Michael)

Therefore:

5. EF (Louis)

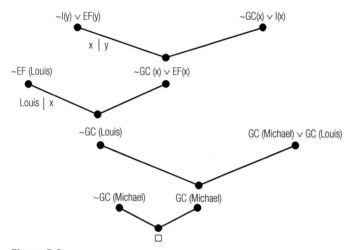

Figure 5.2
Resolution proof —a graphical representation.

Next, we must convert the premises into clause form where no quantifiers can be present. It is easy to remove universal quantifiers because we can assume that all variables are universally quantified. The removal of existential quantifiers (not required for this example) is more involved and will not be discussed in this section. Also, for now, observe that expression 2) below has a distinct variable name (a process referred to as standardization of variable names).

The premises in clause form:
1. ~ GC (**x**) ∨ I (**x**)
2. ~ I (**y**) ∨ EF (**y**)
3. GC (Michael) ∨ GC (Louis)
4. ~ GC (Michael)

Negate the conclusion:
5. ~ EF (Louis)   // already in clause form

We display the search for a contradiction in graphical form in Figure 5.2: The substitutions made are shown on the branches.

Additional examples of unification and resolution proofs can be found in *Logical Foundations of Artificial Intelligence*, by Genesereth and Nilsson.[5]

5.2.3 Converting a Predicate Expression to Clause Form

The following rules can be used to transform an arbitrary predicate logic expression into clause form. The transformation process described here might cause some nuances of meaning to be lost. This loss of meaning can occur because of the substitution process known as skolemization that is used to remove existential quantifiers. This set of transformations does, however, possess one important property—it will preserve a contradiction whenever one exists in the original set of predicate expressions.

a) $(\forall \mathbf{w}) \{[(P_1 (\mathbf{w}) \lor P_2 (\mathbf{w})) P_3 (\mathbf{w})]$
     $\lor [(\exists \mathbf{x}) (\exists \mathbf{y}) (P_3 (\mathbf{x}, \mathbf{y}) \Rightarrow P_4 (\mathbf{w}, \mathbf{x}))]\}$
     $\land [(\forall \mathbf{w}) P_5 (\mathbf{w})].$

Step 1: Eliminate implication. Recall that $\mathbf{p} \Rightarrow \mathbf{q} \equiv \sim \mathbf{p} \lor \mathbf{q}$. Applying this equivalence to a) we obtain:

b) $(\forall \mathbf{w}) \{[\sim(P_1 (\mathbf{w}) \lor P_2 (\mathbf{w})) \lor P_3 (\mathbf{w})]$
     $\lor [(\exists \mathbf{x}) (\exists \mathbf{y}) (\sim P_3 (\mathbf{x}, \mathbf{y}) \lor P_4 (\mathbf{w}, \mathbf{x}))]\}$
     $\land [(\forall \mathbf{w}) P_5 (\mathbf{w})]$

Step 2: Reduce the scope of negation by using the following logical equivalences:

$$i)\sim(\sim\mathbf{a})\equiv\mathbf{a}$$
$$ii)\sim(\exists\mathbf{x})\ P(\mathbf{x})\equiv(\forall\mathbf{x})\sim P(\mathbf{x})$$

Equivalence ii) can be understood as: "If there does not exist a value for x for which the predicate P($\mathbf{x}$) is true, then for all values of x, this predicate must be false."

$$iii)\sim(\forall\mathbf{x})\ P(\mathbf{x})\equiv(\exists\mathbf{x})\sim P(\mathbf{x})$$

Equivalence iii) states that "If it is not the case that P($\mathbf{x}$) is true for all values of $\mathbf{x}$, then there must exist a value for $\mathbf{x}$ which makes P($\mathbf{x}$) false."

$$iv)\sim(\mathbf{a}\wedge\mathbf{b})\equiv\sim\mathbf{a}\vee\sim\mathbf{b}\qquad\text{De Morgan's theorems}$$
$$\sim(\mathbf{a}\vee\mathbf{b})\equiv\sim\mathbf{a}\wedge\sim\mathbf{b}$$

We use the second form of De Morgan's law:

$$c)\ (\forall\mathbf{w})\ \{[\sim P_1\ (\mathbf{w})\wedge\sim P_2(\mathbf{w})\vee P_3\ (\mathbf{w})]$$
$$\vee\ [(\exists\mathbf{x})\ (\exists\mathbf{y})\ (\sim P_3\ (\mathbf{x},\mathbf{y})\vee P_4\ (\mathbf{w},\mathbf{x}))]\}$$
$$\wedge\ [(\forall\mathbf{w})\ P_5\ (\mathbf{w})]$$

Step 3: Standardize variable names. All variables bound by different quantifiers must have unique names. It is therefore necessary to rename some variables.

Step 3 dictates that the variable $\mathbf{w}$ in the last term of c) above must be renamed; we choose $\mathbf{z}$ as the new variable name.

$$d)\ ((\forall\mathbf{w})\ \{[\sim P_1\ (\mathbf{w})\wedge\sim P_2\ (\mathbf{w})\vee P_3\ (\mathbf{w})]$$
$$\vee\ [(\exists\mathbf{x})\ (\exists\mathbf{y})\ (\sim P_3\ (\mathbf{x},\mathbf{y})\vee P_4\ (\mathbf{w},\mathbf{x})]\}$$
$$\wedge\ [(\forall\mathbf{z})\ P_5\ (\mathbf{z})]$$

Step 4: Move all quantifiers to the left, being certain to preserve their order. Step 3 ensures that no confusion will result during this process.

$$e)\ (\forall\mathbf{w})\ (\exists\mathbf{x})\ (\exists\mathbf{y})\ (\forall\mathbf{z})\ \{[\sim P_1\ (\mathbf{w})\wedge\sim P_2\ (\mathbf{w})\vee P_3\ (\mathbf{w})]\vee[(\sim P_3\ (\mathbf{x},\mathbf{y})\vee$$
$$P_4\ (\mathbf{w},\mathbf{x}))]\}\wedge[P_5\ (\mathbf{z})]$$

The expression displayed in e) is referred to as **prenex normal form**, in which all quantifiers form a prefix of the predicate logic expression.

Step 5: All existential quantifiers are now removed. The process referred to above as skolemization is used, in which a name is assigned for something or someone that must exist.

Examples of skolemization:

Rodin was a favorite character in old Japanese monster movies.

- ($\exists\mathbf{x}$) (Monster ($\mathbf{x}$)) Can be replaced by: Monster (Rodin)
  // Rodin is a skolem constant.

- ($\forall\mathbf{x}$) ($\exists\mathbf{y}$) (Favorite _ Pasta ($\mathbf{x},\mathbf{y}$) can be replaced by: ($\forall\mathbf{x}$)
  (Favorite _ Pasta $\mathbf{x}$, fp($\mathbf{x}$))

// fp ( ) is a **skolem function**. The argument(s) of a skolem function will be all the universally quantified variables that occur in front of the existentially quantified variable that is being replaced. Here, the skolem function fp($\mathbf{x}$) returns the favorite pasta of the individual $\mathbf{x}$.

$$=\quad(\forall\mathbf{w})\ (\forall\mathbf{x})\ (\forall\mathbf{y})\ (\exists\mathbf{z})\ (\forall\mathbf{t})\ (\text{Richer}\_\text{than}\ (\mathbf{w},\mathbf{x},\mathbf{y},\mathbf{t}))\ \text{is skolemized to:}$$
$$(\forall\mathbf{w})\ (\forall\mathbf{x})\ (\forall\mathbf{y})\ (\forall\mathbf{t})\ (\text{Richer}\_\text{than}\ (\mathbf{w},\mathbf{x},\mathbf{y},\text{rt}(\mathbf{w},\mathbf{x},\mathbf{y})))$$

//The skolem function **rt( )** has three arguments, **w**, **x**, and **y** which are the three universally quantified variables that precede **z**. Note that the variable **t** is also universally quantified but because it occurs after **z**, it does not appear as an argument in **rt ( )**.

Once e) is skolemized we have:

f) $(\forall \mathbf{w})\,(\forall \mathbf{z})\,\{[\sim P_1\,(\mathbf{w}) \wedge \sim P_2\,(\mathbf{w}) \vee P_3\,(\mathbf{w})] \vee [\sim P_3\,(f(\mathbf{w}),\, g(\mathbf{w})) \vee P_4\,(\mathbf{w},\, f(\mathbf{w}))]\} \wedge [P_5\,(\mathbf{z})]$

// **x** was replaced by the skolem function $f(\mathbf{w})$ and **y** by $g(\mathbf{w})$.

Step 6: Drop all universal quantifiers. This is allowed because it is assumed that all variables are universally quantified.

g) $\{[\sim P_1\,(\mathbf{w}) \wedge \sim P_2(\mathbf{w}) \vee P_3\,(\mathbf{w})] \vee [\sim P_3\,(f(\mathbf{w}),\, g(\mathbf{w})) \vee P_4\,(\mathbf{w},\, f(\mathbf{w}))]\} \wedge [P_5\,(\mathbf{z})]$

Step 7: Convert to **conjunctive normal form (CNF),** in other words, every expression is a conjunction of disjunctive terms. The associative laws and one **distributive law** are reproduced below (from Table 5.8):

$a \vee (b \vee c) = (a \vee b) \vee c$
$a \wedge (b \wedge c) = (a \wedge b) \wedge c$ //associative laws
$a \vee (b \wedge c) = (a \vee b) \wedge (a \vee c)$ //distributive law
$a \wedge (b \vee c)$ //already in clause form

We use the first distributive law and the **commutative law** (consult Table 5.8) to obtain:

h1) $\{[((P_3\,(\mathbf{w}) \vee \sim P_1\,(\mathbf{w})) \wedge ((P_3\,(\mathbf{w}) \vee \sim P_2\,(\mathbf{w}))\,] \vee [\sim P_3\,(f\,(\mathbf{w}),\, g\,(\mathbf{w})) \vee P_4\,(\mathbf{w},\, f\,(\mathbf{w}))]\} \wedge [P_5\,(\mathbf{z})]$

We need to apply the distributive law once again; the substitutions are shown below:

$\{[\ ((P_3\,(\mathbf{w}) \vee P_1\,(\mathbf{w})) \wedge ((P_3\,(\mathbf{w}) \vee P_2\,(\mathbf{w}))\ ]$
---------b--------   ---------c--------
$\vee [\sim P_3\,(f\,(\mathbf{w}),\, g\,(\mathbf{w})) \vee P_4\,(\mathbf{w},\, f\,(\mathbf{w}))]\}$
-----------------a--------------
$\wedge [P_5\,(\mathbf{z})]$

h2) $\{[(P_3\,(\mathbf{w}) \vee \sim P_1\,(\mathbf{w})] \vee [(\sim P_3\,(f\,(\mathbf{w}),\, g\,(\mathbf{w})) \vee P_4\,(\mathbf{w},\, f\,(\mathbf{w}))]\}$
$\wedge \{[(P_3\,(\mathbf{w}) \vee \sim P_2\,(\mathbf{w})] \vee [(\sim P_3\,(f\,(\mathbf{w}),\, g\,(\mathbf{w})) \vee P_4(\mathbf{w},\, f\,(\mathbf{w}))]\}$
$\wedge \{[P_5\,(\mathbf{z})]\}$

Step 8: Each term being AND'ed will become a separate clause:

i1) $[(P_3\,(\mathbf{w}) \vee \sim P_1\,(\mathbf{w})] \vee [(\sim P_3\,(f\,(\mathbf{w}),\, g\,(\mathbf{w})) \vee P_4\,(\mathbf{w},\, f\,(\mathbf{w}))]$
i2) $[(P_3\,(\mathbf{w}) \vee \sim P_2\,(\mathbf{w})] \vee [(\sim P_3\,(f\,(\mathbf{w}),\, g\,(\mathbf{w})) \vee P_4\,(\mathbf{w},\, f(\mathbf{w}))]$
i3) $P_5\,(\mathbf{z})$

Step 9: Standardize the variable names one more time.

j1) $[(P_3\,(\mathbf{w}) \vee \sim P_1\,(\mathbf{w})] \vee [(\sim P_3\,(f\,(\mathbf{w}),\, g\,(\mathbf{w})) \vee P_4\,(\mathbf{w},\, f\,(\mathbf{w}))]$
j2) $[(P_3\,(\mathbf{x}) \vee \sim P_2\,(\mathbf{x})] \vee [(\sim P_3\,(f\,(\mathbf{x}),\, g\,(\mathbf{x})) \vee P_4(\mathbf{x},\, f\,(\mathbf{x}))]$
j3) $P_5\,(\mathbf{z})$

We conclude by commenting that not all nine steps are required in each conversion into clause form but you need to be prepared to use any of the steps that are needed. Additional resolution proofs that entail the skolemization procedure can be found in Chang and Lee's *Symbolic Logic and Mechanical Theorem Proving*.[6]

EXAMPLE 5.6: RESOLUTION EXAMPLE – REVISITED

Suppose, in Example 5.5, "All great chefs are Italian" is replaced by "Some great chefs are Italian." Is the resulting argument still valid? This modified argument is shown below:

1. Some great chefs are Italian.

2. All Italians enjoy good food.

3. Either Michael or Louis is a great chef.

4. Michael is not a great chef.

5. Therefore, Louis enjoys good food.

In predicate logic, using our previous predicates, this modified argument can be represented in the predicate logic as:

1. $(\exists x)\ (GC(x) \wedge I(x))$

2. $(\forall x)\ (I(x) \Rightarrow EF(x))$

3. GC (Michael) $\vee$ GC (Louis)

4. ~GC (Michael)

5. Therefore EF (Louis)

In clause form, the premises are:

1. a) GC (Sam)   //The skolem constant Sam enables us to eliminate $(\exists x)$

1. b) I (Sam)

2. $I(x) \vee EF(x)$

3. GC (Michael) $\vee$ GC (Louis)

4. ~GC (Michael)

and the negation of the conclusion (in clause form) is

5. ~EF (Louis)

No contradiction can be found in this set of clauses, hence this modified argument is not valid.

5.4 ■ SEVERAL OTHER LOGICS

In this Section, we discuss several interesting logics that need thorough understanding of the previously discussed logics. We only outline the basic structure of these logic models, and ask the interested reader to pursue the many references that are available.

5.4.1 Second Order Logic

The predicate logic discussed in Section 5.3 is sometimes referred to as First Order Predicate Logic (FOPL). In the FOPL, quantifiers can be applied to variables but not to predicates themselves. You might have seen induction proofs in your earlier studies. An induction proof has two parts:

i) A basis step in which some assertion **S** is demonstrated to hold for an initial value n_0.
ii) An inductive step in which we assume **S** is true for some value n, we must then show that S holds for $n + 1$.

Gauss's formula for the sum of the first n integers states: $\sum_{i=1}^{n} i = \frac{n(n+1)}{2}$

i) **Basis Step:** When $n = 1$, we have: $\sum_{i=1}^{n} i = \frac{1(1+1)}{2} = 1$

ii) **Inductive Step:** Assume that $= \sum_{i=1}^{n} i = \frac{n(n+1)}{2}$ then $\sum_{i=1}^{n+1} i$, which equals $\left(\sum_{i=1}^{n+1} i\right)$ plus $(n + 1)$. This equals $((n(n + 1))/2) + (n + 1)$, which equals $(n(n + 1))/2 + (2(n + 1))/2$. This last quantity equals $((n(n + 1)) + (2n + 2)/2$, which equals $= n^2 + 3n + 3$, which of course equals $((n + 1)(n + 2))/2$. This last expression shows that the formula is true for $n + 1$. Hence, we have proved that the theorem holds for all natural numbers. To state the proof methodology of mathematical induction we must have:

$$(\forall S)\ [(S\ (n_0) \wedge (\forall n)\ (S\ (n) \Rightarrow S\ (n + 1))] \Rightarrow (\forall n)\ S(n) \qquad (8)$$

We are trying to represent that all assertions are true when an induction proof for S exists. In the FOPL, however, you cannot quantify a predicate. Expression (8) is a well formed formula (WFF) in the **second order predicate logic**. The interested reader might wish to consult Shapiro's excellent text for more details on second order logic.[7]

5.4.2 Non-Monotonic Logic

FOPL is sometimes characterized as **monotonic** (the term monotonic was first encountered in Chapter 3). For example, in Section 5.3.3 we stated the theorem: $\sim (\exists x)\ P\ (x) \equiv (\forall x) \sim P\ (x)$. If there is no value of **x** that makes the predicate: P(x) true, then for all values of **x**, this predicate must be false. Also, you can remain confident that as you learn more about logic, the truth of this theorem will not change. More formally, the FOPL is monotonic, in other words, if some expression Φ can be derived from a set of premises Γ, then Φ can also be derived from any superset Σ of Γ (any set containing Γ as a subset). Real life often does not possess this measure of permanence. As we learn more, we might wish to retract our earlier conclusions. Children often believe in the existence of Santa Claus or the Easter bunny. As many people mature, they no longer hold these beliefs.

Non-monotonic logic has found applications in database theory. Suppose you want to visit Qatar and stay in a 7-star hotel while there. You consult a travel agent and, after consulting their computer, they respond that Qatar has no 7-star hotels. The travel agent is applying (unwittingly) the **closed world assumption**; the assumption is that the database is complete and if such a hotel existed it would appear within the database.

McCarthy was an early researcher in non-monotonic logic. He is responsible for the concept of **circumscription**, which maintains that predicates should be extended only as necessary. For example: "All nonreligious holidays in the United States are observed on the closest Monday to their actual occurrence" (so as to enable a three-day weekend). Only later do you learn that some nonreligious holidays are special (such as July 4 – American Independence Day) and are observed on their actual date. We should not conclude that other nonreligious holidays are special (say New Year's Day) unless we are explicitly told that it is so.

Two problems that are currently intractable for non-monotonic logic are: (1) checking consistency of conclusions and (2) determining which conclusions remain viable as new knowledge is obtained. Non-monotonic logic more accurately reflects the transient nature of human convictions. Computational complexity concerns will need to be addressed if this logic is to find more widespread use. Seminal work in this area of logic has been done by McCarthy,[8] McDermott and Doyle,[9] Reiter,[10] and Ginsberg.[11]

5.4.3 Fuzzy Logic

In the FOPL, predicates are classified as either true or false. In our world, truth and falsehood often come with shades of gray. Some politicians believe that: "All taxes are bad." Is this posit true for a tax on cigarettes—a tax that could possibly cause some smokers to quit smoking, because of the increased price tag on their habit, and thereby live longer? Consider: "New Yorkers are polite." Most probably are, and these people probably will offer directions if they see you consulting a map; yet exceptions do exist. You might wish to maintain "New Yorkers are polite" is true to a certain extent. Fuzzy logic permits this latitude in truth-values. A logical expression can vary anywhere from false (0.0 degree of truth) to certainty (1.0 degree of truth). Fuzzy logic has found many applications in the control of modern conveniences. For example, the wash cycle of a washing machine should be longer if the clothes are especially dirty because dirtier clothes need to be washed longer. The shutter speed should be faster on a digital camera if it is sunny. "It is a sunny day" can vary anywhere from 0.0 to 1.0 in truth-value depending on whether it is nighttime, daytime and cloudy, or it is noon and there is not a cloud in the sky. Fuzzy logic controllers often have simpler logic design than their "non-fuzzy" counterparts. The founding father of fuzzy logic is Lotfi Zadeh.[12] We revisit fuzzy logic in Chapter 8.

5.4.4 Modal Logic

Modal logic is useful in the analysis of beliefs, in settings wherein temporal expressions are used and whenever moral imperatives ("You should brush your teeth before bedtime") are used. Two common modal logic operators are:

Symbol	English Equivalent
□	"It is necessary that…"
◊	"It is possible that…"

We can define ◊ from □ by: ◊A = ~ □ ~A, which says A is possible if ~A is not necessary. You should note the similarity of the equivalence between $(\forall x)\, A\,(x)$ and $(\sim\exists x) \sim A\,(x)$ cited earlier in this chapter.

One axiom proposed by the logician Luitzen Egbertus Jan Brouwer is:

$$A \Rightarrow \Box\,\Diamond\,A \text{ i.e. "if A is true, then A is necessarily possible."}$$

In temporal logic (a type of modal logic), two operators, G for the future and H for the past, are used. Then we would have "If A is a theorem then both GA and HA are theorems as well."

In Section 5.2, we used a truth table to prove that an argument is valid. This approach cannot be used in modal logics, because there are no truth tables to represent: "You should do your homework." Or "It is necessary that you wake up early." We cannot determine the truth-value for □ A from the truth-value for A. For example, if A represents "Fishes are fishes" □ A is true, however when A equals "Fishes are food", □ A is no longer true.

Modal logic has contributed to our understanding of provability in mathematical foundations (where one asks: is a given formula a theorem or not?) A bibliography of early modal logic research can be found in Hughes and Cresswell. [13]

▮5.5▮ CHAPTER SUMMARY

We have seen that logic is a concise language for knowledge representation. Our discussion began with propositional logic because this was the most accessible entry point. Truth tables are a convenient tool to ascertain truth-values for propositional logic expressions.

The FOPL has greater expressive power than the propositional logic. *Resolution* was seen to be a useful procedure for determining *validity* of arguments. In AI we are concerned with both knowledge representation and discovery. *Resolution* is a strategy that enables us to draw valid conclusions from data that can thereby enable us to solve difficult problems.

Section 5.4 discussed various logic models that are more expressive than the FOPL and can enable us to more accurately represent knowledge about the world and to solve some of the conundrums that it often tosses our way.

Questions for Discussion

1. Comment on the difference in expressive power between the propositional logic and the FOPL.

2. What limitations do you believe logic has as an AI knowledge representation language?

3. How might propositional logic be altered if the Law of excluded middle were not a theorem?

4. A fallacy is a type of reasoning that seems to be valid but is not; an example is *post hoc* reasoning, which literally means "after this." In this fallacy, one assumes that an event that occurred first is the cause of a later event. For example, this morning your horoscope might have stated "You will have a conflict today" and then later that same day you have a dispute with a colleague.

   a. Give two additional examples of post hoc reasoning from everyday life.

   b. Comment on the distinction between causality and post hoc reasoning.

5. Another type of faulty reasoning occurs when a premise is stated as a conditional. Consider the following lament all too common from students: "If I don't get at least a B in this course, then life is not fair." Later the student discovers that he has obtained a grade of B+ and concludes: "Therefore, life is fair."

   a. Give an additional example of this type of fallacy.

b.   Comment on the lack of validity in this type of argument

6. "Begging the question" is another form of faulty reasoning. The French comedian Sacha Guitny drew a picture in which three thieves are arguing over the distribution of seven pearls. The shrewdest thief gives two pearls to each of his partners in crime. One of the thieves inquires: "Why do you keep three pearls?" He answers that it is because he is the leader. The other asks "Why are you the leader?" Calmly, he responds "Because I have more pearls."

a.   Comment on the lack of validity in this type of argument.

b.   Give two additional examples of "begging the question."

7. Give three additional types of faulty reasoning. Provide an example for each.

8. Why is skolemization a useful tool even though some meaning can be lost?

9. Give another example in which second order logic has greater expressive power than the FOPL.

The reader who wishes to learn more about fallacious reasoning can consult Fearnside and Holther. [14]

Exercises

1. Use the propositional logic to represent the following English sentences. Choose appropriate propositional logic variables.

a.   Many Americans have difficulty learning a foreign language.

b.   All sophomores must pass an English language proficiency exam in order to continue their studies.

c.   If you are old enough to join the military, then you should be old enough to drink.

d.   A natural number greater than or equal to two is prime if and only if it has no divisors other than 1 and itself.

e.   If the price of gasoline continues to rise, then fewer people will be driving this summer.

f.   If it is neither raining nor snowing, then it is likely there is no precipitation.

2. A logic operator not defined in this chapter is the NAND function; it is denoted by $\uparrow$. NAND is short for "not AND" where $a \uparrow b \equiv \sim (a \wedge b)$.

a.   Give the truth table for the two-input NAND function

b.   Show that the NAND operator can be used to simulate each of the AND, OR, and NOT operators.

3. The NOR function, denoted by $a \downarrow b \equiv \sim (a \vee b)$; i.e., the NOR is true precisely when the (inclusive) OR is false.

a.   Give the truth table for the two-input NOR function.

    b. Show that the NOR operator can be used to simulate each of the AND, OR, and NOT operators.

4. Use truth tables to determine if each of the following is a tautology, a contradiction, or just satisfiable:

    a. $(p \lor q) \Rightarrow \sim p \lor \sim q$

    b. $(\sim p \land \sim q) \Rightarrow \sim p \lor \sim q$

    c. $(p \lor q \lor r) \equiv (p \lor q) \land (p \lor r)$

    d. $p \Rightarrow (p \lor q)$

    e. $p \equiv p \lor q$

    f. $(p \downarrow q)(p \uparrow q)$ // consult exercises 2 and 3.

5. Prove that $\sqrt{2}$ is irrational by using a contrapositive-based proof. *Hint:* if a number n is rational, then n may be expressed as the ratio of two whole numbers p and q, i.e., $n = p/q$; furthermore it can be assumed that p and q are in lowest terms. Examples of fractions *not* in lowest terms: 4/8 and 2/4, whereas 1/2 *is* in lowest terms.

6. State a theorem from one of your prior math classes in which:

    a. the converse is also a theorem.

    b. the converse is not a theorem.

7. Use the theorems in Table 5.8 to determine if the following are tautologies.

    a. $[(p \land q) \lor \sim r] \Rightarrow q \lor \sim r$

    b. $\{[(p \lor \sim r) \Leftrightarrow \sim q] \land \sim q\} \Rightarrow (\sim p \land r)$

8. Use truth tables to determine which of the following arguments are valid:

    a. $p \Rightarrow q$

        $\underline{q \Rightarrow r}$

        $\therefore r$

    b. $p \Rightarrow (q \lor \sim q)$

        q

        $q \Rightarrow r$

        $\underline{\sim q \Rightarrow \sim r}$

        $\therefore r$

    c. $p \Rightarrow q$

        $\underline{\sim q}$

        $\therefore \sim p$

d. $p \Rightarrow q$

$\sim p$
_____

$\therefore \sim q$

e. $p \equiv q$

$p \Rightarrow (r \vee s)$

q
_____

$\therefore r \vee s$

f. $p \Rightarrow q$

$r \Rightarrow \sim q$

$\sim (\sim p \wedge \sim r)$
_____

$\therefore q \vee \sim q$

g. $p \wedge q$

$p \Rightarrow r$

$q \Rightarrow \sim r$
_____

$\therefore r \vee \sim r$

h. The price of oil will continue to rise.

If the price of oil continues to rise then the value of the dollar will fall.

If the value of the dollar falls then Americans will travel less.

If Americans travel less then airlines will lose money.
_____

Therefore: airlines will lose money.

9. Answer question 8 using resolution.

10. Use FOPL to represent the following English sentences. Make up appropriate predicates in each case.

a. Every time I wake up, I want to go back to sleep.

b. Sometimes when I wake up, I desire a cup of coffee.

c. If I do not eat less and go to the gym, then I will not lose weight.

d. If I either wake up late or have a cup of coffee, then I do not want to go back to sleep.

e. If we are going to solve our energy problems then we must either find more sources of oil or develop alternative energy technologies.

f. He only likes women that do not like him.

g. Some of the women that he likes do not like him

h. None of the women that he likes do not like him.

i. If it walks like a duck and talks like a duck, then it must be a duck.

11. Use FOPL to represent the following expressions:

a. He only dines in Italian restaurants.

b. He sometimes dines in Italian restaurants.

c. He always dines in Italian or Greek restaurants.

d. He never dines in restaurants that are neither Italian nor Greek.

e. He never dines in restaurants that are either Italian or Greek.

f. If he dines in a restaurant then his brother will not dine there.

g. If he does not dine in a particular restaurant then his brother will not dine there

h. If he does not dine in a particular restaurant then some of his friends will not dine there.

i. If he does not dine in a particular restaurant, then none of his friends will not dine there.

12. Find the mgu in each pair below or state that unification is not possible.

a) Wines (**x, y**)   Wines (Chianti, Cabernet).

b) Wines (**x, x**)   Wines (Chianti, Cabernet).

c) Wines (**x, y**)   Wines (**y, x**)

d) Wines (Best (bottle), Chardonnay)   Wines (best (**x**), **y**)

13. Use resolution to determine if the following arguments in the FOPL are valid. Use the predicates suggested:

a. All Italian mothers can cook. (M, C)

   All cooks are healthy. (H)

   Either Connie or Jing Jing is an Italian mother.

   Jing Jing is not an Italian mother.

   ───────────────────────

   Therefore, Connie is healthy.

b. All New Yorkers are cosmopolitan. (N, C)

   All cosmopolitan people are friendly. (F)

   Either Tom or Nick is a New Yorker.

   Nick is not a New Yorker.

   ───────────────────────

Conclusion: Tom is friendly.

c.   Anyone who drinks green tea is strong. (T, S)

Anyone who is strong takes vitamins. (V)

Someone at City College drinks green tea. (C)

_____

Therefore, everyone at City College drinks green tea and is strong.

14. Show how resolution can be used to solve the King's Wise Men Problem.

15. **Halmos Handshare Problem**
As is common, academics will occasionally attend dinner parties. Halmos and his wife attended such a dinner party along with four other couples. During the cocktail hour, some of those present shook hands, but in an unsystematic way, with no attempt to shake everyone's hand. Of course, no one shook his or her own hand, no one shook hands with his or her spouse, and no one shook hands with the same person more than once. During dinner, Halmos asked each of the nine other people present (including his own wife), how many hands that person had shaken. Under the given conditions, the possible answers ranged from 0 to 8 hands shaken. Halmos noticed that each person gave a different answer: one person claimed not to have shaken anyone else's hand, one person had shaken exactly one other person's hand, one person had shaken exactly two hands, and so on, to the one person who claimed to have shaken hands with all the others present, except his or her spouse, that is, 8 handshakes in total. So, in summary, of the 10 people present, people gave answers from 0 to 8 hands shaken, i.e. one person had shaken 0 hands, another 1 hand, another 2 hands, another 3 hands, etc., up to 8 hands. How many hands did Halmos' wife shake?[++]

16. **Ten Pirates and Their Gold**—Ten Pirates find a buried treasure of 100 pieces of gold. The challenge is to divide the gold up in some desirable way according to some rules. The first rule is that Pirate 1 is the lead pirate. Pirate 2 is the second in charge. Pirate 3 is the third most powerful and so on. The pirates have a scheme for dividing the money. They agree that the first pirate P_1, will make a proposal for how the money is to be divided. If 50% or more of the pirates agree with P_1's system then it will be put into effect. If not, then P_1 will be killed and the next most powerful pirate becomes the lead pirate. Now, again with one less pirate, the process repeats. Again the new lead pirate, P_2, will now suggest a new process for dividing up the gold. It will be voted on with a 50% vote needed for the leader's suggestion to pass, and less results in the death of this pirate as well.

All the pirates are very greedy and savvy—and will vote against a proposal if they can determine that they will get more gold if a proposal fails – and hence a lead pirate is killed. They will never vote for a proposal that will give them less gold or no gold at all. How Should the Gold be Divided among the Ten Pirates? [++]

_____

[++]*Problems 15 and 16 are from the book "Artificial Intelligence Problems and Their Solutions," Mercury Learning Inc. 2014.*

Programming Exercises

1. Write a program that takes as input an arbitrary propositional logic expression and returns its truth-value. Your program should allow any of the logical connectives from Table 5.2.

2. Write a program that uses a truth table to determine if an arbitrary argument in the propositional logic is valid. Any of the logic connectives from Table 5.2 should be allowed.

3. Use Prolog to solve the jobs puzzle from Section 3 of Chapter 1: Prolog can be downloaded from the Web. SWI Prolog is recommended.

   "There are two people, Michael and Louis. Between them they hold two jobs. Each has one job. These jobs are Post Office Clerk and French Professor. Michael speaks only English, whereas Louis holds a PhD in French. Who holds which job?"

4. Use Prolog to solve the following jobs puzzle:

   "Jim, Jack, and Joan hold three jobs between them. Each has one job. The jobs are schoolteacher, piano player, and secretary. The job of a schoolteacher is held by a male. Jack never went to college and has no musical talent."

   Once again, you need to present Prolog with additional world knowledge. For example, Prolog does not know that Joan is a woman's name or that Jim and Jack are male.

5. Use Prolog to solve The King's Wise Men Problem presented at the beginning of this chapter.

Keywords

antecedent	exclusive-or	normal form
argument	existential quantification	predicate logic
arity	existential quantifier	perfect induction
associative law	fallacy	premises
circumscription	first order predicate logic	prenex normal form
clause form	(FOPL)	propositional logic
closed world assumption	functions	resolution
commutative law	fuzzy logic	resolution refutation
conjunctive normal form	idempotency	Satisfiability Problem (SAT)
(CNF)	inclusive-or	satisfiable
consequent	inverse	second order predicate logic
contradiction	involution	skolem function
contrapositive	Law of Elimination	skolemization
converse	Law of Excluded Middle	statements
De Morgan's law	logical connective	tautology
deduction	modal logic	unification
distributive law	monotonic	universal quantification
domination law	most general unifier (mgu)	universal quantifier
double negation	non-monotonic	validity

References

1. Johnsonbaugh, R. 2005. *Discrete mathematics.* Upper Saddle River, NJ: Pearson-Prentice Hall.

2. Gersting, Judith L. 1999. *Mathematical structures for computer science.* New York, NY: W. H. Freeman.

3. Grimaldi, R. P. 1999. *Discrete and combinatorial mathematics.* Reading, MA: Addison-Wesley.

4. Robinson, J. A. 1965. A machine-oriented logic based on the resolution principle. *Journal of the ACM* 12: 23–41.

5. Genesereth, M. R. and Nilsson, N. J. 1987. *Logical foundations of Artificial Intelligence.* Los Altos, CA: Morgan Kaufmann.

6. Chang, C. L., and Lee, R. C. T. 1973. *Symbolic logic and mechanical theorem proving.* New York, NY: Academic Press.

7. Shapiro, S. 2000. *Foundations without foundationalism: A case for second-order logic.* Oxford: Oxford University Press.

8. McCarthy, J. 1980. Circumscription – A form of non-monotonic reasoning. *Artificial Intelligence* 13:27–39.

9. McDermott, D. and Doyle, J. 1980. Nonmonotonic Logic I. *Artificial Intelligence* 13(1, 2):41–72

10. Reiter. R. 1980. A logic for default reasoning. *Artificial Intelligence* 13:81–132.

11. Ginsberg, M., ed. 1987. *Readings in nonmonotonic reasoning.* Los Altos, CA: Morgan Kaufman.

12. Zadeh, L. 1988. Fuzzy logic. *Computer* 21(4, April):83–93.

13. Hughes, G. and Cresswell, M. 1968. *An introduction to modal logic.* London: Methuen.

14. Fearnside, W. W. and Holther, W. B. 1959. *Fallacy – The counterfeit of argument.* Englewood Cliffs, NJ: Prentice-Hall.

KNOWLEDGE REPRESENTATION

Donald Michie

■ ■ ■ ■ ■

Chapter 6 takes you on a journey from notions of representational choices, with consideration for intentional and extensional approaches, to production systems and object orientation. Minsky's frames and Schank's scripts move us to the conceptual dependency system. The sophistication of semantic networks is complemented by humans' ability to make associations. The chapter is rounded out by presentation of concept maps, conceptual graphs, and other more recent approaches, leading to agent theory with consideration for the future.

Figure 6.0
IROBOT® "NEGOTIATOR."

■6.0■ Introduction

Our information age is composed of computer systems that can process and store vast amounts of information. **Information** comprises **data** and **facts**. There is a hierarchical relationship between data, facts, information, and **knowledge**. The simplest pieces of information are data; from data we can build facts, and from facts we gain information. Knowledge can be defined as the processing of information to enable intelligent decision-making. The challenge of our time is the conversion of information into knowledge, which can be used for intelligent decision-making.

Artificial intelligence is about computer programs that can solve interesting problems and make intelligent decisions based on knowledge. As we have seen in earlier chapters, certain kinds of problems, their solutions, and the choice of language employed are more suited for certain kinds of representations. Games often use search trees, the AI language LISP uses lists, whereas Prolog uses predicate calculus. Information is often most efficiently stored in a table for fast and accurate retrieval. In this chapter, we will describe diverse forms of **knowledge representation** and how they have been developed for use by people and machines. For humans a good representation should have the following characteristics:

1. It should be transparent; that is, easy to understand.

2. It will make an impact on our senses, either through language, vision, touch, sound, or a combination of these.

3. It should tell a story and be easy to perceive in terms of the reality of the world it is representing.

For machines, good representations will exploit their computational power—that is, their vast memories and processing speeds, with the capability of performing billions of computations per second. The choice of a knowledge representation can be so innately tied to a problem solution that the problem's constraints and challenges will be most apparent (and understood) via one representation, whereas they might be hidden, complicated, and remain unresolved via another representation.

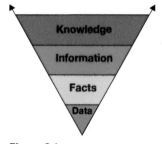

Figure 6.1
The knowledge hierarchy.

Let us consider the hierarchical spectrum from data, facts, and information, to knowledge: Data can be numbers without any meaning or units attached to them. Facts are numbers with units. Information is the conversion of facts into meaning. Finally, knowledge is the higher order expression and processing of information to facilitate complex decision-making and understanding. Figure 6.1 shows the hierarchical relationship of data, facts, information, and knowledge.

Consider the three examples listed in Table 6.1, which show how data, facts, information, and knowledge work together in daily life.

In Example 1, you are trying to determine whether conditions are right for swimming outdoors. The data you have is the integer 70. When you add a unit to the data, you have facts: the temperature is 70° Fahrenheit. To convert these facts into information, add meaning to the facts: The temperature outside is 70° Fahrenheit. By applying conditions to this information, you provide knowledge: If the temperature is over 70° Fahrenheit, then you can go swimming.

In Example 2, you want to explain who is eligible for military service. The data you have is the integer 18. Adding the unit of years to the data, you produce facts: 18 years. To add meaning to the

Table 6.1
Examples of the knowledge hierarchy.

Example	Data	Facts	Information	Knowledge
1. Swimming conditions	70	70 degrees Fahrenheit	The temperature outside is 70 degrees Fahrenheit.	If the temperature is over 70 degrees Fahrenheit, then you can go swimming.
2. Military service	18	18 years old	The age of eligibility is 18.	If you are 18 years old or older, you are eligible for military service.
3. Finding a professor's office	Room 232	Professor Anderson is in Room 232 of Smith Hall	Smith Hall is located on the southwest side of the campus.	Enter the campus from the West Gate, Smith Hall is the second building on your right as you head east. Professor Anderson's office is on the second floor to your right after you. Enter from the main entrance of the building.

facts and convert them to information, you can explain that 18 is the age of eligibility. The knowledge you provide is that if you are 18 year of age or older, you are eligible for military service. A decision (or action) that can be made based on testing for the truth of a condition is known as a *rule* (or If – Then Rule). Rules, or, more formally, production rules (and production systems) will be discussed in Chapter 7, "Production Systems."

Example 2 can be stated as the rule: If the draft is active and you are 18 years of age or older and you have no major chronic ailments, then you are eligible for military service.

In Example 3, you are visiting a college campus where you need to find Professor Anderson. You know he is a professor of mathematics, but that's all you know. The college directory might supply the raw data: Room 232. The facts are that Professor Anderson is in Room 232 of Smith Hall. To add meaning to the facts and convert them to information, you learn that Smith Hall is located on the southwest side of the campus. Finally, you learn enough to gain knowledge: Enter the campus from the West Gate; Smith Hall is the second building, assuming that you are heading east. Professor Anderson's Office is on the second floor to your right after you enter from the main entrance. Clearly the data "Room 232" was insufficient to find the professor's office. Knowing the fact that the office is in Room 232 of Smith Hall doesn't really help much either. Finding Smith Hall from the information provided wouldn't be adequate either, if, for example, there were many buildings in that corner of the campus, or you were unsure from which side of the campus you had entered (north, east, south, or west). However, if the information is carefully processed (engineered) to create a logical, comprehensible solution, you can easily find the professor's office.

You might consider the annual preparation of your income taxes in light of this discussion: Perhaps, every year, you have a shopping bag full of receipts and bank statements in random order (facts). After five hours of sorting this material into meaningful categories, such as earnings, charitable contributions, and educational expenses, you then have meaningful information. Your accountant processes this information and shares with you the (happy) knowledge that you will be receiving a refund.

Now that we can understand the differences between data, facts, information, and knowledge, we can consider the possible elements that knowledge comprises. Knowledge representation systems usually combine two elements: data structures (containing structures such as trees, lists, and stacks) and the interpretive procedures for using the knowledge (such as search, sort, and combine).[1] In other words, there must be a convenient place (structure) to store knowledge and a way to quickly access and process it computationally for problem solving, decision-making, and action.

Feigenbaum and colleagues [2] suggested the following categories for which knowledge should be available:

- **Objects:** Physical objects and concepts (e.g., table structure = height, width, depth).

- **Events:** Time element and cause and effect relationships.

- **Performance:** Information on how something is done (the steps) but also the logic or algorithm governing the performance.

- **Meta-knowledge:** Knowledge about knowledge, reliability, and relative importance of facts. For example, if you cram the night before an exam, your knowledge about a subject isn't likely to last too long.

In this chapter, we will discuss knowledge in terms of its shape and size. We will consider the level of detail (grain size) of a knowledge representation – is it **extensional** (explicit, detailed, and long) or **intensional** (implicit, short, and compact)? Extensional representations will usually show every case, every example, of some information, while intentional representations will often be short; for example, a formula, or an expression that represents some information. A simple example would be as follows:

"The even integers from 2 to 30" (implicit), versus, "the set of numbers: 2, 4, 6, 8, 10, 12, 14, 16, 18, 20, 22, 24, 26, 28, 30" (explicit).

We will also discuss the issue of **executability vs. comprehensibility**. That is, some solutions to problems can be executed (but not understood—either by humans or machines), whereas others are easy to understand, at least by humans. The choice of a knowledge representation for an AI problem solution is invariably related to these issues.

The choice of a knowledge representation is also integral to problem solving. In computer science we all tend to agree on a few common data structures (e.g., tables, arrays, stacks, linked lists, etc.) from which a choice might naturally be made to represent a problem and its solution. Likewise, in artificial intelligence, there are many ways to represent complex problems and their solutions. The types of representation common to *both* computer science and AI, which, for the purposes of this text we will not consider, include lists, stacks, queues, and tables. This chapter will focus on twelve standard types of knowledge representations for AI that have emerged over time:

1. Graphical sketches
2. Graphs
3. Search trees
4. Logic
5. Production systems
6. Object orientation
7. Frames
8. Scripts and the conceptual dependency system
9. Semantic networks

Also, more recent approaches, including:

10.   Concept maps

11.   Conceptual graphs

12.   Agents

6.1   GRAPHICAL SKETCHES AND THE HUMAN WINDOW

A **graphical sketch** is an informal drawing or outline of a setting, a process, a mood, or system. Few AI textbooks classify graphical sketches as a form of knowledge representation. However, a picture can represent knowledge with economy and precision. Although a complete verbal description will perhaps require the proverbial "one thousand words," a pertinent picture or graphic can convey the story or message more succinctly. Furthermore, a verbal description might be incomplete, verbose, or simply unclear.

Consider the graphic shown in Figure 6.2, which illustrates the problems of "computational ecology." You don't have to be a computer expert to understand that there could be situations where computers encounter problems when working in networks. For example, they might have memory problems (hardware), or there might be something wrong with the operating system (software), or there perhaps is an overload in terms of demands on their resources. The extent to which the computer is having trouble is not relevant at this time (too much detail); it is sufficient that we know that the computers in a network are having problems. Hence, the graphic has served its purpose and therefore it is a satisfactory knowledge representation scheme for the information that needs to be conveyed.

The **Human Window** is a region constrained by human memory capabilities and computational limitations. The human window illustrates the limitations of the human brain's ability to process information, and the need for AI solutions to fall within its bounds. The late Donald Michie often credited Michael Clarke [3] for this concept. The key idea is that the solutions to problems of sufficient complexity (AI-type problems) are limited by the amount of computation and memory needed by people to execute the solutions and comprehend them. The solutions to complex problems should also be 100% correct, and their grain size should be manageable. The grain size, again, refers to the computational constraints of humans and the human window shown in Figure 6.3.

Figure 6.3 presents the Human Window as described by Clarke and Michie [4] so we call it the "Clarke–Michie Diagram" or simply "The human window." It has two extremes. At the far left is "L," to represent Sir James Lighthill,

Figure 6.2
The problem of computational ecology.

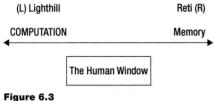

Figure 6.3
The Human Window.
Sources: Clarke[3] and Michie[4].

The Lighthill Report was deemed to be a study of the accomplishments of AI. The study was headed by Sir James Lighthill, an eminent English physicist. He criticized AI for not coming to grips with the combinatorial explosion. (Lighthill, J. 1973. Artificial Intelligence: A general survey. In Artificial intelligence: A paper symposium, Science Research Council.)

whose report criticizing AI stopped all funding of AI research in the 1970s in Great Britain. At the other extreme (no doubt selected by Michael Clarke, who was a strong chess player) is the turn of the twentieth century Bohemian Grandmaster, Richard Reti, who, when asked, "How many moves do you look ahead in a chess position?" is reported to have replied, "One move, the best move." This would be the equivalent of a database lookup.

Of course, humans cannot maintain a complete database of millions of positions in their heads. A four-piece chess ending such as King and Rook vs. King and Knight (KRKN) will have over three million positions. However, with the help of pattern recognition, problem-reduction through symmetry, problem constraints, and some domain-specific knowledge, a human might be able to make sense of such a database.

In his PhD thesis work, Kopec [5] compared five representations of knowledge for the same task. The task was to build a program that correctly determined the result (Win for White, or Draw) for every position in the least mobile of chess endings, King and Pawn against King (KPK). The five representations are illustrated in Table 6.2 as they might fall within boundaries of the human window with respect to their relative costs of requirements for amount of computation and memory size. At the right extreme is the database representation which has 98,304 entries, each representing a unique configuration of the three pieces in KPK. [5] In Chapter 16 and Appendix C, you will read about databases constructed by Stiller (see Bibliography) and Thompson [6] to return the outcome and best move for all chess positions with six pieces or fewer left on the board. Results with both White and Black to move were stored for each configuration. Next was the Don Beal [7] solution for KPK which consisted of 48 decision table rules, again falling to the right extreme by requiring too much memory. Then, falling within the boundary of the human window was Max Bramer's 19 equivalence class solution. [8] Most ideal was the Niblett–Shapiro solution, which consisted of only five rules.

The rules did require two "crib sheets" of patterns that were necessary to be understood in order to execute or understand the rules.

The Niblett–Shapiro solution was developed in Prolog. The other four solutions were developed in either Algol or Fortran (the popular languages of the time). The Harris–Kopec solution consisted of seven procedures, which required too much computation (hence were not executable) to fall within the human window, but they were comprehensible. All five solutions were translated into English and used as "advice texts" for the purpose of evaluating their executability and comprehensibility by chess-novice high school students in Edinburgh, Scotland, in 1980.[5]

Table 6.2
Human window aspects of five solutions to KPK.

Program Name	Correctness	Grain Size	Executable	Comprehensible
Harris–Kopec	(99.11%)	Large	No	Yes
Bramer	√	Medium	Yes	Yes
Niblett–Shapiro	√	Ideal	Yes	Yes
Beal	√	Small	Yes	No
Thompson	√	Very Small	Yes	No

Table 6.2 compares the human window qualities of the five KPK ending computer solutions with regard to **correctness, grain size, executability,** and **comprehensibility.** Some solutions were executable, but not comprehensible, while others were comprehensible but not executable. The Bramer and Niblett–Shapiro solutions were both executable and comprehensible. However, the Niblett–Shapiro was best in terms of the human window, requiring neither too much computation nor too much memory.

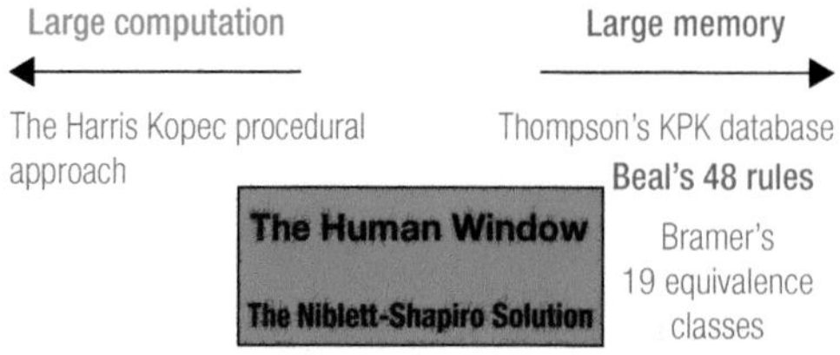

Figure 6.4
Summary of human window compatibility for five KPK solutions.

Figure 6.4 summarizes the human window features of these five solutions to KPK.

NOTE: More details about these diverse knowledge representations as solutions to KPK can be found at this text's companion Web site.

In domains of sufficient complexity, such as computer science, mathematics, medicine, chess, violin playing, among others, it has been estimated that it takes about 10 years of apprenticeship to develop real mastery. [9] It has also been estimated that chess grandmasters store some 50,000 patterns in their heads. [10, 11] In fact, the same approximate number of patterns (rules) has been estimated to be the number of domain-specific facts accrued by a human domain specialist for mastery in any of the above domains.

Little wonder that the secrets of the game of chess and other difficult problems have been studied and determined to be closely related to pattern recognition. However, let us bear in mind that the patterns used by people to represent a problem are not and cannot be the same as the representations that must be used for computer programs using AI techniques.

In Table 6.3, Michie [12] provides useful comparisons that explain some of the human limitations to accessing stored information, performing calculations, and the possibilities for accumulating knowledge over a lifetime. For example, people can transmit 30 bits of information per second, whereas the average computer can transmit trillions of bits per second.

1. Based on Miller. [13]
2. Calculated from 1. above.
3. Stroud, [14] cited by Halstead. [15]
4. 4. 5. and 6., from sources cited by Chase and Simon. [10]
5. Estimated errors can be taken to be around 30%. [13]

Table 6.3
Some information-processing parameters of the human brain.

Activity	Rate or Amount
1. Rate of information transmission along any input or output channel	30 bits per second
2. Maximum amount of information explicitly storable by the age of 50	10^{10} bits
3. Number of mental discriminations per second during intellectual work	18
4. Number of addresses that can be held in short-term memory	7
5. Time to access an addressable "chunk" in long-term memory	2 seconds
6. Rate of transfer from long-term to short-term memory of successive elements of one "chunk"	3 elements per second

Source: D. Michie, Practical Limits to Computation. *Research Memorandum* (1977).

◼6.2◼ GRAPHS AND THE BRIDGES OF KÖNIGSBERG PROBLEM

A **graph** consists of a finite set of **vertices** (nodes) together with a finite set of **edges**. Each edge consists of a distinct pair of vertices. If the edge e consists of the vertices {*u*, *v*} we often write e = (u, v) and say that *u* is joined to *v* (also that *v* is joined to *u*) and that *u* and *v* are adjacent.

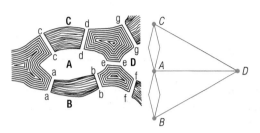

Figure 6.5
The Bridges of Königsberg.[17]

Jan Kåhre claims to have solved this problem, but with two of the bridges missing. See http://mathworld.wolfram.com/KönigsbergBridgeProblem.html *and Kåhre, J. "Königsberg Bridges Solved"* http://www.matheory.info/konigsberg/

We also say that *u* and *v* are incident with the edge *e*. Graphs can be directed or undirected, together with labels and weights. A famous problem is **The Bridges of Königsberg Problem**, shown in Figure 6.5.

The Bridges of Königsberg Problem is a familiar one to mathematics and graph theory, computer science, algorithms, and artificial intelligence. It asks if you can find a single route beginning at any node (point) on a bridge connecting the land regions A, B, C, or D, cross each of the seven bridges only once, and return to the starting point. Königsberg was formerly in Germany; it is now known as Kaliningrad, belonging to Russia, and it spans the River Preger.[16] The famous Swiss mathematician Leonhard Euler, often recognized as the father of graph theory, solved this problem, concluding in the negative, that such a route could not exist in this graph as the degree (number of edges in and out of a node) of every node must be even.

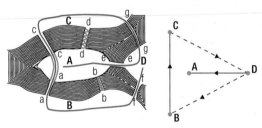

Figure 6.6
Update on the Bridges of Königsberg and their graphical representation.

The geographic map to the left is one representation of the problem in Figure 6.5. Another equivalent representation is the graph on its right, which illustrates the problem as a mathematical graph. For some people, the map on the left is easy to comprehend and is preferable. Others prefer the more formal mathematical representation in the graph. However, in deriving a solution for this problem, few would disagree that the abstract graph on the right facilitates greater insight and better comprehension of the so-called **Eulerian Property** described above.

It seems noteworthy that the bridges bb and dd no longer exist but there is still no **Eulerian Cycle** among the Bridges A, B, C, D. However, there are stairs from A to aacc to connect all bridges. Hence, in the graph on the right in Figure 6.6 we see that there is an Eulerian Trail (a path which hits each of the nodes in the graph but does not originate and finish at the same node), which runs DBCDA.

In summary, graphs are important tools in knowledge representation because they are a natural way to represent states, alternatives, and measurable paths in problems involving the search for a goal state.

◼6.3◼ SEARCH TREES

For problems that require analytical approaches, such as the depth first search and breadth first search (exhaustive approaches), and heuristic searches, such as the best-first search and A* algorithm, a search tree is the most suitable representation. Exhaustive approaches have been discussed in Chapter 2, "Uninformed Search," whereas heuristic approaches were discussed in Chapter 3, "Informed Search." Game trees for Nim, tic-tac-toe, and the Eight Puzzle were presented in Chapter 4, "Search Using Games"; exemplary game trees for checkers, with regard to the minimax and alpha-beta algorithms, will be presented in Chapter 16, "Advanced Computer Games." Other types of search trees used in knowledge representation are decision trees.

6.3.1   Decision Tree

A **decision tree** is a special type of a search tree that can be used to find a solution to a problem by choosing from alternatives starting from a root node. A decision tree will logically split a problem space into separate paths, which can be independently followed in the search for a solution, or for the answer to a question. An example would be to try to determine how many homes there are of self-employed people who earn over \$200K from their businesses (see Figure 6.7). First, we would take the space of all people who are taxpayers in this country and determine who is self-employed, and then we would divide that space into those who earn over \$200K.

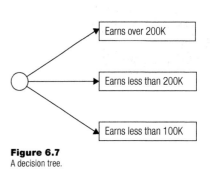

Figure 6.7
A decision tree.

EXAMPLE 6.1: THE TWELVE COINS PROBLEM

Let us return to the problem of the false coin, discussed in Chapter 2. This time, the problem is slightly different: Given a balance scale and 12 coins, determine the irregular coin (or "slug") among them, whether it is heavy or light, and weigh a minimum number of combinations of coins.

This was given as an exercise at the end of Chapter 2.

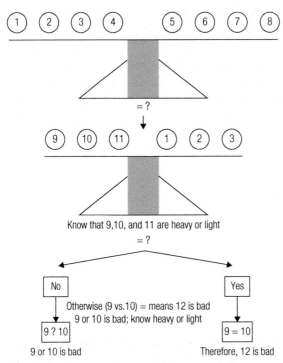

Figure 6.8 illustrates how the solution could be represented in a decision tree: The first two shapes are scales with coins on the scale tray. The first scale has eight coins, numbered 1–8. The second scale has six coins numbered as shown. For the first combination of coins we weigh, we take the example wherein coins 1 to 4 are equal to coins 5 to 8. Then, the second combination of coins weighed balances coins 9, 10, and 11 with coins 1, 2, and 3. If

Figure 6.8
The Twelve Coins Problem.

SIDEBAR

"For A full Discussion of The 12 COINS PROBLEM see Chapter 4 of **Artificial Intelligence Problems And Their Solutions** by D. Kopec, S. Shetty, and C. Pileggi, Mercury Learning Inc., 2014." [60]

they are equal, then we immediately know that coin 12 is bad. Otherwise, we then balance coin 9 against 10 to determine the faulty coin.

Trees tend to grow depth first, especially if the key components are allowed to. The main point is that this problem can be solved by weighing only three sets of coins. However, to minimize the number of times we weigh, we must take advantage of the earlier weighed results to help meet the constraints of the problem. A second hint for the solution is that the second and third times we weigh, comparisons will need to be mixed (especially among coins 9, 10, 11, and 1, 2, 3).

6.4 REPRESENTATIONAL CHOICES

Let us consider a game tree for the familiar Towers of Hanoi Problem, which involves three disks. The goal of the problem is to transfer all three disks from Peg A to Peg C. There are two constraints of the problem: (1) you can transfer only one disk at a time and (2) a larger disk cannot go on top of a smaller disk. This problem is often used in computer science to illustrate recursion, which is illustrated in Figure 6.9. We will consider the solution to this problem from a number of perspectives, particularly with regard to knowledge representation. First let us consider the practical solution to the specific problem of transferring the three disks to Peg C.

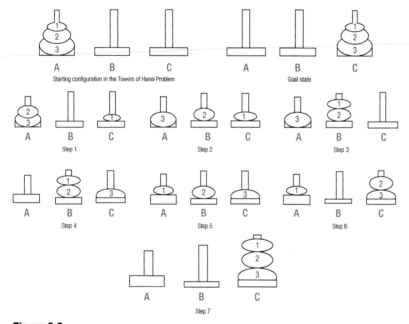

Figure 6.9
The Towers of Hanoi Problem and its solution.

Let us review what has just happened. The solution required seven moves. A description of those moves follows:

1. Move Disk 1 to C
2. Move Disk 2 to B

Table 6.4
Number of moves required to solve the Towers of Hanoi Problem, depending on the number of disks.

Number of Disks	Moves to Temp Peg	Moves from Temp Peg to Goal	"Big" Disk Moved to Goal State	Total Number of Moves
1	0	0	1	1
2	1	1	1	3
3	3	3	1	7
4	7	7	1	15
5	15	15	1	31
6	31	31	1	63
7	63	63	1	127
8	127	127	1	255
9	255	255	1	511
10	511	511	1	1023

3. Move Disk 1 to B

4. Move Disk 3 to C

5. Move Disk 1 to A (unravel)

6. Move Disk 2 to C

7. Move Disk 1 to C

Note that this is also the shortest solution. That is, the minimum number of moves has been made to transform the Start state to the Goal state.

Table 6.4 illustrates the number of moves needed to solve this puzzle, depending on the number of disks involved. The "temp" peg is one that holds a disk temporarily.

Little wonder that as the story goes, Babylonian slaves would need until the end of time to move 65 large concrete slabs and finish constructing a similar tower. For 65 disks, it would take $2^{65} - 1$ moves. Even with concrete slabs moved at 1 slab per second, it would require $2^{65} - 1$ seconds; which is more than 6,418,270,000 years, as described by Alan Bierman in *Great Ideas in Computer Science*.[19] p. 311.

Now we can express the algorithm to solve the problem for any number of disks in words, and then we will examine the solution in terms of the mathematics that is involved.

First, the goal is to isolate the largest disk on the original peg. This allows the largest disk to be moved by itself to the Goal peg (1 move). Next, the remaining $N - 1$ disks on the temporary peg (that is, Peg B—this required $N - 1$ moves) can be "unraveled" and moved to the Goal peg on top of the biggest disk ($N - 1$ moves). Adding these moves, we see that $2 \times (N - 1) + 1$ moves are required in total, or $2^N - 1$ moves are required for N disks to be moved to the Goal peg from the Start peg and for the puzzle to be solved.

Outlining the steps to solve the Towers of Hanoi problem is one way to represent the solution. The steps are an extensional representation because all the steps are explicitly given. Another extensional representation of the steps to solve the Towers of Hanoi problem is provided in the "Example 6.2: Extensional Solution" sidebar.

EXAMPLE 6.2 EXTENSIONAL SOLUTION

For any number of disks, N, if the main goal is to move those N disks from Peg A to Peg C, then you can complete the following steps:

1. Move $N-1$ disks to an intermediary peg (B), which takes $2^{(N-1)}-1$ moves (e.g., for three disks, move two disks ($2^2 - 1$ moves = 3 moves) to peg B).

2. Move the biggest disk from Peg A to Peg C (the Goal).

3. Move the $N-1$ disks from Peg B to Peg C (the Goal, which takes three more moves).

In total, you need 7 moves for 3 discs, 15 moves for 4 disks, 31 moves (15 + 15 + 1) for 5 disks, and 63 moves (31 + 31 + 1) for 6 disks, etc.

Another way to represent the solution is to create an **intensional representation**, which is a more compact ("intensional") description of the solution as shown in the "Intentional Solution" sidebar.

EXAMPLE 6.3: INTENSIONAL SOLUTION

To solve the Towers of Hanoi Problem for N disks, it requires $2^{(N)}-1$ moves comprising $2 \times 2^{(N-1)}-1$ (moving $N-1$ disks to and from peg **B**) + 1 move (for Big to be moved to Peg C).

Another intentional description of the Towers of Hanoi solution would be through the recurrence relation shown in the "Recurrence Relation" sidebar. A **recurrence relation** is a compact mathematical formula that represents the essence of the process occurring (recurring) in terms of the number of steps involved in the solution to a problem. Recurrence relations are often used to analyze the running time of recursive algorithms such as quicksort, mergesort, and selection.

EXAMPLE 6.4: RECURRENCE RELATION

$T(1) = 1$

$T(N) = 2\,T(N-1) + 1$

Which has solution $T(N) = 2^{N-1}$.

The recurrence relation for the Towers of Hanoi Problem sidebar presents a compact intentional solution to the problem.

EXAMPLE 6.5: PSEUDOCODE FOR TOWERS OF HANOI PROBLEM

To describe the Towers of Hanoi problem, you can use the following pseudocode, where:

n is the number of disks

Start is the start peg

int is the intermediate peg

Dest is the goal or destination peg

TOH (*n*, *Start*, *Int*, *Dest*)

```
If n = 1 then move disk from Start to Dest
     Else TOH(n-1, Start, Dest, Int)
          TOH(1, Start, Int, Dest)
          TOH(n-1, Int, Start, Dest)
```

Solving the Towers of Hanoi problem illustrates a number of different forms of knowledge representation, all of them involving recursion, or repetition of a pattern or formula, but with different arguments. Figure 6.9 shows graphical representations of the solution. Example 6.2 lists the seven steps needed to solve the problem explicitly, which provides an extensional solution. Examples 6.3 and 6.4 describe the same steps more intentionally. Example 6.5 is an also an intentional solution that shows the pseudocode you can use to develop a recursively programmed solution to the problem. Determining the best solution depends on who the learner is and how he or she prefers to learn. Note that each of these intentional representations is also an example of **problem reduction**. A problem that seemed large and complex has been broken down into smaller, manageable problems whose solutions are both executable and comprehensible (à la the Human Window, as described in Section 6.1).

6.5 ■ PRODUCTION SYSTEMS

Artificial intelligence is inherently connected with decision making. What sets AI approaches and problems apart from ordinary computer science problems is that they usually require intelligent decisions to be made to solve the problem. For a computer system or person to make intelligent decisions, they need a good way to assess the circumstances (in other words, the problems or conditions) that require a decision to be made. Production systems are often represented by a set of rules of the form,

```
IF [condition] THEN [action],
```

together with a control system, which acts as rule interpreter and a sequencer and a database. The database acts as a context buffer, which enables the recording of the conditions under which the rules are *fired*. Production systems are also often called condition-action, antecedent-consequent, pattern-action, or situation-response pairs. A few production rules follow:

- If [driving and you see a school bus with its STOP sign out], then [pull over quickly to the right and stop].
- If [there are less than two outs and a runner is on first base], then [bunt] // Baseball game //
- If [it is past 2:00 am and you must drive], then [make sure that you drink coffee].
- If [you have a pain in your knees and it has not gone away after taking a few over-the-counter pain relief pills], then [make sure you contact your doctor].

An example of a rule used in a more complex, but typical format:

- If [it is over 70°F outside, and if you have your shorts on and a tennis racket], then [it is recommended that you play tennis].

Chapter 7, "Production Systems," will cover production systems and their application in expert systems in greater detail.

6.6 OBJECT ORIENTATION

In Chapter 1, we discussed a number of contributions from the field of AI that have become absorbed by computer science. One example is the paradigm of **object orientation**, which became the predominant programming paradigm in the 1990s. Computation and simulation were first popularized in the language SIMULA 67, which also introduced concepts of class, object, and message.[20] Alan Kay implemented SmallTalk, the first purely object-oriented programming language in 1969, when he was part of the Palo Alto Research Center (PARC), known as Xerox PARC. The final, standard version of SmallTalk was developed by Alan Kay, Adele Goldberg, and Daniel Ingalls at PARC in 1980, and was known as Smalltalk-80 or just Smalltalk. Smalltalk is considered the purist object-oriented language because every entity is an object.[21]

In contrast, for example, Java does not consider primitive scalar types such as Boolean, character, and numeric types as objects.

Object orientation is a programming paradigm that is designed to be an intuitive and natural reflection of the human experience. It is based on the concepts of **inheritance, polymorphism**, and **encapsulation**.

Inheritance is a relationship among classes, wherein one class shares the structure or behavior defined in an "IsA" hierarchy (see Section 6.9 on Semantic Networks). Subclasses are said to inherit both the data and methods from one or more generalized superclasses. **Polymorphism** *is that feature of a variable that can take on values of several different types of a function that can be executed using arguments of a variety of types.[18] Polymorphism separates the notion of actions on objects from the data type(s) involved.* **Encapsulation** *is the concept that only certain information needs to be known by certain people at certain levels of program development. It is similar to the ideas of data abstraction and information hiding, all important concepts in the object-oriented programming paradigm.*

According to Laudon, "It [object orientation] embodies a way of organizing and representing knowledge, a way of viewing the world that encompasses a wide range of programming activities … ." [19] The desire to allow programmers to define and manipulate abstract data types (ADTs) was the driving force that led to the development of object-oriented programming languages. [20] Foundations for object-oriented languages were provided in languages such as ADA-83, which included packages that describe type specifications and subprograms that can belong to a user-defined ADT. This also led to the development of libraries of code whereby implementation details were separated from a subprogram's interface.

Procedural and data abstraction are combined into the notion of **classes**. Classes describe the data and behavior common to a collection of objects. **Objects** are instances of classes. For example, a typical university program has a class named Students, which contains data pertaining to academic transcripts, tuition bills, and place of residence. An object created from this class might be Joe Smith, a student who is taking two math courses this semester, who still owes $320 on his tuition bill and resides on Flatbush Avenue in Brooklyn. Besides classes, objects can be organized into superclasses and subclasses, which are natural to our hierarchical thinking about the world and how it can be manipulated and changed.

One major AI effort that employed these aspects of the object-oriented paradigm was the work of Seymour Papert at MIT between 1967 and 1981. Through the language LOGO, children learn about objects and how to manipulate them. Papert demonstrated that children can learn about many things through the active, intuitive environment that LOGO offers, including logic, graphics, programming, the laws of physics, and more.[21]

In the 1970s, hardware architecture interfaces, together with operating systems and applications, became more dependent on graphical methods, which lent themselves naturally to the object-oriented paradigm. The same was true of the entity-relationship database model, wherein data is represented as nodes and arcs in a graph.[19]

Ege further states, "Even in knowledge representation, schemes that supported work in artificial intelligence (frames, scripts, and semantic networks), we can see clearly this object-orientation." [18]

The popularity of object-oriented programming languages such as Java and C++ demonstrates that object orientation is an effective and useful way to represent knowledge, especially when used to build up complex information structures whereby common attributes can be exploited.

6.7   FRAMES

Frames, developed by Marvin Minsky, [22] are another effective form of knowledge representation that facilitates the organization of information into a system that can easily be built up to exploit features of the real world. They are intended to provide a straightforward way to represent information about the world. They facilitate the description of stereotypical situations, thereby providing a framework for expressing expectations, goals, and plans. This enables humans and machines to better understand what is going on.

Some examples of these scenarios would be a child's birthday party, a car accident, a visit to the doctor's office, or filling up your car with gasoline. These are common events that vary only by detail. For example, a child's birthday party always involves a child who is turning a certain age; the party is held at a specified place, date, and time. To plan the party, you can create a frame which can include slots for the name of the child, the age of the child, the date, the location of the party, the time of the party, the number of attendees, and the props used. Figure 6.10 shows how such a frame is constructed with its slots, their respective types, and how the slots can be filled with values. Modern-day newspapers quickly generate reports on events that frequently occur by using the "slot and filler" approach to representing events, an essential aspect of frames. Let us construct frames for some of these familiar situations.

From the information in this set of frames we can use *inheritance* to determine that at least two children will attend David's birthday party, and that David's party will be attended by Jill and Paul. We know this because Jill and Paul are attending parties at the same location (Crystal Palace) as the location of David's party on the same date. We also know that at least two children will be at David's party because from Paul's birthday (age) we know that he is a child.

The frame system in Figure 6.11 illustrates how inferences can be made

Slot	Slot Types
Name of child	Character string
Age of child (new)	Integer
Date of birthday	Date
Location of party	Place
Time of party	Time
Number of attendees	Integer
Props	Selection from balloons, signs, lights, and music

Frame Name	Slot	Slot Values
David	IS-A	Child
	Has Birthday	11/10/07
	Location	Crystal Palace
	Age	8
Tom	IS-A	Child
	Has Birthday	11/30/07
Jill	Attends Party	11/10/07
	Location	Crystal Palace
Paul	Attends Party	11/10/07
	Age	9
	Location	Crystal Palace
Child	Age	<15

Figure 6.10
The child's birthday party frame.

Slot	Slot Types
Place	Character string
When	Date/time
Number of cars involved	Integer
Number of people involved	Integer
Number of fatalities	Integer
Number of people injured	Integer
Names of injured	Character string

Frame Name	Slot	Slot Value
Car accident	Place	Coates Crescent
	Date/time	November 1, 8:00am
Car_1	Hits	Car_2
	Cars	2
	People	5
	Fatalities	2
	Injuries	1
Type	Type	SUV

(a) Car accident frame

Frame Name	Slot	Slot Value
Car 1	Type	SUV → SUV Frame
	Number of passengers	3
	Number of fatalities	0
	Number of injuries	1

(b) Car accident frame Car_1

Frame Name	Slot	Slot Value
SUV	Manufacturer	Ford
	Model	Explorer
	Year	2004

(c) Car accident frame Car_1

Frame Name	Slot	Slot Value
Car 2	Type	Sports car → Sports car frame
	Number of passengers	2
	Number of fatalities	2
	Number of injuries	0

(d) Car accident frame Car_2

Frame Name	Slot	Slot Value
Sports Car	Manufacturer	Mazda
	Model	Miata
	Year	2002

(e) Car accident–Car_2

Figure 6.11
Example of multiple inheritance using car accident frames.

Frame Name	Slot	Slot Value
Car accident	Subclass	Number of cars
Occupants	Number of passengers	2
Car driver	Is	Bill
Bill	Passenger	1
Tom	Passenger	1

Figure 6.12
Car accident frame, continued.

based on frames and their data.

The frame system in Figure 6.11 illustrates how inferences can be made based on frames and their data. The information in Figure 6.11(d) indicates that Car_2 was damaged much worse than Car_1 (based on the number of fatalities and injuries). The **slots** and their **fillers** in frames are akin to the instances of classes employed in object-oriented systems. They are facts that describe the accident as the basis for a newspaper report, such as the date, time, and place of the accident. One thing the frame system does not explain, unless explicitly told, is why the SUV had minor injuries to one passenger, and escaped relatively unscathed, (see Figure 6.11) whereas the sports car had two fatalities and was totally destroyed. Additional data could be relevant here—for example, that heavier vehicles generally fare better in accidents.

Figure 6.12 is an example of multiple inheritance. The car driver must also be counted as one of the passengers /occupants of the car. Bill's slot value indicates he is both a passenger and driver of a car.

The fundamental theme behind frames is expectation-driven processing, which is based on the human ability to associate seemingly unrelated facts into complex, meaningful scenarios. Frames are a method of knowledge representation that was commonly used in the development of expert systems in the 1980s and 1990s. Minsky described frames as a network of nodes and relations. Top levels of the frame represent attributes, which are always true about the situation and so remained fixed.[1] The task of AI research is to construct corresponding contexts and trigger them in the appropriate problem environments. Some of the appeal of frames was because of the following characteristics:

1. Default values can be supplied by the program and overwritten by the programmer as information becomes available.

2. Frames lend themselves naturally to query systems. As we've seen above, once an appropriate frame is found, it is straightforward to search the slots for information. In situations where more information is needed, an "IF NEEDED" slot can be used to activate an attached procedure to fill in the slot. This concept of a *procedural attachment* is closely related to the concept of *demons* (ibid.).

Demons are procedures that are activated at any time during program execution depending on conditions evaluated in the demon itself. Examples of demons used in conventional programming include error detection, default commands, and end of file detection (eof).

When a program uses a demon, a list is created wherein all changes of state are recorded. All demons in the demon list check the status list for each change against their network fragment. If changes occur, then control immediately passes to the demon. Self-modifying programs use this approach, which, in turn, is intrinsic to systems that can adapt to new situations and improve their performance with experience. The ability to demonstrate such flexibility is central to the dynamic behavior of programs used for machine learning (ibid.).

Some AI people, however, (particularly Ron Brachman) have also been critical of frames. He notes that those default values, which can be overridden, "...makes one crucial type of representation impossible – that of composite descriptions whose meanings are functions of the structure and interrelation of their parts." [23]

Brachman notes that the "Is-A" could cause as much confusion as "clarification and distinction." [23] His summaries are below (in italics) with our explanations following:

1. *Frames are typically not very frame-like.*

    The world is not always as neatly packaged as frames describe it. A frame that accurately represents an event requires an increasingly detailed and unwieldy hierarchy of frames and slot values.

2. *Definitions are more important than one might think.*

    The more precisely you define frames, slots, and their values, the more accurate the representation can be. Thought must be carefully given to just what the frame categories are.

3. *Cancellation of default properties is more difficult than it looks.*

    Such changes must often be "percolated" throughout the programming system.

6.8 ■ SCRIPTS AND THE CONCEPTUAL DEPENDENCY SYSTEM

In the 1980s, Roger Schank and Robert Abelson developed a series of programs that successfully exhibited natural language understanding in a limited domain with the overall goal of developing cognitive understanding in computers. They developed an approach called **scripts**, which closely resembled frames, but added information that included sequences of events to the goals and plans of the actors involved. Scripts do this so effectively that they can pass the explanation test for computer understanding of stories and newspaper accounts. The success of scripts is their ability to reduce these stories to a set of primitives that can effectively be handled by the conceptual dependency (CD) formalism. [24] The deeper semantic meaning of a story could be represented by scripts. CD theory could be used to answer questions not stated in the story, paraphrase the main issues in the story, and even to translate the paraphrased material into alternate natural languages. CD theory allows one to develop and study scripts of many diverse real-world situations. The theory is versatile and powerful enough to accommodate situations in both the mental and physical world in which we live. For example, familiar human emotions, such as anger, jealously, etc., could be repre-

RESTAURANT FRAME

Specialization_of:		Business_establishment
Types:		(Cafeteria, Seat_yourself,
	Range:	Wait_to_be_seated)
		Wait_to_be_seated
	Default:	IF[plastic_orange_counter]
	If_needed:	THEN[fast_food]
		IF[stack_of_trays]
		THEN[cafeteria]
		IF[wait_for_waitress_sign
		OR reservations made_sign]
		THEN[wait_to_be_seated]
		OTHERWISE seat_yourself
Location:		
	Range:	An ADDRESS
	If_needed:	(Look at the menu)
Name:		
	If_needed:	(Look at the menu)
Food_style:		
	Range:	(Burgers, Chinese, American,
	Default:	Sea_food, French)
	If_added:	American
		(Update alternatives of restaurant)
Time_of_operation:		
	Range:	A Time_of_day
	Default:	Open evenings except Mondays
Payment_form:		
	Range:	(Cash, Credit-card, Cheque,
		Washing_dishes_Script)
Event_sequence:		
	Default:	Eat_at_restaurant script
Alternatives:		
	Range:	All restaurants with same Food_style
	If_needed:	(Find all restaurants with
		same Food_style)

Figure 6.12a
The Restaurant Frame.

EAT_AT_RESTAURANT SCRIPT

Props:		(Restaurant, Money, Food, Menu, Tables, Chairs)
Roles:		(Hungry_persons, Wait_persons, Chef_persons)
Point_of_view:		
		Hungry_persons
Time_of_occurrence:		
		(Times_of_operation of restaurant)
Place_of_occurrence:		
		(Location of restaurant)
Event_sequence:		
	First:	Enter_restaurant script
	Then:	IF[wait_to_be_seated_sign OR reservations]
		THEN [get_maitre_d's_attention script]
	Then:	Please_be_seated script
	Then:	Order_food script
	Then:	Eat_food script UNLESS[long_wait]

Figure 6.12b
Eat at Restaurant Script.

sented, as well as objects in the physical world, such as a person's body, a building, a car, etc. Some of the simple primitives used are shown in Table 6.5.

Figures 6.12a and 6.12b illustrate the differences between a frame and a script. Figure 6.12a represents a basic frame for the situation of eating at a restaurant.

Figure 6.12b is the familiar example, Eat at Restaurant script in Firebaugh[1] (p.295–297), and shows the added sequence of events.

Scripts can be hierarchically organized as we've seen with the examples above. They can also employ production systems in a natural way. It is easy to see that with these solid foundations for representing the world about us, scripts with the CD system of Schank and Abelson can effectively handle questions and demonstrate at least a rudimentary understanding of commonplace settings. Firebaugh concludes as follows:

- Scripts can predict events and answer questions about information not explicitly stated in the story line.

- Scripts provide a framework for integrating a set of observations into a coherent interpretation.

- Scripts provide a scheme for detecting unusual events.[1]

The ability of scripts to perform expectation-driven processing, incorporating the goals and plans of the actors and the expected sequence of events, enables them to significantly improve the explanatory power available for a knowledge representation (ibid., p.298).

Schank, Abelson, and their students developed a number of successful script-based natural language systems. These will be described in Chapter 9, "Expert Systems," and Chapter 13, "Natural Language Processing." They include SAM (Script Applier Mechanism), PAM (Plan Applier

Hubert Dreyfus (1929 –) During the past three decades one of the most ardent critics of AI has been Hubert Dreyfus, a philosopher at Berkeley University. One of his well-known titles is *Mind Over Machine* (1986),[25] which he wrote with his brother Stuart, who is a professor of Industrial Engineering and Operations Research at Berkeley.

The basis of Dreyfus's objection to AI is that neither the physiological, nor psychological aspects of how the human brain works can be mimicked by computers; therefore, AI—as it has been tackled—cannot be achieved. Furthermore, he believes that the way humans think cannot be formalized symbolically, logically, algorithmically, or mathematically. Therefore, in essence, we will never be able to understand our own behavior.

The Dreyfus brothers argue that AI has not really been successful and that many of the purported achievements in AI are really only "microworlds." That is, programs have been developed that seem intelligent but actually are only able to solve problems in very well-defined, limited domains. Hence, they have no general problem-solving ability, no particular theory behind them, and are just specialized problem solvers. Other well-known titles by Dreyfus include: What Computers Can't Do (1972, revised in 1979), and *What Computers Still Can't Do A Critique of Artificial Reason*, a subsequent revision in 1992.

Mechanism), and Memory, Analysis, Response Generation, and Inference on English (MARGIE).

It would be narrow and closed-minded of us not to mention that AI has had its critics over the years, in addition to Lighthill, mentioned in Section 6.1. Please refer to the Human Interest Box about Hubert Dreyfus, who has been among the most vocal in his criticism.

Hubert Dreyfus focuses on the ad hoc nature of scripts. For example, he might question the EAT_AT_RESTAURANT Script with:

- When the waitress came to the table, did she wear clothes?
- Did she walk forward or backward?
- Did the customer eat his food with his mouth or his ear?

If the program is ambiguous about the answers to these questions, then Dreyfus felt that the right answers were attained by tricks or lucky guesses, and it has not understood anything about our everyday restaurant behavior.

Scripts, despite all their positive features, have also been criticized from the perspective of what is called "microworlds." [25] That is, they can be very effective in well-defined settings, but they offer no general solution to the problems of understanding and AI. From that point of view emerged the work of Douglas Lenat [26] and CYC (short for Encyclopedia), with the goal of building a frame-based system with the world's largest database of facts and **common sense knowledge**. Lenat has dedicated much of the past 20 years to this project, which he believes will help solve the kinds of problems with frames and scripts that we have described.

See the Human Interest Box on Lenat, in Chapter 9, "Expert Systems." Further discussion of Lenat's work can also be found in Chapter 9.

6.9 ■ SEMANTIC NETWORKS

Semantic networks were first introduced by Ross Quillian in 1968. They are a versatile form knowledge representation and are intended to be a model of how human associative memory works. They are a convenient formalism that helps to tell a story about an object, concept, event, or situation (represented by nodes—circles or boxes) and lines with arrows (arcs) representing the relationship between nodes. Figure 6.13 is from Quillian's original paper [27] wherein he develops three semantic networks to represent three distinct meanings of the word "plant": (1) a living structure, (2) an apparatus for any structure in industry, and (3) to seed, plant, etc., in earth for growth.

Semantic networks have certainly been useful for computer programmers and AI researchers as a form of knowledge representation, but elements of set membership and precision are missing. These would be more readily available from other forms of knowledge representation, such as logic. An example is shown in Figure 6.14. We see that Mary owns Toby, which is a dog. A dog can be a pet, and so dogs are a subset of pets. So we see multiple inheritance, in that Mary owns Toby, and Mary owns a pet, of which Toby happens to be a member. Toby is a member of the class of objects called Dog. Her dog happens to be a pet, but not all dogs are pets. For example, Rotweilers are dogs that are pets for some people, and for other people they pose a menacing threat.

Is-A relationships are frequently used in semantic networks, though they do not always represent what is true in the real world. Sometimes they might represent set membership and at other times they might mean equality. For example, a penguin Is-A bird, and we know birds can fly, but penguins do not fly. This is because although most birds (superclass) can fly, not all birds can fly

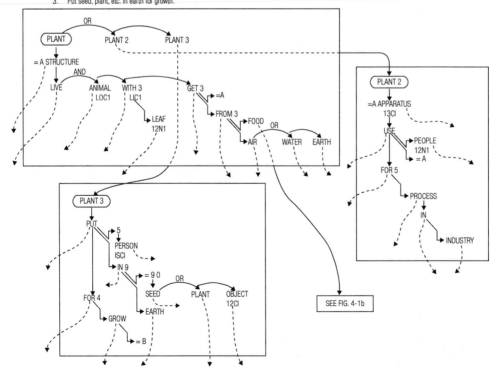

PLANT.   1. Living structure which is not an animal, frequently with leaves, getting its food from air, water, earth.
2. Apparatus used for any process in industry.
3. Put seed, plant, etc. in earth for growth.

Figure 6.13
The semantic networks for the word "plant" from Quillian's original paper in 1968.

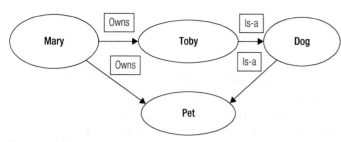

Figure 6.14
Toby is dog; Mary owns a Pet, but not all dogs are pets

Figure 6.15
A penguin is a bird; birds can fly, but penguins can't fly.

(subclass). See Figure 6.15.

Although semantic networks provide an intuitive way of representing the world, they do not represent many details about the real world that must be accounted for.

Figure 6.16 illustrates a more complex semantic network representing a college. The college consists of students, academic departments, administration, and a library. The college might have a number of academic departments, one of which is Computer Science.

Departments consist of faculty and staff. Students *take* classes, *have* records, and *organize* clubs. Students *are required* to do assignments and *receive* grades from faculty who *give* assignments and *give* grades. Students and faculty are joined by classes, class codes, and grades.

Semantic Research is a company that specializes in the development and application of semantic networks in knowledge-processing. They state:

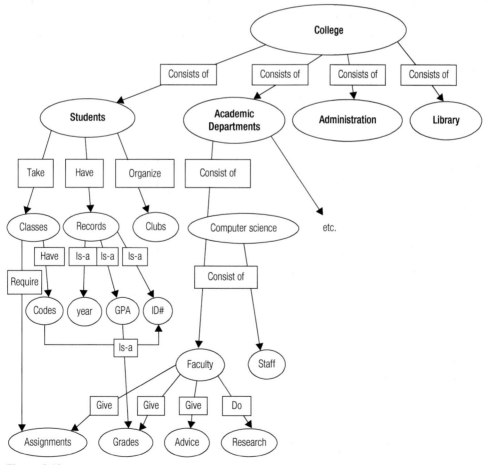

Figure 6.16
Semantic network representation of a college.

"A semantic network is fundamentally a system for capturing, storing and transferring information that works much the same as (and is, in fact, modeled after) the human brain. It is robust, efficient and flexible. It is also the basis for many efforts to produce artificial intelligence. Semantic networks can grow to extraordinary complexity, necessitating a sophisticated approach to knowledge visualization, balancing the need for simplicity with the full expressive power of the network. Semantic networks may be traversed via concept list views, via their relations, or by retracing the user's history."

Source: *http://www.semanticresearch.com/ January 15, 2008*

6.10 ■ ASSOCIATIONS

People are generally adept at making associations. Semantic networks are an attempt to capture some of this ability to associate things, including events. For example, let us share a few of the associations that come from some common life experiences.

- **Association 1:** A man might recall scenes from his youth of being in a 1955 Buick on Sunday nights, with his dad, driving in traffic across a familiar bridge, returning home from a visit to a cousin's house for some holiday. Unfortunately, the trip (on more than one occasion) ended with the car being pushed (or towed) off the bridge because the car had overheated. Only much later did he learn that his dad, who had learned to drive relatively late in life, used to drive with two feet! This, coupled with the car's own tendency to "run hot," helped to explain the car's overheating. Little wonder that our friend, for many years, tended to avoid crossing the bridge (at any time, but especially Sunday nights) and being a passenger in a Buick.

- **Association 2:** Someone else might always remember when she was 15 in the summer of 1969, her first summer away from home, when she spent two months at a college. The associations will always be highlighted by certain people and events, such as the music of the time (The Moody Blues and Merrily Rush); the reading of Darwin's Origin of the Species; sitting, watching swans, by a lily pond on the campus; and the continuous effort for some 24 hours to solve the following crypto-arithmetic problem (offered as an exercise at the end of this chapter).

$$
\begin{array}{r}
\text{SEND} \\
+\ \text{MORE} \\
\hline
\text{MONEY}
\end{array}
$$

It would be easy to conclude that associations are just good or bad memories, based on life's experiences, but they are more than that. They represent the unique ability that people have to assemble seemingly disparate pieces of knowledge (or information) to formulate a theory or a solution, or just to set off special sensations or thoughts, good or bad. It will be a challenge to AI for many years to come to somehow demonstrate this unique ability using the power of the computational resources and methods (discussed in forthcoming chapters) that will perhaps be available.

6.11 ■ MORE RECENT APPROACHES

The advent of the World Wide Web, with improvements in fourth-generation languages, led to the development of systems and languages such as the Apple MacIntosh personal computer and, with its application Hypercard, scripting languages such as HTML and object-oriented languages such as Java.

6.11.1 Concept Maps

Concept maps are a sound educational heuristic developed by Gowin and Novak.[28] Since about 1990, they have been used as the basis for the development of educational software for college-age populations by the author of this text (Kopec) and others. In a paper from the proceedings of the 2001 AMCIS, Kopec [29] states:

> Concept maps are a graphical form of knowledge representation whereby all the important information in a domain can be embedded in nodes (rectangular buttons or nodes in this system) and arcs (the lines connecting nodes). At any time during the use of the system a user can see how he/she arrived at where they are (the path taken through the SmartBook) and where it can lead to. This is indicated by a pictorial representation on the top of each card illustrating how the shaded circle (node) was reached and what circle(s) (nodes) it can lead to. Arrows without circles attached to them represent nodes which exist but are not shown in order to avoid cluttering the screen. These nodes can be found on subsequent screens. "General Text" refers to the node which is currently shaded in a graph on a visible screen.

The paper continues:

> Since 1993 the proliferation of the World Wide Web (WWW) has created a plethora of new opportunities for the delivery of electronic, distance learning systems. However, one might ask, "How many systems facilitated by the existence of the WWW have been proven and tested as sound educational tools?" Between 1988 and 1992 we developed a technology at the University of Maine for building what we called "SmartBooks"™. [30,31,32] The basis of this approach was the use of "concept mapping." The domain of application was education of college-age populations about sexually transmitted diseases (STDs), specifically, AIDS.[33] The importance of developing an anonymous, correct, flexible, and up-to-date source of information and education about this killer disease does not need explanation.

SmartBooks were developed in essentially four stages:

1. Interviews with subject matter experts to develop an effective "concept map" for a domain (possibly involving a number of iterations over several months).
2. Translation of the final concept map into the Hypercard language on the Macintosh (later Toolbook for Windows was also used).
3. Implementation of a working SmartBook.
4. Testing and revision of the working system with undergraduate students.

SmartBooks enable the flexible traversal of nodes in a concept map according to topics of interest to the user. The nodes in Figure 6.17, which shows the AIDS SmartBook, are part of the

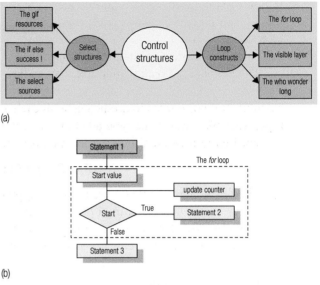

(a)

(b)

Figure 6.18
(a) The control structures concept map for the C language SmartTutor. (b) An excerpt from the For Loop Tutoring Web page. Further details about SmartTutor can be found in an article titled "SmartTutor: A Unified Approach for Enhancing Science Education." [35]

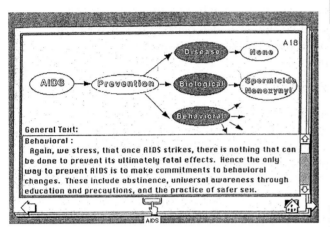

Figure 6.17
A near top-level screenshot of the AIDS SmartBook. [32]

AIDS Concept Map revealing all pop-up windows, which convey vital information and further links when clicked.

More recently, Kopec, Whitlock, and Kogen at Brooklyn College [34] developed a number of programs to enhance the education of science students, which became known as the SmartTutor Project. See Figure 6.18.

SmartBooks and SmartTutor lack the formalism that was available with semantic networks, but at the same time they are not to be confused with formal notions of subsumption (a layered system wherein each layer above subsumes the capabilities of the layers below it; e.g., including formal logic, such as modus ponens, described in Chapter 5, "Logic in Artificial Intelligence"), which could easily be the case with semantic networks. They effectively provide a hierarchical sense of any subject area and are easy to develop using the concept mapping techniques described above combined with subject matter experts and the World Wide Web. They also encapsulate some of the underlying complexities (and details) of a map, because only a few levels need be displayed at any time.

6.11.2 Conceptual Graphs

The person behind the development of **conceptual graphs (CGs)** as a knowledge representation technique is John Sowa. CGs are a system of logic based on the existential graphs of Charles Sanders Peirce [36] and the semantic networks of AI. They express meaning in a form that is logically precise, humanly readable, and computationally tractable. With a direct mapping to language, conceptual graphs serve as an intermediate language for translating computer-oriented formalisms to and from natural languages. With their graphic representation, they serve as a readable, but formal, design and specification language. CGs have been implemented in a variety of projects for information retrieval, database design, expert systems, and natural language processing.

The CG system is able to capture and represent more accurately elements of natural languages than the semantic networks and concept maps described earlier. See Figure 6.19. Typical aspects of language covered are **case relations, generalized quantifiers, indexicals,** and other aspects of natural languages.[37]

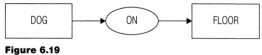

Figure 6.19
Conceptual Graph for "A dog is on the floor."

The items in the rectangular boxes are called concepts, while the items in the circles are called **conceptual relations.** A **formula operator** φ translates conceptual graphs to formulas in predicate calculus. It maps circles to predicates with each arc as one argument, and it maps concept nodes to typed variables, where the type label inside each concept box designates the type.[38]

For Figure 6.18 the following formula is generated:

$$(3\,x\text{: Dog})\ \ (3\,y\text{: Floor})\ \text{on}\ (x,y)$$

The formula means that there is an x of type Dog and a y of type Floor, and x is on y.

Sowa's CG system can represent numerous complex natural language relations and expressions visually, which is more transparent, precise, and compelling than other natural language systems. One can see how it resembles formulations in the logic programming language PROLOG, which is presented on the DVD.

In addition to numerous compelling publications in this area, Sowa has published two major treatises: *Conceptual Structures* [37] and, more recently, *Knowledge Representation*.[38]

6.11.3 Baecker's Work

The work of Ron Baecker seems very novel and worth mentioning. Troudt [39] whose study compares a subject's choice of graphic representations of scenes described by text, reports the following:

> Baecker, et al., began research in 1981 on alternative forms of presenting computer algorithms.[40] Anecdotally, visual animations of algorithms appear to improve students' comprehension of program processes. The authors developed the classroom video *Sorting out Sorting* and other sorting animations. Among the salient features of their representation are: focusing on showing only the data that is crucial at each algorithmic step; simultaneous comparisons of similar algorithms; adopting consistent visual conventions; adding a music track to convey the "feeling of what is going on" (ibid. p.47); and, narrations in sync with motion. (ibid. p.49) The claim is that their 30 minutes of video covers as much material as a 30 page textbook chapter.

Baecker's next claim is that typographic source code presentation improves students' code literacy. Using the SEE Visual Compiler, a print preprocessing system, typically dry source code is turned into what Donald Knuth describes as, "works of literature" (Donald Knuth, as quoted in Baecker, ibid., p. 49). The resulting program books contain a table of contents, indices to points of interest, comments in the margins as opposed to being inline, and descriptive page headers and footers. Special attention is also paid to representing the continuity of logical blocks across multiple pages.

Baecker's software development environment is LogoMedia, which allows him to attach MIDI-based (special files for encoding music) sounds and basic visualizations to running software. In its most sophisticated use, programmers can assign different instruments to variables and monitor the changes to those variables by hearing the instrument play sounds at different pitches. (For example, an infinite loop might have a saxophone play down the scale until the loop becomes stuck at a value, when the saxophone would repeatedly output the same note.)

Baecker claims that auditory representations of code aid in debugging. LogoMedia was tested on a sample group of programmers. The programmers spent two hours learning the software, two hours using it to write their own code, and two hours using it to debug unknown code—during the last two hours, the subjects were asked to "talk aloud" about their thought processes. In all, the test group used the auditory flags in more than half of their test runs. Subjects were generally creative, using sounds, such as explosions and clicking, that melded well with the meaning of a particular code section. Invariably the subjects' vocabulary would shift to describe problems by the sound it made. The authors claim that the methodology frees the screen for other uses, allowing browsing and modification of different sections of the code during the runtime, or fostering debugging on a personal digital assistant (PDA) and similar small-screen devices."

6.12 AGENTS: INTELLIGENT OR OTHERWISE

The **agent** view of AI created a stir since it emerged in the early 1980s. Common notions of the word "agent" are (1) one who acts or who can act, and (2) one who acts in place of another with permission. The second definition subsumes the first. Software agents "live" in computer operating systems, databases, etc. Artificial life agents "live" in artificial environments on a computer screen or in its memory (Langton [41], Franklin and Graesser [42] pp. 185–208).

In this **bottom-up** view of the world, there are layers of specialists who are able to achieve their tasks, and the composite work of the specialists effectively accomplishes a more sophisticated task(s). The possibility of solving complex computational problems by attacking them with tremendous computing resources (possibly in parallel) became feasible (and attractive) with the reduction in size and cost of computer hardware, including increases in the amount of memory feasible via silicon chip technologies and corresponding improvements in CPU speed.

The emergence of agent methods was also in direct contradiction with strong AI methods, which favored the formal knowledge representation approaches described earlier in this chapter. Instead of being concerned with how knowledge is represented, agent methods are concerned with what can be done.

The Laboratory for Computational Intelligence of the Department of Computer Science, at the University of British Columbia in Vancouver, British Columbia, Canada, has even gone as far as to state on its Web site:

> Computational intelligence (also known as artificial intelligence, or AI) is the study of the design of **intelligent agents.**

> An agent is something that acts in an environment—such as a mobile robot, a Web crawler, an automated medical diagnosis system, or an autonomous character in a video game. An 'intelligent' agent is an agent that acts appropriately in order to satisfy its goals. That is, the agent must perceive its environment, decide what action to perform, and then carry out the action. **Perception** comes in many modalities—visual, haptic (touch), speech, textual/ linguistic, etc. **Decision making** also comes in many flavors, depending on whether the agent has complete or partial knowledge of its world, whether it is acting alone or in collaboration/ competition with other agents, etc. Finally, taking actions can have different forms, depending on whether the agent has wheels, arms,

Human Interest Notes

Marvin Minsky [43] (1927–)

Since the 1956 Dartmouth Conference, Marvin Minsky has been one of the founding fathers of AI.

He earned a BA in mathematics from Harvard in 1950, and then a PhD in mathematics from Princeton in 1954, but his field of specialization is cognitive science, to which he has been a contributor through his work at MIT since 1958.

His deep involvement in the field has continued through 2006 and the 50th Anniversary Dartmouth Conference, where this text was first conceived. Professor Minsky founded the MIT Computer Science and Artificial Intelligence Laboratory (CSAIL) in 2003. Minsky won the Turing Award in 1969, the Japan Prize in 1990, the International Joint Conference on Artificial Intelligence Award for Research Excellence in 1991, and the Benjamin Franklin Medal from the Franklin Institute in 2001. He is one of the great pioneers and deep thinkers of AI. He developed the theory of frames (Section 6.8) and many other important contributions to AI from the mathematical, psychological, and computer science perspectives. In recent years he has been affiliated with the MIT Media Lab.

Society of Mind

In 1986 Marvin Minsky [43] made a landmark contribution with his book, *The Society of Mind*, which opened the door to agent thinking and research. A review of the book at *http://www.emcp.com/intro_pc/reading12.htm* highlights the following points.

Minsky's theory as put forth in *The Society of Mind* is the view that the mind comprises collections of enormous numbers of semi-autonomous, intricately connected agents that are themselves mindless. As Minsky puts it,

This book tries to explain how minds work. How can intelligence emerge from nonintelligence? To answer that, we'll show that you can build a mind from many little parts, each mindless by itself. [43]

In Minsky's scheme, the mind is made of many smaller processes which he calls "agents" (see Section 6.12.1). Each agent can only perform simple tasks—but agents when joined to form societies "in certain very special ways" will lead to intelligence.

Minsky's view of the brain is that it is a very complex machine. If we were to imagine replacing every cell in the brain with a computer chip designed to perform the same functions as the brain's agents perform, with the exact same connectivity as in the brain, then, Minsky states,

There isn't any reason to doubt that the substitute machine would think and feel the same kinds of thoughts and feelings that you do—since it embodies all the same processes and memories. Indeed, it would surely be disposed to declare, with all your own intensity, that it is you (ibid. p. 289).

It was around the time of Minsky's landmark work that AI systems were criticized for their inability to exhibit common sense knowledge. Here is what he had to say:

Thousands and, perhaps, millions of little processes must be involved in how we anticipate, imagine, plan, predict, and prevent—and yet all this proceeds so automatically that we regard it as "ordinary common sense" (ibid.).

or is entirely virtual. An intelligent agent should also learn to improve its performance over time, as it repeatedly performs this sense-think-act cycle.

Agents have four qualities:

1. They are **situated**; that is, they are positioned in or part of some environment.

2. They are *autonomous* – that is they can sense the environment that they are part of and act spontaneously upon it.

3. They are *flexible*, able to respond intelligently and *proactive*. Agents are able to respond to environmental stimuli in an appropriate and timely fashion. Agents can also be *proactive* when they are **opportunistic**, goal directed, and resort to alternatives in a given situation. An example would be the traction control agent on a car—it sometimes checks in when there are no traction issues on the road (perhaps due to atmospheric humidity conditions) but it is smart enough not to stay in control continuously, and it reverts to normal driving conditions.

4. Agents are *social*—they can interact with other software or humans appropriately. In this sense they know their responsibilities vis-a-vis the goals of the larger system as a whole. Hence, agents must be "supportive" and "socially responsive" to the needs of the larger system as a whole.

So we come upon the following definition:

> An **autonomous agent** is a system situated within an environment; it senses the environment and acts on it, over time, in pursuit of its own agenda and thereby is able to effect what it senses. [44]

When environments change, agents no longer perform as agents. The distinction between agents and ordinary programs for a specific function (e.g., a financial computation) is that agents keep a temporal continuity. A program that keeps a record of its input and output and possibly learns accordingly is an agent. One that just performs output, would not qualify as an agent. Hence, "All software agents are programs, but not all programs are agents" (ibid.).

The term multi-agent system refers to a variety of software systems that are comprised of multiple semi-autonomous components. These agents have their independent knowledge and it must be tapped and combined in the best way to solve problems that none of the agents can solve alone. The research of Jennings, Sycara, and Woodridge concludes that multi-agent problem solving shares four important characteristics. First, each agent can suffer from a limited viewpoint. Second, there is no global system controller for the entire problem solving. Third, the knowledge and input data for the problem is also decentralized, and fourth, the reasoning processes are often asynchronous. [45, 46]

Franklin and Graesser [42] continue their discussion with development of a taxonomy for defining various kinds of agents based on properties such as being reactive, autonomous, goal-oriented, temporally continuous, communicative, learning, mobile, flexible, and having character, but that is beyond the scope of this text.

6.12.1 A Little Agent History

The notion of **blackboard architectures** is an outstanding feature of the speech understanding system known as "Hearsay II." This is the work of J.L. Erman, F. Hayes-Roth, V. Lesser, and D. Reddy [47] and was the basis for all future research of this kind. Here a number of specialist procedures called **knowledge sources (KSs)** report to a central blackboard that they are available and apply to a problem situation. A control device manages conflicts among the procedures to most efficiently develop a solution to a problem. The work of Kornfeld and Hewitt [48] on Ether relates to problem solving starting from scientific communities. Sprites (akin to KSs) record facts, hypotheses, and demonstrations in a common area similar to that of a blackboard. These hypotheses have *defenders* and *skeptics. Sponsors* also regulate the amount of time that can be spent on each sprite. In general, blackboard architectures enable a set of specialist procedures to declare their availability for completion of a task.

However, limitations of architecture prevent these systems from performing efficiently. One of the first systems developed for problem solving by a community of specialists was the PUP6 System. [49] These software specialists were called "beings," and it was these beings that worked on the synthesis of one specific specialist. This specialist, called Concept Formation, was capable of handling a task by itself. However, this was really only a model or toy system, never fully developed by Lenat. Carl Hewitt [50,] ... "tended to think in terms of distributed systems, considering control structures as patterns of message passing between active entities called *actors.* So he had the idea of viewing problem solving as the activity of an assembly of experts, considering a reasoning process as a confrontation of points of view." [51] One of the most influential, relatively early Distributed Artificial Intelligence Systems (DAI) was the DVMT (Distributed Vehicle Monitoring Test) developed by V. Lesser's team at MIT. [52] It was a significant research project on the perception and recognition of distributed situations. Sensors transmitted data to processing agents implemented in the form of blackboards. The problem for the agents consisted of following vehicles on the basis of data—complex data—much of which was complicated with sound effects. [51] Much further study of multi-agent planning was facilitated by this system.

Since the late 1980s, Rodney Brooks has been building successful robots based on a subsumption architecture, which represents his belief that intelligent behavior emerges from the interactions of organized simpler behaviors. The subsumption architecture is behind the construction of robot control systems including a collection of task-handling behaviors. Robots' behaviors are accomplished through the transitions of a finite state machine that maps a perception-based input into an action-oriented output. A simple set of condition-action production rules (See Section 6.5) define the finite state machines. Brooks' systems do not include a sense of global knowledge, but they do include some hierarchy and feedback between levels of the architecture. Brooks incrementally builds the capabilities of his systems by increasing the number of layers in his architecture. Brooks believes that top-level behavior emerges as a result of the design and testing of the lower levels of the architecture. Experimentation is performed to reveal the best design for the coherent behaviors of layers, and to determine the appropriate communication between and within layers. The simplicity of design of the subsumption architecture has not prevented Brooks from achieving success in several applications (see Brooks, 1989 [53] Brooks, 1991 [54] Brooks, 1997 [55]).

HUMAN INTEREST NOTES

RODNEY BROOKS - REBEL TO REFORM

Rodney Brooks (1954 –) is a multifaceted and interesting person. In the 1980s he burst onto the AI scene as a rebel to the establishment with maverick views of how robot systems should be built. Over the years he has transformed himself into an AI leader, scholar, and visionary. He received a bachelor's degree in pure mathematics from the Flinders University of South Australia and a PhD in Computer Science from Stanford University in 1981. He held research positions at Carnegie Mellon University and MIT, and a faculty position at Stanford before joining the faculty of MIT in 1984. He has established his reputation through work in robotics and artificial life, further diversified via movies, books, and entrepreneurial activities, including the establishment of several companies: Lucid (1984), IROBOT® (1990) (Figure 6.20 (a-d), where he designed the commercially successful Roomba® (see Figure 6.20c below), and its subsidiary Artificial Creatures (1991). He was Panasonic Professor of Robotics at MIT and Director, MIT Computer Science and Artificial Intelligence Laboratory. He has designed and built robots marketed to industry and the military. In 2008 he founded Heartland Robotics whose mission is to bring to market a new generation of robots to improve productivity in manufacturing environments. "Heartland's goal is to introduce robots into places that have not been automated before, making manufacturers more efficient, their workers more productive and keeping jobs from migrating to low-cost regions."

http://www.heartlandrobotics.com/about. html

a)

b)

c)

d)

Figure 6.20 (a – d)
Products from IROBOT Corporation.

6.12.2 Contemporary Agents

Today many agent-based applications serve as specialists for diverse purposes such as communication, transportation, health, and beyond. We will discuss some particularly noteworthy examples.

- **KaZaA**: This software is a peer-to-peer search agent.
- **Spector Pro**: This software is an example of a monitoring agent.
- **Zero Intelligence Plus (Zip)**: Zip is an autonomous adaptive trading agent algorithm developed by Dave Cliff, at Southampton University, and is used by the financial industry to conduct trades of financial instruments such as stocks and bonds.

KaZaA

KaZaA is a peer-to-peer search agent. Unlike traditional search engines with which you query only one database, with KaZaA you can search thousands of interconnected computers that have chosen to share their files. Audio, video, software, and documents are combined as one.

KaZaA is composed of five major sections that you can reach via the five icons in the menu bar: "Start," "My KaZaA," "Theatre," "Search," and "Traffic." You use the Search option to begin searching for files. You can enter the keyword(s) you are looking for, and specify the type of media files (audio, video, image, software, documents) you want. KaZaA is not limited to sharing audio files: as a real digital media library, it lets you find all sorts of documents that have been shared by their owners. After choosing your media type, you can do a simple query (by title or author) or an advanced one (multiple fields such as file size, language, type, category, etc.). The results are displayed in the right window with a lot of information such as the name of the artist and the title, but also some indications about the quality of the document and the expected downloading time.

Monitoring Agent: Spector Pro

Spector Pro is a monitoring agent. Opinions differ about the ethics of computer monitoring. If you use an agent such as Spector Pro to monitor your employees, colleagues, or friends, you might be legally or ethically violating their privacy. On the other hand, you might need to monitor children's activities on the Web, not to limit them, but to protect them. In other cases, you can detect whether someone is using your computer for illegal purposes before you can be held responsible for their acts.

Zero Intelligence Plus (Zip)

The notion of agent-based computing has been adopted enthusiastically in the financial trading community, where autonomous market trading agents are said to outperform human commodity traders by 7%. Michael Luck of the School of Electronics and Computer Science at the University of Southampton and executive director of the EU-funded AgentLink action coordination program explains agent-based computing.

> Agents are a way to manage interactions between different kinds of computational entities, and to get the right kind of behaviour out of large-scale distributed systems.

Luck continues:

> Inevitably, machines can monitor stock market movements much more quickly than humans, and if you can encode the kinds of rules that you want, then it is not unreasonable to imagine that computational traders will be able to outperform humans.

Finally he states:

> I am surprised that the figure is only 7%. This is based on experiments we have carried out, but there are robo-trader programs being used in the market not just to provide information, but to do actual trading. [56]

Since the publication of our first edition smart phones have become even more pervasive in how they are used in almost every aspect of our lives – from checking the latest weather report to determining when the next subway car is leaving from near your campus. These software agents are now ubiquitous as Apps on all smartphone platforms including, for example, restaurant Apps such as Yelp, Savored, and Open Table, traffic Apps such as Waze and Google Maps, shopping Apps such as Overstock.com, Amazon and Quibids. And if you've ever been mesmerized by a tune whose name you cannot recall, you may be familiar with Shazam. And the list can go on and on.

HAL: The Next Generation Intelligent Room

Hal is a highly interactive environment that uses embedded computation to observe and participate in the normal, everyday events occurring in the world around it. An offshoot of the MIT AI Lab's Intelligent Room, Hal has cameras for eyes, microphones for ears, and uses a variety of computer vision, speech, and gesture recognition systems to allow people to interact naturally with it. Hal is the next generation of the Intelligent Room, designed to support the kind of human-computer interaction that up until now has only been science fiction.

6.12.3 The Semantic Web

The Semantic Web is a project which Tim Berners-Lee, the inventor of the World Wide Web, has been developing since the late 1990s. The Semantic Web is a vision of information that is understandable and manageable by computers, so that they can perform more of the tedious work involved in finding, sharing, and combining information on the Web that humans need and computers can provide.

The types of tasks that the Semantic Web would be able to accomplish would be to find the French word for "horse," to make reservations for a concert performance, or to be able to find the cheapest hotel room in a city with our particular requirements (e.g., nonsmoking room, king-size bed, first floor).

For example, a computer might be instructed to list the prices of flat screen televisions that are greater than or equal to 40" wide, or local restaurants that can offer Italian food, with a menu that offers courses between $10 and $15 per plate, and are open after 10 pm on a Tuesday night. Present-day conditions would require search engines that are individually tailored to every Web site being searched. The semantic web provides a common standard (RDF) for Web sites to publish the relevant *information* in a form that may more readily be processed and integrated by machine.

Tim Berners-Lee originally expressed the vision of the semantic web as follows:

> I have a dream for the Web [in which computers] become capable of analyzing all the data on the Web—the content, links, and transactions between people and computers. A 'Semantic Web', which should make this possible, has yet to emerge, but when it does, the day-to-day mechanisms of trade, bureaucracy and our daily lives will be

handled by machines talking to machines. The 'intelligent agents' people have touted for ages will finally materialize.[57]

6.12.4 The Future – According to IBM

IBM, for most of the twentieth century the largest and most successful computer corporation in the world, has dedicated a number of programs to the study and development of agents. Following is a statement from its Web site, exemplary of IBM's commitment to this perspective:

"Today, we are witnessing the first steps in the evolution of the Internet towards an open, free-market information economy of software agents buying and selling a rich variety of information goods and services. We envision the Internet some years hence as a seething milieu in which billions of economically-motivated software agents find and process information and disseminate it to humans and, increasingly, to other agents. Agents will naturally evolve from facilitators into decision-makers, and their degree of autonomy and responsibility will continue to increase with time. Ultimately, transactions among economic software agents will constitute an essential and perhaps even dominant portion of the world economy.

The evolution of the Internet into an information economy seems as desirable as it does inevitable. After all, economic mechanisms are arguably the best known way to adjudicate and satisfy the conflicting needs of billions of agents – human agents. It is tempting to blindly wave the Invisible Hand and assume that the same mechanisms can be applied successfully to software agents. However, automated agents are not people! They make decisions and act on them at a vastly greater speed. They are immeasurably less sophisticated, less flexible, less able to learn, and notoriously lacking in "common sense." Given these differences, it is entirely possible that agent-based economies will behave in very strange and unfamiliar ways." [58]

6.12.5 Author's Perspective

We live in times that depend on various kinds of agents. We have personal training agents, real estate agents, automobile agents, literary and sports agents, and more. We also have various special-purpose devices that perform as our personal assistants. Examples would include watches, cell phones, electronic address books, personal computers, geographic information systems, thermometers, blood pressure machines, blood-sugar monitors, and so forth. It is easy to foresee a time in the not-so-distant future when we will carry upon our person a small, integrated multi-agent system that will offer all these features and more. The device will be truly multifunctional, easy to understand, and easy to operate. It could comprise: (1) communication systems, (2) transportation systems, (3) body systems, (4) personal information systems, and (5) knowledge systems. Imagine performing your day-to-day living with the aid of such a personal agent? Knowledge systems would be akin to our present-day computers with the benefit of the Internet. They could help us solve problems, answer questions intelligently and quickly, and enable real dynamic learning. Personal information systems could address our personal needs—appointments, personal

Gift of Fire has already been published in its third edition (2008), and it has become a standard and classic for the course, "Computers and Society"; its focus is that computers can be viewed as having both positive and negative effects on society, as did fire when it was first introduced to mankind.

records, health, finances, and much more. Communication and transportation systems would solve those traditional problems. What a wonderful opportunity and, as you can imagine, none of the components we have mentioned are beyond our technical capabilities today. It is all a matter of successfully building integrated multi-agent systems. Naturally, once such a wonderful system would exist, we need to concern ourselves with security—yes, with the good comes the bad (á la Sara Baase's wonderful text, *Gift of Fire* [59]), and that is where this discussion ends.

6.13 CHAPTER SUMMARY

This Chapter focuses on a topic which is very integral to AI—*knowledge representation.* Before you can begin any problem solving you must have some sense of how the problem can best be represented. Considerations might include: will the solution to the problem involve decision-making? Will it involve search? Will the solution be precise or within some range of acceptable values? All these factors contribute to the choice of an appropriate knowledge representation, in addition to the predilections of the learner. Does the learner feel comfortable with a graphic representation, or would he/she prefer mathematical expression?

The discussion in the early sections of this chapter focuses on the hierarchy of information processing involving the transitions from *data, facts,* and *information* to the highest level—knowledge. Then the key issue becomes how can the knowledge best be represented?

Section 6.1 considers graphical sketches and introduces the notion of the Human Window. Another often-used method of knowledge representation is a graph, and this topic is presented through the famous *Bridges of Königsberg Problem* (Section 6.2), why it cannot be solved given its inability to satisfy the *Eulerian Property,* and how the bridges have actually changed in recent years is explained.

Discussion then moves to search trees, decision trees, and is further illustrated through The Twelve Coins Problem (Section 6.3). The variety of possible choices for a problem solution is highlighted through the famous Towers of Hanoi Problem (Section 6.4). In this section there are graphical sketches of the solution, as well as tables, comprising explicit descriptions (*extensional representations*); we also provide pseudocode and *recurrence relations* comprising implicit (*intensional representations*) solutions to the problem.

Production Systems (Section 6.5) have been an important and effective method of knowledge representation for many decades, and are also the subject of Chapter 7. *Frames* (Section 6.7), with their *slots* and *fillers,* introduced by Marvin Minsky in 1975, are an important contribution to AI and a forerunner to what later became a whole paradigm for programming languages in computer science and the subject of Section 6.6, "Object Orientation." A whole school of AI using scripts and the *conceptual dependency* (CD) *system* (Section 6.8) emerged from Yale University in the 1980s, led by Roger Schank and his students. *Semantic networks* (Section 6.9) were introduced by Quillian in 1968. They seem to naturally lend themselves to knowledge representation for language processing, simultaneously allowing for sufficient flexibility through graphics and enabling sufficient formality and precision through the use of language and its implicit meaning and the parsing of phrases and sentences. *Associations* (Section 6.10) are a skill germane to humans and how our brains might be wired for relational thinking, interpretation, and problem solving—this perhaps is something that can be developed in computers (i.e., the work of Doug Lenat in CYC) but it does not come naturally to them.

More recent approaches such as *concept maps, conceptual graphs*, and *Baecker's Work* whereby the senses, particularly employing visualization and sound, are used to convey meaning, are the focus of Section 6.11.

Agents (Section 6.12) are an entirely different approach to developing problem-solving paradigms. They stem from the early work of Marvin Minsky and later led by the efforts of Rodney Brooks (subsumption architecture), both at MIT. This *bottom-up approach* concerns itself with what can be accomplished through combined efforts of layered specialists exploiting the possibility of powerful computational resources. Some of the qualities of agents include being (1) situated, (2) autonomous, (3) flexible, and (4) social. A well-known forerunner to the agent approach were the *blackboard architectures* of the speech understanding system, Hearsay II, which employed *knowledge sources* (KSs), highlighted by the work of Hayes-Roth, Erman, Lesser, and Reddy.

Section 6.12.2 presents some contemporary agents including KaZaA for peer-to-peer searching, Spector Pro for monitoring, and the trading agent, Zero Intelligence Plus.

Sections 6.12.3 and 6.12.4 look from the present to the future via the Semantic Web by Tim Berners Lee (1999) and how IBM views the world (http://www.research.ibm.com/infoecon).

Finally, Section 6.12.5 portrays an author's view of our future world under the control of personal multi-agents that will serve and facilitate day-to-day life for humans in many possible ways.

Questions for Discussion

1. Describe the important features of good knowledge representations.

2. Distinguish between data, facts, information, and knowledge.

3. What is the notion of grain size?

4. What is meant by the Human Window?

5. What is an intentional representation vs. an extensional representation?

6. What do frames and object-oriented programming have in common?

7. What does it mean for a program to be comprehensible?

8. What are some of the good features of scripts?

9. What are some of negative features of scripts?

10. How would you describe the functionality of frames?

11. What are some of the negative features of frames?

12. Develop a script for a common scenario that frequently occurs, e.g., "The Getting Dressed Script"; "The Go to Work Script"; "The Go Shopping for Food Script."

13. Develop a semantic network for the following facts and relations:

    a. Joe and Sue are the parents of Tom and Debi. Tom and Debi are brother and sister. Kim is the child of Tom; Jill is the child of Debi.

    b. Bill, Betty, and Bob are siblings; they live in Baltimore, Maryland. They are the children of Don and Carol.

14. How are semantic networks different for Conceptual Graphs and Concept Maps?

15. What is the notion of an agent?

16. Describe four properties of agents.

17. What are the contributions of Marvin Minsky to the subject of this chapter?

18. What are some of the accomplishments of Rodney Brooks?

Exercises

1. Describe some of the elements of a good knowledge representation.

2. Trace the history of knowledge representation in AI as discussed in the chapter.

3. Discuss some of the pros and cons of frames, semantic networks, and scripts.

4. Develop a frame representation for the college depicted in the semantic network in Figure 6.16.

5. Develop a semantic network for the car accident frames in Figure 6.11.

6. Describe some arguments by Hubert Dreyfus against the value of scripts as knowledge representation.

7. Develop production rule, frame, and semantic network-based representations of the decisions made as to what to wear on a given day; e.g., on a workday or holiday, wear a suit, if it is a weekend, wear casual clothes, if it is rainy, if it is sunny and hot, etc.

8. Write a research paper describing the achievements of one of the following people: Ross Quillian, Marvin Minsky, John Sowa, Roger Schank, Robert Abelson, or Rodney Brooks.

9. You are trying to describe the game of baseball to someone. Which knowledge representation method would be most suitable? Try to build a baseball system using your preferred choice.

10. Try to solve the following famous crypto-arithmetic problem. Each letter can stand for one and only one digit. What is a most suitable knowledge representation choice for deriving a solution to this problem? ++

$$
\begin{array}{r}
\text{SEND} \\
+\quad\text{MORE} \\
\hline
\text{MONEY}
\end{array}
$$

BEG SIDEBAR

60

END SIDEBAR

++*This problem and crypt-arithms comprise Chapter 5 of Artificial Intelligence Problems and Their Solutions, Mercury Learning Inc. 2014.*

11. Consider the map in Figure 6.21. Explain whether knowing the instructions represents information or knowledge. If your answer is "information," then explain what would be needed to "upgrade" it to knowledge.

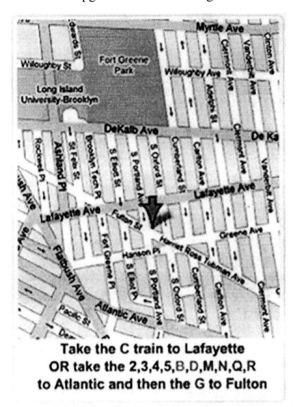

**Take the C train to Lafayette
OR take the 2,3,4,5,B,D,M,N,Q,R
to Atlantic and then the G to Fulton**

Figure 6.21
Subway map.

12. We have presented a number of problems to this point that have a common feature including: The Missionaries and Cannibal Problem, The Twelve Coins Problem, The Knight's Tour, The Eight Puzzle, and the Cryptarithm above. What do these problems share in common?

13. In this Chapter we introduced the concept of the Human Window. Consider your solutions to the above problems and other exercises and problems we have posed in the book. How "Human Window" like are your solutions? That is, do they require too much memory or computation for humans? Are they 100% correct? Have a suitable grain size?   Executable? Comprehensible? [++]

14. This Chapter introduced the concept of how "Intensional" or "Extensional" a solution to a problem is. Consider representations of solutions to problems that you have produced above, in our text, and elsewhere – Are these solutions extensional or intensional? Who would prefer an intensional solution? Who would prefer an extensional solution? Which would most people prefer? [++]

Keywords

agent	Eulerian Cycle	meta-knowledge
associations	Eulerian Trail	multi-agent system
autonomous agent	events	multiple inheritance
blackboard architecture	executability	object
bottom-up	expectation-driven processing	object orientation
Bridges of Königsberg Problem	extensional	opportunistic
case relations	extensional representation	perception
class	fact	performance
common sense knowledge	fillers	polymorphism
comprehensibility	formula operator	problem reduction
concept	frame	recurrence relation
concept map	generalized quantifiers	script
conceptual dependency (CD) system	grain size	semantic networks
	graph	Semantic Web
conceptual graph (CG)	graphical sketch	situated
conceptual relation	indexicals	slot
correctness	information	slot value
data	inheritance	SmartBook
decision making	intelligent agent	sprite
decision tree	intensional	subsumption architecture
demon	intensional representation	The Human Window
edge	knowledge	The Twelve Coins Problem
encapsulation	knowledge representation	Towers of Hanoi Problem
Eulerian Property	knowledge source (KS)	vertices

References

1. Firebaugh, M. 1988. *Artificial intelligence: a Knowledge-based approach.* Boston, MA: PWS-Kent.

2. Feigenbaum, E. A., Barr, A., and Cohen, R., eds. 1981–1982. *The handbook of artificial intelligence. Vol 1–3.* Stanford, CA: HeurisTech Press / William Kaufmann.

3. Clarke, M. R. B. 1980. The construction of economical and correct algorithms for KPK, in *Advances in Computer Chess 2*, ed. M. R. B. Clarke. Edinburgh: Edinburgh University Press.

4. Michie, D. 1982. Experiments on the mechanization of game-learning: 2 – rule- based learning and the human window. *The Computer Journal* 25(1):105–113.

5. Kopec, D. (1983). Human and machine representations of knowledge. *PhD thesis*, Machine Intelligence Research Unit, University of Edinburgh, Edinburgh.

6. Thompson, K. 1986. Retrograde analysis of certain endgames. *International Computer Chess Association Journal* 8(3):131–139.

7. Beal, D. 1977. The construction of economical and correct algorithms for king and pawn against king. Appendix 5 In *Advances in Computer Chess 2*, ed. Beal & Clarke, 1–30. Edinburgh: Edinburgh University Press.

8. Bramer, M. A. 1980. Correct and optimal strategies in game playing. *The Computer Journal* 23(4): 347–52.

9. Reddy, R. 1988. The foundations and grand challenges of artificial intelligence. AAAI President's Address: aaai.org/Library/President/Reddy.pdf.

10. Chase, W. G. and Simon, H. A. 1973. Perception in chess. *Cognitive Psychology* 4:55–81.

11. Nievergelt, J. A. 1977. Information content of chess positions. *ACM SIGART* April: 13–15.

12. Michie, D. 1977. Practical limits to computation. Research Memorandum, MIP-R-116. Edinburgh: Machine Intelligence Research Unit, Edinburgh University.

13. Miller, G. A. 1956. The magical number 7, plus or minus 2: Some limits on our capacity for processing information. *Psychological Review* 63:81–97.

14. Stroud, J. M. 1966. The fine structure of psychological time. *Annals of the NY Academy* 623–631.

15. Halstead, M. H. 1977. *Elements of software science*. New York, NY: Elsevier.

16. Kraitchik, M. 1942. §8.4.1 in *Mathematical recreations*. New York, NY: W. W. Norton, 209–211.

17. Bierman, A. 1990. *Great ideas in computer science*. Cambridge, MA: MIT Press.

18. Ege, R. 200 The object-oriented language paradigm, In *The Computer Science Handbook*, 2nd ed. Allen Tucker, Chapter 91, 1–27, Boca Raton, Florida: CRC, Chapman and Hall.

19. Laudon, K. 2003. *Programming language: Principles and practice*, 2nd ed. Boston, MA: Thomson / Brooks/Cole.

20. Budd, T. 2001. *The introduction to object-oriented programming*. Reading, MA: Addison-Wesley.

21. Papert, S. 1980. *Mindstorms: Children, computers and powerful ideas*. New York, NY: Basic Books.

22. Minsky, M. 1975. A framework for representing knowledge. In *The Psychology of Computer Vision*, ed. P. Winston, 211–277. New York, NY: McGraw-Hill.

23. Brachman, R. J. 1985. I lied about the trees – Or, defaults and definitions in knowledge representation. The *AI Magazine* 6:80–93.

24. Schank, R. C. and Abelson, R. P. 1977. *Scripts, plans, goals, and understanding*. Hillsdale, NJ: Lawrence Erlbaum.

25. Dreyfus, H. A. 1981. From micro-worlds to knowledge representation. In *Mind Design*, ed. John Haugeland. Cambridge, MA: MIT Press.

26. Lenat, D. and Guha, R. V. 1990. *Building large knowledge-based systems: Representation and inference in the CYC project*. Reading, MA: Addison-Wesley.

27. Quillian, M. R. 1968. Semantic memory. In *Semantic information processing*, ed. M. Minsky. Cambridge, MA: MIT Press.

28. Novak, J. D. and Gowin, D. B. 1985. *Learning how to learn*. Cambridge: Cambridge University Press.

29. Kopec, D. 2001. SmartBooks: A generic methodology to facilitate delivery of post-secondary education. In *Proceedings AMCIS 2001 Association for information systems 7th Americas conference on information systems*. Boston, August 2–5, Curriculum and Learning Track; (CDROM).

30. Kopec, D., Wood, C. and Brody, M. 1991. An educational theory for transferring domain expert knowledge towards the development of an intelligent tutoring system for STDs. *Journal of Artificial Intelligence in Education* 2(2):67–82.

31. Kopec, D., Wood, C. 1994. *Introduction to SmartBooks* (Booklet; to accompany interactive educational software AIDS SmartBook). Boston, MA.: Jones and Bartlett. Also published as United States Coast Guard Academy, Center for Advanced Studies *Report No. 23–93*, December, 1993.

32. Kopec, D., Brody, M. Shi, C., and Wood, C. 1992. Towards an intelligent tutoring system with application to sexually transmitted diseases. In *Artificial intelligence and intelligent tutoring systems: Knowledge-based systems for learning and teaching*, eds. D. Kopec and R. B. Thompson, 129–151. Chichester, England: Ellis Horwood Publishers.

33. Wood, C. L. (1992). Use of concept maps in micro-computer based program design for an AIDS knowledge base. *EDD Thesis,* University of Maine, Orono.

34. Kopec, D., Whitlock, P., and Kogen, M. 2002. SmartTutor: Combining SmartBooks™ and peer tutors for multi-media online instruction. In *Proceedings of the international conference on engineering education*, University of Manchester, Manchester, England, UMIST, (CDROM), August 18–21, 2002.

35. Eckhardt, R., Harrow, K., Kopec, D., Kobrak, M., and Whitlock, P. 2007 SmartTutor: A unified approach for enhancing science education. *The Journal of Computing Sciences in Colleges* 22(3):29–36.

36. Peirce, C. S. 1958. *Collected Papers (1931 – 1958)*. Cambridge, MA: Harvard University Press.

37. Sowa, J. 1984. *Conceptual structures: Information processing in mind and machine.* Reading, MA: Addison- Wesley.

38. Sowa, J. 2000. *Knowledge representation: Logical, philosophical, and computational foundations.* Boston, MA: Brooks/Cole / Thomson Learning.

39. Troudt, E. 2014. *Automated Learner Classification Through Interface Event Stream and Summary Statistics Analysis.* Ph.D Thesis. CUNY, New York, NY: The Graduate Center.

40. Baecker, R., DiGiano, C., Marcus, A. 1997. Software visualization for debugging; *Communications of the ACM* 40(4).

41. Langton, C. G. 1989. *Artificial life: Santa Fe Institute studies in the sciences of complexity,* VI. Reading, MA: Addison-Wesley.

42. Franklin, S. and Graesser, A. 1996. Is it an agent, or just a program? : A taxonomy for autonomous agents. In *Proceedings of the third international workshop on agent theories, architectures, and languages.* New York, NY: Springer-Verlag.

43. Minsky, M. 1986. *The Society of Mind.* New York, NY: Simon and Schuster.

44. Durfee, E. H. and Lesser, V. 1989. Negotiating task decomposition and allocation using partial global planning. In *Distributed artificial intelligence, Vol II*, ed. L. Gasser and M. Huhns. San Francisco: Morgan Kaufman.

45. Jennings, N. R., Sycara, K. P., and Woolbridge, M. 1998. A roadmap for agent research and development. *Journal of Autonomous Agents and Multiagent Systems* 1(1):17–36.

46. Luger, G. 2005. *Artificial intelligence: Structures and strategies for complex problem solving,* 5th ed. Reading, MA: Addison-Wesley.

47. Erman, J. L., Hayes-Roth, F., Lesser, V., and Reddy, D. 1980. The HEARSAY II speech understanding system: Integrating knowledge to resolve uncertainty. *Computing Surveys* 12(2):213–253.

48. Kornfeld, W. 1979. ETHER: A parallel problem solving system. In *Proceedings of the 6th international joint conference on artificial intelligence,* 490–492. Cambridge, MA, August 1979.

49. Lenat, D. 1975. BEINGS: Knowledge as interacting agents. In *Proceedings of the 1975 international joint conference on artificial intelligence,*126 – 133.

50. Hewitt, C. 1977. Viewing control structures as patterns of message passing. *Artificial Intelligence* 8(3):323 – 374. \

51. Ferber, J. 1999. *Multi-agent systems.* Reading, MA: Addison-Wesley.

52. Lesser, V. R. and Corkill, D. D. 1983. The distributed vehicle monitoring testbed. *AI Magazine* 4(3):15–33.

53. Brooks, R. A. 1989. A robot that walks; Emergent behaviors from a carefully evolved network. *Neural Computation* 1(2):254–262.

54. Brooks, R. A. 1991. Intelligence without representation. *Artificial Intelligence* 47(3): 139–159.

55. Brooks, R. A. 1997. The cog project. *Journal of the Robotics Society of Japan, Special Issue Mini on Humanoid,* ed. T. Matsui. 15(7).

56. Sedacca, B. 2006. "Best-kept secret agent revealed. *Computer Weekly* http://www.computerweekly.com/Articles/2006/10/12/219087/best-kept-secret-agent-revealed.htm.

57. Berners-Lee, T. and Fischetti, M. 1999. *Weaving the web.* San Francisco: Harper.

58. *http://www.research.ibm.com/infoecon*

59. Baase, S. 2008. *A gift of fire: Social, legal, and ethical issues for computing and the Internet,* 3rd ed. Saddle Brook, NJ: Prentice Hall.

60. Kopec, D., Shetty, S., and Pileggi, C. 2014. *Artificial Intelligence Problems and Their Solutions.* Dulles, VA: Mercury Learning, Inc.

PRODUCTION SYSTEMS

John von Neumann

This Chapter starts with a discussion of weak vs. strong AI methods and includes a practical example—The CarBuyer. This production system is thoroughly analyzed together with the advantages and methods of the production system approach. Methods of inference, including forward and backward chaining, together with conflict resolution, are illustrated with a number of examples. The chapter concludes with an introduction to cellular automata, stochastic processes, and Markov Chains.

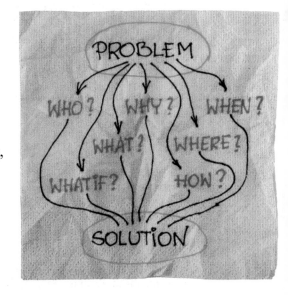

7.0 ■ INTRODUCTION

"I prefer to be a productionist rather than a perfectionist." Perhaps the opening quotation needs some further explanation. In essence we are suggesting that perfection, although a noble goal, is rarely achieved or achievable in any arena, be it science, academics, sports, business, government, or others. In many disciplines it is desirable to produce results, albeit imperfect, but representing our best efforts, and still provide valuable contributions to society. You perhaps have heard it said "Perfection is the enemy of the good." We leave it to the reader to decide.

7.1 ■ BACKGROUND

In some sense the discussion of production vs. perfection is integral to the notion of artificial intelligence in the strong or traditional sense. That is, if we were able to discover or derive algorithms that represent all human behaviors, decisions, and problem-solving activities, then there would be no need for the discipline of artificial intelligence. Instead we must guess, estimate, and make informed, statistically sound decisions, based on what we have learned. Production systems can be viewed as a link to, or an attempt at a translation of, what is in a human-domain specialist's head and how that knowledge would look if converted to instructions for a computer to follow and execute.

Production systems can essentially be viewed as synonymous with "IF – THEN Rules." That is, given that certain conditions specified under the "IF" are matched, then we reach certain conclusions, make certain decisions, and take certain actions accordingly. However, there is no intelligent human behavior that can be "perfectly" reduced to a set of IF – THEN rules. Attempts to better represent reality with probabilities of certainty in reaching specific decisions or conclusions can be helpful, but at present are not capable of fully replicating human decision-making processes.

The notion of production systems has considerable history and is led by research in the area of human problem solving by Allen Newell and Herb Simon (1972). They viewed production systems as a paradigm for how the brain processes information. That is, given a particular set of circumstances, we trigger certain actions, decisions, or knowledge. Production systems are also called **Situation – Action Systems, Antecedent – Consequent, and Rule-Based Systems, Inference Systems,** or simply productions.

Early developments were inherently tied to the notion of a symbol on the left side generating a symbol, or group of symbols, on the right side, for example, $A \geq BC$. In 1943, Emil Post introduced the system in a famous paper, "Formal Reductions of the General Combinatorial Decision Problem." [1]

Formally speaking, a **Post Tag Machine** is a **finite state machine** that consists of a tape that is essentially a *first in first out* (FIFO) *queue* of unbounded length, such that, in each transition, the machine (1) reads the symbol at the head of the queue, (2) deletes a fixed number of symbols from the head, and (3) appends a pre-assigned symbol-string substitution string to the deleted symbol.

Alphabet: {x, y, z, H}

Production rules:

$x \rightarrow zzyxH$

$y \rightarrow zzx$

$z \rightarrow zz$

$H \rightarrow halt$

The basic idea of a **Post Production System** is to read the first symbol, delete a fixed number of symbols from the head of the queue, and append the substitution string for the deleted symbol to the end of the queue. We will be deleting two symbols; our case is a 2-tag system.

Later, in 1957, Noam Chomsky [2] reintroduced production systems as a series of rewrite rules that can be used as transformation rules for representing formal grammars in natural language systems (See Section 13.3).

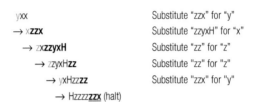

Initial word: yxx

yxx	Substitute "zzx" for "y"
→ x**zzx**	Substitute "zzyxH" for "x"
→ zx**zzyxH**	Substitute "zz" for "z"
→ zzyxH**zz**	Substitute "zz" for "z"
→ yxHz**zzz**	Substitute "zzx" for "y"
→ Hzzzz**zzx** (halt)	

Figure 7.1
Example of a Post Production System

Production systems are very appealing and attractive to AI researchers from a number of perspectives:

- *As a powerful form of knowledge representation*. They are very enticing as a model for how humans think about the world—either formally or informally. Although any attempt to build complete systems with regard to a particular human knowledge domain either will be too detailed (for the purpose of representing what truly goes on in an expert's head), or will fall short of telling the entire truth by being too simplistic. Production systems can be conveniently used to represent decisions and, consequently, action(s).

> *Production systems, akin to Post Production Systems, can, in their full generality, be demonstrated to be the equivalent of a Universal Turing Machine. Any working computer program (in any computer language) can, theoretically, be translated to one that performs on a Turing Machine.*

- *As a bridge connecting AI research to expert systems while embodying strong AI methods*. Production systems are a very natural means of expression for conveying knowledge, for expressing the major rules of a problem domain, and for building an expert system.

- *As a way of presenting heuristics and as a model for human behavior*. As we've emphasized throughout this text, humans operate by heuristics. Unlike computers, humans are not capable of consistently executing formal algorithms (recall the notion of the Human Window presented in Chapter 6, "Knowledge Representation") but are very comfortable in developing and employing heuristics. Production systems are an excellent way to represent heuristics and therefore serve as a model for human behavior.

- *As excellent models for pattern matching and situation – action scenarios*. The satisfying of conditions acts as a trigger for deciding what action(s) to take. This is a very natural way to represent a wide range of human and natural situations. Rules can range from being very simple, straightforward, general, and clear, to more complex and very domain specific.

7.1.1 Strong Methods vs. Weak Methods

The dichotomy between the *strong* and *weak* approaches to AI research was presented in Chapter 1, "Overview of Artificial Intelligence." The main point was that strong AI methods rely on domain-specific knowledge that has been accumulated, organized, refined, and employed to obtain working systems that can be helpful to mankind. A good example is computer chess: despite the apparent strength of the top programs today, most of the success in the discipline has not been achieved by strong AI methods. Strong AI methods would involve the accumulation of all the

Strong AI is akin to the limitations of memory and calculation power which humans must cope with by applying knowledge to play strong chess—looking at a relatively small number of positions and not very deeply, compared with computer programs.

relevant knowledge about chess (such as positional concepts, pawn structures, all that is known about openings, middle-games, and endings, etc.) and have it combined into one "knowledge soup," as Sowa has called it.[3] Strong AI methods would employ all the knowledge that can be accumulated for programs to produce strong, winning chess moves.

Instead, we have programs that seem to play on a par with the best human players in the world, but don't necessarily have a huge amount of chess-specific knowledge, at least with respect to Reddy's 50,000 or so estimated chess-specific concepts, which might be accumulated by age 50 by a human grandmaster.[4] That is because the programs employ what are called "weak" AI methods, which routinely search trees comprised of hundreds of billions of possible future board positions, in contrast to the 50–200 positions that humans will search in the quest to find the best move in a given position. The approach of logicians (see Chapter 5, "Logic in Artificial Intelligence"), through the framework of the predicate calculus, with complex symbol manipulation, would be considered a relatively weak AI method. In contrast, expert systems (Chapter 9, "Expert Systems") constructed from hundreds of domain-specific rules, are examples of strong AI methods. Other examples of weak methods are the neural approaches of Chapter 11, "Neural Networks," and the evolutionary approaches described in Chapter 12, "Search Inspired by Mother Nature." Which approach is to be preferred? Discerning the answer entails considering the fine balance between the demands for performance vs. competence. For example, it would seem that in the particularly "human" domain of natural language processing, strong AI methods would be preferred. Results with statistically-based approaches, which would seem like hybrids comprising both strong and weak AI methods, have proven particularly promising, however.[5]

7.2 ■ BASIC EXAMPLES

As described before, production systems are a very versatile way of representing the world about us. They follow the basic form we have discussed previously:

IF [condition] THEN [action]

A number of examples follow:

EXAMPLE 7.1: A SIMPLE RULE (LAW)

IF [you are operating a motor vehicle] THEN [don't drink alcohol]

EXAMPLE 7.2: ANOTHER RULE (LAW)

IF [you are driving a car AND you want to use your cell phone]

THEN [make sure you are using a hands-free device]

EXAMPLE 7.3: COMMON SENSE RULE / HEURISTICS

IF [driving AND heavy thunderstorm AND visibility is poor]

THEN [pull over]

EXAMPLE 7.4: MORE COMPLEX DOMAIN-SPECIFIC EXAMPLE

IF [Car does not start AND Battery is OK AND Starter is OK

AND there is gas]

THEN [Check Alternator]

Meta-knowledge is knowledge about a domain that is useful in specific situations where one might identify a problem. Following is an example using meta-knowledge to suggest a change in teaching strategy that would perhaps lead to better results.

EXAMPLE 7.5: USING META-KNOWLEDGE

Meta-Rule 1:

IF [student cannot answer a question]

THEN [try asking the student a more fundamental question which he/she

is more likely to be able to answer successfully]

Example of Meta-Rule 1:

Question 1: How many people are there in the world?

Answer: I have no idea.

Question 2: How many people live in China?

Answer: 1.3 Billion

Meta-Rule 2:

IF [student can answer the more fundamental question]

THEN [ask a follow-up question which might serve as a "bridge" to

answering the original question].

Example of Meta-Rule 2:

Question 3: So how many people would you guess there are in the world?

One of the earliest and most successful expert systems was MYCIN, developed by Buchanan and Shortliffe at Stanford University in 1976.[6] MYCIN tries to determine which urinary tract infection might be present in a patient. The following is one of the most often quoted excerpts from MYCIN:

IF [the stain of the organism is gramneg AND the morphology of the organism is rod AND the patient is a compromised host]

THEN [there is suggestive evidence (0.6) that the identity of the organism is pseudomonas]

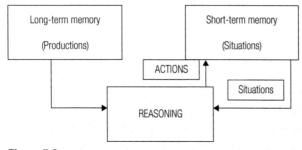

Figure 7.2
Production Systems Model.

MYCIN, developed by doctors and a computer scientist, comprises some 400 rules. This example illustrates its very deep domain-specific knowledge and is intended to illustrate MYCIN's conclusion (chain of reasoning) after evaluating the answers it has received to a series of questions. MYCIN is able to "explain" how it reached its conclusions by stating the facts it has accrued and its level of confidence (in this case .6) for the conclusion it has reached.

Recall that productions are a paradigm for how human problem-solving works, developed by Newell and Simon at Carnegie-Mellon University.[7] They argued that humans used productions stored in long-term memory when solving certain problems. When certain problem conditions or situations are recognized in short-term memory, a production or rule is said to be **fired** in long-term memory. The prescribed actions (or consequents) are then added to **short-term (working) memory**. As a result, new productions in long-term memory can be fired. This dynamic process is said to be a model for human reasoning, in that new information can be inferred from existing information. As we will soon see, given that a set of circumstances (antecedents, conditions) stored in short-term memory are matched, there could be more than one plausible action to take; rule-based systems are designed with the notion that there is a most appropriate action (decision) to take. This process is called **conflict resolution.** Short-term memory matches situations in long-term memory and then chooses the best matching rule to determine appropriate action(s). Figure 7.2 illustrates how this process works.

This leads us to the notion of Rule-Based Expert Systems. These are systems that combine productions (or rules) in a knowledge base, with domain-specific information contained in working memory, and an inference engine that can infer new information from existing information. Durkin[8] gives the following definition, from Expert Systems: Design and Development (p.168):

> A computer program that processes problem-specific information contained in the working memory with a set of rules contained in the knowledge-base, using an inference engine to infer new information.

Figure 7.3 illustrates the interaction between these three fundamental components of a rule-based or production system. Here, the **global database** is the equivalent of the short-term memory. It is the main data structure of **production systems** and consists of lists, small matrices, relational databases, or indexed file structures. It is a dynamic structure, which continually changes as a result of actions by production rules, and can be referred to as context or working memory. From a computer science perspective, it is the difference between RAM and hard disk or permanent memory. The knowledge base comprises production rules, and the control structure is the equivalent of the inference engine defined above.

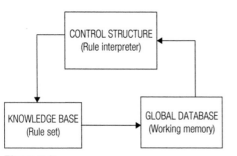

Figure 7.3
A production system with its three fundamental components: Knowledge Base, Global Database, and Control Structure.

7.3 ■ THE CARBUYER SYSTEM

We will now present a system (See Table 7.1) that provides a set of production rules to help us choose an appropriate car to buy, based on the most pertinent factors, such as CLASS (or body type/size), PRICE, whether the car is NEW or USED, the car's MILEAGE (if the car is used), and the AVGCMPG (the car's average combined miles per gallon). If the car is USED, then other typical factors would include the car's MILEAGE and the YEAR the car was manufactured.

We have tried to build this system to be as realistic as possible while developing a small model that is representative of the car buying decisions that are most applicable today. Probably the most significant factor in choosing a car at the time of this writing (May 2008) would be the car's CLASS, closely followed by the PRICE, followed by the AVGCMPG. By CLASS we mean one of the following: compact, subcompact, midsize, large, SUV, sports car, and so forth.

- ON_WM x Tests if a property x is in WM (working memory)
- PUT_ON WM x Puts property x in WM

We built the Car Buyer Production System by developing production rules based on what we know about car features that are important when making a buying decision. We have included only 32 cars in this model or toy system (we ask that readers not be offended if their favorite car model is missing).

Rule 1: IF [ON_WM MILEAGE = 0]

THEN [PUT_ON_WM_ **NEW**]

Rule 2: IF [ON_WM MILEAGE > 0]

THEN [PUT_ON_WM_ **USED**]

Rule 3: IF [ON_WM PRICE ≥ 30K]

THEN [PUT_ON_WM_ **LUXURY**]

Rule 4: IF [ON_WM PRICE ≥ 20K]
THEN [PUT_ON_WM_ **STANDARD**]

Rule 5: IF [ON_WM PRICE > 5K]
THEN [PUT_ON_WM_ **ECONOMY**]

Rule 6: IF [ON_WM **NEW**] **AND** [ON_WM 8cyl]

THEN [PUT_ON_WM **LUXURY**]

Rule 7: IF [ON_WM AVGCMPG ≥ 25]

THEN [PUT_ON_WM Excellent-MPG]

ELSEIF [ON_WM AVGCMPG > 16]

THEN [PUT_ON_WM Medium-MPG]

ELSEIF [ON WM AVGCMPG ≤ 16]

THEN [PUT_ON_WM Low-MPG]

Rule 8:   IF [ON_WM **LUXURY**]

THEN [PUT_ON_WM **SUV**] **AND** [PUT_ON_

WM_ **Cadillac**] AND [PUT_ON_WM **Lincoln**] AND

[PUT_ON WM **Mercedes**]

Rule 9:   IF [ON_WM **FOREIGN**]

THEN [PUT_ON_WM **Toyota**] **AND**

[PUT_ON_WM **Mercedes**] **AND** [PUT_ON_WM **Honda**]

AND [PUT_ON WM **Hyundai**]

Rule 10:   IF [ON_WM **NEW**] **AND** [ON_WM **SUB-COMPACT**]

THEN [PUT_ON_WM **Honda Civic**]

Rule 11:   IF [ON_WM **NEW**] **AND** [ON_WM **COMPACT**]

THEN [PUT_ON_ WM **Honda Civic**] **AND**

[PUT_ON_ WM **Ford Focus**]

Rule 12:   IF [ON_WM **NEW**] **AND** [ON_WM **MIDSIZE**]

AND [ON_WM **ECONOMY**]

THEN [PUT_ON_ WM **Hyundai**]

Rule 13:   IF [ON_WM **NEW**] **AND** ON_WM **MIDSIZE**]

AND [ON_WM **STANDARD**]

THEN [PUT_ON_WM **Toyota**] **AND**

[PUT_ON_WM **Chevrolet**]

Rule 14:   IF [ON_WM **NEW**] **AND** [ON_WM **MIDSIZE**]

AND [ON_WM **LUXURY**]

THEN [PUT_ON_WM **Cadillac**] **AND**

[PUT_ON_WM **Lincoln**]

Rule 15:   IF [ON_WM **USED**] **AND** [ON_WM **LARGE**]

THEN [PUT_ON_ WM **Lincoln**] **AND**

[PUT_ON_ WM **Cadillac**] **AND**

[PUT_ON_ WM **Ford**]

Rule 16:   IF [ON_ WM **USED**] **AND** [ON_WM SUV]

THEN [PUT_ON_ **WM Toyota**] **AND**

[PUT_ON_ WM **Ford**] **AND**

[PUT_ON_ WM **Chevrolet**] **AND**

[PUT_ON_ WM **Cadillac**] **AND**

[PUT_ON_ WM **Hyundai**]

Rule 17:   IF [ON_ WM **USED**] **AND** [ON_WM **Sub-Compact**]

THEN [PUT_ON_ WM **Chevrolet**] **AND**

[PUT_ON_ WM **Ford**]

Rule 18:   IF [ON_WM **USED**] **AND** [ON_WM **Compact**]

THEN [PUT_ON_ WM **Toyota**] **AND**

[PUT_ON_ WM **Hyundai**]

Rule 19:   IF [ON_ WM **USED**] **AND** [ON_ WM **Midsize**]

THEN [PUT_ON_ WM **Honda**] **AND**

[PUT_ON_ WM **Cadillac**]

Rule 20:   IF [ON_ WM **USED**] **AND** [ON_ WM **Sports/Conv**]

AND [ON_WM_Price $\geq$ **$20K**]

THEN [PUT_ ON WM **LUXURY**] **AND**

[PUT_ON_ WM **Mercedes**]

These 20 rules cover all of the 32 cars in our database, at least in terms of being possible candidates for consideration. Although in some cases they will not result in the choice of a single vehicle, they will always succeed in reducing the database of cars to a much smaller list. Now we will present the rule interpreter, also known as the **control system** (or structure), which will systematically work through the rules to identify the car(s) that would best match the desired features. The control system works as follows:

1. Scan the production rules from first to last for those that have been activated or deemed applicable, i.e., those whose IF condition evaluates to TRUE. The result of this step is a list of active rules (which could also be the null or empty list).

2. If more than one rule is applicable (active), then deactivate (remove from working memory) those rules which would duplicate characteristics already stored on WM. This prevents redundancy of features on WM.

3. Fire the LONGEST ACTIVE production rule (in terms of "IF conditions). If there are no applicable rules, Exit the loop. The best match for the desired vehicle(s) will be the item at the top of WM.

4. Turn the IF part of all production rules to FALSE and go to Control Statement (1). This enables the control structure to iterate until a best solution is found.

There are two clearly distinct purposes for the control system. One purpose is to examine working memory (our database) to *answer questions* such as: "What used economy cars are available?" or "What new luxury cars are available?" **Rule 2** and **Rule 5** would answer the question about what used **Economy** cars are available. **Rule 6** would tell which **New Luxury** cars are available. The second purpose of the control system is to *add knowledge* about a possible car sought in the database by making logical inferences through the process of firing production rules which might apply. For example, **Rule 7** tells us that **Luxury** cars in our database are **SUVs, Cadillac, Lincoln,** and **Mercedes. Rule 3** adds further knowledge that Luxury cars cost over $30,000. **Rule 13** adds further specifications in that if we want a **New, Midsize, Luxury** car then Cadillac and Lincoln are our possible choices. Finally, if we are looking for a **USED Luxury** car then **Rule 20** makes the exception (a luxury car for less than $30,000) and offers us the **Mercedes Sports Convertible.** At any point in this process, the working memory can be examined to list the original data that has been obtained from rule matches and inferences.

The iterative nature of the control system is noteworthy. It entails a four-step process, which is repeated until no more matching rules can be found (fired). Step 3 is where exit from the loop structure can conveniently occur with the resulting best match left at the top of working memory. Hence, we summarize that the first phase of the iterative process performs pattern-matching to identify candidate rules, whereas the second phase performs conflict resolution to identify the best matching rules. The purpose of the third phase is to decide which car(s) are the best candidates for the desired features and then to provide action, which, in this case, means decisions.

Let us now explore how the system might work. Let us suppose that we are searching for a MIDSIZE car that is NEW or USED and costs under $20K. Let us iteratively run through the rules and see which can apply:

Clearly **Rule 5** applies, as does **Rule 12** and **Rule 19**.

For the reader, we note that this puts the following cars on WM:

Rule 12 → Hyundai; Rule 19 → Honda, Cadillac

Gas prices fluctuate; although they returned to more stable levels in 2010, it is not inconceivable that at any time they could again reach the $4/gallon level, or perhaps soar even higher.

It is noteworthy that the **LUXURY** car, **Cadillac,** is on the same list with the **ECONOMY** cars, **Hyundai** and **Honda.** This demonstrates that automobile manufacturers must adjust to changing economic conditions. In the United States, there was, a few years ago, a sharp rise in gasoline prices to well over $4 per gallon. This means that a major consideration for automobile purchases is AVGCMPG.

We have added **Rule 7** to represent this situation where the goal is high **AVGCMP.** As we can see, **Rule 7** results in the choice of the NEW (2008) Hyundai Elantra ($16K, 28 AVGCMPG), the Honda 2003 Accord V6 ($11K, 24 AVGCMPG), and Honda 2003 Accord V4 ($15K, 28 AVGCMPG).

For a difference of only $1000 in price, (and given that the three cars are all foreign) it seems that the system should be able to choose the new Hyundai Elantra at only $16K. The fact that the 2003 Honda V4 has 111K miles makes the decision easy for humans. How does this logical choice get represented in the computer? **Rule 12**, which is longer than **Rule 19**, turns out to be a tie-breaker on the grounds of the conflict resolution strategy (step 3 of our control system), which favors the longest active rule.

7.3.1 Advantages of Production Systems

As we have seen, production systems can be a very desirable way for developing an expert system and for expressing the rules in a specific domain. If we want to be very specific, then we just add many specific rules. If we want to be general, then we do not develop too many rules that are

Table 7.1
The CarBuyer database.

#	BRAND	CATEGORY	New/Used	PRICE ($K)	US?	AVGCMPG	MILE (K)	Doors	Engine	Year	Car Chosen
1	Cadillac	Midsize	new	31	US	20	0	4	3.6L 6cyl	2008	Cadillac CTS
2	Lincoln	Midsize	new	33	US	22	0	4	3.5L 6cyl	2008	Lincoln MKZ
3	Mercedes	Sports/Conv	new	96	Foreign	14	0	2	5.5L 8cyl	2009	Mercedes-Benz SL-Class
4	Chevrolet	Midsize	new	23	US	25	0	4	2.4L 4cyl gas/electric hybrid	2008	Chevrolet Malibu Hybrid
5	Honda	Sub-Comp	new	18	Foreign	29	0	4	1.8L 4cyl	2008	Honda Civic
6	Toyota	Midsize	new	26	Foreign	34	0	4	2.4L 4cyl gas/electric hybrid	2009	Toyota Camry Hybrid
7	Ford	Compact	new	17	US	28	0	2	2.0L 4cyl	2008	Ford Focus
8	Honda	Sub-Comp	new	21	Foreign	29	0	2	2.0L 4cyl	2008	Honda Civic
9	Honda	Compact	new	27	Foreign	45	0	4	4.0L 4cy	2008	Honda Civic Hybrid
10	Hyundai	Midsize	new	16	Foreign	28	0	4	2.0L 4cyl	2008	Hyundai Elantra
11	Cadillac	SUV	new	56	US	14	0	4	6.2L 8cyl	2008	Cadillac Escalade
12	Toyota	SUV	new	49	Foreign	14	0	4	5.7L 8cyl	2008	Toyota Sequoia
13	Mercedes	SUV	new	53	Foreign	15	0	4	5.5L 8cyl	2008	Mercedes-Benz M-Class
14	Chevrolet	Sports/Con	used	18	US	20	83	2	8cyl	2000	Chevrolet Camaro Z28 Convertible
15	Mercedes	Sports/Conv	used	20	Foreign	24	66	2	4cyl	2003	Mercedes-Benz SLK230 Convertible
16	Chevrolet	Sports	used	14	US	21	42	2	8cyl	2002	Chevrolet Camaro Z28 Coupe
17	Ford	Sports	used	13	US	20	23	2	8cyl	2004	Ford Mustang GT Coupe
18	Honda	Midsize	used	11	Foreign	24	60	2	6cyl	2003	Honda Accord EX V6 Coupe
19	Honda	Midsize	used	15	Foreign	28	111	4	4cyl	2003	Honda Accord EX Sedan
20	Lincoln	Large	used	11	US	14	97	4	8cyl	2002	Lincoln Continental
21	Lincoln	Large	used	13	US	15	45	4	8cyl	2002	Lincoln LS V8
22	Toyota	Compact	used	16	Foreign	24	102	4	6cyl	2003	Toyota Avalon XLS
23	Toyota	Compact	used	15	Foreign	24	66	2	6cyl	2004	Toyota Solara
24	Toyota	SUV	Used	17	Foreign	19	36	4	6cyl	2004	Toyota 4Runner SR5
25	Ford	SUV	used	11	US	25	29	4	6cyl	2003	Ford Escape XLT
26	Ford	Large	used	9	US	20	59	4	8cyl	2004	Ford Crown Victoria LX
27	Ford	Sub-Comp	used	17	US	20	51	2	8cyl	2003	Ford Mustang GT
28	Chevrolet	SUV	used	15	US	16	45	2	6cyl	2004	Chevrolet Blazer
29	Cadillac	SUV	used	18	US	14	57	4	8cyl	2003	Cadillac Escalade AWD
30	Cadillac	Large	used	10	US	21	65	4	8cyl	2004	Cadillac De Ville
31	Cadillac	Midsize	used	15	US	20	50	2	8cyl	2001	Cadillac Eldorado ESC
32	Hyundai	SUV	Used	19	Foreign	23	40	4	6cyl	2005	Hyundai Tucson 4x4
33	Hyundai	Compact	used	7	Foreign	28	90	4	4cyl	2001	Hyundai Elantra GLS Sedan

overly specific. In addition, the rules themselves can all be inclusive or exclusive, as, for example, Rule 7, which breaks down all cars that could be purchased into three possible price categories. This is achieved by the multi-clause nested IF – THEN – ELSEIF structure.

Again, we stress that the system we have developed is just a small model, whereas a real system might have thousands of cars in its database and could contain several hundred rules. If possible, we wish to avoid the "diminishing returns effect," whereby a small percentage of the rules handle most of the problem space, but more and more rules must be added to handle "special cases." In building expert systems, it is common for 10% of the rules to cover 90% of the problem space, and then the other 90% of the rules must handle exceptional cases.

Summarizing the advantages of production systems:

1. *Ease of expression* – production systems are a natural way for people (human domain-specialists or experts) to express themselves and to represent their great amounts of knowledge.

2. *Intuitive in nature* – the IF – THEN (or antecedent – consequent) nature of production systems is a very intuitive way for humans to express themselves. such systems are a sound paradigm for representing the thinking and decision-making processes by which human experts operate.

3. *Simplicity* – Production rules are very easy to develop and modify. They are also easy to understand (transparent) and consistent with English (or natural) language forms of expression.

4. *Modularity and modifiability* – We have seen how easy it is to build a production system. A production system is a superb example of how knowledge is neatly and distinctly separated from control. Knowledge can easily be modified; it can be expanded, reorganized, or deleted as necessary, and is said to possess **modularity**. This is a very distinct aspect of production systems, expert systems, and AI in general; it is sometimes called "separation of concerns." Furthermore, it is important that, as knowledge is added to the system, rules are easily reviewed and considered in terms of what has or has not been "covered."

5. *Knowledge Intensive* – The separation of concerns addressed above is **knowledge intensive**; it allows the knowledge engineer to focus on developing production rules and to concentrate on the rules rather than to become distracted by the operational aspects of the control structure. It becomes cumbersome if the system developer must reconsider how the control structure works each time a rule is added. The ease of expression also facilitates development of clusters of rules, which can systematically cover a problem space.

■7.4■ PRODUCTION SYSTEMS AND INFERENCE METHODS

The overall purpose of production systems as a form of knowledge representation and as a method of embodying heuristics is to facilitate the decision-making process. As we have already described, situations will often arise when more than one rule could be applicable unless an a priori tie-breaking system has been decided on. That tie-breaking system is called conflict resolution and is discussed in the next section. During the history of production systems, two main approaches to traversing rules have been developed and employed for the purpose of problem solving. One is a system of reasoning called forward chaining and the other **backward chaining**.

These are explored in Sections 7.4.2 and 7.4.3 to follow.

HUMAN INTEREST NOTES

HERB SIMON

Herb Simon (1916 – 2001). Perhaps the most significant reason a student of artificial intelligence would be interested in the work of Herbert Simon and his close associate, Allen Newell, is because these two men represented the most human side of the field. They made tremendous contributions to the field, but always maintained the Carnegie-Mellon University perspective, which has had a distinct cognitive science slant—hence, strong AI, as discussed in Chapter 6, and earlier in this chapter.

Dr. Simon won the Nobel Prize in Economics in 1978, "for his pioneering research into the decision-making process with economic organizations," and the ACM's Turing Award in 1975 jointly with his PhD student Allen Newell, for making "basic contributions to artificial intelligence, the psychology of human cognition, and list processing." He also won the National Medal of Science (1986) and the American Psychological Association's Award for Outstanding Lifetime Contributions to Psychology (1993). He joined the Psychology Department at CMU in 1949, where he remained until his death in 2001. He is considered to be one of the founding fathers of the fields of both cognitive psychology and artificial intelligence. Simon and Newell were two of the main proponents of the pattern-based, heuristic approach to problem-solving and developing models for human thinking.

He attained The Academy Medal of Honor for his theory of bounded rationality, wherein the notion is simply that people make rational decisions based on the limitations of their knowledge or analytical abilities rather than seeking the optimal choice/commodity at the best price. People make the choice(s) that "satisfices" (a Simon word), or, is good enough. (*http://www.postgazette.com/regionstate/20001016simon2.asp*)

Writes Jones (1999; see first entry, Selected References, below):

Bounded rationality asserts that decision makers are intendedly rational; that is, they are goal oriented and adaptive, but because of human cognitive and emotional architecture, they sometimes fail, occasionally in important decisions . . . .

Although most political scientists are aware of Simon's contributions, many fail to appreciate that bounded rationality was the first, and because of its ripple effects in so many disciplines, the most important idea (even academic school of thought) that political science has ever exported.

The broadness and deep respect for the quality of his contributions is further represented by the following statement, issued by Royal Academy of Sciences in 1978:

Herbert A. Simon's scientific output goes far beyond the disciplines in which he has held professorships: political science, administration, psychology and information sciences. He has made contributions in the fields of science theory, applied mathematics, statistics, operations research, economics and business and public administration (and), in all areas in which he has conducted research, Simon has had something of importance to say.

– Official Nobel Prize announcement of the Royal Academy of Sciences in Sweden.

The CMU Computer Science Department tribute to Professor Simon included the following words:

> The thread of continuity through all of his work was his interest in human decision-making and problem-solving processes and the implications of these processes for social institutions. He made extensive use of the computer as tool for both simulating human thinking and augmenting it with artificial intelligence.

(*http://www.cs.cmu.edu/simon/bio. html*).

Simon studied social sciences and mathematics at the University of Chicago, earning a BA in 1936 and a PhD in Political Science in 1943. As Simon states in his autobiography:

> . . . the descriptive study of organizational decision-making continued as my main occupation. … Our work led us to feel increasingly the need for a more adequate theory of human problem-solving if we were to understand decisions. Allen Newell, whom I had met at the Rand Corporation in 1952, held similar views.

(*http://nobelprize.org/nobel_ prizes/economics/laureates/1978/ simon-autobio.html*)

Around 1954 Newell and Simon conceived the idea "that the right way to study problem-solving was to simulate it with computer programs" (ibid.).

Gradually, computer simulation of human cognition became his central research interest for the rest of his life.

In an interview in 2000 with Byron Spice, Simon was asked how computers will continue to shape the world. His response was that, in essence, although computers will embody great power, the outcomes of how this power is embraced and used will continue to be up to people. Stating …

> So we're going to have to think about how you group people up who find exciting things to do when there's nothing that has to be done. We're dangerously close to that for half our society right now. But here again, you see, technology may create a condition, but the questions are what do we do about ourselves. We better understand ourselves pretty clearly and we better find ways to like ourselves…

(*http://www.post-gazette.com/ regionstate/20001016simon2.asp*)

Selected References

Herb Simon published over 1000 papers. Only a small sample is represented below.

Jones, B. D. 1999. "Bounded rationality" *Annual Review of Political Science* 2:297–321.

Political Science

Simon, H. 1957. "A behavioral model of rational choice." In *Models of Man, Social and Rational: Mathematical Essays on Rational Human Behavior in a Social Setting.* New York, NY: Wiley.

Simon, H. 1990. A mechanism for social selection and successful altruism. *Science* 250 (4988):1665–8.

Simon, H. 1991. "Bounded rationality and organizational learning." *Organization Science* 2(1):125–134.

Psychology

Zhu, X., and Simon, H. A. 1987. "Learning mathematics from examples and by doing." *Cognition and Instruction* 4:137–166.

Larkin, J. H., and Simon, H. A. 1987."Why a diagram is (sometimes) worth 10,000 words." *Cognitive Science* 11:65–100.

Langley, P., Simon, H. A., Bradshaw, G. L., and Zytkow, J. M. 1987. *Scientific discovery: Computational explorations of the creative processes*. Cambridge, MA: The MIT Press.

Qin, Y., and Simon, H. A. 1990. "Laboratory replication of scientific discovery processes." *Cognitive Science* 14: 281–312.

Kaplan, C., and Simon, H. A. 1990. "In search of insight." *Cognitive Psychology* 22:374–419.

Vera, A. H., and Simon, H. A. 1993. "Situated action: A symbolic interpretation." *Cognitive Science* 17:7–48.

Richman, H. B., Staszewski, J. J., and Simon, H. A. 1995. "Simulation of expert memory using EPAM IV." *Psychological Review* 102(2):305–330.

Computer Science and AI

Simon, H. A. 1973. "The structure of ill-structured problems." *Artificial Intelligence* 4:181–202.

Newell, A., and Simon, H. A. 1972. *Human problem solving*. Englewood Cliffs, NJ: Prentice-Hall.

Baylor, G. W., and Simon, H. A. 1966. "A chess mating combinations program." *Proceedings of the 1966 Spring Joint Computer Conference* 28:431–447.

Simon, H. A. 1963. "Experiments with a heuristic compiler." *Journal of the Association for Computing Machinery* 10:493–506.

Newell, A., and Simon, H. A. 1961. "GPS: A program that simulates human thought". In *Lernende automaten*, ed. H. Billings, 109–124. Munchen: R. Oldenbourg.

Newell, A., Shaw, J. C., and Simon, H. A. 1958. "Chess-playing programs and the problem of complexity." *IBM Journal of Research and Development* 2:320–335.

Newell, A., and Simon, H. A. 1956. "The logic theory machine." *IRE Transactions on Information Theory* IT-2(3):61–79.

Scientific Discovery

Simon, H. A. 1996. *The Sciences of the Artificial*, 3rd ed. Cambridge, MA: The MIT Press.

Okada, T., and Simon, H. A. 1995. "Collaborative discovery in a scientific domain." In *Proceedings of the 17th Annual Conference of the Cognitive Science Society*, ed.J. D. Moore and J. F. Lehman, 340–345. Hillsdale, NJ: Erlbaum.

Shen, W., and Simon, H. A. (1993). "Fitness requirements for scientific theories containing recursive theoretical terms." *British Journal for the Philosophy of Science*, 44:641–652.

Kulkarni, D., and Simon, H. A. 1988. "The processes of scientific discovery: The strategy of experimentation." *Cognitive Science* 12:139–176.

Langley, P., Simon, H. A., Bradshaw, G. L., and Zytkow, J. M. 1987. *Scientific discovery: Computational explorations of the creative processes*. Cambridge, MA: The MIT Press.

Simon, H. A., and Kotovsky, K. 1963. "Human acquisition of concepts for sequential patterns". *Psychological Review* 70:534–546.

Web References

http://www.cs.cmu.edu/simon/bio.html

http://www.princeton.edu/~smeunier/JonesBounded1.pdf

http://nobelprize.org/nobel_prizes/economics/laureates/1978/simon-autobio.html

http://www.post-gazette.com/regionstate/20001016simon2.asp November 3, 2010

7.4.1 ■ Conflict Resolution

As we have seen, when several rules are candidates for matching the antecedent [If] conditions of a production, then there must be a strategy for choosing the most appropriate rule among them. This is called conflict resolution, and it can be accomplished several ways.

This topic will also be addressed in Chapter 16, "Advanced Computer Games," and the work of Arthur Samuel on the game of checkers. There we will introduce Samuel's notions of forgetting and refreshing. Forgetting refers to the aging or lack of use of a heuristic, whereas refreshing gives heuristics added importance, if they have recently been used, by dividing their age (time unused) by two.

Conflict Resolution Strategies:

1. **Fire the first rule that matches the contents of memory.**

   Example:

   Rule 1: If I have a significant amount of money I go out to eat.

   Rule 2: If I have limited funds, then I stay home and cook dinner.

   Using the conflict resolution rule above, one would go out to dinner if one had funds. It could turn out that the real thrust is that a person might have adequate funds to go out to eat but doesn't have the time! And that person is perhaps also a poor cook. So the resolution of the conflict might be to go out to eat—but for fast food nearby, which was not specified by Rule 1. To resolve such a conflict, more rules and more specific rules could be needed.

2. **Fire the rule with the highest priority.**

   Rules can be assigned priorities. That is, some rules are perhaps deemed more important than others. Clearly, in our CarBuyer system, the rules related to the PRICE of the car are more important than the CATEGORY or whether the car is NEW or USED. The reason is that you cannot buy what you cannot afford. That is why those rules have been put at the top of the list, although the list is not technically prioritized. We have tried to construct the list of rules in a way that would be representative of buyers' priorities. You might ask, then why is NEW or USED at the top of the list? That is because we believe the decision (NEW or USED) is the first one that affects a buyers' initial searches. Later, as buyers become more knowledgeable in their search processes, and as they learn what kinds of vehicles are available at what prices, buyers could indeed decide that price is the most important factor. In addition, the choice of NEW or USED quickly splits the list into two conveniently sized lists of 12 and 20 cars, respectively!

3. **Fire the most specific rule.**

   If two rules essentially cover the same set of possibilities, it is likely that the more specific rule will represent the case we are looking for. That is, the more specific rule contains more information than the more general one. Earlier we saw that **Rule 12** was "resolved" over **Rule 19**, because it was the more specific rule. The additional information contained in this rule was that an **Economy** car (that is, one which costs less than $20K) was desirable. It is not coincidental that the longest rule will almost always be the most specific rule.

4. **Fire the most recently used rule.**

   This approach is called refreshing, and it is a logical way of adding significance to concepts that have been used before and have been proven valuable. For a depth first search, as used in chess and checkers, this strategy encourages exploration of paths with greatest activity.

5. **Fire the most recently added rule.**

   This **cycling** approach to heuristics is particularly suitable for dynamic knowledge bases which can be quickly changing. Its purpose is to give a fair chance to heuristics that might otherwise not be used. An example of applying this conflict resolution rule would again be production **Rule 7** in the CarBuyer system, which was actually added only after the 19 other rules had been developed. The reason was to enhance the importance of the concept of a car's AVGCMPG, given the recent economic developments. As it turned out, that rule was quickly applied and was the deciding factor in the choice of a car with the appropriate desired features.

6. **Don't fire a rule that has already fired.**

   This rule prevents looping (redundancy) and means that only new rules will be fired and put on working memory.

Conflict resolution strategies enable control over which rules will fire. There could be situations wherein certain heuristics will be favored over others. For this purpose, conflict resolution strategies can be designed to facilitate certain groups or clusters of heuristics to fire. This encourages experimentation and the study of the process behind certain results.

7.4.2 Forward Chaining

Forward chaining refers to a very natural form of inference (thinking) that humans perform regularly. We accumulate facts that enable us to reason and reach a conclusion. Not all the facts that are accumulated will contribute to our conclusion. Some might be irrelevant while others could be part of a line of reasoning that might lead to certain conclusions. Another term for forward chaining is **fanning in**.

Examples of Forward Chaining

EXAMPLE 7.6

1. I am feeling weak

2. I have a head cold

3. I have a fever

Conclusion: Weakness, having a cold, and fever are all indicative of flu-like symptoms.

Remedy: Rest in bed, drink plenty of fluids, take aspirin or Tylenol.

EXAMPLE 7.7

1. The dog got into the garbage and made a mess.

2. We came home and saw the mess in the kitchen.

3. There was an unpleasant smell emanating from the basement.

4. We found the dog lying on the floor in the basement not far from the smell in the basement.

Conclusion: The dog got sick from what it ate in the garbage.
The conclusion seems very viable based on the facts.

EXAMPLE 7.8

1. **THE CAR WILL NOT START**

> Then **Check the Battery**

> If the Headlights work

>> Then Conclude *Battery is OK*

> **Check the Starter**

> If Car turns over

>> Then Conclude *Starter is OK*

Check the Alternator

If Alternator is connected and operational

> Then Conclude *Alternator is OK*

Check Fuel Pump

> If Pump is Operational

>> Then **Check Fuel Line**

> If Fuel Line is damaged

>> Then *Replace Fuel Line*

Else Seek Professional Help

The above is a standard protocol for trying to understand why a car might not be starting properly, or might be starting and then stalling. We see how each fact leads to a logical conclusion and a logical follow up. In situations involving starting problems, it is normal to **check the battery**, check the starter, check the alternator, and finally to check the fuel pump. To a mechanic there is also a hierarchical logic as to which questions are asked first. In other words, we do not first consider a possible failure in the alternator or even the starter. The most common problem associated with cars not starting is the battery. Once we have established that a car's battery is sufficiently charged, we consider a possible failure in the car's starter. Only when we know that the battery and starter are properly functioning do we consider that the alternator is perhaps not functioning properly. Finally, if we have established that the battery, starter, and alternator are not at fault, then we consider the fuel pump. Again, in terms of probability, the fuel pump is the least likely of these parts to be responsible for this kind of problem.

Figure 7.4 illustrates the reasoning that is being used in forward chaining. Here we see evidence E1 and E2 supporting hypothesis H1, evidence E3 and E4 supporting hypothesis H2, and evidence E5 and E6 supporting hypothesis H3.

Essentially, forward chaining works by accumulating data (evidence, facts) and then can lead to a hypothesis (or several hypotheses) and subsequently could lead to one or more conclusions. Forward chaining is particularly suitable for problems requiring planning, monitoring, control, and interpretation. Each of these kinds of problems involves making decisions based on the accumulation of a significant amount of data.

7.4.3 Backward Chaining

Backward chaining is another standard way of drawing inferences with production systems. Backward chaining retraces events from a known goal or outcome and tries to ascertain which facts/knowledge/events (evidence) led to the result.

Backward chaining is often used to diagnose, analyze, troubleshoot or to prove some goal or hypothesis by working backward through the available evidence and facts that might be suggestive of some condition.

When backward chaining is performed, we are said to be fanning out from the goal or conclusion to the supporting facts or evidence. Figures 7.5a, 7.5b, and 7.5c illustrate this.

$$H1 \leftarrow E1$$
$$H1 \leftarrow E2 \leftarrow E3$$

Here we see hypothesis H1 supported by evidence E1; hypothesis H1 is also supported by evidence E2 which itself is supported by evidence E3.

$$H2 \leftarrow E1$$
$$H2 \leftarrow E4$$
$$H2 \leftarrow E5$$

Here hypothesis H2 is supported by evidence E; evidence E4 also supports H2, as does evidence E5.

$$H3 \leftarrow E2$$
$$\leftarrow E5 \leftarrow E6 \leftarrow E7$$

Here, H3 has four pieces of evidence: E2, E5, E6, and E7.

A typical example would be trying to solve a crime mystery. We know that a certain criminal event has occurred and try to work backward, employing all the facts and evidence to solve the mystery. For example, if a bank robbery has occurred, we try to obtain as much evidence as possible surrounding the robbery.

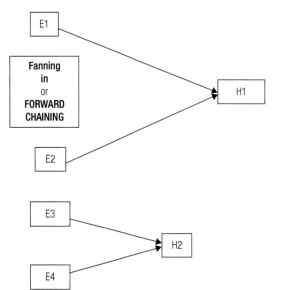

Figure 7.4
Forward Chaining or fanning in.

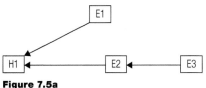

Figure 7.5a
Fanning out with backward chaining.

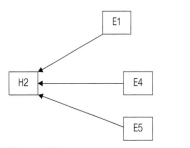

Figure 7.5b
Fanning out; hypothesis H2 is supported by each of evidence E1, E4, and E5.

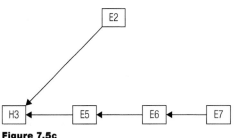

Figure 7.5c
Backward chaining with linked evidence E5, E6, E7.

Examples of Backward Chaining

EXAMPLE 7.9: HEART ATTACKS

Fact: A person has had a heart attack.

E1: Smoking causes hardening of the arteries.

E2: Hardening of the arteries will result in a heart attack.

E3: High cholesterol is likely to be conducive to a heart attack.

This example essentially matches pattern 1 in Figure 7.5a.

$H1 \leftarrow E3$

$E1 \rightarrow E2$

If the person who had a heart attack was a smoker and had high cholesterol, Then it was very plausible that these factors were causes of the heart attack.

EXAMPLE 7.10: CAR REPAIR

Facts:

1. One day I backed into a tree with my car; no apparent damage.

2. A few days later I noticed that my indicator lights for braking and right hand turns were not working.

Analysis:

1. One possibility was that it was the flashers—which are the electrical device under the dashboard that controls turning and breaking indicators in a car.

2. Then apply "backward chaining" Fact 1 to the indicator lights. Indeed, the problem was just that some bulbs were damaged from the impact of hitting the tree.

Summary:

Flashers in a car will break after about 100,000 miles of driving or a number of years. It was logical to "causally" connect the failure of the indicator lights (by backward chaining) to hitting the tree a few days earlier. Failure of the flashers was a much less likely event.

EXAMPLE 7.11: RETROGRADE ANALYSIS

There is a whole field of logic that is used to analyze the history of a chess position. The form of analysis tries to answer questions such as "what piece fell off the board on a particular square" or "how did the pawn get to a certain square on the chessboard?" By performing a logical historical (retrograde or backward) analysis of what could have occurred, based on at least a knowledge of the rules of the game in certain peculiar positions, such questions can be answered. The person most associated with the field of retrograde analysis in chess is Professor Raymond Smullyen, logician, mathematician, and philosopher. Again, retrograde analysis in chess is performed by working backward from an outcome (a position) through a database of facts known about the position and the game of chess.

EXAMPLE 7.12: ACCIDENT ANALYSIS

Whenever a major catastrophic event, such as a plane crash or railroad accident occurs, there will be a careful reconstruction of the events that occurred leading up to the accident. The Air or Rail Safety Transportation Board will send personnel who are expert analysts of such scenes. These experts will know everything that is important to know about the vehicles involved in the accident, everything about the accident scene, as well as the relevant safety factors. They will also know how and what to study and investigate in terms of developing an understanding of the events leading up to the accident and for building a causal analysis. Again, this is an example of backward chaining through the evidence and facts to try to reach a conclusion about what has happened.

EXAMPLE 7.13: RECOVERING A LOST ITEM

Almost all of us have, on occasion, lost or misplaced something of value; perhaps a wallet, purse, or keys. Usually, the only way to recover something that has been lost or misplaced is to work backwards.

Perhaps you have had an experience similar to this: It's a Sunday and you are casually dressed in your comfy sweats. You have stopped to eat and relax a bit at a restaurant in the course of doing some window shopping and a couple of errands, and you stop at a bank ATM; when you return to where your car is parked, you reach into your pocket and can't find your car keys—nor your house keys! You must retrace your steps, and you must also backtrack in your mind, considering where you had been, on which side of the street you had walked, and other details, until . . . lucky you! You find your keys on the counter at the bank ATM—the last place you had stopped. In fact, in the course of backtracking, you consider several specific details, or facts, such as (1) because you're wearing sweat pants, your keys had been in the same pocket with your wallet; (2) you clearly remember taking your keys out of your pocket every time you retrieved your wallet. (3) You have not made any purchases, so you used your wallet at the restaurant and (4) at the bank; it was Sunday, so the bank lobby was closed and you had to retrieve your ATM card so you could use the ATM; (5) you remember taking your keys out of your pocket at that time.

Clearly, this is an example of backward chaining. An event happens and we try to figure out why and how it happened. The more detail we can recall, as we piece facts together, the greater the chance we have of recovering what we have misplaced.

It seems worth mentioning that if the keys been taken by someone, what would be your chances of recovering them? Well, there are two security matters that would probably have protected me (but not without some inconvenience and uncertainty) – one is that most banks today will have security cameras, and secondly, to get inside a bank on a Sunday (note the evidence given) one would need an ATM card to open the door.

In considering the above possibilities I did learn something. There are occasions when one visits the bank in off hours when another person who also uses that bank ATM arrives at nearly the same time. If you use your ATM card and let that person in too, then you are in effect lowering bank security, and had something peculiar happened, that ATM card would be an important piece of evidence.

Human Interest Notes

Allen Newell (1927–1992) was one of the great early AI researchers who made a number of significant contributions to the fields of problem solving, knowledge representation, and cognitive science. For this he was awarded the ACM's AM Turing Award in 1975 together with his long-time colleague Herbert Simon.

Two of the early programs that Newell developed were The Logic Theorist (1956) and The General Problem Solver (1957).

He received a bachelor's degree from Stanford University in 1949, and then he studied mathematics at Princeton University where he learned about the work of von Neumann and Morgenstern in the area of game theory and economics. From his early experience at RAND Corporation in the 1950s in areas such as Air Traffic Control and simulation of organizations, Newell learned about information processing using card-programmed calculators.

According to Simon (*http://www.nap.edu/html/biomems/anewell.html*),

Newell described himself as "a scientist." His early experiences provided an excellent background and pedigree for his development; influenced by the likes of Polya (see Chapter 3, "Informed Search") at Stanford, von Neumann, and others at RAND, he became focused on solving the problem of "How do humans think?" After a seminar run by Oliver Selfridge at RAND in 1954, Newell became convinced that "intelligent adaptive systems could be built to accomplish things more complex than anything yet done (Newell, 1986)."

Hence, his interest turned to developing heuristics for complex problem-solving such as is found in the game of chess, and to developing a better understanding of how the human mind works.

In 1955, Newell joined Herb Simon in Pittsburgh, where he had been relocated by the RAND Corporation. His interest in chess evolved to building a Logic Theory Machine (LTM), which was to discover theorems in the propositional calculus, then used to perform hand simulations (in 1955) and then a running program in 1956. LTM and its successor, General Problem Solver (GPS) laid the foundations for AI programs for the next decade. Newell eventually obtained a PhD from Carnegie-Mellon in Industrial Management. "The LTM was a program of research to understand complex information-processing systems, but was the first, only partially successful, attempt at automating protocol analysis (Newell, 1971)."

GPS was a primary example of the study of "means ends analysis"—the attempt to minimize the distance between a current state in a problem situation and a goal state. GPS was able to identify its own small set of primitives and to learn which operators were relevant for reducing differences (ibid).

Dr. Newell's *Human Problem Solving* (1972, with Cliff Shaw and Herb Simon) was a monumental contribution toward furthering our understanding of how humans perform problem solving in a number of domains. He tried to develop *Unified Theories of Cognition* (his final work, 1990), which could be experimentally modeled and tested with the system Soar, which he developed in the 1980s. The intent was a broad theoretical framework for how the mind works.

Simon (*url above*) summarizes Newell's Soar project as follows:

> When existing unified theories are viewed closely, each can be seen to be built around a core cognitive activity, which is then extended to handle other cognitive tasks. In Anderson's Act* the core is semantic memory; in EPAM, perception and memory; in connectionist models, concept learning. In Soar as in GPS the core is problem solving, and the central GPS concept of problem space is taken over and expanded to allow the system to use multiple problem spaces in solving a single problem. The Soar program is a production system. To this were added two key components developed in collaboration with graduate students: learning by chunking (Rosenbloom and Newell, 1982), which produced a wide variety of kinds of learning obeying the empirically observed power law, and a universal weak method (Laird and Newell, 1983), which incorporated a method for universal subgoaling.

The essence of Soar was the demonstration that a powerful learning mechanism, chunking (an accepted theory of how memory works, Rosenbloom and Newell, 1982), coupled with learning by adaptive production systems, can provide a consistent, viable, working theory of learning. Soar has continued to attract researchers from a number of universities since Newell's death.

Selected References

Primary Source: Simon, H. A. *Biographical Memoir, Allen Newell*. n.d. National Academies Press. *http://www.nap.edu/html/biomems/anewell.html* May 5, 2011

Newell, A., and Simon, H. A. 1956. The logic theory machine: A complex information processing system. *IRE Transactions on Information Theory* IT 2:61–79.

Bell, C. G., and Newell, A. 1971. *Computer structures: Readings and examples*. New York, NY: McGraw-Hill.

Bell, C. G., Broadley, W.Wulf, W., Newell, A., Pierson, C., Reddy, R., and Rege, S. 1971. "*C.mmp: The CMU multiminiprocessor computer: Requirements, overview of the structure, performance, cost and schedule*." Technical Report, Computer Science Department, Carnegie Mellon University, Pittsburgh.

Newell, A., and Simon, H. A. 1972. *Human problem solving*. Englewood Cliffs, NJ: Prentice-Hall.

Newell, A. (1982). "The knowledge level." *Artificial Intelligence* 18:87–127.

Rosenbloom, P. S., and Newell, A. 1982. "Learning by chunking: Summary of a task and a model." In *Proceedings of AAAI-82 National Conference on Artificial Intelligence*. AAAI, Menlo Park, CA.

Newell, A (1986) American Psychological Association, 1986 Award for Distinguished Scientific Contributions, *American Psychologist*, 41, pp.337-52, p.348.

Newell, A. 1990. *Unified theories of cognition*. Cambridge, MA: Harvard University Press.

Newell, A. 1992. "Unified theories of cognition and the role of Soar." In Soar: *A cognitive architecture in perspective*, eds. J. A. Michon and A. Anureyk. Dordrecht: Kluwer Academic Publishers.

7.5 ■ PRODUCTION SYSTEMS AND CELLULAR AUTOMATA

In the classic AI movie "Bi-Centennial Man" (starring Robin Williams), the robot was trying to replicate itself; it was running a factory for the construction of robot parts.

Closely related to artificial intelligence is the field of artificial life and the question: Can machines replicate themselves? This was the interest of John von Neumann, one of the founders of computer science, at Princeton University in the 1950s. Could a robot-like machine, with vision, be able to follow a program in the form of a Turing Machine and be able to assemble a copy of itself from the basic component parts? [9]

Los Alamos mathematician Stanislaw Ulam [10] suggested to von Neumann that he could construct an abstract model of this universe on a grid of squares (cells) to test his hypotheses.

Here is the standard set of production rules for the Game of Life:

R1: If $[N = 2]$

THEN [cell maintains status quo]

R2: If $[N = 3]$

THEN [cell is on (lives) in next generation]

R3: If $[N = 0$ OR $N = 1$ OR $N = 4$ OR $N = 5$ OR $N = 6$ OR

$N = 7$ OR $N = 8]$ THEN [cell is off (dies) in next generation]

Where N = number of live neighbors (range is $0 - 8$).

The seven cases of R3 can be described in terms of what goes on in life. If a cell has 0 or 1 neighbors it dies of "loneliness." If a cell has more than 3 neighbors it dies from overcrowding. Some states are stable, some disappear, and some oscillate and will effectively explode. Following these simple rules we can see what happens to the patterns in Figure 7.6.

HUMAN INTEREST NOTES

JOHN CONWAY

Von Neumann was sufficiently impressed by Ulam's cellular automata idea that he developed a prototype model. The model included 29 "game pieces" that could reside on any square of the cellular grid. These 29 cells fell into three categories: one an unexcited state (perhaps the empty cell), twenty quiescent (or dying) states, and eight excited or reproductive states. "A pulsar (or construction arm) would pass over these cells and help them get into the state that the automaton wanted. With these twenty-nine states for the cells, it would theoretically be possible to do anything logical or constructive or operative that was required. These automata would be able to construct other automata, certainly including automata like themselves." [11] Von Neumann's ideas were far ahead of the machinery of his time and were at the forefront of his thinking at the time of his death in 1957. [12]

Many of von Neumann's ideas were implemented in The Game of Life by John Conway, also of Princeton University. [13] Here again we have a square board of cells on which patterns can be randomly generated by either a computer program or a human player. What happens to every cell in the "the next generation" is determined by how many live neighbors (N) a cell has.

The top line shows five patterns in Generation 0. The bottom line shows what has happened to these patterns by the time Generation 3 is reached. The first two patterns have disappeared, while the third pattern becomes a "blinker" as it alternates between generations, and the fourth and fifth patterns have already stabilized.

Figure 7.6
The Game of Life patterns.

The Game of Life demonstrates how production systems can be used to simulate interesting and complex real-life situations based on some very simple rules.

In Chapter 12, we will see examples of how some simple initial states can produce interesting results.

Human Interest Notes

John von Neumann (1903 – 1957) is a legendary figure in the history of mathematics, high-speed computing machines, the mathematical theory of games, economics, logic, quantum physics, and a number of other fields.

He was born in Budapest, Hungary, one of three sons in a well-to-do Jewish family. At a very early age it was clear that he had prodigious talents, such as his memory of phone numbers and addresses. He also had the ability to perform tremendous computations quickly and possessed the ability to divide two eight-digit numbers in his head.

By seventeen, he was dissuaded from studying mathematics by his father for financial reasons; this led to his obtaining a diploma in chemistry in Berlin (1921 – 1923) a diploma in Chemical Engineering from the Zurich Technical University (ETH) and a PhD in Mathematics from The University of Budapest (1926). He made contributions to set theory and logic in mathematics; however, some of his ideas were shaken by those of Kurt Godel.

He was a visiting lecturer at Princeton University in 1930 (at the age of 27), and by 1933 he helped found the Institute for Advanced Study where he was one of its six original professors in the School of Mathematics. Von Neumann knew how to enjoy life in America; there were frequent parties at his home.

Von Neumann produced over 150 papers, about 60 of them in pure mathematics, including set theory, logic, topological groups, measure theory, ergodic theory, operator theory, and continuous geometry. There were also about 20 papers in physics, and about 60 in applied mathematics, including statistics, game theory, and computer theory. In game theory, one of his early contributions was the theory of minimax (see Chapter 4, "Search Using Games"), which led to his famous co-authored authoritative book on the subject with Oscar Morgenstern.

He is generally credited with designing the first computer architecture; his stored-program concept is the backbone for serial architectures to this day. He was interested in what machines could remember, questions of self-reproduction for automata, and the use of machines to perform a large number of probabilistic experiments.

Much of his greatness could be attributed to "…the extraordinary rapidity with which he could understand and think and the unusual memory that retained everything he had once thought through…"(Halmos, 1973).

Paul Halmos, the late esteemed mathematician, his student, and the author of an article, "The Legend of John von Neumann," which formed much of the basis of our summary here, felt that it was von Neumann's ability to stick to "axiomatic methods" that helped make him so great—his repeated clarity, speed, and depth of thought.

Selected Reference

Halmos, P. 1973. "The legend of John von Neumann." *The American Mathematical Monthly* 80(4). *http://www.jstor.org/stable/2319080 May 5, 2011*

7.6 STOCHASTIC PROCESSES AND MARKOV CHAINS

As we study the real world and systems about us, we learn that the manner in which a system performs will differ depending on the state that the system is in at that time. That is, the probability of making a transition to a certain new state or condition will vary depending on the current state. Processes that depend on time states are very common today. In Chapter 16, we will introduce the notion of "temporal difference learning," which is the process by which most contemporary strong backgammon programs have been developed. It depends on the backgammon programs learning the differences (by probabilities) between the quality of a given current state and a possible future state. So "time" and "timing" do make a difference.

There are a number of familiar real-world examples in which time is of critical importance. In such cases, there will be a series of discrete states and associated probabilities of making a transition from one state to another; the processes are called **stochastic processes**. Stochastic processes will usually have a number of random variables involved and will tend to be statistical in nature. Examples include the stock market, medicine, equipment, weather, voting, and genetics, among others. Markov Systems will be concerned only with the probability of getting from a current state to a future state, not with *how* we arrived at where we are. That is why we introduce them here.

Let us consider the example of weather. Early work in computing using Markov Chains was done by Kemeny, Snell and Thompson.[14] Consider this famous example:

The Land of Oz is blessed by many things, but not by good weather. They never have two nice days in a row. If they have a nice day, they are just as likely to have snow as rain the next day. If they have snow or rain, they have an even chance of having the same the next day. If there is change from snow or rain, only half of the time is this a change to a nice day. We take as states the kinds of weather R, N, and S. From the above information we determine the transition probabilities. These are most conveniently represented in a square array as:

	R	N	S
R	(1/2	1/4	1/4)
N	(1/2	0	1/2)
S	(1/4	1/4	1/2)

From this description, it is easy to interpret the probabilities for weather represented in the matrix. It is called a **matrix of transition probabilities**, or the **transition matrix**. For example, row two indicates that a nice day can never be followed by another nice day since there is a 50% chance of rain and a 50% chance of snow on the next day. And a rainy or snowy day has only a 25% chance of being followed by a nice day.

So the challenge becomes to compute the probability of the weather two days from now. If it is raining today then tomorrow three kinds of whether can follow: Raining (probability of .50), Nice (probability of .25), and Snowing (probability of .25). So if it is raining today the probability of snow two days from now is the disjoint union of three events: (1) rain tomorrow followed by snow, (2) nice tomorrow followed by rain, and (3) snow tomorrow followed by more snow.

This can be done by computing the probability of the product $\mathbf{p}_{11}\mathbf{p}_{13}$ in the transition matrix which gives,

$$\mathbf{P}_{13}^{(2)} = \mathbf{p}_{11}\mathbf{p}_{13} + \mathbf{p}_{12}\mathbf{p}_{23} + \mathbf{p}_{13}\mathbf{p}_{33},$$

which is the dot product of the first row times the third column of the transition matrix. Using computer programs, it is easy to compute the probability of weather many days in the future for the entire matrix. Statistical methods in natural language processing such as Markov Chains combined with AI techniques will be explored further in Chapter 13.

7.7 ■ CHAPTER SUMMARY

Chapter 7 presents the background, history, key concepts behind, as well as applications of *production systems*. It begins with an introduction to *Post Production Systems* and works its way historically to presenting how and why production systems are such attractive paradigms for representing the way the human brain and intelligent systems work. In this regard, the work of Newell and Simon is emphasized. Chapter 7 also discusses how *strong* AI methods are distinct from *weak* methods.

Much of the chapter gets its inspiration from the following excellent treatises: *Human Problem Solving*,[7] *Artificial Intelligence: A Knowledge-Based Approach*,[15] and *Expert Systems: Design and Development*.[8] For their time, we found both the Firebaugh and Durkin texts very readable, profound, and comprehensive. Also very helpful, comprehensive, and highly recommended is the text by Joseph Giarratano and Gary Riley, *Expert Systems: Principles and Programming*.[16]

The CarBuyer System, as developed and presented in Section 7.3, was inspired by the example of the "Naturalist" as presented by Firebaugh in Chapter 10 of his excellent text. The Naturalist has been has been successfully used as a classroom example of the topic of production systems, *working memory* and *conflict resolution* in expert systems. We hope that readers will find the CarBuyer System equally useful as an example of how a small expert system works and will find it somewhat practically useful as well.

We have dedicated a complete Section, 7.3.1, to the important topic of conflict resolution, discussing, through a number of examples, ways in which this can be done. Sections 7.3.2 and 7.3.3 cover the equally important fundamental methods of making *inferences* while traversing a *knowledge base, forward chaining and backward chaining*. Included are a number of examples illustrating how each approach would possibly be more suitable for certain kinds of problems.

Section 7.6 re-introduces cellular automata, a form of production system and an introduction to evolutionary systems that we will investigate more closely in Chapter 13, "Natural Language Understanding." Section 7.7 presents stochastic processes and Markov Chains, which represent an important aspect of statistical approaches to artificial intelligence.

Questions for Discussion

1. Describe briefly the history of production systems.

2. Why are production systems an important AI topic?

3. Give five synonyms for production systems.

4. Describe the components of a rule-based expert system.

5. How might production systems be a metaphor for the human brain?

6. Give five advantages of production systems for building an expert system.

7. In what kinds of situations would it be desirable to use forward chaining and when might backward chaining be more appropriate?

8. What is conflict resolution?

9. What is *aging, refreshing, and recycling* in terms of conflict resolution? Describe three other conflict resolution techniques.

10. Who was the famous Princeton computer scientist who first studied cellular automata? Who inspired him and what was the ultimate theoretical goal of his research in this area?

11. What is the Game of Life, who devised it and what is the premise behind it?

12. What is a stochastic process and give some examples.

13. What is the purpose of Markov Chains, how are they related to production systems, and what would a transition matrix represent?

14. What is the "diminishing returns effect" in terms of expert systems or rule bases?

Exercises

1. Production systems are equivalent to the single IF – THEN case, the two alternative IF - THEN - ELSE, and multiple alternative IF – THEN – ELSE-IF or CASE structure of many programming languages. How is what was presented in this Chapter different from those straightforward applications of programming language constructs?

2. Consider and discuss the problems of a conflict resolution strategy that would say "Fire All Rules."

3. How is the Global Database illustrated in Figure 7.3 different from conventional database systems used today?

4. Consider the effects that ordering of rules can have in expert systems.

5. If there were no conflict resolution strategy in an expert system what would two possible affects be? Why can't the knowledge engineer just develop rules so that every possible case is covered?

   Hint: Consider scaling effects for the above question.

6. Implement the CarBuyer System in your favorite programming language? Does it work? Are there cars in the database that will never be selected with the existing set of 20 rules?

7. a. Are there any improvements to the CarBuyer System that you can see? Are there any rules that you would add or remove?

   b. What would you need to add to the system to make it more realistic?

8. Intuitiveness, modularity, and ease of expression are three features of production systems that are often given as advantages.

   Discuss briefly how production systems facilitate these advantages. Develop a small set of rules for something that you are trying to express.

9. What if von Neumann's results had indicated that it is impossible to build a cellular automaton that is self-replicating. How would that affect the possible construction of a self-replicating machine in the 3-dimensional world?

10. Let us say you notice the following market trends. You are considering buying a house. How would you Backward Chain to a conclusion to buy or not?

Rule 1   IF the price of homes is down
THEN buy a house.

Rule 2   IF Interest rates are increasing
THEN the price of homes is up.

Rule 3   IF Interest rates are decreasing
THEN the price of homes is down.

Rule 4   IF Gas prices are rising
THEN the stock market is down.

Rule 5   IF Gas prices are decreasing
THEN the stock market is up.

11. Let us say that another rule is added, as below, how would the rule system in Question 10 above be affected if traversed in a Forward Chaining style?

Rule 6   IF you have job instability
THEN invest in bonds.

12. Given

1. $A \mathrel{\&} B \Rightarrow F$

2. $C \mathrel{\&} D \Rightarrow G$

3. $\quad E \Rightarrow H$

4. $B \mathrel{\&} G \Rightarrow J$

5. $F \mathrel{\&} H \Rightarrow X$

6. $G \mathrel{\&} E \Rightarrow K$

7. $J \mathrel{\&} K \Rightarrow X$

And that Facts B, C, D and E are True, how would a program deduce that X is true?

(Reference: "Expert Systems", by Donald Michie, The Computer Journal, V 23, No. 4, 1980)

13. Write a five page paper summarizing the accomplishments of one of the following people: John von Neumann, Allen Newell, Herb Simon, and John Conway.

Keywords

aging
antecedent – consequent
backward chaining
bounded rationality
conflict resolution
control system
cellular automata
cycling
fanning in
fanning out
finite state machine
fired
forgetting

forward chaining
global database
inference systems
knowledge base
knowledge intensive
Markov Chains
matrix of transition
    probabilities
meta-knowledge
modularity
pattern-matching
Post Production Systems
Post Tag Machine

productions
production systems refreshing
retrograde analysis
rule-based systems
situation – action systems
short-term (working memory)
stochastic processes
The Game of Life
transition matrix

References

1. Post, E. 1943. "Formal reductions of the general combinatorial decision problem." *American Journal of Mathematics* 65: 197–215.

2. Chomsky, N. 1957. *Syntactic structures.* The Hague: Mouton.

3. Sowa, J. 1984. *Conceptual structures: Information processing in mind and machine.* Reading, MA: Addison- Wesley.

4. Reddy, R. 1988. "Foundations and grand challenges of artificial intelligence": AAAI Presidential Address. *AI Magazine* 94: 9–21.

5. Charniak, E. 2006. "Why natural-language processing is now *statistical* natural language processing." In *Proceedings of AI at 50*, Dartmouth College, July 13–15.

6. Buchanan, B. G. and Shortliffe, E. H. 1984. *Rule-based expert systems.* Reading, MA: Addison-Wesley.

7. Newell, A. and Simon, H. A. 1972. *Human problem solving.* Englewood Cliffs, NJ: Prentice-Hall.

8. Durkin, John 1994. *Expert Systems: design and development.* New York, NY: MacMillan.

9. Von Neumann, J. 1956. "The general and logical theory of automata." *The World of Mathematics*, ed. James R. Newman, New York, NY: Simon and Schuster.

10. Ulam, S. M. 1976. *Adventures of a mathematician.* New York, NY: Charles Scribner's Sons.

11. Macrae, N. 1992. *John von Neumann.* New York, NY: Pantheon Books. (A Cornelia and Michael Bessie Book.)

12. Von Neumann, J. 1958. *The computer and the brain.* New Haven, CT: Yale University Press.

13. Conway, John. 1970. "The game of life." *Scientific American* 223(October): 120–123.

14. Kemeny, J. F., Snell, J. L., and Thompson, J. 1974. *Introduction to finite mathematics*, 3rd ed. Englewood Cliffs, NJ: Prentice-Hall.

15. Firebaugh, M. 1988. *Artificial Intelligence: a knowledge-based approach.* Boston, MA: Boyd and Fraser.

16. Giarratano, J. and Riley, G. 2005. Expert systems: *Principles and programming*, 2nd ed. Boston, MA: Thomson/Cengage Learning.

■ ■ ■ ■ ■

This Part presents and explores well-trodden and proven success stories for AI. Some 50 years ago when Lofti Zadeh discovered Fuzzy Logic, little did he know how powerful and pervasive this concept would become. Fuzzy Logic, fuzzy sets, and fuzzy inferences coupled with probability theory and uncertainly comprise Chapter 8.

Expert Systems are one of the genuine success stories of AI. Since the 1980's, thousands of these systems have proven cost-effective with human experts in many diverse disciplines. Methods for efficiency, case-based reasoning systems and more recent approaches are also explored (Chapter 9).

Chapter 10 begins our discussion of Machine Learning. Decision trees with an introduction to entropy are studied. Our discussion of Machine Learning continues with Neural approaches. Neural Networks are a domain that was introduced more than a half century ago and abandoned by AI for many years before theoretical and hardware advances enabled computational power feasible for practical application. The Perceptron Learning Rule, The Delta Rule, and Backpropagation are discussed. Implementation concerns, discrete Hopfield nets, and diverse application areas round out Chapter 11.

It is natural for AI researchers to seek alternate ways to search and solve problems. These are explored through genetic algorithms, genetic programming, ant colony optimization and tabu search (Chapter 12).

UNCERTAINTY IN AI

Lotfi Zadeh

Conclusions reached in inference systems often are not certain. Your doctor might feel that you have a cold or you could be suffering from allergies. Fuzzy logic and probability theory are two methods for coping with such uncertainty.

Figure 8.0
Most modern automobiles are equipped with traction control systems which "kick-in" under varying precipitation conditions. Fuzzy logic controls these systems.

8.0 INTRODUCTION

Uncertainty is an inevitable component in everyone's life. The morning weather report informs us that there is a 30% chance of evening showers. The business section in your newspaper reports that there is a 50% chance that the housing foreclosure crisis in your community will get worse before it improves. Your doctor has said that if you continue to overeat and avoid exercise, your chances for a long life are not certain. Naturally, if our AI systems are going to be robust, they must possess the capability to contend with such uncertainties.

Fuzzy logic and probability theory are two often-used tools. Fuzzy logic assigns grayness levels to events that were previously declared to be black or white. For example, when it is raining, the traction control system on your new car should engage. Suppose there is a light drizzle, then it is raining to *a certain extent*. Fuzzy logic supplies the wherewithal to contend with such uncertainties.

You want to buy a new car but you are strapped for cash. You apply for a bank loan. The bank's loan officer wants to know the size of your savings account, your yearly income, the remaining mortgage on your house or your monthly rent, your credit history, and other financial considerations. Essentially, the bank is trying to determine the probability that you will repay the loan based on your present circumstances. Probability is often used in situations when outcomes are not entirely predictable.

8.1 FUZZY SETS

Suppose your instructor asked you to raise your hand if you are male then asked you to put your hands down. Next you were asked to raise your hand if you are female. Undoubtedly, each student in your class raised their hands once and only once. The following sets:

$$M = \{x \mid x \text{ is a male student in your class}\}$$

$$F = \{y \mid y \text{ is a female student in your class}\}$$

are examples of **crisp sets** in that each student in your class belongs to one and only one set. The intersection of these two sets is empty, i.e.

$$M \cap F = \varnothing \text{ meaning that no element is a member of both sets.}$$

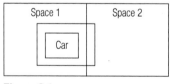

Figure 8.1
A car partially parked in two different spaces.

Imagine next that everyone in your class has a job; your instructor now asks you to raise your hand if you are satisfied with your jobs. Then you are asked to raise your hand if you are dissatisfied with your job. It is likely that some hands went up both times. [1] Some hands may have even been only somewhat raised in each case. Job satisfaction can be thought of as a **fuzzy concept** in that most people are not entirely happy or unhappy with their jobs. Another example can be taken from spaces in a parking lot (consult Figure 8.1). Frequently we find that people, in a rush for whatever reason, will haphazardly park their cars in such a way as to take two different, adjoining spaces.

Fuzzy logic was developed by Lotfi Zadeh.[2] Let $\mathbf{X} = \{x_1, x_2, x_3, \ldots, x_n\}$ be a finite set. Let $\mathbf{A}$ be a subset of X, written $\mathbf{A} \subseteq \mathbf{X}$ consisting of x_2 alone; then $\mathbf{A}$ can be denoted by a membership vector of dimension n:

$$\mathbf{Z}(A) = \{0, 1, 0, \ldots, 0\}.$$

Whenever x_i equals 1, then x_i is an element of the set **A**. The subset **B** of **X** that contains x_2 and x_3 is denoted by

$$\mathbf{Z(B)} = \{0, 1, 1, …, 0\}.$$

The other crisp subsets (there are $2^n - 2$ others) can be similarly represented.

Consider next the **fuzzy set** C:

$$\mathbf{Z(C)} = \{0, 0.5, 0, …, 0\}.$$

This represents an impossible scenario in classical (i.e., crisp) set theory. Does x_2 belong to **C** or does it *not*? In **fuzzy set theory**, the element x_2 belongs to the set **C** to a *certain extent*. [3] This degree of membership is represented by a real number in the interval [0, 1].

Another example of a fuzzy set is the set of all tall people. If you watched the opening ceremonies of the 2008 Beijing Olympics, then you may have seen Yao Ming, the 7'6"-tall basketball star carrying the flag for the Chinese contingency of athletes. Beside him was Lin Hao, an elementary school student who helped rescue classmates from rubble after an earthquake in Sichuan Province in May 2008. No one would argue with the premise that Yao Ming is tall and Lin Hao is *not*.

What should be said of individuals who are 5'10"? Well, you can say they are tall *to a certain extent.*

"Tallness" is seen to be a 'fuzzy concept.' To represent the degree of membership in a fuzzy set we can draw a **membership function** as in Figure 8.2.

A person who is 5' tall (or shorter) is not a member of the set of tall people. A person who is 6' tall might have a degree of membership of 0.65 in this set; we would write this as $\mu_t (6') = 0.65$, where $\mu_t ( )$ is the **membership function** for this set. You certainly would agree that $\mu_t (7' 6'') = 1.0$, i.e., Yao Ming certainly qualifies for full membership in this set. [4]

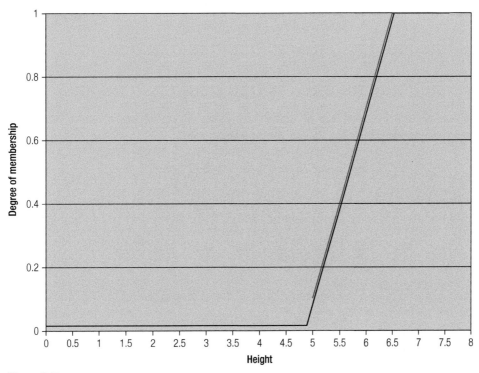

Figure 8.2
Membership function for the set of tall people.

Let **X** be a classical universal set.

A real function $\mu_A : \mathbf{X} \rightarrow [0, 1]$ is the membership function for the set **A**. The set of all pairs $(x, \mu_A(x))$ defines the fuzzy subset **A** of **X**.

A membership function completely specifies a fuzzy set. The set of all elements x that belong to **X** where $(x, \mu_A(x))$ belongs to **A** and $\mu_A(\mathbf{x}) > 0$ is called the **set of support** of the fuzzy set A. For the set **t** of all tall people (as described in Figure 8.2), the set of support consists of all people 5' in height or taller. If **A** is a set with a finite set of support $\{a_1, a_2, .., a_m\}$ then this can be represented as

$$\mathbf{A} = \mu_1 / a_1 + \mu_2 / a_2 + \ldots + \mu_m / a_m,$$

where $\mu_i = \mu_A(a_i)$, $i = 1, \ldots, m$. Note, the "/" and "+" symbols are being used as delimiters, no divisions or additions are being performed. For example, if $\mathbf{X} = \{x_1, x_2, x_3\}$ where **A** and **B** are the two (crisp) subsets: $\mathbf{A} = \{x_1, x_3\}$ and $\mathbf{B} = \{x_2, x_3\}$, then these sets can be represented as

$$\mathbf{A} = 1 / x_1 + 0 / x_2 + 1 / x_3$$
$$\mathbf{B} = 0 / x_1 + 1 / x_2 + 1 / x_3.$$

The union of two sets A and B denoted $\mathbf{A} \cup \mathbf{B}$, is the set of all elements that lie in either **A** or **B** (or both). $\mathbf{A} \cup \mathbf{B}$ can be computed by taking for each x_i, the *maximum* of its membership in either set, i.e., $\mathbf{A} \cup \mathbf{B} = 1 / x_1 + 1 / x_2 + 1 / x_3$. This methodology easily generalizes to the case in which the sets are fuzzy. For example, if

$$\mathbf{C} = 0.2 / x_1 + 0.5 / x_2 + 0.8 / x_3$$
$$\mathbf{D} = 0.6 / x_1 + 0.4 / x_2 + 0.2 / x_3,$$

Then the fuzzy union of C with D is

$$\mathbf{C} \cup \mathbf{D} = 0.6 / x_1 + 0.5 / x_2 + 0.8 / x_3.$$

The fuzzy intersection of two sets can be defined by using the *minimum* instead of the maximum of each degree of membership. So, for our previous example,

$$\mathbf{C} \cap \mathbf{D} = 0.2 / x_1 + 0.4 / x_2 + 0.2 / x_3$$

The *complement* of the crisp set **E**, i.e., $\mathbf{E}^c$ is the set of all elements that lie in the universal set (**X** in this example) but not in **E**. The complement $\mathbf{E}^c$ where **E** is a fuzzy set can be computed by

$$\mu_{\mathbf{E}}^c(x) = 1 - \mu_{\mathbf{E}}(x), \forall x \in \mathbf{X}.$$

For example, if **E** is the *fuzzy* subset,

$$\mathbf{E} = 0.3 / x_1 + 0.1 / x_2 + 0.9 / x_3,$$

then the complement of **E** equals

$$\mathbf{E}^c = 0.7 / x_1 + 0.9 / x_2 + 0.1 / x_3.$$

Observe that, in general, when **A** is a fuzzy set, the union of **A** with its complement does not equal the universal set, and the intersection of **A** with its complement does not equal the empty set, as is the case for crisp sets. For the fuzzy set E we have

$$\mathbf{E} \cup \mathbf{E}^c = 0.7 / x_1 + 0.9 / x_2 + 0.9 / x_3$$

$$\mathbf{E} \cap \mathbf{E}^c = 0.3 / x_1 + 0.1 / x_2 + 0.1 / x_3$$

8.2 FUZZY LOGIC

In "ordinary" propositional logic (consult Chapter 5, "Logic in Artificial Intelligence"), an expression is either true or false. For example, it is either raining or it is *not* raining. In fuzzy logic, an expression can be true *to a certain extent*. One can define fuzzy counterparts to logical operations, where for the fuzzy OR operation ($\triangledown$) we use the maximum, for fuzzy AND ($\triangle$), the minimum is used, and for fuzzy complementation ($\rightsquigarrow$) replace x with $1 - x$. So suppose that proposition **A** has a truth value of 0.8, where 0 denotes false and 1 means true with certainty, and proposition **B** has a truth value of 0.3. Then $\mathbf{A} \triangledown \mathbf{B}$ has truth value equal to max (0.8, 0.3) = 0.8 and $\mathbf{A} \triangle \mathbf{B}$ is true with a truth value equal to min (0.8, 0.3) = 0.3.

Notice that $\mathbf{A} \triangle \rightsquigarrow \mathbf{A} = $ min (0.8, (1 − 0.8)) = 0.2. In ordinary propositional logic, the truth value of an assertion and its complement is always false. So that $p \triangle p$ where p can represent "It is raining," is always a contradiction. Also, observe that $\mathbf{A} \triangledown \rightsquigarrow \mathbf{A} = $ max (0.8, (1−0.8)) = 0.8, whereas $p \triangledown p$ ("It is raining" or "It is not raining") is always true in ordinary propositional logic. This last claim is known as the **Law of the Excluded Middle** and was accepted as evident by Aristotle.

The fuzzy OR operator obeys boundary conditions, and is commutative, associative, monotonic, and idempotent. Consult Table 8.1.

The fuzzy AND function is monotonic, commutative, and associative. The boundary conditions are: $0 \triangle 0 = 0$; $1 \triangle 0 = 0$; $0 \triangle 1 = 0$; $1 \triangle 1 = 1$.

Fuzzy negation obeys the following conditions:

- $\rightsquigarrow 0 = 1$
- $\rightsquigarrow 1 = 0$ boundary conditions
- If $a \le b$, then $\rightsquigarrow b \le \rightsquigarrow a$ monotonicity
- $a = \rightsquigarrow \rightsquigarrow a$ involution

Table 8.1
Properties for the fuzzy OR function.

$0 \triangledown 0 = 0$	Boundary Conditions
$1 \triangledown 0 = 1$	
$0 \triangledown 1 = 1$	
$1 \triangledown 1 = 1$	
$a \triangledown b = b \triangledown a$	commutativity
$a \triangledown (b \triangledown c) = (a \triangledown b) \triangledown c$	associativity
If $a \le a'$ and $b \le b'$, then $a \triangledown b \le a' \triangledown b'$	monotonicity
$a \triangledown a = a$	idempotency

To illustrate the monotonic property, for the fuzzy OR function assume the following truth values: $a = 0.3$, $b = 0.6$, then $\rightsquigarrow b$ has a truth value of $1 − 0.6 = 0.4$, and the truth value of $\rightsquigarrow a$ equals $1 − 0.3 = 0.7$ and $0.4 \le 0.7$ as expected.

8.3 FUZZY INFERENCES

Production systems were discussed in Chapter 7, "Production Systems." Chapter 9, "Expert Systems," will show how knowledge-based systems can be used to solve real-world problems, such as why your car won't start or what disease you might have contracted. Fuzzy measures can be applied to production rules to reflect the vagueness that is present in the world. For example, perhaps your car will not start because the battery is dead, or maybe the fuel tank is empty, or, if it's too cold, the motor could have frozen.

Fuzzy production rules have the same structure as their more traditional counterparts, introduced in Chapter 7, for example,

$$\text{Rule1: If } (\mathbf{A} \veebar \mathbf{B}), \text{ then } \mathbf{C}.$$

$$\text{Rule2: If } (\mathbf{A} \barwedge \mathbf{B}), \text{ then } \mathbf{D}.$$

Suppose that the truth values of **A** and **B** are 0.1 and 0.8, respectively. Then

$$\mathbf{A} \veebar \mathbf{B} = (0.1, 0.8) = 0.8$$

$$\mathbf{A} \barwedge \mathbf{B} = \min (0.1, 0.8) = 0.1$$

Rules 1 and 2 can be applied only to *some extent*. Rule 1 is applied 80% and Rule 2 is applied 10%, in order that a combination of actions (or deductions) **C** and **D** will occur.

EXAMPLE 8.1: DEGREE OF MEMBERSHIP

Suppose that you work in a tea factory as a taster for bottled tea and your job is to ensure that bottles of tea being produced have the correct degree of sweetness.

There is a pump that sprays sugar into the vat holding the tea. The pump's operation is governed by three rules that depend upon your appraisal of sweetness:

R1: If (tea is not sweet enough), then spray more sugar.

R2: If (tea is satisfactory), then maintain sugar spray.

R3: If (tea is too sweet), then spray less sugar.

Your evaluations on sweetness are integer values that range from −5 to +5, where a sweetness evaluation $x = +2$ indicates that the batch is 2% too sweet, whereas when $x = -3$, you thought the tea was 3% less sweet than ideal. Assume that your evaluation of sweetness is $x = +1$ for this measurement:

Degree of membership of 0.14 in the set of *too sweet*.

Degree of membership of 0.5 in the set of *tea that is fine*.

Degree of membership of 0.0 in the set *tea that is not sweet enough*.

We express this information as a fuzzy category:

$$X = \frac{\text{too sweet}}{0.14} + \frac{\text{fine}}{0.5} + \frac{\text{not sweet enough}}{0.0}$$

Based on this information, some action is taken. We obtain the following fuzzy inference:

$$\text{Action} = \frac{\text{reduce sugar spray}}{0.14} + \frac{\text{Maintain system}}{0.5} + \frac{\text{increase sugar spray}}{0.0}$$

To be useful, however, this action must be converted into a crisp value; reduce sugar spray (or increase it) and by how much.

To express fuzzy categories graphically, triangular or trapezium-shaped membership functions are frequently used. Figure 8.3 displays a triangular-shaped membership function.

Figure 8.4 shows a trapezium-shaped graphical representation of a membership function.

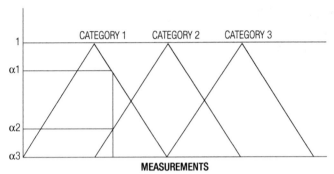

Figure 8.3
Categories with triangular-shaped membership functions.

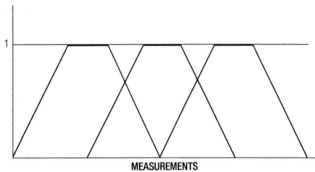

Figure 8.4
Categories with trapezium-shaped membership functions.

We return to Example 8.1

EXAMPLE 8.1: REVISITED:

The membership functions for the bottled tea factory example are drawn in Figure 8.5

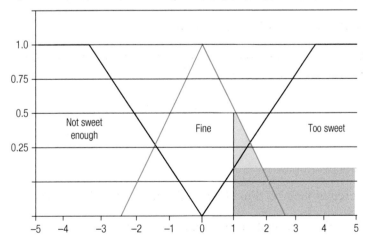

(a)

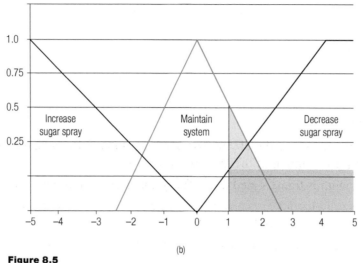

(b)

Figure 8.5
Membership functions for the bottled-tea factory example; (a) sweetness evaluation; (b) percentage change in sugar spray from pump.

Observe that in Figure 8.5b, the action reduce sugar spray is valid to 0.12 and maintain sugar spray is valid to 0.5. The regions of the two respective categories are shaded. To transform the fuzzy action prescribed above into a crisp action, we must find the horizontal component for the "center of gravity" of the shaded region in Figure 8.5. This corresponds to a value approximately equal to 0.1, hence sugar flow should be reduced by 1%.

The so-called "center of gravity" is technically known as the **centroid** of the shaded region. Algorithms for computing the centroid of a region can be found in many advanced calculus texts.

If our goal is to produce artificial intelligence at or near (above?) the human level then we should be concerned with biological plausibility. The human eye can be viewed as a fuzzy system. Light of different wavelengths comes to rest on the human retina—a typical eye responds to light energy in the range of 380 nm (violet) to 750 nm (red) (this is usually expressed in angstrom units, where 1 angstrom unit($\mathring{A}$) = 0.1nm) or 3800 to 7500 angstrom units. The eye, however, contains receptors that are specialized for the colors blue, green, and red. Consult Figure 8.6

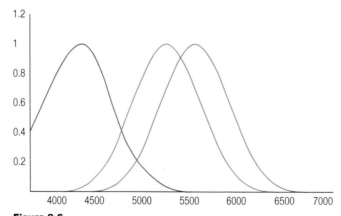

Figure 8.6
Reponses of the three receptors in the human retina. The maximum excitation for the blue receptor is 4300Å, for green it is 5300Å, and 5600Å for red.

- Monochromatic color will excite all three receptor types. The output of each receptor class depends on wavelength.
- Maximum excitation for each receptor:

  Blue~4300 Å

  Green~5300 Å

  Red~5600 Å

- Monochromatic light is thereby transformed into three different excitation levels, i.e., into a relative excitation of the three receptor types.
- The wavelength is transformed into a fuzzy category, just as with fuzzy controllers.
- The three excitation levels measure the degree of membership in each of the three color categories: *blue*, *green*, and *red*.
- Coding of the wavelength using three excitation values reduces the number of rules needed in subsequent processing.
- Sparseness of rules in fuzzy controllers has a counterpart in the sparseness of the biological components.

Ordinary light will excite each of the three receptors *to some extent*, the light is thereby being transformed into a fuzzy category. Fuzzy systems are noteworthy for the sparseness of the rule set. This attribute of fuzzy systems is in harmony with the need for biological frugality.

Fuzzy logic has been incorporated into the control mechanism for many devices. Imagine you are taking photos with friends and it is somewhat cloudy. Should you use a flash? The instructions that came with your camera say that if it is not sunny, use a flash . . . however, it is sunny—to a *certain extent*. It is no surprise that many digital cameras incorporate fuzzy logic into their control.

Now, imagine that you are doing your laundry and you are setting the wash cycle. Machine instructions recommend that if clothes are especially dirty, then you should select a long wash cycle. Naturally, your clothes are dirty *to a certain extent*. Many washing machine models use fuzzy logic. Fuzzy logic is finding applicability in vacuum cleaners, automobile ABS brakes, and traction systems. Additionally, we cannot be certain of many of the conclusions we reach in real life. Are you sneezing because you have a cold or are you suffering from an allergy attack? It is no surprise that fuzzy logic is used in Expert Systems (Chapter 9). In Chapter 11, "Neural Networks," we discuss artificial neural networks (ANN), an information processing paradigm based on the structure of animal nervous systems. Unfortunately, ANNs cannot explain their results. Many researchers have combined ANNs with fuzzy logic to produce systems that possess an explanatory capability.

8.4 ■ PROBABILITY THEORY AND UNCERTAINTY

Some would contend that probability theory witnessed its inception in 1654. A friend of Blaise Pascal was interested in gambling problems—what resulted was a series of mathematical communications between Pascal and Pierre de Fermat. It should come as no surprise then, that probability theory plays a prominent role in handling uncertainty. One impediment, however, to its achieving even wider acceptance is that most people are subjective (rather than analytical) in their evaluations

HUMAN INTEREST NOTES

LOTFI ZADEH

Lotfi Zadeh

Lotfi Zadeh (1921–) was born in Baku, Soviet Azerbaijan, but he is also of Iranian descent, and has long lived in the United States; like the famous concept that he created, his background is across boundaries—he is an international person. "The question really isn't whether I'm American, Russian, Iranian, Azerbaijani, or anything else," he'll tell you. "I've been shaped by all these people and cultures and I feel quite comfortable among all of them." (*http://azer.com/aiweb/categories/ magazine/24_folder/24_articles/24_ fuzzylogic.html*) April 15, 2011.

When Zadeh was 10 years old, his family, under persecution from Stalin, decided to move back to Iran, which was his father's homeland. In 1942, he graduated from the University of Tehran with a degree in electrical engineering. During World War II, his family moved to the United States; he obtained an MS degree from MIT in 1946, and a PhD from Columbia University in 1949.

In 1959 he joined the Electrical Engineering Department at Berkeley, where he became chair in 1963 and chair of the Computer Science Division (EECS) as well.

Following is a segment of an interview Betty Blair conducted with Lotfi Zadeh.

Zadeh was asked:

Back in 1965 when you published your initial paper on Fuzzy Logic, how did you think it would be accepted?

Zadeh responded:

Well, I knew it was going to be important. That much I knew. In fact, I had thought about sealing it in a dated envelope with my predictions and then opening it 20–30 years later to see if my intuitions were right. I realized this paper marked a new direction. I used to think about it this way—that one day Fuzzy Logic would turn out to be one of the most important things to come out of our Electrical Engineering Computer Systems Division at Berkeley. I never dreamed it would become a worldwide phenomenon. My expectations were much more modest.

(*http://azer.com/aiweb/categories/ magazine/24_folder/24_articles/24_ fuzzylogic.html*)

From that interview it seems clear that Zadeh felt that fuzzy logic would have wide application in many fields, such as economics, psychology, philosophy, linguistics, politics, and other of the social sciences. He has been surprised at how few social scientists have exploited its possibilities. Back in 1965, Zadeh did not expect that fuzzy logic would primarily be used by engineers for industrial process control and in "smart" consumer products. Examples of the latter include hand-held camcorders, in which fuzzy logic compensates for spurious hand movements, and microwaves that enable us to cook food perfectly by pressing a single button.

Zadeh further confirmed that he decided on the term "fuzzy logic" because he felt it most accurately described what was going on in the theory. Other terms, such as "soft," "unsharp," "blurred," and "elastic" were considered, but he didn't feel they more accurately portrayed what his methods did.

The fact that fuzzy logic is a "coarse" rather than a "refined" way of doing things means that it is less expensive and easier to accomplish than traditional forms of computing. He gives the example of parking a car: if one had to find a car in a parking lot within the space of 1/10th of an inch it would be a very difficult task, but since we don't have to do so, more "coarse" methods can be used.

In preparing an article on fuzzy logic, Mark Hopkins received a wide response and found the following list of applications: finances, geography, philosophy, ecology, agricultural processes, water treatment, baggage handling at Denver International Airport, remote sensing images from satellite images, recognition of handwriting and nuclear science, the stock market, and weather. Boeing in Seattle reported that it has incorporated fuzzy logic in a controller for Navy #6 autopilots, which trails a long wire antenna for communications with submarines.

Further examples that Hopkins found include the following: biomedical applications are being used to diagnose breast cancer, rheumatoid arthritis, postmenopausal osteoporosis, and heart disease; to monitor anesthesia, blood pressure, and insulin for diabetes; as a postoperative pain controller; to produce magnetic resonance images of the brain; and to set up intelligent bedside monitors and hospital communication networks.

To date, the countries applying fuzzy logic most prevalently are Japan (#1), Germany (#2), and the United States (#3). The possibilities are limitless, because the concept is broad and can be applied to almost any field.

References

http://azer.com/aiweb/categories/magazine/24_ folder/24_articles/24_fuzzylogic.html

Zadeh, L. A. 1965. Fuzzy sets. Information and Control 8:338 – 353.

of risk. For example, people are often more fearful of air travel than driving. It is a well-known fact, however, that statistically you are much safer in an airplane than you are driving in your car.

The starting point for any discussion of probability theory begins with an experiment which is some process that is carried out. For example, consider the experiment of tossing a fair coin twice.

We considered this example in Chapter 4, where some rudiments of probability theory were needed to properly analyze games involving chance. The sample space for an experiment **S** is the set of all possible outcomes (an outcome is sometimes referred to as a set of **sample points**). In our case, **S**, in which a coin is tossed twice, equals {(**H, H**), (**T, T**),(**T, H**),(**H, T**)}.

Notice that we are distinguishing between a head followed by a tail and the outcome in which the lone tail occurs first. An *event* **E** is a subset of **S**. The sample space S consists of four sample points, hence 2^4 or 16 events are possible:

E_1 = {(**T, H, (H, T**)} which corresponds to one head and one tail occurring,

E_2 = {(**T, T**), (**H, H**)}, the event in which each toss resulted in the same side landing up,

E_3 = {(**T, T**), (**T, H**)}, the event in which the first toss is a tail, and so on.

Finally, the *probability* of an event E_i is defined as:

$P(E_i)$ = the number of ways in which E_i can occur, divided by the total number of possible outcomes.

For example, the probability of event E_3 (just described) equals:

$P(E_3)$ = 2/4 or 1/2, as when a fair coin is tossed, two sample points correspond to this event, whereas $|S|$ equals 4.

There are three basic axioms of probability measures:

- For any event E : $P(E) \geq 0$
- $P(S) = 1$ // when two coins are tossed, *some* outcome is certain to occur.
- If the events E_1 and E_2 are mutually exclusive, then $P(E_1 \cup E_2) = P(E_1) + P(E_2)$

// For example, if E_1 equals two heads occurring when a coin is tossed twice, and E_2 corresponds to two tails occurring, then $E_1 \cup E_2$ is the event corresponding to either two heads or two tails occurring. The probability of this event equals

$$P(E_1 \cup E_2) = P(E_1) + P(E_2) = 1/4 + 1/4 = 1/2.$$

A function that satisfies these three axioms is referred to as a probability function.

EXAMPLE 8.2:

There are nine marbles in an urn, three are blue, three dark pink, and three red. Two marbles are drawn randomly from the urn at the same time (your eyes are closed). What is the probability that both marbles are red?

$$P(2r) = (3C2) / (9C2) = 3/36 = 1/12.$$

The numerator represents the number of ways in which two red marbles can be drawn. Number the red marbles: r_1, r_2, and r_3. Then two red marbles are drawn for each of these events :$\{r_1, r_2\}$, $\{r_1, r_3\}$, and $\{r_2, r_3\}$. The denominator corresponds to the total number of outcomes when two marbles are drawn, i.e., $\{r_1, r_2\}$, $\{p_1, p_2\}$, $\{p_1, p_3\}$, etc.

Suppose we could not derive the probability in Example 8.2 analytically; what you could do instead is to conduct the following series of experiments: Draw two marbles from the urn, ten successive times (replacing the marbles after each attempt). Draw the two marbles from the urn, 100 times, then 1000 times, and so on. As the number of times that the experiment is repeated grows relatively larger and larger, we believe that the frequency of obtaining two red marbles approaches the probability of this event. A more formal statement of this observation is known as the **Law of Large Numbers**. In fact, we use this perspective on probability later (Chapter 12, "Search Inspired by Mother Nature") in a Monte Carlo exercise to approximate the value of π.

Suppose that E_1 is the event that a head occurs on the first toss when a fair coin is tossed twice and E_2 is the event that a tail occurs on the second toss when a coin is tossed twice, then the joint probability of both E_1 and E_2 occurring is the event (E_1,E_2) equal to {**H,T**}, that is, a head and then a tail occur when a fair coin is tossed twice $P(E_1,E_2) = P(H$ on first toss) * $P(T$ on second)

$$= 1/2 * 1/2 = 1/4$$

Consider Example 8.2 once again. Suppose you know that both marbles drawn are the same color and you wish to calculate the probability that both marbles are red. In essence, the sample space has shrunk from (9C3) to 3 * (3C2); what you wish to calculate is the conditional probability:

P (two red | both marbles the same color).

P (2r | both same color) = (3C2) / (3*(3C2)) = 1/3.

Probability theory enters into many situations in real life. A bank is (or should be) interested in the probability that a home owner will repay their mortgage. A doctor weighs the probabilities of several conflicting diagnoses when treating a patient with some symptoms. A person considers the odds when placing a bet on a horse at the racetrack.

An important result when considering conditional probabilities is Bayes' theorem. Suppose the probability of some event **B** > 0, then **P** (A|B) can be calculated by

P (A|B) = [**P** (B|A) * **P** (A)] / **P** (B)

....

EXAMPLE 8.3: BAYES' THEOREM

A brief physical exam is administered to all new inmates at a prison. Suppose that 80% of all healthy individuals pass this exam, 60% of all individuals with minor ailments pass, and 30% of all prisoners with serious ailments also pass. Suppose that 25% of these new prisoners are actually in good health (event E_1), 50% have minor ailments (E_2), and 25% have major health issues (E_3). Given that an inmate passes this physical (event B), what is the conditional probability that the inmate is in good physical condition?

$P(B|E_1) = 0.8, P(B|E_2) = 0.6, P(B|E_3) = 0.3, P(E_1) = P(E_3) = 0.25, P(E_2) = 0.50$

Using Bayes' Theorem we obtain that:

P (inmate is healthy | passes health exam) = **P** (E_1 | **B**)

$$= P (B | E_1) * P (E_1) / \sum_{i=1}^{3} P (B | E_i) * P (E_i)$$

$$= [(0.8) (0.25) / (0.8) (0.25) + (0.6) (0.5) + (0.3) (0.25)] = 0.35$$

Originally we might have suspected that a randomly chosen new inmate would be in good health with a probability of 0.25. However, after passing this health exam, our conviction has risen to 0.35

....

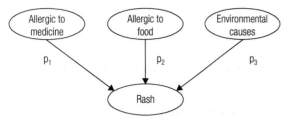

Figure 8.7
A Bayesian network to analyze a symptom.

Bayesian networks are often used to contend with uncertainty. Suppose you have a skin rash for which you consult your doctor; in order to properly treat you, your doctor must determine what is causing this rash. Common causes include allergic reaction to a medicine or food product or contact with an object (perhaps even a pet).

Your doctor might view the situation as shown in Figure 8.7:

This is a Bayesian network in which nodes represent variables. The three variables that could be causing the condition have arrows leading to the resulting condition. Probabilities p_1, p_2 and p_3 are probabilities labeling these arcs. Where do these probabilities come from? They are a subjective evaluation of the situation based on the doctor's previous experience with this malady. The incidence of allergies (MSG, peanuts, corn starch) and environmental factors (cats, dogs) is relatively common, hence your doctor will likely conclude that p_1 is much less than either p_2 or p_3.

8.5 ■ CHAPTER SUMMARY

This chapter has provided a brief glimpse at two tools used for handling uncertainty in AI. As we have seen, life is not just black or white; there are many shades of gray as well. For example, when is an individual considered mature? A person can enter the military in the United States at the age of 18; however, to order a drink in a bar in New York State, you must be 21 years of age. To run for president, you must be at least 35. Maturity is seen to be a fuzzy concept. Fuzzy logic has achieved widespread applicability in the control for many modern applications from digital cameras to washing machines.

Probability theory has its origins with the desire to understand the odds involved in games of chance. It is a tool employed by pharmaceutical firms in testing the effectiveness of their products. Many expert systems (Chapter 9) employ probability to contend with the uncertainty inherent in drawn inferences of these systems. This chapter is in no way meant to be complete. In fact, there is a third approach to handling uncertainty in AI systems that we have not discussed. Dempster-Shafer theory [11] measures the confidence one has in probabilities that have been assigned to events. The belief for some event **E**, bel (**E**) $\leq$ **P** (**E**), is defined as the sum of all outcomes in which **E** results. The plausibility of this event E, pl (E) is the sum of all outcomes in which E is not contradicted, hence $P(E) \leq p_l(E)$. This methodology is often used in sensor fusion. For example, an astronomer observing a distant star may use an optical telescope, a spectrometer, and a radio telescope. The observations achieved by these tools could be in conflict with one another. Dempster-Shafer theory provides a calculus for contending with contradictory evidence.

Questions for Discussion

1. Name five things from everyday life that correspond to fuzzy sets.

2. **a.** Let **S** be a crisp set with *n* elements. How many subsets will **S** have?

   b. How many subsets will **S** have if **S** is a fuzzy set with *n* elements?

3. Give an example of a fuzzy inference from everyday life.

4. Fuzzy logic and probability are essentially the same thing. Discuss this assertion.

5. **A ~ B** represents set difference, or, the set of all elements in **A** but not in **B**.

   Choose an appropriate metric to calculate the set difference between two sets (i.e., max, min, etc).

6. Let **X** = {*a*, *b*, *c*}. List all subsets of **X** using membership function notation.

7. Do you believe fuzzy logic should be preferred to probability theory (or vice versa) when analyzing the following situations:

   a. The effectiveness of a new medicine.

   b. Evaluating highway safety.

   c. The accuracy of a weather report.

   d. The risk involved in buying a lottery ticket.

   e. The risk involved in buying a stock.

   f. Analyzing pollution levels in a nearby lake.

8. Give an example from your everyday life in which you use conditional probability (perhaps unknowingly).

Exercises

1. Let **X**={x_1, x_2, x_3} be a universal set. Consider the following sets:

   $$A = 0.2 \ /x_1 + 0.1 \ /x_2 + 0.2 \ /x_3$$
   $$B = 0.2 \ /x_1 + 0.4 \ /x_2 + 0.7 \ /x_3$$

   a. $A \cup B = ?$

   b. $A \cap B = ?$

   c. $A^c \cap B^c = ?$

2. Draw the fuzzy membership function for each of the following:

   a. Person **X** is considerably heavier than 100 pounds.

   b. Star **Y** is considerably larger than our Sun.

   c. Car **Z** costs approximately $30,000.

   d. $\mu_{A(x)} = 0$ for $x \leq 5$ and $1 + (x - 5)^{-2}$ when $x > 5$.

3. Consider the example of tallness discussed in this chapter. Draw the membership function for the set of:

   a. Very tall person.

   b. A person who is *not* tall.

4. a. Draw the membership functions for the following sets:

M: mature people

Y: young people

O: old people

b. Classify a person who is

    i. 18 years old

    ii. 21 years old

    iii. 42 years old

    iv. 61 years old

c. Explain how you would defuzzify your answer for part b. iii. above (i.e., obtain the age of 42 from your fuzzy categorization).

5. a. A television can be viewed as "domestic" or "foreign" in different ways. For example, many components for American televisions are manufactured in Mexico or Asia. Similarly, there can be instances in which a television with a foreign name is actually manufactured in your country. Draw two fuzzy membership functions, one for foreign TV sets ($\mu_F(x)$) and one for domestic brands ($\mu_D(x)$). What are $\mu_F(x)$ and $\mu_D(x)$ for 60%?

b. Assume the following rules have the same membership functions as above:

Rule 1: If a TV set is domestic then maintain tariffs (a tax imposed on imports).

Rule 2: If a TV set is foreign then raise tariffs.

What inference would you make for a TV set that is 40% foreign?

6. Suppose that the people attending a resort have a long-term chance of 1 in 100 of having skin cancer (from too much sun exposure). The resort maintains a clinic to help detect this disease. Suppose that the screening used at this clinic has a false positive rate of 0.2 (that is 20%) of people without skin cancer will test positive for cancer) and that it has a false negative rate of 0.1 (10% of people with skin cancer will test negative). Suppose that a person has just tested positive for skin cancer. What is the probability that he actually has the disease?

7. A gambling bet is considered fair if the individual making the bet considers that they will break even in the long run. Which of the following bets would be considered fair?

a. A fair coin is flipped. You pay $1 to guess the outcome and receive $2 in return if your guess is correct.

b. You pay $5 to toss two dice. If the total is 7 or 11 you receive $20 in return.

8. A *Dutch Book* is some mix of wagers, which can be shown to result in a sure loss (according to the bettor's beliefs). Consider this situation (The three-card problem): there are three cards, one is red on both sides (RR), the second is red on one side and white on the other (RW), and the third card is white on both sides (WW). A single card is drawn (eyes closed) and tossed into the air.

a. P (RR card selected) = ?

b. P (W-showing) = ?

c. P (not - RR|R - showing) = ?

d. Are the following fair bets or a Dutch Book:

    i. You pay \$1 – to guess a card

      You win \$3 – if correct

    ii. R-showing

      You pay \$1 – to guess card

      You win \$2 – if correct

    iii. Win \$1– if R-showing and not RR

      You lose \$1– if R-showing and RR

Keywords

crisp sets	**joint probability**	**sample space**
fuzzy concept	**Law of the Excluded Middle**	**sample points**
fuzzy set	**Law of Large Numbers**	**set of support**
fuzzy set theory	**membership function**	

References

1. Halpern, J. 2003. *Reasoning about uncertainty*. Cambridge, MA: MIT Press.

2. Zadeh, L. A. 1965. Fuzzy sets. *Information and Control* 8:338–353.

3. Korb, K. B. and Nicholson, A. E. 2004. *Bayesian artificial intelligence*. London, England: Chapman & Hall/CRC.

4. Jensen, V. F. 1995. *An introduction to Bayesian networks*. New York, NY: Springer-Verlag.

Bibliography

1. Rojas, R. *Neural Networks A Systematic Introduction*. Berlin, Germany: Springer, 1996.

EXPERT SYSTEMS

Edward Feigenbaum

This chapter presents Expert Systems, one of the domains of AI considered most successful with regard to its contributions to computer science and the real world in general. Herein we discuss typical features of expert systems, how they are built, and some of the most successful systems that have been built during the more than 30-year history of the field. Examples of systems employing case-based reasoning and some of the most recent expert systems are also presented.

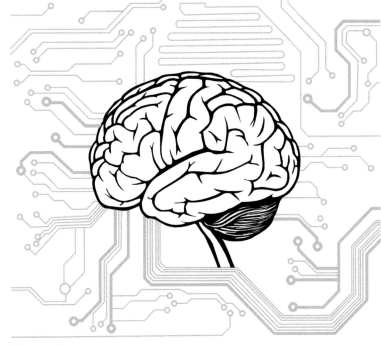

Figure 9.0
Brain on IC.

9.0 ■ INTRODUCTION

The development of expert systems could be viewed as the single most important accomplishment of artificial intelligence. They emerged in the 1970s at a time when the whole field of artificial intelligence was stifled by the disparaging report by Sir George Lighthill (See Chapter 6, "Knowledge Representation"). AI was criticized for not producing real-time, real-world working systems. Some important insights were gained in the fields of computer vision and, hence, robotics from the work of R. J. Popplestone.[1] The toy system *Freddy* was built to perform simple tasks such as the assembly of a toy car or the placing of a coffee cup on a saucer. Soon thereafter came the famous thesis work of Terry Winograd[2] at MIT; SHRDLU, or *Blocks World*, lent further insight into understanding natural language (see Chapter 13, "Natural Language Understanding"). AI had also gained a certain degree of interest and notoriety from early systems such as GPS in 1972 ("Overview of Artificial Intelligence," Chapter 1, Section 1.8.8) and the famous ELIZA system which fooled many people into believing it was intelligent.[3]

9.1 ■ BACKGROUND

As we have discussed in Chapters 1, "Overview of Artificial Intelligence," and 6, "Knowledge Representation," we live in times when knowledge is at a premium. In earlier times, such as during the Industrial Revolution of the 1800s, a society's progress could be measured by its ability to convert natural resources such as minerals and iron ore into energy and man-made products. In the twentieth century, more typical measures of progress were the facility and speed in communication and transportation. In communications we have gone from the telephone in the late 19th century to Google, Facebook, and Twitter in the 21st century. In transportation we have progressed from steam-driven ships to landing man on the moon. Technological progress was also in part driven by World War I, and to a greater extent by World War II, with the burgeoning of the Computer Age. In America, the development of the Electronic Numerical Integrator and Computer (ENIAC) was the driving force of the technological age, and in England, it was the attempt to solve the Enigma Codes through the construction of the Colossus by Turing and his aides at Bletchley Park in 1943.

In addition to putting a man on the moon in 1969, technological progress was based on **microminiaturization** coupled with microchip technologies. In the 1980s, with the proliferation of the personal computer, the transition to an **"information society"** began.

More and more homes could afford personal computers, and the computer took on increasingly diverse and important roles in peoples' lives. In the 1990s, the World Wide Web was introduced by Tim Berners-Lee, offering an entirely new forum for business, leisure, travel, work, study, and for that matter, just about anything else. By the end of the first decade of the new Millennium the challenges for the "knowledge-society" that we live in are to efficiently manipulate and transfer vast amounts of information and convert it to knowledge for useful and important decision-making that will benefit society.

Presper Eckert and John Mauchley are credited for the ENIAC at around 1946.

The Enigma codes were secret codes that the Germans sent to submarines during World War II. The Colossus (Turing, et al.) was built primarily to help break the Enigma Codes. It did indeed succeed in accomplishing this task.

The use of microchip technologies reduced the size and increased the speed of operation of computers and their corresponding chips; this led directly to the advent of Moore's Law, through which it was realized that smaller components meant the possibility of greater speed. Hence, it was also discovered that the speed of microprocessors corresponded directly to the speed of computers—and for many years improved chip technology with microminiuaturization had enabled the speed of microprocessors to double every 18 months.

A good example of a system that is very sensitive to tremendous, abundant, and varied information sources is the stock market. For example, the stock market's position at the time of this writing is highly affected by the supply and demand for oil. In the course of a very short time we have seen the price of oil jump from $60 per barrel to nearly $150 per barrel and more recently drop to below $100 per barrel. What is the true value of a barrel of oil today and how should it be reflected at the gas pumps? A truly intelligent expert system would be able to take into consideration a number of factors in order to predict the correct value (within a range) for oil in both the short and long term.

9.1.1 Human and Machine Experts

The goals of early systems, labeled the "power strategy" by Goldstein and Papert,[34] were to develop general and powerful methods that could be applied to diverse problem-solving areas. Early programs, such as DENDRAL,[5] proved weak in terms of their power of generality. The behavior of the best general problem solvers we know, human problem-solvers, is weak and shallow, except in those areas where the human problem-solver is a specialist (ibid.).

Contrary to early beliefs, most humans are experts in only their own specialized fields; they do not possess some kind of magic that enables them to quickly generate the finest and most cogent set of rules for an arbitrary problem domain. Hence, a chess grandmaster, who might have some 50,000 rules (patterns) which have been accumulated and developed over many decades of praxis and study (see Michie [6] and Reddy [7]), will more than likely not be a grandmaster in the creation of heuristics, rules, methods, or anything else in life for that matter. The same is probably true for a PhD mathematician, medical doctor, or a lawyer. Each is expert in handling information within his/her sphere, and that skill doesn't assure any particular expertise in the handling of information in general or to other spheres of expertise. What we do know is that a long apprenticeship is required before any particular domain can be mastered.

Brady [8] noted that there are a number of ways human experts combat the combinatorial explosion:

> Firstly to impose structure on the knowledge base, to enable the solver to operate within a relatively narrowly specified context. A second approach is to make explicit the knowledge one has about the way in which domain specific knowledge can best be used; so-called *meta-knowledge*. The uniformity of knowledge representation really begins to pay off here, as one can turn the full power of the problem solver onto the meta-knowledge in exactly the same way as one applies it to the base knowledge. …
> Thirdly, one attempts to exploit the redundancy which seems ever present and crucial for human problem solving and perception. There are several ways in which this might be achieved, but mostly they amount to the exploitation of constraints.

Often one can make explicit a number of conditions, none of which uniquely specify a solution, but whose simultaneous satisfaction is unique.

Here, for "redundancy present in human problem solving and perception," we believe that Brady really means one word: PATTERNS. Again we return to the example of finding your car in a vast parking lot. Knowing what floor your car is on or what numbered area will make a huge difference with regard to how quickly you retrieve it. Furthermore, having knowledge about the position (central row, outer row, middle or end of row, etc.), the features of your car (its color, shape, style, etc.), and the area within the parking lot where you left it (near a building, an exit, a column, a wall, etc.), will make a huge difference in how quickly you find it. There are three distinct approaches humans will use:

1. Depending on the information (the numbers on your receipt, ticket, and the information provided in the lot). With this approach, a human is not using any intelligence, just as one might use a car's navigation system to a destination without having any geographical understanding of where one is going.

2. Using a combination of the information on the ticket/receipt provided and some patterns about the car and its location. For example, your ticket says your car is in Area 7B, but you also remember it is not very far away from where you are, that your car is bright yellow and that it is huge; there aren't many large yellow cars, and it stands out from all other cars. (See Figure 9.1.)

3. A fragile approach whereby a human relies entirely on memory and patterns, rather than any specific information.

Figure 9.1
Patterns and information can help us identify things.

All three approaches illustrate the advantages humans have in processing information. Humans have built-in random access and associations (Section 6.11). To get to a car on Level 3, we do not need to explore Levels 1 through 3 linearly. A robot would have to be explicitly taught to skip the Levels below Level 3. Our memories allow us to exploit constraints about our vehicle (e.g., it was yellow, it was large, it was an old car). There are not too many of those cars around. Patterns coupled with information can help reduce our search (akin to the constraints and meta-knowledge that Brady refers to above). So we know our car is on a certain level (the ticket says so), but we also recall how we parked it (neatly or sloppily), what cars might have been nearby, and other notable features of the spot we selected. When humans become totally dependent on information systems, they could deprive themselves of their fundamental, innate intelligence, and this will perhaps lead to critical situations. Little wonder that we hear stories of a couple who let a GPS system lead them to the precipice of a mountain!

Before we go any further in our discussion of human expertise it would seem appropriate to mention the thoughts of the philosopher brothers at Berkeley, Hubert, and Stuart Dreyfus (see Chapter 6, 'Human Interest Box'). One of their main criticisms is that human "know-how" is hard to explain or develop in a machine. We know how to ride a bicycle, we know how to drive a car, and many other fundamental things such as walking, talking, and so forth, but when we try to explain how these actions are accomplished, our performance degrades quickly. The Dreyfus brothers also make the distinction between "knowing that" and "knowing how." Knowing that refers to factual knowledge, such as a set of instructions or steps to follow, but it is not the same as knowing how. Developing know-how is not something that we want to explain because it is very difficult. When know-how is attained, it becomes something that is hidden in the subconscious. Practice is required to avert memory failure. For example, you perhaps used to record TV programs with a VCR. You learned the necessary steps—they were both intuitive from the controls on the VCR, and you also understood that the TV had to be set on a particular channel. You could both execute and comprehend the necessary steps to record a TV program (know-how). That was a long time ago, however. Now there are DVDs, and systems have changed. So now you might have to admit that you have lost the know-how for how to record a TV program.

Dreyfus and Dreyfus [9] focus much of their discussion of expertise on the premise that there are five stages of skill acquisition in the progression from novice to expert:

1. Novice
2. Advanced Beginner
3. Competent
4. Proficient
5. Expert

Stage 1: The novice just follows rules and has no coherent understanding of the task domain. There is no context to the rules, no understanding, just the ability to follow rules to accomplish a task. One example would be to follow a sequence of steps to get somewhere when driving. Another is following some instructions for example – assembling a new product, or typing in a computer program from a paper copy.

Stage 2: The **advanced beginner** starts to learn more from experience and is able to employ contextual clues. For example, when learning to make coffee with a coffee machine, we follow the instructions, however, we also use our sense of smell to tell us when the coffee is indeed ready. In other words, we learn from clues that we can perceive in the task environment.

Stage 3: The **competent** skill performer no longer needs to just follow rules, but also has a clear understanding of the task environment. He is able to make decisions, draw upon a hierarchy of rules, and to recognize patterns (which Dreyfus and Dreyfus call a "small set of factors" or a "constellation of those elements" [9]). Competent performers might be goal-oriented and can alter their behavior according to conditions. For example, a competent driver knows how to alter his driving according to weather conditions, including speed, the gear, windshield wipers, mirrors, and so forth. At this point, the performer will have developed intuition or know-how. A performer at this level is still analytical, able to combine elements to make the best decisions based on his experience.

Stage 4: The **proficient** problem-solver will not only be able to recognize what the situation and appropriate choices are, but will also be able to deliberate the best way to implement a solution. An example is the doctor who knows what a patient's signs and symptoms suggest, and will carefully consider what the possible choices of treatment are.

Stage 5: The **expert** "generally knows what to do, based on mature and practiced understanding." [9] When the expert copes with his environment, he does not see problems as detached from his effort to solve them, nor does he worry about the future and devise elaborate plans. "We usually do not make deliberative decisions when we walk, talk, drive, or carry on most social activities." [9] Hence, Dreyfus and Dreyfus suggest that experts become one with the environment or tableau they are working on. The driver is not just driving a car, but is "driving," the pilot is not flying a plane, but is "flying," and the chess grandmaster is not just playing chess, but rather becomes a participant "in a world of opportunities, threats, strengths, weaknesses, hopes and fears." [9] Dreyfus and

Dreyfus further state: "*When things are proceeding normally, experts don't solve problems and don't make decisions; they do what normally works*" (ibid., p. 30). The main point Dreyfus and Dreyfus make is that "those who are proficient or expert make judgments based upon their prior concrete experiences in a manner that defies explanation" (ibid., p. 36). They conclude that "*experts act irrationally*"; that is, action without conscious analytic decomposition and recombination.

Dreyfus and Dreyfus argue that machines are inferior to the human mind in many ways, including the way in which the human mind works holistically, for vision, for interpretation and judgment, and that without this ability machines will always be inferior to human beings (the brain/ the mind). Although machines might be excellent symbolic manipulators (logic machines or inference engines), they lack the ability to holistically recognize and distinguish among similar images that humans have. For example, in facial recognition, machines cannot capture all the features that a human will, neither explicitly nor implicitly. The Dreyfus brothers cite Hofstader, in *Gödel, Escher, Bach: An Eternal Golden Braid* [10] who argued that machines are required to recognize letters from their basic parameters (font, length, width of serifs, etc.) and basic features, opposed to holistically using judgment of similarity. Hofstader states "Nobody can possess the 'secret recipe' from which all the (infinite many) members of a category such as 'A' can in theory be generated. In fact, my claim is that no such recipe exists." [10]

One wonders how impressed Hofstader and the Dreyfus brothers would be by progress in this domain in recent years.

Firebaugh [11] discusses the fact that experts have certain characteristics and techniques that allow them to perform at a high level in their problem domain. One key distinguishing feature is that they get the job done, hence, *performance*. To accomplish this they are able to

- **Solve the problem** – this is fundamental, and without this ability the expert would not be an expert.

  Unlike some other AI Techniques (neural nets, genetic algorithms, consult Chapters 11 and 12) expert systems are able to explain their decision-making process. Consider a medical expert system which determines that you have six months to live; You certainly would like to know how this conclusion was attained.

- **Explain the result** – experts must be able to serve in an advisory capacity and explain their reasoning. Hence, they have a deep understanding of their task domain. Experts understand the underlying principles, how the principles relate to the problem at hand, and can apply them to new problems.

- **Learn** – human experts continuously learn and thereby can improve their abilities. Perhaps this is the single most difficult aspect of human expertise that those in the field of AI aspire to for machines.

- **Restructure Knowledge** – this is a unique feature of humans who can adapt their knowledge to a new problem environment. In this sense, expert human problem-solvers can be flexible and adaptive.

- **Break rules** – exceptions, in some instances, are the rule. The real human expert knows the exceptions in his discipline. For example, a pharmacist knows what drugs or medications will not interact well with the prescribed drug when he fills a prescription for a patient.

- **Know their limitations** – human experts know what they can and cannot do. They don't accept tasks beyond their capabilities or too far afield from their standard areas.

- **Degrade gracefully** – human experts do not just break down when confronted with difficult problems. That is they do not "crash"; likewise, this is unacceptable in expert systems.

Let us consider and compare these features in expert systems:

- **Solve the problem** – expert systems are certainly capable of solving problems in their domains. Sometimes they even solve problems that human experts could not solve, or come up with solutions that the human expert did not consider.

- **Learn** – learning is not a main feature of expert systems, but they can be taught by changes to their knowledge base or inference engine if necessary. Machine learning is another topic area and will be explored in Chapter 10, Machine Learning: Part I, Chapter 11, Machine Learning Part II: Neural Networks and 12, "Search Inspired by Mother Nature."

- **Restructure knowledge** – although this capability might exist in expert systems, in essence it calls for a change in representation, and this is difficult for machines.

- **Break rules** – for machines to break rules in the intuitive, informed way that a human expert might, is difficult. Instead, new rules will be added to existing rules as exceptions.

- **Know their limitations** – perhaps aided by the World Wide Web, when a problem is beyond their realm of expertise, expert systems and programs in general today are able to refer to other programs wherein solutions can be found.

- **Degrade gracefully** – instead of the computer screen just freezing or going blank, expert systems will usually explain where they are stuck or having problems, what they are trying to determine, and what they have ascertained to that point.

An example of an expert who understands the rules of his discipline and their exceptions can be taken from the violent movie Casino. Recall Robert De Niro at the end, when he cites a special protective feature of his 1980 Cadillac that prevented its explosion despite a bomb being attached to the ignition!

Other typical features of expert systems include the following:

- **Separate the inference engine and the knowledge base.**
  This is important in order to avoid duplication and to maintain efficiency of the program.

- **Use as uniform a representation as possible.**

  Too many representations could lead to combinatorial explosion and "obscure the actual operation of the system."

- **Keep the inference engine simple.**
  This prevents the programmer from getting bogged down and it is easier to determine what knowledge is critical to the system's performance.

- **Exploit redundancy.**
  By bringing together as much diverse and relevant information as possible, incomplete and inexact knowledge can be avoided. (ibid., p. 374–375).

Giarratano and Riley (2005) [12] summarize the advantages of expert systems as follows:

- Increased availability
- Cost efficiency
- Embodiment of multiple sources of expertise

- Multiple information sources
- Fast Response

Despite all of these advantages, it seems appropriate to mention that there are a few well-known weaknesses of expert systems. First, their deep subject-matter understanding, in a causal sense, as alluded to earlier, is shallow. Second, they lack common sense. For example, they might know that water boils at 212°F, but they don't have any idea that boiling water can turn into steam, which can be used to run turbines. Hence, the efforts of Lenat, [13] who is building the largest encyclopedia of common-sense knowledge, Cyc. Third, they cannot demonstrate deep subject matter understanding. Even great expert systems with thousands of rules do not have a deep understanding of their subject matter. e.g. MYCIN (See Section 9.5.3) does not have a deep understanding of human physiology.

HUMAN INTEREST NOTES

DOUGLAS LENAT

Douglas Lenat

Douglas Lenat (1950 –) is CEO of CyCorp and one of the preeminent AI researchers. Lenat received his PhD in Computer Science in 1976 from Stanford University, under the supervision of Edward Feigenbaum.

His early work with the programs AM and Eurisko quickly gained him notoriety. AM, developed in LISP, stands for Automated Mathematician and was one of the first discovery programs, which in 1977 led to Lenat being awarded the IJCAI (International Joint Conference on Artificial Intelligence) Computers and Thought Award. AM generated and modified short LISP programs, which were interpreted to represent mathematical concepts. An example would be a program that could learn the notion of mathematical equality by comparing the length of two lists and discovering that they are equal.

The program was sophisticated in the number and kinds of heuristics available, but also quite complicated. AM always chose the top task on its priority list, but this could become quite convoluted when combined with an intricate set of preconditions for rules. AM also was a good example of meta-knowledge—the use of knowledge about knowledge—in its complex infrastructure of rules. Lenat attracted some controversy when he claimed that AM had solved Goldbach's Conjecture (a famous unsolved mathematics problem) and the Unique Prime Factorization Theorem, which others disputed.

Eurisko (Greek for "discover"), which Lenat began in 1976, was intended to extend the domain of discovery of his program beyond mathematics, the limited domain of AM. Eurisko's purpose was discovery of heuristics across a broad spectrum of domains, and in this sense it has been a great success, receiving the support of the Defense Advanced Research Projects Agency (DARPA).

One prevailing criticism of AI systems in the 1980s was that, although they had domain-specific knowledge, they lacked more general "common sense" knowledge necessary to tackle more general problems. In 1986, Lenat set out to build the largest database of common-sense knowledge, Cyc, and this has been his mission ever since. In Cyc, Lenat hopes to combine a powerful inference engine with millions of pieces of common-sense knowledge of over 100,000 concepts, with thousands of links between concepts embodying relationships such as inheritance and "Is-A," as discussed in Chapter 6. Lenat has also stated: "Once you have a truly massive amount of information integrated as knowledge, then the human software system will be superhuman, in the same sense that mankind with writing is superhuman compared to mankind before writing."

References

Lenat, D. "Hal's Legacy: 2001's Computer as Dream and Reality. From 2001 to 2001: Common Sense and the Mind of HAL".

Cycorp, Inc.
http://www.cyc.com/cyc/technology/halslegacy.html

This section has explored human and machine expertise from a number of perspectives. In the next two sections, we will focus on how machine expertise is accomplished.

9.2 CHARACTERISTICS OF EXPERT SYSTEMS

The first question that arises when one considers building an expert system is whether the domain and problem are suitable. Giarratano and Riley [12] have a series of questions that one should consider before embarking on the construction of an expert system:

- *"Can the problem be solved efficiently by conventional programming?"* If the answer is YES then an expert system is probably not the best choice." Ill-structured problems where there are no efficient algorithms are most suited for the construction of an expert system.

- *"Is the domain well-bounded?"* A well-defined domain is most suitable, if problems in the domain draw upon expertise in other domains. For example, an astronaut must know a great deal more about her mission than she does about outer space, such as the mechanics of flight, nutrition, computer controls, electrical systems, etc.

- *"Is there a need and a desire for an expert system?"* There must be users (or a market) for the system, and the experts must also be in favor of building the system.

- *"Is there at least one human expert who is willing to cooperate?"* Without this, it is certainly not possible to proceed. The expert(s) must be in favor of the system and be willing to dedicate many hours to its construction. The expert(s) must be aware of the amount of time and cooperation that will be necessary.

- *"Can the expert explain the knowledge so that it is understandable by the knowledge engineer?"* This is a kind of litmus test. Can the two people work together? Can the expert be sufficiently clear in terms of his use of technical terms for the knowledge engineer to understand them and translate them into computer code?

- *"Is the problem-solving knowledge mainly heuristic and uncertain?"* Such domains, based on knowledge and experience and the kind of "know-how" we have described above, are particularly suitable for expert systems.

Note that the main differences are that expert systems tend to deal with uncertainty and inexact knowledge. That is, they might work correctly only part of the time, and the input data might be incorrect, incomplete, inconsistent, or have other flaws. Sometimes expert systems will even just give some answer—even a bad one. They note that at first this will perhaps seem very surprising and perhaps disturbing, but upon further consideration, it is consistent with notions of what an expert system is all about.

Expert systems have been built for many purposes including those on the following list (based on Durkin): [14]

- **Analyze** – to determine the cause of a problem given data

- **Control** – to ensure that systems and hardware perform according to specifications

- **Design** – to configure systems under certain constraints

- **Diagnosis** – to be able to make inferences about system malfunctions

- **Instruction** – to analyze, debug, and provide suggestive instruction for student errors

- **Interpretation** – to infer a situation description from data

- **Monitor** – to compare observations to expected values

- **Plan** – to design actions according to conditions

- **Predict** – to predict likely consequences of a given situation

- **Prescript** – to recommend a solution to system malfunction

- **Select** – to identify the best choice from a number of possibilities

- **Simulate** – to model interactions between system components.

Expert systems have been built in a number of domains; Table 9.1 lists some of the most common.

See Appendix D.1 presenting a number of well-known, successful expert systems that have been developed across several domains. Thousands of expert systems have been built worldwide to date.

Table 9.1
Major application areas of expert systems.

Major Application Areas of Expert System		
Agriculture	Environment	Meteorology
Business	Finance	Military
Certification	Geology	Mining
Chemistry	Image Processing	Power Systems
Communications	Information Management	Science
Computer Systems	Law	Security
Education	Manufacturing	Space Technology
Electronics	Mathematics	Transportation
Engineering	Medicine	

9.3 KNOWLEDGE ENGINEERING

Knowledge is the key to the power of any expert system. Knowledge will often arrive in a crude, inexact, incomplete, and poorly specified form. Like human amateurs, experts do not develop instantly, but must be built incrementally over time. Knowledge will be inexact for probabilistic sciences such as medicine, geology, weather, and certain other disciplines, yet the techniques for propagating uncertainties have been highly developed (see Section 9.5.5) and expert systems can do this much more systematically, quickly, and accurately than humans can. Perhaps surprisingly, human experts often find it difficult to express the logic, intuition, and heuristics they use to analyze data when it comes under their management. Recall the introduction to Chapter 1, wherein this phenomenon was described through the example of the professor of mechanics and the unicyclist; both are fine doing what they do expertly, however, once they try to understand and explain their expertise, their performance dramatically degenerates. The unicyclist can't explain her abilities and, likewise, the professor's knowledge of the laws of mechanics won't make him a successful unicyclist!

In reporting on *Themes and Cases of Knowledge Engineering*, Feigenbaum [15] noted that the keys to building successful systems use the following approaches:

1. **Generate and Test** – This approach is used not for any particular advantage that it has, but simply for the reason that it has been tried, tested, and employed for several decades. We hear of employing generate and test in the development of the heuristic DENDRAL program.

2. **The use of situation–action rules** – Also known as production rules (Chapter 7, "Production Systems"), or knowledge-based systems, this representation facilitates effective construction of expert systems with ease of modification of knowledge, ease of explanation, and so forth. "The essence of our approach is that a rule must capture a 'chunk' of domain knowledge that is meaningful, in and of itself, to the domain specialist" (ibid.).

3. **Domain-specific knowledge** – Knowledge is the key, not the inference engine. The knowledge plays a critical role in organizing and constraining search. Knowledge in the form of rules and frames is easy to represent and manipulate.

4. **Flexibility of the knowledge base** – The knowledge base comprises rules whose grain sizes (see Chapter 6) are chosen appropriately. That is, small enough to be comprehensible and large enough to be meaningful to the domain specialist. In this way, the knowledge is flexible enough to be easily modified in terms of changes to, addition to, and subtraction of knowledge.

5. **Line of reasoning** – The construction of knowledge whose meaning, intention, and purpose is clear to the domain specialist seems to be an important organizing principle in the construction of intelligent agents.

6. **Multiple sources of knowledge** – The integration of multiple sources of seemingly unrelated items of knowledge is necessary for the development and maintenance of a line of reasoning.

7. **Explanation** – The ability for the system to explain its line of reasoning is important (and necessary for system debugging and extension). This is considered an important knowledge engineering principle and must be given considerable thought. The structure of explanations and their appropriate level of complexity is also very important.

In order to gain credibility from both the scientific and business world, AI needed systems that worked properly and were economical. Here is what Donald Michie [6] summarized as "practical insights" into the requirements for an expert system:

1. The market for consultancy demands specialists, not generalists: this applies to automated consultancy too.

2. Real-time operation is, in some applications, not just desirable, but essential.

3. A consultant's skill consists to an important degree in asking the client the right follow-up questions, as the outlines of the case take shape.

4. Unless the program can do this, and can also explain its steps on demand, client confidence suffers.

5. An expert system acts as a systematizing repository, over time, of the knowledge accumulated by many specialists of diverse experiences. Hence, it can and does ultimately attain a level of consultant expertise exceeding that of any single one of its "tutors."

6. Program text in the ordinary sense is an unsuitable and unpopular medium for the description and communication by human experts of their expertise; "advice languages" are needed.

Figure 9.2 illustrates the main components of a rule-based expert system. Expert systems, due to their complexity, can be driven from either direction, (e.g., MYCIN), but Michie (ibid., p. 370) refers to them as "data-base driven."

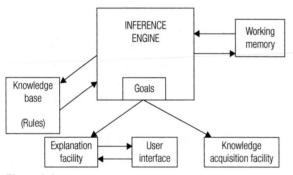

Figure 9.2
Typical structure of a rule-based expert system.

In Chapter 7 we described how AI systems, particularly production systems and expert systems based on them, are distinct from traditional computer science programs because they tend to separate the computational components from the knowledge-based components. Hence, in terms of expert systems, the inference engine is distinct from the knowledge base. In Chapter 7 (Section 7.4) we also introduced concepts of top-down (procedural approaches) and bottom-up (data-driven) approaches.

Their database typically comprises rules "invoked by pattern-match with features of the task-environment which can be added to, modified, or deleted by the user." Databases of this type are called knowledge bases. Users can employ knowledge bases in three typically distinct fashions:

1. Getting answers to problems – *user as client*

2. Improving or increasing the system's knowledge – *user as tutor*

3. Harvesting the knowledge base for human use – *user as pupil* (ibid.)

The people who use expert systems in mode 2 are known as **domain specialists**. It is not possible to build an expert system without the help of a domain specialist. The person who extracts the knowledge from a domain specialist and formulates it as a knowledge base is known as the knowledge engineer. "The process of extracting the knowledge from the domain specialist's head (a very important process) is known as **knowledge acquisition**."

The process of constructing the knowledge base via a series of interactions between the domain specialist and the knowledge engineer is known as **knowledge engineering**.[16] Often this process will involve a number of iterations and refinements of the rules over time by the knowledge engineer as he becomes more familiar with the domain specialist's rules.

The knowledge engineer is always searching for the best tools available for representation and solution of the problem at hand. He tries to organize knowledge, to develop methods of inference, techniques for structuring symbolic information. He works closely with the domain specialist to try to build the best possible expert system. Knowledge and its representation in the system is re-conceptualized as necessary. The human interface to the system is improved and "linguistic transactions" of the system are made more comfortable for the human user. The system's inference processes are made more understandable to the user.[5]

9.4 ■ KNOWLEDGE ACQUISITION

The task of eliciting the knowledge from the expert and organizing it into a usable system has always been viewed as a difficult one. It is also most important to the power of an expert system and, in essence, represents the expert's understanding of the problem. Knowledge acquisition is the formal name of this task, and it is the biggest challenge to building an expert system.

Although sources of knowledge can be books, databases, reports, or records, the single most important source for most projects is the domain specialist or expert.[14 (p. 519)] The process of getting the knowledge from the expert is called knowledge elicitation. **Knowledge elicitation** can be a long and arduous task involving a number of tedious sessions. These sessions could be in the form of interactive discussion with exchange of ideas or in the form of interviews or case studies. In the latter form, the expert is observed as she tries to solve a real problem. Whatever the method, the goal is to uncover the expert's knowledge and gain better insight into her problem-solving skills. People have wondered why the expert cannot simply be probed by questions for her knowledge. Let us not forget the following characteristics of experts:

1. They tend to be very specialized in their domain and will tend to use language that is domain specific.
2. They have largely heuristic knowledge, which is uncertain and imprecise.
3. They have difficulties in expressing themselves.
4. They bring to bear many sources of knowledge to achieve their performance.

Duda and Shortliffe [17] give their position on this issue by stating:

> The identification and encoding of knowledge is one of the most complex and arduous tasks encountered in the construction of an expert system ... the effort required to produce a system that is ready for serious evaluation (well before contemplation of actual use) is more often measured in man-years.

Hayes-Roth et al.[18] employed the famous term "bottleneck" in describing the construction of expert systems:

> Knowledge acquisition is a bottleneck in the construction of expert systems. The knowledge engineer's job is to act as a go-between to help build an expert system.

Since the knowledge engineer has far less knowledge of the domain than the expert, however, communication problems impede the process of transferring expertise into the job.

Of course, since the 1970s, there have been many attempts to automate the process of knowledge acquisition with techniques such as machine learning, data mining, and neural nets, among others (see Chapter 11). In certain cases, these have proven successful. For example, there is the famous case of soybean crop diagnosis [19] wherein, starting with a set of primitive descriptors from the human expert pathologist (Jacobsen) and a training set of values for diseased plants with confirmed diagnoses, the program synthesizes a set of diagnostic rules. The unexpected discovery was that a machine-synthesized set of rules out-performed those developed by the plant pathologist, Dr. Jacobsen, who acted as domain specialist. Jacobsen provided the original set of descriptors and then tried to improve his rules with partial success, as shown in Figure 9.3. With the machine's rules 99% accurate, however, he abandoned this effort and adopted the machine-synthesized rules as the basis for his professional work.

AQ11 in PL1	120 K byes of program space
Soybean data:	19 diseases
	35 descriptors (domain sizes 2-7)
	307 cases (descriptor-sets with confirmed diagnoses)
Test set:	376 new cases
	> 99% accurate diagnosis with machine rules
Machine runs using	83% accuracy with Jacobsen's rules
Rules of different origins	93% accuracy with interactively improved rule.

Figure 9.3
Experiment by Chilausky, Jacobsen, and Michalski.[19]

There are five major classifications of knowledge:

1. **Procedural knowledge** – rules, strategies, agendas, and procedures
2. **Declarative knowledge** – concepts, objects, and facts
3. **Meta-knowledge** – knowledge about the other types of knowledge and how to use them
4. **Heuristic knowledge** – rules of thumb
5. **Structural knowledge** – rule sets, concept relationships, concept to object relations [14]
    (p. 521)

The sources of these diverse forms of knowledge might be experts, end users, multiple experts, reports, books, regulations, online information, programs, and guidelines.

The processes of collecting and interpreting knowledge could require only several hours, but interpreting, analyzing, and designing a new model of the knowledge might, in contrast, require many hours (ibid., pp. 524–25).

We have already addressed some of the difficulties that can possibly be encountered when dealing with experts. Experts will tend to compile their problem-solving knowledge into a compact form that enables efficient problem-solving. They will also make mental leaps that go far beyond what the nonexpert knowledge engineer can appreciate or understand. Experts perhaps describe such leaps as intuition, but they could, in fact, be the result of some very complex reasoning based on deep knowledge (ibid. p. 527). Waterman [20] labels this dilemma the **knowledge-engineering paradox**, stating, "The more competent domain experts become, the less able they are to describe the knowledge they used to solve problems!"

The process of converting *shallow knowledge* (which might be based on intuition) into *deep* or *deeper knowledge* (which might be hidden in the expert's subconscious) is called the **knowledge compilation problem**. Developing skill in knowledge elicitation can help to facilitate the knowledge-acquisition process.

9.5 CLASSIC EXPERT SYSTEMS

Expert systems with hundreds to several thousand rules have been built for over 40 years. In this section we will explore a few of the best-known systems and present their background, history, main features, and main accomplishments.

9.5.1 DENDRAL

The story of DENDRAL, its longevity, and its overall importance as an example of expert-systems development, is almost as magnificent and old as the history of AI. The program is a success story from many perspectives, involving numerous chemists and computer scientists at Stanford University for many years, beginning in 1965. Many ideas pertinent to the development of AI, both in an experimental sense and in a formal analytic and scientific sense, were initiated with this project. For example, DENDRAL was an early and strong testament to the validity of the generate-and-test algorithm, as well as the rule-based approach to building expert systems.

The main developers of the system were Edward Feigenbaum (computer scientist), Joshua Lederberg (chemist, Nobel prizewinner in genetics), Bruce Buchanan (computer scientist), and Raymond Carhart (chemist), all at Stanford University.[5]

DENDRAL's task was to enumerate plausible chemical structures (atom-bond graphs) for organic molecules, given two kinds of information: (1) analytic instrument data from a mass spectrometer and a nuclear magnetic resonance spectrometer, and (2) user-supplied constraints on the answers, derived from any other source of knowledge (instrumental or contextual) available to the user. Feigenbaum [21] explained it as follows:

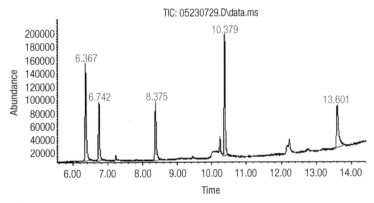

As Feigenbaum [21] noted. There was no algorithm for mapping the mass spectrograph of an unknown compound into its molecular structure. Hence, the task was to incorporate the experience, skill, and expertise of a human expert

Figure 9.4
Typical mass spectrum for unknown organic compounds.

(Lederberg) into a program that could perform at a human-expert level. In the process of developing DENDRAL, Lederberg had to learn a great deal about computing, as Feigenbaum had to learn about chemistry. It became apparent to Feigenbaum that in addition to many specific rules related to chemistry, chemists use a vast amount of heuristic knowledge based on experience and guessing.[11]

The input to DENDRAL typically consisted of the following information on the compound under study:

- The chemical formula, e.g., $C_6H_{12}O$
- The mass spectrum for unknown chemical compounds (see Figure 9.4)
- Nuclear magnetic resonance spectroscopy information

(*www.fda.gov/Food/scienceresearch/laboratorymethods/drugchemicalresiduesmethodology/ucm113209.htm*)

DENDRAL then performs a heuristic search in three stages without feedback called: plan – generate – test.

1. **Plan** – This stage reduces the answer from the set of all possible configurations of atoms to those consistent with the constraints derived from the mass spectrum. Constraints can be applied to select molecular fragments that must appear in the final structure and those that must not appear (ibid.).

2. **Generate** – A program called CONGEN was then used to generate possible structures. "Its foundation is a combinatorial algorithm (with mathematically proven properties of completeness and non-redundant generation) that can produce all the topologically legal candidate structures. Constraints supplied by the use or by the 'Plan' process prune and steer the generation to produce the plausible set (i.e., those satisfying the constraints) and not the enormous legal set." [5]

3. **Test** – This final stage ranks the output of the structures generated according to the quality of fit between the hypothesized mass structure and the experimental one.

DENDRAL would quickly reduce from hundreds of possible structures to several or possibly one. If several possible structures were generated, then they would be listed with probabilities attached.

Summary: DENDRAL demonstrated that computers could perform on a par with human experts in a restrictive domain. In chemistry it performed on a par or above a PhD chemist. The program was largely written in a dialect of Lisp called Interlisp. Subroutines such as CONGEN were written in Fortran and Sail. It was widely marketed and used by chemists throughout the United States. Feigenbaum [5 (p.11)] further states,

> DENDRAL's structure elucidation abilities are, paradoxically, both very general and very narrow. In general, DENDRAL handles all molecules, cyclic, and tree-like. In pure structure elucidation under constraints (with instrument data), CONGEN is unrivaled by human performance. ... Within these areas of knowledge-intensive specialization, DENDRAL's performance is usually not only much faster but also more accurate than expert human performance.

9.5.2 MYCIN

There can be little doubt that the most famous and most quoted expert system is MYCIN. It also was started and developed at Stanford University, as the PhD thesis of Edward Shortliffe. [22] This rule-based expert system was designed for diagnosis and therapy recommendations for infectious blood diseases caused by bacteria in the blood and meningitis (bacterial disease that causes inflammation of the membrane surrounding the brain and spinal cord). Such diseases can be quickly fatal if not treated early. MYCIN required some 20-person years to develop, uses backward chaining, and is comprised of more than 400 rules. Like DENDRAL, it was primarily written in Interlisp.

Clearly, due to the life-threatening nature of possible illnesses, it was important to be able to quickly diagnose the particular infection present and to quickly be able to decide on an appropriate course of drug intervention. There was, therefore, a need for such a system, and this was consistent with the direction that AI was taking in the 1970s.

Furthermore, if the system was going to be accepted and successful, then it had to be interactive and closely resemble interactions between physicians and resident blood infection experts. It should be able to answer doctors' queries and in general be accommodating (rather than removed or obstructive) to physicians' needs.

MYCIN is the most written about, studied, and modeled program. Durkin [14] dedicates a whole chapter (Ch. 5, pp.131–62) to MYCIN and provides some very interesting insights to the system's background, methods, performance, and evaluation. He notes that at the time (1970s), treatment procedures led to a misuse or overuse of antibiotics. He notes the study of Roberts and Visconti,[23] which "suggested that 66% of therapies selected by physicians were inadvisable and of these, over 62% used inappropriate combinations of antibiotics" (p.132). He notes that it was a time when the introduction of penicillin led to the introduction of a large number of antibiotics. These drugs, though very effective when properly prescribed and used, could have harmful side effects. A standard desk reference, *The Physician's Desk Reference*, was necessary and helpful. Furthermore, there was a shortage of expertise in the area of blood diseases. Hence, according to Durkin, for the reasons above, it seemed like a very good idea to develop the MYCIN program.

To prove its conclusion and be able to explain it, MYCIN works backward through its rule base, searching for confirming evidence. Using backward chaining, MYCIN could perform on a par with human experts. It confirmed that the power of experts' abilities comes from their knowledge and not some clever tricks.

The important results that MYCIN represented, based on Durkin,[14 (pp.134–140)] are as follows:

- *Knowledge is separated from control* – a hallmark of all expert systems, and MYCIN was one of the earliest examples of this. If the rules change you don't have to change the inference engine.

- *Incorporates meta-rules* (rules about rules) – when to break rules for special cases or situations.

- *Employs inexact reasoning* – MYCIN's certainty factor (CF) ranged from −1 (definitely false) to +1 (definitely true). Another term is "degree of belief."

- *Remembers prior sessions* – like a good human expert, every experience in his sphere has an impact on expert knowledge.

- *Accommodates the user* – the program has to be user friendly and transparent to the user/physician.

- *Natural language interaction* – MYCIN interacts with the physician in a natural fashion.

- *Provides explanations* – MYCIN can explain HOW and WHY it reached a particular conclusion.

- *Can provide alternative recommendations* – MYCIN tries to provide alternatives for the physician to choose from. In doing this, the program is being cooperative rather than directive; hence the physician can feel that she is being helped rather than dictated to or controlled.

EXAMPLE 9.1: HYPOTHETICAL EXAMPLES OF HOW AND WHY IN A MEDICAL SYSTEM

Two samples of the MYCIN program are represented in Figures 9.5a and 9.5b. Figure 9.5a shows a WHY and HOW to determine the suitability of surgery as a course of treatment for an elderly patient.

SYSTEM: How old is the patient?

USER: WHY

SYSTEM: This will aid in determining if the patient is a good candidate for surgery.

> Rule 057
> IF The patient is over 80 years old
> AND The patient is frail
> THEN The patient is probably not a good
>   candidate for open heart surgery.

SYSTEM: I recommend that the patient is not a good candidate for surgery.

USER: HOW

SYSTEM: I used rule 048 to conclude that patient should not undergo surgery:

> Rule 048
> IF The patient is frail (weak)
> THEN Recommend against surgery.

> I used Rule 057 to conclude the patient's condition
> IF The patient is over 80 years old
>   AND The patient is frail
> THEN The patient is probably not a good
>   candidate for open heart surgery.

Figure 9.5a
Illustrates a sample WHY and HOW plan from MYCIN.

My therapy recommendations will be designed to treat for organisms that are either very likely or, although less likely, would have a significant effect on therapy selection if they were present. It is important to cover for the following probable infection(s) and associated organism(s):

INFECTION-1 is CYSTITIS
<Item 1> PSEUDOMONAS-CEPACIA [ORGANISM-5]
<Item 2> CITROBACTER-DIVERSUS [ORGANISM-4]
<Item 3> E.COLI [ORGANISM-3]

INFECTION-2 is UPPER-RESPIRATORY-INFECTION
<Item 4> LISTERIA [ORGANISM-2]

INFECTION-3 is BACTEREMIA
<Item 5> ENTEROCOCCUS [ORGANISM-1]

[REC-1] My preferred therapy recommendation is as follows:
In order to cover for items <1 2 3 4 5>:
Give the following in combination:
1) KANAMYCIN
Dose: 750 mg (7.5 mg/kg) q12h IM (or IV)
    for 28 days
Comments: Modify dose in renal failure
2) PENICILLIN
Dose: 2,500,000 units (25,000 units/kg)
    q4h IV for 28 days

Figure 9.5b
Illustrates a sample diagnosis and treatment plan from MYCIN.

Figure 9.5b shows a recommendation for therapy that would rely on treatment for an infection through the use of drugs.

Summary: MYCIN is the most famous and successful expert system ever developed.

Its purpose is to diagnose and recommend treatment of blood infections, and it was eventually used as a training program for medical interns. As a model, it is exemplary of many good features and reasons for why one would like to build an expert system. MYCIN employs probabilities, it has an explaination facility, it tries to communicate in a friendly and useful manner for physicians, and it has more than 400 rules.

9.5.3 EMYCIN

MYCIN proved to be such a successful expert system that it was determined that it should be generalized. William van Melle used the MYCIN inference engine and a 1975 Pontiac Service Manual to build a 15-rule system for diagnosing problems with the car horn circuit. This toy system provided the basis for the development of the first expert system shell, EMYCIN. The acronym, which was suggested by Joshua Lederberg, stands for "Essential" or "Empty" MYCIN. A shell is a special-purpose tool designed for certain types of applications in which the user must supply only

the knowledge base. In the case of EMYCIN the shell was made by removing the medical knowledge base of the MYCIN expert system.[12 (p. 28),24] Van Melle [25] wrote, "One ought to be able to take out the clinical knowledge and plug in knowledge about some other domain."

The goal was naturally to retain the excellent features of MYCIN, including the representation of domain-specific knowledge, ability to traverse the knowledge base, the ability to support uncertainty, hypothetical reasoning, explanation facilities, and so forth.

EMYCIN supported both forward and backward chaining and led to the development of many expert systems, including PUFF,[26] an application for the diagnosis of pulmonary problems. It was a very important development for expert-systems technology because it provided a tool whereby expert systems could be built "cost effectively," which we noted in Section 9.3 was a requirement for their success as listed by Donald Michie. EMYCIN served as the model for all future expert-system shells.

9.5.4 PROSPECTOR

PROSPECTOR was an early expert system designed for decision-making problems in mineral exploration. It was noted for using a structure called an **inference network** to represent its database. The program was written in 1978 by Richard O. Duda, who, at the time, was at Stanford Research Institute (SRI).[27] We summarize its most important features as represented in Firebaugh. [11 (p. 345)]

- The system represents fuzzy input on a range from −5 = *certainly false* to +5 = *certainly true* and produces conclusions with associated uncertainty factors.

- The system's expertise is based on the hand-crafted knowledge of 12 major prospect-scale models and 23 smaller regional-scale models. The prospect-scale models describe major ore deposits:
  - ○ Massive Sulfide Deposit, Kuroko Type
  - ○ Mississippi-Valley-Type Lead-Linz
  - ○ Western States Sandstone Uranium

- Prospector doesn't *understand* the rules in its knowledge base, but *can explain* the steps used in reaching its conclusions.

- The knowledge acquisition system KAS was developed for easy editing and expansion of the inference network structure in which the knowledge base is stored.

- PROSPECTOR performs at the level of an expert hard-rock geologist and was successful at prospecting. It predicted a molybdenum deposit near Mt. Tolman in Washington State, which was later confirmed by core drilling as having a value of $100 million.

Prospector uses a knowledge representation scheme called an **inference network** which is a form of semantic networks described in Chapter 6. Next, we will summarize the main features of inference networks and their correspondence to the elements of a semantic network.

Nodes – correspond to propositional assertions rather than a single noun. A typical model contains about 150 nodes. A node might consist of the following assertions:

- There is a pervasively biotized hornblende.

- There is a cretaceous dike.

- There is an alteration favorable for the potassic zone of a porphyry copper deposit.

Arcs – Akin to semantic networks, arcs specify the relationship between nodes. In particular, they represent the inference rules that specify how the probability of one assertion affects the probability of another assertion. A typical model contains about 100 arcs.

Inference trees – The nodes and arcs are organized in an inference tree with the following structure:

- Top-level hypotheses – no outgoing arcs

- Intermediate factors – both incoming and outgoing arcs

- Evidential statements – no incoming arcs

PROSPECTOR works like a bottom-up tree, using evidence to forward chain to a location that suggests further exploration. The program is designed to run in three modes: compiled execution, batch processing, or interactive consultation. The user's answers range from −5 (assertion absolutely false) to +5 (assertion absolutely true).

At any point in the interaction the user may ask WHY to ask the system for an explanation of the rationale for a question. Thereby the skilled geologist can follow PROSPECTOR's line of reasoning. Other commands can provide tracing inferences, change assertions, and list the best "current estimate" of the prospect. The program also has graphics capability and can produce a map with probability distributions for success and failure in an area.

For further information regarding the data listed in Table 9.2, see the following:
Nokleberg et al., 1987. "Significant metalliferous lode deposits and placer districts of Alaska." U.S. Geological Survey Bulletin 1786, p. 104.
Cox, D. P., and Singer, D. A., eds. 1986. Mineral deposit models: U.S. Geological Survey Bulletin 1693, p. 379.

Table 9.2 illustrates the effectiveness of the Prospector II expert system. Of 124 deposits classified by a panel of geologists, 103 were classified the same by Prospector II.

"By combining Prospector II's first and second choices as indicating a match with the classifications made by the panel, there was agreement in 111 out of the 119 deposits classified – that is, a 93 percent agreement."

Table 9.2 Comparison of classification between Prospector 11 and panel of geologists using the Cox-Singer deposit classification for 124 metalliferous lode deposits in Alaska.

Deposit type (classified by panel of geologists)	Frequency of ranking (classified by Prospector 11)				
	1st	2nd	3rd	4th	5th
1. Gabbroic Ni-Cu deposits (7a)	4	0	1	0	1
2. Podiform chromite deposits (8a)	1	0	0	0	0
3. Serpentine-hosted asbestos deposits (8d)	1	0	0	0	0
4. Alaskan-pge (9)	5	0	0	0	0
5. W skarn deposits (14a)	1	0	0	0	0
6. Sn skarn deposits (14b)	2	0	0	0	0
7. Sn vein deposits (15b)	1	0	1	0	0
8. Sn greisen deposits (15c)	1	0	0	0	0
9. Porphyry Cu deposits (17)	4	1	0	0	0
10. Cu skarn deposits (18b)	2	0	1	0	0
11. Zn-Pb skarn deposits (18c)	2	0	0	0	0
12. Fe skarn deposits (18d)	4	1	0	0	0
13. Porphyry Cu-Mo deposits (21a)	1	0	2	0	0
14. Porphyry Mo, low F deposits (21b)	1	0	0	0	0
15. Polymetallic vein deposits (22c)	14	3	0	0	0
16. Basaltic Cu deposits (23)	0	0	1	0	0
17. Cyprus massive sulfide deposits (24a)	0	0	1	0	0
18. Besshi massive sulfide deposits (24b)	3	0	0	0	0
19. Epithermal vein deposits (25b, 25c, 25d, 25c)	2	0	0	0	0
20. Hot-spring Hg deposits (27a)	3	1	0	0	0
21. Sb-Au vein deposits (27d, 27e)	5	0	0	0	0
22. Kuroko massive sulfide deposits (28a)	9	0	0	0	0
23. Sandstone U deposits (30c)	1	0	0	0	0
24. Sedimentary exhalative Zn-Pb deposits (31a)	2	0	0	0	0
25. Bedded barite deposits (31b)	2	0	0	0	0
26. Kipushi Cu-Pb-Zn deposits (32c)	1	0	0	0	0
27. Low-sulfide Au quartz vein deposits (36a)	25	1	0	0	0
Totals	103	8	7	0	1

Source: McCammon, R. Numerical Mineral Deposit Models, Table 4. Available at *http://pubs.usgs.gov/bul/b2004/html/bull2004numerical_mineral_deposit_models.htm May 15,* 2011
NOTE: Alphanumeric characters in parentheses refer to model numbers in Cox and Singer (1986).

9.5.5 Fuzzy Knowledge and Bayes' Rule

Geology and mineral exploration is a classic domain for the use and discussion of uncertainty. Fuzzy knowledge (as discussed in Chapter 8, "Uncertainty in AI") deals with making good decisions when dealing with uncertainty. PROSPECTOR works with rules of the form:

IF E, THEN H (to degree LS, LN)

where

H = a given hypothesis
E = evidence for the hypothesis
LS = measure of support for hypothesis if E present
LN = measure of discredit to hypothesis if E missing

The values of LS and LN are defined when the model is built and remain constant during the analysis. A small portion of the set of rules might read:

R1: IF E_1 AND E_2,   THEN H_2(LS_1, LN1)
R2: IF H_2,   THEN H_1(LS_2, LN2)
R3: IF E_3 THEN H_1(LS_3, LN3)

This net incorporates R1 – R3 from Figure 9.6 and indicates how evidence is used in reaching the hypotheses. H1 is the top level hypothesis or "conclusion" of this portion of the net.

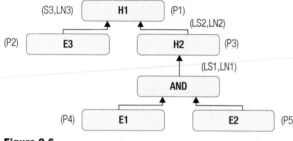

Figure 9.6
Portion of inference net from PROSPECTOR.

Prospector was the first expert system to incorporate Bayes' Theorem for evidence for computing P (H | E) and propagating uncertainties through the system. See Chapter 8 for a discussion of this rule.

In addition to using Bayes' rule for computing probabilities, PROSPECTOR uses heuristics from the theory of fuzzy sets to propagate uncertainties based on logical contributions of assertions (A_1, A_2, ... A_K), in either a conjunctive or disjunctive form:

Conjunction: $A = A_1$ AND A_2 AND ... A_K

Disjunction: $A = A_1$ OR A_2 OR ... A_K,

Assuming that we know the probabilities P (A_i|E) associated with assertions A_i for the case in which evidence E is presented. The challenge is to propagate the probability of A being true in light of this evidence. Lotfi Zadeh (See Chapter 8) proposed the following set of heuristic equations which were applied in PROSPECTOR:

Conjunction: $P(A|E) = MIN_i (P A_i|E)$

Disjunction: $P(A|E) = MAX_i (P (A_i|E)$

In brief, the Conjunction (AND) of assertions depends on the assertion with minimum fuzzy measurement of the assertions, while the Disjunction (OR) of assertions depends on the maximum fuzzy measurement of the assertions. Let us turn this **fuzzy logic** example into a real-world problem you can probably relate to:

We want to determine the probability that someone whom you are about to meet will like you. Here are the pieces of evidence with probabilities:

Evidence = e = You will meet

E_1 = You communicate easily = 0.80

E_2 = You matched well on the computer dating survey = 0.84

E_3 = Your life situations match = 0.80

E_4 = You are pretty busy = 0.50

Fuzzy logic will generate a conclusion of .50 that you will like each other. This might seem "unfair" since all the other pieces of evidence look good. (High matching, high probabilities. Keep in mind, however, that all the reasons you might *not* like each other haven't been listed either! Maybe your match has some habits you really don't like? Maybe your match is a workaholic? Maybe this person has reasons for desiring a courtship that are different from yours? Anyway, dating, like love, cannot be just a probabilistic thing!

On the other hand, let's consider the Disjunction of Evidence Formula:

$$\text{If } E_1 \text{ Or } E_2 \text{ Or } E_3 \text{ Or } \dots E_n, \; p(E|e) = \text{Max}[p(E_i|e)].$$

What is the probability that you will fall in love when you meet your match?

E_1 = She contacted me (Nice!) = 0.80
E_2 = We matched high on the computer dating survey = 0.80
E_3 = We have never met = 0.50
E_4 = We carry a large amount of life's "baggage" into a relationship = 0.85

Here, the Fuzzy Logic rule of Disjunction will go by E_4. In reality, this is probably a good representative value, and PROSPECTOR used an approach similar to this.

Summary: It is noteworthy that thousands of prospective mineral deposits are usually explored before one is found that could lead to a profitable mine. The PROSPECTOR Project was funded by SRI, the U.S. Geological Survey and the National Science Foundation. Many of the researchers involved went on to join or develop successful commercial efforts with expert systems.

9.6 ■ METHODS FOR EFFICIENCY

As expert systems grew and became more complex, it became evident that methods were needed to handle rules efficiently in terms of search, conflict resolution and activation, and general management. In Section 7.4.1 of Chapter 7, we discussed conflict resolution strategies. In this section we will address two methods that have been developed for handling rules in critical situations and for efficiency.

9.6.1 ■ Demon Rules

Demon rules are a way that expert system designers combine forward and backward chaining. Durkin [14] defines a *Demon Rule* as:

A rule that fires whenever its premises match the contents of working memory.

The concept is that these "friendly demons" are there, sitting among backward-chaining rules, but without participating in the backward chaining process. Instead they remain in the background, until "called upon" by information that appears in working memory. When called, the demon will fire and enter its conclusion into working memory. The new information it generates could support backward-chaining rules, or "it might set into motion other demon rules that collectively act like a series of forward chaining rules" (ibid.). Demons thereby allow systems to be self-modifying, an essential aspect of applications that need to adapt to new situations.[14 (p. 115)]

We present the notion of demons through the hypothetical example of nuclear power station fire alarms. Alarms will be set off when there is too much heat. Too much heat means that machines should be shutdown. If machines are shutdown, then the building should be evacuated. Using backward chaining will help a complete system shutdown so that diagnosis of the problem can be done.

Demon 1 Generator Heat Problem
    IF POWER IS OFF
    AND TEMPERATURE IS > 500,
    THEN PROBLEM = GENERATOR HEAT PROBLEM

Demon 2 Emergency Situation / Sound Alarms
    IF PROBLEM = TANK PRESSURE,
    THEN SITUATION = EMERGENCY / SOUND ALARMS

Demon 3 Evacuate
    IF SITUATION = EMERGENCY,
    THEN RESPONSE = EVACUATE PERSONNEL

We can see how these demons work together (in a backward chaining style) to handle this potential emergency situation. Heat will set off alarms and alarms will lead to the evacuation of the building.

9.6.2 The Rete Algorithm

The Rete Algorithm involves efficient negotiation of a number of component procedures of expert systems that we have already discussed in Chapter 7 (including Markov Chains) and in our present discussion. Once one gets into the construction of fairly large expert systems of dozens to hundreds of rules, matters of efficiency become rather important. That is, we need a procedure that knows which rules will apply without having to test each of them sequentially.

In his PhD thesis on the OPS (Official Production System) Shell, (1979 at Carnegie Mellon University), Charles Forgy developed a solution to this problem. Forgy's concept was that the net could hold much information

The word "Rete" means "net" in Latin.

about rules and rule firings, and this could significantly reduce the amount of searching needed. The Rete Algorithm is a dynamic data structure, which can be reorganized once search proceeds.

Giarratano and Riley [12 (p.38)] state,

> The Rete Algorithm is a very fast pattern matcher that obtains its speed by storing information about the rules in a network in memory. The Rete Algorithm is intended to improve the speed of forward-chained rule systems by limiting the effort required to re-compute the conflict set after a rule is fired.

The algorithm is costly in terms of memory space requirements, but this is not a problem because memory has become very inexpensive. The Rete, as it is known, takes advantage of two empirical observations that were used to come up with its data structure, as Giarratano and Riley further state:

1. **Temporal Redundancy** – The firing of a rule usually changes only a few facts, and only a few rules are affected by each of these changes.

2. **Structural Similarity** – The same pattern often appears in the left-hand side of more than one rule (ibid.).

In the 1970s, when computers were much slower, and with expert systems having thousands of rules, The Rete Algorithm was an important practical tool which could facilitate fast execution.

On every cycle of its execution, the algorithm looks only for changes in matches of rules. This greatly speeds up the matching of facts to antecedents over trying to match facts against every rule on every recognize-act cycle. See Figure 9.7

The Rete Algorithm has been an important contributor to the practical and efficient application of expert systems.

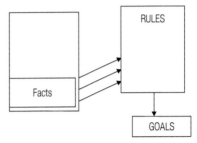

Figure 9.7
An interesting feature of the Rete Algorithm is the discovery of the notion that it is more efficient to match a few facts maintained in the inference cycle against antecedents of rules, than to check rules for facts.

■9.7■ CASE-BASED REASONING

This section introduces **case-based reasoning** (CBR), an approach to problem-solving that really is the basis for many of the fundamental ways civilized man functions and makes decisions. The essence is that we learn from experience—the experiences others have had and our own experiences. It is on this basis that we make decisions. Naturally, these experiences must somehow be documented, otherwise their usefulness is limited. You may have heard the saying: "What is the purpose of history if we don't learn from it?"

Lawyers, doctors, teachers, mechanics, sportsmen, or trades-people—people make decisions based on their previous experiences. For lawyers it is precedent. How have cases with similar circumstances in the past been resolved? What is the tendency of the particular judge we are dealing with? Is he conservative or liberal? What kind of decisions is the judge likely to make, based on the precedents in similar cases? The medical profession is similar; most decisions doctors make are actually based on probabilities— the kinds of Bayesian probabilities that you learned about in Chapter 8. Given the particular signs and symptoms that a patient has had, and given the patient's age, medical history, and other known relevant factors (e.g., existing conditions, previous surgeries, allergies to drugs, medical insurance) a doctor is able to make the decision(s) most likely to result in a favorable outcome. Furthermore, today's doctors must also be aware of how their decision(s) might result in a malpractice suit! For a teacher, the circumstances are similar. We use techniques that have worked in the past. If a certain course has gone well with a certain text book or a certain order of topics or with certain materials, we will tend to use them again. If not, we will vary and try things out according to our experience. It is the same for auto mechanics and other trades people; people in all walks of life learn from experience and know how to ply their trades.

Very little that one can read in books can entirely compensate for the knowledge gained by experience. Rules are good to know, for example, you should not drive a brand new car at full speed for the first 1000 miles; but possibly, rules of thumb, heuristics, are even more important— for example, "don't drive a large luxury sedan as you would drive a sports car"— are even more im-

SIDEBAR

Example: Baseball CBR

Let us imagine that we could represent any baseball game situation with a 6-tuple. The 6-tuple would consist of: (1) the inning, (2) the number of outs, (3) the number of base runners, (4) the score (5) the batter, and (6) what the case-based reasoning system suggests should be done (swing, take a pitch, bunt). The top of the inning is represented by positive numbers and the bottom of the inning by negative numbers. The number of base-runners and their positions can be represented as follows 0 = no one on base, 1 = runner on 1st base, 2 = runner on 2nd base, 3 = runner on 3rd base, 4 = runners on 1st and 2nd, 5 = runners on 1st and 3rd base, 6 = runners on 1st, 2nd, and 3rd base (bases loaded). The score can embed whether we are winning or losing, for example, +6 4 means we are winning 6 – 4, whereas −6 4 means we are losing 6 – 4.

So let us say we have the following 6-tuple representing a game situation for the New York Yankees in 2010: (−8, 0, 4, −2 3, 13, 3). This 6-tuple translates to: (1) We are in the bottom of the 8th inning; (2) there is no one out; (3) there are runners on 1st and 2nd; (4) the Yankees are losing 3–2; (5) Number 13 is at bat, and (6) the system recommends a bunt. This means that the superstar Alex Rodriguez (one of the best and highest paid players in baseball) is batting. The percentage play that the CBR should discover for most players, and the best suggestion in the circumstance, is to bunt the runners over to 2nd and 3rd bases, and there would be one out. That is why well over 50% of the situations in which there are runners on 1st and 2nd with no one out result in a run scored. Here, however, is where the CBR system would have to demonstrate some a priori knowledge or intelligence for the 2010 New York Yankees—*Alex Rodriguez never bunts*. A study of a database of previous cases would reveal that he has bunted very rarely in his career and in similar previous situations has not been asked to bunt, even though this is by far the best recommended percentage play. There are three other players on the present-day New York Yankees Team who are never asked to bunt in similar situations. They are: Jorge Posada (20),[†] Mark Texeira (25), and Robinson Cano (24)[‡]. Each of these players is considered such big slugger that he is never asked to bunt, in any situation. Our CBR would have to recognize the general case and distinguish the special cases of Rodriguez, Posada, Texeira, and Cano batting (via their numbers −13, 20, 25, 24).

I (DK) did a little research and discovered that my suggested strategy that one should bunt with runners on first and second and no one out in a close game is considered a bit archaic. Most baseball analysts do not think so cautiously, but the key is the probability of generating a run – The contemporary thinking is that it very much depends on who is batting. A very interesting discussion can be found at: http://baseballanalysts.com/archives/2006/07/empirical_analy_1.php June 15, 2010. [a]

[†]Now retired
[‡]Now (2014) playing for Seattle Mariners

portant. Why? Because, such rules of thumb tend to cover a greater number of situations. It is most important, however, that whatever kinds of rules or heuristics we follow, we understand the underlying reasoning behind them and therefore know why and when to invoke them. One might ask, "Why did I pay the mechanic for the little job he did? He only tightened a screw— anyone could have done that." The answer, of course, is: "You paid him for his know-how— the fact that he knew which screw to tighten!"

Finally, let us consider the case of athletes or sportspeople. Almost everything they do is based on statistics and trying to match or improve on past performance. In baseball, it might be how well does a batter do against a particular pitcher? Nearly all decisions by the manager are based on precedent or statistics. What outcomes are most likely to be brought about by certain actions in certain situations?

In essence, this is what (CBR) is all about. That is, building AI systems that are able to match cases of solutions according to precedent; in other words, trying to solve new problems by matching them to solutions of old problems. Hence, it is about building knowledge-based systems that learn from previous situations.[28] The main element of a CBR system is the case base; a structure that stores the problems, elements (cases), and its solutions. Therefore, a **case base** can be visualized as a database where a collection of problems is stored, keeping a relationship with the solutions to every problem stored, which gives the system the ability to generalize in order to solve new problems.[29]

The learning capabilities of CBR systems are defined by the result of their own structures, typically composed of four phases: **retrieval, reuse, revision,** and **retention.**[30] The first phase, (retrieve) consists of finding the case most similar to the proposed problem, and retrieving it from the case base. Once a series of cases are extracted from the case base, the second phase (reuse) adapts the selected case to fit the current problem. Once the system finds a solution to the problem it is revised and checked to see whether it is indeed a solution to the problem. Once the proposed solution is confirmed as appropriate, it is retained and can serve as a solution to future problems.[29]

One of the main issues for CBR design is the choice of a data structure. Data structures can range from simple tuples, which store the cases to be matched and their solutions, to complex proof trees. Most typical are a large number of situation–action rules, whereby the rules are the most salient features to be matched, and the operators comprise transformations to be used in new situations.

The most difficult decision for CBR systems is the choice of the most salient features of cases for indexing and retrieval.[29] Kolodner suggests that it is most important for cases to be organized by the goals and needs of the problem solver; this requires careful analysis of the case descriptors in the context of how they will be used in the problem solution.[30]

Kolodner offers the following set of possible preference heuristics to facilitate the storage and retrieval of cases:

1. *Goal-directed preference.* Organize cases at least in part by goal descriptions. Retrieve cases that have the same goal as the current situation.

2. *Salient-feature preference.* Prefer cases that match the most important features or those matching the largest number of important situations.

3. *Specify preference.* Look for cases that match features as closely as possible, before considering more general matches.

4. *Frequency preference.* Check first the most frequently matched cases.

5. *Recency preference.* Prefer case used most recently.

6. *Ease of adaptation preference.* Use first cases most easily adapted to the current situation (Luger, p. 307–308).

The notion of "similarity" becomes a more important and subtle issue. Selecting and defining the vocabulary that determines similarity is an important factor. As the number of cases for matching increases, good and bad factors arise; that is, more cases offer the opportunity for better matching, but the process of matching also becomes more complex and time consuming.

CBR is not a new area of AI and is often used when the domain rules are incomplete, ill-defined, or inconsistent.[31] Case-based approaches can be useful in enabling an expert system to learn from previous experiences by storing solutions that have worked or failed in the past. This can greatly curtail the overall problem-solving process. Long before expert systems were developed, an early example of learning from experience was the building of signature tables of heuristics for checkers programs by Arthur Samuel.[32] His work, which tried to identify and store good and bad board situations, will be presented in detail in Chapter 16, "Advanced Computer Games," and will be applicable to this discussion.

During the past 20 years, CBR has drawn a great deal of attention via the large number of successful commercial and industrial computer applications that have been developed using this approach. Systems commonly in daily use include applications assisting in customer support, sales support, diagnostics, and help-desk systems as described by Watson.[33, 34] The earliest CBR systems were developed nearly 30 years ago. One of the first systems was developed by Rissland and was designed to support legal arguments.[35] CASEY and PROTOS were early CBR systems that exploited case histories of patients and interns' experiences with other patients. [36, 37]

Human Interest Notes

Janet Kolodner

Janet L. Kolodner

Janet L. Kolodner (1954 –) is a Regents' Professor in the School of Interactive Computing at Georgia Tech and founding editor in chief of *The Journal of the Learning Sciences*, an interdisciplinary cognitive science journal that focuses on learning and education. She obtained a BS degree in Mathematics and Computer Science from Brandeis University, and then an MS and a PhD (1980) from Yale. During the 1980s, she pioneered CBR with a number of publications in the field, also demonstrating how CBR could be linked with analogy. Her book, *Case-Based Reasoning* [38] synthesizes work across the field of CBR from its inception to 1993. The notion of a case-based design aid (CBDA), an indexed library of design cases with the kinds of information in them that can help with design decisions, comes from her lab, which was the originator of the first CBDA, Archie-II.

During the late 1980s and early 1990s, Kolodner used the cognitive model implied by CBR to address issues in creative design. Automated case-based reasoners from her lab have focused on CBR for situations of real-world complexity. She has developed an approach to education called "Learning by Design," and it is incorporated into the published middle-school science curriculum called Project-Based Inquiry Science (PBIS).

Kolodner was founding director of Georgia Tech's EduTech Institute, whose mission was to use what we know about cognition to inform the design of educational technology and learning environments. EduTech's major efforts, under her direction, were in the areas of design education and software in support of collaborative learning.

As described earlier, auto mechanics and experts in hardware diagnosis in general will bring extensive theoretical knowledge of electronic and mechanical systems, including recall of successful and failed experiences, to the process of solving a new problem. CBR has proven to be an important component of many hardware diagnostic systems. Skinner and Luger used CBR on the maintenance of signal sources and batteries in earth-orbiting satellites.[39] Later, this was applied to failure analysis of discrete component semiconductors.[40] Automated explanation for why a particular case is chosen as the best match is desirable but difficult to achieve. Perhaps more importantly, any degree of sophistication in the explanation of how and why a particular case is chosen is particularly difficult, though not necessarily of importance. In the case of recurring weak satellite signals, CBR could not discern their causes, and this introduces an example of a different approach to problem solving: model-based reasoning, which was able to accomplish the task of identifying the cause of weak satellite signals.[39, 28 (p.309)]

APPLICATION BOX

CBR FOR FINDING OIL SLICKS

Recently (June 2010), in the Gulf of Mexico, there occurred the worst oil spill ever known. The cost amounted to billions of dollars, and there ensued far-reaching effects on the ecological life and economic welfare of the entire region, and the potential for disastrous consequences for the entire Eastern seaboard.

In 2008, Aitor Mata and Juan Manuel Corchado published a paper titled "Forecasting the Probability of Finding Oil Slicks Using a CBR System," [41] which addressed how such disasters could be avoided. Given complex oceanic conditions, numerous variables and elements, this is a difficult problem. The basis of such an effort is the gathering of data from previous spills, including measuring numerous variables, piecing them together using satellite images to obtain the precise position of slicks. The basis for the study by the authors is the Prestige Oil Spill generating data from November 2002 to April 2003. The program generates a probability of between 0 and 1 of finding an oil slick after an oil spill. Once an oil spill occurs, it is important to determine if an area will be contaminated. The more data available on how oil slicks behave, the better we can determine how they *will* behave, and this is done by obtaining Synthetic Aperture Images (SAR) images by satellite. Areas where there appear to be no waves are indicative of oil spills. Figure 9.8 illustrates an SAR image which shows oil spills (ibid., p. 8240). In this way, normal sea variability can be distinguished from oil slicks. The distinction between the surface of an oil slick and normal quiet waters, however, is sometimes difficult to distinguish, however, by applying a series of computational tools this can be resolved. In addition, once a slick is identified, collecting various atmospheric, maritime, and weather condition data can help explain how slicks evolve.

Then Oil Slick CBR (OSCBR, as the system is known) combines the capabilities of CBR and the power of artificial intelligence techniques. As part of the pre-processing, historical data is collected and then principal components analysis (PCA) is used to reduce the number of variables and therefore the number of candidate cases. Then a technique called Growing Cell Structures (GCS) is used to organize cases by their similarity and proximity. Mata and Corchado state:

"When a new cell is introduced in the structure, the closest cells move towards the new one, changing the overall structure of the system, as shown in in (2) and (3).

Figure 9.8
NASA Satellite image showing an oil slick.

The weights of the winning, Wc, and its neighbors, Wn, are changed. The changed value is represented by Wc $(t+1)$ and Wn $(t+1)$ respectively. The terms εc and εn represent the learning rates for the winner and χ, the value of the input vector.

$$Wc(t+1) = Wc(t) + \varepsilon c \,(\chi - Wc)$$

$$Wn\,(t+1) = Wn\,(t) + \varepsilon n\,(\chi - Wn)$$

The pseudocode of the insertion process is shown below

```
Growing Cell Structure Insertion Pseudocode:

(1)  The most similar cell to the new one is found.

(2)  The new cell is introduced in the middle of the connection between the
     most

(3)  similar cell and the least similar to the new one.

(4)  Direct neighbors to the closest cell change their values by approximating
     to

(5)  the new cell and specified percentage of the distance between them and
     the new cell."
```

(ibid. p. 8243).

This takes care of the first phase of CBR, retrieve. The problem of finding the most relevant candidate cases uses the GCS again. The similarity between cases is determined by calculating a multidimensional distance. Then the problem of predicting the future probability of finding oil slicks in an area is generated using an artificial neural network with a hybrid learning system. Radial basis functions are a type of neural network (See Chapter 11), which is efficient in training to identify the most similar cases in the case base to the proposed problem (ibid.). This addresses the problem of reuse.

A set of square colored areas appear and the intensity of their color corresponds with the possibility of finding an oil slick in that area. The proposed solution is to check with a human user, and the system provides an automatic method of revision that must be checked by an expert. *Explanations* for the proposed solution are reviewed, and its proximity is compared with other selected cases. As long as the proposed solution does not seem too far afield, it is accepted. Once accepted, the solution is considered good and retained and added to the case base for future use with new problems.

The OSCBR system, using a combination of AI techniques with CBR, has proven to be close to 90% accurate in predicting oil slicks as the number of cases increases. The burning question, however, is "What can the OSCBR system been able to do future oil spoils?"

▣ 9.8 ▣ MORE RECENT EXPERT SYSTEMS

More recent expert systems integrated other well-known and tested approaches to dealing with large amounts of domain-specific data, including databases, data mining, machine learning, and CBR. **Hybrid-intelligent approaches** have been used in many diverse areas, such as speech/natural language understanding, robotics, medical diagnosis, fault diagnosis of industrial equipment, education, assessment, and information retrieval. In this section, we will briefly present and describe some examples of these systems.

▣ 9.8.1 ▣ Systems for Improving Employment Matching

Kouremenos Drigas et al. have developed a number of expert systems during the past two decades, but particularly suitable for times of a suffering economy was their development of a system for matching jobs with the skills of the unemployed in more than a rudimentary Boolean way. [42] An earlier expert system that tried to match qualified individuals with small companies was the Skills Analyzer Tool.[43] It combined neural networks (see Chapter 11) with rule-based analysis to match employees with certain jobs on new projects. Collaboration filtering techniques were used in a later system (CASPER) to help enforce intelligence in the search engine of the JobFinder Web site (*www.jobfinder.com*).[43,44] CASPER consisted of a user profiling system, an automated collaborative filtering engine for recommendation services, and a personalized retrieval engine. Mobile Agents Technology (see Chapter 6, Section 6.12) has been applied to the EMA employment agent and is a typical recommender agent.[45] The methods of CASPER and EMA have been extensively used in recommendation and information retrieval, but one could hardly call them experts in job matching.

The system for job matching developed by Drigas et al. employed the following features:

1. Connectivity with a corporate database contains the unemployed, employers, and offered jobs records

2. Use of neurofuzzy techniques (see Chapters 8 and 11) for the inductive training (through examples) of complex fuzzy terms, also used in the final evaluation phase

3. Supervised retraining of the neuro-fuzzy network when recommended by the administrator

4. Fuzzy models that design and develop the fuzzy inference engine

5. Combination processing of the fuzzy elements for the final data evaluation

6. Flexible and friendly user interface in Visual Basic [42]

Large training sets of old historical records of unemployed who belonged to the same social class, previously rejected or approved at several posts, were used to define the weights of the system parameters. Retraining was performed after a standard number of new cases became available. The output was a measure of the suitability for certain jobs by the unemployed (ibid.).

▣ 9.8.2 ▣ An Expert System for Vibration Fault Diagnosis

One of the important roles of expert systems is fault diagnosis. In the case of expensive, high-speed, critical machinery, early and accurate detection of faults is very important. In the case of machinery, a common indicator of abnormal conditions is vibration in rotating machinery. Upon detection of a fault, the maintenance engineer is able to identify symptomatic information, interpret various error messages and indications, and come up with the correct diagnosis. That is, the components that might have caused the fault and the reasons the component(s) has failed. [45]

Machinery will tend to have hundreds of parts and be highly complex. It will require domain-specific expertise to diagnose and repair machinery. A decision table (DT) is a compact, fast, accurate way to solve problems (see the CarBuyer Example in Chapter 7).

The VIBEX Expert System combines decision table analysis (DTA) constructed on known cases and a DT constructed for the purpose of making classifications using the inductive knowledge acquisition process. The VIBEX DT, coupled with machine learning techniques (See Chapters 11 and 12), makes diagnoses more efficiently than the VIBEX (VIBration Expert) TBL, dealing with 14 vibration causes and cases where the probability is high.[46] The DTA is constructed in cooperation with a human expert, resulting in a set of rules that compose the knowledge base of the system. The Bayesian algorithm (Chapters 7 and 8) is then used to establish certainty factors for the rules. The DT analysis then employs the C4.5 Algorithm [47] as a convenient way to systematically break down and classify the data. This requires definition of the classes that represent the vibration cause, and attributes that represent the vibration phenomena required for sets of samples to enable machine learning. The C4.5 uses inductive inference from examples to build the decision tree. Thereby, it plays a role itself as a vibration diagnostic tool. VIBEX embeds the cause-result matrix, comprising some 1800 confidence factors suitable for monitoring and diagnosing the rotating machinery.

9.8.3 Automatic Dental Identification

For forensic reasons, it is very important to be able to quickly and accurately assess dental records. Given the abundance of data available, particularly as a result of mass disasters such as wars, natural disasters, and terrorist attacks, the automation of identification of dental records is both necessary and very useful.

In 1997 the Criminal Justice Information Services (CJIS) division of the FBI created a Dental Task Force (DTF) to foster the creation of an Automated Dental Identification System (ADIS). The purpose of ADIS was to provide automated search and matching capabilities for digitized radiographs and photographic images, in order to generate a short list for dental forensic agents.[48] The philosophy behind the architecture of the system is to exploit high-level features for fast retrieval of a candidate list. A potential match's search component uses this list and then refines the candidate list, using low-level image features reducing to a short match list. Hence the architecture includes (1) a Record Preprocessing component, (2) a Potential Matches Search component, and (3) an Image Comparison component. The record preprocessing component handles the following five tasks:

1. Record cropping into dental films
2. Enhancement of films to compensate for possible poor contrast
3. Classification of films into bitewing, periapical, or panoramic views
4. Segmentation of teeth from films
5. Annotating of teeth with labels corresponding to their location

There are three modes of operation for the Web-ADIS: (1) configuration mode, (2) identification mode, and (3) maintenance mode. Configuration mode is for tuning, Identification Mode is used by the client to get the mechanics for the submitted record.

The Maintenance Mode is used for uploading the database server with new reference records and also to enable updating of the preprocessing server. The system has achieved a genuine acceptance rate of 85%.

9.8.4 More Expert Systems Employing Case-Based Reasoning

Now we will briefly discuss some more recent systems that employ CBR. The work of He et al.[49] addressed interface design of Web-based CBR retrieval systems. They note that although there exist a number of systems that assist with customer support, sales support, diagnostics, and help-desk systems, most have focused on functional capability and implementation, rather than interface design. Interface design is an important component of systems design, and, as He et al. (ibid.) argue, more effort needs to be devoted to the study of users' mental models for searching a CBR system. Conceptual descriptions with conceptual schemas can be provided by the CBR retrieval system to enable users to receive training to achieve higher levels of learning and problem solving. [50] The value of a hybrid approach combining CBR with a rule-based approach for domain independent decision support in an ICU was demonstrated by Kumar, Singh, and Sanyal (2007). [51] The case base consisted of several domains such as poisoning, accident, cancer, viral diseases, and others. Flexibility was induced by giving more importance to the CBR system and making sure that the rule base consists of rules that are common for all domains of the ICU.

9.9 CHAPTER SUMMARY

Chapter 9 discusses one of the oldest, most well-known, and most favorably recognized fields of AI – expert systems. They are ideal for domains that are well defined, in which there is a large corpus of human expertise and knowledge, yet the knowledge is mainly heuristic and uncertain. Although expert systems do not necessarily perform in the same manner that human experts will perform, they are built on the premise that they are somehow mimicking or modeling the decision-making and problem-solving skills of human experts. An important feature of expert systems, which sets them apart from typical programs, is that they will usually include an *explain facility*. That is, they will try to explain how they reached their conclusions, in other words, what kind of chain of reasoning did they use to reach a conclusion?

Section 9.1 provides a background on what kinds of inventions in the late nineteenth and early twentieth centuries led up to the development of expert systems. Section 9.1.1 discusses some of the essential differences between human and machine expertise. Some of the key abilities of human experts include the ability to: (1) solve the problem correctly, (2) explain their results and how they were attained, (3) learn from experience, (4) restructure knowledge, (5) break rules, (6) know their limitations, and (7) degrade gracefully. Some features that expert systems do offer include: knowledge that is separate from the inference engine, an inference engine that is simple, redundancy that can be exploited, increased availability, reduced cost, reduced danger, multiple expertise, and so forth.

Section 9.2 discusses the characteristics, variety of uses of expert systems, and the wide areas of application of expert systems, including, for example, communications, medicine, engineering, analysis, advice, control, decision-making, design, instruction, monitoring, planning, prediction, prescription, selection, and simulation.

Section 9.3 introduces *knowledge engineering* and describes how this is a craft in itself. The acquisition, harvesting, and exploitation of knowledge leading to the construction of a knowledge base and subsequently to an expert system is the focus of this section.

Section 9.4 presents the subject of *knowledge acquisition* and discusses how this in itself is a challenge to knowledge engineers. How do we best extract what is in an expert's head? How do we know that we have correctly and accurately represented what is in the expert's head? As expert systems grew in size and complexity it became more important to develop techniques to efficiently process knowledge, hence, *demon rules* and the *Rete Algorithm* of Section 9.6 has become more important.

There follows a presentation of some of the classic expert systems, in Section 9.5 and its subsections, including DENDRAL, MYCIN, EMYCIN, and PROSPECTOR.

Then we introduce the notions of fuzzy logic and Bayes' Theorem reminding us that expert systems, although very capable and possibly rich with domain-specific knowledge, are still founded on handling uncertainty.

This segues to a very important active area of expert systems development, *case-based reasoning* (CBR, Section 9.7). A number of CBR systems are discussed, including an example of a CBR system for helping to recognize oil slicks. Section 9.8 presents some more recent expert systems and investigates how the domain has evolved with *hybrid-intelligent* approaches.

Questions for Discussion

1. Explain how expert systems fit into the advances in technology in the time during which they were developed.

2. Explain how a domain specialist might have some 50,000 concepts in his skill domain.

3. Explain how humans can compete with programs in performance of activities in which programs perform millions of computations.

4. Describe the Five Stages of Skill Acquisition.

5. What was Dreyfus & Dreyfus's main position on the limitations of AI?

6. Describe 10 characteristics of human experts.

7. Describe 10 characteristics of expert systems.

8. List 10 purposes expert systems have been built for.

9. List 10 application areas for expert systems.

10. Name 5 different expert systems in five different areas.

11. Describe the process of knowledge engineering.

12. Explain why knowledge acquisition is the "bottleneck for AI."

13. Describe the main purpose and main method of DENDRAL.

14. Why was MYCIN such an important program?

15. What is a Demon Rule?

16. What is the Rete Algorithm?

17. What is the idea behind case-based reasoning (CBR)?

18. Name four typical aspects of constructing a CBR System?

19. Describe several problems in building a CBR?

20. Name three expert systems built in the last decade and their application domains.

21. Describe some of the *hybrid intelligent* techniques used to build these systems.

Exercises

1. Consider a domain you might want to build an expert system for. What characteristics should the domain possess in order to be a good candidate?

2. Try to build an expert system using CLIPS in your domain of interest.

3. Evaluate your system. How good is its performance? How could it be improved? Can it be used as a practical tool?

4. Did you use/need a domain specialist for your problem domain? If not, consider how a domain specialist might help you. If so, consider the knowledge engineering process that took place between you and the domain specialist.

5. What is a Demon Rule? Develop prototype demon rules for your expert system.

6. Do you believe expert systems can outperform human experts? If not, explain why not. If so, give some examples and describe what these can do that a human expert cannot do.

7. Why is a procedure such as the Rete Algorithm important to expert systems development?

8. Why is it important for an expert system to be cost effective?

9. Explain why expert systems are different from conventional programs?

10. Explain the difference between procedural knowledge, declarative knowledge, and meta-knowledge.

11. Explain why MYCIN was such an important program to all future expert systems and shells.

12. Who owns expert systems? Expert systems have long been considered a major success story from the field of artificial intelligence; however, they have also become somewhat standard and common. Should expert systems be considered a computer science technology or do they strictly belong to AI?

13. One of the criticisms of expert systems has been that they are conducive to the creation of microworlds (e.g. by Professor Hubert Dreyfus, see Chapter 6, Section 6.8, p.185). Explain why you do or do not agree.

14. How would expert systems need to perform to pass the Turing Test?

15. Research expert systems built in the past 5 years. What are their features?
How are they different from earlier expert systems described in this chapter?

Keywords

advanced beginner
assessment phase
case base
case-based reasoning
competent
declarative knowledge
demon rules
design phase
documentation phase
domain specialist
expert
fuzzy logic
heuristic knowledge
hybrid-intelligent approaches
inference engine

inference network
information society
knowledge acquisition
knowledge acquisition phase
knowledge compilation prob-
    lem
knowledge elicitation
knowledge engineer
knowledge engineering
knowledge base
knowledge-engineering
    paradox
maintenance phase
meta-knowledge
microminiaturization

novice
procedural knowledge
proficient
retention
retrieval
reuse
revision
structural knowledge
structural similarity
testing phase
temporal redundancy
the five stages of skill
    acquisition

References

1. Popplestone, R.J. 1969. Freddy in Toyland. In *Machine intelligence,* Vol. 4, ed., B. Meltzer and D. Michie, 455–462. New York, NY: American Elsevier.

2. Winograd, T. 1972. *Understanding natural language,* New York: Academic Press. Also published in *Cognitive Psychology* 3(1).

3. Weizenbaum, J. 1976. *Computer power and human reason.* San Francisco: W. H. Freeman.

4. Goldstein, I. and Papert, S. 1977. Artificial intelligence, language and the study of knowledge, *Cognitive Science* 1(1).

5. Feigenbaum, E.A., Buchanan B.G., and Lederberg J. 1971. On generality and problem solving: A case study using the DENDRAL program. In *Machine Intelligence,* Vol 6, ed., B. Meltzer and D. Michie, 165–190. New York, NY: American Elsevier.

6. Michie, D. 1980. Expert systems. *The Computer Journal* 23(4).

7. Reddy, R. 1988. Foundations and grand challenges of artificial intelligence: AAAI presidential address. *AI Magazine* 94:9–21.

8. Brady, M. 1979. Expert problem solvers opening remarks from the chair at AISB, summer school. In *Expert Systems in the Micro-electronic Age,* ed., D. Michie, 49. Edinburgh: Edinburgh University Press.

9. Dreyfus, H. L. and Dreyfus, S. E. 1986. *Mind over machine.* New York, NY: MacMillan, The Free Press.

10. Hofstadser, D. 1979. *Godel, Escher, Bach: An eternal golden braid.* New York, NY: Basic Books.

11. Firebaugh, M. 1988. *Artificial intelligence: A knowledge-based approach.* Boston, MA: PWS-Kent.

12. Giarratano, J. C. and Riley, G. D. 2005. *Expert systems: Principles and programming.* Boston, MA: Thompson/Cengage.

13. Lenat, D. 1995. Cyc: A large scale investment in knowledge infrastructure. *CACM* 38:33–38.

14. Durkin, J. 1994. *Expert systems: Design and development.* New York, NY: Macmillan.

15. Feigenbaum, E. A. 1979. Themes and case studies of knowledge engineering. In *Expert systems in the micro-electronic age*, ed., D. Michie, 3–33. Edinburgh: Edinburgh University Press.

16. Michie, D., ed. 1979. *Expert systems in the micro-electronic age*. Edinburgh: Edinburgh University Press.

17. Duda, R. O. and Shortliffe, E. 1983. Expert systems research. *Science* 220(4594, April): 261–268.

18. Hayes-Roth, F., Waterman, D. A, and Lenat, D. B, eds. 1983. *Building expert systems*. Reading, MA: Addison-Wesley.

19. Chilausky, R., Jacobsen, B., and Michalski, R. S. 1976. An application of variable-valued logic to inductive learning of plant disease diagnostic rules, In *Proceedings of the 6th annual international symposium on multi-varied logic*. Utah.

20. Waterman, D. A. 1986. *A guide to expert systems*. Reading, MA: Addison-Wesley.

21. McCorduck, P. 1979. *Machines who think*. Boston, MA: W. H. Freeman.

22. Shortliffe, E. 1976. *MYCIN: Computer-based medical consultations*. New York, NY: Elsevier Press.

23. Roberts, A. W. and Visconti, J. A. 1972. The rational and irrational use of systemic microbial drugs. *American Journal of Pharmacy* (29): 828–34.

24. Buchanan, B. G. and Shortliffe, E. H. 1984. *Rule-based expert systems*. Reading, MA: Addison-Wesley.

25. van Melle, W. 1979 A domain-independent production-rule system for consultation programs. In *Proceedings of the international Joint Conference on Artificial Intelligence '79*, 923–925.

26. Aikens, J. S., Kunz, J. C., and Shortliffe, E. H. 1983. PUFF: An expert system for interpretation of pulmonary function data. *Computers and Biomedical Research* 16: 199–208.

27. Duda, R.O. and Reboh, R. 1984. AI and decision making: The PROSPECTOR experience. In *Artificial intelligence applications for business*, ed., W. Reitman, Ablex Publishing Corp.

28. Luger, G. 2005. *Artificial intelligence 5th edition: Structures and strategies*. Reading, MA: Addison-Wesley.

29. Aamodt, A. 1991. A knowledge-intensive, integrated approach to problem solving and sustained learning. *Ph.D. diss.*, Knowledge Engineering and Image Processing Group, University of Trondheim,, Norway.

30. Kolodner, J. L., ed. 1988. *Proceedings: Case-based reasoning workshop*. San Mateo, CA.: Morgan Kaufmann.

31. Koton, P. A. 1988. *Using experience in learning and problem Solving*. Boston, MA: MIT Press.

32. Samuel, A. 1959. Some studies in machine learning using the game of checkers. *IBM Journal of Research and Development* 3:210–229.

33. Watson, I. 1997. *Applying case-based reasoning, Techniques for enterprise systems*. San Francisco, CA: Morgan Kaufman.

34. Watson, I. 2003. *Applying knowledge management: Techniques for building corporate memories*. Boston, MA: Morgan Kaufman.

35. Ashley, K. D. and Rissland, E. L. 1988. A case-based reasoning approach to modeling legal expertise. *IEEE Expert* 33:70–77.

36. Koton, P. 1988. Reasoning about evidence in causal explanations. In *Proceedings of the seventh national conference on artificial intelligence*, 256–261. Saint Paul, MN.

37. Bareiss, E., Porter, B., and Weir, C. 1988. PROTOS: An exemplar-based learning apprentice. *International Journal of Man-Machine Studies* 29(5):549–61.

38. Kolodner, J. L. 1993. *Case-based reasoning*, San Mateo, CA: Morgan Kaufmann.

39. Skinner, J. M., and Luger, G. F. 1992. An architecture for integrating reasoning paradigms. *Knowledge Representation* 4:753–761.

40. Stern, C. R. and Luger, G. F. 1997. Abduction and abstraction in diagnosis: A schema-based account. In *Situated Cognition: Expertise is Context*, ed., Ford et al. Cambridge, MA: MIT Press.

41. Mata, A. and Corchado, J. M. 2009. Forecasting the probability of finding oil slicks using a CBR system. *Expert Systems with Applications* 36(4):8239–8246.

42. Drigas, A., Kouremenos, S., Vrettos, J., Vrettaros, J., and Koremenos, D. 2004. An expert system for job matching of the unemployed. In *Expert systems with applications,* 26:217–224. The Netherlands: Elsevier.

43. Labate, F. and Medsker, L. 1993. Employee skills analysis using a hybrid neural network and expert system. *In IEEE international conference on developing and managing intelligent system projects*. Los Alamitos, CA, USA: IEEE Computer Society Press.

44. Rafter, R., Bradley, K., and Smyth, B. 2000. Personalised retrieval for online recruitment services. In *Proceedings of the 22nd annual colloquium on IR research*. Cambridge: UK.

45. Gams, M., Golob, P., Karaliø, A., Drobniø, M., Grobelnik, M., Glazer, J., Pirher, J., Furlan, T., Vrenko, E., and Krizman, R. 1998. EMA – zaposlovalni agent, *http://www-ai.ijs.si/~ema/EMA_Info-e.html*

46. Yang, B. S., Lim, D. S., and Tan, A. C. C. 2005. VIBEX: An expert system for vibration fault diagnosis of rotating machinery using decision tree and decision table. *Expert Systems with Applications* 28:735–742.

47. Quinlan, J. R. 1993. C4.5: *Programs for machine learning*. Canada: Morgan Kaufmann.

48. Ammar, H., Howell, R., Muttaleb, M. Jain, A. 2006. Automated dental identification System ADIS. In *Proceeding of the 2006 International Conference on Digital Government Research*, Poster Session, 369–370. San Diego, CA.

49. He, W., Wang, F. K, Means, T., Xu, L. D. 2009. Insight into interface design of web-based case-based reasoning. *Expert Systems with Applications* 36:7280–7287.

50. Moore, J., Erdelez, S., and He, W. 2006. Retrieval from a case-based reasoning database. *American Exchange Quarterly* 104:65–68.

51. Kumar, A. Singh, Y. and Sanyal, S. 2007. Hybrid approach using case-based reasoning and rule-based reasoning for domain independent clinical decision support in ICU *Expert Systems With Applications*, Elsevier. [doi:10.1016/j. physletb.2003.10.071] April 15, 2011

Bibliography

Duda, R. O., *The PROSPECTOR System for Mineral Exploration*, (Final Report, SRI Project 8172). Menlo Park, CA: SRI International, Artificial Intelligence Center, 1980.

Haase, K. W. *Invention and Exploration in Discovery* (PDF). MIT, 1990–02, archived from the original on 2005-01-22,

Heuristic Programming Project Report HPP-76-8, Stanford, California: AI Lab, Stanford University, and Published in *Knowledge-Based Systems in Artificial Intelligence* together with Randall Davis's PhD Thesis, McGraw-Hill, 1982.

Kolodner, J. L., ed. *Case-Based Learning.* Dordrecht, Netherlands: Kluwer Academic Publishers, 1993.

Kolodner, J. L. *Retrieval and Organizational Strategies in Conceptual Memory: A Computer Model*. Hillsdale, NJ: Lawrence Erlbaum, 1984.

Kolodner, J. L. "Towards an Understanding of the Role of Experience in the Evolution from Novice to Expert." *International Journal of Man-Machine Systems*, 19 (Nov. 1983): 497–518.

Lenat, D. B., "AM: An Artificial Intelligence Approach to Discovery in Mathematics as Heuristic Search," *Ph.D.* Thesis, AIM-286, STAN-CS-76-570. 1976. Stanford University.

Lenat, D. and Brown, J. S. "Why AM and EURISKO Appear to Work." Artificial Intelligence 23(1984): 269–294.

Lenat, D. B., Ritchie, G. D., and Hanna, F. K. "AM: A Case Study in AI Methodology." *Artificial Intelligence* 23, 3(1984): 249–268.

van Melle, W., Scott, A. C., Bennett, J. S., and Peairs, M. *The EMYCIN Manual.*

Report No. HPP-81-16, Computer Science Department, Stanford University.1981.

Zadeh, L. "Commonsense Knowledge Representation Based on Fuzzy Logic." *Computer* 16(1983): 61–65.

Understanding Computers: Artificial Intelligence. Amsterdam: Time-Life Books, 1986. *http://web. archive.org/web/20050122170922/ http://web. media.mit.edu/~haase/thesis/*. Retrieved December 13, 2008.

MACHINE LEARNING: PART I

Classroom

This chapter begins our discussion of learning. We start with machine learning and an explanation of the inductive paradigm. Decision trees are a widely used inductive learning approach. They had fallen out of favor for a decade or so as they did not generalize well and hence were bad at prediction. However, if we take many trees, we are able to remove much variance. The so-called random forests (or decision forests) that result have led to a recent renaissance in this learning approach. Finally, we explain entropy and the relation that this mathematical measure has to decision tree construction.

▮10.0▮ INTRODUCTION

Learning enables people to improve their performance in an area of study—whether it is dentistry or violin playing. Students in dental school become more proficient at repairing teeth whereas a violinist attending the Juilliard School in New York City is likely to play a Mozart violin concerto with greater artistry after several years of training. Similarly, **machine learning** is the process whereby a computer distills meaning by exposure to training data. Earlier in our studies, we posed the question: Can machines think? If we were to discover algorithms wherein computers were enabled to perform the analytical reasoning entailed in learning (beyond the application of deductive principles outlined in Chapter 5), this would go a long way toward resolving this question—as most people believe that learning is an essential component of thinking. Furthermore, many view machine learning as the *holy grail* of AI, since machine learning would undoubtedly help to overcome the knowledge and commonsense bottlenecks that we have identified as major roadblocks to the development of human-level AI.

▮10.1▮ MACHINE LEARNING: A BRIEF OVERVIEW

Machine learning can trace its roots to Arthur Samuel.[1] He spent two decades at IBM (starting in 1949) teaching computers to play checkers. One aspect of his programs was rote learning—i.e., the programs would memorize good moves from previous games. More interesting, perhaps, was the incorporation of strategy into his checker playing programs. Samuel obtained his insights into the game by interviewing human checker players. Guidelines included:

- Always strive for center control of the checkerboard.
- Jump your opponent's pieces wherever possible.
- Seek to achieve Kings.

To achieve superior game playing ability in some game, humans play that game repeatedly. Similarly, Samuel had various versions of his programs play against one another. The loser of a game would borrow heuristics from the winner. This pioneering work is described in detail in Chapter 16.

Five major Machine Learning (ML) paradigms are listed below.

1. neural networks
2. case-based reasoning
3. genetic algorithms
4. rule induction
5. analytic learning [2]

This listing is in no sense meant to be exhaustive but rather serves as an entry point for our discussion. The subject of ML would easily fill an entire volume. The interested reader is encouraged to consult one of the many excellent texts on this subject.[3,4,5]

The artificial neural network-focused ML community received their inspiration from the *metaphor* with the human brain and nervous system, which is perhaps the most intelligent vestibule of natural intelligence on this planet. In an artificial neural network (ANN), artificial neurons are connected with links in some prescribed topology. An input signal to the network often results in a change in the interconnection strengths and culminates with the production of an

A metaphor is a figure of speech in which two things that are in reality different are compared with one another. The properties of the second are thereby transferred to the first. For example: "He eats like a horse."

output signal. A **training set** is a carefully selected set of input examples that is used to teach a concept to a neural network. Chapter 11 is entirely devoted to this approach to Machine Learning.

In case-based reasoning, it is the analogy with human memory that is at play. This approach maintains a file of past cases or scenarios that are effectively indexed to permit ready access. A metric is used to measure similarity with some present case. For example, a doctor examines a patient complaining of severe headaches and exhibiting partial aphasia with some peripheral vision loss. The doctor may recall a similar case in which the diagnosis was viral meningitis; appropriate anti-seizure meds were administered and the eventual outcome was favorable. Having a file of previous cases that have already been handled enables the doctor to reach a speedier diagnosis in the current case. Naturally, some tests must still be performed to rule out other diseases exhibiting similar symptomology but with vastly different causation and/or outcomes. For example, the doctor might order an MRI to confirm brain swelling and also rule out the presence of a tumor. A spinal tap might even be performed to preclude the presence of bacterial meningitis. Further discussion of case-based reasoning may be found in Chapter 9.

In genetic algorithm-based ML, natural evolution is the inspiration for this learning. Darwin developed his theory of natural selection in the mid-nineteenth century. Changes in a species—whether flora or fauna—that provide advantages for survival will appear with greater frequency in offspring. In early nineteenth-century London, for example, light-colored moths possessed an ecological advantage over their darker-colored brethren. Birch trees were prevalent in London and its environs at the time and were light in color, thus affording the lighter-colored moths natural camouflage from birds, their predators. Once the industrial revolution was underway, pollution became widespread. Consequently, trees in England became darker, and the camouflage advantage went to the darker moths, whose proportion in the population increased. Genetic algorithms and genetic programs are discussed in Chapter 12.

Rule induction is that branch of ML that relies upon production rules and decision trees—two topics that were introduced in Chapters 6 and 7. One production rule appropriate for teaching a robot to bag groceries is:

IF [item is frozen food]

THEN [place item in freezer bag before placing item in shopping bag] [6]

We will soon discover a similarity between the information content in each of these production rules and decision trees. Figure 10.1 depicts a part of a decision tree for our robot grocery bagger.

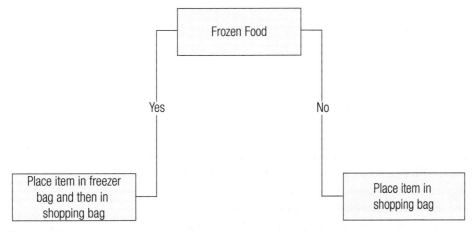

Figure 10.1
A decision tree for a robot grocery bagger. Note the similarity with the production rule given in the text.

The impetus in rule induction is from heuristic search. Decision trees are studied extensively in this chapter.

10.2 THE ROLE OF FEEDBACK IN MACHINE LEARNING SYSTEMS

This quote is from the 1988 movie Bull Durham directed by Ron Shelton. The reader by now has certainly observed that both of the authors are baseball fans.

Suppose we have an agent that wishes to play baseball at the major league level. Training for this profession can easily require 15 or more years. This is a lengthy learning period in spite of the maxim:

"Throw the ball, catch the ball, hit the ball."

One thing our agent must learn early in this training is that a baseball game has many possible states.

1. Is our team leading?
2. If I am on defense and the ball has been hit to me, then I must know: Is the player now running to first base a fast runner? If so, then I must rush my throw.
3. Does the opposing pitcher throw a knuckleball (this pitch is hard to hit!)? Then perhaps I should feign an illness today.

The type of **feedback** *this young agent receives is central to the learning process. In machine learning there are three types of feedback:*

- Supervised learning
- Unsupervised learning
- Reinforcement learning

Learning a function with **supervised learning** is the most straightforward approach. The agent is provided with appropriate feedback immediately after he performs some action. For example, if he takes his time throwing the ball to first base when a fast runner has grounded a ball at him, he will be reminded within minutes of the need for haste in these situations. In Chapter 11, we discover how a neural network uses supervised learning to learn a Boolean function. The network is provided with a table that lists the correct outputs for each possible input.

With **unsupervised learning** no specific feedback is provided during the training. If learning is to occur, however, then our agent must receive *some* feedback. Suppose that our agent has had a miserable day on offense, i.e., he had no base hits. Defense was a different story—he made two diving catches and robbed an opponent of a homerun. It was a close game and his team won. After the game, he is congratulated by his teammates, thus concluding that good defense is also appreciated.

Figure 10.2
Balancing an umbrella, small incremental moves in the x-y plane are required to keep the umbrella balanced.

With **reinforcement learning** there is no teacher providing right answers to our agent. In fact, the agent may not even know the consequences of an action in advance. To further complicate matters, even when the impact of an action is known, the value of the impact may not be, and must therefore be learned by trial and error. It is difficult to ascertain the goodness of an action as rewards are delayed. Anyone who has attempted to balance an umbrella (closed) on their index finger understands the basics of reinforcement learning. Consult Figure 10.2.

If the umbrella is leaning left, a corresponding large move to the left on your part will not be discovered as an overcorrection until a few moments later. Let us return to our baseball agent for a moment. Suppose he is a pitcher with a penchant for throwing the baseball at opposing batters when they have hit a homerun off him. Several innings later when the opposing pitcher throws a 90-mph fastball at his legs, he will need to make a connection between his aching knee cap and his perhaps overly aggressive style of play. We will restrict our discussion in this text to supervised learning. An excellent discussion of unsupervised learning and reinforcement learning may be found in Ballard.[7]

With supervised learning, you are presented with a set of ordered pairs:

$$\{(\bar{x}^{(1)}, \bar{t}^{(1)}),(\bar{x}^{(2)}, \bar{t}^{(2)})...(\bar{x}^{(r)}, \bar{t}^{(r)})\}$$

known as a training set. $\bar{x}^{(i)}$, $i=1,...,r$ is an input vector in n-dimensional space, i.e., $\bar{x}^{(i)} = (x_1^{(i)}, x_2^{(i)},...,x_n^{(i)})$) whereas $\bar{t}^i$ is the value of this function at $\bar{x}^{(i)}$, that is to be learned. The function f maps each input vector into the correct output response. Generally $\bar{t}^{(i)} = (t_1^{(i)}, t_2^{(i)}, ..., t_m^{(i)})$ in m-dimensional space. Each component t_k, $k = 1, ..., m$ is from a prescribed set, i.e., the set of integers, reals, etc. (the sets for inputs and outputs may be different).

10.3 INDUCTIVE LEARNING

The task in inductive learning is to find that function h that most closely agrees with the true function $f()$. We refer to h as a hypothesis for $f()$. The **Hypothesis Space** H is the set of functions that the learning algorithm considers as approximators of the correct function $f()$. The goal in this learning is to find h that agrees with f at all points in the training set. This endeavor is known as curve fitting. Refer to Figure 10.3.

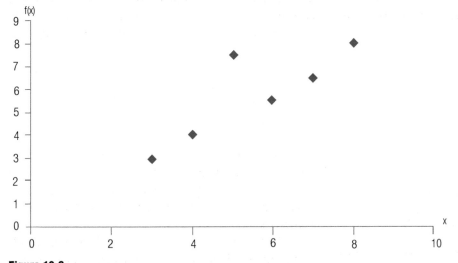

Figure 10.3
The hypothesis h is said to be consistent if it agrees with f on all points.

Three different hypotheses are drawn in Figure 10.4. At first glance it appears that h_3 is the best hypothesis. And it is important for us to keep in mind that the purpose of learning is not for us to score perfectly on the training set but rather for the agent to perform well on the validation set.

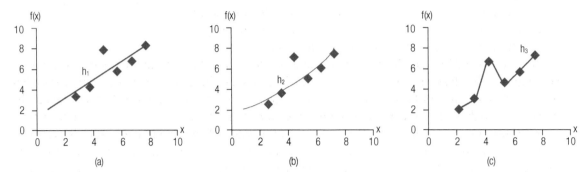

Figure 10.4
Three Different Hypotheses. Note that only h_3 is consistent with *f* as it passes through all six points.

The validation set is a set of examples upon which the agent is tested. If the agent has truly learned some concept, then it should not merely have memorized the input-output correspondence, but rather it should have attained the ability to generalize, i.e., to provide appropriate responses to inputs it has never before encountered. Often a hypothesis that performs flawlessly on the training set has been *overtrained* and will not generalize well. One way to achieve generalization is to alternate training and validation, and note that during validation the agent's learning mechanism is turned off. Training terminates when the validation error—and *not* the training error—is minimized. This training methodology is explained thoroughly in Chapter 11, in the context of backpropagation learning with neural networks. We refer one last time to our baseball agent. If he has truly learned how to play the game of baseball well, then he should respond appropriately even when encountering a game situation for the first time, e.g., participation in his very first triple play, in which three outs are made during one play.

Refer once again to Figure 10.4 (c). The function passes through all six points. We can use Lagrange Interpolation to find many other functions with this property, e.g., polynomials of degree 7, 8, 9, etc. A guiding principle in the learning community—both machine and human learning—is that when there are multiple explanations for the same observed phenomenon, it is wise to choose the simplest. This principle is known as **Occam's Razor**. Here are several examples of this guideline:

1. A small bright light is seen moving in the distant sky. Explanation a): It is an airplane either taking off from or readying to land at a nearby airport. Explanation b): A star has left its galaxy and is preparing to enter ours. Explanation a) is the likelier one.

2. You wake up early on Christmas morning and observe snow on the street outside your window—snow that was not there last night when you went to sleep. Explanation a): Santa Claus commissioned his elves to shovel snow from the North Pole to your neighborhood because you behaved extraordinarily well this year. Explanation b): It snowed while you were sleeping. Explanation b) is more likely.

3. You walk past Bleecker Street and 6th Avenue in Manhattan one September morning some years ago. You witness thousands of New Yorkers walking north heading away from the downtown section of the city. Explanation a): There was an electrical malfunction on the subways and the trains were not running. Explanation b): Terrorists hijacked two airplanes and crashed them into the World Trade Center Towers. Explanation a) is

more likely but as we unfortunately remember, the correct explanation was b).

One of authors (SL) was late for an appointment that Tuesday morning in 2001 and failed to listen to a morning news broadcast.

Most scientists would agree that when there are two theories to explain the same phenomenon, the simpler one is preferable; however, as we know, this does not always guarantee correctness. It may just be a better starting point until new evidence is discovered.

There is one additional characterization that is often applied to learning methods; they can be classified as either lazy or eager. A **lazy learner** is deemed so because it delays generalization beyond the training data until a new query is made. No effort is made to compress data; consequently, all data is available when the model is invoked. Contrast this with **eager learners**, which abstract general rules that can be applied when a new query is made. The training data itself, however, is no longer retained. Training lazy learners is generally faster; however, using them requires more time. Eager learners adhere to a single hypothesis and are therefore less flexible than lazy learners.

Case-based reasoning (consult Chapter 9) is classified as a lazy learner. The advantage in this is that the entire case is available and hence may have more general applicability. Neural networks, on the other hand, are classified as eager learners. The weights in a backpropagation network (BPN) represent the network's learning and may be considered a compressed version of the training data. To apply a BPN to a new sample, you need simply apply the new query as inputs to the network. The previous data that was used to train this network, however, is no longer retrievable.

10.4 ■ LEARNING WITH DECISION TREES

Decision trees are a widely used inductive approach for concept learning. Nodes in the decision tree correspond to queries made regarding some attribute. Branches emanating from a node denote the values that an attribute has assumed. Refer to Figure 10.5.

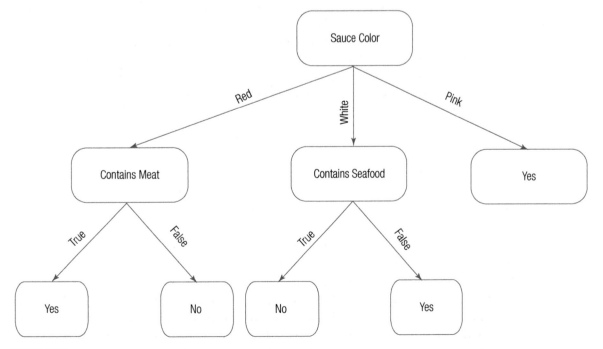

Figure 10.5
Decision tree depicting Italian pasta preferences for one of the authors (SL).

This tree may be used to classify instances of pasta into two distinct classes—those that are liked by SL and those that are not. Queries always commence at the root of the tree and terminate at leaf nodes where class labels are found. Consider the following list of pasta dishes:

1. ***Spaghetti and Meatballs***—Meatballs and pasta in a red tomato sauce.
2. ***Spaghetti Arrabbiata***—Spaghetti with spicy red marinara sauce.
3. ***Linguine Vongole***—Linguine with clams in red sauce.
4. ***Linguine Vongole***—Linguine with clams in white sauce.
5. ***Rigatoni alla Vodka***—Rigatoni in a pink creamy vodka sauce.

To classify Spaghetti and Meatballs from this list, we begin at the root in Figure 10.5. The sauce of this dish is red, hence we go left in the tree. The root of the left subtree asks if this dish contains meat, and of course it does. The tree classifies Spaghetti and Meatballs as a pasta dish liked by SL. Why not trace the other four instances using this same decision tree? After doing so you will have observed that all five pasta recipes are classified into one of two distinct classes:

Class 1—Pasta dishes liked by SL contains instances 1, 4 and 5.

Disclaimer—One of the authors (SL) chose these attribute values for pedagogical reasons alone. SL grew up in New York City's Little Italy in lower Manhattan and, unfortunately (for his waistline), he likes just about every pasta dish! In fact, he has tasted most of the dishes cited at two of his favorite restaurants—Puglia's located at 189 Hester Street and DaNico's at 164 Mulberry Street in Little Italy.

Class 2—Pasta dishes disliked by SL consists of instances 2, 3.

Any path down the decision tree in Figure 10.5 that begins at the root and ends at a leaf node represents the conjunction (**AND**ing) of attribute values on that path. For example, the path followed in the classification of Spaghetti Arrabbiata is (sauce = red) ∧ (meat = no). The concept of pasta dishes liked by SL corresponds to the disjunction (**OR**ing) of all conjunctive terms that follow a path culminating in a yes node. In our example, we have:

[(sauce = red) ∧ (meat = yes)] ∨ [(sauce = white) ∧ (seafood = no)] ∨ [(sauce = pink)].

10.5 PROBLEMS SUITABLE FOR DECISION TREES

Problems that work well with decision tree learning are characterized by the following:

1. Attributes assume a small number of values, e.g., sauce = red, white, or pink. Instances are represented by a set of attribute values, e.g., for instance = Spaghetti and Meatballs, we have attributes with values Sauce is ***red***, and meat present = ***yes***.
2. Target function should generally have a small number of discrete values. In our Italian pasta example, the values were yes and *no*.
3. Errors may be present in the training data. Decision trees perform well when errors occur in either attribute values or instance classification (contrast this robustness with neural network learning in Chapter 11).

These are ideal conditions. By consulting the literature in this field, you will learn of ways to bypass many of these limitations.

Missing attribute values may occur in training data. For example, it might be assumed that the user of a decision tree knows that Spaghetti Arrabbiata contains no meat and this attribute might be missing.

Many real-world problems satisfy the constraints imposed by the previous list. In medical applications, attributes correspond to visible symptoms or patient complaints: skin color = yellowish, nose = runny, headache is present, or test results: temperature is elevated, blood pressure or blood sugar levels are high, heart enzymes are abnormal. The target function in a medical application would likely indicate the presence of a disease or condition: patient has hay fever, hepatitis, or trouble with a recently repaired heart valve. Decision trees are widely used by medical practitioners.

In the financial arena, applications range from credit card worthiness decisions to the favorability of real estate investments. A fundamental application in the business world is option trading—i.e., where an option is a contract that gives a person the right to buy or sell some asset (e.g., a stock) at a given price or by a certain date.

10.6 ENTROPY

Entropy quantifies the homogeneity present in a collection of samples. To simplify our discussion, we assume that the concept to be learned is binary in nature—e.g., a person either likes a pasta dish or does not. Given a set S, the entropy of S relative to this binary classification is:

$$\text{Entropy} = -p(+) * \log_2 p(x) - p(-) * \log_2 p(-)$$

where $p(+)$ represents the portion that is favorably disposed, i.e., likes the pasta dish and $p(-)$, the portion that dislikes it. In discussions of entropy, logarithms are always taken base 2, even when the classification is not binary as it is here.

The decision tree in Figure 10.5 describes pasta preferences. Suppose that we have a set of four pasta dishes and they are all liked—we denote this by [4(+), 0(−)]. The entropy contained in this set is:

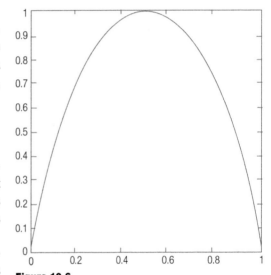

Figure 10.6
The entropy function for a binary classification as the proportion of positive samples varies over the interval [0,1].

Entropy $[4(+), 0(-)] = -4/4 * \log_2 (4/4) - 0/4 * \log_2 (0/4)$
$= -1 * \log_2 (1) - 0 * \log_2 (0)$
$= -1 * 0 - 0 * 0$
$= 0.$

If two pasta dishes are liked and two are disliked, then:

Entropy $[2(+), 2(-)] = -2/4 * \log_2 (2/4) - 2/4 * \log_2 (2/4)$
$= -1/2 * (-1) - 1/2 * (-1)$
$= 1/2 - (-1/2)$
$= 1.$

We observe that when all members belong to the same set, the entropy of this collection is 0. This value of 0 indicates there is no impurity in the set as all members in this example are positive. The entropy achieved its maximal value of 1 in the second example when half the members were positive and half negative. In a binary classification, the entropy of a set ranges from 0 to 1 (see Figure 10.6).

The entropy of a set may be viewed as the number of bits required to determine which class a selected item is from. For example, for the set [2(+), 2(−)], one bit is needed to specify which class an item is chosen from, where 1 could mean that the item is liked and 0 that it is not. Conversely, no bits are necessary to label an item in the set [4(+), 0(−)] with entropy 0 as all items are liked.

10.7 CONSTRUCTING A DECISION TREE WITH ID3

Quinlan developed ID3 in 1986. It has been one of the most widely used algorithms for decision tree learning. A decision tree is constructed by ID3 in a top-down manner. It begins by searching for that attribute which most nearly partitions the training set into equal subsets. If we are to successfully use decision trees, we must understand how they are constructed. In our pasta example, there are three attributes: sauce color, meat is contained, seafood is contained. See Table 10.1.

Table 10.1
Data used for our decision tree learning.

	Pasta	Sauce Color	Contains Meat	Contains Seafood	Like
1	Spaghetti with Meatballs	Red	True	false	yes
2	Spaghetti Arrabbiata	Red	False	false	no
3	Linguine Vongole	Red	False	true	no
4	Linguine Vongole	white	False	true	no
5	Rigatoni alla Vodka	Pink	False	false	yes
6	Lasagne	Red	True	false	yes
7	Rigatoni Lucia	white	False	false	yes
8	Fettucine Alfredo	white	False	false	yes
9	Fusilli Boscaiola	Red	False	false	no
10	Ravioli Florentine	Pink	False	false	yes

There are three different attributes, hence there are different choices for which attribute is to appear first. Consult Figure 10.7.

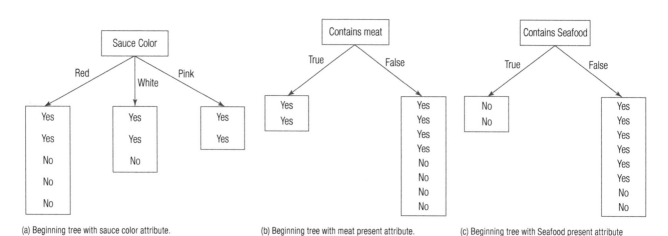

(a) Beginning tree with sauce color attribute.

(b) Beginning tree with meat present attribute.

(c) Beginning tree with Seafood present attribute

Figure 10.7
There are three attributes the decision tree may begin with. In part a) when the sauce color is red, two pasta dishes are liked and three are not. The other boxes may be similarly interpreted.

An attribute is deemed *good* if the sample is dichotomized based upon the value of that attribute, i.e., for one attribute value we have all instances positive and for the other value, all negative. Contrawise, an attribute is considered useless when it contains no discriminative value. In our example, this would mean that for each attribute value we have the same number of *likes* and *dislikes*.

ID3 uses **information gain** for the placement of attributes. It will place an attribute closer to the root of the decision tree if that attribute yields the greatest expected reduction in entropy. To determine which of the three subtrees in Figure 10.7 should be selected first, ID3 calculates the average information for each of the subtrees illustrated. The tree that results in the greatest information gain is then selected where:

The information gain yielded by attribute A is the reduction in entropy that results from the partitioning of the set S induced by A.

$$\text{Gain}\,(S, A) = \text{Entropy}\,(S) - \sum_{V \subseteq \text{values}\,(A)} \frac{|S_v|}{|S|} * \text{Entropy}\,(S_v)$$

where v is a value that attribute A can assume. This formula will sum S_v (which is the subset of S with value v) over all values for v. Consult Figures 10.8 through 10.10 to follow the calculations that ID3 must complete.

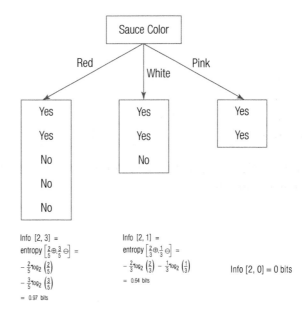

Figure 10.8
Information Gain if *Sauce Color* is chosen first equals 0.29.

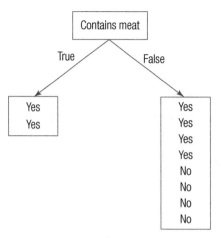

info [2,0] = 0 bits info [4,4] = 1.00 bit

Average weighted info of the subtree = $\left(0 * \frac{2}{10}\right) + \left(1.00 * \frac{8}{10}\right)$ = 0.80

Info of all training samples S = 0.97
Gain (S, Contains Meat) = 0.97 - 0.80 = **0.17**

Figure 10.9
Information Gain if *Contains Meat* is Chosen first.

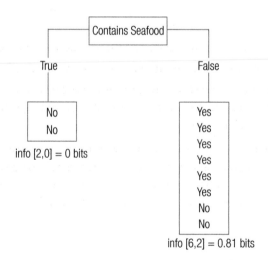

info [2,0] = 0 bits

info [6,2] = 0.81 bits

Average weighted info of the subtree = $\left(0 \times \frac{2}{10}\right) + \left(0.81 \times \frac{8}{10}\right)$ = 0.65

Info of all training samples S = 0.97
Gain (S, contains seafood) = 0.97 - 0.65 = **0.32**

Figure 10.10
Information gain if *Contains Seafood* is chosen first equals 0.32.

Perusing Figures 10.8, 10.9, and 10.10, it is evident that ID3 selects Contains Seafood as the first attribute in the decision tree, as its associated information gain of 0.32 is the largest of the three.

Next, ID3 must choose between the two trees drawn in Figure 10.11.

Once the second attribute is chosen, the attribute not selected is applied next where needed. You will be asked to complete these computations in the exercises.

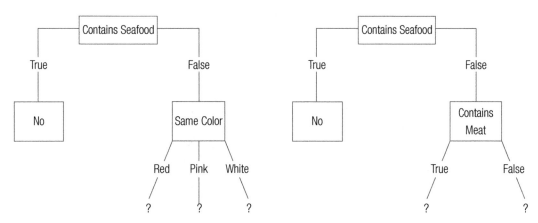

Figure 10.11
ID3 must select which attribute is second—either *Sauce Color* or *Contains Meat*.

10.8 ■ ISSUES REMAINING

This chapter is intended as an introduction to Inductive Learning with decision trees. There are additional issues listed below:

1. Overfitting the data—this may occur when you do not possess sufficient training data to adequately cover the entire hypothesis space.

2. How does one handle attributes with continuous values, e.g., temperature, income, stress?

3. How do you train when certain attributes are missing?

4. What if some attribute values are more costly or inconvenient to obtain? For example, taking a patient's temperature is less intrusive than performing an MRI (especially when the patient is claustrophobic).

Machine Learning is a huge and vastly important area of research. Hopefully this chapter has encouraged you to consult some of the excellent references listed at the end of this chapter and also to read Chapter 11 on neural approaches to Machine Learning, as well as Chapter 12, which can serve as springboard to evolutionary approaches on the subject.

10.9 ■ CHAPTER SUMMARY

This chapter has introduced the field of machine learning. We have emphasized the importance of some form of feedback to the system. With supervised learning the agent is provided with immediate feedback so that it knows at once if it has been correct. With unsupervised learning no feedback is provided while training is ongoing; however, eventually the agent will know if it is performing well. Finally, with reinforcement learning, interpreting received feedback correctly is the most problematic.

Our discussion has emphasized inductive learning, wherein a hypothesis is found that most accurately reflects a set of observations. We cited Occam's Razor as a useful principle when formulating an explanation; when several hypotheses explain an observed phenomenon, it is often wise to choose the simplest one (at least as a starting point).

Decision trees were seen to be a useful tool for classifying data. We also explained the information-theoretic concept of entropy, which is a measure of the amount of disorder in a set. Quinlan's

ID3 program utilizes entropy in a manner that favors shorter decision trees. Decision trees have long been used in both the medical community and the financial area. Our discussion of machine learning continues in Chapter 11 with neural networks. Consult the many fine machine learning texts to learn about AdaBoosting, an algorithm that strengthens the performance of decision trees.

Questions for Discussion

1. What is machine learning and why is it such an important subfield of AI?

2. List several ML paradigms.

3. Describe three different forms of feedback in ML systems.

4. Why is feedback important to an agent?

5. Describe inductive learning.

6. When performing curve fitting, why is a function that passes through all the points in a training set not necessarily the best hypothesis?

7. a. What is Occam's Razor?

   b. Does it claim that the shortest hypothesis is always the best?

8. Give an example of where you have used Occam's Razor in your everyday experience.

9. Look on the web and find several other areas where decision trees are used.

10. When calculating the entropy of a set, why are logarithms calculated with a base equal to 2?

11. Why does choosing that attribute with the largest information gain favor construction of shorter decision trees?

12. Suggest a possible method to handle attributes with continuous values.

13. Are decision trees a lazy or eager learner? Explain your answer.

Exercises

1. Design a decision tree for the following Boolean functions:

   a. $a \vee (b \wedge \sim c)$

   b. majority (x, y, z)

2. Calculate the entropy for each of the following sets:

   a. $[6(+), 11(-)]$

   b. $[1(+), 9(-)]$

   c. $[2(+), 12(-)]$

3. Entropy is also defined when classification is into three or more classes.

The entropy of a set S relative to n distinct classes is defined as:

$$\text{Entropy (S)} = \sum_{i=1}^{n} -p_i \log_2 p_i$$

where p_i is the proportion of the Set S in class i,

with $i = 1, \ldots, n$. Notice that logarithms are still calculated base 2.

Calculate the entropy of the set S, where $p_1 = 6/20$, $p_2 = 9/20$, and $p_3 = 5/20$.

Programming Exercises

1. Use ID3 to confirm the final form of the decision tree for pasta preferences in Section 10.7.

2. Add some noisy data to the tree construction program above.

   Comment on what happens. For example:

   Sauce = red, contains meat = true, and contains seafood = false, but likes = no.

   Penne with Bolognese sauce would yield these attribute values.

   Go on-line to find several other "noisy" examples.

3. Test your trees from programming exercises 1 and 2 with:

   Spaghetti carbonara where sauce = white, contains meat = true, and contains seafood is false.

   What result did you obtain? Is it what you expected? Explain.

4. Table 10.2 contains data about two medical conditions:

   A person has a cold vs. a person has the flu. Use ID3 to build a decision tree to determine which affliction a person suffers from based upon their symptomology.

   Cold and **Flu**.

   Table 10.2

Fever or Chills	Sore Throat	Cough	Headache or Body ache	Stuffy or Runny Nose	Fatigue	Fever	Diagnosis
Mild	yes	moderate	None	yes	mild	None	Cold
Medium	no	extreme	Severe	no	extreme	higher	Flu
Extreme	no	none	Moderate	yes	mild	slight	Flu
No	no	mild	Moderate	yes	none	slight	Cold
Extreme	yes	moderate	Severe	no	extreme	higher	Flu
No	yes	moderate	None	yes	none	None	Cold
Medium	no	moderate	Severe	no	extreme	higher	Flu
No	yes	mild	None	no	mild	slight	Cold

5. Refer first to exercise 3. Design a decision tree to distinguish between bronchitis, pneumonia, and TB.

Table 10.3

Cough	Fever	Phlegm	Shaking Chills	Shortness of Breath	Weakness or Fatigue	Diagnosis
bad	no or low	yes	No	yes	yes	Bronchitis
yes	mild or high	yes	Yes	yes	yes	Pneumonia
yes	Yes	yes	Yes	yes	yes	TB

6. If your decision tree does not converge, what is needed here?

   i. More input data?

   ii. Attributes that do a better job of separating hypotheses?

Keywords

eager learners	**ID3**	**reinforcement learning**
entropy	**information gain**	**supervised learning**
feedback	**lazy learner**	**training set**
homogeneity	**machine learning**	**unsupervised learning**
hypothesis space	**Occam's Razor**	

References

1. Samuel, A. 1959. Some studies in machine learning using the game of checkers. *IBM Journal of Research and Development* 3: 210–229.

2. Langley, P. and Simon, H. A. 1995. Applications of machine learning and rule induction. *Communications of the ACM* 38 (11): 54–64.

3. Mehryer, M., Rostamizaden, A., and Talwalker, A. 2012. *Foundations of Machine Learning*. Cambridge, MA: MIT Press.

4. Murphy, K. P. 2012. *Machine Learning*: *Probabilistic Perspective*. Cambridge, MA: MIT Press.

5. Marsland, S. 2009. *Machine Learning: An Algorithmic Perspective*. United Kingdom: Chapman and Hall/CRC.

6. Winston, P. H. 1992. *Artificial Intelligence*, 3rd ed. Reading, MA: Addison-Wesley.

7. Ballard, D. H. 1999. *An Introduction to Natural Computation*. Cambridge, MA: MIT Press.

8. Quinlan, J. R. 1993. *Programs for Mach ine Learning*. San Mateo, CA: Morgan Kaufman.

Bibliography

Darwin, C. 1959. *Origin of Species*. New York, NY: Bantam.

Heath, M. T. 1997. *Scientific Computing—An Introductory Survey*. New York, NY: McGraw-Hill.

Kolodner, J. L., ed. 1988. *Proceedings: Case-Based Reasoning Workshop*. San Mateo, CA: Morgan Kaufman.

Quinlan, J. R. 1986. Induction of decision trees. *Machine Learning* 1: 81–106.

MACHINE LEARNING PART II: NEURAL NETWORKS

John Hopfield.

■ ■ ■ ■ ■

This chapter continues our discussion of machine learning. Algorithms are presented that are modeled on the human brain and nervous system. These so-called artificial neural networks (ANN) have exhibited remarkable performance in pattern recognition, economic forecasting, and many other applications.

Colored stock ticker on black.

11.0 INTRODUCTION

In this chapter and parts of Chapter 12 we shift gears somewhat. At the onset of this text we stated that intelligent systems (natural or artificial) must be able to represent their knowledge, search for answers when necessary, and learn from experience. In this chapter we begin our discussion of learning. Whenever you wish to design a system to perform some activity, it is a good idea to begin by asking yourself if a solution already exists in nature. For example, imagine the year was 1902 (before the Wright brothers' successful flights in 1903), and you wanted to design an artificial flying machine (an airplane). You would observe that natural flying "machines" do in fact exist (birds). Your airplane design would probably incorporate two large wings. So it seems natural that if you want to design artificially intelligent systems (as we do) that you begin your studies by analyzing one of the most naturally intelligent systems on this planet—the human brain and nervous system.

The human brain consists of 10–100 billion neurons that are highly connected to one another. Some neurons communicate with several or perhaps several dozen neighboring neurons, whereas others have thousands of neurons with which they share information. Drawing inspiration from this natural paradigm, researchers have designed artificial neural networks (ANN) over the past decades. Applications have ranged from stock market forecasting to autonomous control of automobiles.

The human brain is an adaptive system that must respond to the vagaries of existence. Learning takes place by modifying the strengths of connections between neurons. In a similar manner, artificial neural network weights must change to take on this same adaptability. In one ANN paradigm—supervised learning—learning rules assume responsibility for this task by comparing a network's performance against desired responses and then modifying the system's weights accordingly. Three learning rules are described: The Perceptron Learning Rule, the delta rule, and backpropagation. It is the latter rule that has the wherewithal to contend with multilayer networks and has encountered widespread success across numerous applications. Some of these successes are described in Section 11.8.

Familiarity with various network architectures and learning rules is not enough to guarantee the success of your models. You also need to know how your data should be encoded and how long your network training should last, as well as how you should handle difficulties if your network fails to converge. These and other issues are discussed in Section 11.6.

Artificial network research underwent a dry spell during the 1970s. Government funding was not as available, and the field produced few new results. John Hopfield, the Nobel Prize laureate in physics, rekindled enthusiasm in this discipline with his research. His model, the so-called Hopfield network, has found widespread applications in optimization. Discrete Hopfield models are briefly introduced in Section 11.7.

11.1 RUDIMENTS OF ARTIFICIAL NEURAL NETWORKS

McCulloch and Pitts [1] developed the first model for artificial neurons. They were attempting to understand (and to simulate) the behavior of animal nervous systems. Present day biologists and neurologists do understand how individual neurons communicate with one another inside a living being. Animal nervous systems are composed of thousands or millions of these interconnected cells; in humans, it is billions. The way in which parallel collections of neurons form functional units, however, is still a mystery. Before plunging into a discussion of artificial neural networks (ANN), we need to understand the relationship to their biological counterparts. A biological neuron is shown in Figure 11.1.

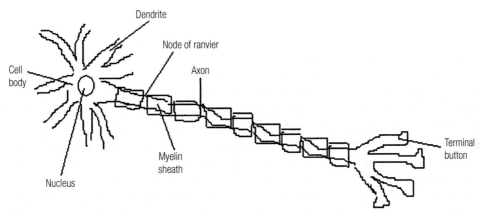

Figure 11.1
Basic design of a biological neuron.

Electrical signals flow into the cell body via dendrites, which are hair-like filaments. The cell body (or soma) is where "processing" occurs. When sufficient excitation is present, the neuron fires; in other words, it sends a small electrical signal (measured in milliwatts) down the cable-like protrusion known as an axon. A neuron will usually have a single axon but will possess many dendrites. By sufficient excitation we mean in excess of some predetermined threshold.[1] The electrical signal flows through the axon until it reaches the end bulb (refer to the bottom right corner of Figure 11.1). The axon-dendrite (or axon-soma or axon-axon) contact between an end bulb and a cell it encroaches on is called a synapse. There is actually a small gap between two neurons (that almost touch)—this is called a synaptic gap. This gap is laden with a conductive fluid that permits the flow of interneuronal electrical signals. Brain hormones (or ingested drugs such as caffeine) affect the degree of conductivity that is present.

There are four elements that AI has adopted from this biological model:

Biological model	Artificial neurons
• Cell body	• Cell body
• Axon	• Output channel
• Dendrites	• Input channel
• Synapses	• Weights

As seen above, real-valued weights play the role of synapses. The value of a weight reflects the conductive level of a biological synapse and serves to mediate the degree of influence that one neuron has on another. An abstract neuron (sometimes called a unit or node or just a neuron) is depicted in Figure 11.2.

The input to a neuron is a real-valued vector $\bar{x} = (x_1, x_2,...,x_n)$ with n components. A weight vector $\bar{w} = (w_1, w_2,...,w_n)$, also real-valued, is the counterpart to a synapse in a biological neuron. These weights govern the effect that the inputs will have on the unit. The body of a neuron computes a primitive function **f**. Finally, the output

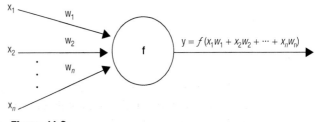

Figure 11.2
A model of an abstract neuron.

$$y = f(x_1 w_1 + x_2 w_2 + \cdots + x_n w_n)$$

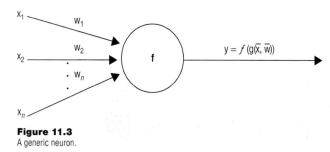

Figure 11.3
A generic neuron.

of this unit **y** is equal to the function **f** applied to the dot product of $\bar{x}$ with $\bar{w}$. More generally, the network computes some function **g** of the inputs and weights. Figure 11.3 illustrates the more general situation. Here, **g** is a function of the inputs $\bar{x}$ and $\bar{w}$ and **f** is the output or **activation function**. Recall from Chapter 1, "Overview of Artificial Intelligence," that the dot product of two vectors, $\bar{x}$ and $\bar{w}$, denoted by $\bar{x} \cdot \bar{w}$, is their component-wise product. That is,

$$\bar{x} \cdot \bar{w} = x_1 * w_1 + x_2 * w_2 + \ldots + x_n * w_n,$$

which equals a scalar (a real number without direction).

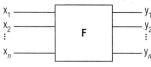

Figure 11.4
A neural network as a black box.

An artificial neural network (ANN) (in the text of this chapter, we always mean an *artificial* neural network; on those rare occasions when we are referring to "real" neurons, we will use the adjective *biological*) is a collection of abstract neurons arranged in some topology. An ANN computes a function F, where F is from R^n into R^m, or F: $R^n \rightarrow R^m$ with R being the set of real numbers. An ANN can be viewed as a *black box* (refer to the discussion on abstraction in Chapter 1) as seen in Figure 11.4.

Certain input vectors $\bar{x}$ should produce specific outputs $\bar{y}$. To accomplish this feat, the network must adjust its weights in a self-organizing process.

11.2 McCULLOCH-PITTS NETWORK

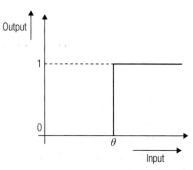

Figure 11.5
Diagram of a McCulloch-Pitts neuron.

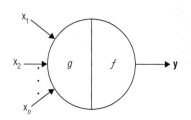

Figure 11.6
The step function for a McCulloch-Pitts neuron with threshold θ

The earliest models for neurons were by McCulloch and Pitts.[1] Marvin Minsky introduced the notation for the so-called McCulloch-Pitts units shown in Figure 11.5.

The input to this neuron $\bar{x} = (x_1, x_2, \ldots, x_n)$ and the output *y* are binary signals, in other words, either **0** or **1**. Edges are either **excitatory** or **inhibitory**. The latter are marked with a small circle just near the unit. The threshold value is θ. The inputs x_1, x_2, ..., x_n enter the neuron through *n* excitatory edges. There can also be inputs v_1, v_2, ..., v_m entering the unit through *m* inhibitory edges; if any inhibitory inputs are present, then the neuron is inhibited and its output **y** will equal **0**. Otherwise, the total excitation $g(\bar{x}) = x_1 + x_2 + \ldots + x_n$. If $g(\bar{x}) \geq \theta$ then the unit fires, and **y = 1**. The **activation function f** which produces the output of this unit is a **step** (or **threshold**) **function** (see Figure 11.6).

Note that when the total excitation $g(\bar{x}) < \theta$, the output is 0. McCulloch-Pitts units that function as two-input Boolean AND and OR gates (consult Chapter 5, "Logic in Artificial Intelligence") are shown in Figure 11.7.

In Figure 11.7(a), the output of the AND gate, $y = g(\bar{x}) = x_1 x_2$, equals 1 only when both x_1 and x_2 are equal to 1. For the (inclusive) OR gate in 11.7(b), the output **y** equals 1 when either x_1 or x_2 (or both) are

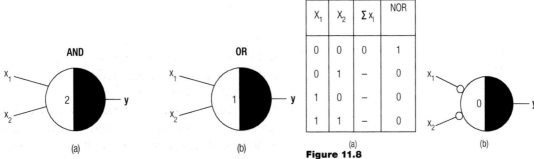

Figure 11.7
McCulloch-Pitts implementations for two-input (a) AND gate and (b) OR gate.

Figure 11.8
(a) Truth table for a two-input NOR function and (b) McCulloch-Pitts implementation of this function.

equal to 1. Figure 11.8 shows the truth table for a two-input NOR function and a McCulloch-Pitts implementation.

The function equals 1 when both inputs equal 0. When either (or both) inputs equal 1, the inhibitory inputs of the McCulloch-Pitts unit (depicted by little circles) cause the correct output of 0 to be produced.

A decoder is a switching circuit that is true for one or more **minterms**. A minterm is a product term (terms that are ANDed together) in which every variable is present in complemented or uncomplemented form. For example, three minterms over the variables x_1 and x_2 are $x_1'x_2, x_1x_2'$, and x_1x_2 (the AND operation is implicit and is therefore not shown). A decoder for $x_1x_2'x_3$ (sometimes denoted by 101 when the variables are understood) is shown in Figure 11.9.

Confirm that the output of this unit will equal 1 only when $x_1 = x_3 = 1$ and $x_2 = 0$. The truth table for the two-input XOR function is shown in Figure 11.10a (refer to Chapter 5). A McCulloch-Pitts neuron that implements the XOR function is provided in Figure 11.10b.

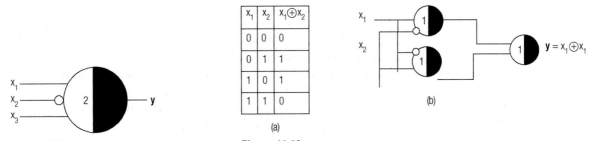

Figure 11.9
A decoder for the minterm x_1x_2', x_3.

Figure 11.10
(a) Truth table for the two-input XOR function. (b) McCulloch-Pitts implementation using decoders.

11.3 THE PERCEPTRON LEARNING RULE

The limitation of the McCulloch-Pitts model is that there are no weights. Neurons are not adaptive and, hence, no learning can take place unless the network topology is transformed or the threshold is altered. We saw that an ANN can be viewed as a black box (refer once again to Figure 11.4). Suppose that we present a network with a series of input vectors $\bar{x}_1, \bar{x}_2, \ldots, \bar{x}_r$. For each input vector $\bar{x}_i$ there is a desired output vector $\bar{t}_i$, where **t** is short for target (something we aim for). Naturally, the actual output of the network $\bar{y}_i$, can be different from $\bar{t}_i$. Associated with each input in this model is a weight; these weights are the free parameters of the system. Our task is to adjust the weights so as to minimize (or eliminate) the difference between $\bar{y}_i$ and $\bar{t}_i$. The process that governs the adjustment of system weights is called a **learning rule**. In this section we discuss the

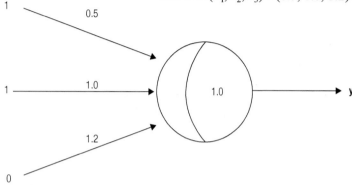

Figure 11.11
An abstract neuron referred to as a
Threshold Logic Unit (TLU).

Perceptron Learning Rule, which was developed by the psychologist Frank Rosenblatt in 1958. [2] We begin our discussion by considering networks consisting of one neuron. An abstract neuron was discussed in Section 11.1 and appears as in Figure 11.11.

We will refer to this device as a **Threshold Logic Unit (TLU).** We let the excitation function of a TLU, or $g(\overline{x}, \overline{w})$ equal to $\overline{x} \cdot \overline{w} = x_1 * w_1 + x_2 * w_2 + \ldots + x_n * w_n$. As an example, consider a TLU with threshold $\theta = 1.0$ and with $\overline{x} = (x_1, x_2, x_3) = (1,1,0)$ and $\overline{w} = (w_1, w_2, w_3) = (0.5, 1.0, 1.2)$ as shown in Figure 11.12.

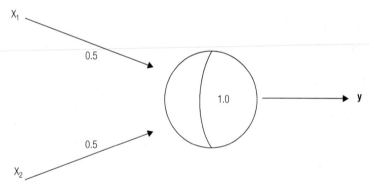

Figure 11.12
A Threshold Logic Unit with threshold input vector $\overline{x} = (1, 1, 0)$ and weight vector $\overline{w} = (0.5, 1.0, 1.2)$.

The excitation to this neuron is $\overline{x} \cdot \overline{w} = x_1 * w_1 + x_2 * w_2 + x_3 * w_3 = (1*0.5) + (1*1.0) + (0*1.2) = 1.5$. Whenever $\overline{x} \cdot \overline{w} \geq \theta$, the activation function **f** specifies that the output **y** will equal 1. Since the excitation $\overline{x} \cdot \overline{w}$ in this example equals 1.5 and the threshold θ equals 1.0, the output of the unit **y** equals 1.

We have seen that whenever the excitation equals or exceeds the threshold, the TLU has an output of 1; when this quantity is less than θ, **y** equals 0. We examine the case in which $\overline{x} \cdot \overline{w}$ equals θ. Consult Figure 11.13. The TLU in this figure has a threshold $\theta = 1.0$, and weight vector $\overline{w} = (0.5, 0.5)$.

By setting $\overline{x} \cdot \overline{w} = \theta$ we obtain: $x_1 * w_1 + x_2 * w_2 = \theta$. We solve for x_2 in terms of

$$x_1, w_1, w_2 \quad \text{and} \quad \theta,$$

yielding:

$$x_2 * w_2 = \theta - x_1 * w_1.$$

Figure 11.13
A TLU with two inputs.

Some algebraic manipulation gives us:

$$x_2 * w_2 = -x_1 * w_1 + \theta$$

$$x_2 = -\frac{w_1}{w_2} * x_1 + \frac{\theta}{w_2}.$$

Recall that the equation of a straight line is: $y = m * x + b$ where m is the slope (m equals $\frac{\Delta y}{\Delta x}$, or the change in y divided by the change in x), and b is the y-intercept. Hence, we have a straight line whose slope equals $-\frac{w_1}{w_2}$ and intercept equals $\frac{\theta}{w_2}$. Substituting the values for w_1, w_2, θ, shown in Figure 11.13 we have: $x_2 = -x_1 + 2$. This line is shown in Figure 11.14.

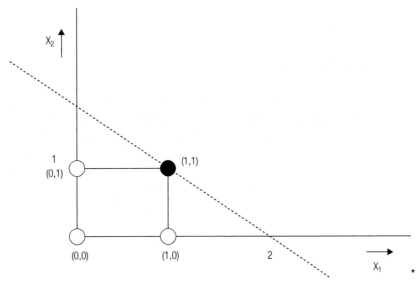

Figure 11.14
The straight line obtained from the TLU in Figure 11.13 when the excitation equals the threshold.

Inputs to a neural network are sometimes referred to as patterns. Inputs are presently restricted to binary values, therefore the four patterns for the TLU in Figure 11.13 are $(0, 0)$, $(0, 1)$, $(1, 0)$, and $(1, 1)$. The n-dimensional space representing all input patterns is referred to as the **pattern space**; Figure 11.14 shows the pattern space for this TLU. Figure 11.15 displays the outputs for the TLU in Figure 11.13 for each input pattern.

We observe that this TLU is behaving as a 2-input AND gate. The set of patterns that produce the same output is referred to as a **pattern class**. From Figure 11.15 we surmise that $\{(0, 0), (0, 1), (1, 0)\}$ result in an output of 0, whereas $\{(1, 1)\}$ produces a 1 as output. We refer to the former as pattern class zero, or $\mathbf{C_0}$, and the latter as pattern class one, or $\mathbf{C_1}$. In Figure 11.14, members of $\mathbf{C_0}$ are represented by circles that are unshaded, whereas the sole element in $\mathbf{C_1}$ is denoted by a darkened circle. Referring once again to the straight line in Figure

x_1	x_2	$\bar{x} \cdot \bar{w}$	y
0	0	0.0	0
0	1	0.5	0
1	0	0.5	0
1	1	1.0	1

Figure 11.15
Input/output behavior for the TLU in Figure 11.13.

11.14, we notice that members of $\mathbf{C_0}$ lie entirely below this line whereas the element in $\mathbf{C_1}$ lies at (or above) the line. This straight line, which is called a **discriminant**, separates the two pattern classes from one another. In this example, the patterns lie in 2-dimensional space and the discriminant is a straight line. More generally, when the dimension of the pattern space is n, the discriminant will have dimension $n-1$. An $(n-1)$-dimensional "surface" is referred to as a hyperplane. ANNs perform pattern recognition by producing discriminant(s) that separate the n-dimensional pattern space into convex subspaces bounded by discriminating hyperplane(s). How are these discriminants produced? The Perceptron Learning Rule does so by a series of iterative corrections. To understand how these corrections are made, we return to the concept of the dot product of two vectors.

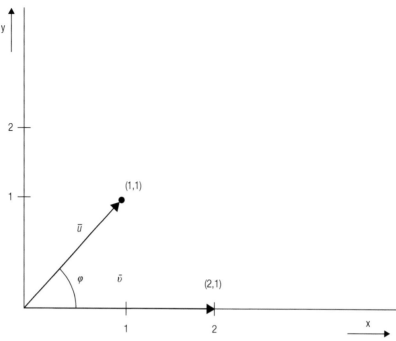

Figure 11.16
Two vectors $\bar{u}$ and $\bar{v}$ separated by an angle φ.

The magnitude of a vector $\bar{U} = (u_1, u_2,...,u_n)$, denoted by $|U|$ equals $\sqrt{u_1^2 + u_2^2 + ... + u_n^2}$. Figure 11.16 illustrates this concept for a vector with two components.

The magnitude of $\bar{u}$, denoted $|\bar{u}|$ equals $\sqrt{u_1^2 + u_2^2} = \sqrt{1^2 + 1^2} = \sqrt{2}$. The magnitude of $\bar{v}$, in other words, $|\bar{v}|$, equals $\sqrt{v_1^2 + v_2^2} = \sqrt{2^2 + 0^2} = \sqrt{4} = 2$. We stated that $\bar{x} \cdot \bar{w}$ is the component-wise product of the input vector $\bar{x}$ with weight vector $\bar{w}$, in other words, $\bar{x} \cdot \bar{w} = x_1 * w_1 + x_2 * w_2 + ... + x_n * w_n$. Alternatively, $\bar{x} \cdot \bar{w}$ can be defined as $|x| * |w| * \cos \varphi$, where φ is the angle between the two vectors. Calculating the dot product of $\bar{u}$ and $\bar{v}$ using our first formula yields:

$$\bar{u} \cdot \bar{v} = u_1 * v_1 + u_2 * v_2 = 1 * 2 + 1 * 0 = 2.$$

Employing the second formula for the dot product of two vectors yields the same result (as expected):

$$\bar{u} \cdot \bar{v} = |u| * |v| * \cos \varphi = \sqrt{2} * 2 * \cos 45° = 2 * \sqrt{2} * \frac{\sqrt{2}}{2} = 2.$$

The definition and graph for the cosine function are shown in Figure 11.17.

You can observe in this figure that the cosine function achieves its maximal value when the angle φ equals 0°. At 90°, $\cos \varphi$ equals 0, and at 180°, the cosine equals −1, then at 270° it again equals 0°, and at 360° the value of the cosine once more returns to 1. As Figure 11.17 shows, the cosine function is periodic and hence the aforementioned values repeat modulo 360°.

We are almost poised to derive the Perceptron Learning Rule. One final observation remains, one that concerns the equivalence of the two TLUs drawn in Figure 11.18.

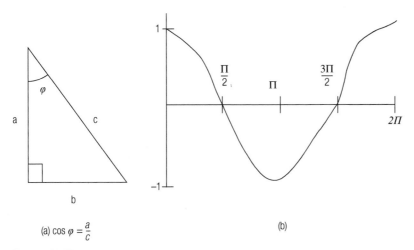

(a) $\cos \varphi = \dfrac{a}{c}$

(b)

Figure 11.17
Graph of the cosine function.

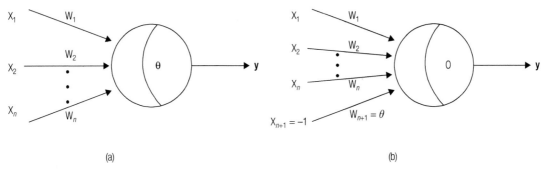

(a)

(b)

Figure 11.18
The threshold of a TLU can be treated as an additional weight.

In 11.18(a), the output **y** equals 1 whenever $\overline{x} \cdot \overline{w} \geq \theta$. Observe that the TLU in 11.18(b) has a 1 as an output whenever $\overline{x} \cdot \overline{w} + (x_{n+1} * w_{n+1}) \geq 0$. By setting x_{n+1} to -1 and w_{n+1} to θ, we obtain: $\overline{x} \cdot \overline{w} + (-1) * \theta \geq 0$. By adding θ to both sides we have that this occurs precisely when $\overline{x} \cdot \overline{w} \geq \theta$. Hence, the two models of TLU's are equivalent. We refer to the input vector $(x_1, x_2, ..., x_n, x_{n+1},$ where $x_{n+1} = -1$) as the **augmented input vector**, which we denote by $\hat{x}$. Similarly, the **augmented weight vector** $\hat{w}$ equals $(w_1, w_2, ..., w_n, w_{n+1},$ where $w_{n+1} = \theta$).

Suppose now that we present an augmented input $\hat{x}$ to the TLU in Figure 11.18(b) and that the output **y** is 0 but the target output t is 1. We know that $\hat{x} \cdot \hat{w}$ is less than 0 (or else **y** would have been equal to 1). Consult Figure 11.19(a).

The TLU has produced the wrong output. The output **y** equals 0 because the excitation of the TLU, $\hat{x} \cdot \hat{w}$, is less than 0. Therefore, we seek to increase this dot product; to do so, we rotate $\hat{w}$ in the direction of $\hat{x}$. The angle between these two vectors, φ, is thereby decreased to φ'. Since $\varphi' < \varphi$, $\cos \varphi' > \cos \varphi$ and hence $\hat{x} \cdot \hat{w}_{new} > \hat{x} \cdot \hat{w}_{old}$. We continue rotating $\hat{w}$ toward $\hat{x}$ in subsequent steps until $\hat{x} \cdot \hat{w}$ exceeds 0 and the correct output is produced, or until **y** equals **t**. Rotating the vector $\hat{w}$ toward $\hat{x}$ is equivalent to adding a fraction (α) of $\hat{x}$ to $\hat{w}$. So that when

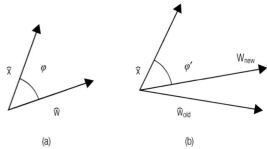

(a)

(b)

Figure 11.19
(a) The angle between $\hat{x}$ and $\hat{w}$ equals φ. (b) The vector $\hat{w}$ is rotated toward $\hat{x}$.

$$\mathbf{y} = 0 \quad \text{and} \quad \mathbf{t} = 1, \ \hat{w}_{new} = \hat{w}_{old} + \boldsymbol{\alpha}^* \ \hat{x}. \tag{1}$$

You are asked to verify that when

$$\mathbf{y} = 1 \quad \text{and} \quad t = 0, \text{ the proper corrective action is provided by}$$

$$\hat{w}_{new} = \hat{w}_{old} - \boldsymbol{\alpha}^* \ \hat{x}. \tag{2}$$

In this situation, $\bar{w}$ is being rotated away from $\bar{x}$. The constant $\boldsymbol{\alpha}$ is referred to as the learning rate of the algorithm. This quantity is a small positive constant with $0 < \boldsymbol{\alpha} \leq 1$. Combining Equations 1 and 2 we obtain:

$$\hat{w}_{new} = \hat{w}_{old} + \boldsymbol{\alpha}^* \ (\mathbf{t} - \mathbf{y}) \ * \ \hat{x}. \tag{3}$$

Observe that the *quantity* $\mathbf{t} - \mathbf{y}$ always provides the proper sign for the corrective term. Pseudocode for the Perceptron Learning Rule is given in Figure 11.20. The vector $\hat{w}_{new}$ has $n + 1$ components; accordingly Equation (3) may also be expressed as:

$$\Delta w_i = \alpha^*(\mathbf{t} - \mathbf{y}) * x_i, \ i = 1 \text{ to } n + 1.$$

```
1. Inputs:  X̂₁, X̂₂, ..., X̂ₚ              // the input patterns.

2. t̄₁, t̄₂, ..., t̄ₚ                        // the desired outputs for each pattern.

3. Ŵ_new = Ŵ_old = (W₁, W₂, ..., Wₙ, Wₙ₊₁)   // augmented weight vector which
                                              is randomly generated.

4. i = 1                                  // an index that selects pattern.

5. while (not-all equal)                  // i.e. ȳᵢ ≠ t̄ᵢ for some pattern Xᵢ.

6. for i = 1 to p

7. if  ȳᵢ ≠ t̄ᵢ then { Ŵ_new is corrected according to Equation 3

     not_all_equal = true}

8. // end if

9. // end for

10. if not_all_equal = false then return that the TLU has

     successfully been trained and Ŵ = Ŵ_new.

11. else continue

12. //end while
```

Figure 11.20
Pseudocode for the Perceptron Learning Rule.

The Perceptron Learning Rule is an iterative procedure. It begins with a random weight vector $\bar{w} = w_1, w_2,..., w_n$, in which each w_i is a small (close to 0) random number. You might be asking what happens when the driver for the while loop in line 5 is never satisfied, or when some network output y_i always differs from the target t_i? When this occurs, the algorithm will cycle endlessly, confined within this while loop. The algorithm converges and a discriminant is produced when the pattern classes are **linearly separable**, in other words, can be separated by a straight line (see Figure 11.25(d) for the two-input OR function). We return to the issue of separability later in this section.

More accurately, the Perceptron Learning Rule should be classified as a procedure because an algorithm is always guaranteed to halt.

We observe that the input patterns $\hat{x}_1...,\hat{x}_p$ and derived outputs, $\bar{t}_1, \bar{t}_2,..., \bar{t}_p$ are inputs to this algorithm. Two comments are in order here—first that in general, a TLU can have more than a single output, hence, each target value $\bar{t}_i$ and each actual output $\bar{y}_i$ can be viewed in general as vectors (we shall drop the "(–)" above the variables when the TLU has a single output). Second, the Perceptron Learning Rule is an instance of what is called **Supervised Learning** or **Learning with a Teacher**, in that the network is supplied a priori with the correct input-output correspondence.

EXAMPLE 11.1: USE THE PERCEPTRON TRAINING RULE TO TRAIN A TLU TO LEARN THE 2-INPUT INCLUSIVE OR FUNCTION.

Observe from Figure 11.22, and 11.23 that we let the learning rate $\alpha = \frac{1}{2}$ and $\hat{w} = (0,0,0)$.

We build a table as shown in Figure 11.22.

Observe in this figure that the set of all possible inputs to the OR function are listed in the first four rows of columns 1 and 2. Column 3 contains x_3, the augmented input which always equals –1. The augmented weight vector, $\hat{w}$, is contained in columns 4, 5, and 6. Notice that w_3 the augmented weight which equals θ, is treated in the same manner as the original weights w_1 and w_2. All three components of $\hat{w}$ are initialized to 0 in this example. Column 7 contains the excitation to the neuron; when this quantity equals or exceeds 0, then the corresponding entry in column 8—the output of this unit y—will equal 1, and otherwise **y** will be set to 0. Column 9 contains the target output for each

x_1	x_2	$x_1 + x_2$
0	0	0
0	1	1
1	0	1
1	1	1

Figure 11.21
Two input inclusive OR functions.

input pattern. Finally, columns 10, 11, and 12 hold the quantities by which the components of $\hat{w}$ should be adjusted. We refer to the set of all input patterns as an epoch. After one **epoch**, the table for this example appears as in Figure 11.23.

In row one of the table, $\hat{x} \cdot \hat{w} = (0,0,-1) \cdot (0,0,0)$, which equals 0 (column 7). Because $0 \geq 0$, column 8 contains a "1." However, the target output in row one is "0." Hence, weights are adjusted according to Equation 3. Only w_3 is changed as each of x_1 and x_2 are 0. $\Delta w_3 = 0.5 * (0 - 1)*(-1) = 0.5$ (column 12). Therefore, when pattern $\bar{x}_2 = (0, 1)$ is presented (row 2), w_3 equals 0.5. As a result of the calculations in the second row, w_2 will be increased by $\Delta w_2 = 0.5$

(1)	(2)	(3)	(4)	(5)	(6)	(7)	(8)	(9)	(10)	(11)	(12)
x_1	x_2	x_3	w_1	w_2	$w_3 = \theta$	$\hat{x} \cdot \hat{w}$	y	t	Δw_1	Δw_2	Δw_3
0	0	−1	0	0	0			0			
0	1	−1						1			
1	0	−1						1			
1	1	−1						1			

Figure 11.22
Table employed for the Perceptron Learning Rule.

(1)	(2)	(3)	(4)	(5)	(6)	(7)	(8)	(9)	(10)	(11)	(12)
x_1	x_2	x_3	w_1	w_2	$w_3 = \theta$	$\hat{x} \cdot \hat{w}$	y	t	Δw_1	Δw_2	Δw_3
0	0	−1	0	0	0	0	1	0	0	0	0.5
0	1	−1	0	0	0.5	−0.5	0	1	0	0.5	−0.5
1	0	−1	0	0.5	0	0	1	1	0	0	0
1	1	−1	0	0.5	0	0.5	1	1	0	0	0

Figure 11.23
Parameter values after one epoch of Perceptron Training.

and w_3 will be decreased by $\Delta w_3 = -0.5$. The stopping condition for this learning rule is that an entire epoch must be processed with no weight changes.

The entire table for this example is shown in Figure 11.24.

The training required four epochs. The correct weights were found during Epoch III, however, an additional epoch was required to verify that the values were correct.

	(1) X_1	(2) X_2	(3) X_3	(4) W_1	(5) W_2	(6) $W_3 = \theta$	(7) $\hat{x} \cdot \hat{w}$	(8) y	(9) t	(10) ΔW_1	(11) ΔW_2	(12) ΔW_3
Epoch I	0	0	−1	0.0	0.0	0.0	0.0	1	0	0	0	0.5
	0	1	−1	0.5	0.0	0.5	−0.5	0	1	0	0.5	−0.5
	1	0	−1	0.0	0.5	0.0	0.0	1	1	0	0	0
	1	1	−1	0.0	0.5	0.0	0.5	1	1	0	0	0
Epoch II	0	0	−1	0.0	0.5	0.0	0.0	1	0	0	0	0.5
	0	1	−1	0.0	0.5	0.5	0.0	1	1	0	0	0
	1	0	−1	0.0	0.5	0.5	−0.5	0	1	0.5	0	−0.5
	1	1	−1	0.5	0.5	0.0	1.0	1	1	0	0	0
Epoch III	0	0	−1	0.5	0.5	0.0	0.0	1	0	0	0	0.5
	0	1	−1	0.5	0.5	0.5	0.0	1	1	0	0	0
	1	0	−1	0.5	0.5	0.5	0.0	1	1	0	0	0
	1	1	−1	0.5	0.5	0.5	0.5	1	1	0	0	0
Epoch IV	0	0	−1	0.5	0.5	0.5	−0.5	0	0	0	0	0
	0	1	−1	0.5	0.5	0.5	0.0	1	1	0	0	0
	1	0	−1	0.5	0.5	0.5	0.0	1	1	0	0	0
	1	1	−1	0.5	0.5	0.5	0.5	1	1	0	0	0

Figure 11.24
The entire Perceptron Training Procedure for Example 11.1.

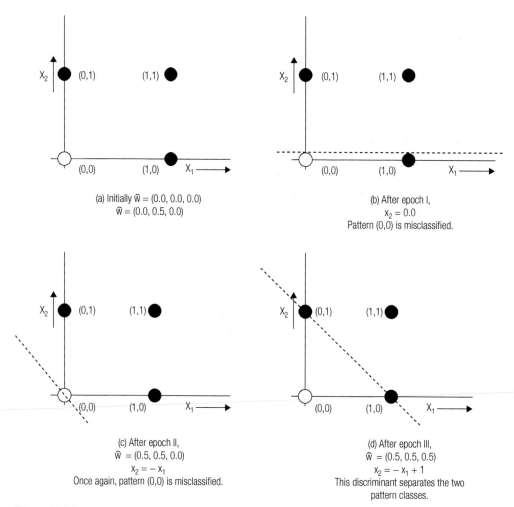

Figure 11.25
(a) The initial discriminant, (b) in other words, (c) before training begins. (d) After each of epochs I, II, and III.

Figure 11.25 depicts the discriminant at four stages during the training process.

As this figure illustrates, the discriminant in 11.25(d) correctly separates pattern class $0 = \{(0, 0)\}$ from pattern class $1 = \{(0, 1), (1, 0), (1, 1)\}$. All points in C_0 lie below the discriminant, while all members of C_1 lie on (or above) this line.

We have chosen to represent inputs and outputs as binary numbers, in other words, 0 or 1. Because weight updates in the Perceptron Learning Rule prescribe that $\Delta w_i = \alpha * (t - y) * x_i$, a glance at Figure 11.24 confirms that in many instances where y and t differed, no weight adjustments were made. This occurs because the corresponding input, or x_i, equals 0. It is for this reason that bipolar values are often chosen to represent neural net inputs and outputs. Bipolar values are −1 and 1, where −1 corresponds to 0, and 1 is represented as itself. The two-input inclusive-OR function represented with bipolar values appears in Figure 11.26. Compare this figure with Figure 11.21. A training rule that employs bipolar values often converges sooner.

We stated earlier that the Perceptron Learning Rule will successfully converge and produce a discriminant when the pattern classes are linearly separable. There are 2^4 or 16 Boolean functions on two variables. All but two are linearly separable. One function that is not is the two-input exclusive-OR function illustrated in Figure 11.10a and reproduced for convenience in Figure 11.27a.

Figure 11.27(b) depicts the pattern space for the 2-input XOR function.

Pattern class 0 consists of (0, 0) and (1, 1) whereas pattern class 1 contains (0, 1) and (1, 0). You should convince yourself that it is impossible to separate C_0 from C_1 with a single straight line; the 2-input XOR function is *not* linearly separable. Therefore, the Perceptron Learning Rule will loop forever when this function is input. The Perceptron Learning Convergence Theorem states that this learning rule will halt with a solution when a solution exists; alternatively, it will loop forever when one does *not*. It must be understood that the 2-input XOR function does not represent a death sentence for the utility of ANN. This function *can* be implemented—however, to do so will require multilayer networks, the subject of Section 11.5.

X_1	X_2	$X_1 + X_2$
−1	−1	−1
−1	1	1
1	−1	1
1	1	1

Figure 11.26
The two-input inclusive-OR function represented with bipolar values.

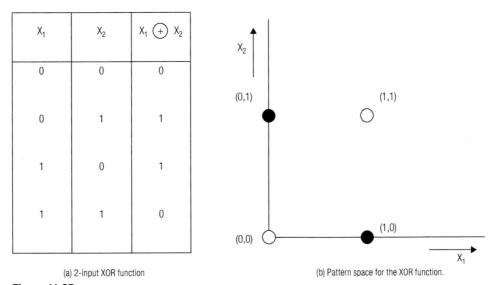

X_1	X_2	$X_1 \oplus X_2$
0	0	0
0	1	1
1	0	1
1	1	0

(a) 2-input XOR function

(b) Pattern space for the XOR function.

Figure 11.27
(a) The truth table for the 2-input Exclusive Or function. (b) The associated pattern space.

11.4 THE DELTA RULE

The Perceptron Learning Rule fails to converge whenever the input patterns are not linearly separable; this limitation manifests itself even when outliers represent a small fraction of the inputs. Consult Figure 11.28.

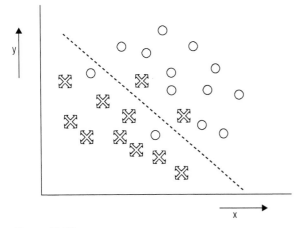

Figure 11.28
Two pattern classes (⊠ and ○). The dashed line correctly classifies most of the inputs.

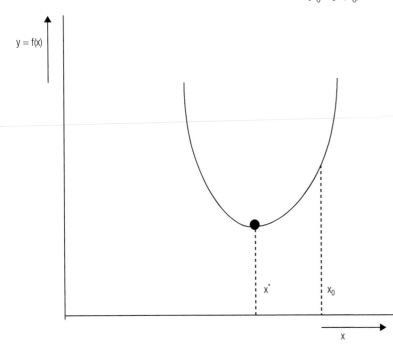

Figure 11.29
Finding the minimum of the function $y = f(x)$.

The Perceptron Rule would not converge in this example; however, the Delta Rule, which we define here, successfully classifies the vast majority of the inputs. The Delta Rule and backpropagation, which is discussed in Section 11.5, both rely on **gradient descent**.

Gradient descent is a calculus-based method used to find the minimum of a function. Suppose that the variable y depends on a single variable x, or $y = f(x)$. We refer to x as the **independent variable** and y as the **dependent variable**. Refer to Figure 11.29. We are searching for that value x^* for which y is minimum; $f(x^*) \leq f(x), \forall x$.

Let x_0 be the current value for x, in other words, we are at position $P_0 = (x_0, y_0)$ on the graph, where $y_0 = f(x_0)$. Consult Figures 11.29 and 11.30.

We are searching for x^*, that value that minimizes $y = f(x)$. We travel in the direction that minimizes this function, in other words, we proceed either to $x_0 + \Delta x$ or $x_0 - \Delta x$ for some small step Δx. You perhaps recognize this as a form of hill climbing (Chapter 3, "Informed Search"). We need to know the resulting change in y for these changes in x; in other words, we require the slope $m = (\Delta y/\Delta x)$ of the straight line L (known as the tangent line), which just touches the graph at the point P_0. If the graph is drawn carefully, then Δx and Δy can be measured directly from the graph. You might recall from the first course in calculus that as Δx and Δy get smaller and smaller then the ratio $(\Delta y/\Delta x)$ approaches the derivative of the function at the point P_0; in other words, $\dfrac{\Delta y}{\Delta x} \approx f'(x_0)$. In Figure 11.30,

observe that δ_y and δ_x are also drawn. The ratio of these quantities represents the rate at which the function $f(x)$ is changing at the point $P_0 = (x_0, y_0)$; in other words, the derivative $f'(x)$, and not the rate at which the tangent line to the point P_0 is changing. When Δx is sufficiently small, then $\delta_y = \Delta y$, or the change in height of the function equals the change in y-value of the tangent line. We employ some algebra:

$$\delta_y = \Delta y \qquad\qquad \text{// } \Delta x \text{ sufficiently small}$$

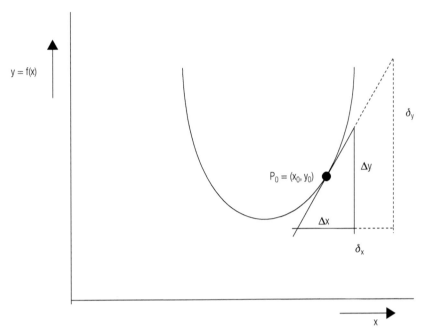

Figure 11.30
The slope of a function.

$$\delta_y = \left(\frac{\Delta y}{\Delta x}\right) * \Delta x \qquad \text{// we multiplied the right hand side (rhs) by } (\Delta x/\Delta x)$$

$$\delta_y \approx \Delta y \qquad \text{// for small } \Delta x$$
$$\therefore \delta_y = slope\ of\ tangent\ \text{line} * \Delta x$$

$$\text{and } \delta_y = \left(\frac{dy}{dx}\right) * \Delta x \qquad (*)\text{// where } (dy/dx) \text{ is the instantaneous rate of}$$
$$\text{// change of } y \text{ with respect to } x,$$
$$\text{// or the derivative of the function } f(x).$$

If the function f is differentiable, then calculate the derivative of $f(x)$, in other words, $f'(x)$. Set:

$$\Delta x = -\alpha * \left(\frac{dy}{dx}\right) **,$$

where α is a positive constant, small enough so that .
When (**) is substituted into (*), we have

$$dy \approx -\alpha \left(\frac{dy}{dx}\right)^2 (***)$$

Because $\left(\frac{dy}{dx}\right)^2$ must be positive, the rhs of *** $-\alpha \left(\frac{dy}{dx}\right)^2$ is negative. $\therefore \delta_y < 0$. We have therefore taken a step down the curve. If this process is repeated, we should eventually arrive at the function minimum $f(x^*)$. This iterative process is known as gradient descent.

The gradient of a function f (denoted grad f or ∇f, read as del of f) is a vector that points in the direction in which f increases most rapidly. So strictly speaking, we are traveling down f in the direction opposite to the gradient of f.

If y is a function of the n variables: $x_1, x_2,..., x_n$, or, $y = f(x_1, x_2,..., x_n)$, then the above argument can be generalized. One can speak of the rate of change of the function f with respect to each of the variables. The partial derivative $\partial f/\partial x_i$ is the instantaneous rate of change of the function f with respect to the variable x_i, the "variables" $x_1, x_2, ..., x_{i-1}, x_{i+1}, ..., x_n$ are treated as constants. The counterpart to equation (**) in the n-dimensional case is

$$\Delta x_i = -\alpha * \left(\frac{\delta_y}{\delta_{x_i}} \right) \quad \text{for each} \quad i = 1, ..., n .$$

We now apply gradient descent to find the minimum of the error function for a single TLU. This discussion culminates with a second rule for supervised learning—the Delta Rule—a rule that can be viewed as more robust than the Perceptron Learning Rule in that a few inputs may violate the linear separability restriction imposed by the latter rule. For this discussion we redraw a simple threshold logic unit in Figure 11.31.

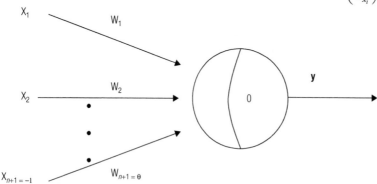

Figure 11.31
A TLU.

This abstract neuron is presented with an input pattern $\bar{x}^p$ and where $\bar{t}^p$ is the associated target output. Whenever the TLU's output $\bar{y}^p$ does not equal $\bar{t}^p$, the system's weights must be adjusted. The blame for any discrepancy between $\bar{y}^p$ and $\bar{t}^p$ lies with $\hat{w}$, the augmented weight vector. Any function E that expresses the error of this unit must have $\hat{w}$ as an argument, in other words, $E(\hat{w}) = E(w_1, w_2,..., w_{n+1})$. Our task is to find an appropriate expression for this error function $E(\ )$ and to use gradient descent to minimize it.

Suppose we present N patterns to the TLU and we set E to the average error:

$$E = \frac{1}{N} * \left(\sum_{p=1}^{N} e^p \right), \quad \text{where} \quad e^p = t^p - y^p,$$

or, the system error encountered for pattern p. However, when $t^p = 1$ and $y^p = 0$, the error will be calculated as larger than when $t^p = 0$ and $y^p = 1$. One is tempted to use: $e^p = (t^p - y^p)^2$ instead. However, gradient descent requires that the function involved be smooth and differentiable. The TLU's activation function is discontinuous at the point $x = \theta$, with an abrupt jump in output as x increases to θ, y experiences a sudden leap from 0 to 1 (consult Figure 11.35a). The equation that is used is

$$e^p = \frac{1}{2} * \left(t^p - \hat{x}^p \cdot \hat{w} \right)^2,$$

where bipolar $\{-1, 1\}$ instead of binary values $\{0, 1\}$ are used. The average or **mean square error** (MSE) over all N patterns is

$$E = \frac{1}{N} \sum_{p=1}^{N} \frac{1}{2} * \left(t^p - \hat{x}^p \cdot \hat{w} \right)^2 .$$

This error E depends on all of the patterns, as does each partial derivative $\partial E / \partial w_i$. Hence, all of the N patterns must be presented *before* any weight changes are mandated; this is referred to as **batch training** but is computationally intensive. Instead, what is done in practice is to present a network with a pattern p and then make adjustments based on $\dfrac{\partial e^p}{\partial w_i}$, which is used as an estimate for $\partial E / \partial w_i$. This minimization process is noisy, and sometimes weight changes are made that actually increase the error E. The error produced when pattern p is presented to the TLU is

$$e^p = \frac{1}{2} * \left(t^p - \hat{x}^p \cdot \hat{w} \right)^2,$$

where the dot product $\hat{x}^p \cdot \hat{w}$ equals

$$x_1^p * w_1 + x_2^p * w_2 + \ldots + x_{n+1}^p * w_{n+1}.$$

Therefore, $\dfrac{\partial e^p}{\partial w_i} = -\left(t^p - \hat{x}^p \cdot \hat{w} \right) * x_i^p,$

where x_i^p is the ith component of the input pattern p. The chain rule is employed to obtain this result. Remember that the w's are variables in this expression and the x terms are constants. Weight adjustments are made according to

$$\Delta w_i = \alpha * \left(t^p - \hat{x}^p \cdot \hat{w} \right) * x_i^p, \quad (\#)$$

where α is the learning rate. The learning rule based upon this minimization process is the Widrow–Hoff Rule,[3] often referred to as the Delta Rule (or δ rule). Pseudocode for the Delta Rule is given in Figure 11.31a.

```
Repeat
        For each training vector pair (x̄, t̄)
                Calculate the excitation x̂·ŵ when x̂ is
                        presented as input to the TLU
                Make weight adjustments according to #
        End for
    Until the rate of error change is sufficiently small
    End
```

Figure 11.31a
Pseudocode for the Delta Rule.

The Delta Rule converges when the learning rate α is sufficiently small. That is, the weight vector $\hat{w}$ approaches $\hat{w}^*$ where $E\left(\hat{w}^* \right)$ is minimum. When the pattern classes are not linearly separable then some error will remain, in other words, some patterns will be misclassified ("x"s that lie above the discriminant in Figure 11.28 will be incorrectly classified as "0"s and vice versa; the Perceptron Learning Rule would never have converged for these input patterns). The Delta Rule will always make changes (unless your program forces an exit from the loop) because $\hat{x} \cdot \hat{w}$ will never exactly equal t which is either 0 or 1.

EXAMPLE 11.2

Use the Delta Rule to train a two-input TLU to learn the two-input inclusive OR function with initial weights $\overline{w} = (0, 0.2)$ and threshold $\theta = 0.25$ using a learning rate $\alpha = 0.10$.

We illustrate the requisite calculations during the first epoch in Figure 11.32.

w_1	w_2	$w_3 = \theta$	x_1	x_2	x_3	$\hat{x} \cdot \hat{w}$	t	$\alpha * (t - \hat{x} \cdot \hat{w})$	δw_1	δw_2	δw_3
0.0	0.2	0.25	0	0	−1	−0.25	−1	−0.075 a)	0.0	0.0	0.075
0.0	0.2	0.33	0	1	−1	−0.13	1	0.113 b)	0.0 c)	−0.113 d)	0.113 e)
0.0	0.09	0.44	1	0	−1	−0.44	1	0.144	0.144	0.0	−0.144
0.14	0.09	0.30	1	1	−1	−0.07 f)	1	0.107	0.107	0.107	−0.107

Figure 11.32
Sample training with the Delta Rule. Recall that bipolar inputs and outputs are being used.

After the first epoch, $w_1 = 0.25$, $w_2 = 0.20$, $w_3 = \theta = 0.19$. Details for several of the results are given as follows:

(a) Row 1: $\alpha * (t - \hat{x} \cdot \hat{w}) = 0.1 * (-1 - (-0.25)) = 0.1 * (-0.75) = -0.075$

Note that rounding off to two decimal places has occurred *after* the calculations are made.

(b) Row 2: $\alpha * (t - \hat{x} \cdot \hat{w}) = 0.1 * (1 - (-0.13)) = 0.1 * (1.13) = 0.113$

(c) $\delta_{w_i} = \alpha * (t - \hat{x} \cdot \hat{w}) * x_1$
In Row 2, $x_1 = 0$
$\therefore \delta w_1 = 0$.

(d) $\delta_{w_2} = \alpha * (t - \hat{x} \cdot \hat{w}) * x_2 = 0.1 * (1 - (-0.44)) = 0.1 * (1.44) = 0.144$

(e) $\delta_{w_3} = \alpha * (t - \hat{x} \cdot \hat{w}) * x_3 = 0.1 * (1 - (-0.44)) * (-1)$ // x_3 is always −1

$= 0.1 * (1.44) * (-1) = -0.144$.

(f) In Row 4

$\hat{x} \cdot \hat{w} = (1,1,-1) \cdot (0.14, 0.09, 0.30)$
$= (1 * 0.14) + (1 * 0.09) + (-1 * 0.30)$
$= 0.14 + 0.09 + (-0.30) = -0.07$

Widroff and Hoff first produced this training method in 1960. They trained ADALINES (short for **adaptive linear elements**) which are similar to TLUs, except that bipolar values (or {−1, 1}) are used for both inputs and outputs.

11.5 BACKPROPAGATION

We have described three paradigms for neural networks. McCulloch-Pitts neurons were seen to be capable of implementing arbitrary Boolean functions; their drawback, however, is that the functions they implemented are "hard-wired" and cannot consequently be modified without over-hauling the network topology. Both the Perceptron Learning Rule and the Delta Rule overcome this handicap, thus these models behave as **adaptive systems**: systems capable of responding to their environment. The limitation of these approaches is that the function being implemented must be linearly separable and for complex pattern spaces this can be a draconian requirement. The Delta Rule is somewhat more flexible; however, implementation of arbitrary functions remains unten-able. Backpropagation is the learning rule described in this section; it is robust enough to work on multilayer networks, and as we shall see, this rule overcomes the aforementioned drawbacks.

A multilayer neural network is drawn in Figure 11.33.

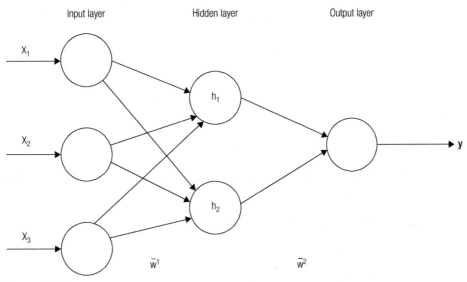

Figure 11.33
A multiple layer neural network.

This network consists of six neurons arranged in three layers. Neurons in the same layer lie at the same distance from the input signals x_1, x_2, and x_3. In this figure, there are three neurons in the **input layer**, two neurons in the **hidden layer**, and the **output layer** consists of a single unit. Input neurons are connected directly to input signals and output signals emanate directly from output neurons. Since neither the inputs nor outputs from the middle layer are directly accessible, they are referred to as **hidden units**. There is some disagreement in the literature as to how the neural net-work in Figure 11.33 should be classified. You could argue that it is a 3-layer network (for obvious reasons); however, neurons in the input layer of a multilayer network behave merely as input sites. The learning in a network takes place in the weights. A quick glance at Figure 11.33 confirms that two layers of weights are present—those connecting input neurons to hidden neurons are denoted by $\bar{w}^1$, and those weights from the outputs of hidden units to the inputs of output units are labeled as $\bar{w}^2$. Hence, this neural network is often classified as a 2-layer network. We adopt the latter characterization in this text.

We have commented on the inconsistencies in the notation. Some sources reverse the definition of feed forward and layered networks provided here. When consulting other sources, be sure to understand how those authors define their terms.

In the network depicted in Figure 11.33 every neuron in layer i (counting from left to right) is connected only to neurons in layer j where $j = i + 1$; additionally, there are no intra-layer connections. This network topology is referred to in general as a feed forward network; the specific network illustrated is a $3 - 2 - 1$ feed forward network, as these numbers designate the number of neurons in each layer. When intra-layer connections are also present, then the network is referred to as a layered network.

We comment here that in a fully connected, $\mathbf{n} - \mathbf{r} - \mathbf{m}$ feed forward network, $\overline{w}^1$ is an $n \times r$ matrix of weights and $\overline{w}^2$ has dimension $r \times m$.

Training in a multilayer network is somewhat more involved. Refer to Figure 11.34.

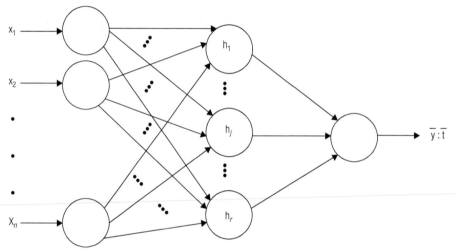

Figure 11.34
An n − r − m feed forward network.

An input pattern $\overline{x}_i = (x_1, x_2, \ldots, x_n)$ is presented to the network. Each input x_i, where $i = 1, \ldots, n$ is connected to every hidden unit h_j, $j = 1, \ldots, r$. Additionally, each of the hidden units is connected to every one of the m output neurons (for clarity we have taken $m = 1$). In response to this input $\overline{x}$, the network produces an output $\overline{y}_i$, which is then compared to the target $\overline{t}_i$. An error term e_i is computed, which measures the disparity between the actual and desired outputs. This process of presenting an input pattern $\overline{x}_i$ to the network and then calculating the resulting error $\overline{e}_i$ is repeated N times, where N is the number of patterns in the training set. This process yields E, the average error produced by the network where $E = \dfrac{1}{N} \sum_{i=1}^{N} e^i$. Armed with this information, the network must assign blame to every one of the l weights in the network where $l = (n \times r) + (r \times m)$ (l corresponds to the sum of the number of entries in the weight matrices $\overline{w}^1$ and $\overline{w}^2$. As a precursor to this assignment of responsibility to each weight, the partial derivatives $\dfrac{\partial E}{\partial w_l}$ must be calculated for all $l = 1, \ldots$ $(n \times r) + (r \times m)$. These partial derivatives specify the instantaneous rates of change of the error term with respect to each weight in the network. In Section 11.3, we saw an example where the Perceptron Learning Rule with a training set of size four required three epochs; in backpropagation it is common to have training sets of hundreds or even thousands of patterns and for training to require thousands of epochs. Even before the exact details of the backpropagation algorithm are presented, it is apparent that the procedure will be computation intensive. Backpropagation was "discovered" on several occasions [4, 5, 6, 7] but it was not until the 1980s that computers had become fast enough to handle the requisite calculations that backpropagation entails.

Backpropagation requires that the activation function be continuous and differentiable (just as the Delta Rule did). The threshold function shown in Figure 11.35(a) is discontinuous and hence unacceptable. The Sigmoid function in 11.35(b) is often used with backpropagation networks. The Sigmoid function $S_c: \mathbb{R} \to (0, 1)$ is given by $S_c = \dfrac{1}{1+e^{-c*x}}$, and the parameter c is referred to as the slope of the function; for larger values of c this function resembles the step function. The input to a sigmoidal unit will be $\hat{x} \cdot \hat{w}$, in other words, when the input is $\overline{x} = (x_1, x_2, ..., x_n)$, the output prescribed by this activation function is $\dfrac{1}{1+exp\sum_{i=1}^{n} w_1 * x_i - \theta}$. Recalling the reciprocal rule, the

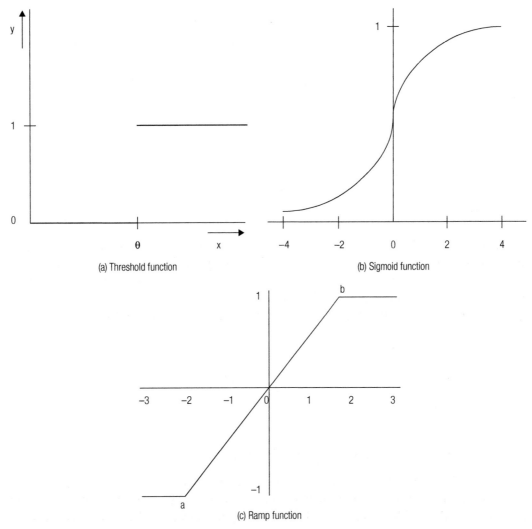

Figure 11.35
Several common activation functions (a) the step or threshold function (b) sigmoid function (c) ramp function .

derivative of the sigmoid with respect to x is: $\frac{d}{dx}S(x)=\frac{e^{-x}}{\left(1+e^{-x}\right)^2}=S(x)(1-S(x))$. This quantity will prove useful later when we derive the rule for backpropagation learning.

The ramp function in Figure 11.35(c) is defined by $r(x)=\begin{cases} cx,\ a\le x\le b \\ 1,\ x\ge b \\ -1,\ x\le a \end{cases}$

This activation function is useful when scaling of input quantities is required. You must use care when $x = a$ or $x = b$, as $r(x)$ is not differentiable at these points.

The learning problem for a **backpropagation network (BPN)** can be characterized as follows:

- Each neuron j in the network evaluates a function of its inputs $f(g(\overline{x}))$where $g(\overline{x})$ is usually the dot product of the unit's inputs with its weights, or $g(\overline{x}) = \overline{x}\cdot\overline{w}$, and $f_j(**)$ is an activation function that is continuous and differentiable; f_j determines the neuron's output. The weights of the network are initialized to small random numbers.

- The network implements a composite function F, called the **network function**.

- The **learning problem** consists in finding the set of weights: w_1, w_2, ..., w_t such that F is as close as possible to F_d (desired function). However, F_d is not given explicitly. Rather, you are provided with a training set $\{(\overline{x}_1,\overline{t}_1),(\overline{x}_2,\overline{t}_2),...,(\overline{x}_N,\overline{t}_N)\}$, wherein each input pattern $\overline{x}_i$ is an n-dimensional vector and each target output $\overline{t}_i$ is an m-dimensional vector.

- An input $\overline{x}_i$ is presented to the network. The BPN produces an output $\overline{}$, which is then compared to the target output $\overline{t}_i$.

- The aim of the **learning rule** is to make $\overline{y}_i = \overline{t}_i$ for every pattern i in the training set. This is done (exactly or approximately) by minimizing the network error function

$$=\frac{1}{2}\sum_{i=1}^{N}(\overline{y}_i-\overline{t}_i)^2.$$ E is minimized by using gradient descent (described in Section 11.4).

The gradient of E is calculated: $\nabla E=\left(\frac{\partial E}{\partial w_1},\frac{\partial E}{\partial w_2},...,\frac{\partial E}{\partial w_l}\right)$. The weights are then updated

according to: $\Delta w_i=\alpha\left(\frac{\partial E}{\partial w_i}\right)$ $i = 1$, ..., l where the learning rate is $0 < \alpha \le 1$. When the

error is minimized, $\nabla E = 0$, though we will rarely be this fortunate and some error will

remain.

To derive the backpropagation algorithm, we use the two-layered network in Figure 11.36.

A glance at this function confirms that there are $(n + 1) * r$ weights between input sites and hidden units and $(r + 1)* m$ weights between the network's hidden and output units. Therefore, $\hat{w}_1$ is an $(n + 1) \times r$ weight matrix and $\hat{w}_2$ has dimension $(r + 1) \times m$. As usual, $\overline{x}=(x_1,x_2,...,x_n)$ represents the n-dimensional input. The augmented input $\hat{x}$ equals $(x_1, x_2, ..., x_n, -1)$. The excitation of the jth

hidden unit we denote by g(h_j), where $g(h_j)=\sum_{i=1}^{n+1}\hat{x}_i\hat{w}_{ij}^{(1)}$. The output of hidden unit j, or $f(g(h_j))$ we

(a)

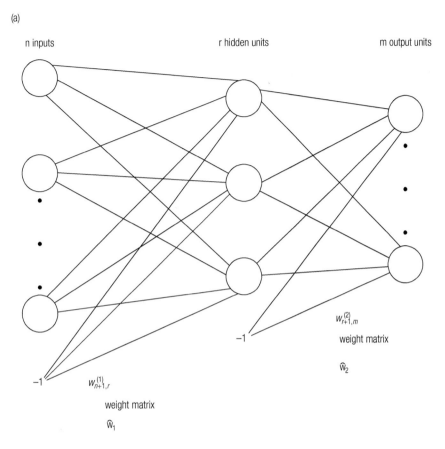

n inputs   r hidden units   m output units

$w_{r+1,m}^{(2)}$

weight matrix

$\hat{w}_2$

−1

$w_{n+1,r}^{(1)}$

−1

weight matrix

$\hat{w}_1$

(b)

n input units.
location n + 1 is a constant −1 input.
m output units.

$w_{ij}^{(1)}$ denotes a weight between input i and hidden unit j.

$w_{ij}^{(2)}$ denotes the weight between hidden unit i and output j.

$w_{n+1,j}^{(1)}$ the weight between the constant input of −1 and hidden unit j (equals θ for j = 1, ..., r).

$w_{r+1,j}^{(2)}$ the weight between the constant input of −1 and output unit j. (equals θ for j = 1, ..., m).

Figure 11.36
(a) A two layered network. (b) Explanation of notation employed.

denote (for clarity) by $x_j^{(1)}$. Because we are using sigmoid functions for the activation functions of all units, we have that

$$x_j^{(1)} = s\left(\sum_{i=1}^{n+1} \hat{x}_i w_{ij}^{(1)}\right).$$

The excitation of all units in the hidden layer = $\hat{x} \cdot \hat{w}_1$.

The vector is represented by $\bar{x}^{(1)}$, whose components are the outputs of the hidden units; it is calculated by

$$\bar{x}^{(1)} = s\left(\hat{x}\hat{w}_1\right).$$

The excitation of units in the output layer is computed using $\hat{x}^{(1)} = \left(x_1^{(1)},\ldots,x_r^{(1)},-1\right)$. Finally, the output of the network is an m-dimensional vector:

$$\bar{x}^{(2)} = s\left(\hat{x}^{(1)}\hat{w}_2\right).$$

The Backpropagation Algorithm can be viewed as a four step procedure:

Step 1: Feed forward computation

Step 2: Backpropagation to the output layer

Step 3: Backpropagation to the hidden layer

Step 4: Update the weights

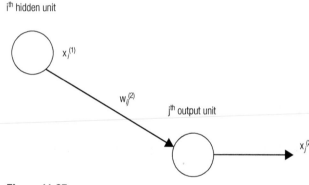

ith hidden unit

$x_i^{(1)}$

$w_{ij}^{(2)}$

jth output unit

$x_j^{(2)}$

Figure 11.37
Hidden unit i connected to output unit j.

The stopping criteria are similar to those for the Delta Rule: either the number of epochs has exceeded our limit or the error E of the network has become sufficiently small. We will return to this issue in Section 11.7.

During the feed forward step, the input pattern $\bar{x}$ is presented to the network. Next, the vectors $\bar{x}^{(1)}$ and $\bar{x}^{(2)}$ are computed. In Step 2, the partial derivatives $\dfrac{\partial E}{\partial w_{ij}^{(2)}}$ are calculated. Figure 11.37 illustrates the path from hidden unit i to output unit j.

The output at output node j is $x_j^{(2)}$ and the jth component of the target is t_j. Hence, the error at output node j is $\dfrac{1}{2}\left(x_j^{(2)}-t_j\right)^2$. The partial derivative

$$\frac{\partial E}{\partial w_{ij}} = x_j^{(2)}\left(1-x_j^{(2)}\right)\left(x_j^{(2)}-t_j\right)x_i^{(1)}.$$

$\dfrac{d}{dx}s(x) = s(x)*\left(1-s(x)\right)$ coefficient of weight w_{ij} (the input to this weight)

The backpropagation error at output unit j is equal to the product of the first three terms above, in other words,

$$\delta_j^{(2)} = x_j^{(2)}\left(1-x_j^{(2)}\right)\left(x_j^{(2)}-t_j\right).$$

Therefore, we may simply $\dfrac{\partial E}{\partial w_{ij}}$ write as $\delta_j^{(2)}x_i^{(1)}$.

In Step 3, we compute $\dfrac{\partial E}{\partial w_{ij}^{(1)}}$. That is, we assign blame proportionally to each weight on the left side of the network for the errors that occur at the output units. Consult Figure 11.38.

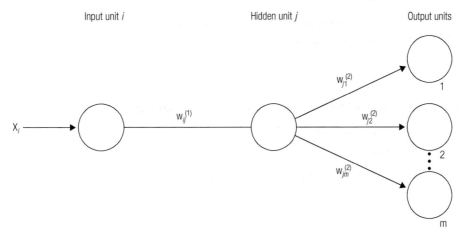

Input unit i Hidden unit j Output units

Figure 11.38
The error caused by a weight leading into hidden unit j.

Each hidden unit j is connected to each unit q in the output layer with an edge whose weight is $w_{jq}^{(2)}$ for $q = 1, \ldots, m$. The backpropagated error at hidden unit j is denoted by $\delta_j^{(1)}$ where:

$$\delta_j^{(1)} = x_j^{(1)}\left(1 - x_j^{(1)}\right)\sum_{q=1}^{m} w_{jq}^{(2)}\delta_q^{(2)}.$$

The partial derivative that expresses the rate at which the error E would change with changes in weight $w_{ij}^{(1)}$ is

$\dfrac{\partial E}{\partial w_{ij}^{(1)}} = \delta_j^{(1)}x_i$, where, as Figure 11.38 shows, x_i is the input along weight w_{ij}.

In Step 4, weight adjustments are made. Weights in the right portion of the network—in other words, weights connecting hidden units to output units—are adjusted according to

$$\Delta w_{ij}^{(2)} = -\alpha x_i^{(1)}\delta^{(2)} \text{ for } i = 1, \ldots, r + 1 \text{ and } j = 1, \ldots, m.$$

And weights on the left side of the network, or weights connecting input neurons to hidden units, are adjusted according to

$$\Delta w_{ij}^{(1)} = -\alpha x_i\delta_j^{(1)}, \text{ for } i = 1, \ldots, n + 1 \text{ and } j = 1\ldots r,$$

where α is the learning rate of the network and $x_{n+1} = x_{r+1}^{(1)} = -1$.

Corrections should be made to the weights only after the backpropagation error has been computed for all units. We have calculated the error that a single input pattern will induce in the BPN. In general, the training set will consist of N patterns, necessitating the following series of corrections:

$$\Delta_1 w_{ij}^{(1)}, \Delta_2 w_{ij}^{(1)}, \ldots, \Delta_N w_{ij}^{(1)}.$$

When batch (or offline) updates are made, then each weight will be corrected only after all N patterns have been presented $\Delta w_{ij}^{(1)} = \Delta_1 w_{ij}^{(1)} + \Delta_2 w_{ij}^{(1)} + \ldots + \Delta_N w_{ij}^{(1)}$ with backpropagation applications, the number of patterns N in the training set can often be in the thousands. Hence, weight adjustments are often made after each input is presented (online training). This is not true of gradient descent; however, the noise that is thereby introduced often facilitates training in that the training is less prone to settle at a local optimum of the function.

Consider the network in Figure 11.39.

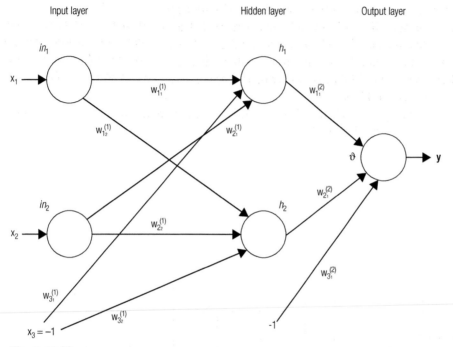

Figure 11.39
Backpropagation network to implement the two-input XOR function.

This network includes all components in one implementation of the two-input XOR function. Use a random number generator to initialize all weights to random numbers between −0.5 and +0.5. Then, to test your understanding of backpropagation, train this network for one epoch by hand (with the aid of a pocket calculator). For ease of computation, let the learning rate $\alpha = 0.1$.

11.6 IMPLEMENTATION CONCERNS

We have spent a good deal of time in this chapter discussing neural networks—the biological units that provide the infrastructure for naturally intelligent entities, and the artificial units that are the building blocks for learning networks. However, if we are to design useful ANN applications, our intellectual armamentarium must possess more than a rudimentary knowledge of linear algebra, calculus, and learning rules. We must also know how to represent appropriate data and, more importantly, how to obtain it. Finally, we must know how to train a network. For both the Delta Rule and backpropagation, we have cited one stopping condition: "the error E of the network has become sufficiently small." We must be more specific than this if our applications are to succeed. How should the output of an individual neuron or even an entire layer in this structure be interpreted? The outputs themselves in an ANN have no intrinsic meaning—it is the user who supplies the external semantics to the system.

For example, how different are the following binary patterns:

$$x = 0111010010111101100001110$$
$$y = 0111001010010100110101110$$

The reader is referred to an excellent text by David M. Skapura that treats the issues of data representation and training methodology in depth.

What metric should we employ to measure distance? One common measure used to measure dissimilarity in binary patterns is Hamming distance, where this distance is defined as the number of bits in which two signals differ. For example, the Hamming distance between 110 and 000, in other words H(110,000), equals two, as these patterns differ in both the first and second bits.

Hamming distance is a common metric in algebraic coding theory—the theory behind error detection and error correction in computer data.

In our example, $H(x, y)$ equals 7. How is this to be interpreted? Suppose that x and y are viewed as 2-dimensional patterns (consult Figure 11.40).

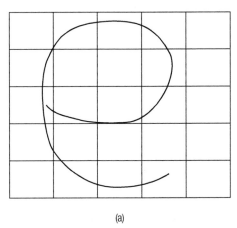
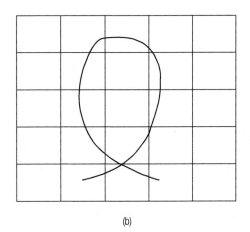

(a) (b)

Figure 11.40
The letter "e" in (a) block form and (b) cursively.

The letter "e" is written in both block form and cursively on a 5 × 5 grid. The boxes considered are numbered in row major order. The ith component of a vector equals 1 if the letter occupies the corresponding block (to some extent), and 0 otherwise.

Pattern Representation is a critical issue. Suppose that you designed an application to model the behavior of iron as its temperature varies from 2780°F to 2820°F (the melting point of iron is 2800°F). Should you scale directly? Recall that ANN inputs and outputs vary in magnitude over (0, 1), or sometimes over (−1, 1). It would make more sense to model the difference in temperatures (2820 − 2780 = 40) rather than the temperatures themselves, so that 2780°F could be represented by 0, 2790°F by 0.25, 2800°F by 0.50, and so on. Also, the sigmoid function does not scale well (Section 11.5), so that the use of the ramp function as an activation function is recommended.

Another concern is any interrelationship between parameters that might be present. For example, if you are designing an ANN for weather prediction, you should expect a correlation between precipitation type (e.g., rain, snow, sleet, hail, etc.) and temperature. You must also be wary of interrelationships among data—in fact, duplicated data may be present.

Skapura in Building Neural Networks *has an excellent example of a network for this purpose.*

Binary patterns are the easiest to represent; you can allow 1 to represent the presence of a feature, say the possession of a checking account, and 0 to represent its absence. Sometimes, however, there is a third possibility—a don't care condition. In Chapter 4, we discussed simple adversarial games such as Nim and tic-tac-toe. How would you represent a tic-tac-toe board to an ANN? A square can be occupied with an X, an O, or it can be vacant. You can represent an X by 100, an O by 010 and a vacant square by 001. These representations are orthogonal (the dot product of any two of these equals zero); this aids the network in distinguishing between them. Nine independent subpatterns can then be concatenated together to form a vector of length 27, which represents the state of an entire tic-tac-toe game. Figure 11.41(a) illustrates a row major ordering convention that can be used to represent each square in the game, and Figure 11.41(b) depicts an arbitrary state in a game and its vector representation.

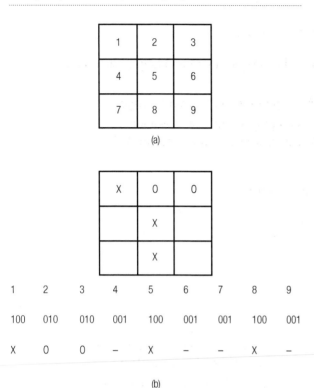

Figure 11.41
(a) The squares in a tic-tac -toe grid numbered in row major order. (b) Representation of a game state by a binary vector with 27 components.

Many other issues arise in data representation. For example, how would you represent an image that is moving? Anyone who intends to become a serious user of the technology of ANN is advised to consult the excellent texts on this subject. [8, 9, 10, 11, 12]

EXAMPLE 11.3

Propose a design for a backpropagation network (BPN) to help graduate advisors make admission decisions to a graduate program in Computer Science (CSc).

Discuss the appropriate inputs and outputs to your BPN. What data representations do you recommend, and what type of activation functions would you use? Use your own real-world knowledge to help your network balance conflicting aims: a student's desire to be granted admission vs. a department's limited resources, which make it incumbent to admit only students who are likely to succeed. Indicate where the necessary training data will come from, and propose an initial architecture for your BPN.

Inputs to the network are as follows:

• Student name and address—this is text and is not to be weighted.

- Undergraduate major—there are literally dozens of possible undergraduate (ug) majors—you might group them as suggested:
  - science/math/engineering   input 1
  - liberal arts/humanities/social sciences   input 0
- with the rationale that students with technical ug majors are more likely to succeed in a CSc program.
- Undergraduate grade point average (GPA) —grades in most schools range
  - from A, B, C, D, F; many institutions employ + and – on these letters as well. We employ numeric $0 \to 4$ scaled, where 4 represents an A, 3 a B, etc.

- GPA in CSc courses—scaled numeric data, also from 0–4.
- Financial ability to pay—   if no, then input equals 0
                                           if yes, then input equals 1
- This would not be an admission criterion unless scholarship funds are limited.
- English proficiency—Many American graduate students in CSc come from foreign countries. TOEFL exam scores measure English proficiency. Input is scaled numeric.
- Recommendation letters: if excellent, then input equals 1
                                           if average, then input equals 0.5
                                           if bad, then input equals 0
- Quality of ug school attended: if excellent, then input equals 1
                                           if average, then input equals 0.5
                                           if not so excellent   0.0
                                           (scaled from 0 to 1)

The output of this network is either: deny represented by 0
                                                           admit by 1.

The output is scaled between these values based on the strength of the conclusion. Numeric data that must be scaled should use a ramp activation function; a sigmoid unit suffices in other cases.

There are a total of eight inputs to this network. A good rule of thumb (heuristic) is that the number of hidden units should equal about 20% of the input units. Therefore, the initial architecture for this application is an $8 – 2 – 1$ feed forward BPN depicted in Figure 11.42.

Training data could be obtained from the Registrar's Office. Because this data is from past years, you also have access to the ultimate success of these students.

Input layer   Hidden layer   Output layer

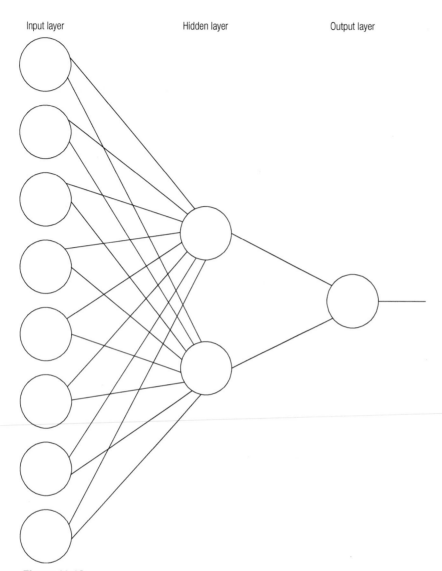

Figure 11.42
Proposed BPN architecture for the graduate CSc admission application.

11.6.1 Pattern Analysis

Considering Example 11.3, suppose the Registrar's Office contains records for only American students who have applied to your graduate program in the past; however, presently, the vast majority of your applicants are from Europe and Asia. You cannot expect your network to produce valid results. Suppose that you were designing a network for weather prediction and you had the following two patterns in your training set:

Current weather conditions: cloudy and cold

Tomorrow's weather: rain

Current weather conditions: cloudy and cold

Tomorrow's weather: sunny

No learning rule could reconcile this disparity. You need to eliminate this inconsistency from your patterns, or network convergence is impossible. Either remove these patterns or find other factors (say an approaching warm or cold front) that explain the different outcomes.

Suppose you are designing a BPN application for Optical Character Recognition (OCR). OCR devices have numerous applications; the Post Office routinely uses these devices to automatically sort first class mail. Those letters that cannot be classified by machine must still be routed by postal clerks. When designing your training set, you should follow the 50:50 rule. Half of your input patterns should be valid examples, such as a, a, A, **A** for the letter "A." The other half should be null patterns, in other words, inputs that do not belong to any of the (26) valid pattern classes, for example, Δ, <, and ξ.

11.6.2 Training Methodology

How long should training with an ANN continue? If the Perceptron Learning Rule is being used, the answer is easy: stop once (if) the network weights have remained constant for an entire epoch. For BPN the answer is more subtle. Consult Figure 11.43. In 11.43(a) all patterns have been correctly classified, whereas the application in 11.43(b) incorrectly classifies several patterns. You might be misled into believing that the network in Figure 11.43(a) does a better job at classification, when, in fact, it has memorized the training set and will exhibit poor generalization. The network in Figure 11.43(b) has several errors but performs better on a validation set. A **validation set** is a collection of input patterns that the network has not seen previously. This set, as the name suggests, is used to measure how well the network has learned the "essence" of its task (i.e., how well has it identified features that are key to identifying a pattern).

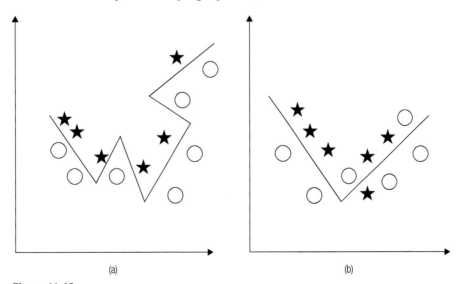

(a)   (b)

Figure 11.43
Two examples of network training in pattern space: (a) overtraining and (b) generalization.

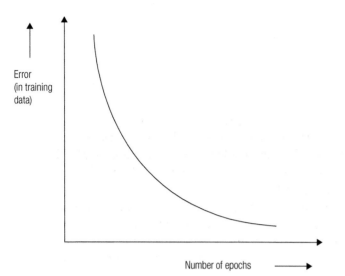

Figure 11.44
In a BPN, the error in the training set continues to decrease.

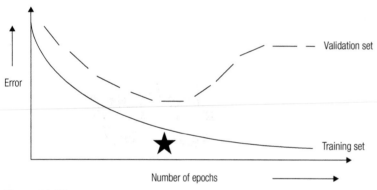

Figure 11.45
Training error vs. validation error in a BPN.

If you have chosen your exemplar set properly, and no contradictions remain in your training data, then you should expect that the error of a BPN will decrease as the number of epochs increases (Figure 11.44).

However, this is not so; instead, once the training error is minimized, you will likely have overtrained your network, and it will fail to perform well on validation data. Your goal in training a BPN should be to minimize the *validation error* (Figure 11.45). After some number of epochs in the training process, the validation error (denoted with a dashed line) begins to rise (the point marked by ★ in this figure), while the training error continues to fall.

Remember that the reason for developing a neural network is to use it in the real world and *not* on the training set. It is therefore a good idea to alternate training with validation (be sure to disable weight changes during validation) and stop training once the validation error exhibits an upturn.

What should you do if you begin training your network but the error fails to decrease? It is likely that inconsistencies remain in your data. What now? It is infeasible to manually examine several thousand (or more) training patterns. Instead, you can use a binary search of the exemplar set. Divide your training set in half and train two copies of your network independently on each half of the data. The half that contains contradictory data will fail to converge. Continue this splitting process until the spurious pattern(s) are sufficiently isolated so that manual inspection becomes feasible. However, the network's failure to converge might be due to the network itself. It could be necessary to add or delete hidden units from your design. A graphical tool that is useful here is a Hinton diagram that permits visual inspection of interconnection weights while training is occurring (consult Skapura [8]).

You might desire additional guidance on when network training can cease. Interleaving training and validation data can be time-consuming. Another approach is to train the BPN until the error falls below 0.2. Recall the epoch and save the value of all network weights. Continue training until the error falls below 0.1. If the additional number of epochs required to reach this halving of error is ≤ 30% of the original number of epochs, then repeat this process and try for an error of 0.05. If not, then overtraining is occurring and you should return to the previous state of the network.

If validation is to occur after training, then two approaches can be used. In validation, the network is presented with patterns that are not in the training set. You can choose to withhold a number of patterns randomly; exercise caution, however, that the network is not sensitive to the order in which the training patterns are presented. A more robust procedure is known as **Hold-one-out training**; however, training the network N times is then required, and when the training set is large, this method can be time-consuming.

11.7 DISCRETE HOPFIELD NETWORKS

In this section, we discuss the **Discrete Hopfield Network**, which was proposed by John Hopfield, a Nobel Prize laureate in physics. It is not surprising that an energy function is associated with this model. A Hopfield network always finds a local minimum of the energy function. Hopfield networks are a type of associative network that have proven useful in combinatorial optimization and in finding approximate solutions for NP–complete problems.

Discrete Hopfield Networks are a type of associative network. In an associative network, patterns are associated that are similar or perhaps opposites of one another. In some cases, a pattern is recalled from a part of a pattern or from a noisy (distorted) version of it. Human memory often functions as an associative network. How often have you heard a song on the radio and immediately recalled a special evening from your past?

Two types of associative networks are autoassociative and heteroassociative. In autoassociative networks the input patterns used for training and the target outputs are identical. Often these networks are used to retrieve distorted or partial inputs. An example of an autoassociative network "at work" is shown in Figure 11.46.

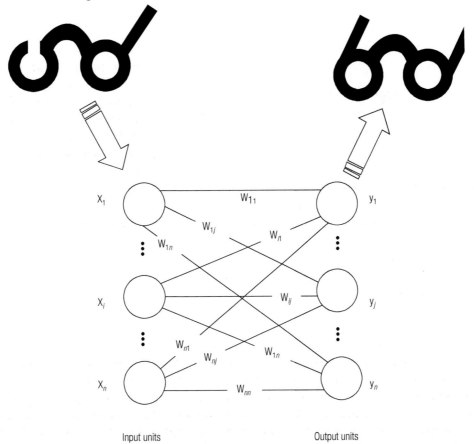

Figure 11.46
An autoassociative network.

Heteroassociative networks, as the name suggests, associate patterns from different pattern classes. A sample heteroassociative application is depicted in Figure 11.47.

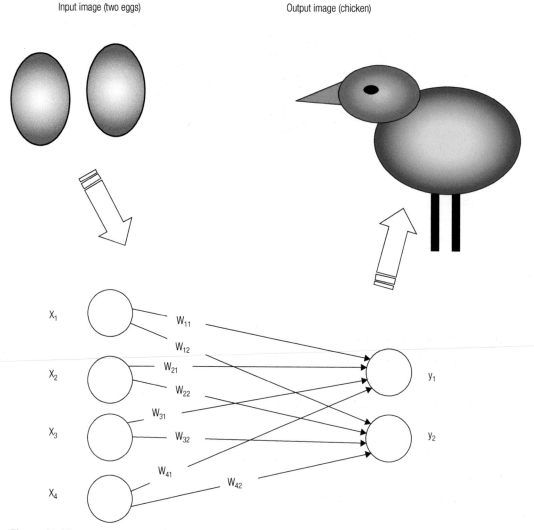

Input image (two eggs)

Output image (chicken)

Figure 11.47
A heteroassociative network.

The reader who has taken a course in switching theory can see the analogy with sequential circuits that also remember some of their outputs.

Associative networks are often trained using **Hebb's learning rule**.[13] Hebb postulated that two neurons that are active at the same time should be more actively engaged (i.e., should be joined by a larger weight) than those neurons not correlated via the same processing task. For an input neuron x_i and an output neuron y_j, Hebb's rule prescribes that weight updates should be made by: $\Delta w_{ij} = \alpha x_i y_j$. Excellent examples of learning for associative networks can be found in *Fundamentals of Neural Networks* by Laurene V. Fausett.[14]

A Discrete Hopfield Network is an autoassociative network with feedback, in other words, a recurrent autoassociative network (see Figure 11.48). The outputs of the network at time t form inputs to the system at time $t + 1$.

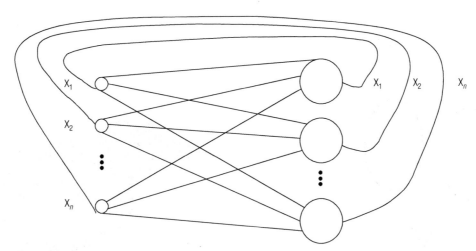

Figure 11.48
An autoassociative network with feedback.

However, in a Discrete Hopfield Network, no self-loops are present (Figure 11.49).

The architecture of a Discrete Hopfield Network has the following attributes:

i. Every unit in the network is connected to every other unit except itself.

ii. The network is symmetric: $w_{ij} = w_{ji} \ \forall i, j$.

iii. Each unit can assume the state 1 or −1.

iv. Only one unit is selected for update at a time and selection is random.

v. A necessary (but not sufficient) condition for the network to lead to a stable state $\left(\bar{x}^{t+1} = \bar{x}^{t} \ \forall t \geq t_{*}\right)$.

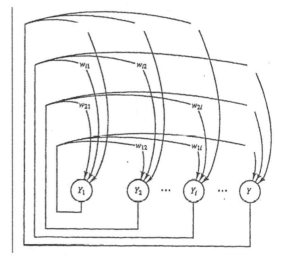

Figure 11.49
A Discrete Hopfield Network.

A Discrete Hopfield network with two units is drawn in Figure 11.50.

The number drawn inside a unit represents that unit's threshold, hence $\theta_1 = \theta_2 = 0$. Also, observe that $w_{12} = w_{21} = -1$. Suppose further that the network is initialized to $x_1 = 1$ and $x_2 = -1$. The excitation to unit 1 is then $x_2 * w_{21} = (-1) * (-1) = 1$. Because this is greater than the unit's threshold, unit 1 remains in state $x_1 = 1$ (note, we are assuming a threshold activation function). Meanwhile, unit 2 experiences an excitation equal to $x_1 * w_{12} = (1) * (-1) = -1$. This excitation is less than θ_2, which is 0, hence unit 2 remains in state $x_2 = -1$. The state $(1, -1)$, written this way for convenience, remains in this state and is therefore referred to as a **stable state**. Verify that $(-1, 1)$ is a second stable state. Next, consider what happens if the initial state is $(-1, -1)$? Assume that unit 1 is chosen first for updating. This unit experiences an excitation equal to $x_2 * w_{21} = (-1) * (-1) = 1$. This excitation of 1 is greater than $\theta_1 = 0$,

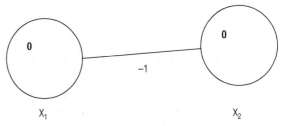

Figure 11.50
A Discrete Hopfield Network with two units.

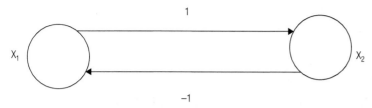

Figure 11.51
A network with asymmetric weights ($w_{12} \neq w_{21}$).

therefore unit 1 will change its state to x_1 = 1. The network is now in state (1, −1); the state (−1, −1) is therefore referred to as an unstable state. What if unit 2 had been chosen first for updating above? You may wish to confirm that (1, 1) is also an unstable state for this network.

What would happen if we relax condition ii) above, which requires that weights in a Discrete Hopfield Network be symmetric? Consult Figure 11.51.

Let the thresholds θ_1 and θ_2 each once again equal 0. Verify that the state (1, −1) will change to (1, 1), and that (−1, 1) → (−1, −1) → (1, −1) and so on. We conclude that symmetric weights are a necessary condition if stable states are to exist.

Hopfield defines an energy function for these networks (also known as a Lyaponov function). If $\bar{w}$ denotes the $n \times n$ weight matrix of a Hopfield network with n units $\bar{\theta}$ and is a row vector of dimension n, representing the units' thresholds, then the energy $E(x)$ of a state $\bar{x}$ is given by

$$E(\bar{x}) = -\frac{1}{2}\overline{x}\overline{w}x^T + \bar{\theta}\,x^T$$

Alternatively, this energy function can be computed as

$$E(\bar{x}) = -\frac{1}{2}\sum_{j=1}^{n}\sum_{i=1}^{n}w_{ij}x_ix_j + \sum_{i=1}^{n}\theta_ix_i$$

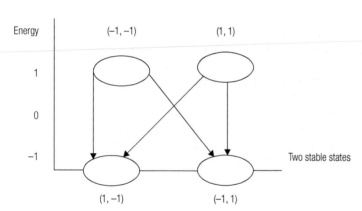

Figure 11.52
State transitions for the network in Figure 11.51.

The terms $w_{ij}\,x_i\,x_j$ and $w_{ji}\,x_j\,x_i$ will both occur in this double sum, therefore a coefficient of (1/2) is used. Hopfield networks are often used to solve combinatorial problems. Because a Hopfield network will always find a local minimum of the energy function, the solutions obtained are sometimes only approximate solutions. Consider the two-state Hopfield network in Figure 11.52. The energy is calculated for each of the four states below.

Unstable: $E(1,1) = E(\bar{x}) = -\frac{1}{2}\left(w_{12}x_1x_2 + w_{21}x_2x_1 + \theta_1x_1 + \theta_2x_2\right) =$

$-\frac{1}{2}\left[(-1)*1*1 + (-1)*1*1 + 0*1 + 0*1\right] = -\frac{1}{2}\left[(-1) + (-1)\right] = 1$

Stable: $E(1,-1) = -\frac{1}{2}\left[(-1)*1*(-1) + (-1)*(-1)*1 + 0 + 0\right] = -1$

Stable: $E(-1,1) = -\frac{1}{2}\left[(-1)*(-1)*1 + (-1)*1*(-1) + 0 + 0\right] = -1$

Unstable: $E(-1,-1) = -\frac{1}{2}\left[(-1)*(-1)*(-1) + (-1)*(-1)*(-1)\right] = 1$

Figure 11.52 illustrates state transitions when each of unit 1 or unit 2 is chosen for updating. Observe that stable states correspond to those with minimal energy.

EXAMPLE 11.4: USE THE HOPFIELD NETWORK TO SOLVE THE MULTIFLOP PROBLEM.

A multiflop is a binary vector with n components, each of which equals 0 except for a single 1. For example, if $n = 4$, then one solution to this instance of the problem is (1, 0, 0, 0). Consider the Hopfield network in Figure 11.53.

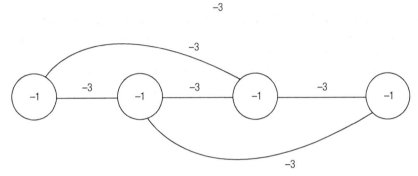

Figure 11.53
A Hopfield network to solve the multiflop problem when $n = 4$.

If a unit is set to 1, this unit will inhibit the other units through edges with weights equal to -3. Suppose the network is started with all units set to zero (in this example, binary values are allowed). Any unit that is randomly chosen for update will flip its state to 1, as the excitation will be 0, which is greater than $\theta_1 = -1$. Suppose that unit 1 is updated to 1, then it will prevent any other unit from changing its state to 1. This example appears somewhat innocuous; however, in the exercises we see how, by using the networks similar to the one illustrated in Figure 11.53, we can tackle formidable problems encountered in earlier chapters, such as the n-Queens problem and the TSP.

11.8 APPLICATION AREAS

Neural networks have been widely applied over the last three decades to solve problems in several areas:

- Control
- Search
- Optimization
- Function approximation
- Pattern association
- Clustering
- Classification
- Forecasting

In control applications there is a device that requires inputs so that desired outputs can be produced. A recent example of a control application is with Lexus, the Toyota luxury line of auto-mobiles, which comes equipped with rear back-up cameras, sonar devices, and a neural network that automatically parallel parks the car for you.[15] Actually, this is an example of what is known as the inverse problem, in that the route the car must take is known, and what must be calculated is the requisite force and the steering wheel displacements involved. An earlier example of inverse control is that of a truck backing up.[16] An example of forward identification (the forces are known and the behavior must be identified) is that of robot arm control.[17]

Search is a critical component of any intelligent system. The basic problem in applying neural networks to search is representation of the state space. If a suitably trained network were presented with the input vector in Figure 11.41(b) representing a state in the game of tic-tac-toe, we would hope that the network's response would be $\bar{y} = 001\ 001\ 001\ 001\ 001\ 001\ 001\ 001$ 010 - place an "0" in the lower right square so as to block the "X" player. Neural networks have been applied to blackjack,[18] backgammon,[19] checkers,[20] and numerous other games, including tic-tac-toe.

In optimization, the goal is to minimize or maximize some objective function. A classic optimization problem is the TSP (Chapters 2, 3, 12). Discrete Hopfield Networks can yield approximate solutions that are often useful.[21] Bharitkar et al. describe how the Hopfield network can be used to optimize word width in the control memory of a computer.[22]

In function approximation you are trying to map numerical inputs (domain elements) into appropriate outputs (range elements). Many problems can be recast in this framework. For example, you can view the states in a tic-tac-toe game as the domain of some function and optimal moves as the range of this function.

We have already seen that associative networks are adept at pattern association. Some patterns, perhaps noisy versions of photo images (the photographer may have moved during filming), form the inputs to such a network, and crisp versions of these photos are outputs. Associative networks have also been successful in OCR applications (consult Section 11.6.1).

With clustering, you are trying to map patterns into clusters so that each pattern in the same cluster shares commonality in the values of some feature(s) while patterns in different clusters differ in these values. For example, flowers can be mapped into clusters based on color or petal length. Often the features that govern membership within a cluster are not known a priori and the network must discover these on its own.

In pattern classification, input patterns are grouped according to membership in a particular pattern class. We have encountered examples of classification in our discussion of Boolean functions and supervised learning algorithms. For example, does $\bar{x} = (0, 1)$ belong to pattern class 0 or 1 for the 2-input inclusive OR function? A seminal work in this research area was NETtalk by Terry Sejnowski and Charles Rosenberg.[23] NETtalk can be viewed as a talking typewriter. Written text is converted into sequences of phonemes; these phonemes are then fed into a speech synthesizer to produce spoken words. The relationship between text and sounds in English is complex and sometimes contradictory. Why is "tough" pronounced with an "f" sound while "dough" is not? Why is the "e" in the words "head" and "heat" pronounced differently? If English is your second language, then you can probably volunteer dozens of additional examples. Critical to correct pronunciations is the way in which vowels are spoken; their pronunciation is dependent upon the surrounding characters.

Letters are input to NETtalk in a neighborhood consisting of the three preceding and three succeeding letters. The letters are first converted into binary vectors of length 29:

Residents of New York City will identify a problem in that "Houston," a city in Texas, is pronounced differently than "Houston" as in a street in NYC.

- One of N encoding is used
- 26 uppercase English characters, i.e., A…Z
- Three inputs for punctuation characters that influence pronunciation

Training data consisted of 5,000 English words together with the correct phonetic sequence for each word. Each input pattern had length 203 (29 bits per character * 7 characters per letter neighborhood). The training set for NETtalk consisted of 30,000 examples (5,000 words * average word length ≈ 6 characters). The BPN architecture for NETtalk is drawn in Figure 11.54.

The classification produced by this network is converted to a phoneme, which is then used as input to a speech synthesizer. The sounds produced by NETtalk during the course of its training can be likened to those made by a child upon first learning to read.

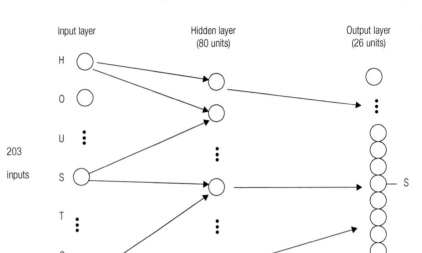

Figure 11.54
BPN architecture for NETtalk application.

- Before training—the network produced random sounds.
- After 100 epochs—proper segmentation began.
- After 500 epochs—vowel and consonant sounds could be distinguished.
- After 1,000 epochs—words were distinguishable from one another but still not phonetically correct.
- After 1,500 epochs—phonetic rules appeared to have been learned. Pronunciation was correct but the sound was somewhat mechanical.

When training was completed, NETtalk was presented with 200 words from the validation set. It is estimated that NETtalk can read English text with accuracy ≈ 95%.

In forecasting one desires the measure of a phenomenon at some point in the future. Forecasting can be viewed as function approximation, where the function's domain is time and its range is the future performance of the phenomenon under investigation. Neural networks have succeeded in arenas ranging from prediction of sunspot activity [24, 25] to Standard & Poors (S & P) 500 Index performance.[26]

It is the latter application, that of economic forecasting, that excites most people. Which of us would not be delirious to know tomorrow's stock prices with certainty? Are stock prices chaotic, in other words, a complex phenomenon and hence too elusive to be predictable? Neural networks have met with some success in this area.

The Dow Jones Industrial Average is a single number that provides the scaled average of the 30 most widely held public companies in the United States. This single number reflects the state of the American stock market. This average, however, varies continuously and therefore needs to be modified before it can serve as a neural network input. A technique known as discrete time sampling is employed, in which this continuously varying signal is sampled at regular time intervals. A single pattern consists of *n* samples that are concatenated together. Figure 11.55 shows the Dow Jones Industrial Average over six months.

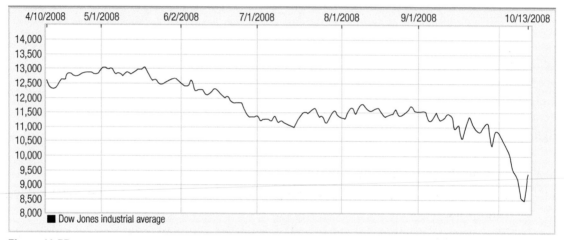

Figure 11.55
The Dow Jones Industrial Average from April 2008 to October 2008.

Each bar represents the range of values during the day, and tick marks indicate the closing price that day. We cannot use the Dow Jones average by itself as input to a neural network, because by itself it provides very little predictive value.

Financial analysts often use so-called economic indicators to gain insights into the way the stock market in general or a particular stock is moving (up or down). There are three common indicators:

- ADX—a market intensity indicator
- MACD (moving average convergence/divergence)—provides optimal buy and sell signals when the market is trending
- Slow Stochastic Analysis—works well in conjunction with MACD

The ADX compares the high and low values of the market at present with the high and low values at a previous time. Figure 11.56 will prove useful in defining this metric.

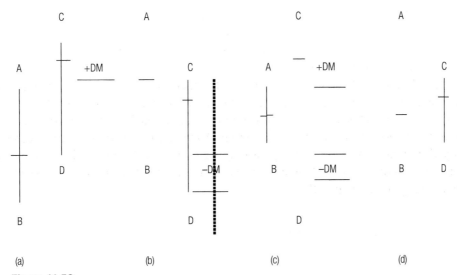

Figure 11.56
Illustration of directional movement (DM) of a stock: (a) Positive DM, (b) negative DM, (c) current trading is outside the range of previous time, and (d) DM = 0.

In Figure 11.56 vertical lines represent the high and low prices of a stock (or stock index) during a day, and tick marks indicate the closing value for that day. Four cases arise:

1. The directional movement is positive (+DM) when the current high price is above that for the previous time unit.

2. DM is negative (−DM) because the previous high price is above the current day's high price.

3. The current trading is outside the range of the previous time; in this case DM = max ($|1 + DM|$, $|1−DM|$).

4. The trading range for today lies within the range at the previous time. The DM = 0.

The Directional Indicator (DI) [27] provides a method to scale the DM. The DI is the percentage of the price range that is directional for a time period.

$$DI = \frac{DM}{TR},$$

where TR is the actual range exhibited. The TR is defined as the largest of

- The difference between the current high and low values
- The difference between the current high and the closing value at the previous time
- The difference between the current low and the closing value at the previous time

The DI can be positive or negative. Wilder [25] defines two indicators, one for each case.

- +DI reflects a time interval with positive DI.
- −DI uses the absolute value of DI where DI is negative.

Finally, the ADX is a smoothed moving average of the DI values across an interval consisting of n time periods. Financial analysts often find it useful to convert the DI to a Directional Movement Index (DMI), which reflects the magnitude of the trend on a scale from 0 to 100. The ADX is then computed as an n-period moving average of the DMI. Figure 11.57 exhibits the value of the ADX in making timely buy and sell decisions.

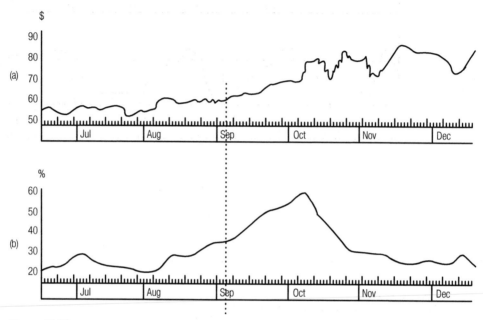

Figure 11.57
(a) Behavior of a stock on the New York Stock Exchange (NYSE) over a period of six months.
(b) ADX for this stock over this same six-month period.

Observe that the ADX peaks at the same time that the stock growth trend diminishes.

A **Stochastic Oscillator** is a signal whose purpose is to predict sudden market reversals.[25, 27, 28] Wall Street insiders know that a market top or high point for a stock is often reflected in daily closing values that cluster around the stock's high value, whereas a market bottom is reflected in daily closing values that cluster around a stock's low value. Stock prices tend to reverse their trends during a top (or bottom) period. If we can detect when a stock is close to its limit, then predicting a reversal becomes possible. To develop such an indicator, you compare the closing price of a stock with its highest high and lowest low values over a period of time. Lane's indicators[28] do so over an interval of 5–14 days. His notation for a 14-day interval is %K, and %D is a 3- day average of the %K indicator. Consult Figure 11.58.

A stock is considered *overbought* when the stochastic indicator goes over 80% (a good time to sell) and *oversold* (a good time to buy) when the indicator goes below 20%.

The Moving Average Convergence / Divergence (MACD) measures the trend of a stock over a period of time (Figure 11.59)

Referring to this figure, note that Buy signals tend to precede periods in which stock prices are increasing, and *Sell* signals precede those in which stock prices are decreasing.

Fishman, Bar, and Loick[27] developed a successful BPN for predicting the Standard & Poors (S&P) index five days into the future. Their network had two layers (though a 3-layer network was

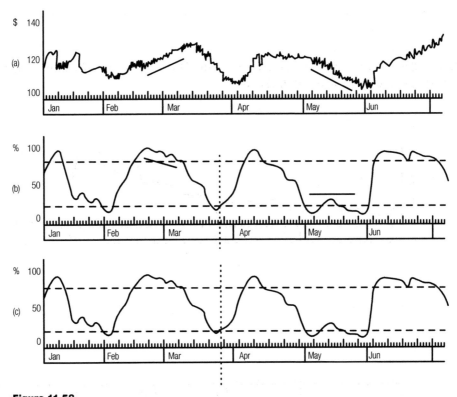

Figure 11.58
(a) Sell periods are indicated by a stochastic (straight lines).
(b) Buy period shown at right. Indicators have gone below 20%. (c) Data smoothed by %D indicator.

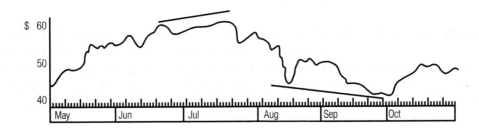

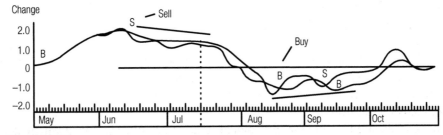

Figure 11.59
The usefulness of the MACD. (a) The closing price of a stock. (b) MACD over the same period.

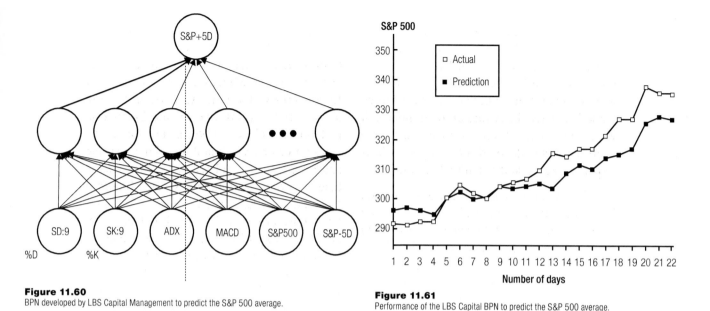

Figure 11.60
BPN developed by LBS Capital Management to predict the S&P 500 average.

Figure 11.61
Performance of the LBS Capital BPN to predict the S&P 500 average.

also developed). The network had *n* inputs, where *n* corresponded to the number of economic indicators used. The output of their network was a single unit scaled so as to predict the change in the S&P five days from the present. The architecture of one of their networks is shown in Figure 11.60. This network has six inputs, as depicted, and one output unit.

Getting specific architectural details for a successful model for a (or more recent) BPN such as the S&P index is not an easy chore. Successful models are usually hidden from the public.

Training examples were obtained from past market data. The performance of their network is shown in Figure 11.61.

This figure compares the actual S&P average with that predicted by their network. Performance is formidable for periods of 9–10 days into the future. At that juncture, it makes sense to retrain with more recent data than to depend on less reliable predictions. This extended foray into economic forecasting should forewarn you that to develop a successful neural network in a particular domain requires that you (or colleagues) possess extensive knowledge in neural networks *and* that application area.

HUMAN INTEREST NOTES

DONALD MICHIE.

Donald Michie

Donald Michie (1923–2007) was an exceptional scientist whose accomplishments spanned four different fields: the biological sciences, medicine, computing, and artificial intelligence. Born in Burma in 1923, he graduated from Balliol College, Oxford, with an MA in Human Anatomy and Physiology, and a D.Phil. in Mammalian Genetics. During World War II, he worked with Alan Turing and the Enigma code-breaking group at Bletchley Park. He later founded the Turing Institute (in 1984) at the University of Strathclyde, where he was Chief Scientist and was Chairman of the Board of Trustees of the A. M. Turing Trust (1975–1984).

Professor Michie's scientific publications include authorship of five books and some 170 academic papers, and he has edited the 14 volumes of the *Machine Intelligence* series as well as several other books. His best known work has been in Artificial Intelligence, in which his seminal efforts made enormous contributions in the fields of Computer Chess, Expert Systems, and Machine Learning.

His awards and affiliations include: Scientific Fellow, Zoological Society of London (1953); Founder and Director, Experimental Programming Unit, University of Edinburgh (1965); Founder, Professor Emeritus and first Chairman, Department of Machine Intelligence and Perception, University of Edinburgh (1967); Fellow of the Royal Society of Edinburgh (1969); Fellow of the British Computer Society (1971); Visiting Lecturer, USSR Academy of Sciences (1973 and 1985); Director, Machine Intelligence Research Unit, University of Edinburgh (1974–1984); Founder, British Computer Society Specialist Group in Expert Systems (1980); Pioneer Award, International Embryo Transfer Society (1988), jointly with Dr. Ann McLaren for work in the 1950s; Founding Fellow, American Association for Artificial Intelligence (1990); Founder, Human-Computer Learning Foundation (1995); recipient, Feigenbaum Medal of the World Congress on Expert Systems (1996) and of the International Joint Conference on Artificial Intelligence Award for Research Excellence (2001); and Foreign Honorary Member of the American Academy of Arts and Sciences (2001).

An outstanding speaker who was in regular demand, Professor Michie was invited to give many honorary lectures including: the Herbert Spencer Lecture, Oxford University (1976); the Samuel Wilks Memorial Lecture, Princeton University (1978); the Royal Institution Lecture *Co-operating Robots* (1982); the Technology Lecture, Royal Society (1984); the G. A. Miller Lecture, University of Illinois (1983); the S. L. A. Marshall Lecture to the US Army Institute for the Behavioral and Social Sciences (1990); and the C. C. Garvin Lecture, Virginia Polytechnic Institute and State University (1992). Professor Michie held visiting appointments at: Stanford University (1962, 1978, 1991); Syracuse University (1970, 1971); Oxford University (1971, 1994, 1995); Virginia Polytechnic Institute and State University (1974, 1992); University of Illinois (1976, 1979, 1980, 1981, 1982); McGill University (1977); and University of New South Wales (1990, 1991, 1992, 1994, 1998).

He was awarded honorary doctorates by: the UK National Council for Academic Awards (1991); The University of Salford (1992); Stirling University (1996); The University of Aberdeen (1999); and The University of York (2000).

He also consulted for several corporations and public bodies including: Stanford Research Institute (1973); The Sloan Kettering Institute and Memorial Hospital (1976); Rand Corporation (1982); IBM Scientific Centers at Palo Alto and Los Angeles (1982–1985); and The Westinghouse Corporation (1988).

Professor Michie was at once charming, intelligent, profound, and a world-renowned visionary. Friends and colleagues who were disciples of Professor Michie include Daniel Kopec, Alen Shapiro, David Levy, Austin Tate, Andrew Blake, Larry Harris, Ivan Bratko, and Tim Niblett, amongst many others, many of whom have made important contributions to the field of computing sciences and AI.

⬛ **11.9** **CHAPTER SUMMARY**

This chapter has introduced the rudiments of Artificial Neural Networks. We began by high-lighting the similarities between artificial neural networks and their biological counterparts. In fact, McCulloch and Pitts used their artificial network models to gain insights into biological units. Their models, however, were not adaptive because weights were fixed a priori, and hence, were incapable of learning.

Three learning rules were introduced that turned ANNs into adaptive systems. The Perceptron Learning and the Delta Rule are rules that can function on single-layer networks to learn functions that are linearly separable. Backpropagation is a more robust algorithm, in that multilayer networks can be trained to learn arbitrary functions, and many successful applications have been developed using this framework. Finally, Discrete Hopfield networks were introduced. These networks are adept at solving combinatorial optimization problems.

This introduction to the subject has in no way been meant to be complete. Many omissions were made due to time and space constraints. For example, Radial Basis Function (RBF) networks have been shown to be astute function approximators[29] and have also met with some success in forecasting applications. [12] Also, our survey has focused on Supervised Learning. In some applications, **Unsupervised Learning** is used when the network is not supplied with the "right answers" but must find them on its own. One example is Adaptive Resonance Theory (ART) models, which are proficient at clustering applications. [30] With Competitive Learning (another Unsupervised Learning Paradigm), units that respond most strongly to an input pattern squelch the responses of other units in the network. This approach has biological plausibility in that the brain must conserve its resources; allowing more neurons to respond to a stimulus than is necessary is wasteful. Competitive networks have been successful in performing Vector Quantization (VQ), a technique useful in the compression of image and speech signals. The so-called Self Organizing Map (SOM) developed by Kohonen[31] has found widespread applicability.[12]

A major disadvantage of neural networks is that they are *opaque*, in other words, they cannot explain their results. One area of research is that of combining ANN with fuzzy logic (Chapter 8, "Uncertainty in AI") to produce neural fuzzy networks that have the learning capability of ANNs combined with the facility for explanation, possessed by fuzzy logic. Negnevitsky [32] provides a nice introduction to these so-called hybrid systems. In fact, a recent research area is devoted to making ANNs more transparent (able to explain their results). Cloete and Zurada[33] have an entire text devoted to the subject of knowledge-based neurocomputing.

The holy grail of ANN research would, of course, be to design a network with the same information processing capabilities as the human brain; a goal that certainly, for the foreseeable future, must remain as a dream. Some researchers have attempted to model a cat's brain. [31] Meanwhile, Carver Mead, taking a more bottom-up approach, has successfully modeled networks capable of seeing and hearing. Kurzweil predicts [34] that by the year 2050, neurobiologists will have a complete understanding of the human brain. He also predicts that it will be feasible to build a highly connected network consisting of 10 billion components. If and when these predictions come to fruition, will the creation of human-level artificial intelligence finally become a reality?

Questions for Discussion

1. In Section 1 we portray an ANN as a black box. What limitations does this opaqueness impose on their utility?

2. In a linear system, the output is proportionally related to the input, in other words, small changes in the input produce correspondingly small changes in output and similarly for large input changes. Describe two systems in nature that are examples of linear systems.

3. Nonlinear systems do not obey the proportionality relation between input and output changes as do linear systems. Consider an artificial neuron with a threshold $\theta = 0.50$. Argue that this neuron is a nonlinear system.

4. Why might stress in humans be considered a nonlinear phenomenon?

5. A single-layer neural network cannot implement a function that is not linearly separable. Is this a serious drawback? Explain.

6. The learning rate is a constant between 0 and 1, in other words, $0 < \alpha \leq 1$. Since a larger learning rate results in faster learning, why not use large values for α?

7. What information does the dot product of $\bar{x}$ with $\bar{w}$ provide in an ANN? How is this information used in the following:

   a. The Perceptron Learning Rule?

   b. The Delta Rule?

   c. Backpropagation?

8. The backpropagation algorithm is often referred to as the generalized Delta Rule. Why do you think this is so?

9. Why will both the Delta Rule and backpropagation continue to have some error, whereas the Perceptron Learning Rule halts when there is no error present?

10. What is the difference between offline and batch training?

11. The human brain consists of between 10 billion (10^{10}) and 100 billion (10^{11}) neurons. Once we understand the workings of the human brain [1] and we construct full-scale software and/or hardware simulations, what do you predict will occur?

   Kurzweil predicts (Kurzweil 1999) that this will occur by the mid-21st century.

12. What are the differences between biological and artificial neurons (neural networks) in terms of both structure and functionality?

13. Contrast supervised and unsupervised learning.

Exercises

1. Draw a McCulloch-Pitts network to implement the sum function S for a full adder where $S(ABC_i) = A'B'C_i + A'BC_i' + AB'C_i' + ABC_i$.

2. Design a McCulloch-Pitts network for the three-input minority function where $Min(x_1,x_2,x_3)$ equals 1 whenever only one or none of the inputs equal 1, in other words, $Min(x_1, x_2, x_3) = x_1'x_2'x_3' + x_1'x_2'x_3 + x_1'x_2x_3' + x_1x_2'x_3'$.

3. What function F is computed by the McCulloch-Pitts network in Figure 11.62?

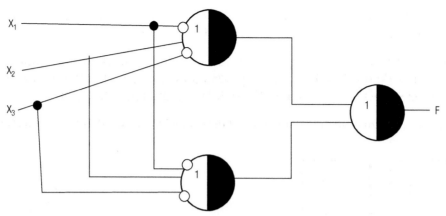

Figure 11.62
A McCulloch-Pitts network to implement the function F.

4. It is a well-known physiological phenomenon that if a cold stimulus is applied to a person's skin for a very short period of time, the person will perceive heat. However, if the same stimulus is applied for a longer period, the person will perceive cold. The use of discrete time steps enables the McCulloch-Pitts network drawn below to model this phenomenon. Neurons x_1 and x_2 represent receptors for heat and cold, respectively, and neurons y_1 and y_2 are the counterpart perceptors. Neurons z_1, z_2 are auxiliary neurons. As shown, each neuron has a threshold of 2. Input to the system will be (1, 0) if heat is applied and (0, 1) if cold is applied. Verify that this network correctly models this phenomenon—in other words, if a cold stimulus is applied for only one time step, heat will be perceived. However, if the cold is applied for two time steps, then cold will indeed be perceived. Notice, we allow this network to possess weights.

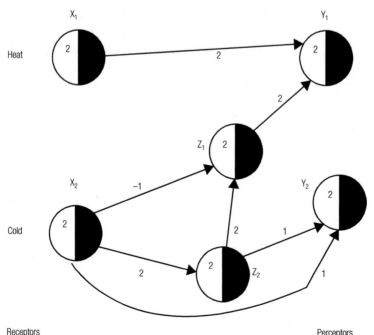

Figure 11.63
A McCulloch-Pitts network that models human perception of hot and cold stimuli.

5. Prove that the two-input XNOR function cannot be implemented with a single perceptron. Your proof should use a system of inequalities.

6. a. Use the Perceptron Learning Rule to train a neuron to learn the two-input function depicted in Figure 11.64. Use an augmented input vector. Let the initial weight values be $w_1 = 0.1$, $w_2 = 0.4$ and $\theta = 0.3$. Use a learning rate $\alpha = 0.5$.

   b. Give the equation of the discriminant and draw this line in two-dimensional pattern space.

x_1	x_2	$f(x_1, x_2)$
0	0	0
0	1	0
1	0	1
1	1	1

Figure 11.64
A two-input function.

7. Use the Perceptron Learning Rule to learn the majority function on three inputs where the second input x_2 is held fixed at 1. $Maj(x_1, x_2, x_3) = 1$ whenever two or three of x_1, x_2, and x_3 are equal to 1, then $Maj(x_1, x_2, x_3) = 1$. All inputs are binary and the initial weight values are $(w_1, w_2, w_3, \theta) = \left(\frac{3}{4}, -1, \frac{3}{4}, \frac{1}{2}\right)$. The learning rate $\alpha = \frac{1}{2}$.

8. A TLU is being trained using the Perceptron Learning Rule. Input vector and weight vector appear as in Figure 11.65.

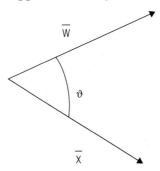

Figure 11.65
Input and weight vectors for a TLU during training.

The target t for the current pattern = 1, however, the actual output of the unit y equals 0. Which way should $\bar{w}$ be rotated with respect to $\bar{x}$? Explain your answer.

9. Suppose that you have a single TLU with n inputs; in other words, unaugmented input vector $\bar{x}_i$, will have n components, and you are performing Perceptron Learning. How many epochs must you wait before you can be certain that the algorithm will not halt (that is, that the patterns are not linearly separable)?

10. Which of the following sets of points are linearly separable?

    a. Class 1: {(0.5, 0.5, 0.5), (1.5, 1.5, 1.5)}

       Class 2: {(2.5, 2.5, 2.5), (2.5, 2.5, 2.5)}

    b. Class 1: {(1, 1, 0), (2, 3, 1), (3, 2, 1.5)}

       Class 2: {(1, 1, 2), (2, 3, 2.5), (3, 2, 3.5)}

    c. Class 1: {(0, 0, 18), (2, 1, 10), (7, 5, 4)}

       Class 2: {(0, 1, 16), (2, 5, 9), (6, 8, 1)}

    d. Class 1: {(0, 0, 5), (1, 2, 4), (3, 5, 8)}

       Class 2: {(0, 0, –2), (1, 2, 5), (3, 5, –1}

11. a. Solve Exercise 6 using the Delta Rule. Train the neuron for one epoch.

     b. What is the stopping criterion for this learning rule?

12. a. Propose a design for a BPN to help make health insurance premium decisions for an insurance company. Prospective clients for health insurance are to be classified as low-risk or high-risk candidates, where high-risk clients are to be charged a higher premium or may even be refused insurance. Carefully, discuss the appropriate inputs and outputs to your BPN. What data representation do you recommend and what type of activation function would you use? What is the initial architecture of your network?

     b. Indicate where the necessary training data would come from.

     c. In light of advances in computer and genetics technology, discuss some of the ethical and legal problems that could arise.

     d. Describe your training methodology. Include a discussion of the types of problems that can occur and recommend possible remedies in each case. When should training stop?

     e. Describe several approaches to validating your BPN. Give an advantage and disadvantage for each approach.

13. The n-Rooks Problem is to place n rooks on an $n \times n$ chessboard so that these pieces are nonattacking. A rook can attack any piece on the same row or column. A solution to the 4–rooks problem is shown in Figure 11.66.

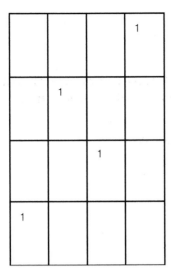

Figure 11.66
A solution to the 4–rooks problem.

Specify the architecture of a Discrete Hopfield Network to solve this problem.

14. The *n*-Queens Problem was discussed extensively in Chapter 2. Specify the architecture of a Discrete Hopfield Network to solve this problem when $n = 4$.

15. The TSP was also discussed extensively in both Chapters 2 and 3. Specify the architecture of a Discrete Hopfield Network to solve a small instance of this problem, say $n = 4$ cities. Hint—use an $n \times n$ Boolean matrix to represent your tour. A "1" should be placed in column j of row i if city j is visited after city i.

16. Consider the Hopfield network drawn in Figure 11.67. Calculate the energy for each state and draw the state transition diagram for this network. Identify the stable states (if any).

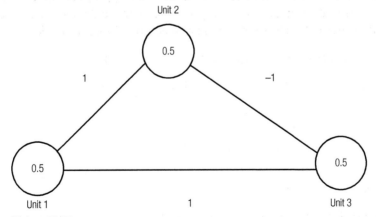

Figure 11.67
A Hopfield network with 3 neurons.

Programming Exercises

1. Generate 20 triples of random numbers (60 in total) where each number $\in [0, 1]$. Each triple corresponds to a point in the unit cube. Generate these numbers so that ten triples lie in Class 1 and ten lie in Class 2 and these classes are linearly separable. Use the Perceptron Learning Rule on this data with a learning rate $\alpha =$ (a) 0.01 (b) 0.1 (c) 0.25 (d) 0.50 (e) 1.0 (f) 5.0. Comment on the performance of the learning algorithm in each case.

2. There are 2^4 or 16 Boolean functions of 2 variables. Use the Perceptron Learning Rule to determine how many of these are linearly separable.

3. Use the Delta Rule to complete the training for the two-input OR function in Example 11.2.

4. Write a program to implement the backpropagation algorithm to train the two-layer network in Figure 11.38 for the XOR function.

5. Write a program that can apply the backpropagation algorithm to any two-layer feed forward network.

6. Use your program in Programming Exercise 5 to approximate the function that provides the weight in *mg* of Wild Australian Rabbits as a function of age (in days). Withhold every third data item in this table for validation purposes. [See DVD, Appendix D.2.1]

7. Use your program in Programming Exercise 5 to predict the next week's gold price based upon the following data. Use the last 25% of the data for validation. [See DVD, Appendix D.2.1]

8. Use your program in Programming Exercise 5 to classify irises into three classes—Setosa, Versicolor, and Virginia. [See DVD, Appendix D.2.1]

9. Write a program to solve the 4–Queens problem using a Discrete Hopfield Network (consult Exercise #14). Run your program 10 times choosing different units for update on each run. Discuss your results. (Recall that the Hopfield network finds a local energy minimum, and therefore you should expect at times to obtain "approximate" solutions.)

10. Write a program to solve the TSP when $n = 10$ cities, using a Discrete Hopfield network (consult Exercise #15). As in the previous program, run your program 10 times and discuss your results.

Keywords

activation function	discriminant	inhibitory
adaptive systems	epoch	input layer
augmented input vector	excitatory	learning problem
augmented weight vector	gradient descent	learning rule
backpropagation network (BPN)	Hebb's learning rule	Learning with a Teacher
	hidden layer	linearly separable
batch training	hidden units	mean square error
dependent variable	Hold-one-out training	minterms
Discrete Hopfield Network	independent variable	network function

output layer
pattern class
pattern space
Perceptron Learning Rule
stable state

step function
Stochastic Oscillator
Supervised Learning
threshold function
Threshold Logic Unit (TLU)

unstable state
Unsupervised Learning
Validation set

References

1. McCulloch, W. S. and Pitts, W. H. 1943. A logical calculus of the ideas immanent in nervous activity. *Bulletin of Mathematical Biophysics* 5: 115–133.

2. Rosenblatt, F. 1958. The perceptron: A probabilistic model for information storage. *Psychological Review* 65: 386–408.

3. Widrow, B. and Hoff, M. 1960. Adaptive switching circuits. In *1960 IRE WESCON Convention Record*, volume 4, 96–104. New York, NY: Institute of Radio Engineers (now IEEE).

4. Robenblatt, F. 1961. *Principles of Neurodynamics: Perceptrons and the Theory of Brain Mechanisms.* Washington, DC: Spartan Book.

5. Werbos, P. 1974. Beyond Regression: New Tools for Prediction and Analysis in the Behavioral Sciences. PhD thesis, Harvard University.

6. Parker, D. 1982. Learning logic. Invention Report S81-64, File 1, Stanford University, Office of Technology Licensing.

7. LeCun, Y. 1988. A theoretical framework for back-propagation. In *Proceedings of the 1988 Neural Network Model Summer School*, edited by Touretzky, D., Hinton, G., and Sejnowski, T. Pittsburgh, PA: Carnegie Mellon.

8. Skapura, D. M. 1995. *Building Neural Networks.* New York, NY: ACM Press.

9. Bose, N. K. and Liang P. 1996. *Neural Networks Fundamentals with Graphs, Algorithms, and Applications.* New York, NY: McGraw-Hill.

10. Haykin, S. 1999. *Neural Networks: A Comprehensive Foundation*, 2nd ed. Englewood Cliffs, NJ: Prentice Hall.

11. Rojas, R. 1996. *Neural Networks: A Systematic Introduction.* New York, NY: Springer-Verlag.

12. Mehrotra, K., Mohan K., and Chilukuri, R. S. 2000. *Elements of Artificial Neural Networks.* Cambridge, MA: The MIT Press.

13. Hebb, D. O. 1949. *The Organization of Behaviour.* New York, NY: John Wiley & Sons.

14. Fausett, L. 1994. *Fundamentals of Neural Networks: Architecture, Algorithms, and Applications.* Upper Saddle River, NJ: Prentice-Hall.

15. Healey, J. December 4, 2006. Parallel parking a pain? Your car can do it for you as auto-park systems arrive. *USA Today.*

16. Nguyen, D. and Widrow, B. 1990. Reinforcement learning. In *Proceedings of the IJCNN*, 3, 21–26. Retrieved from *http://www.cs.montana.edu/~clemens/nguyen-widrow.pdf.*

17. Guez, A., Eilbert, J., and Kam, M. 1988. Neural network architecture for control. *IEEE Control Systems Magazine* 40 (9): 22–25.

18. Sipper, M., Mange, D., and Uribe, A. P. 1998. Evolvable systems: From biology to hardware. In *Proceedings of the Second International Conference on Evolvable Systems*, ICES 98, Lausanne, Switzerland, September 23–25. New York, NY: Springer-Verlag.

19. Tesauro, G. 1995. Temporal difference learning and TD-Gammon. *Communications of the ACM* 383: 56–68.

20. Fogel, D. and Chellapilla, K. 2002. Verifying Anaconda's expert rating by competing against Chinook: Experiments in co-evolving a neural checkers player. *Neurocomputing* 42 (1–4): 69–86.

21. Hopfield, J. and Tank, D. 1985. 'Neural' computation. *Biological Cybernetics* 52:141–152.

22. Bharitkar, S., Kazuhiro, T., and Yoshiyasu, T. 1999. Microcode optimization with neural networks. *IEEE Transactions on Neural Networks* 10 (3): 698–703.

23. Sejnowski, T. J. and Rosenberg, R. 1987. Parallel networks that learn to pronounce English text. *Complex Systems* 1: 145–168.

24. Li, M., Mehrota, K. G., Mohan, C. K., and Ranka, C. 1990. Sunspot numbers forecasting using neural networks. *Proceedings of the IEEE Symposium on Intelligent Control* 1:524–529.

25. Wilder, W. J. 1978. *New Concepts in Technical Trading Systems.* McLeansville, NC: Trend Research.

26. Weigend, A. S., Huberman, B. A., and Rumelhart, D. E. 1990. Predicting the future: A connectionist approach. *International Journal of Neural Systems* 1: 193–209.

27. Fishman, M. B., Barr, D. B., and Loick, W. J. 1991. Using neural nets in market analysis. *Technical Analysis of STOCKS & COMMODITIES* 9 (April): 18–21.

28. Lane, G. C. 1984. Stochastics. *Technical Analysis of STOCKS & COMMODITIES* 4 (May/June).

29. Girosi, F., Poggio, T., and Caprile, B. 1990. Extensions of a theory of networks for approximation and learning. *Proceedings of Neural Information Processing Systems.* 750–756.

30. Carpenter, G. A. and Grossberg, S. 1998. The ART of adaptive pattern recognition by a self-organizing neural network. *IEEE Computer* 21 (3): 77–88.

31. Kohonen, T. 1988. *Self-Organizing and Associative Memory.* New York, NY: Springer-Verlag.

32. Negnevitsky, M. 2005. *Artificial Intelligence: A Guide to Intelligent Systems,* 2nd ed. Reading, MA: Addison-Wesley.

33. Cloete, I. and Zurada, J. M. 1999. *Knowledge-Based Neurocomputing.* Cambridge, MA: The MIT Press.

34. Kurzweil, R. 1999. *The Age of Spiritual Machines.* New York, NY: Penguin Putnam.

SEARCH INSPIRED BY MOTHER NATURE

Giant Tiki.

This chapter continues our discussion of learning. We describe several approaches that take their inspiration from the work of Charles Darwin—so-called evolutionary methods. Tabu search is an algorithm motivated by social mores. Finally, the behavior of ants gives rise to ant colony optimization.

Figure 12.0
Currency Exchange.

12.0 INTRODUCTION

Search is an essential component of any intelligent system. You have already seen that complete search through a state space can be a daunting challenge. Chapter 3, "Informed Search," demonstrated the ways heuristics enable you to search through the most auspicious portions of search trees. The inspiration for these heuristics derives from our insights into a problem, for example: How many tiles must be moved to solve an instance of the 8-Puzzle? In this chapter, inspiration is provided by natural systems—both living and nonliving.

It is a fairly well-known fact that diamonds are made from compressed coal. Coal and diamonds are each composed of carbon; what distinguishes one from the other is the arrangement of the carbon molecules, which are pyramidal in the former and plane-like in the latter. This insight—that the physical properties of a substance depend not only on its composition but also upon the arrangement of its molecules, and that this arrangement can be modified—is the impetus behind annealing. In annealing, a metal is first heated until it liquefies and is then slowly cooled until it re-solidifies. The resulting metal is often stronger after undergoing annealing. Simulated annealing is a search algorithm modeled after this physical process. It is described in Section 12.1.

Some of you might have seen the episode of the 1951–57 television series Superman, in which Superman converts a plain lump of coal into a lavish diamond by merely compressing it in his hand. The episode "Jungle Devil," in which this phenomenon took place, aired originally in 1953.

In 1859, Charles Darwin's magnum opus *The Origin of Species* was first published. In this work he presents his theory on how populations of living systems evolve, through a process known as natural selection. When individuals mate, their offspring display traits garnered from each of their parents. Progeny that possess characteristics favorable to survival are also more likely to reproduce. Over time these favorable traits are likely to occur with greater frequency. A well-studied example is that of gypsy moths in England. In the early nineteenth century, most gypsy moths were light gray, as this afforded natural camouflage from their predators. The industrial revolution, however, was well underway at this time, and immeasurable quantities of pollutants were spewed into the environment of industrialized countries. Trees, which had been pristine and light colored, were coated with soot and became dark. Light gray gypsy moths could no longer depend on their coloration for protection. Over the course of several decades, gray-black Gypsy Moths evolved to become the norm. [1] Inside a computer program we can perform "artificial evolution." Genetic Algorithms form the subject matter of Section 12.2.

The example of the gypsy moths is often cited in the literature. However, selection usually requires thousands and even tens of thousands of years before changes in a population are evident.

In "The Elves and the Shoemaker," a fairy tale by The Grimm Brothers, a poor shoemaker leaves leather on his workbench at night and awakens each morning to observe shoes that have seemingly made themselves. He soon discovers that two talented elves are responsible for the handiwork. Would we not all wish to possess software that (magically) writes itself to solve the problems we are confronted with? In Section 12.3, we discuss Genetic Programs, software that employs evolutionary strategies (rather than elves) to design itself.

Section 12.4 describes **tabu search**, a search based upon societal practices. A tabu (or taboo) is behavior that society believes should be forbidden. What we learn about human behavior is that over time, things change. For example, at one time it was considered tabu for a man to wear earrings. Obviously, that prohibition no longer exists. A tabu search maintains a tabu list of recently made moves; these moves are forbidden from being reused for some period of time. This proscription fosters exploration as already visited portions of the state space are temporarily out of bounds. Tabu search does not entirely ignore exploitation because forbidden moves *are* allowed if they would take the search to a destination whose objective function is superior to any visited previously; this latter "reprieve" is dubbed an **aspiration criterion**. Tabu search has met with great success in the solution of scheduling problems.

Inspiration for Section 12.5 comes from insect colonies—more specifically, colonies of ants. Ants are social insects that exhibit remarkable cooperation and adaptability. Ants communicate indirectly by depositing pheromones (chemical scents) in a process referred to as **stigmergy**. Ant colonies exhibit rare acumen for solving optimization problems, such as finding a shortest path to a food source, and also for the clustering entailed in cemetery formation. It is suspected that stigmergy plays a key role in these behaviors. Computer scientists simulate this behavior in distributed algorithms to solve difficult combinatorial problems and to perform useful data-clustering procedures.

12.1 ■ SIMULATED ANNEALING

Simulated annealing (SA) capitalizes on the analogy between the energy level of the molecules within a physical substance and a search algorithm in which some objective function is to be optimized.

In metallurgy, metals are often subjected to molecular realignment in a process known as annealing. The molecules in a metal are arranged in a local energy minimum. In order to rearrange these molecules at a lower energy, it is first necessary to heat the metal until it liquefies. The molten metal is then slowly cooled until it solidifies; annealed metals exhibit many desirable properties, for instance, they are stronger and often more pliable.

We mentioned earlier that Superman affected molecular realignment of the carbon molecules in coal by compressing the coal in his hand. In nature this transformation of coal to diamonds is achieved by subjecting the coal to tons of pressure over millions of years.

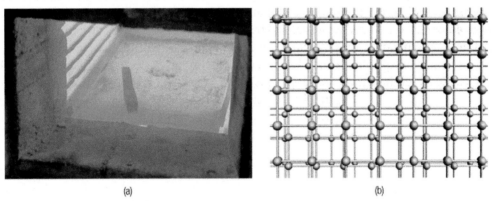

(a)   (b)

Figure 12.1
Molecular rearrangement in a metal that has occurred due to annealing. (a) Iron in a furnace, being heated to its melting point.
(b) A lattice arrangement of molecules often exhibits more strength.

SA is a probabilistic search that sometimes allows counterintuitive moves so as not to become trapped in a local optimum. Recall that hill climbing (Chapter 3) sometimes fails to find a global optimum. This drawback of hill climbing is illustrated in Figure 12.2. A search that begins at x_0 will culminate at x_*, even though the true global optimum lies at x_{best}.

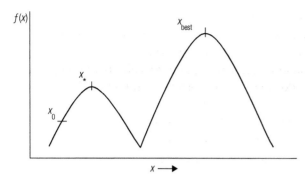

Figure 12.2
Hill climbing sometimes gets stuck in a local optimum. A search that begins at x_0 will get stuck at x^*. Observe that $f(x_{best}) > f(x^*)$.

There are two components to any search algorithm: **exploitation** and **exploration**. Exploitation employs the maxim that good solutions are likely to lie close to one another. Once a good solution is found, you examine its neighbors to determine if a better solution is present. Exploration, on the other hand, relies upon the adage, "Nothing ventured, nothing gained"; in other words, better solutions can lie in unexplored regions of the state space, so do not confine your search to one small region. An ideal search algorithm must strike the proper balance between these two conflicting strategies. Hill climbing makes advantageous use of exploitation to find x_*, the *local optimum* in Figure 12.3.

In this example, however, if the global maximum located at x_{best} is to be found, then some use of exploration is required as well. Consult Figure 12.4 and assume that x_3 is the present location. SA would permit a jump to x_6 even though this constitutes a "backward jump." Note that any search that fails to explore the rightmost peak in this example will never find a *global optimum*.

SA was discovered by S. Kirkpatrick, C. D. Gelatt, and M. P. Vecchi in 1983[3] and independently by V. Cerny in 1985.[4] SA is based upon the Metropolis-Hastings algorithm.[5]

In SA there is a global temperature parameter T. At the beginning of the simulation, T is high; as the simulation progresses, T is lowered. The manner in which T is decreased is referred to as the **cooling schedule**. Two widely used methods are **geometric cooling** and **linear cooling**. In geometric cooling, $T_{new} = \alpha * T_{old}$ with $\alpha < 1$, whereas with linear cooling, $T_{new} = T_{old} - \alpha$ with $\alpha > 0$. Whenever $f(x_{new}) > f(x_{old})$ SA will allow this jump. However an SA also permits counterintuitive or backward jumps with a probability P, which is proportional to

$$e^{-[(f(x\_old) - f(x\_new))/T]}. \tag{1}$$

Observe that when T is high, jumps that result in a lower objective function will occur with a greater probability. Consulting Figure 12.4 once again, this means that a jump from x_3 to x_6 is more likely to occur at the beginning of the simulation, when T is much higher, rather than later. Hence, the early stages of SA favor exploration, whereas exploitation is preferred in later stages of the

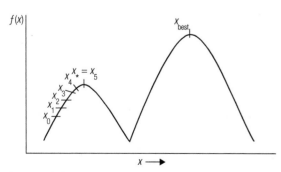

Figure 12.3
Hill climbing relies heavily upon exploitation.

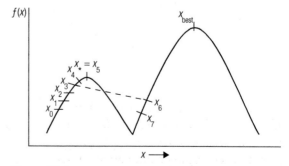

Figure 12.4
If a search is to find the global maximum at x_{best}, then it perhaps will have to use exploration as well as exploitation. Simulated annealing would allow a jump from x_3 to x_6 even though $f(x_6) < f(x_3)$. (Ignore x_7 for the present.)

search. Referring once again to the above equation, we observe that even though counterintuitive jumps are allowed, as the difference between $f(x_{old})$ and $f(x_{new})$ increases, that is, as the new value of x becomes less and less favorable, the probability of going there decreases. This last observation dictates that if each of x_6 and x_7 in Figure 12.4 are possible successors to x_3, the probability of going to x_6 is greater than to x_7 as $f(x_7)$ is less than $f(x_6)$. Pseudocode for SA is provided in Figure 12.5.

```
1. Choose x₀ as initial solution      // Usually done randomly

2. Calculate f(x₀)                     // Objective function

3. Place in memory                     // Solution = [x₀, f(x₀)]

4. x_old = x₀

5. f(x_old) = f(x₀)

6. Count = 0

7. T = T₀                              // Initial temperature T₀ is high

8. while Count < maxcount and progress being made and ideal solution
   not found.                          // Number of iterations permitted

9. Count = Count + 1

10. choose x_new from neighborhood of x_old

11. calculate f(x_new)

12. if f(x_new) = f(x_old) or rand [0,1] = e*[[f(x_old) = f(x_new)]/T] then
    x_old = x_new
    Solution = [x_old, f(x_old)]

13. // end if

14. T_new = cooling_schedule (count, T_old) // geometric or linear cooling
    can be adaptive, greater decrease if a large improvement is made

15. // end while

16. Print Solution                     // Best solution so far.
```

Figure 12.5
Simulated annealing pseudocode.

Line 8 in the code reminds us that a search cannot run forever. After some maximum number of iterations you must end the search and output your results. Line 10 in the algorithm specifies that each possible new point in our search x_{new} must be reachable from x_{old} (i.e., lie in the neighborhood of x_{old}). For example, if you are trying to solve an instance of the TSP, then the neighborhood of one solution can consist of all tours that result when **d** cuts are permitted, and the specified edges are reconnected (as shown in Figure 12.6). Line 12 in this code confirms that x_{new} is selected whenever $f(x_{new}) \geq f(x_{old})$, thereby encouraging exploitation. However, x_{new} can be accepted even when $f(x_{new})$ is less than $f(x_{old})$. The probability

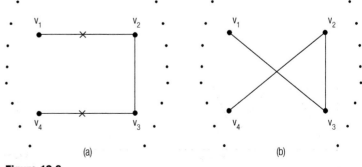

Figure 12.6
Possible neighborhood function for an instance of the TSP. Assume we permit **d** = 2 cuts on the current solution in (a) and then rearrange the cited edges as in (b).

of this acceptance hinges on both the difference between $f(x_{old})$ and $f(x_{new})$ and the temperature T. Exploration is encouraged more fervently early in the simulation; modest decreases in the objective function are more acceptable than precipitous drops throughout the search. And finally, the comment in Line 16 reminds us that SA does not guarantee a global optimum. There are two ways that the likelihood of obtaining a global optimum can be increased. The first is to let the simulation run longer (increase maxcount). The second is to conduct several restarts, in other words, reset all variables and begin a new SA, commencing at a different place in the search region (compare this to restarts in backpropagation in neural networks in Chapter 11, "Neural Networks"). SA searches have been successful at solving combinatorial optimization problems.

12.2 ■ GENETIC ALGORITHMS

Figure 12.7
The *HMS Beagle*. Charles Darwin spent five years on this ship gathering physical samples of flora, fauna, and fossils from around the world.

In August 1831, the HMS *Beagle* departed London to begin its voyage around our planet; its mission was to collect plant, animal, and fossil samples. Charles Darwin, a young naturalist (physical anthropologist) was on board. The voyage lasted five years and vast numbers of physical samples were collected. The adventures encountered by the *Beagle's* crew are vividly described in Darwin's *The Voyage of the Beagle*.[6] Consult Figure 12.7.

Darwin spent much of the next several decades analyzing the samples from this voyage. In the 1840s he began to communicate his emerging theory on evolution via letters to colleagues. He admitted, with some trepidation, that he feared the world would deem him insane. Finally, in 1857 he published his theory of evolution.[7] In 1859 his *Origin of Species* was published.[8] It is in this volume that the term "survival of the fittest" was coined. Darwin postulated that populations of living entities (both fauna and flora) adapt, in other words, those traits that make a living organism more suited to its environment will occur with greater frequency over the course of many generations; this tendency he called natural selection. You can view **natural selection** as a type of *learning* in which the species (rather than an individual within that species) learns to better adapt itself to its environment.

John Holland developed Genetic Algorithms (GA) at the University of Michigan in the later 1960s. He popularized the field with *Adaptation in Natural and Artificial Systems*,[9] and he explains that his inspiration came from the work of Darwin.

In GA, a solution is represented by a string. In canonical GA this string is binary, in other words, a sequence of 0s and 1s, though real numbers and other representations are possible.[10] This string is often referred to as a chromosome. Suppose that we wish to design a GA to learn the two-input NAND function depicted in Table 12.1 (consult Chapter 5, "Logic in Artificial Intelligence").

John Holland.

There are several ways to represent the information contained in this table. You can choose a 12-bit representation in which the contents of Table 12.1 are written in row-major order (the contents of row 1 followed by row 2, and so on) as: 001011101110. Alternatively, you might choose to write just the contents of the rightmost columns yielding 1110, where the ith bit represents the NANDing of the operands in the ith row; for example, the third bit in 1110 is a "1," which is the result of NANDing 1 with 0 (the third row operands). GAs are parallel algorithms so that you begin with a so-called population of strings. Also, canonical GAs are an instance of a blind search algorithm (consult Chapter 2, "Uninformed Search") in that no domain knowledge is presumed; this latter condition also characterizes GA as a so-called weak method (Chapter 7, "Production Systems"). We will employ a population size of four; each string will consist of four bits and will be randomly generated.

Table 12.1
Two-input NAND function.

X_1	X_2	$X_1 \uparrow X_2$
0	0	1
0	1	1
1	0	1
1	1	0

String	Fitness
1010	3
0000	1
1101	2
0110	3

Figure 12.8
A population of four 4-bit numbers that have been randomly generated. The fitness of each string is also shown.

Central to the operation of GA is a **fitness function** (or payoff function). The fitness of a string is a measure of how well the string solves our problem.

If a fitness function is to be useful, it should do more than indicate merely whether a string solves a problem or not, rather, it should also provide some indication of how close the string comes to an ideal solution. A natural metric in our problem is to award one point to a string for each row of the NAND function table that it represents correctly.

Consulting Figure 12.8, we observe that the fitness of the first string 1010 is three; this is because 1010 correctly contains the results of rows one, three, and four in Table 12.1. Only the result of row two is incorrect as **0** NANDed with **1** should equal **1** and not **0**. GAs are an **iterative procedure**. The algorithm proceeds through a sequence of stages and in each stage it (hopefully) converges toward a solution. The strings that you begin with, in other words, those that have been randomly generated, are referred to as the initial population. Hence, in Figure 12.8 you observe that the initial population, denoted here by P_0, equals {1010, 0000, 1101, 0110}. In each stage (or iteration) you apply genetic operators to the strings to produce a new population of strings that is likely to contain a better (or ideal) solution to the problem. Therefore, GAs produce a sequence of populations: P_0, P_1, P_2, ... P_i, ..., $P_{maxcount}$. You stop the GA when $P_{maxcount}$ contains an ideal solution or one that is adequate. Alternatively, the algorithm may have exceeded its time constraints.

Some authors distinguish between the evaluation of a string (how well it solves the problem) vs. fitness (how much this string should be favored in reproduction); to be explained shortly (Vafaie et al.1994).

Other stopping criteria are possible. You might wish to stop the GA if little or no improvement is observed for several generations.

Three popular genetic operators are **selection, crossover (recombination)**, and **mutation**. These operators are applied to population P_i to produce the next population, P_{i+1}. Selection chooses the individuals (i.e., strings or chromosomes) that are to participate in the formation of the next population. One selection method is **roulette wheel selection**, in which the ith string, S_i, is chosen to help form the next population with a probability equal to $f_i / \Sigma f$, where f_i is the fitness of string i and Σf is the total fitness of the current population. So S_i is selected with a probability proportional to the percentage of the population's fitness that it possesses.

You might wish to consult the discussion of expected values in Chapter 4, "Search Using Games."

Consult Figure 12.9. If $p(S_i) = 0.5$ and we select four strings, then the expected number of occurrences of string i would equal two.

String	Fitness	$p(s_i)$ probability of selection of string $= f_i / \Sigma f$	Expected count $= f_i / \bar{f}$	Actual count (via roulette wheel selection)
S_1: 1010	3	3/9	3/(9/4) = 4/3	1
S_2: 0000	1	1/9	1/(9/4) = 4/9	0
S_3: 1101	2	2/9	2/(9/4) = 8/9	1
S_4: 0110	3	3/9	3/(9/4) = 4/3	2
	Total fitness = 9 Max fitness = 3 Avg fitness $\bar{f} = 9/4 = 2.25$			

Figure 12.9
Initial population for the NAND problem. The probability of selecting a string and the expected number of times a string is selected are also shown.

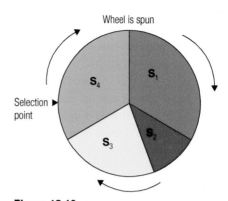

Figure 12.10
Roulette wheel selection. The probability of selecting S_i is proportional to $f(S_i) / \Sigma f$. $P(S_1) = (3/9)$, $P(S_2) = (1/9)$, $P(S_3) = (2/9)$, $P(S_4) = (3/9)$.

The half-closed, half-open interval from 0 to 1 is [0,1). Zero is included, however one is not. Consult any calculus text for further discussion.

Strings selected from initial population	Mating Partner (selected randomly)	Crossover point (selected randomly)	Population after crossover	New population (mutation has been applied)	F(S_i) fitness of new population
S_1: 1010	2	1	1110	1110	4
S_2: 0110	1	1	0010	0110	3
S_3: 1101	4	3	1100	1100	3
S_4: 0110	3	3	0111	0111	2
				Tot fitness = 12 Max fitness = 4 Avg fitness = 3	

Figure 12.11
Formation of the next population. Note that we begin with two copies of S_4 and one each of S_1 and S_3 from P_0. However, for easy reference, the strings are renumbered S_1 through S_4.

To simplify the discussion, we are ignoring discussion of dominant and recessive traits. For example, brown eyes are a dominant trait in humans whereas blue eyes are recessive (both parents must carry this gene). Consult any standard text on genetics for more details.

In roulette wheel selection, you can imagine that the strings constituting the present population are placed around a roulette wheel with arc lengths proportional to their fitness (Figure 12.10).

Naturally, in a GA no roulette wheels are spun, rather random numbers over (0,1) are generated.

Imagine that you have selected four strings randomly, as shown in the rightmost column of Figure 12.9; in other words, strings 1 and 3 occur one time each, and two copies of string 4 are chosen.

You are now ready to form the next population from the intermediate pool of strings seen in the leftmost column of Figure 12.11. To do so, crossover will be applied to these strings. Crossover is a genetic operator that produces offspring from parent strings via a sharing of genetic material. For example, if a human male with a long nose marries a woman with a petite nose, it is expected that their children will have medium length noses.

In one form of crossover, two mates are randomly selected. Next, a single crossover point is randomly generated. Finally, two offspring are produced, as shown in Figure 12.12.

Suppose that the crossover point selected is k = 4. Then the first child will be identical to parent$_1$ before the crossover point (bits 1–4) and equal to parent$_2$ after the crossover point (bits 5–7). Similarly, the second child shares genetic material from parent$_2$ before the crossover point and from parent$_1$ after this point. After crossover, you have the strings in the 4th column of Figure 12.11. Once crossover is completed, then mutation is applied to each bit in the population. Mutation inverts each bit with a small probability. A "1" is changed to a "0" or vice versa with a probability equal to approximately 0.001. In nature, mutation helps to ensure genetic diversity. Most traits that occur via mutation are not productive and, hence, quickly vanish, however, occasionally mutation does result in some survival advantage and such traits will become more prevalent in subsequent generations. In our "toy" example, we let the probability for mutation equal 0.1.

Observe from Figure 12.11 that the second bit in S_2 has been mutated, changing 0010 to 0110 (fifth column, second row). The fitness of the new population is contained in the rightmost column. Notice that the average, maximum, and total fitness of population P_1 have all increased from P_0. Also, note that the fittest string in P_1, in other words, S_1 equal to 1110, with a fitness of four, solves the problem and, hence, P_1 is the final population. Recapitulating, we have seen that GAs have the following characteristics:

- parallel
- probabilistic
- iterative
- blind

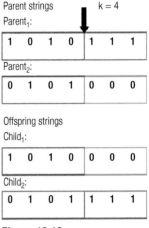

Figure 12.12
Crossover between two parent strings with crossover point **k** = 4.

A toy example is one used to explain a concept or process and should not be taken as indicative of a realistic application.

The solution to a problem is encoded as a string to which a fitness function is applied. The fitness of a string is a measure of how well that string solves the problem. You begin with a population of strings that are randomly generated. The genetic operators of selection, crossover, and mutation are then applied to form subsequent populations until a string in some generation solves the problem exactly or satisfactorily, or the GA is observed not to be making satisfactory progress toward a solution. Figure 12.13 illustrates the parallel nature of GA.

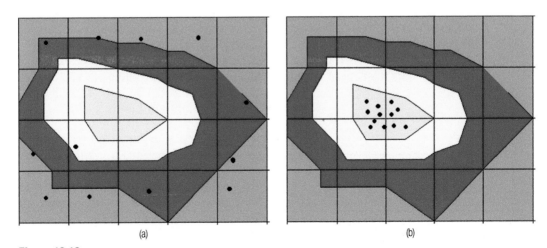

(a)   (b)

Figure 12.13
GA search illustrated. (a) Randomly generated points are distributed throughout the search space. (b) We observe that the points are converging to a global optimum after some number of iterations.

Pseudocode for GA is contained in Figure 12.14.

Genetic algorithm search

1. Randomly generate S_1, S_2, ..., S_n from state space. // Initial population of strings – P_0.

2. Calculate the fitness for each string – $f(S_1)$, $f(S_2)$, ..., $f(S_n)$.
3. Count = 0
4. While count **< maxcount and progress being made and ideal solution not found.**
5. Count = Count + 1
6. Select mates from the current population
7. Apply crossover
8. Apply mutation
9. Calculate the fitness for this new population of strings
10.   // end while

/*Print the string with the highest fitness from the last population. If fitness equals ideal fitness (best possible), indicate that the solution is exact, otherwise state that it is the best possible. If no progress is made for several generations, specify that GA is not converging toward an exact solution. */

Figure 12.14
Pseudocode for GA.

Consult the Sidebar for an example of a GA search that directs a robot to a goal.

EXAMPLE 12.1: GA TO DIRECT ROBOT TO A GOAL.

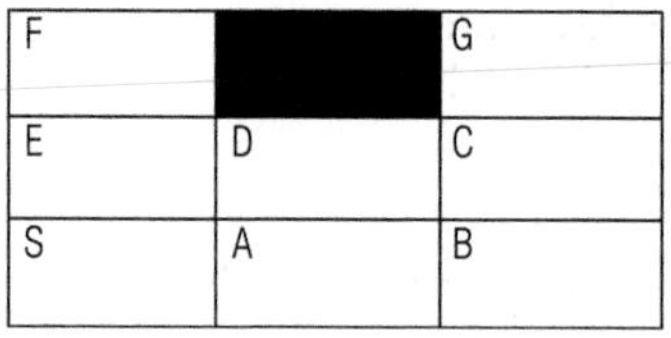

Figure 12.15
A robot must get from square S (Start) to G (Goal).

Suppose that a robot starts at square S in Figure 12.15 and must reach goal square G.

The robot can move one square at a time in each of the directions: North, South, East, or West. A legal move is one that is not prevented by the constraints of the board, for example, the robot cannot move West from square E, East from Square F, or South from square A. One of the first steps in a GA is to encode the solution as a string. We encode the moves North, South, East, and West, respectively, by the strings 00, 01, 10, and 11. Suppose that we suspect that the Goal can be reached in four moves; then a series of four moves can be represented by a string of length eight. This is a small problem, so you can let the population size be four (consult the leftmost column in Figure 12.16).

The next step is to decide on an appropriate fitness function. A natural choice is to use the Manhattan distance from the goal for this purpose. However, better strings would then be allocated lower fitness measures. We generally desire that strings that more accurately solve a problem be allotted higher fitness values. This condition is satisfied by the function $f(s_i) = 4$ – distance from the Goal

Initial population	Fitness	$P(s_i) = f_i/\Sigma f$	Expected count $= f_i/\bar{f}$	Actual count
S_1: 10101111	0	0	0	0
S_2: 10100001	2	1/3	4/3	2
S_3: 00010000	2	1/3	4/3	1
S_4: 10111000	2	1/3	4/3	1
	Total fitness = 6			
	Max fitness = 2			
	Avg. fitness = 1.5			

Figure 12.16
Initial population P_0 for the robot problem.

that the string Si takes the robot to. For example, in Figure 12.16, the string S₃ has a fitness of two, as $S_3 = 00010000$ takes the robot one square North, then one square South (the robot is back in square S) followed by two squares North, leaving the robot in Square F. Recall that the Manhattan distance from square F to G is an *estimate* of remaining distance between the two squares (and not the *actual* distance). The fitness of S₃ is therefore seen in Figure 12.16 to equal two. The remaining fitnesses are calculated in a similar manner.

Strings selected from initial population	Mating partner (selected randomly)	Crossover point (selected randomly)	Population after crossover	F(s₁) fitness of new pop.
S₁: 10101111	2	4	10100000	4
S₂: 00010000	1	4	00011111	0
S₃: 10100001	4	6	10101000	0
S₄: 10111000	3	6	10110001	0
			Tot fitness = 4 Max fitness = 4 Avg fitness = 1	

Figure 12.17
Constructing the second population in our simulation.

Observe in Figure 12.16 that two copies of string two and one each of strings three and four are selected to help construct the next population. Figure 12.17 shows the details of this process. In this example, we have chosen a more realistic probability for mutation of 0.001; as a result, notice that mutation does not play a role in this simulation. In the fourth column, first row, observe that the problem has been solved by string 1, whose fitness is four. Also notice that something curious has occurred in this population. Confirm that S₁ does indeed take the robot to square G. This has occurred in spite of the fact that both the total and average fitness of this population have decreased. We will comment on this anomaly shortly.

At this point in our discussion, you might be asking yourself: "Why should GA work?" "Why should randomly generated strings subjected to repeated selection, crossover, and mutation converge toward the global optimum of some function?" Holland's explanation for GA convergence involves the concept of **schemata**. [11] To simplify this discussion, we assume that binary strings represent GA chromosomes.

If a chromosome has string length L, then the GA has a state space consisting of the 2^L points in L-dimensional space. To concretize matters, we consider L = 3; the state space then consists of the eight vertices of the cube depicted in Figure 12.18. A *schema* is a string over the extended alphabet {0, 1, *} where * is a *don't care* symbol (i.e., * matches 0 or 1). For example **0, 1*1, and 110 are three schemata (the plural for schema). The *order* of schemata is the number of original alphabet symbols they contain. Our three sample schemata have order one, two, and three, respectively. Holland [11] and Goldberg [12] describe the way in which a schema can be viewed as representing a subspace of the state space. For example, consult Figure 12.18(c) to confirm that schema 0** matches each of 000, 010, 001, and 011 and represents the front plane of the cube, while schema 1*1 matches 101 and 111 and represents the right rear vertical edge, whereas 110 represents just itself. Each population in a GA uncovers more information than is contained in just those points themselves. Each string provides information about all of the hyperplanes (and subspaces) corresponding to the numerous schemata in which each point is contained; this property is referred to in the literature as **implicit parallelism** and could help to explain the robustness of GA. More information is thereby obtained in each generation to help guide the search.

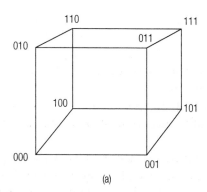

(a)

Order 0 schemata		Order one	Order two	Order three
***(corresponds to the space itself)		**0 **1	*00 0*0 00*	000 100
		0 *1*	*01 0*1 01*	001 101
		0** 1**	*10 1*0 10*	010 110
			*11 1*1 11*	011 111

(b)

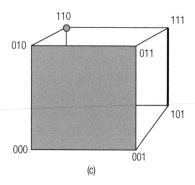

(c)

Figure 12.18

(a) The state space for a GA when chromosome length equals three. (b) All schemata when string length L = 3. (c) Subspaces for three schemata. Subspace represented by schema 0** (front plane), schema 1*1 (right rear vertical edge), and 110 just the left rear vertex.

The defining length of a schema, Δ(H) is the distance between the rightmost and leftmost occurrence of a 0 or 1. For example, the schema 1***0 has length 5 − 1 = 4 whereas 010** has length two. The probability that a schemata of length L will be decoupled by one-point crossover is Δ(H) / (L−1). Observe that schemata with short defining lengths are less likely to be disturbed. Highly fit schemata of short defining length are called **building blocks**. Goldberg describes how these building blocks combine to form optimal solutions. [12] He likens this process to brainstorming in a business meeting where each person has a notion of how the problem under discussion is to be solved; notions are alternately rejected, accepted, and combined with other notions, ultimately to form an idea that the meeting participants agree upon. Suppose that a GA must minimize the function $f(x) = x^2$, where x is an integer between 0 and 127. The chromosomes will consist of 7 bits (*why?*). And you might suspect that 000****, *000***, and **00*** are schemata with relatively high fitness. The GA would work with these building blocks (and others), combining them at times, much as notions are combined during brainstorming. The mathematical justification for GA is provided by the *Schema Theorem* which states that schemata with above average fitness can be expected to become more frequent in the next generation (see [11] or [12] for a more concise statement of this theorem and a proof). It is quite reasonable in the short run, however, to witness the average or total fitness take several backward steps (refer to Example 12.1).

Several points still need to be clarified. In the toy problems we considered earlier, population size was four. Realistic GA applications will typically use several hundred to several thousand chromosomes; calculating the fitness for each of these strings through many generations requires considerable computing prowess. It should come as no surprise that the emerging popularity of GA in the late 1980s coincided with the tremendous increases in processor speeds that occurred at that time.

We mentioned only one model for selection—that of roulette wheel selection. Other paradigms are available. One is elitist selection, in which the best or several of the best strings are guaranteed to be included in the formation of the next generation. However, you must be careful to avoid **premature convergence**, in which "superfit" individuals reproduce abundantly; population diversity is thereby decreased and convergence to a local optimum results. In nature this is referred to as

genetic drift and in nature it is not a problem, as animals or plants need only possess an adequate mode for survival—optimal traits are not mandatory. To control genetic drift, you can utilize scaled selection, in which reproduction is based on a statistical comparison to the average fitness of the population. You can allow selection strength to increase over the course of the simulation (note the similarity to the temperature parameter T in an SA). Finally, in **tournament selection**, a population is partitioned into subgroups. Members of each subgroup compete against one another with the winner from each subgroup included in the formation of the next generation (compare this with Olympic tryouts on a nation-by-nation basis).

GAs have found widespread acceptance over the past several decades with numerous applications. GAs have been used for stock market prediction and portfolio planning. Kurzweil [13] states that GAs are currently responsible for 10% of all stock purchase decisions, and this percentage will soar dramatically as we approach mid-century. They have also been used to predict the exchange rates of foreign currencies. GAs are especially well suited to scheduling problems. You might recall how television reports from abroad would fade on our television screens as orbiting satellites fell out of range. E. A. Williams, W. A. Crossley, and T. J. Lang in 2001 [14] used GAs to help schedule telecommunication satellite orbits so as to minimize such fade-outs. GA has also reduced airport landing delays by 2–5% at London's Heathrow airport. [15] GAs have been successful at both finding appropriate weights for backpropagation networks as well as formation of appropriate network topologies. Consult the discussions in Negnevitsky [16] and Rojas. [17] We cited earlier that a fitness function should not only indicate whether or not a string solves a problem but also how close it comes to doing so. Recent work by Chellapilla and Fogel [18] is noteworthy in that they employed a GA to help evolve ANN to play the game of checkers. Their fitness function indicated merely whether a win or draw resulted. The network itself was left the task of discovering game strategy. Their program, Anaconda, played competitively but not entirely successfully against both Chinook (Chapter 16, "Advanced Computer Games") and human competitors. Its rating was about 2045 (expert-level play).

12.3 GENETIC PROGRAMMING

In GA, a problem is encoded as a string. Genetic operators guided by a fitness function iteratively modify a population of these strings until some string (hopefully) solves the given problem. With Genetic Programming (GP), a string is used to encode a program that solves the problem. The genetic operators (similar to those described in the

More recent work has focused on Linear Genetic Programming, in which imperative languages such as C++ or Java are used.

last section) act on the programs themselves. The programs, through a process akin to computational introspection, evaluate themselves based on how well they solve a problem and rewrite themselves to do better. GP works with programs that are encoded as trees rather than strings. GP works well with LISP (and other functional languages), which is based on lists.

The function $f(x, y, z)$, for example, can be encoded as (f x y z); the function f is followed by its list of arguments. When the program is run, the function is computed. In LISP, a list can consist of both terminals and functions. Examples of terminals are X, Y, Z, 1, 2, and 3, whereas <, +, •, and IF are functions. A LISP program can be written as a nested list whose semantics correspond to a tree. For example, (* x (* y z)) computes x * (y * z) and + ((* x y)(/ y z)) corresponds to (x * y) + (y / z), as shown in Figure 12.19.

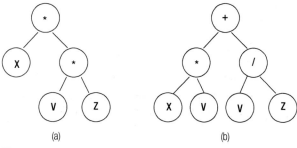

Figure 12.19
Two programs and their interpretations.

As these examples demonstrate, the format of instructions in LISP is that of functions applied to arguments.

Common genetic operators in GP are crossover, inversion, and mutation. To apply these operations you must identify a fracture point in the list where modification can occur. A fracture point can occur at the beginning of a sublist or at a terminal.

Following these steps to perform crossover:

- Choose two programs in the current population.
- Select two sublists randomly, one from each parent.
- Switch these sublists in their offspring.

Consult Figure 12.20.
The steps to perform inversion are as follows:

- Randomly choose an individual from the population.
- Select two fracture points within this individual program.
- Switch the indicated subtrees.

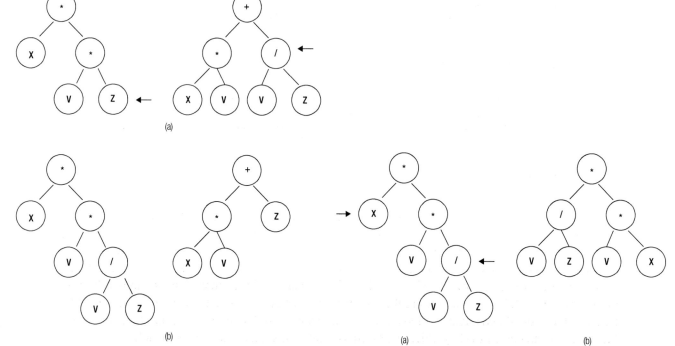

Figure 12.20
Crossover in a Genetic Program. (a) Fracture points (←) chosen in two parents; (b) offspring after crossover.

Figure 12.21
Inversion acts on one parent to produce a single offspring. (a) Two fracture points (→; ←) chosen in a program; (b) new program after inversion.

Refer to Figure 12.21.

And finally, follow these steps to perform mutation:

- Select an individual program from the population.

- Randomly replace any function symbol with another function symbol

OR—

any terminal symbol with another.

Mutation is depicted in Figure 12.22.

To avoid errors when performing

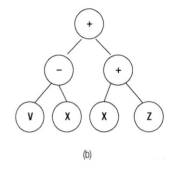

Figure 12.22
Mutation modifies an individual parent to produce one offspring. (a) Individual before mutation, chosen node also shown; (b) after mutation. Note that the multiplication operation has been changed to subtraction at the selected node.

mutation, type checking must be performed. For example, you must check if the operands should be numeric or logical.

Pseudocode for GP is provided in Figure 12.23.

```
Genetic Programming


1. Randomly generate S₁, S₂,..., Sₙ // initial population of programs
2. // For a realistic problem, population can easily be in the
   thousands
3. Calculate the fitness for each program, i.e.: How well does each
   program solve the problem? - f(S₁),f(S₂),..., f(Sₙ)
4. Count = 0
5. While Count < maxcount and progress is still being made and ideal
   solution not found.
6. Count = Count + 1
7. Select individuals from the current population
8. Apply crossover
9. Apply inversion
10.Apply mutation
11. Calculate the fitness for this new population of strings
12. // end while

/*Print the string with the highest fitness from the best population.
If the program provides an ideal solution for the problem indicate that
the solution is exact, otherwise state that it is the best possible.
If no progress is made for several generations then specify that the GP
is not converging toward an exact solution.*/
```

Figure 12.23
Pseudocode for GP.

Line 1 of the GP pseudocode merits a good deal of explanation. In a GP, we cannot generate random strings, binary or otherwise, as we did with GA. The nodes in a tree that represent an individual program can either contain a function or a terminal; these contents are often referred to as genes. If a GP is to achieve success, then genes should be chosen carefully. As a toy example, we consider a full adder circuit (FA). This is a circuit that has three binary inputs and two binary outputs (Figure 12.24.) The inputs are the two numbers to be added (represented by x and y respectively)—the addend and augend—and a carry in (C_i) from a similar unit to its right. The outputs are the Sum (S) and carry out (C_o) which is passed as a carry in signal to the FA on its left.

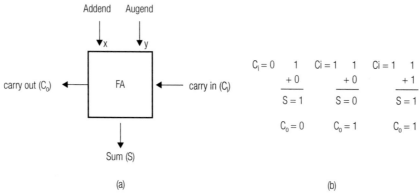

Addend Augend

carry out (C₀) ← FA ← carry in (Cᵢ)

Sum (S)

(a)

$$C_i = 0 \quad 1 \qquad Ci = 1 \quad 1 \qquad Ci = 1 \quad 1$$
$$\underline{+\ 0} \qquad\qquad \underline{+\ 0} \qquad\qquad \underline{+\ 1}$$
$$S = 1 \qquad\qquad S = 0 \qquad\qquad S = 1$$

$$C_0 = 0 \qquad\quad C_0 = 1 \qquad\quad C_0 = 1$$

(b)

Figure 12.24
Full adder circuit; (a) schematic diagram of an FA; (b) three sample additions.

X	Y	C_i	S	C_0
0	0	0	0	0
0	0	1	1	0
0	1	0	1	0
0	1	1	0	1
1	0	0	1	0
1	0	1	0	1
1	1	0	0	1
1	1	1	1	1

Figure 12.25
Truth table for an FA.

X	Y	+
0	0	0
0	1	1
1	0	1
1	1	1

(a)

X	Y	•
0	0	0
0	1	0
1	0	0
1	1	1

(b)

X	X′
0	1
1	0

(c)

Figure 12.26
Truth tables; (a) the OR function, (b) the AND function, and (c) the NOT function.

Figure 12.25 gives a truth table for an FA, in other words, for every set of inputs, this table specifies the correct outputs. Naturally, to do addition in many computers, we require that 32 FAs be joined in tandem (where 32 is the word size of the machine).

We desire a GP to construct a program that performs as an FA. One appropriate set of genes is {0, 1, +, •, '}. The 0 and 1 represent the terminals and +, •, and ' represent the OR, AND, and NOT functions (refer to Figure 12.26).

We note that any set of functions capable of simulating the behavior of {+, •, '} would suffice. For example, the NAND function (↑) introduced in Chapter 5 would also work.

Koza is often cited as the "father" of GP. He recommends three strategies for creation of a random population: grow, full, and ramped-half-and-half. He also advises that no duplicates be allowed in the initial population. With the *grow* method, a tree can be of any depth up to some specified value **m**.

Every node is chosen randomly to be either a terminal or a function. Naturally, leaf nodes (nodes at the "bottom" of the tree) must be terminals. If a node is selected to be a function, then its direct descendants must be terminals, and there must be a number of these, equal to the arity of the function. For example, + would have two children whereas – (for minus) would have only one. Suppose we let maximum depth **m** = 3. Then possible trees in the initial population for our toy FA problem appear in Figure 12.27.

In the *full* method, every tree has a depth equal to a prespecified depth **d**. For example, if depth **d** = 2, then every tree would consist of three levels or have depth **d** = 2, as does the fifth tree from the left in Figure 12.27.

Finally, Koza describes the *ramped-half-and-half* method that he uses to maintain increased variation within the initial population. Population is divided into **m * d** – 1 parts. The composition of each part is produced half by the grow method, and half by the full method. Consult Figure 12.28.

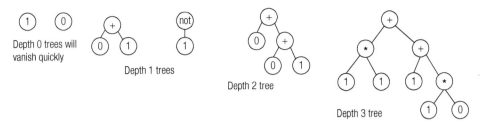

Figure 11.27
Possible trees in the initial population using the grow method with bound **m** = 3 (AND is represented by the symbol *).

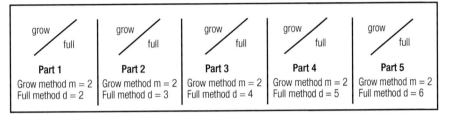

Figure 12.28
Composition of the initial population for GP when the ramped-half-and-half method is used. In this example, **m** = 2 and **d** = 3.

GPs have been successfully applied in numerous fields: the design of antennas [19] and field programmable gate arrays, pattern recognition, [20] and robotics. [21] Koza has cited the same functionality in already patented devices and also in new inventions that have been discovered. [22]

12.4 TABU SEARCH

In this chapter, we have explored search paradigms based on nature. Simulated annealing takes its impetus from annealing—a metallurgical process that attempts to place the molecules in a material at an energy minimum. Evolutionary algorithms (GA and GP) use operators inspired by natural selection to, respectively, find solutions for problems or to construct programs that solve these problems. The search paradigm described in this section seemingly mirrors societal mores.

A tabu (or taboo) is cultural behavior that is frowned upon, if not outright forbidden. Over the course of time, though, behavior that was once

Tabu Search Revisited.

tabu (morally repugnant) might become acceptable. For example, it was once tabu for an older woman to date a younger man; a casual glance at the Hollywood gossip columns should convince anyone that such behavior is now acceptable.

Tabu Search (TS) was developed by Fred Glover in the 1970s [23] and employs two types of lists: **tabu lists** and **aspiration lists**. Recall that to prevent convergence to a local optimum, SA uses a temperature parameter T that permits backward jumps with some probability. TS also allows backward jumps; tabu lists are present to prevent the search from revisiting previous points in the search

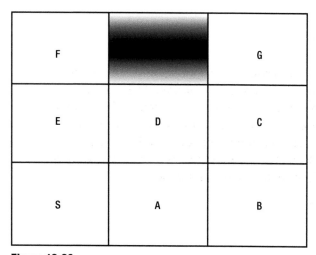

Figure 12.29
A robot must get from square S (Start) to G (Goal).

space and also to prevent cycling. A move to x* that is tabu may nonetheless be allowed, *if* this move appreciably increases the objective function: $f(x)$; say, for example, that $f(x^*) \geq$ any previously visited point; the aspiration list monitors such conditions.

We revisit a problem from Section 12.2 to illustrate a simplified form of TS. Once again, a robot must get from square S (Start) to G (Goal). Figure 12.15 is reproduced as Figure 12.29.

A TS can begin its search by randomly selecting a starting point or by using a greedy-based method. We represent a possible solution to this problem by a sequence of size four, over the alphabet {"N," "S," "W," "E"} where the alphabet symbols represent a move of one square in the directions: north, south, west, or east, respectively. We start the search with a random feasible solution—one that does not take the robot off the board (consult Section 12.2 for further clarification). Our starting point will be: $x_0 =$ ENWS. Once again we use the fitness function: $f(x_i) = 4 -$ Manhattan distance to the goal after the move contained in sample point x_i is executed. TS terminology refers to this function $f()$ as an objective function, and solutions in TS need not necessarily be strings; hence, we use x_i rather than s_i. In our example, x_0 takes the robot one square east, then one square north, then west one and south one, leaving it where it started, in square S. The objective function $f(x_0)$ therefore equals $4 - 4 = 0$.

If there is some biological underpinning to TS, it lies with the importance of memory in decision-making; decision-making should improve with experience. TS uses both **short-term memory** and **long-term memory**. Short-term memory is incorporated into the search in terms of a recency-based tabu list. States in the state space that have been recently visited cannot be revisited for a period of time referred to as the **tabu tenure**. Actually, it is the moves m that transform one point xi into another x_j (where $x_i + m = x_j$) that are tabulated. This strategy encourages exploration. Long-term memory is reflected in the use of aspiration criteria. We mentioned earlier that one aspiration criteria is to visit x* even if forbidden by the tabu list, if $f(x^*)$ is superior to any previously visited point x_i. Other aspiration criteria include the following:

- *Aspiration by default*; if all moves are tabu, then select the oldest move.

- *Aspiration by direction* favors moves that have led to improved values of $f(x)$ in the past. This heuristic fosters exploitation.

- *Aspiration by influence* favors moves that lead to unexplored regions of the state space. This heuristic favors exploration. [24]

Long-term memory also includes a frequency-based tabu list; this list monitors how often each move has been used since the search began.

We now return to our toy problem. We stated that $x_0 =$ ENWS and that $f(x_0) = 0$. We let a move correspond to the alteration of a single step. When selecting moves, we need to ensure that a path exists from x_0 to an optimal solution. There is no concern with this simple problem, but this latter proviso cannot be ignored when more realistic problems are encountered. We observe that there are 4^4, or 256, points in the state space of this problem; many of these points correspond to infeasible solutions (take the robot off the grid). The neighborhood of a sample point x_j : $N(x_j)$, corresponds to all points reachable from x_j via one move. More accurately, we should refer to the neighborhood of x_j at time k or $N(x_j, k)$, because the neighborhood changes as the search progresses (and various tabu and aspiration criteria are modified). It is no surprise that memory usage can become a concern for TS on moderate to large problems. The neighborhood of x_0 at time 0 (the search just beginning), $N(x_0, 0)$ contains 12 additional sample points (i.e., in addition to x_0 itself). To see this, just observe that any one of the four directional steps can be changed to any of the three remaining directional steps. We comment that some of these 12 sample points are not feasible, for example, ENNS attempts to enter the barrier between squares F and G. Any move that is made is reflected in a recency-based tabu list (RTL). Initially, this list will have the following format:

1	2	3	4	RTL
0	0	0	0	

$RTL(i) = j$ indicates that step i of a sample point was last modified at time j. Observe that the list is initialized to all zeroes as no moves have yet been made.

Suppose that at time 1 we choose x_1, which belongs to N(ENWS, 0) equal to ENWN. Note that $f(x_1) = f(\text{ENWN}) = 2$ as ENWN leaves the robot in square D, which is a Manhattan distance of two from G. The recency-based tabu list now equals:

1	2	3	4	
0	0	0	1	RTL

The "1" in RTL (4) reflects that this step was last modified at time 1. Any move that takes place will remain tabu for k time units, in other words, this move cannot be made again until sufficient time has elapsed. This quantity k is referred to as the tabu tenure and must be specified. We shall let $k = 3$, hence step 4 cannot be modified again until three time periods have elapsed, in other words, until time 4. What can occur if tabu tenure is set too high, say $k = 4$ or 5, in this example?

At time 2, we modify $x_1 = \text{ENWN}$ to $x_2 = \text{EEWN}$ as no other move brings us closer to square G. We have modified the second step from N to E. Observe that EEWN also brings the robot to square D, hence $f(x_2)$ still equals 2. RTL appears as:

1	2	3	4	RTL
0	2	0	1	

At time 3, we observe that steps 2 and 4 cannot yet be modified (they are tabu). By converting step 3 from W to N we obtain $x_3 = \text{EENN}$. Our final tabu list equals:

1	2	3	4	RTL
0	2	3	1	

More importantly, however, the fitness of this proposed solution, $f(x_3) = 4 - 0 = 4$, and therefore the problem has been solved as EENN sends the robot to square G. It is difficult to construct a toy problem for TS that uses frequency-based tabu lists and aspiration. The reader who wishes to use TS to solve real-world problems is therefore encouraged to consult references by Glover [25] and Glover and Manuel. [26] Pseudocode for TS appears in Figure 12.30.

```
1. Randomly choose an initial solution x₀. // A Greedy method can also
   sometimes be used to get started.

2. Calculate f(x₀)  // Objective function.

3. Initialize tabu list // Fill in RTL with all 0's.

4. Count = 0

5. while Count < maxcount and progress being made and ideal solution
   not found.

6. Count = Count + 1

7. Choose xₜ in N(x, t) - (tabu elements)  // Observe that the
                          neighborhood changes with time

8. Calculate f(xₜ)

9. Update the tabu list RTL

10.  //  end while

/*Output the last solution xₜ and indicate whether this represents an
ideal or approximate solution. */
```

Figure 12.30
Pseudocode for tabu search.

TS has successfully been applied to the solution of many scheduling and optimization problems, VLSI design, pattern classification, and many additional problem domains. [27, 28, 29]

12.5 ANT COLONY OPTIMIZATION

In Chapter 1, we defined intelligence as the ability to cope with the demands of daily living and to solve problems that arise. We concluded by stating that intelligence was not a binary attribute in an entity, in other words, either present or absent, but rather, existed in degrees. If we were to rate the most intelligent creatures on this planet, it is doubtful that ants would be on anyone's "Top Ten list." And yet, ant colonies exhibit remarkable intelligence. The intelligence exhibited by ant colonies is an example of **emergent behavior**, unforeseen behavior at one level that arises from a lower level. An example from our discipline is human consciousness. Beteem ten billion (10^{10}) and hundred billions (10^{11}) neurons form the human brain; these neurons are arranged to process visual and auditory inputs and to control breathing, locomotion, and other biological functions. There seem to be no rules for consciousness, and yet it is present in our sense of "I". This is also an example of **bottom-up design**, where rule-based organization at a lower level yields unexpected behavior at a higher level.

The emergent behavior that serves as impetus here is the apparent intelligence that arises from ant colonies. Ants can be viewed as agents—entities capable of sensing the environment, communicating with other agents, and responding to the vagaries of their environment. M. Dorigo was the first to recognize the applicability of ant colony behavior to combinatorial optimization. [30]

One behavior of interest to us is that of ant foraging. If a food source is introduced near an ant colony, a trail will be formed to enable colony ants to locate and retrieve this nourishment (see Figure 12.31).

In Figure 12.31(a) you observe that forager ants eventually discover the food source. These "scouts" then recruit colleagues by forming a chemical trail on the return trip to the nest; they

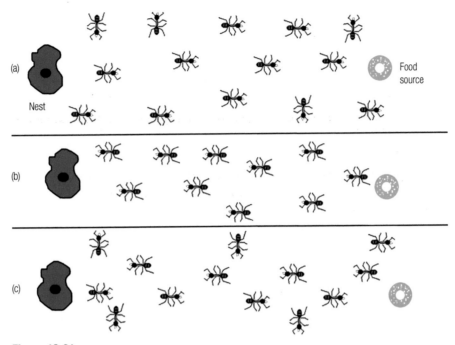

Figure 12.31
Ants establishing and then following a trail from their nest to a food source. (a) Forager ants eventually discover the food source; (b) these "scouts" then recruit colleagues; and (c) not every ant is following the prescribed trail.

do so by depositing pheromones, lightweight chemicals that are produced in an ant's guts or in special glands. This indirect communication among insects is called stigmergy and has several advantages:

1. One insect need not know the location of the others with whom it is communicating.
2. The communication will outlast the sender should it perish.

The pheromone trail encourages exploitation by other colony members. Observe, however, in Figure 12.31(c) that not every ant is following the prescribed trail; this apparently random behavior by the foragers fosters exploration—in this context, the search for alternate food sources.

We mentioned that ant colony behavior was applicable to combinatorial optimization. The phenomenon of trail laying and following just discussed enables some species of ants to find a shortest path between a food source and their colony. Goss and colleagues [31] and Deneubourg and colleagues [32] conducted several experiments that demonstrate this facility for optimization. In Figure 12.32(a) we see a food source separated from an ant home by two paths of different lengths; initially the nest is blocked. Once the barricade is removed in Figure 12.32(b) we observe no preference for either path. In 12.32(c), however, after the ants have had some time to travel along both pathways, a clear preference for the shorter path is evident.

Once again some ants continue to traverse the longer path, which is a form of exploration. One further comment about pheromone; over time this chemical will evaporate. Does this last remark help you to answer why ants in this experiment display a clear preference for the shorter path?

There are biological advantages to choosing a shorter path. Ants expend less energy in food collection and thereby finish this task faster; this enables them to avoid competition from other

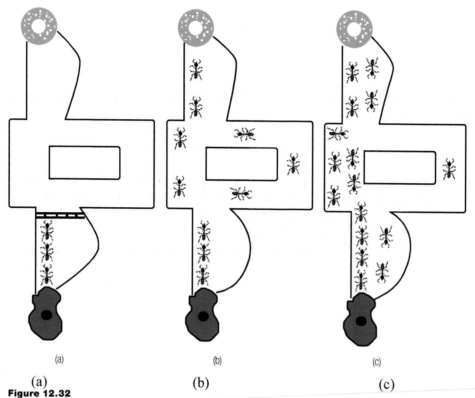

(a)   (b)   (c)

Figure 12.32
Ants finding a shortest path from their home to a food source. Initially the nest is isolated. The barrier is removed. We witness traffic on both paths that appears random. The shortest path to the food source exhibits heavier traffic (exploitation), whereas some foragers are found on the other path (exploration).

colonies and possible confrontations with predators. Dorigo and colleagues [33] employed artificial ants with artificial pheromone trails to solve instances of the Traveling Salesperson Problem (TSP; Chapters 2 and 3). In their simulations, a colony of artificial ants travels from city to city; journeys are made independently and randomly; however, pheromone is deposited on the trail. The quantity of pheromone deposited is inversely proportional to the overall length of a particular tour. Because of pheromone evaporation, shorter tours will contain more pheromone than longer ones. Ants make this trip a number of times; on subsequent journeys, those tours with more pheromone will be visited by more ants. In what is termed a simple ant colony optimization algorithm (S-ACO), each edge (i, j) in a graph has some quantity of artificial pheromone $\tau_{i,j}$. Each agent (artificial ant) is capable of depositing pheromone on a trail and can also sense deposits left by other agents. Each agent can probabilistically decide the next node to visit according to

$$p_{ij}^{k}(t) = \begin{cases} \dfrac{\tau_{ij}(t)}{\sum_{j \in N} \tau_{ij}(t)} & \text{if } j \in N \\ 0 & \text{o.w.} \end{cases}$$

The probability that ant k, situated at node i during time t, will choose to visit node j is represented by $p_{ij}^{k}(t)$; the pheromone level of edge $[i, j]$ at time t is $\tau_{i,j}(t)$; and N_i is the set of adjacent nodes. While an agent is traversing an edge (i, j), it deposits some quantity of pheromone $\Delta\tau$. Hence, pheromone levels are updated as follows:

$$\tau_{i,j}(t) \leftarrow \tau_{i,j}(t) + \Delta\tau.$$

More robust results, however, were obtained when pheromone evaporation was also employed as a parameter, yielding

$$\tau_{i,j}(t) \leftarrow (1-p)\,\tau_{i,j}(t) + \Delta\tau,$$

where the pheromone decay rate is represented by p in $[0, 1]$. [34] Most early work for ACO has focused on discrete optimization. ACO has successfully solved the vehicle routing problem (VRP) [35, 36, 37], network routing, graph coloring (consult exercises in Chapters 2 and 3), machine scheduling, and the shortest common super sequence problem. [38]

Other behavior of ant colonies that has attracted attention by researchers is that of dead body clustering. In several ant species, it has been observed that worker ants will gather dead ants (and ant parts) and form clusters similar to cemeteries.[39, 32] Figure 12.33 illustrates this phenomenon.

Initially corpses are randomly distributed. Several hours later, you can observe that worker ants are beginning to pile the corpses. Worker ants have formed clusters of corpses.

It is believed that the clustering that occurs is the result of an attraction between corpses, facilitated by worker ants. As small clusters of corpses grow, more worker ants are attracted to deposit more corpses. This form of positive feedback is responsible for the formation of larger and larger

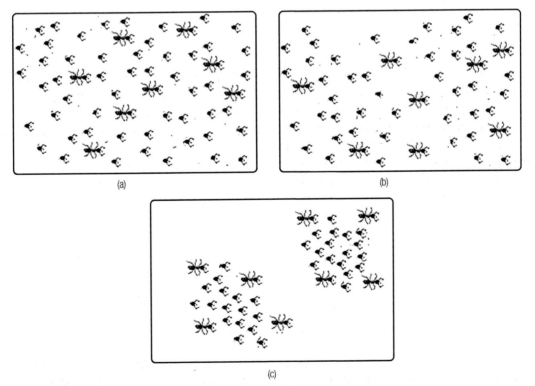

(a)

(b)

(c)

Figure 12.33
Cemetery formation in ants.

clusters. A related behavior is that of larval sorting by one species of ants, in which worker ants gather larvae. Broods are arranged with smaller larvae in the center and larger larvae around the outside. [40] These two behaviors have led to applications in data clustering (ant clustering algorithms or ACA).

Videos of this work in the area of swarm robotics can be viewed at http://www.nature.com/nature/journal/v406/n6799/extref/406992ail.mov and http://www.cs.ualberta.ca/~kube. Looking several decades into the future, one can envision useful applications for micro bots and nano bots in surgery and for the internal dispensing of medicines.

Ants are not alone as social insects. Bees, wasps, and termites have also been studied extensively. One can use the word *swarm* to refer to any structural collection of cooperating agents.[41] Hence, a flock of birds can also be considered a swarm. Swarm intelligence refers to intelligence that emerges from a collection of cooperating agents that work in close proximity to one another. In this section we have discussed ant colonies as an example of swarm intelligence. A new field of research is **swarm robotics**, in which autonomous robotic agents, governed by relatively simple rules, behave much as a community of ants. Collections of these small robots have recreated the behavior of ants in the following areas: foraging for food, clustering of dead bodies, collective prey retrieval, and clustering around a food source. Food foraging simulations were conducted by Krieger, Billeter, and Keller [41] and by Krieger and Billeter. [42] Research on object clustering was performed by Beckers and colleagues. [43] Work on cooperative box-pushing, in which miniature robots cooperate to move a box that is beyond the capability of any individual robot, was conducted by Kube and Zhang [44, 45, 46] and by Kube and Bonabeau.[47]

12.6 ■ CHAPTER SUMMARY

We have seen that artificial intelligence researchers can glean useful search paradigms from the world around us. Many of the optimization algorithms discussed earlier—for example, hill climbing (Chapter 3) and gradient descent (Chapter 11)—suffer from a propensity to converge to a local optimum.

Simulated annealing draws its inspiration from the metallurgic process of annealing. If the molecules in a metal are to be brought to an energy minimum, they must first be excited via heating and then be allowed to slowly cool. In SA, reaching a global optimum might first involve jumping to points in the state space with lower objective values.

GA and GP borrow the genetic operators of selection, crossover, and mutation to facilitate the convergence of strings toward a problem's solution, much as living systems converge toward adaptation with their environment. Evolution of living organisms is inherently a parallel process as it occurs across an entire population. Additionally, adaptation of a species to an (ever-changing) environment requires many generations. This adaptation is necessarily blind because no individual in a population can consciously change itself to facilitate its fitness.

Lamarck was a French botanist who subscribed to the theory that traits acquired by an individual could be transmitted to his or her descendants. His theories are not held in high regard by modern geneticists.

Evolutionary algorithms such as GA and GP are therefore parallel, iterative, and blind procedures.

Tabu search capitalizes on the changing state of human beliefs to design a search that fosters exploration. Portions of the state space that have been recently visited remain forbidden until some time has elapsed. This tabu can be overlooked if the payoff is sufficient; these "free passes" are contained in an aspiration list.

The social behavior of ants in ant colonies, wherein communication occurs indirectly via chemical transmission, is the impetus behind ACO and ACA algorithms. Intelligence that emerges from a large population of communicating and autonomous agents in close proximity is referred to as swarm intelligence. This is a model for intelligent behavior that has been successfully applied to colonies of small robots (swarm robotics) and holds promise for the future, once advances in miniaturization have occurred.

There are several research disciplines in so-called Natural Computing that we have not discussed:

- Immunocomputing—Agents are modeled after an animal's immune system. There has been some success in speech identification and computer virus detection systems.

- A-life—Simulations that model the behavior of living systems yield insight into these systems.

- Quantum computing—The U.S. government expects to have a viable model of a computer based upon quantum physics in the not too distant future (interactions at the subatomic level do not obey the traditional physical principles of everyday life). Such computers are expected to be highly parallel for certain search problems.

- DNA Computing—Computer systems modeled after the algorithms involved in human DNA transcriptions. These computers would have the capacity to replicate processors when more computing prowess is required.

Questions for Discussion

1. What is the relationship between annealing and SA?

2. Define exploitation and exploration in search algorithms.

3. What is the disadvantage of favoring exploitation over exploration in a search (hint: think of hill climbing)?

4. How does the temperature parameter T help SA to balance exploitation and exploration?

5. Explain the genetic operators: selection, crossover, and mutation used in GA.

6. Which operator do you believe is more useful to a GA—crossover or mutation? Defend your assertion.

7. One selection algorithm not discussed is that of miser selection, in which the *worst* member of a population is selected to participate in reproduction. What advantages do you foresee for this approach?

    a. What advantages do you foresee in increasing the population size in a GA?

    b. What disadvantages?

8. Suppose that you are using a GA to solve an instance of the TSP. What precautions must be taken when performing crossover?

9. A genetic operator not discussed for GA is inversion. Choose two sites randomly on a chromosome: 10^0100^11, and then reverse all characters between these two points as: 10001012.

   a. First, what possible problem do you believe inversion is trying to correct?

   b. Second, what is wrong with the way we have addressed this operation?

10. What is the major distinction between GA and GP?

11. What problems do you foresee in selection of tree heights in GP? How does Koza's ramped-half-and-half method address this problem?

12. a. In tabu search, do tabu lists encourage exploitation or exploration?

    b. Same question for aspiration lists?

13. List three aspiration criteria in tabu search and explain why they are helpful.

14. What is stigmergy? Why is this a useful means of communication?

15. Explain the role that pheromone evaporation plays in the shortest path example explained in Section 5.

16. Observe that in Figure 12.32, some ants do not follow the shortest path from the nest to a food source. What useful purposes do these supposedly misguided foragers play?

17. What possible applications do you envision for the cemetery formation example?

18. Cite several future applications for swarm robotics at both the macroscopic and microscopic level.

Exercises

The search methods in this chapter employ probability to some extent (there is a stochastic version of TS that we did not discuss). Monte Carlo simulation uses probabilistic tools to approximate "difficult" functions. Imagine that you are playing darts on the following dartboard.

1. Drawn on the dartboard is ¼ of a circle as shown. You throw 100 darts at the board. Assume that all darts land randomly somewhere on the board. How can you use this experiment to approximate the value of π?

Figure 12.34
A square dartboard, 1 foot on each side.

2. Design a GA solution for the 4-Queens problem (Chapter 2). Be sure to specify your representation and your fitness function.

3. Design a GA solution for the Missionaries and Cannibals problem (Chapter 2). How does your fitness function measure closeness to the goal? How does it prevent unsafe states from occurring?

4. Design a GA solution for determining the chromatic number of a graph (Chapter 2). How does your fitness function avoid infeasible solutions? How does it reward solutions using fewer colors?

5. Design a GA solution for the 15-puzzle.

6. How would you formulate a GA that is capable of playing tic-tac-toe?

7. How would you design a GA-based strategy for the iterated Prisoner's Dilemma (Chapter 4)?

8. Design a GP to determine the chromatic number of a graph (see Exercise 12.3). You will need to use functions that

   a. Assign a color to a node.

   b. Change the color of a node when necessary.

   c. Keep count of the number of colors used.

9. Until Darwin's theory of evolution, people believed that living systems were designed by God (or a God-like figure). William Paley was a theologian who proposed in the 1802 book *Natural Theology*[48] his watchmaker argument: A watch is a complex artifact. If you were to find a watch on the side of the road and carefully examined its internal workings, it is likely you would conclude that some human watchmakers designed it. Similarly, he argued that living systems are also complicated. It is natural to conclude that God must be responsible for *their* design: Are you convinced by Paley's argument? You might wish to first consult the book by Richard Dawkins *The Blind Watchmaker*[49] before answering. Dawkins argues that evolution via natural selection can be viewed as a *blind watchmaker*.

Programming Exercises

1. Write a program that uses Monte Carlo simulation to approximate the value of π. (See Exercise 1 above). Use pairs of random numbers over [0, 1) instead of darts.

2. Write a program to have a GA solve the 4-Queens problem (see Exercise 2).

3. Write a program to have a GA solve the Missionaries and Cannibals problem (see Exercise 3).

4. Write a program to have a GA determine the chromatic number of a graph (see Exercise 4). Test your program on the graphs depicted in Figures 2.39 and 2.40.

5. Write a program to have a GA solve the 15-puzzle. The input to your program is a random arrangement of the tiles. The output is the tiles in order or a message that a solution is not possible (recall that half of the arrangements will not be reachable).

6. Write a program for a GA-based tic-tac-toe player.

7. Write a program that uses a GA to develop a strategy for the iterated Prisoner's Dilemma.

   Use Koza's ramped-half-and-half method to form the initial population for each of problems 8 and 9. Experiment with various values of **m** and **d**.

8. Write a program that uses GP to construct a full adder.

9. Write a program that uses GP to determine the chromatic number of a graph. Test your program on the graphs depicted in Figures 2.39 and 2.40.

10. Write a program that uses GP to solve the Tower of Hanoi Problem (consult Chapter 6) for $n = 3$ discs.

11. The minimum *k*-tree problem is to find a tree T in a labeled graph such that T has *k* edges and the total cost is minimal. For the graph shown in Figure 12.35, minimum 3-tree has a cost = 9.

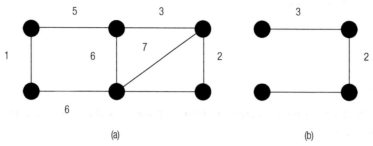

Figure 12.35
(a) A graph G and (b) A minimum 3-tree with cost = 2 + 3 + 4 = 9.

12. Write a program that uses TS to find a minimum k-tree in a graph. Test your program on the graph shown in Figure 12.36, with k = 4.

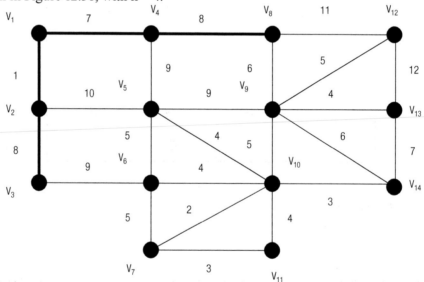

Figure 12.36
Test input for your TS program.

Your program begins with a greedy-based solution that selects the minimal cost edge first and 3 additional edges that are adjacent to this edge (depicted by bold edges in Figure 12.36). Moves in this search consist of the addition of an adjacent edge and the deletion of a single edge from the tree. You may wish to consult "Tabu Search" by Fred Glover and Manuel Laguna. [50]

13. Write a program that uses S-ACO to solve the shortest path problem described in Chapter 2. Test your program on the map of northern China depicted in Figure 2.14(a). Experiment with various pheromone deposit levels. Also, compare results obtained when pheromone evaporation is not (is) employed.

14. In the Euclidean TSP, vertices are randomly placed in some square box (see Figure 12.37). No cost matrix is provided, as the distance between two points, P_1 and P_2, can be calculated by: $d(P_1, P_2) = sqrt((x_2 - x_1)^2 + (y_2 - y_1)^2)$. Write a program to solve an instance of the Euclidean TSP when $n = 25$ by using

   a. SA

   b. GA

   c. Tabu Search

   d. Experiment with various values of d (the number of cuts—consult discussion in Section 12.1).

   e. Try various population sizes for Part b of this question. Discuss your results.

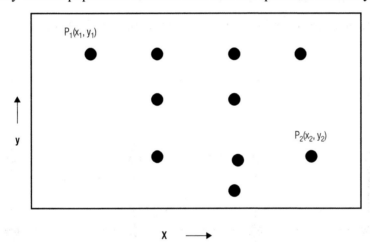

Figure 12.37
An instance of the Euclidean TSP with $n = 10$ cities.

Keywords

aspiration criterion
aspiration lists
bottom-up design
building blocks
cooling schedule
crossover
elitist selection
emergent behavior
exploitation
exploration
fitness function
genetic drift

geometric cooling
implicit parallelism
inversion
iterative procedure
linear cooling
long-term memory
mutation
natural selection
positive feedback
premature convergence
recombination
roulette wheel selection

scaled selection
schemata
selection
short-term memory
stigmergy
swarm intelligence
swarm robotics
tabu lists
tabu search
tabu tenure
tournament selection

References

1. Sambamurty, A. V. S. 2005. *Genetics*, 2nd ed. Oxford: Alpha Science Int'l Ltd.

2. Kirkpatrick, S., Gelatt, C. D., and Vechi, M. P. 1983. *Simulated annealing. Operations Research* 39: 378–406.

3. Cerny, V. 1985. Thermodynamical approach to the traveling salesman problem: An efficient simulation algorithm. *Journal of Optimization Theory and Applications* 45: 44–51.

4. Metropolis, N., Rosenbluth, A., Rosenbluth, M., Teller, A., and Teller, E. 1953. Equation of state calculations by fast computing machines. *Journal of Chemical Physics* 21: 1087–1092.

5. Darwin, C. 2001. *The Voyage of the Beagle*. New Ed. New York, NY: Random House.

6. Darwin, C. 1994. The correspondence of Charles Darwin, Volume VI. *The English Historical Review* 109: 1856–1857.

7. Darwin, C. 1859. *Origin of Species*. New York, NY: Bantam.

8. Holland, J. 1992. *Adaptation in natural and artificial systems,* 2nd ed. Cambridge, MA: MIT Press.

9. Molfetas, A. and Bryan, G. 2007. Structured genetic algorithm representation for neural network evolution. *Proceedings of Artificial Intelligence and Applications*, Innsbruck, Austria, Feb.12–14, 519–524.

10. Holland, J. 1975. *Adaptation in Natural and Artificial Systems*. Ann Arbor, MI: University of Michigan..

11. Goldberg, D. E. 1989. *Genetic Algorithms in Search, Optimization, and Machine Learning*. Reading, MA: Addison-Wesley.

12. Kurzweil, R. 1999. *The Age of Spiritual Machines*. New York, NY: Penguin Books.

13. Williams, E. A., Crossley, W. A., and Lang, T. J. 2001. Average and maximum revisit time trade studies for satellite constellations using a multiobjective genetic algorithm. *The Journal of the Astronomical Sciences 49: 385–400.*

14. Beasley, J., Sonander, J., and Havelock, J. 2001. Scheduling aircraft landings at London Heathrow using a population heuristic. *Journal of the Operation Research Society* 52: 483–493.

15. Negnevitsky, M. 2005. *Artificial Intelligence: A Guide to Intelligent Systems*, 2nd ed. Reading, MA: Addison-Wesley.

16. Rojas, R. 1996. *Neural Networks: A Systematic Introduction. Berlin: Springer.*

17. Chellapilla, K. D. and Fogel, B. 2002. Anaconda's expert rating by computing against Chinook experiments in co-evolving a neural checkers. *Neurocomputing* 42: 69–86.

18. Koza, J. R., Comisky, W., and Jessen, Y. 2000. Automatic synthesis of a wire antenna using genetic programming. *Conference on Genetic and Evolutionary Computation, Las Vegas, Nevada.*

19. Teredesai, A. 2003. *Active Pattern Recognition Using Genetic Programming*. PhD dissertation, SUNY at Buffalo.

20. Messom, C. H. and Walker, M. G. 2002. Evolving cooperative robotic behavior using distributive genetic programming. *Seventh Int'l Conference on Control, Automations, Robotics, and Vision ICARCV'02,* Singapore.

21. Koza, J. R., Keane, M. A., Streeter, M. J., Mydlowec, W., Yu, J., and Lanza. G. 2003. *Genetic Programming: Routine Human-Competitive Machine Intelligence.* New York, NY: Springer.

22. Glover, F. 1995. Tabu search fundamentals and uses. *Technical Report.* University of California at Davis.

23. Nascaoui, O. 2005. Class notes on tabu search. Dept. of Computer Engineering and Computer Science, Speed School of Engineering, University of Louisville, KY.

24. Glover, F. 1997. *Tabu Search.* New York: Springer.

25. Glover, F. and Manuel, L. 1997. Tabu search, September 22, 2008. Retrieved from *http://www. dei.unipd.it/~fisch/ricop/tabu_search_glover_laguna.pdf.*

26. Tung, C. and Chou, C. 2004. Pattern classification using tabu search to identify the spatial distribution of groundwater pumping. *Hydrogeology Journal* 12: 488–496.

27. Emmert, J. M., Lodha, S., and Bhatia, D. K. 2004. On using tabu search for design automation of VLSI systems. *Journal of Heuristics* 9: 75–90.

28. Kazuhiro, A. 2005. Tabu search optimization of horizontal and vertical alignments of forest roads. *Journal of Forestry Research* 10: 275–284.

29. Dorigo, M. 1992. *Optimization, learning and natural algorithms.* PhD thesis, Dipartamento ai Electronica Politecnio di Milano, Italy.

31. Goss, S., Aron, S., Deneubourg, J.-L., and Pasteels, J. M. 1989. Self-organized shortcuts in the Argentine ant. *Naturwissenschaften* 76: 579–581.

31. Deneubourg, J.-L., Goss, S., Franks, N., Sendova-Franks, A., Detrain, C., and Chretien, L. 1991. *Simulation of Adaptive Behavior: From Animals to Animats.* Cambridge, MA: MIT Press/Bradford Books.

32. Dorigo, M., Maniezzo, V., and Calorni, A. 1996. The ant system: Optimization by a colony of cooperating agents. *IEEE Transcriptions on Systems, Man and Cybernetics* 26: 26–41.

33. Dorigo, M., Di Caro, G. A., and Gambardella, L. M. 1999. Ant algorithms for discrete optimization. *Artificial Life* 5 (2).

34. Bullnheimer, B., Hartl, R. F., and Strauss, C. 1999a. An improved ant system algorithm for the vehicle routing problem. *Annals of Operations Research* 89: 319–328.

35. Bullnheimer, B., Hartl, R. F., and Strauss, C. 1999b. Applying the ANT system to the vehicle routing problem. In *Meta-Heuristics: Advances and Trends in Local Search for Optimization.* Boston, MA: Kluwer Academic Publishers.

36. Bullnheimer, B. 1999. *Ant Colony Optimization in Vehicle Routing.* PhD thesis, University of Vienna.

37. Dorigo, M. and Stutzle, T. 2004. *Ant Colony Optimization. Cambridge,* MA: MIT Press.

38. Chretien, L. 1996. *Organisation Spatiale du Materiel Provenant de l'Excavation du Nid Chez Messor Barbarus et Agregation des Caduares d'Ouvrieres Chez LAsius Niger Hymenoptera: Formicidae.* PhD Thesis, Department of Animal Biology, Universite Libre de Bruxelles, Belgium.

39. Franks, N. R. and Sendova-Franks, A. B. 1992. Brood sorting by ants: Distributing the workload over the work surface. *Behavioral Ecology and Sociobiology* 30: 109–123.

40. Krieger, M. B., Billeter, J. B., and Keller, L. 2000. Ant-task allocation and recruitment in cooperative robots. *Nature* 406: 992–995.

41. Krieger, M. B. and Billeter, J. B. 2000. The call of duty: Self-organized task allocation in a population of up to twelve mobile robots. *Robotics and Autonomous Systems* 30: 65–84.

42. Beckers, R., Holland, O. E., and Denenbourg, J. L. 1994. From local actions to global tasks: Stigmergy and collective robotics. In *Artificial Life IV:* Proceedings of the 4th International Workshop on the Synthesis and Simulation of Life, edited by R. A. Brooks and P. Maes., Cambridge, MA: MIT Press.

43. Kube, C. R. and Zhang, H. 1992. Collective robotic intelligence. In *From Animals to Animats: International Conference on the Simulation of Adaptive Behavior,* 460–468.

44. Kube, C. R. and Zhang, H. 1994a. Collective robotics: From social insects to robots. *Adaptive Behavior* 2: 189–218.

45. Kube, C. R. and Zhang, H. 1994b. Stagnation recovery behaviors for collective robotics. In *1994 IEEE/RSJ/GI International Conference on Intelligent Robots and Systems,* 1893–1890.

46. Kube, C. R. and Bonabeau, E. 2000. Cooperative transport by ants and robots. *Robotics and Autonomous Systems,* 30: 85–101.

47. Paley, W. 2003. *Natural Theology. Kessinger Publishing.*

48. Dawkins, R. 1996. *The Blind Watchmaker: Why the Evidence of Evolution Reveals a Universe without Design.* New York, NY: W. W. Norton.

49. Glover, F. and Laguna, M. 1997. *Tabu Search.* Boston: Kluwer.

Bibliography

Corne, D., Dorigo, M., and Glover, F. 1999. *New Ideas in Optimization*. New York, NY: McGraw Hill.

Galdone, P. 1986. *The Elves and the Shoemaker*, 2nd ed. Clarion Books.

Kube, C. R. and Zhang, H. 1997. Multirobot box-pushing. *IEEE International Conference on Robotics and Automation*, video proceedings, 4 minutes.

Vafaie, H. and Iman, I. F. 1994. Feature-Selection Methods: Genetic Algorithms vs. Greedy-like Search. *Technical Report*.

PART **IV**

ADVANCED TOPICS

Chapter 13
**Natural Language
Understanding** · · · · · · · · · · 403

Chapter 14
Automated Planning · · · · · · 457

Natural language understanding has long been a goal of AI researchers. Early researchers in machine translation did not realize the difficult challenges posed by both syntax and semantics in language. Formalisms were used leading to grammars that helped to make significant progress in the 1970s and 80s. But real breakthroughs came with the development of corpus linguistics coupled with statistical approaches including Markov methods. Great progress has been made in recent years and this is illustrated by examples of several question–answer systems) as well as significant progress in speech understanding systems (Chapter 13).

Planning is an old area of AI which has enjoyed much progress in design, development, and application during the past few decades. Future systems are being designed to tackle such monumental tasks as industrial automation and space exploration coupled with robotics (Chapter 14).

NATURAL LANGUAGE UNDERSTANDING

Eugene Charniak.

Having computers understand the written and spoken language of humans has been the goal of some research disciplines for many years. Here we trace that history leading to the knowledge-based approaches of the 1970s and 80s. The development of language corpora led directly to successful statistical approaches to language which have prevailed for the past two decades. We present some of the more interesting commercial and technical systems of the past decade.

Figure 13.0
Communications icons.

13.0 ■ INTRODUCTION

One of the oldest, most researched, and most demanding fields of AI is speech and language understanding. Any attempt at developing intelligent systems ultimately seems compelled to address what form of communication will be the standard. Language communication is often the preferred choice over, for example, graphical or data-based systems. Early attempts at tackling language with Machine Translation in the 1950s and 60s proved futile. However, the foundations for natural language understanding were established in the 1940s and 50s with work on **finite automata, formal grammars,** and probability. There followed trends toward **symbolic** and **stochastic** approaches into the 1970s. This chapter will explore developments in Natural Language Processing (NLP) leading to present approaches using stochastic processes, machine learning, information extraction, and question-answering amongst others, with a view to the future.

13.1 ■ OVERVIEW: THE PROBLEMS AND POSSIBILITIES OF LANGUAGE

Today there are many systems in which machines perform language related functions (both spoken and textual / interactive) that are difficult to distinguish from humans. It is not uncommon to be at once both frustrated and impressed with these systems. We may be frustrated by the number of simple decisions that we must endure in interacting with a machine to route our calls, but sometimes the machine seems capable of making decisions that we had previously thought were special to humans.

- Today travelers can make reservations and check the status of their transportation plans using conversational agents that provide them with most of the choices a human can offer.

- Remarkable advances have been made in automobile navigational systems, which provide textual, graphical, and speech guides to the driver, including typical destinations, points of interest such as gas stations, restaurants, stores, banks, etc., as well as tourist attractions. The important thing is that these satellite-based systems (which can come factory-installed in newer vehicles and can be easily purchased for $100–$300) is that they will get you where you want to go efficiently while providing great amounts of useful information.

- Video search companies provide search services for millions of hours of video on the Web by using speech technology to capture the words in the desired sound track.

- Google, as we know, can perform amazing information retrieval tasks. For example, it can perform cross-language information retrieval and translation services whereby a query is made in one's native language, then is translated to other languages (e.g., to search for a collection); the relevant pages are found and then translated back to the native language.

- Large educational publishers and the Educational Testing Service have developed automated systems that can analyze thousands of student essays, grading and assessing them in a manner indistinguishable from human graders.

- Interactive virtual agents, emulating animated characters, can serve as tutors for children learning to read (Wise et al. 2007).

- In addition to great advances in information retrieval, there is text analysis whereby automated measurement of opinion, importance, preferences, and attitudes is possible.

Wise, B., Van Vuuren, S., and Byrne, B. 2005–2010. National Institutes of Health, 5 p50 HD27802, Response to Computer-Assisted Instruction for Reading Difficulties. Wise, B., PI, Project V in Differential Diagnoses of Learning Disabilities Center, Olson, R., PI.

The contemporary standard text on this subject is *Speech and Language Understanding, by D. Jurafsky and J. Martin,*[1] and a number of the above points are based on their "State of the Art" (p.8–9).

Language is diabolical. Spoken and written language is somewhat special to human beings (although there can be no doubt that other animals communicate through sound and language). Language affords us many opportunities for detailed communication—and great misunderstanding! The opportunities and advantages of language (both spoken and written) are somewhat obvious, yet we feel they are worth explaining here. Spoken language enables us to have a synchronous conversation through which we can communicate interactively with one or more people. This is probably the most common and oldest form of language communication between human beings. It is easy to do, allows us to be most expressive, and most importantly, we can also listen to each other. Although spoken language offers the opportunity for precision, there are few people who can and do use language as precisely as it can be used. Spoken language can lead to misunderstanding when the two or more parties are not speaking the same language, have different interpretations of language, or the words are not properly understood; sounds may be slurred, blurred, muffled, or are subject to regional dialects. Perhaps most importantly, spoken language rarely leaves any official record, unless there is an actual effort to record it.

On the other hand, textual language has the obvious advantage of providing a record (whether it is a book, a document, an email, or other form) but it lacks the spontaneity, fluidity, and interactivity that spoken language affords.

In this chapter, we will present some techniques that will provide insights into how computers can be programmed to handle language as text.

13.1.1 Ambiguity

One need not go far to see some of the possibilities for misunderstanding and misinterpretation of language. Consider some of the following modern methods of communication and how they can be used normally but could result in miscommunication(s):

Telephone – sound(s) could be unclear, a person's words may be misunderstood, and language comprehension between the two parties poses its own set of unique problems. Many possibilities for misinterpretation, misunderstanding, and incorrect recall exist.

Handwritten Letter – may be illegible, various kinds of writing errors can easily occur; could be lost by the post office. Origin and date may be omitted.

Typed Letter – Not sufficiently fast and the source and real meaning behind a letter may be misunderstood and may not be sufficiently formal.

Email – requires the Internet; it is easy to misunderstand context and misinterpret intent.

Instant Message – precise, fast, may be synchronous, but still not as smooth as talking. Records can be kept.

Text Message – requires phone, limited size, and can be hard to produce. (e.g., small keyboard, not to be done while driving, during class, etc.)

Language is unique for the very reason that it offers opportunities for both precision and vagueness; it can be used precisely in terms of (for example) legal or scientific language, or it can be used in a deliberately "artistic" way, for example, as poetry or a novel. As a form of communication, written or spoken language can be ambiguous. Let us consider a few examples:

EXAMPLE 13.1 "I'LL MEET YOU AFTER THE CONCERT, IN THE BAR."

The intent of this sentence is clear, although there are many details missing that could help make this rendezvous more likely to be successful. What if the concert hall has more than one bar? Could the concert be in the bar and we are meeting after it? What time exactly was the meeting to take place and how long are you willing to wait for the meeting to take place? The statement "after the concert" shows intent but is ambiguous. What will the two parties do after a certain amount of time has passed and they have not yet met each other?

EXAMPLE 13.2. "TURN RIGHT AT THE THIRD LIGHT."

Again here, the intention is good but a lot of details have been omitted.

How far apart are the lights? They could be a few blocks apart or they could be miles apart. More precision about distance, landmarks, and so forth would be helpful in terms of driving instructions, when directions are given.

EXAMPLE 13.3. "HOW ARE YOU DOING? WE'RE ALL SET."

These two sentences demonstrate contextual ambiguity. What are the referents set for? Set to depart? Is the dinner table set up? Or they're not in any need for counseling. Part of the problem here is the possible multiple meanings of the word "set." Is it a noun (a set of kitchenware), a verb (to set up), or perhaps another kind of word usage?

From the examples above, it should be clear that there are many possible ambiguities in language. Therefore, if this is the case with language in communications between humans, one can well imagine the problems that language understanding can pose for machines.

13.2 HISTORY OF NATURAL LANGUAGE PROCESSING (NLP)

Jurafsky and Martin [1] identify six major periods in the history of Natural Language Processing, which we present in Table 13.1. We will briefly try to describe each of these periods. The subsections in this history roughly correspond to the titles for these periods provided by Jurafsky and Martin.

Table 13.1
The six periods of NLP (based on Jurafsky and Martin, 2008, pp 9–12).

Period Number	Period Name	Years
1	Foundations	1940s and 1950s
2	Symbolic vs. Stochastic Approaches	1957–1970
3	Four Paradigms	1970 – 1980
4	Empiricism and Finite State Models Redux	1983–1993
5	The Field Comes Together	1994–1999
6	The Rise of Machine Learning	2000–2008

13.2.1 Foundations (1940s and 1950s)

The history of natural language processing can be traced back to the foundations of computer science itself. The field of computer science was built on the groundwork of Turing's model of algorithmic computation.[2] After this initial foundation, many subfields emerged in computer science, each of which provided fertile ground for further research. Natural language processing is a subfield in computer science that has drawn on the conceptual groundwork of Turing's ideas.

Turing's work led to other models of computation, such as the McCulloch-Pitts neuron.[3] The McCulloch-Pitts neuron was modeled on the human neuron, taking several inputs and producing output only if the combined input exceeded a threshold value.

See Chapter 11, "Neural Networks," for further discussion.

These models of computation were closely followed by the work of Kleene on **finite automata** and regular expressions;[4] they would play a major role in computational linguistics and theoretical computer science.

Shannon added probability to finite automata, making these models more powerful in their representation of ambiguity in language.[5] These probabilistic finite automata were based on Markov models in mathematics, and they played a crucial role in the next major development in natural language processing.

Noam Chomsky drew on the ideas of Shannon, and Chomsky's work on formal grammars was a major influence shaping computational linguistics.[6] Chomsky used finite automata to describe formal grammars, and he defined languages in terms of the grammars that generated them. Based on formal language theory, a language could be considered a set of strings, and each string could be considered a sequence of symbols produced by a **finite automaton.**

Together with Chomsky's work in shaping the field, Shannon provided the other major influence on the early work in natural language processing. In particular, Shannon's noisy channel model was crucial to the development of probabilistic algorithms in language processing. In the noisy **channel model**, it is assumed the input has been obscured by noise, and the original word must be recovered from the noisy input. Conceptually, the input is treated as if it had been passed through a noisy communication channel. Based on this model, probabilistic methods were used to find the best match between the input and possible words.

13.2.2 Symbolic vs. Stochastic Approaches (1957–1970)

From these early ideas, it became clear that natural language processing could be considered from two different perspectives: (1) the **symbolic** and (2) the **stochastic**. The symbolic approach was exemplified by Chomsky's formal language theory. Based on this view, a language contained sequences of symbols, and these sequences had to follow the rules of syntax of their generative grammar. This perspective simplified linguistic structure into a set of clearly defined rules, allowing each sentence and word to be broken into structural components.

Parsing algorithms were developed to break an input into smaller units of meaning and structure. Work in the 1950s and 1960s led to several different strategies for parsing algorithms, such as top-down parsing and bottom-up parsing. Zelig Harris developed the Transformations and Discourse Analysis Project (TDAP), an early example of a parsing system. Later work on parsing algorithms used the concepts of dynamic programming, storing intermediate results in a table to build the best possible parse.[7]

Thus, the symbolic approach emphasized linguistic structure and the parsing of an input into its units of structure. The other major approach, the stochastic, was more concerned with probabilistic methods to represent the ambiguity in language. Taken from mathematics, Bayesian methods were used to represent conditional probabilities. Early applications of this approach included optical character recognition, and an early text-recognition system was built by Bledsoe and Browning.[8] Given a dictionary of words, the likelihood of each letter sequence was computed by multiplying the likelihood of each included letter.

13.2.3 The Four Paradigms: 1970–1983

The next period was dominated by four paradigms:

1. **Stochastic methods,** particularly in speech recognition systems. Earlier work on the noisy channel model was applied in speech recognition and decoding, and Markov models were modified into Hidden Markov models (HMMs) to allow further ambiguity and uncertainty to be represented. AT&T's Bell Laboratories played a key role in these developments in speech recognition, as did IBM's Thomas J. Watson Research Center, and Princeton University's Institute for Defense Analyses. The stochastic approach began to dominate in this period.

2. The **symbolic approach** also made key contributions, and **natural language understanding** was another strand of development that continued the classic symbolic approach. This area of research could be traced back to the earliest work on Artificial Intelligence (AI), including the workshop known as the 1956 Dartmouth Conference organized by John McCarthy, Marvin Minsky, Claude Shannon, and Nathaniel Rochester where the term "Artificial Intelligence" was coined (See Section 1.5.3). AI researchers began to emphasize the underlying reasoning and logic used by the systems they built, such as Newell and Simon's Logic Theorist and the General Problem Solver. In order for these systems to "reason" their way to a solution, the systems had to "understand" the problem in terms of language. Thus, natural language understanding found an application in these AI systems, allowing these systems to answer questions by recognizing text patterns in the input problems.

3. **Logic-based systems** used formal logic as a way to represent the computations involved in language processing. Notable contributions included the work of Colmerauer and colleagues on metamorphosis grammars,[9] Pereira and Warren's work on Definite Clause Grammars,[10] Kay's work on functional grammar,[11] and Bresnan and Kaplan's work on Lexical Functional Grammar (LFG).[12]

Natural language understanding had its most productive period in the 1970s with Winograd's SHRDLU system.[13] This system was a simulation in which a robot moved toy blocks into different positions. The robot responded to commands from the user, moving the appropriate blocks on top of each other. For example, if the user asked the robot to move the blue block onto the larger red block, the robot would successfully understand and follow the command. This system pushed natural language understanding to a new level of complexity, pointing the way to more advanced uses of parsing. Rather than focusing simply on syntax, parsing could be used on the level of meaning and discourse, allowing the system to interpret commands more successfully.

Similarly, Roger Schank and his colleagues at Yale University built more conceptual knowledge of meaning into their systems. Schank used models such as scripts and frames to organize the information available to the system.[14, 15] For example, if the system was supposed to answer questions about restaurant orders, the system would be provided with the typical information associated with restaurants. The script would capture the typical details associated with well-known settings and these associations would be used by the system to answer questions about those settings (see Section 13.9.3).[16] Other systems, such as LUNAR (used to answer questions about moon rocks), combined natural language understanding with logic-based methods, using predicate logic as a semantic representation.[17, 18] Thus, these systems incorporated more semantic knowledge, expanding the power of the symbolic approach from syntactic rules to semantic understanding.

4. The **discourse modeling paradigm** was featured in the work of Grosz; she and her colleagues introduced and concentrated on substructure in discourse and **discourse** focus,[19] while Sidner[20] introduced anaphora, but other researchers such as Hobbs also made contributions to the field.[21]

13.2.4 Empiricism and Finite-State Models

In the 1980s and early 1990s, the symbolic approach continued with a revival of earlier ideas such as finite-state models. These models had fallen out of favor after their initial use in the early years of natural language processing. Their revival was brought about by Kaplan and Kay's work on finite-state phonology and **morphology,**[22] and Church's work on finite-state models of syntax.[23]

The second trend in this period was called "the return of empiricism." This approach was highly influenced by the work at IBM's Thomas J. Watson Research Center employing probabilistic models in speech and language processing. Probabilistic models coupled with data-driven approaches moved to studies of part-of-speech tagging, parsing, attachment ambiguities, and semantics. The empirical approach also led to a new focus on model evaluation, with development of quantitative metrics for evaluation. Emphasis was on comparison of performance with previously published research.

13.2.5 The Field Comes Together: 1994–1999

The changes in this period indicate that probabilistic and data-driven approaches became the standard in NLP Research in all aspects of speech, including algorithms for parsing, part-of-speech tagging, **reference resolution,** and discourse processing. It incorporated probabilities and employed evaluation methods borrowed from speech recognition and information retrieval. This was all somewhat coincidental with increases in computer speed and memory enabling commercial exploitation of various subareas of speech and language processing. In particular, these subareas included speech recognition with spelling and grammar correction. Equally important, the rise of the Web emphasized the need and possibilities for language-based retrieval and **information extraction** (ibid., p. 12).

13.2.6 The Rise of Machine Learning

The early 2000s were marked by a key development: the availability of huge collections of written and spoken material, provided by organizations such as the Linguistic Data Consortium (LDC). Collections such as the **Penn Treebank** [24] annotated the written material with syntactic and semantic information. The value of this resource was immediately evident in the development of new language processing systems. New systems could be trained by comparing the correctness of their parses with the annotations. Supervised machine learning became a major part of solving traditional problems such as parsing and semantic analysis.

This development was accelerated by the availability of high-performance computing systems, as computers continued to grow in speed and memory. With more computing power available to a large number of users, speech and language processing technology could be used in commercial applications. In particular, speech recognition with spelling/grammar correction tools became more commonly used in a variety of environments. The Web was another major driving force for these applications, as information retrieval and information extraction became essential parts of using the Web.

In very recent years, *unsupervised statistical approaches* began to receive renewed attention. These approaches were effectively applied to perform machine translation on unannotated data alone. [25, 26] The cost of developing reliably annotated corpora became a limiting factor for the use of supervised learning approaches. We refer the reader to Jurafsky and Martin [1] for more detail about each period.

13.3 SYNTAX AND FORMAL GRAMMARS

Language can be analyzed on several different levels of structure. These levels include syntax, morphology, and semantics. We now present some of the key terms in the study of language:

Morphology – The study of form and structure of a word and its relationship to its roots and derived forms

Syntax – The manner in which words are put together to form phrases and sentences; usually concerned with the formalities of structure of sentences

Semantics – The study or science of meaning in language

Parse – To break a sentence down into its component parts of speech with an explanation of the form, function, and syntactical relationship of each part; rules of the grammar determine how the parse is done

Lexical – Relating to the vocabulary, words, or morphemes (atoms) of a language; derived from *lexicon*

Pragmatics – The study of the use of language in context

Ellipsis – The omission of a portion of a sentence necessary syntactically but for which the semantics are clear from the context

In this section, we begin with syntax, and in Section 13.4 we continue with semantics and an analysis of meaning.

13.3.1 Types of Grammars

A good way to approach the study of language and how it can be taught to computers is through the study of *grammar*. Feigenbaum et al. define the grammar of a language as "A scheme for specifying the sentences allowed in the language, indicating the syntactic rules for combining words into well-formed phrases and clauses." [27]

MIT linguist Noam Chomsky [28] did the seminal work in the systematic and mathematical study of language **syntax,** and this essentially initiated the field of computational linguistics. He defined formal language as a *set of strings* composed of a *vocabulary of symbols* according to *rules of grammar*. The set of strings correspond to the set of all possible sentences, which may be infinite in number. The vocabulary of symbols corresponds to a finite alphabet or lexicon of words. He defined the four rules of grammar as follows:

1. Syntactic categories serving as variables or nonterminal symbols are defined. Examples of syntactic variables include <VERB>, <NOUN>, <ADJECTIVE>, and <PREPOSITION>.

2. Natural language words from the vocabulary are considered *terminal symbols* and are concatenated (strung together) to form sentences according to rewrite rules.

3. The relationships between particular strings of terminal and nonterminal symbols are specified by *rewrite rules* or *productions* (see Chapter 7, "Production Systems"). In the context of this discussion:

   <SENTENCE> → <NOUN PHRASE> <VERB PHRASE>

   <NOUN PHRASE> → the <NOUN>

   <NOUN> → student

   <NOUN> → expert

   <VERB> → reads

   Note that the variables are enclosed in <...>, and terminal symbols are lowercase.

4. The start symbol, S, or <SENTENCE>, is distinguished from the productions and initiates the generation of all possible sentences according to the productions specified in (3) above. This set of sentences is called the *language generated by the grammar*. The simple grammar defined above would generate the following sentences:

   The student reads.

   The expert reads.

The rewrite rules to generate these sentences by substituting words for sentences would be applied as follows:

<SENTENCE> →

<NOUN PHRASE> <VERB PHRASE>

The <NOUN PHRASE> <VERB PHRASE>

The student <VERB PHRASE>

The student reads.

It is easy to see how a grammar can therefore act as a "machine" to "crank out" all possible sentences that would be allowed by rewrite rules. All that is necessary is a given vocabulary and a set of productions. Similarly, using this approach, the grammar and "structure" of all programming languages has been developed using the Backus-Naur production rules. From these sentences it is possible to perform the first phase of all NLP programs—parsing—and work backward to put the sentences into their syntactic categories without ambiguity.

Chomsky demonstrated that there are essentially four types of grammars that can be generated by his formal language theory. The grammar is defined as the quadruplet (VN, VT, P, S),

where

V = vocabulary

N = nonterminal symbols from the vocabulary

T = terminal symbols from the vocabulary

P = productions of the form X → Y

S = the start symbol.

Type 0: Recursively Enumerable Languages

This type of language has no restrictions on the form of the productions and consequently is too general to be useful. Sentences generated by languages of this type can be recognized by a Turing machine, which is the theoretical basis for all modern-day computers.

Type 1: Context-Sensitive Languages

This type of grammar generates productions of the form X → Y, with the restriction that the right-hand side Y must contain at least as many symbols as the left-hand side, X. Hence, productions look like:

u X v → uYv

where X = single nonterminal symbol

u, v = arbitrary strings including the null string

Y = nonempty string over vocabulary V.

This form of production (rewrite rule) is equivalent to saying "X can be replaced by Y in the context u, v."

So, for example, the grammar:

Rule 1 S → xSBC

Rule 2 S → xBC

Rule 3 CB → BC

Rule 4 xB → xy

Rule 5 yB → yy

Rule 6 yC → yz

Rule 7 zC → zz

where   S = Start symbol

A, B, C = Variables

x, y, z = terminal symbols.

Substituting according to the rewrite rules of this grammar, we are able to derive the following sentence:

$$S \rightarrow$$

Rule 1: xSBC

Rule 2: xxBCBC

Rule 3: xxBBCC

Rule 4: xxyBCC

Rule 5: xxyyCC

Rule 6: xxyyzC

Rule 7: xxyyzz

After some analysis, it shouldn't take readers long to convince themselves that this grammar generates strings of the form xyz, xxyyzz, and so on.

Type 2: Context-Free Languages

In **context-free grammars**, the left-hand side must contain only a single nonterminal symbol. Context-free means that each word in the language occurs with rules applied to it independent of the context in which the word(s) are used. This grammar most closely represents natural language.

The productions S → aSb

S → ab

generate strings of the form ab, aabb, aaabbb, and so on.

Let us see an example of how a context-free grammar can generate natural language sentences with the following rewrite rules:

<SENTENCE> → <NOUN PHRASE> <VERB PHRASE>

<NOUN PHRASE> → <DETERMINER> <NOUN>

<NOUN PHRASE> → <NOUN>

<VERB PHRASE> → <VERB> <NOUN PHRASE>

<DETERMINER> → the

<NOUN> → dogs

<NOUN> → cat

<VERB> → chase

This derivation tree or the parse tree (from sentences to grammar) is as follows:

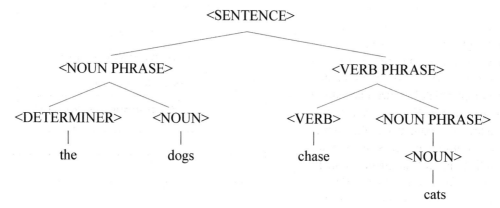

This context-free grammar has generated the sentence:

The dogs chase cats.

However, following the same rules, the sentence,

The cats chase dogs,

can also be generated by the same grammar. This demonstrates that syntax is only concerned with structure and that semantics is an entirely different matter.

Type 3: Regular Languages

This class of language is also called a finite-state grammar and generates sentences according to the productions,

$$X \rightarrow aY$$
$$X \rightarrow a$$

where

X, Y = single variables
a = single terminal.

The following regular grammar: $S \rightarrow 0S \,|\, 0T$
$$T \rightarrow 1T \,|\, \varepsilon$$

would generate the language consisting of at least one "0" followed by any number (including zero) of "1s."

Note that as we go from Type 0 to Type 3 languages, we move from more general to more restrictive grammars. That is, every regular grammar is context-free, every context-free grammar can generate context-sensitive sentences, and every context-sensitive grammar is of Type 0 because it is essentially unrestricted. Hence, the more restrictive the rewrite rules, the simpler the generated language becomes.

Figure 13.1 shows that the hierarchy is slightly augmented with a fifth class called "Mildly Context-Sensitive Languages." Such grammars can be defined by a number of different grammar formalisms (including Post Production Systems introduced in Section 7.1) which are, however, beyond the scope of our discussion here.

At this point it is important to emphasize that although context-free grammars are useful in the design of programming languages and for deciphering large segments of natural languages, Chomsky himself felt that they could not completely represent natural languages such as English. Again, this emphasizes the conclusion that while syntax / grammar is necessary for understanding natural language, it in itself is not sufficient. Firebaugh [29] notes the analogy between grammar for language interpretation and propositional logic for problem solving. Although either may be adequate in certain well-defined situations, neither is adequate in large, general problem situations. [29]

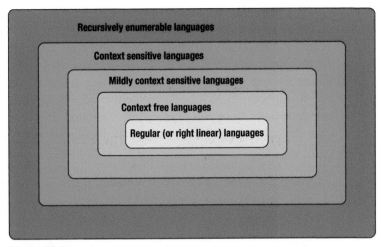

Figure 13.1
Reproduced from Jurafsky and Martin (2008, p. 530) illustrates what is called the **"Chomsky hierarchy"** in a Venn diagram.

13.3.2 Syntactic Parsing: The CYK Algorithm

The syntactic structure of natural languages is often represented in the form of a parse tree. Sentences are often ambiguous and can be parsed in many different ways, so finding the best parse is a key step in representing the correct meaning and intent of the sentence.

One way of finding the best parse is to approach parsing as a search problem. The search space contains all possible parse trees for the input sentence, and the best parse must be found by searching this space. Using this approach, there are two main strategies that can be pursued: top-down search, and bottom-up search.

Top-down search begins at the start symbol S and tries to build all parse trees that will produce the input sentence as the leaves of the tree. Beginning with S as the root node, this strategy builds a separate parse tree for each production rule in the grammar, with S on the left-hand side. Thus, after the first stage of the process, there will be a separate parse tree for each production rule that expands S in the grammar. Continuing onto the next level of the tree, the left-most symbol produced by S will be expanded next. Each possible expansion of this symbol will lead to a separate parse tree. This process continues until all parse trees have been explored to their final level, and the leaves are compared to the input sentence. Incorrect parses are rejected and pruned from the search, while the correct parses are retained as successful parses of the input sentences.

In contrast, bottom-up search begins with the words of the input sentence, trying to build a tree from the leaves upward. This strategy tries to match a word in the input with the nonterminal symbols that could be expanded to produce this word. If a word can be produced from a nonterminal symbol, then the nonterminal symbol is used as the parent node of the word in the parse tree. If the word can be produced from several different nonterminal symbols, then separate parse trees must be constructed for each of these possible expansions. Continuing from the leaves to the next higher level, this strategy moves upward until it reaches S as the root node. The parse trees that cannot reach S are pruned from the search.

The problem with both of these search strategies is the large amount of memory needed to store all the possible parse trees. These memory demands are impractical, and a more realistic alternative is to use a backtracking strategy (see Section 2.2.1). A parse tree is explored until it successfully reaches a solution, or it can no longer continue as a viable solution. Then the search moves back to an earlier state in the search space, returning to build a tree from a state which is yet to be expanded.

Backtracking has its own problems with efficiency, mainly because large portions of the trees are duplicated from one expansion to the next. If a tree fails to reach a solution, it is discarded, even though much of the tree will be duplicated in the next possible solution. This inefficiency can be avoided by using dynamic programming algorithms. The dynamic programming approach stores intermediate results in a table so they can be reused. Subtrees are stored in the table, allowing them to be looked up each time they are needed for a possible solution.

To learn about the CYK algorithm in more detail, the interested reader should see Kasami, T. 1965. An efficient recognition and syntax-analysis algorithm for context-free languages. Scientific report AFCRL-65-758, Air Force Cambridge Research Lab, Bedford, MA.

The CYK algorithm (developed by Cocke, Kasami, and Younger) is a dynamic programming algorithm (see Chapter 3, "Informed Search") and one of the most frequently used techniques in syntactic parsing.

To use the algorithm, the input's grammar must be in **Chomsky Normal Form,** which means that the production rules must take one of two forms: $A \rightarrow BC$, or $A \rightarrow x$. The right-hand side must have two nonterminals, or it must have a single terminal. Chomsky Normal Form is useful in this application because it ensures each nonterminal node will have two children, or it will have a single child, which will be a terminal symbol and a leaf of the tree.

Once the grammar is in Chomsky Normal Form, the CYK algorithm builds a $(n + 1) \times (n + 1)$ matrix, where n is the number of words in the input sentence. Each cell $[i, j]$ in the table contains information about the span of words from position i to position j. Specifically, each cell contains the set of nonterminal symbols that could have produced the words from position i to position j.

The cell $[0, 1]$ contains nonterminal symbols that can produce the first word in the sentence. Similarly, the cell $[1, 2]$ represents the second word in the sentence (the word between position 1 and position 2). This cell contains the nonterminals that could have produced the second word in the sentence.

More complex is the calculation of the cell $[0, 2]$. This cell represents the span between positions 0 and 2. This combined span of words can be broken up into two parts: the first part from position 0 to position 1, and the second part from position 1 to position 2. These two parts are represented by the cells $[0, 1]$ and $[1, 2]$ respectively. The nonterminals in both of these cells are combined in every possible combination, and the algorithm searches for any production rule that could have produced these combinations. If such production rules exist, the nonterminals on the left-hand sides of the rules are placed in the cell $[0, 2]$.

Similarly, the cell $[0, 3]$ describes the span between positions 0 and 3. However, the value for this cell is more difficult to compute because this span can be broken in several different ways. Either it can be broken after position 1, separating it into two parts: the first part between positions 0 and 1, and the second part between positions 1 and 3. Or it can be broken after position 2, separating it into a first part between positions 0 and 2, and a second part between positions 2 and 3.

If it is broken after position 1, then we will use the cells $[0, 1]$ and $[1, 3]$ and combine their nonterminal symbols. If it is broken after position 2, we will use the cells $[0, 2]$ and $[2, 3]$ and combine their nonterminal symbols. We must use both of these partitions to get the total number of nonterminals for cell $[0, 3]$. Continuing in this way, we build the table by using intermediate results from previous cells, until we reach $[0, n]$. This cell represents the words between positions 0 and n, which compose the entire input sentence. Thus, the cell $[0, n]$ contains all the nonterminal symbols that could be used to begin a parse tree for the input sentence. We can use back-pointers in the table to connect the final cell with the intermediate cells that produced it, yielding the correct sequence of nonterminal symbols in a parse of the sentence.

13.4 SEMANTIC ANALYSIS AND EXTENDED GRAMMARS

Chomsky [30] was well aware of the limitations of formal grammars and proposed that language must be analyzed at two levels: the **surface structure,** which can be analyzed and parsed grammatically, and the underlying structure (**deep structure),** which holds the sentence's semantic information. Professor Michie summarized the distinction between surface and deep understanding by analogy to a medical example, with regard to complex computer systems:

> A patient may have a boil (a surface level problem) on his or her bottom and lancing will do to remove the boil. However, if the patient's problem is a cancer (a deep problem) which is rapidly spreading, then no amount of lancing will remedy this problem.[31]

The solution that researchers settled on for this problem was the addition of more knowledge. Knowledge about the deeper structure of sentences, knowledge about the purpose of sentences, knowledge about the case of words, and even knowledge through the exhaustive enumeration of all possible meanings of a sentence or phrase. Possibilities for such complete enumerations became more realistic with the continuing multifold rise in computer speed and memory during the past few decades. We will summarize the extensions to **phrase-structure grammar** (called **extended grammars**) in the following sections.

13.4.1 Transformational Grammar

The task of a **transformational grammar** is to connect the two levels of understanding: syntactic and semantic. Transformational grammars were introduced to make adjustments between tenses, between singular and plural objects, and between active and passive tenses. The method often employed is a dictionary (lexicon) which is used with a context-free grammar to parse the surface structure, together with transformation rules, in order to convert the surface structure to a deep structure.

Sentences that may have distinct structures but are identical in semantic meaning (deep structure) are identified through queries and answered intelligently. In order to accomplish this, two additional components are needed:

Phonological component – that is, the sentence is transformed back from its deep structure to its surface structure in order to sound correct.

Semantic component – this element determines meaning from the deep structure representation.

Recall from Chapter 6: SAM (Script Applier Mechanism), PAM (Plan Applier Mechanism), and MARGIE (Memory, Analysis, Response Generation, and Inference on English; also the name of Roger Schank's mother).

The entire framework, which tries to draw meaning by using transformational grammars, is called **interpretive semantics**. This is not an easy task to accomplish and has drawn some criticism in the past. It will reappear soon in our presentation of Schank's conceptual dependency systems **MARGIE, SAM, and PAM** (see also Chapter 6, "Knowledge Representation").

13.4.2 Systemic Grammar

When we think about how easily natural language can be misunderstood, we often return to the notion of context. Sentences can have distinctly different meanings and interpretations depending on the context in which they occur. One of the early systems to address context was by Michael Halliday of the University of London.[32] The key notion of a systemic grammar is the function or purpose of the language under consideration. This field, focusing on the functional context of language, is called pragmatics. Halliday defined three functions that every sentence normally serves:

1. **Ideational Function – What is the main idea the sentence is trying to convey?**
   In order to accomplish this, several key questions are answered:

   - Who is the actor (object)?
   - What kind of process does the clause describe?
   - Are there other participants such as direct or indirect objects?
   - Are time and place of conditions described?

This approach tries to apply a series of hierarchical choices called "systems" to determine the

2. Structure and mood of a sentence and

3. Sentences are considered from their "interpersonal function," in other words, what the *mood* of the sentence is (often aided by punctuation); and from their "textual function," for example, knowledge of what has come before, the theme of the question or statement, and knowledge of what is new and what is given.

Halliday further classified his grammar by four categories:

1. Units of Language (e.g., clause, group, word, and morpheme)
2. Structure of Units (e.g., subject or predicator)
3. Classification of Units (e.g., role such as verbal for the predicator, and nominal for the subject)
4. System, as described earlier, hierarchical breakdown of sentence components

This approach to language, the study of pragmatics for the context of language, helped make understanding of the meaning of sentences clearer and helped to remove much of the ambiguity inherent in language. Systemic grammar's embedding of a sentence's units within the grammar is called **generative semantics** and was used by Winograd in his highly successful SHRDLU program.

13.4.3 Case Grammars

The case of a noun is determined by the ending which is applied to it. Cases can include nominative, genitive, accusative, dative, and ablative. These endings help the reader identify the function a noun plays in a sentence (e.g., the subject, the direct object, possession, and so on). Nouns therefore carry their own "tag" within a sentence, revealing how they are used. This makes the word order of a sentence less important. This approach (**case grammars**) to the study of language was an extension of Chomsky's transformational grammar and was introduced by Fillmore.

Fillmore, C. J. 1968. "The case for case." In Universals in linguistic theory, ed., E. Bach and R. Harms. New York, NY: Holt, Rinehart, and Winston.

He proposed that noun phrases are always related to verbs in uniquely identifiable ways that indicate the "deep case" of the noun phrase. Fillmore proposed the following deep cases:

Agent – the instigator of the event

Counteragent – the force or resistance against which the action is carried out

Object – the entity that moves or changes or whose position or existence is in consideration

Result – the entity that comes as a result of the action

Instrument – the stimulus or immediate physical cause of an event

Source – the place from which something moves

Goal – the place to which something moves

Experience – the entity which receives or accepts or experiences or undergoes the effect of an action

Verbs were designated as having **case frames**. For example, verbs such as "grow" can be framed as:

[(OBJECT) (INSTRUMENT) (AGENT)]

Case frames for verbs resemble the predicates with associated argument lists in predicate calculus (Chapter 5, "Logic in Artificial Intelligence," and Prolog).

The verb will be "framed" appropriately for how it is used, and this can serve as a template for how sentences are interpreted.

Case frames helped to resolve certain ambiguities that had eluded previous grammars. Contributions of this approach included the following:

1. Ordering of cases so that it is clear which noun is the subject of a sentence (highest ranking).

2. Recognizing legitimate sentence structures, e.g., *I am toasting* and *the bread is toasting* are legitimate, but the sentence *I and the bread are toasting* is not legitimate. This is recognized because *I* and *bread* will belong to different cases.

3. Distinguishing similarities, but not reciprocal (inverse) nature of verb pairs, e.g., *buy* and *sell*, or *learn* and *teach*. Again, case frames helped with this.

Deep cases helped to extract correct and same meaning of sentences that would be structured differently, for example, *The cat knocked over the garbage* and *The garbage was knocked over by the cat*. Case frames did bring some progress, but they also helped to illustrate the difficulties in trying to derive meaning from grammar.

13.4.4 Semantic Grammars

Hendrix, G. and Sacerdoti, E. 1981. "Natural language processing, the field in perspective", Byte 6(9):304–352. Peterborough, New Hampshire.

Semantic Grammar is the work of Gary Hendrix in building the natural language tool LIFER (Language Interface Facility with Ellipsis and Recursion) and the database query system LADDER (Language Access to Distributed Data with Error Recovery), described by Hendrix and Sacerdoti.[33]

Semantic Grammar is represented by three major features:

1. The domain is restricted – thereby LIFER can provide the front end to a variety of applications such as information retrieval and database management.

2. Integrate semantics into the syntax – this is accomplished by the user restricting the range of sentences that can be used for natural language queries. In addition, nonterminal symbols are restricted to a narrowly defined set such as <PERSON> and <ATTRIBUTE>, rather than broad categories such as <NOUN>. After the categories are drawn, an exhaustive enumeration is done for possible terminal substitutions.

3. Excellent user interface – LIFER had a very friendly user interface and included features such as spelling correction, ellipsis, and paraphrase generation.

Questions to LIFER were of the form

(GETPROP 'PERSON 'ATTRIBUTE).

Using a complex search of numerous databases, LIFER could handle a wide range of questions:

- How many home runs did Roger Maris hit in 1961?

- When was Abraham Lincoln born?

- How wealthy is Bill Gates?

- Who founded Apple Computer?

- What hurricane hit New Orleans in 2005?

The performance of these systems was impressive and is a result of the encoding of semantic knowledge directly into its grammar and associated functions. This was accomplished by restricting the problem domain to a large but manageable database.

We conclude our discussion of semantic analysis and its role in NLP by noting that the more specific the knowledge that was added to the system, the better the performance that could be achieved. So, for example, the use of a semantic grammar to write a natural language interpreter would require producing a list of all possible cases for each word. This returns to where we started by noting that language is diabolical—it can be used and analyzed precisely, but some may prefer it to remain deliberately vague and open to interpretation—for example, as in poetry!

13.4.5 Schank's Systems

In Section 6.8, we introduced and discussed Roger Schank's conceptual dependency (CD) system. We discussed how the CD can be used to develop natural language representations for many real-world situations, abstract, mental, and physical transfers, mental concepts, physical states, causality, and more.

MARGIE

The first product of Roger Schank's CD theory was MARGIE. It was developed with Schank's students at Stanford University and combined a parser, a generator, and an inference engine.[30]

The parser could take an English sentence and convert it to a semantic primitive representation. The generator reviewed an internal representation and returned valid English paraphrases of the statement. The inferencer, using 16 rules of inference, generated the implications of the statement in semantic primitive language, and this was sent to the generator, which converted the inferences into English.

Margie could operate in two modes, paraphrase mode and inference mode.

Samples from each mode are shown below:

Inference Mode

INPUT: John told Mary that Bill wants a book.

OUTPUT1: A book about what?

OUTPUT2: Mary knows that Bill wants a book.

OUTPUT3: Bill wants to come to have a book.

OUTPUT4: Bill wants someone to cease to have a book.

OUTPUT5: Bill wants to read a book.

INPUT: John gave Mary an aspirin.

OUTPUT1: John believes that Mary wants an aspirin.

OUTPUT2: Mary is sick.

OUTPUT3: Mary wants to feel better.

OUTPUT4: Mary will ingest aspirin.

Paraphrase Mode

INPUT: John advised Mary to drink the wine.

OUTPUT: John told Mary that drinking the wine would benefit her.

The system might paraphrase the following Input:

INPUT: It is a warm cloudy day.

OUTPUT: The sky is not clear and temperature is high.

For its time MARGIE was an impressive program, but its most serious flaws were:

- It could process only single sentences.
- It demonstrated the problem of "inference explosion." That is, inferences drawn from the original statement could be expanded ad infinitum.

SAM

By 1974, Schank moved to Yale University, where he and Robert Abelson (Professor of Psychology) developed *scripts* (Chapter 6). Scripts helped to solve both of the above mentioned problems with MARGIE. Scripts enabled the easy expansion of sentences into stories. The explosion of inferences was remedied by providing *context* through which some inferences could be validated and others removed. These ideas were implemented in the program SAM and were the PhD thesis work of Richard Cullingford. The internal structure consisted of four parts:

1. A modified version of MARGIE's parser was used to convert the story sentences to CD formalism.
2. A modified version of MARGIE's generator was used to convert CD representations back into correct English.
3. A script applier checked the consistency of the CD representation with that specified in the script.
4. A question-answerer module was included.

Using automobile accident scripts, SAM was capable of reading, paraphrasing, translating, and answering questions on newspaper reports of accidents. An excerpt from a script illustrating this follows: [29]

INPUT

```
Friday evening a car swerved off Route 69. The vehicle struck a
tree. The passenger, a New Jersey man, was killed. David Hall,
27, was pronounced dead at the scene by Dr. Dana Blanchard,
medical examiner. Frank Miller, 32, of 593 Foxon Rd., the driver,
was taken to Milford Hospital by Flanagan Ambulance. He was
treated and released. No charges were made. Patrolman Robert
Onofrio investigated the accident.
```

ENGLISH SUMMARY

```
An automobile hit a tree near Highway 69 four days ago. David
Hall, age 27, residence in New Jersey, the passenger, died. Frank
Miller, 32, residence at 593 Foxon Rd. in New Haven, Connecticut,
the driver, was slightly injured. The police department did not
file charges.
```

SPANISH SUMMARY

Un auto choco contra un arbol cerca de la carretera 69 el viernes
al anochecher. David Hall, de 27 anos, que vivia en New Jersey,
el pasagero, se murio. Frank Miller, de 32 anos, que vivia en 593
Calle Foxon en New Haven, Connecticut, el chofer, quedo un poco
herido. El departamento de policia no acuso a nadie.

QUESTION-ANSWERING OUTPUT

Q1: Was anyone killed?
A1: Yes, David Hall died.

Q2: Was anyone hurt?
A2: Yes, Frank Miller was slightly injured.

Q3: Why was Miller hurt?
A3: Because the automobile hit the tree.

Q4: Did Miller go to the hospital?
A4: Yes, he was in the Milford Hospital.

Q5: How did Miller get to the hospital?
A5: The Flanagan Ambulance Company took him to the Milford
    Hospital.

For its purpose, SAM was excellent, but it could only work with very restrictive stories. The Yale University group's efforts then led to the development of PAM to address these issues.

PAM

PAM, by Robert Wilensky, was a hybrid of the ideas of SAM and TALE-SPIN.[33] In TALE-SPIN, Schank and his students gave the characters of a story certain goals and simulated human planning to meet those goals. The program was then allowed to write its own stories based on the information it had been given.

PAM had its own generator and special vocabulary to enhance the sophistication of its conversations. In addition, because PAM had the plans and goals of each of its main characters available to it, PAM could narrate story summaries from various points of view!

One more CD-based program seems worth mentioning—CYRUS.

CYRUS (Computerized Yale Reasoning and Understanding System) was the PhD work of Janet Kolodner. It was the culmination of the previous CD-based programs, and had some very impressive capabilities and accomplishments:

- It was an attempt to model the memory of a particular individual, the diplomat Cyrus Vance.

- It could learn, that is, continuously change on the basis of new experience.

- It continually reorganized itself to best reflect what it knew. This feature resembles the human capability of "self-awareness."

- It had the capability of "guessing" about events of which it had no direct knowledge.[33]

HUMAN INTEREST NOTES

ROGER SCHANK

Roger Schank (1946 –) is a visionary in Artificial Intelligence, learning theory, cognitive science, and the building of virtual learning environments. He is CEO of Socratic Arts, a company whose goal is to design and implement learning-by-doing, story-centered curricula in schools, universities, and corporations.

Roger Schank.

In the early 1970s, while an assistant professor at Stanford, Schank was the first to get computers to be able to process typewritten everyday English language sentences. In order to do this, Schank developed a model for representing knowledge and the relationships between concepts that enabled his programs to predict what concepts might be coming next in a sentence. This spawned an entire field in psychology devoted to determining how people make inferences from what they hear.

After moving to Yale in 1974, Schank worked on developing computers to read newspaper stories. His work was heavily funded by the U.S. Department of Defense, which was interested in trying to make computers able to predict world trouble spots by reading the news and analyzing it. He built the first newspaper-story-reading program in 1976. Five years later, Schank was made Chairman of Computer Science at Yale and ran their Artificial Intelligence lab.

In order to enable computers to know enough about the world to comprehend the semantics of a sentence, Schank came up with the notion of a script. Scripts were needed to keep the inferences that computers made from exploding exponentially. For example, a computer could understand that what you order is what you eat in a restaurant if it had a set of expectations about what happened in a restaurant (the script). Scripts were a powerful idea that enabled Schank's machines to read about any subject that was well structured. Psychologists began testing people to see if they operated with scripts, as Schank had suggested, and the evidence was overwhelming that Schank had discovered something important about people even though he was working in computer science. This work culminated in a book, written with Robert Abelson, on the subject utilized by social scientists to this day—*Scripts, Plans, Goals and Understanding: An Inquiry into Human Knowledge Structures*.

Schank's most famous book, *Dynamic Memory: A Theory of Reminding and Learning in Computers and People*, dealt with learning through the remembrance of events and their results. This theory of learning via a "schema" was in opposition to traditional learning theory.

Schank had a successful career in academia and business in the 1990s and 2000s. After founding AI related-Departments at Northwestern University and Carnegie Mellon University, as well as running the Department of Computer Science at Yale University, Schank became the Distinguished Career Professor in the School of Computer Science at Carnegie Mellon University and the Chief Educational Officer of Carnegie Mellon West. Dr. Roger Schank is the Executive Director and founder of Engines for Education. He is also the Chairman and CEO of Socratic Arts, a company that delivers Story-Centered Curricula to schools and businesses. In an advisory capacity, he is also Chief Learning Officer of Trump University.

13.5 STATISTICAL METHODS IN NLP

Previous sections of this chapter focused on sentence parsing techniques (e.g., syntax, Section 13.3) and attempts to decipher meaning (semantics, Section 13.4). These methods are often insufficient, however, to process ambiguous sentences. For example, a sentence can have several different parse trees, making it difficult to choose the best parse and infer the correct meaning.

One way of approaching this problem is to assign probabilities to each parse, choosing the parse tree with the highest probability. Thus, probabilistic and statistical methods have become the norm in language processing over the last two decades.

During the past 25 years or so, NLP research has adopted statistical methods as the dominant approach to solving long-standing problems in the field. Eugene Charniak (See Section 13.9), a leading researcher at Brown University, calls it a "statistical revolution" in his wonderful paper at *Artificial Intelligence at 50,* Dartmouth College, July 13–15, 2006.[34]

13.5.1 Statistical Parsing

Probabilistic parsers assign a probability to each parse, choosing the most likely parse for a particular input sentence. To do this, context-free grammars can be augmented with conditional probabilities for each production rule.

For example, if the grammar includes a nonterminal symbol A, and it is the left-hand side of three production rules in the grammar, then each of these production rules can be assigned a probability, based on the likelihood of each expansion of A. The sum of the three probabilities must be 1, and similarly, for any other nonterminal B, the sum of probabilities for B's production rules must be 1.

Thus, for a production rule A → CD [p], the conditional probability p represents the likelihood of A being expanded to produce CD. In other words, p is the probability of the expansion CD, given the left-hand side A.

Extending this concept to parse an entire sentence, we can calculate the probability of a parse by multiplying the probabilities for each rule used to expand the nodes in the parse tree. If there are *n* nonterminal nodes in the parse tree, then there are *n* production rules that were used to produce these nodes. For each of these *n* production rules, there is an associated probability, and we multiply these n probabilities together to calculate the total probability of the parse:

$$P(\pi, s) = \prod_{c \in \pi} p(rule(c))$$

To use probabilistic parsers, we must know the probability for each production rule in the grammar. There are two ways of assigning probabilities to the rules of a grammar. If a treebank such as the Penn Treebank is available, we can simply count the number of times a nonterminal symbol A was expanded with a particular production rule. For example, for the production rule A → CD, the probability could be calculated with the equation,

$$\frac{Count\ (A \to CD)}{Count\ (A)}$$

If a treebank is not available, then we must train the system on a corpus of sentences. The parser starts off with equal probabilities for each rule, parsing the sentences in the corpus and calculating the probabilities for these parses. Based on the results of the first parse, the parser adjusts the probabilities for each rule, using the adjusted parameters to parse the sentences again, and so on, until the parser is trained with the most appropriate probabilities for each rule.

Currently, most probabilistic parsers have been augmented to take other syntactic and semantic features into consideration. Of particular note is the Collins parser, [35] which belongs to more complex types of systems known as probabilistic lexicalized parsers. In a lexicalized grammar, each nonterminal is marked with a lexical head and the head's part-of-speech tag. The head is the most important word in the phrase produced by a nonterminal.

Essentially, the lexicalized grammar is an augmented version of a context-free grammar, in which each nonterminal is made specific to its headword. By having so many more nonterminals, the lexicalized grammar can make each production rule specific to the headword it produces. Thus, there are many copies of a simple production rule, one copy for each possible headword and head tag combination.

As an example of **lexicalized statistical parsing**, Charniak gives the following example: Consider the probability of the rule: "VP → VERB NP NP." This construction represents sentences in which there is a verb followed by two nouns. For example, "Tom gave Jill a racket." The probability of the rule $p(VP \rightarrow VERB\ NP\ NP\ |\ VP, V=racket) = 0.003$, a very low probability. However, the probability of the main verb "gave" is nearly a factor of 10 higher, giving: $p(VP \rightarrow VERB\ NP\ NP\ |\ VP, V=gave) = 0.02$. Here we can see how combined probabilities can effectively contribute to the ability to make correct parses. Probability is, in effect, being converted to knowledge.

Parsers of the kind discussed here were known to be about 73% accurate, but with additional information of the kind referred to in the example above, they are now able to achieve an accuracy of well over 90%. The next section describes how a statistical "advantage" is sought when dealing with language as sound (speech) understanding.

13.5.2 Machine Translation (Revisited) and IBM's Candide System

During earlier periods, **machine translation** was done mainly by nonstatistical approaches. The three main methods of translation were: (1) **direct translation**, which is the word-by-word translation of the source text; (2) **transfer approaches**, which use structural knowledge and syntactic parsing; and (3) **interlingua approaches**, which translate the source sentence into a general representation of meaning before translating this representation into the desired language. None of these approaches was very successful.

The transition to statistical methods began in the early 1990s with the development of IBM's Candide system. This project was hugely influential in shaping subsequent research in machine translation, and statistical methods began to dominate the field in the following years. IBM used probabilistic algorithms, which they had already developed in the context of speech recognition, applying these algorithms to their research in machine translation.

The statistical approach to machine translation is based on ideas from the noisy channel model. Using this approach, a sentence in the source language is considered to be a noisy version of a sentence in the target language. We must calculate the most probable sentence in the target language that corresponds to the noisy input of the source sentence. For example, if we are translating from French into English, then French is the source language and English is the target language. Therefore, we will calculate the probability $P(E|F)$, or the probability of a particular English sentence, given the noisy input of the French sentence.

Using Bayes' Rule (see Chapter 8, Section 8.4), we can express this probability by the equation,

$$P(E|F) = \frac{P(F|E)P(E)}{P(F)} .$$

We want to maximize this probability by choosing the most probable English sentence from all possible English translations. We can disregard the denominator P(F) because the French sentence will be fixed as a constant for each possible English translation.

$$P(E|F) = \text{argmax}_E \, P(F|E) \, P(E)$$

Now using this equation, we only need to calculate two things:

- P(F|E), which is the probability of the French sentence, given the English translation,
- and P(E), which is the probability of the English sentence.

P(E) is the likelihood of the sentence occurring in English, and this can be estimated by using probabilistic N-gram models with a large corpus of English text. P(F|E) is the probability of the French sentence, given the English sentence, and it requires a phrase-by-phrase alignment between French sentences and English sentences. Phrase-alignment algorithms used by IBM were defining influences on the research in machine translation, providing it with the statistical methods to move beyond the less consistent approaches of earlier research.

13.5.3 Word Sense Disambiguation

Statistical methods are also used in word sense **disambiguation**, a crucial task in natural language processing. Words can have many different meanings, depending on the context, and this ambiguity is the source for much of the difficulty in natural language processing.

For example, the word *table* can be used to describe a piece of furniture, or it can be used to refer to a graphical representation of data. Countless other ambiguous examples can be found (see Section 13.1.1), and the correct meaning of the word must be inferred from the context in which it occurs. Ide and Veronis[36] point out that word sense disambiguation was first articulated by Weaver with regard to machine translation:

> If one examines the words in a book, one at a time as through an opaque mask with a hole in it one word wide, then it is obviously impossible to determine, one at a time, the meaning of the words. [...] But if one lengthens the slit in the opaque mask, until one can see not only the central word in question but also say N words on either side, then if N is large enough one can unambiguously decide the meaning of the central word. [...]
>
> The practical question is: "What minimum value of N will, at least in a tolerable fraction of cases, lead to the correct choice of meaning for the central word?" [1, p. 640]

Using supervised learning algorithms, systems can be trained to recognize the correct sense of a particular word. With a large training set of text, the system can learn the associations between a word and the context clues which typically surround it. For example, the word table will tend to have a certain set of words around it when it is used to refer to furniture, as compared to another set of words around it when it is used to describe a tabular representation of data.

Feature extraction is the process by which the key features of the accompanying text are identified for their predictive value in determining the correct sense of the word. Often, the context clues occur at very specific positions relative to the word in question. For example, the word *remote* can often be found one position before the word *control*, combining to form *remote control*. Similarly, the word *table* can often be found two positions before the word *contents*, forming the phrase *table of contents*. A **collocation** is a word or sequence of words typically found at a set position relative to the word in question. These positions can be noted by the system as it learns the typical associations between words, helping the system to overcome the difficulties of word sense disambiguation.

13.6 PROBABILISTIC MODELS FOR STATISTICAL NLP

Statistical methods involve the computation of a probabilistic model, and the model is used to assign probabilities to each possible outcome for a given task. For example, in statistical parsing, each production rule is assigned a probability by counting its occurrence in a corpus of text.

In this section, we provide an example of a probabilistic model used in NLP applications, together with the algorithm that computes the most likely outcome based on the model.

13.6.1 Hidden Markov Models

Hidden Markov Models (HMMs) are statistical models used in many NLP applications. Like finite state automata, HMMs are represented as directed graphs in which vertices represent different states of the computation, and the arcs represent transitions between states. Similar to weighted finite state automata, HMMs include probabilities for each arc, representing the probability of moving from one state to another.

A Markov chain is a weighted finite state automaton, in which the input uniquely determines the transitions through the automaton. In other words, each input produces exactly one path through the automaton. The probability of this input is calculated by multiplying the arc probabilities in the path.

We are able to multiply the probabilities because of the **Markov property** of these models. The Markov property allows us to disregard preceding events when estimating the probability of a transition. The probability of a transition depends only on the current state (state 2) and the following state (state 3), and does not depend on previous transitions in the sequence. This simplifies the estimates of probability, and it allows us to calculate the total probability of a sequence by multiplying the probabilities along each arc.

Like Markov chains, HMMs are specified by a set of states, and a set of transition probabilities describing the probability P_{ij} of moving from state i to state j for each i and j. When describing a path through the model, however, we do not know the sequence of states. We can only describe a path in terms of the output produced along the path.

HMMs include a set of output observations O, and a set of observation probabilities B. For each observation and each state, there is an associated probability $b_i(o_t)$, expressing the likelihood of the observation o_t being produced at time t as output from state i. Less formally, the observations are the output that can be produced, and the observation probabilities represent the likelihood of generating a particular output from a particular state. We make the simplifying assumption that there is one output observation produced for each state transition. Thus, if the output consists of five observations, then we know five states must have been included in the path, because there are five output symbols produced.

To make this more concrete, we can use a real-life example in which the underlying "states" are hidden and must be inferred from the observable output. Imagine a student who is answering questions on a computer-generated standardized test. The computer produces questions of varying difficulty, mixing together simple questions with more difficult questions. The student does not know if a question is intended to be simple or difficult, and he tries to infer the difficulty of a question from the amount of time he spends to find an answer.

For example, if he takes only 1 minute to answer a question, he is reasonably confident the question was intended to be simple. However, if he takes 3 minutes to answer a question, he feels the question was intended to be more difficult. He can only infer the intended level of difficulty from the amount of time he spends on a question.

In this example, the hidden states are **Simple** and **Difficult**, and the observable output is the number of minutes taken on a question. The output observations are the set $\{1, 2, 3\}$, representing 1 minute, 2 minutes, or 3 minutes to answer a question.

Figure 13.2 shows the two states **Simple** and **Difficult**, together with the start state and the end state.

The model includes the transition probability for each arc between states. To complete the model, we need to include the observation probabilities:

$P(1|\text{Simple}) = 0.8$

$P(2|\text{Simple}) = 0.1$

$P(3|\text{Simple}) = 0.1$

$P(1|\text{Difficult}) = 0.1$

$P(2|\text{Difficult}) = 0.2$

$P(3|\text{Difficult}) = 0.7$

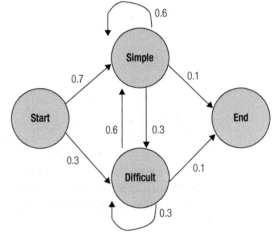

Figure 13.2
HMM for test questions.

These numbers are the conditional probabilities of spending a certain number of minutes on a question, given the intended level of difficulty. For example, the probability P(1|Simple) is the probability of spending 1 minute on a simple question. Similarly, P(3|Difficult) is the probability of spending 3 minutes on a difficult question.

If we are given a sequence of output observations 2 1 1 3, we find the most likely sequence of states by calculating the probability for each sequence and choosing the one with highest probability. Because there are two states and four observations in this sequence, there are 2^4 or 16 possible sequences of states.

One possible sequence of states is **Simple Simple Simple Difficult**. The probability for this sequence of states can be calculated by multiplying the transition probabilities for the path:

$$P_{\text{startS}} \times P_{SS} \times P_{SS} \times P_{SD} \times P_{\text{DEnd}} = .7 \times .6 \times .6 \times .3 \times .1 = 0.00756$$

P_{startS} is the transition probability of moving from the start state to the **Simple** state, P_{SS} is the transition probability of looping from the **Simple** state to the **Simple** state again, P_{SD} is the transition probability of moving from the **Simple** state to the **Difficult** state, and so on.

Once we multiply the transition probabilities, we need to take the observation probabilities into account for this sequence. The observation probabilities in this sequence are as follows:

$$P(2|Simple) \times P(1|Simple) \times P(1|Simple) \times P(3|Difficult) = .1 \times .8 \times .8 \times .7 = 0.0448.$$

For the total probability, we multiply the product of observation probabilities by the product of transition probabilities:

$$P_{startS} \times P_{SS} \times P_{SS} \times P_{SD} \times P_{DEnd} \times P(2|Simple) \times P(1|Simple) \times P(1|Simple) \times$$
$$P(3|Difficult) = 0.7 \times 0.6 \times 0.6 \times 0.3 \times 0.1 \times 0.1 \times 0.8 \times 0.8 \times 0.7$$

$$= 0.000338688.$$

This product is the probability for one possible sequence of states **Simple Simple Simple Difficult**. We do not know if this is the correct sequence of states, and we must try all the different sequences that are possible.

Real-world applications have many more states and many more observations, and these calculations become impractical for such large numbers. More feasible methods involve dynamic programming algorithms, in which intermediate results are stored in a table so calculations do not have to be duplicated.

13.6.2 The Viterbi Algorithm

The **Viterbi algorithm** is a dynamic programming algorithm used to find the most probable sequence of states in an HMM. This algorithm creates a table in which each cell represents the probability of being in a particular state after seeing a certain number of output observations.

In our example, the states can be numbered so that the start state is state 0, the **Simple** state is state 1, the **Difficult** state is state 2, and the end state is state 3. Now the table can be represented with a two-dimensional array Viterbi [ ] [ ].

In this array, a cell such as Viterbi [1] [1] represents the probability of being in state 1 after seeing the first output observation. Remembering that our output sequence was 2 1 1 3, the first output symbol in this sequence is 2. Thus, this cell represents the probability of producing a 2 as the first output observation while reaching state 1, the **Simple** state.

To calculate Viterbi [1] [1], we use the transition probability P_{startS} for the transition from the start state to the **Simple** state, and we multiply P_{startS} by the observation probability P(2|Simple), which is the probability of producing a 2 as output from the **Simple** state:

$$Viterbi [1] [1] = PstartS \times P(2|Simple) = .7 \times .1 = 0.07$$

Similarly, the cell Viterbi [2] [1] represents the probability of being in state 2, the **Difficult** state, after producing the first observation. This probability is the product of PstartD and P(2|Difficult):

$$Viterbi [2] [1] = P_{startD} \times P(2|Difficult) = .3 \times .2 = 0.06$$

Once these initial cells have been calculated, we store these values in the table, using them to calculate the remaining cells. In the next column, Viterbi [1] [2] represents the probability of producing the second output observation from state 1. The second observation in this sequence is a 1, so this cell represents the probability of producing a 1 as the second observation while reaching state 1, the **Simple** state.

To calculate this cell, we multiply the probability stored in each cell in the preceding column by the transition probability from its state to the **Simple** state. Then we multiply each of these products by the observation probability of producing a 1 from the **Simple** state. We place the maximum of these values in Viterbi [1][2]:

$$\text{Viterbi [1] [1]} \times \text{PSS} \times \text{P(1|Simple)} = 0.07 \times 0.6 \times 0.8$$

$$= 0.0336.$$

$$\text{Viterbi [2] [1]} \times \text{PDS} \times \text{P(1|Simple)} = 0.06 \times 0.6 \times 0.8$$

$$= 0.0288.$$

Thus, Viterbi [1] [2] will contain 0.0336, the maximum of these 2 computations. More generally, in a HMM with n states, we make n computations, one for each state in the previous column, and we place the maximum in the current cell. When we reach the cell representing the final observation and the end state, this cell will contain the total probability of the most likely sequence of states.

We can trace through this sequence of states by keeping a backpointer [ ] [ ] array to store our path so far. This trace will give us the sequence of states with the highest probability of producing the output sequence.

13.7 LINGUISTIC DATA COLLECTIONS FOR STATISTICAL NLP

Statistical methods require large amounts of data in order to train probabilistic models. In language processing applications, large collections of text and spoken language are used for this purpose. These collections consist of huge numbers of sentences labeled with syntactic and semantic information by human annotators. In this section, we describe the most important collections used in statistical NLP over the last decade.

13.7.1 The Penn Treebank Project

As we have learned in earlier sections, given a context-free grammar it is possible to parse every sentence. That is, we can build a **corpus** in which every sentence is syntactically annotated with a parse tree. A systematically annotated corpus such as this is called a **treebank**. Treebanks have proven very useful in empirical studies of syntactic phenomena.[1, p.404]

A number of treebanks have been created during the past 40 years that can automatically parse sentences, following which humans contribute with hand-correction (e.g., the Brown corpus described in Section 13.2). The Penn Treebank has produced treebanks from the Brown, Switchboard (for standard telephone conversations), ATIS, and Wall Street Journal corpora of English. Treebanks have also been produced in other languages such as Arabic and Chinese. Other treebanks include: the Prague Dependency Treebank for Czech, the Negra treebank for German, and the Susanne treebank for English.[1, p. 404]

In Marcus et al. (1993) it is stated: "A distinction is sometimes made between a corpus as carefully structured set of materials gathered together to jointly meet some design principles, and a collection, which may be much more opportunistic in construction. We acknowledge that from this point of view, the raw materials of the Penn Treebank form a collection."

```
(S1 (S (NP (DT The) (NNP Bush) (NN administration))
(VP (VBD said)
(NP (NNP Wednesday))
(SBAR
(SBAR (IN that)
(S (NP (DT the) (NNP United) (NNPS States))
(VP (MD would)
(VP (VB join)
(NP (DT the) (NNPS Europeans))
(PP (IN in)
(NP (NP (NNS talks))
(PP (IN with) (NP (NNP Iran)))
===> (PP (IN over)
(NP (PRP$ its) (JJ nuclear) (NN program)))))))))))
(, ,)
(CC but)
(SBAR (ADVP (RB only))
(IN if)
(S (NP (NNP Tehran))
(ADVP (RB first))
(VP (VBD suspended)
(NP (NP (PRP$ its) (NN uranium) (NNS activities))
(, ,)
(SBAR (WHNP (WDT which))
(S (VP (AUX are) (VP (VBN thought)
(S (VP (TO to)
(VP (AUX be)
(NP (NP (DT a) (NN cover))
(PP (IN for)
(S (VP (VBG developing)
(NP (JJ nuclear) (NNS arms))))))))))))))))))
(. .)))
```

Figure 13.3
Parse for the lead sentence of the June 1, 2006 edition of the NYT.

The Penn treebank project started around 1989 and has produced treebanks in multiple languages at various stages. There have been Treebank I,[24] Treebank II,[37] and Treebank III releases for the English language.

Treebank 1 consists of 4.5 million words and was constructed between 1989 and 1992 for part-of-speech (POS) tagging. It has also been annotated for skeletal syntax syntactic structure.

Charniak [34] gives an impressive practical example of how far NLP with these treebanks has gone. He gives the following sentence from the June 1, 2006 edition of the New York Times:

The Bush administration said Wednesday that the United States would join the Europeans in talks with Iran over its nuclear program, but only if Tehran first suspended its uranium activities, which are thought to be a cover for developing nuclear arms.

Charniak [34] summarizes what the Penn WSJ parser has done in Figure 13.3 with the following comments:

Given current parser accuracy (92%) and length of the sentence (44 words and punctuation) we would expect several errors. The only mistake is the attachment of the clause which starts "only if…" We believe it should be conjoined with the 'S' that starts "the United States…" not the SBAR that starts "that the United…".

This latter analysis is the one found by the parser. It is also reasonable, but to our mind not as plausible.

The next few sections describe more recent systems that exploit the capabilities of database, statistical, and web technologies.

13.7.2 WordNet

WordNet is a lexical database that stores words organized in synsets, or sets of synonyms. Each synset represents one lexical concept, accompanied by a short definition of the concept it expresses, and is linked to all semantically related synsets.[38] WordNet is a popular tool, widely used in the field of AI and NLP in particular. The WordNet database and software tools have been licensed and are available online at *http://wordnet.princeton.edu*. The English version of WordNet has served as a basis for databases for other languages such as EuroWordNet, MultiWordNet, and BalkaNet.

Bentivogli and colleagues propose to extend WordNet with a new data structure called *phraset* that will represent a set of free combinations of words (as opposed to lexical units), which are frequently used to express a certain concept. Bentivogli and colleagues think that phrasets will be useful for knowledge-based word alignment of parallel corpora to find correspondence between lexical units in one language. This will free combinations of words in another language and word sense disambiguation in both monolingual and multilingual environments.

Two basic lexical units that compose WordNet's synsets are words and multiwords, which are idioms or restricted collocations. An idiom is a term or phrase, the meaning of which cannot be understood from the literal definitions of its constituents. None of the constituents of an idiom can be substituted with a synonym. A restricted collocation, on the other hand, is "a sequence of words which habitually co-occur and whose meaning can be derived compositionally."[38] Idioms and restricted collocations are different from free combinations of words, which are simply combinations of words that follow the general rules of syntax.[39] Free combinations are not considered lexical units and therefore do not compose synsets in WordNet.

There are phrases in every language that are frequently used to represent a single concept, and which are not idioms or restricted collocations. Examples include such Italian phrases as "andare in bicicletta," which means "to bike" in English and "punta di freccia," which means "arrowhead." Bentivogli and colleagues propose to extend the WordNet model with phrasets to include such phrases. The members of a phraset are referred to as recurrent free phrases. Phrasets could be extremely useful in a multilingual environment when the source language uses a lexical unit to express a concept whereas the target language does not, or vice versa.

13.7.3 Models of Metaphor in NLP

For a Natural Language Processing system to be effective, it must be able to deal with metaphors. This task can be divided into two parts: metaphor recognition and metaphor interpretation. In the literature of linguistics and philosophy, we can find four main views on the theory of metaphor. Katerina Shukova [40] did a thorough study of models of metaphor in NLP. She studied a number of models including:

1. the comparison view [41]
2. the interaction view [42, 43]
3. the selectional restrictions violation view [44, 45] and
4. the conceptual metaphor view. [46]

One of the first attempts to implement a system to identify and interpret metaphorical expressions automatically was done by Dan Fass. The system was called met* (pronounced met star) and was able to distinguish between literalness, metonymy, metaphor, and anomaly. Metonymy is figure of speech in which a thing or concept is called the name of something related in meaning with that thing or concept. While a metaphor works by drawing a similarity between the two concepts across different domains, metonymy works by drawing a contiguity (association) between them within the same domain. For example, "Hollywood" is a metonym for the US film industry. This district of Los Angeles contains most of the major American film studios, but there's nothing similar between the location itself and the film industry. Met* works in three stages: first it would determine the literalness of a phrase using selectional preference violation as an indicator. This refers to the Preference Semantics approach for word-sense disambiguation as developed by Yorick Wilks, where the "most coherent" interpretation of a sentence is determined based on the maximum number of internal preferences of its parts. If it was found to be nonliteral, the phrase would be tested for metonymy using a hand-coded set of metonymic relationships. If it fails to find a metonymy, then a knowledge base is searched for a suitable analogy to distinguish a metaphorical relation from an anomalous one. One problem with the selectional preference approach is that while some expressions may be metaphorical, they may still not violate preference selection. For example, the sentence "Idi Amin is an animal" is literally valid and will not violate the preference selection, but is clearly meant metaphorically. And on the other hand, a sentence may violate preference selection, but may be neither metaphorical nor metonymical.

Some other approaches to metaphor identification are worth mentioning. Goatly came up with a system for identifying metaphors by picking up on language cues such as "so to speak." By itself, it may not be sufficient, but could be a part of a larger system. Peters and Peters [47] mined WordNet, an English lexical database, looking for systematic polyseme, which they found has a strong correlation to metaphorical or metonymic expressions. While Fass' work relied on a hand-coding of metonymic and metaphoric relationships, Zachary Mason's CorMet system [48] was the first attempt to automatically discover source-target domain mappings. CorMet analyzes large corpora of domain-specific documents and learns the preferences of the characteristic verbs of each domain for a particular type of argument in a particular role. For example, CorMet would collect texts from the LAB domain and a FINANCE domain in both of which "pour" is a characteristic verb. "Pour" selects strongly in the LAB domain for objects of liquid type and in the FINANCE domain for money. From this a concept mapping liquid-money is inferred. Birke and Sarkar [49] developed a TropFi system which uses a sentence clustering approach for nonliteral language recognition. This idea originates from a similarity-based word sense disambiguation method developed by Karov and Edelman. [50] The method employs a set of seed sentences with annotated senses. It then computes the similarity between a sentence containing the word to be disambiguated and all of the seed sentences and then selects the sense corresponding to the annotation in the most similar seed sentences.

While Birke & Sarkar and Fass focus strictly on verbs, Krishnakumaran and Zhu's [51] approach deals with verbs, nouns, and adjectives. For nouns, they use the hyponym (is-a) relationship in WordNet to check if a phrase is metaphorical. If it is not hyponymous, then the phrase is tagged as metaphorical. At the same time, they also calculate bigram probabilities of verb-noun and adjective-noun pairs, but also consider all the hyponyms/hypernyms of the nouns. If the pair is not found in the data with a frequency above a certain threshold then the phrase is tagged as metaphorical. At the same time that Fass was working on metaphor recognition with met*, Martin [52] developed a Metaphor Interpretation, Denotation and Acquisition System (MIDAS). MIDAS relies on a database of conventional metaphors organized into a hierarchy. Given a metaphorical expression, it searches for it in the database. If it's not able to find it, it abstracts to more general concepts and performs the search again. If found, it attaches the sought-after metaphor to the parent in the hierarchy. In 2008, Veal and Hao developed a knowledge base called Talking Points and an associated reasoning framework called SlipNet. Talking Points is comprised of a set of characteristics of concepts belonging to source and target domains and related facts about the world mined from WordNet and the web. SlipNet is a framework that allows insertions, deletions, and substitutions of such characteristics in order to find a connection between the source and target domains.

The trend of metaphor research has followed the same path as the field of NLP in general, that is to to move away from the hand-coded knowledge methods of the 80s and early 90s to more robust corpus-based statistical methods. The latest developments in the lexical acquisition technology will in the near future enable fully automated corpus-based processing of metaphor. Future research would benefit greatly from a standardized metaphor annotation procedure and creation of a large publicly available metaphor corpus.

13.8 ■ APPLICATIONS: INFORMATION EXTRACTION AND QUESTION ANSWERING SYSTEMS

In the previous section, we described statistical methods in NLP, contrasting these methods to the symbolic approach of formal syntax and semantics. Often, both approaches are used in tandem, and a single application must make use of both symbolic and statistical methods.

Perhaps the most well-known application of NLP methods is in information extraction (IE) and question answering systems, now commonly used for searching the web. Let us consider an example:

Before you would make the decision to buy AIG's stock, however, you would want to locate articles on the Internet that will back up your "belief" that AIG's stock will go up. In order to do this you will have to find text that includes "AIG," "Government Bailout," stock, and a number of other keywords that will help you to find the relevant information about what AIG's stock future is likely to be.

> **SIDEBAR**
>
> **EXAMPLE**
>
> In 2008 the US government bailed out the multinational insurance conglomerate AIG (American International Group) to the tune of $85 billion. You assume that since none other than the US government has supported such a large company (essentially ensured its survival), it might be a good time to buy its stock which has dropped from $70 a share to $2 a share. You are fairly confident that the government bailout will guarantee that AIG's stock value will rise from $2.

This is precisely the kind of task that is suitable for an information extraction system to solve. IE is actually a combination of a number of techniques that we have already addressed, including finite state methods, probabilistic models, and syntactic chunking. In this section, we describe the techniques used to build an information extraction and question answering system.

13.8.1 Question Answering Systems

Question answering systems find the best answer to a user's query by searching through a collection of documents. Often, the collection of documents can be as large as the Web, or it can a set of related documents owned by a particular company. Because the number of documents can be huge, it is essential to find and rank the most relevant documents, breaking these files down into the most relevant passages, and finding the correct answer to the question by searching within these passages.

Thus, question answering systems must accomplish three tasks: (1) process the user's question, turning it into a suitable input query for the system; (2) retrieve the documents and passages most relevant to the query; and (3) process these passages to find the best answer to the user's question.

In the first step, the user's question is processed by identifying keywords and eliminating non-essential words. Initially, a query is formed from the keywords, and then the query is expanded to include any synonyms of the keywords. For example, if the user's question included the keyword car, the query would be expanded to include *automobile* along with *car*. In addition, morphological variants of keywords are also included in the query. If the user's question included the word *drive*, then the query would also include *driving* and other morphological variants of the verb *drive*. By expanding the list of keywords in the query, the system maximizes the chances of finding relevant documents.

Retrieving these documents is the second step in the process. This task is known as information retrieval (IR), and IR can be performed with a vector space model, in which vectors are used to represent word frequencies. For example, let's use a small document for the purposes of explanation, and let's assume there are three words in this document. The word frequencies in this document can be represented by the vector (w_1, w_2, w_3), in which w_1 is the frequency of the first word, w_2 is the frequency of the second word, and so on. If the first word occurs 8 times, and the second word occurs 12 times, and the third word occurs 7 times, then the vector for this document would be (8, 12, 7).

Of course, in a real-world example, there would be thousands of words, not just three words as in our small document. In real applications, the vector has thousands of dimensions, one dimension for each word in the collection of documents. Each document is assigned a vector to represent the words that occur within the document. Many entries will be 0 in this vector, because many words will not occur in a particular document. Similarly, a query from the user is assigned a vector, and most of the entries will be 0, because the query does not contain many words compared with the entire collection of documents. However, many of these 0s do not have to be stored in the vectors because hashing and other forms of representation are used to simplify the vectors.

Once a vector is assigned to a query, this vector is compared to the vectors of all the documents in the collection. The closest matches are found by viewing the vectors in multidimensional space. To calculate the distance between two vectors, we use the angle between them, and we compute the cosine of this angle.

The cosine of the angle between two vectors can be calculated by using the normalized dot product of the two vectors. A higher value denotes a closer match between the query vector and a document vector. When the two vectors are identical, the cosine is equal to 1, and when the two vectors are completely different from each other with nothing in common, the cosine is equal to 0. Thus, the documents most relevant to the query are identified by finding the highest values for the cosine function, using the angle between the query vector and the document vector.

Once the most relevant documents have been retrieved, these documents are divided into passages of manageable size. Passages that do not contain any keywords or potential answers are discarded, and the remaining passages are ranked by their likelihood of containing an answer.

At this stage, we are ready for the third and final step of the question answering process: extracting an answer from the ranked passages.

HUMAN INTEREST NOTES

LARRY R. HARRIS

Larry Harris.

Larry R. Harris (1948–) has a long history of involvement with and contributions to AI database systems and natural language processing. His "diffusion of AI research techniques into commercial products," as he calls it, began with his PhD thesis at Cornell University (1970) titled *A Model for Adaptive Problem Solving Applied to Natural Language Acquisition*. His early publications include: *The Bandwidth Heuristic Search,*

User-Oriented Data Base Query with the ROBOT Natural Language Query System, and Experience with INTELLECT: Artificial Intelligence Technology Transfer. Harris developed ROBOT in 1975, when he founded the AI Corporation which eventually employed over 80 people. INTELLECT, the successor to ROBOT, provided a unique English language interface to enable the query of database systems. The approach of ROBOT called for mapping English language questions into a language of database semantics that is independent of the content of the database. In this way, the system worked in a "movable mini-world" because the semantic primitives were fixed, but the area of discourse varied with the content of the database. Thus, by making only dictionary changes, a student grade file could be interfaced with an employee file and a data dictionary.

He was also the chief architect of KBMS (Knowledge-Base Management System), an expert system tool, and InfoHub, a relational engine for accessing nonrelational mainframe data.

Harris was a professor in the Mathematics Department at Dartmouth College in 1972; there was no computer science department at that time. He was instrumental (together with this author) in developing the Dartmouth Computer Chess Program, which (in 1973) was the first program to not lose to Northwestern University's Program (NUCHESS), the then-dominant computer chess program in the United States in the 1970s (see Chapter 16 for more on Computer Chess).

He founded EasyAsk as Linguistic Technology Corporation (LTC) in 1994, and is the author of its EasyAsk and English Wizard products. EasyAsk, which was spun off from Progress Software in early 2009 and is now a standalone corporation once again, focused on the continuation of Dr. Harris' vision to innovate and take a leadership role in the areas of e-Commerce, Operational Business Intelligence, and Search, while using natural language to create a user experience that makes its products truly usable by knowledge workers and end users alike.

Dr. Harris had the following to say, as early as 1984 in the AAAI Magazine:

> Our orientation is product-based; we want to sell the same product repeatedly. We want it to be general purpose so that it can be used in a wide variety of application domains and we want to remove as much of the AI mystique as possible from the process of using it. In terms of market positioning we have

made the commitment to be market-driven, to find out what the real needs of the marketplace are in terms of the problem we are trying to solve, and to choose the appropriate technology to solve that problem. We also made the commitment to interface to existing software and to work within the common commercial data processing structure, but, at the same time, not to try to reproduce the existing data base technology, graphics technology, and so forth.

The perspective described above demonstrates a deep appreciation of what AI systems need to be able to do in order to serve the business and commercial world effectively.

Relevant Publications by Larry R. Harris:

1. (1977). A system for primitive natural language acquisition. *International Journal of Man-Machine Studies* 9:153–206.

2. (1978). ACM SIGART Bulletin Status report on the Robot natural language query processors. 66 (August): 3–4.

3. (1977). User oriented database query with the ROBOT natural language query system. *International Journal of Man-Machine Studies* 9:697–713.

4. (1981). INTELLECT on demand. *Datamation* 27(12):73.

5. (1980). Using the database as a semantic component to aid in the parsing of natural language database queries. *Journal of Cybernetics* 10:77–96.

6. ROBOT: a high performance natural language processor for data base query, ACM SIGART Bulletin [doi>10.1145/1045283.1045309] April 20, 2010.

7. (1984). Experience with INTELLECT: Artificial Intelligence Technology Transfer. *AI Magazine* 5(2): 43–50.

APPLICATION BOX

EASYASK

One of Dr. Larry Harris' contributions to AI was the founding of EasyAsk® in 1994. EasyAsk delivers software for information discovery and analysis. EasyAsk e-Commerce is the retail industry's most intuitive Web site search, navigation, and merchandising software. It helps merchandisers to deliver immediate ROI through increased conversion rates, sales revenue, and customer satisfaction.

EasyAsk is widely adopted by business users and consumers who use the business language they employ every day to find pertinent information, regardless of the information source or location.

EasyAsk technology is used today by leading retailers, manufacturers, financial services institutions, government agencies, and pharmaceutical and healthcare organizations around the globe.

EasyAsk allows business users to ask ordinary English questions to get answers from relational databases. Common business questions can often require complex SQL, so it is often the case that users cannot be self-sufficient in getting the answers they need without the help of a natural language system. The following three examples are very simple business questions that happen to require complex SQL. Figures 13.4 (a), (b), and (c) present an example of how EasyAsk works:

Problem: Find customers that are returning products at a much higher rate than other customers. The challenge here is that you must look at returns in both an absolute and a relative basis. The customers you really want to find are those that order a great deal and return a great deal. (See Figure 13.4c)

The complexity of the SQL comes from the need to use a "Having clause" to restrict on a subtotal and the need to express the sum of a ratio (the percent returned) as a ratio of the sums.

Note: The user's English input is shown on the upper left of the screen with the answer below it. The SQL generated by EasyAsk is shown at the bottom. The Report matches on the right side of the screen represent reports, possibly from other systems, that EasyAsk feels might also be relevant to the user's question.

Problem: Sales of one product are often related to sales of related product. Effective marketing campaigns can be directed at customers who are buying the first product but not the related product. For example, if we could ask "What customers bought tables, but not chairs?" we could market chairs to them. Unfortunately, this requires SQL with subselects, which are too difficult for business users to deal with on their own. Oddly, conventional query tools don't help users put together queries with subselects. It's a major advantage of natural language systems that they can expand a user's range to include questions that require this complexity.

Problem: Every business loses customers; it is extremely helpful to find these customers so that they can be marketed to and to help prevent them from leaving the customer base. An answer to "What customers had an order in the last 12 months but didn't have an order in the last 12 weeks" would provide a list of customers that a company might be losing. Unfortunately, answering this question also requires a query with subselects.

```
SQL   ECHO

SELECT DISTINCT "CustomerName" as "Customer" FROM "Customers" WHERE exists(SELECT * FROM "Products", "InvoiceLineItems", "ProductSubCategories" WHERE
("SubCategoryName"="Tables") and "Customers"."CustomerKey"="InvoiceLineItems"."CustomerKey" and "Products"."ProductKey"="InvoiceLineItems"."ProductKey" and
"ProductSubCategories"."SubCategoryCode"="Products"."SubCategoryCode") and not exists(SELECT * FROM "Products", "InvoiceLineItems", "ProductSubCategories"
WHERE ("SubCategoryName"="CHAIRS") and "Customers"."CustomerKey"="InvoiceLineItems"."CustomerKey" and "Products"."ProductKey"="InvoiceLineItems"."ProductKey"
and "ProductSubCategories"."SubCategoryCode"="Products"."SubCategoryCode")
```

Figure 13.4a
Example of interactive EasyAsk.

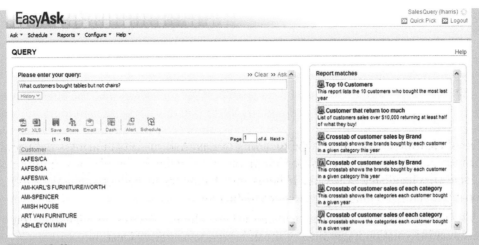

Figure 13.4b
Example of interactive sales query with EasyAsk.

Business problems:
Too many products are being returned
Sales of one product are fine, but sales of a companion product are too low
Some sales reps are underperforming
Losing too many customers

Dashboard showing that returns are high
Too many products are being returned
customer returns – 2 reports
    Note: report search & ad hoc query
    Note: help with date item names & questions Look at both reports: return rate is key
show the sales, returns and return rate last year of each customer with sales over $10,000
show the sales, returns and return rate last year of each customer with sales over $10,000 and a return rate above 50%
share this report: Find it by "customer returns"
Line graph returns monthly last year for HENNEN (/ALEXANDRIA)
show the sales, returns and return rate this year of each brand
    Note: share this report
    Diffculty: all other systems sum(return rate)!
    EasyAsk transforms sum of a ratio into ratio of the sums
Rumor. sales of chairs is down, relative to tables
Compare the unit sales of tables to chairs last year/quarter/month.
What customers bought tables but not chairs?
    Show SQL
    Diffculty: SQL requires a subselect
Some sales reps are underperforming
Show the growth in sales of each sales rep from last year to this year.
    Diffculty: SQL requires temp tables to compute % growth!
Rumor: Losing too many customers
What percent of customers didn't have an order in the last year?
How many customers had an order in the last 12 months but had no order in the last 12 weeks.
Diffculty: SQL requires 2 sub-selects!
Add to dash board

Figure 13.4c
Business report for EasyAsk.

13.8.2 Information Extraction

To extract an answer, we search through these passages, looking for specific patterns that are typically found in text surrounding the answer. Often, answer phrases are related to question phrases in clearly recognizable patterns in a sentence.

For example, let us assume the user asked the question: *What is a syllogism?* The query is made up of the keyword *syllogism*, and we will perhaps be able to find this keyword next to possible answers in very specific patterns and locations. A common pattern is: **<AP> such as <QP>**, in which AP represents an answer phrase, and QP represents a question phrase. This pattern is a regular expression that can be used to search through the passages for possible answers.

Basically, we will search for sentences in which the word *syllogism* is preceded by '*such as*,' and we will be reasonably confident that 'such as' will be preceded by an answer. For example, let's assume we find the following sequence of words in a passage: A *logical argument such as syllogism*. This sequence contains the question keyword syllogism, and this keyword is preceded by the answer phrase *A logical argument*. Thus, the pattern captures a common relationship between an answer and the question keyword: often the keyword is defined by an answer phrase followed by *such as*, followed by the question keyword.

Many other patterns can be used. In another commonly found pattern, the answer phrase is an appositive separated by commas from the question phrase: **<QP>, a <AP>**. This pattern may be found in a sequence of words such as *Syllogism, a form of deductive reasoning*, in which the answer phrase is an appositive separated by commas from *syllogism*. Based on the answer phrases we found, we know syllogism is *a logical argument* and *a form of deductive reasoning*, and we can begin to combine these phrases into an answer to the user's question.

13.9 PRESENT AND FUTURE RESEARCH (ACCORDING TO CHARNIAK)

Eugene Charniak [34] notes that there is ongoing work to extend capabilities in many directions. Efforts to make parsing more accurate have been somewhat successful, with the record for the Penn WSJ treebank now at 92%. This means about one in three errors have been eliminated with no loss in speed. Other research associated with speed has accelerated parsing from 0.7 seconds a sentence to 0.2 seconds a sentence. Research is spreading to languages other than English, although few treebanks have the size of Penn WSJ. Other languages tend to depend more on case endings (See Section 13.4.3) of nouns and this may require new techniques. Now that syntactic parsing has been accomplished with some degree of success, more attention can be paid to "deep structure" issues.

Charniak believes that the future of NLP must be to concentrate on meaning. Hence, there must be a shift from concentrating on the correct parse of a sentence to the correct meaning of a sentence. This will still require many years of work, with the likelihood that efforts will continue to go into a long series of representations, each adding information about aspects of meaning, while other components of a sentence that are not necessary for meaning can be removed.

Charniak concludes, "Statistics has taken over AI because it works." [34, p. 7] It has worked for machine parsing and speech recognition, and even for where this chapter began—machine translation. He notes that Google® already has a pretty good machine translation from Arabic and Mandarin to English, with other languages soon to follow, all by statistical methods. Charniak predicts that in the future, AI will be dominated by statistical approaches. That is because he believes that probability theory is the best way to make use of multiple sources of information. Examples of AI areas successfully employing statistical approaches include machine learning and robotics, and they are likely to spread to other areas.

13.10 SPEECH UNDERSTANDING

Speech Understanding is a functionality that enables a system to understand spoken input from a microphone and respond back correctly. These systems are also known as voice recognition systems. There are several different types of Speech Understanding systems that exist, and during the past two decades or so there have been dramatic improvements. As of today, many of us live surrounded by such software and devices. It is remarkable to witness how far speech understanding systems have progressed. A reason for this progress may be that speech understanding was one of the first areas studied in artificial intelligence and also that it is in high demand. This section is prepared by Mimi Lin Gao based on a thesis by Sona Brahmbhatt.[58]

Speech recognition software may be so popular because it is easier for us to speak than to type. Speaking commands is faster than clicking buttons with a mouse or a touch pad. To open a program such as "Notepad" in Windows would require a click on Start, then Programs, Accessories, and finally Notepad. Four or five clicks can easily be required. Speech recognition software allows the users to simply say, "Open Notepad" and the program opens, saving time and sometimes frustration.

The development of speech understanding systems began with ideas from machine translation. However, attempts at solving basic problems in syntax proved more challenging than had been assumed; this was before problems in semantics, accent, and inflexion were tackled. Three early methods of speech translation are **direct translation**, **transfer**, and Interlingua. The direct translation method interprets "word by word" of the source as words, attempting to translate them. The transfer method uses structural knowledge and syntactic parsing. The Interlingua method first translates the sentence into a representation of the meaning and then translates the sentence into the preferred language.[1]

13.10.1 Speech Understanding Techniques

There are several techniques used for recognizing speech understanding patterns. The Pattern Recognition approach is a combination of pattern training and pattern comparison. The Hidden Markov Model (see Section 13.6.1) is applied to sounds or words to accomplish accurate pattern training recognition. The direct comparison approach occurs when unknown words are tested with the patterns learned from training the system, using algorithms such as The Viterbi algorithm (Section 13.6.2) and the Feature Extraction approach.[54]

Part-of-Speech Tagging

A Hidden Markov Model uses **Part-of-Speech Tagging (POST)**. The eight part-of-speech tags are noun, verb, pronoun, preposition, adverb, conjunction, participle, and article. The importance of part-of-speech tagging is that it provides much information regarding a word and its context. It is usually applied to a sequence of words using a microphone. "Knowing whether a word is a possessive pronoun or a personal pronoun can tell us what words are likely to occur in its vicinity" [1, p. 123]. POST is valuable when a portion of a sentence or word is distorted. Voice recognition software can use part-of-speech tags to find the best match for the missing word. This enables us to estimate the best tag sequence. [54, p. 133–139]

Bayesian Inference

Bayesian inference (see Section 8.4, Example 8.3) is a special case where part-of-speech tagging is used for the Hidden Markov Models. Bayesian inference is used to determine part-of-speech tagging for the observations usually in order of words or a sentence. In other words, each word of the sentence is classified for proper tagging. To correctly classify a word, all possible sequence tags are applied. Out of all tags, one tag will be rated the most probable for that word.

Bayesian inteference uses Bayes' Rule (See Figure 13.5) to calculate a probability equation that returns the prior probability and the probability of likelihood that the word's POST is correct. "The two terms are the prior probability of the sequence $P(t_1^n)$ and the likehood of the word string $P(w_1^n | t_1^n)$" (ibid., p. 139–140).

$$\text{Bayes' Rule} = r_1^n = \arg\max_{t_1^n} \overbrace{P(w_1^n | t_1^n)}^{\text{likelihood}} \overbrace{P(t_1^n)}^{\text{prior}} \quad {}^{55,\ p.\ 140}$$

Figure 13.5
Bayes' Rule

There are two "simplifying assumptions" made by an HMM tagger once Bayes' Rule is computed. The first is that the word is independent and does not depend on its surrounding words. The second assumption is that the word is dependent on previous tag words. The HMM tagger helps estimate the highest probable tag-sequence.[55]

Bigram Equation

A Bigram equation is formulated by using the HMM "simplifying assumptions." This equation includes tag **transition** probabilities and word **likelihood**, which help determine the most probable tag. The tag transition probability equation is $P(t_i | t_i - 1|)$ which stands for the "probability of a tag given the previous tag" (ibid. Computing the likelihood by employing a Corpus would help us determine the probability for the tag transition. The **Corpus equation** which is used to calculate the tag transition is $P(t_i | t_i - 1|) = P(NN|DT)$, in which NN stands for common nouns and DT stands for Determiners, which refers to words such as "a, the." The Corpus equations use words labeled with their part of speech to count the number of determiner words before nouns that are followed by determiners.[55]

The Feature Extraction Approach

The **feature extraction approach** determines the predictive value of a word by identifying key features of the accompanying text. Feature extraction helps overcome disambiguation with words by extracting relevant information from the speech.

The feature extraction approach uses sets of **feature vectors**, the product of analog-to-digital conversion, to understand sounds for proper sound labeling. These vectors signify the data of a signal in a little time window.[54]

Analog sound waves are captured through a microphone where the analog waves are converted into digital signals. **Sampling Rate** and **Quantization** are the two steps involved during the conversion of analog to digital. When a signal's amplitude is measured at a certain time, it is called *Sampling rate.* There must be at least two sampling rates taken to accurately measure a sound wave. Thus, each cycle of a sound wave has a negative and a positive state. [1, p. 295].

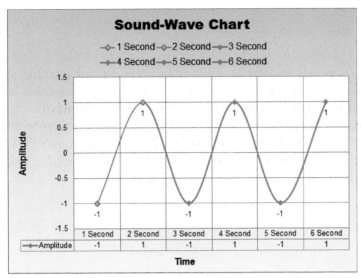

Figure 13.6
Sound wave chart.

In the Sound Wave chart (Figure 13.6), the 1st to the 2nd second is one cycle. It is better to have more than two samples in a cycle to increase amplitude accuracy. The **Nyquist Frequency** represents the maximum frequency for a particular sampling rate. In human speech, the frequency is usually below 10,000 Hz. Thus, a sampling rate of 20,000 Hz is needed for accuracy. Telephone frequency is less than 4,000 Hz, since speech is transmitted by switching networks; therefore, a sampling rate of 8,000 Hz is needed to transmit frequency on a telephone bandwidth. Microphone speech uses wideband to transmit a frequency at a 16,000 Hz sampling rate. (ibid., p. 295).

Amplitude measurements are stored in 8-bit to 16-bit integers where quantum size and the values that appear closer to this quantum size are signified as identical. This process is called Quantization. The quantized waveform equation is x[n] (see Figure 13.7) representing a digitized sample.

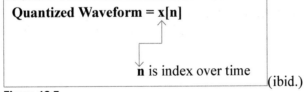
(ibid.)

Figure 13.7
Quantized waveform equation.

Mel Frequency Cepstral Coefficient

The most well-known and respected feature extraction technique is the Mel Frequency **Cepstral Coefficient (MFCC)**. There are seven steps to complete the MFCC process: (1) Preemphasis, (2) Window, (3) Discrete Fourier Transform, (4) Mel Filter Bank, (5) log, (6) Inverse Discrete Fourier Transform, and (7) Deltas and Energy as illustrated in Figure 13.8. [56] We will now discuss each of these features.

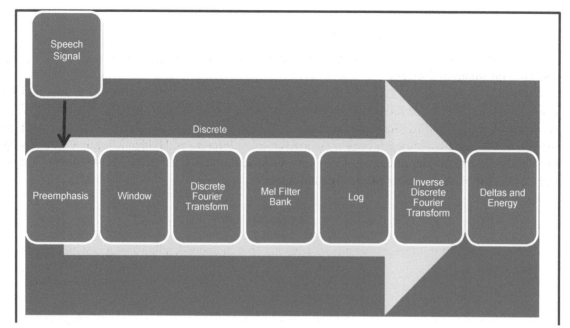

Figure 13.8
MFCC: Process

1. **Preemphasis** boosts the energy to the maximum value. In the voice spectrum, vowel segments have a greater amount of energy in a lower frequency than in a higher frequency, called *spectral tilt*. Boosting the high frequency improves the results of the acoustic model and phone recognition accuracy.

2. *Windowing* allows the extraction of the spectral features of a part of a conversation. Since speech is made of non-stationary signals, the spectrum rapidly changes. Windowing actually stationizes the signals that are captured in a small window. This portion of the window consists of a zero and a non-zero region where waveforms are extracted. MFCC extraction employes a *Hamming Window* where the values near the window boundaries are leveled out to zero. This avoids signals that are cut off shortly at each end which usually happens in a rectangular-shaped window.

3. The *Discrete Fourier Transform* extracts spectral data from the window. This process identifies the signal's energy level at each frequency band at a discrete time [1, p. 298].

4. The *Mel Filter Bank* collects the energy for each band of frequency including ten filters less than 1,000 Hz. The rest of the filters are above 1,000 Hz. One thousand hertz is an important number in a Mel Filter, since humans are not able to hear frequencies higher than 1,000 Hz. (ibid., p. 299).

5. Log is a process which takes the log of each mel spectrum result. The log process helps the feature estimates reduce the level of sensitivity created by the voice input device. It is also caused by the distance between a user and the voice input device. (ibid.)

6. Inverse of the Discrete Fourier Transform helps to increase speech recognition accuracy by detecting all the filters in a waveform. Filters represent the actual position of the vocal tract.

7. **Deltas** demonstrate the change between each frame and are added to each of the features to improve accuracy, since a speech signal is not constant. (ibid., p. 301)

It is straightforward to envision that extracting these seven features will help improve the speech understanding process.

In summary, we can see that Speech Understanding Systems entail a number of factors in their evaluation including voice recognition, adaptation, dictation, commands, personalization, training, costs, and system features. Some of the common techniques used to develop Speech Recognition Systems include Part-of-Speech Tagging using Bayesian Inferences, Hidden Markov Chains using the Viterbi algorithm, identification of Bigrams, Feature Extraction using the Mel Frequency Cepstral Coefficient with a number of prerequisite substeps.

13.11 APPLICATIONS OF SPEECH UNDERSTANDING

This section features three examples of working speech understanding systems which illustrate the tremendous progress that has been made in this field during the past few decades. The first versions of such systems developed in the early 1990s cost thousands of dollars and were prohibitively expensive for most individuals. A dramatic indication of the progress in this area is the fact that today it is possible to buy such a system for under $100, and it will be nearly 100% accurate with a voice that has been trained.

HUMAN INTEREST NOTES

DR. JAMES MAISEL AND ZYDOC

James M. Maisel, MD
Chairman, Zydoc Medical Transcription.

Since its inception in 1993, ZyDoc's mission has been to increase the efficiency of physicians through the use of software technology and services to improve patient care and outcomes, lower malpractice risk, and maximize reimbursement. In 1993, ZyDoc released one of the first multimedia electronic medical records (EMR) as envisioned by the Institute of Medicine. The prototype was purchased by the Department of Defense and helped serve as a paradigm for the industry. ZyDoc immediately recognized the problem of the data-entry bottleneck inherent in the EMR and has been pursuing solutions since then. The founder, James Maisel, M.D., a retina surgeon, became involved in medical informatics and served as the Chairman of Healthcare Open Systems and Trials (HOST) in 1998. ZyDoc left the EMR arena in 2000 to develop other solutions that would be more efficient for physicians.

Early on, ZyDoc promoted speech-recognition technology and created language models for every medical specialty. These were bundled and sold by Dragon Systems Naturally Speaking 4.0 Medical in 2000 and are widespread in the industry. Realizing that speech recognition was only a tool that needed to be embedded within other applications, ZyDoc developed an award-winning multimodal EMR solution in conjunction with Toshiba that allowed physicians to enter information via dictation, touch screens, keyboard, or mouse. Usability and support issues for speech recognition limited the success of this EMR, and in 2002 ZyDoc turned its attention to medical transcription. ZyDoc's medical transcription infrastructure platform was ranked third in competition at TEPR in 2004, and has been licensed to public and private transcription companies. Leveraging this platform for its own use, ZyDoc has grown its transcription business to a nationwide level with a reputation for ease-of-use, high accuracy, fast turnaround time, and full-featured service backed by a 24/7 ZyDoc Operations Center.

Recognizing an industry-wide problem for medical informatics due to tremendous increase in security concerns and difficulty in software implementation in physician and hospital environments, ZyDoc.com, the software division of the company, released Bulletproof Messenger (BPM) in 2009. BPM is a new generation of file transfer software that obviates the need for administrative privileges and bypasses network, security, and firewall constrictions within offices. This application allows physicians with no technology expertise to transmit audio, imaging, and other data files up to 2 GB in size securely and easily. When used in combination with ZyDoc's proprietary TrackDoc Web-based object management services, workflow is customizable to accommodate the file transfer requirements of virtually any size healthcare facility. Over 2000 physicians completed beta testing of the software that was released at the HIMSS meeting in April 2009.

13.11.1 Dragon's NaturallySpeaking System and Windows' Speech Recognition System

For her 2013 MSc thesis in Management of Information Systems, Sona Brahmbhatt did a comparative study of Dragon's NaturallySpeaking System and Microsoft's Windows Speech Recognition System. [58] Below is a summary of her work prepared by Mimi Lin Gao.

Today, almost everyone owns a smartphone with an Apple or Android operating system. These devices have speech recognition functionality, giving users the capability to speak their text messages without typing a single letter. Navigation devices have also added speech recognition capabilities, allowing users to speak destination address(es) or just say "home" to navigate to their home, instead of typing. This is very helpful if one is unable to use a keypad on a small window due to spelling difficulties or vision problems.

Two leading commercially available speech recognition systems are Nuance's **Dragon NaturallySpeaking Home Edition™** software, which understands dictation and follows customized commands by providing the user with capabilities for navigation, interpretation, and website browsing; and Microsoft's **Windows Speech Recognition™** software, which understands spoken commands and is also used as a navigation tool. It allows users the ability to select links and buttons, and choose from a numbered list.

In her thesis,[58] Sona Brahmbatt compared and evaluated these two systems based on their positive features, weak points, and their profile customization, as well as a voice training tutorial provided for first-time users.

User Profile Creation and Voice Training

The user profile process is very important since a user's voice is learned and adapted to by his/her accent. This also allows the system to only focus on the user's voice and channel out most of the background noises. Dragon NaturallySpeaking and Microsoft Speech Recognition both allow the user to create multiple profiles for different people using the computer.

Dragon NaturallySpeaking (DNS) User Profile

The DNS profile creation process asks for name, age, region, accent, and the type of speech device that will be employed. This process also adjusts the user's microphone and performs a quality check on the microphone sound for better accuracy.

The training prompts the user to read a passage onscreen to test sound levels, voice, and accent so that the system is able to recognize the user's voice by picking a passage that he/she reads.

The accuracy training process goes through the user's applications such as Word and Outlook to add a personalized vocabulary. It scans for unknown words from sent e-mails, documents, and contact names.

Microsoft's Speech Recognition (MSR) User Profile

Microsoft's Windows 7 Professional Speech Recognition System requires the same steps to set up a user profile that are required by the DNS System. They primarily include setting up the microphone and performing voice training. The interface is not as user-friendly as the DNS interface, but it gives the user a chance to access and modify many settings. The wizard screen allows the user to choose the most appropriate microphone for best results in a given setting and to adjust the volume of the microphone. The last step necessary to complete a profile is Speech Recognition Voice Training, allowing the system to adapt to the way a user speaks.

Dragon NaturallySpeaking Interactive Tutorial

The DNS Interactive Tutorial process helps users understand the basics in order to dictate and increase efficiecy. This tutorial is broken down into segments which explain the basics on Dictating, Correction Menu, Spelling Window, Editing, and Learning More.

Microsoft Speech Recognition Training

The tutorial is broken down into segments which are also broken in sections. The process prompts the user to use the commands after every segment of the tutorial and to complete a final lab that requires all the learned commands. This tutorial asks the user to delete a word or correct a sentence during the tutorial so that he/she is more likely to remember more commands and know how to use them better.

Positive Features and Weak Points

The DNS interface is user-friendly (Figure 13.9). The left panel of the figure displays all the commands that can be used, and it is very helpful for users who are new to the software and do not remember all the commands. The panel also displays tips for usage and can be minimized if not needed. There is a panel on the top bar that displays messages and what has been said, and it's very helpful when correcting mistakes. The top panel also gives access to Profile, Tools, Vocabulary, Modes, Audio, and Help.

DNS is able to format text by saying "Select <word>", "bold," or "underline" using Excel or Microsoft Word. It is relatively easily to open Firefox and browse yahoo.com by saying, "Open Firefox," "Search Web for Yahoo.com" using DNS. The DNS system weak point is that it takes about two minutes to load the user profile.

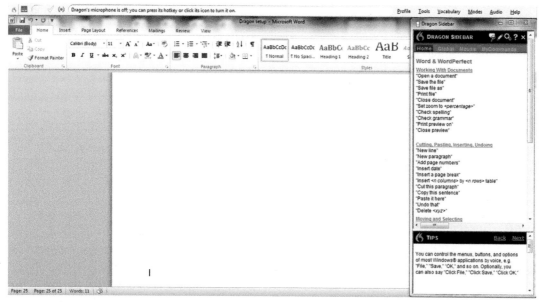

Figure 13.9
Dragon NaturallySpeaking Interface

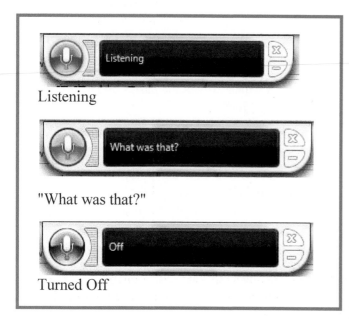

Listening

"What was that?"

Turned Off

Figure 13.10
Microsoft speech recognition panel.

The MSR panel is very simple and easy to understand. All the messages are displayed within the panel. The microphone icon (Figure 13.10) on the panel lets the user turn on and off speech recognition. The panel is small and can be easily moved to diverse locations on the screen or minimized when not needed. This interface is not as user-friendly as DNS, since very few options are provided on the panel.

In MSR, the user would have to select the word, say "Font Tab" and then say "bold" or "underline." In MSR, the user has to say "Open Firefox" and spell out the entire website URL. However, MSR is fast when loading the user profile. Also, "Show Numbers" is a positive feature in MSR in which all application options are numbered and easier to navigate through by just selecting the number of the application.

Overall we found that DNS was more user-friendly in terms of its interface, although MSR was more efficient when in training mode.

APPLICATION BOX

13.11.2 CISCO's VOICE SYSTEM

Speech Enabled Auto Attendant (SEAA) Design: Using Application Intelligence to Deliver Superior Voice Recognition

Business owners and employees today conduct business worldwide 24 hours a day using seemingly infinite combinations of tools: phones, voice messaging, e-mail, fax, mobile clients, and rich-media conferencing. However, these tools are often not used as effectively as they could be due to various reasons such as Information Overload, Misdirected Communications, Technical Difficulties, and Insufficient Training. As unified communications solutions integrate applications, phones, and computers, speech recognition plays an increasingly important role in the way we interact with these devices and applications. Speech recognition frees our hands and lets us control our unified communications experience with spoken commands instead of memorized, menu-controlled clicks, keystrokes, and button pushing.

Yet speech recognition solutions, for a variety of reasons, have failed to evolve to maximize the effectiveness of unified communications solutions. In particular, many Automated Attendant products have added speech recognition to improve the user experience and increase customer satisfaction by allowing customers to use natural language to command the attendant to direct their calls. However, the many alternative solutions contain underdeveloped application intelligence which does not deliver a time-saving, customer-satisfying experience. Some of the shortcomings in many SEAA solutions can be attributed to the fact that there are numerous approaches to designing the solution. A typical SEAA solution is made up of three key components:

1. Speech-enhanced user interface
2. Speech engine
3. The directory (or grammar)

The Cisco solution contains six components:

1. Speech-enhanced user interface	4. Advanced disambiguation
2. Speech engine	5. Names-tuning linguists
3. The directory (or grammar)	6. Dynamic dictionary

Advanced Disambiguation

This is a process to validate the dialogue which a caller uses when making a request through the system. A user tells the system he would like to reach an employee named "Jim Smith." When multiple employees have the same name, the speech engine begins the "advanced disambiguation" process.

1. Jim Smith (Marketing, Chicago, Ill.
2. Jim Smith (Marketing, San Jose, Calif.
3. Jim Smith (Manufacturing, location unknown
4. Jim Smith (Product Management, San Jose, Calif.

Advanced disambiguation adds intelligence to the user interface, learning from past disambiguations and applying reason to reduce your time spent (and level of frustration) connecting with the people you are trying to reach.

Competing SEAA Products

Presents these results to you through a dialogue such as "Press 1 for Jim Smith in Marketing, Press 2 for…" or "Did you mean Jim Smith in Chicago? Press 1…" This approach fails in most organizations, not because you have to work your way through all four results the first time you participate in this dialogue, but because there is no change in the procedure after the 100th time you are presented with this dialogue. For as long as you speak "Jim Smith," you will always have to tolerate the same interaction. Before long you will fall back to dialing numbers, meaning the SEAA product failed to deliver any value.

Name-Tuning Linguists

This product collects the results of disambiguations along with your actions, sorting the information and routing the records to linguists. A linguist can then accurately determine the source of the error—whether information might have been missing from the grammar, the name was mispronounced, or noise contributed to the problem. Timely corrections can then be made and transmitted back to the grammar, tuning the directory.

Dynamic Dictionary

As employees join your organization, move locations, and add new contact numbers, the application will allow administrators to easily reflect these changes in the master dictionary in real time.

Figure 13.11
SEAA architecture with advanced disambiguation, names tuning, and dynamic dictionary.

http://www.cisco.com/en/US/prod/collateral/voicesw/ps6789/ps5745/ps2237/white_paper_c11-468855.html

Reference

Cisco Systems, Inc. 2008. Speech enabled auto attendant design: Using application intelligence to deliver superior voice recognition. Cisco.com. <http://www.cisco.com/en/US/prod/collateral/voicesw/ps6789/ps5745/ps2237/white_paper_c11-468855.html >.

13.12 ■ CHAPTER SUMMARY

Chapter 13 covers the exciting challenges posed by trying to program a computer to understand natural language. First the problems of language and ambiguity are introduced (Section 13.1). The history of the field is covered across the past seven decades in Section 13.2, based on the periodic breakdown presented in the classic work by Jurafsky and Martin. [1]

Formal grammars introduced by Chomsky in the 1950s, which are important for sentence parsing and their implications, are explained in Section 13.3. In addition, the complexities of understanding meaning are described with examples of semantic analysis and extended grammars (Section 13.4).

The transition from symbolic methods to statistical NLP is explained in Section 13.5, involving the use of probabilistic models such as HMMs (Section 13.6), and requiring large collections of linguistically annotated data (Section 13.7).

We revisit several of these methods as exemplified in information extraction and question answering systems, a defining example of an NLP application (Section 13.8). The chapter continues with a discussion of the present and future of NLP according to Professor Eugene Charniak.

The authors would like to express sincere thanks to Professor Dragomir Radev of the University of Michigan for his suggestions on how this chapter could be improved, and which systems and methods were important to include, and how it could be more pertinent to contemporary developments in the field. This led to inclusion of certain specific subsections of Sections 13.5, 13.7, and 13.8. We would also like to thank and acknowledge Harun Iftikhar (Columbia University) for writing Section 13.2 and Section 13.6, as well as Sections 13.3.2 and 13.5.1.

Inclusion of a number of the specific topics covered in 13.2 and 13.5—Noisy Channel Models (13.2.1) and Machine Translation (Revisited) and IBM'S Candide System (13.5.2), as well as the CYK Algorithm (13.3.2) and the Collins Parser (13.5.1) —were specific suggestions of Professor Radev's.

New additions to this chapter are Sections 13.7.3 on Metaphor prepared by Daniil Agashiyev, Section 13.10 on Speech Understanding prepared by Mimi Lin Gao (basen on Sona Brahmbhatt's 2013 thesis), and the Applications Boxes in Section 13.11 prepared by Mimi Lin Gao (13.11.2 on Nuance's Dragon NaturallySpeaking and Microsoft's Speech Recognition System) and CISCO's Speech Recognition System (SEAA) prepared by Oleg Tosic.

Questions for Discussion

1. Describe some of the typical ambiguities of language.

2. Explain why language can be diabolical.

3. What were the goals of machine translation?

4. Have they been accomplished after some 50 years?

5. Research what Henri Kucera did to build the Brown Corpus.

6. Describe briefly the six periods of Natural Language Processing.

7. Describe five classes of understanding in terms of language.

8. Describe the Chomsky Hierarchy of Grammars.

9. Give an example of a regular grammar.

10. Describe two features of Prolog that make it suitable for NLP.

11. What is a transformational grammar?

12. What is a systemic grammar?

13. What is a case grammar?

14. What is a semantic grammar, who developed it, and for what system?

15. Describe the features of a finite state transition network.

16. What is the CYK Algorithm and how does it work?

17. What is an HMM and how is it different from a Markov chain?

18. What were the features of Schanks' MARGIE, SAM, and PAM systems?

19. Describe when and how statistical systems became prevalent in NLP systems.

20. What was one of the main efforts that led to the success of this approach?

21. What is the noisy-channel model?

22. Describe some of the main elements of Information Extraction.

23. Describe the Penn Treebank Project.

24. What does Charniak see as the future of NLP and AI?

Exercises

1. Explain the kind of difficulties that machine translation encountered.

2. Write two context-free grammars to generate this sentence: "Time flies like an arrow."

3. Have a field day in parsing two of Yogi Berra's famous phrases:

   "It's getting late early"; and "That place is getting too crowded so nobody goes there anymore."

   What are the syntactic and semantic issues here?

4. What was the concept behind the development of extended grammars?

5. Describe how natural language processing has turned from the early ideals of AI researchers—clearly trying to distinguish syntax from semantics—to more recent approaches?

6. Obtain a copy of the early ELIZA program and run several pages of conversation with her. You should include reference to "computers," family (mother, father, etc.), and perhaps use harsh language.

   What patterns do you observe?

7. Winograd observes that the problem of determining the correct time context can be seen with the following sentences:

   a. Many rich people made their fortunes during the depression.

   b. Many rich people lost their fortunes during the depression.

   c. Many rich people worked in restaurants during the depression.

   Consider the question: "When were the people rich?" and justify your answer for each of the sentences.

8. Experience indicates that the average programmer produces N lines of documented, debugged code per day, on the average, for which N is some number less than 10. High-level code is typically n_1 times as efficient as assembly code (i.e., a given job requires $1/n_1$ times as many lines of code as lower level code) and Prolog is typically n times as efficient as high-level language where n_1 and n_2 are in the range 4 to 10. Find evidence supporting these

numbers and interpret your results in terms of the implications of NLP for programming productivity.

9. Write as many interpretations as you can of the sentence:

"Tom saw his dog in the park with the new glasses."

10. Bar-Hillel was astonished that no one had ever pointed out that in language understanding there is a world-modeling process going on in the mind of the listener. In what ways is this observation related to the basic hypothesis of conceptual dependency theory?

11. Identify the different senses of the verb "roll" in the following sentences, and give an informal definition of each meaning. Try to identify how each different sense allows different conclusions to be made from each sentence (you may use a dictionary).

We rolled the log onto the river.

The log rolled by the house.

The cook rolled the pastry with a large jar.

The ball rolled around the room.

We rolled the piano to the house on a dolly.

12. Consider the following CFG that generates sequences of letters:

```
S -> a X c
X -> b X c
X -> b X d
X -> b X e
X -> c X e
X -> f X
X -> g
```

a. If you had to write a parser for this grammar, would it be more efficient to use a top-down or bottom-up approach? Explain why.

b. Trace the approach of your choice on the input bffge.

13. Consider the following grammar and the sentential forms it could produce. Draw a parse tree to demonstrate how the output strings below may be generated.

$S \rightarrow aAb \mid bBA$ $A \rightarrow ab \mid aAB$ $B \rightarrow aB \mid b$

a. aaAbb

b. bBab

c. aaAbBb

14. Explain the difference between traditional Markov Chains and the Hidden Markov Model.

15. Explain the trends in NLP during the past 10–20 years. What are the challenges of Information Extraction?

Keywords

case frames	Hamming Window	parse
case grammars	HMM	Penn Treebank
Chomsky hierarchy	ideational function	phonological component
Chomsky Normal Form	information extraction	phrase-structure grammars
collocation	interlingua	pragmatics
context-free grammars	interpretive semantics	preemphasis
corpus	inverse of discrete Fourier	probabilistic
corpus equation	Transform	quantization
deep structure	lexical	reference resolution
deltas	lexicalized statistical parsing	SAM
determiners	logic-based systems	sampling rate
direct translation	machine translation	semantic component
disambiguation	MARGIE	semantics
discourse	Mel Filter Bank	spectral tilt
discourse modeling	Mel Frequency Cepstral	stochastic
discourse modeling paradigm	Coefficient (MFCC)	surface structure
discrete Fourier Transform	Met*	syntax
ellipsis	mildly context sensitive	transfer
enrollment	languages	transformational grammar
extended grammars	morphology	transition probability
feature extraction approach	natural language understanding	treebank
feature vectors	noisy channel model	Viterbi Algorithm
finite automaton	PAM	windowing
generative semantics	part-of-speech tagging (POST)	

References

1. Jurafsky, D. and Martin, J. 2008. *Speech and Language Processing,* 2nd ed. Upper Saddle River, NJ: Prentice Hall.

2. Turing, A. M. 1936. On computable numbers, with an application to the Entscheidungsproblem. *Proceedings of the London Mathematical Society* 42: 230–265. Read to Society in 1936, but published in 1937. Correction in 43: 544–546.

3. McCulloch, W. S. and Pitts, W. 1943. A logical calculus of ideas immanent in nervous activity. *Bulletin of Mathematical Biophysics, 5: 115–133. Reprinted in Neurocomputing: Foundations of Research, edited by J. A. Anderson and E. Rosenfeld. Cambridge, MA: MIT Press, 1988.*

4. Kleene, S. C. 1951. Representation of events in nerve nets and finite automata. In *Automata Studies,* edited by C. Shannon and J. McCarthy. Princeton: Princeton University Press.

5. Shannon, C. E. 1948. A mathematical theory of communication. *Bell Systems Technical Journal* 27: 373–423.

6. Chomsky, N. 1956. "Three models for the description of language. *IRE (now IEEE) Transactions on Information Theory* 23: 113–124.

7. Harris, Z. S. 1962. *String Analysis of Sentence Structure.* The Hague: Mouton.

8. Bledsoe, W. W. and Browning, I. 1959. Pattern recognition and reading by machine. In *1959 Proceedings of the Eastern Joint Computer Conference,* 225–232. New York: Academic Press.

9. Colmerauer, A. 1970. Les systemes-q ou un formalisme pour analyzer et synthetiser des phrase sur ordinateur. *Internal Publication* 43, Departement d'informatique de l'Universite de Montreal.

10. Pereira, F. C. N. and Warren, D. S. 1980. Definite clause grammars for language analysis—A survey of the formalism and a comparison with augmented transition networks. *Artificial Intelligence* 133: 231–278.

11. Kay, M. 1980. Functional grammar. In *Proceedings of the Berkeley Linguistics Society Annual Meeting, 142–158. Berkeley, CA.*

12. Bresnan, J. and Kaplan, R. M. 1982. Introduction: Grammars as mental representations of language. In *The Mental Representation of Grammatical Relations,* edited by J. Bresnan. Cambridge, MA: MIT Press.

13. Winograd, T. 1972. *Understanding natural language.* New York, NY: Academic Press.

14. Schank, R. C. and Abelson, R. P. 1977. *Scripts, Plans, Goals and Understanding.* Hillsdale, NJ: Lawrence Erlbaum.

15. Shank, R. C. and Riesbeck, C. K, eds. 1981. *Inside Computer Understanding: Five Programs Plus Miniatures.* Hillsdale, NJ: Lawrence Erlbaum.

16. Lehnert, W. G. 1977. A conceptual theory of question answering. In *Proceedings of the international joint conference on artificial intelligence '77:* 158–164. San Francisco, CA: Morgan Kaufmann.

17. Woods, W. A. 1967. *Semantics for a question-answering system.* PhD thesis, Harvard University.

18. Woods, W. A. 1973. Progress in natural language understanding. In *Proceedings of NFIPS National Conference,* 441–450.

19. *Grosz, B. A. 1977. The representation and use of focus in a system for understanding dialogs. In Proceedings of the International Joint Conference on Artificial Intelligence '77,* 67–76. San Francisco, CA: Morgan Kaufmann.

20. Sidner, C. L. 1979. Focusing in the comprehension of definite anaphora. In *Computational Models of Discourse, edited by M. Brady and R. C. Berwick,* 267–330. Cambridge, MA: MIT Press.

21. Hobbs, J. R. 1978. Resolving pronoun references. Lingua 44: 311–338.

22. Kaplan, R.M. and Kay, M. 1981. *Phonological rules and finite-state transducers. Paper presented at the Annual Meeting of the Linguistics Society of America,* New York.

23. Church, K. W. 1989. *On memory limitations in natural language processing.* Master's thesis, MIT. Distributed by the Indiana University Linguistics Club.

24. Marcus, M. P., Marcinkiewicz, M. A., and Santorini, B. 1993. Building a large annotated corpus of English: The Penn Treebank. *Computational Linguistics* 192: 313–330.

25. Brown, P. F., Cocke, J., Della Pietra, S. A., Della Pietra, V. J., Jelinek, F., Lafferty, J. D., Mercer, R. L., and Roossin, P. S. 1990. A statistical approach to machine translation. *Computational Linguistics* 162: 79–85.

26. Och, F. I. and Ney, H. 2003. A systemic comparison of various statistical alignment models. *Computational Linguistics* 29 (1): 19–51.

27. Feigenbaum, E., Barr, A., and Cohen, P., eds. 1981–1982. *The Handbook of Artificial Intelligence* 1–3: 229. Stanford, CA: HeurisTech Press/William Kaufmann.

28. Chomsky, N. 1957. *Syntactic Structures.* The Hague: Mouton.

29. Firebaugh, M. 1988. *Artificial Intelligence: A Knowledge-Based Approach.* Boston, MA: PWS-Kent.

30. Chomsky, N. 1965. *Aspects of the Theory of Syntax.* Cambridge, MA: MIT Press.

31. Kopec, D. and Michie, D. 1982. Mismatch between machine representations and human concepts: Dangers and remedies. *Report to the EEC,Subprogram FAST,* Brussels, Belgium.

32. Halliday, M. 1985. *A Short Introduction to Functional Grammar.* London, UK: Arnold.

33. Wilensky, R. 1983. *Planning and Understanding: A Computational Approach to Human Reasoning.* Reading, MA: Addison-Wesley.

34. Charniak, E. 2006. Why natural-language processing is now *statistical* natural language processing. In *Proceedings of AI at 50,* Dartmouth College, Hanover, NH, July 13–15.

35. Collins, M. J. 1996. A new statistical parser based on bigram lexical dependencies. In *Proceedings of the 34th Annual Meeting on Association for Computational Linguistics*. Morristown, NJ: Association for Computational Linguistics.

36. Ide, N. M. and Veronis, J., eds. 1995. *Computational Linguistics: Special Issue on Word Sense Disambiguation.* Vol. 24. Cambridge, MA: MIT Press.

37. Marcus, M., Kim, G., Marcinkiewicz, M. A., MacIntyre, R., Bies, A., Ferguson, M. Katz, K., and Schasberger, B. 1994. The Penn Treebank: Annotating predicate-argument structure. In *Advanced Research Projects Agency Human Language Technology Workshop.* Plainsboro, NJ: Morgan Kaufmann.

38. Bentivogli, L. and Pianta, E. 2003. Beyond lexical units: Enriching wordnets with phrasets. In *Proceedings of European Chapter of the Association for Computational Linguistics '03,* Budapest, Hungary.

39. Benson, M., Benson,E., and Ilson, R. 1986. *The BBI Combinatory Dictionary of English: A Guide to Word Combinations.* Philadelphia, PA: John Benjamins Publishing Company, Philadelphia.

40. Sukova, E. 2010. *Models of Metaphor in NLP.* Computer Laboratory, Cambridge, England: University of Cambridge.

41. Gentner, D. 1983. Structure mapping: A theoretical framework for analogy. *Cognitive Science 7: 155–170.*

42. Black, D. 1962. *Models and Metaphors.* Cornell University Press.

43. Hesse, M. 1966. *Models and Analogies in Science.* Notre Dame University Press.

44. Wilks, Y. 1975. A preferential pattern-seeking semantics for natural language inference. *Artificial Intelligence* 6: 53–74.

45. Wilks. Y. 1978. Making preferences more active. *Artificial Intelligence* 11 (3): 197–223.

46. Lakoff, J. and Johnson, M. 1980. *Metaphors We Live By.* University of Chicago Press, Chicago.

47. Peters, W. and Peters, I. 2000. Lexicalised systematic polysemy in wordnet. *In Proceedings of LREC 2000,* Athens.

48. Mason, Z. J. 2004. Cormet: A computational, corpus-based conventional metaphor extraction system. *Computational Linguistics* 30 (1): 23–44.

49. Birke, J. and Sarkar, A. 2006. A clustering approach for the nearly unsupervised recognition of nonliteral language. *In Proceedings of EACL-06,* 329–336.

50. Karov, Y. and Edelman, S. 1998. Similarity-based word sense disambiguation. *Computational Linguistics* 24 (1): 41–59.

51. Krishnakumaram, S. and Zhu, X. 2007. Hunting elusive metaphors using lexical resources. *In Proceedings of the Workshop on Computational Approaches to Figurative Language,* Rochester, NY, 13–20.

52. Martin, H. 1990. *A Computational Model of Metaphor Interpretation.* San Diego, CA: Academic Press Professional, Inc.

53. Veale, T. and Hao, Y. 2008. A fluid knowledge representation for understanding and generating creative metaphors. In *Proceedings of COLING 2008*, Manchester, UK, 945–952.

54. Santosh, B. W. Y. and Gaikwad, K. 2010. *A Review on Speech Recognition Techniques.* Retrieved from http://www.ijcaonline.org/volume10/number3/pxc3871976.pdf.

55. Juang, L. A. B. 2014. *An Introduction to Hidden Markov Models.* Retrieved from http://luthuli.cs.uiuc.edu/~daf/courses/Signals%20AI/Papers/HMMs/01165342.pdf.

56. Lindasalwa, M., Mumtaj, B., and Elamvazuthi, I. 2010. Voice recognition algorithms using Mel Frequency Cepstral Coefficient (MFCC) and Dynamic Time Warping (DTW) techniques. *Journal of Computing* 2 (3). Retrieved from http://arvix.org/ftp/arvix/papers/1003/1003.4083.pdf.

57. BBC. August 23, 2011. Voice recognition software—An introduction. Retrieved from http://www.bbc.co.uk/accessibility/guides/factsheets/factsheet_VR_intro.pdf.

58. Brahmbhatt, S. 2013. *Speech Understanding: History, Techniques, Leading Systems and Future Directions.* MIS thesis, Brooklyn College: Brooklyn, N.Y.

AUTOMATED PLANNING

Austin Tate.

▪ ▪ ▪ ▪ ▪

The needs and ideas for planning in AI are not new. This chapter explores traditional problems, methods, and approaches transitioning to newer approaches. With numerous successful industrial applications, it is clear that the field has come a long way and is very important to future developments in a number of areas of AI including industrial robotics, communication, and transportation.*

Figure 14.0
A futuristic robot space lab.

*The authors are indebted to Dr. Christina Schweikert for assistance in the editing and preparation of this chapter.

14.0 INTRODUCTION

As was the case with Natural Language processing (the subject of Chapter 13), planning is an activity that is normally considered germane to human beings. Planning is unique to humans because it represents a very special indicator of intelligence, that is, the ability to make adjustments to activities in order to achieve goals.

Planning has two characteristics that are quite distinct:

1. In order to complete a task, a defined series of steps will possibly need to be completed.
2. The sequence of steps that define a solution to a problem will possibly be conditional. That is, the steps that comprise a plan might be revised according to conditions (this is called **conditional planning**).

Hence, the ability to plan represents a certain consciousness, and consequently, self-consciousness, that makes us human.

Tate (1999) states,

> Planning is the process of generating (possibly partial) representations of future behavior prior to the use of such plans to constrain or control that behavior. The outcome is usually a set of actions, with temporal and other constraints on them, for execution by some agent or agents.[1]

Planning can also be defined as follows:

> Planning is an essential component of intelligent agents and systems; it enhances their independence and ability to adapt to a dynamic environment. In order to accomplish this, agents must be able to represent the current state of a world and be able to predict the future. Intelligent agents utilize planning to generate sequences of actions that lead to a goal. Planning has been an active area of research in artificial intelligence; areas in which planning algorithms and techniques have been applied include: robotics, process planning, web-based information gathering, autonomous agents, animation, and multiagent planning.

14.1 THE PROBLEM OF PLANNING

Planning, usually considered a subfield of reasoning within the general area of problem solving, is one of the earliest areas of interest of artificial intelligence. Some typical planning problems in AI include the following: [2]

- Representing and reasoning about time, causality, and intentions
- Physical and other kinds of constraints on acceptable solutions
- Uncertainty in the execution of plans
- How the "real world" is sensed and perceived
- Multiple agents who may cooperate or interfere

There has been particularly great progress in the field during the past 20 years or so, concurrent with advances in machine capabilities and in the field of machine learning.

It is common to see planning and scheduling listed as common types of problems, but there is a fairly clear distinction: Planning is concerned with "figuring out what actions need to be carried out," whereas scheduling is concerned with "figuring out when to carry out actions." [3] In a general sense, planning focuses on choosing and proper sequencing of actions in order to accomplish a goal, whereas scheduling focuses on resource constraints (including timing). In this chapter, we will consider scheduling problems as a special case of planning problems.

14.1.1 Planning Terminology

The essence of all planning problems in AI is the challenge of transforming a current (possibly initial) state into a desired goal state. The plan generated is comprised of a sequence of steps within a domain to perform this transformation. The sequence of steps followed to solve a planning problem is called operator schemata. **Operator schemata** characterize *actions* or *events* (terms that are used interchangeably). Operator schemata characterize a *class* of possible variables, which can be replaced by values (constants) comprising operator *instances* that describe specific actions. The term *operator* can be used synonymously for operator schemata and operator instances. Common usage in the AI literature is to refer to Stanford University Institute Problem Solver (STRIPS) operators (one of the oldest planning programs of Fikes et al.) [4, 5] STRIPS operators are used to describe an action by three components: a **precondition formula**, an add-list, and a **delete-list** (see Figure 14.1).

An operator's precondition formula (or simply the operator's preconditions) provides facts that must hold true before the operator can be applied. Whenever an action occurs, the add-list and the delete-list help to define that specific action. The application of an operator means that the add-list and delete-list produce a new state. The new state is produced with the deletion of all the formulas in the delete-list and the addition all the formulas in the add-list. The first state considered is the initial state, and repeated operator application produces intermediate state descriptions until a goal state is reached. At this stage, a plan can be called a solution to the specified problem.

PICKUP (x)

Precondition : ONTABLE(X) ∧

HANDEMPTY ∧

CLEAR(x)

Delete List: ONTABLE(X)

HANDEMPTY

CLEAR(x)

Add List: HOLDING(x)

Figure 14.1
PICKUP(x) – A typical STRIPS operator.

Plans that work from the initial state to a goal state are called **progressions**, whereas those that work backward from a goal state are called **regressions**, akin to the *forward chaining* and *backward chaining* discussed in Chapter 7, "Production Systems."

Repeated analysis will determine if all the operators in a plan can be applied in the order specified by a plan. Such an analysis is referred to as **temporal projection**.

14.1.2 Examples of Planning Applications

Planning has found familiar applications in discrete puzzles such as Rubik's cube, sliding block puzzles such as the 15-puzzle in Chapter 4, "Search Using Games," including chess and bridge, and scheduling problems. These areas are very suitable for developing and applying planning algorithms because of the regularity and symmetries involved in the moving parts.

Chapter 16 makes the distinction between strategy and tactics in chess. In games, strategic play is really synonymous with planning. It does not usually involve interaction of forces, but rather, long-term thinking, which will result in measurable improvements in terms of positioning of forces.

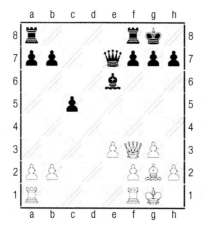

Figure 14.2
Capablanca – Marshall, 1909.

The actual interplay of forces resulting in captures (in chess and checkers) is usually synonymous with tactical play. Figure 14.2 presents a very famous position from the 23rd and final game of the chess match between Jose Raul Capablanca and Frank Marshall in New York City in 1909. Marshall was a gifted tactician but lacked depth in his strategic play, whereas Capablanca was a **complete** player who went on to become World Champion (1921–1927). Capablanca won the match with 8 wins, 1 loss, and 14 draws.**

Marshall's continuation 16.Rfc1? led to one of the most famous examples of how to win with a queenside pawn majority whereas the correct plan was for White to play 16.e4 followed by Qe3, f4, and a general kingside pawn advance.

Figure 14.3 shows an excerpt from Bridge Baron, the 1997 World Championship bridge program.[6]

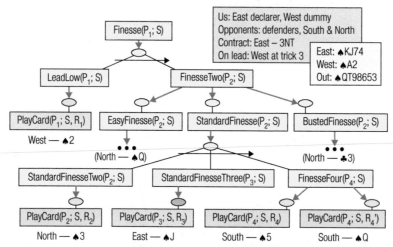

Figure 14.3
An example of plan declaring by Bridge Baron.

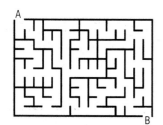

Figure 14.4
A typical maze problem. The robot not only needs to get from A to B, but it also needs to be able to recognize walls and deal with them appropriately.

In Chapter 16, it is demonstrated how search and thinking in computer chess and checkers is different from how humans play the game. In contrast, the Bridge Baron emulates the plan declarer in Bridge. (See Appendix D.3.1). Bridge Baron uses an adaptation of the Hierarchical Task Network (HTN) planning to accomplish its play. We shall discuss how this is done in Section 14.3.

Equally common was the problem of trying to get a robot to move through a maze by recognizing walls and obstacles but at the same time navigating successfully to its goal. This was a typical problem in the field of computer and robot vision. Figure 14.4 illustrates the kind of maze problem that robots have been solving for many years.

The task in Figure 14.5 is to use three mobile robots with manipulation arms mounted on them to move a grand piano across a room that has furniture as obstacles. Humorously labeled *The Piano Mover's Problem*, collisions between robots and other pieces of furniture must be avoided. This is a typical contemporary planning problem.

** The Marshall Chess Club on 23 W 10th Street in New York City celebrates its 100th Anniversary in 2015.

In design and manufacturing applications, planning is applied to solve problems of assembly, maintainability and mechanical part disassembly. Motion planning is used to automatically compute a collision-free path for removing a part from an assembly. The illustration in Figure 14.6 demonstrates the removal of a pipe from a complex machinery room without any collisions.[7]

There are many potential opportunities for the video game programmer and AI planner communities to combine efforts to produce wonderful, unique, humanlike characters. There is also a broad interest in developing virtual humans and computer-generated animations. The goal of animators is to develop characters with the features

Figure 14.5
Illustrates the familiar Piano Mover's Problem.

special to human actors while being able to design high-level descriptions of motions that can to be performed by agents. Otherwise, this remains an extremely detailed and laborious, frame-by-frame process, which animators hope can be curtailed through the development of planning algorithms.

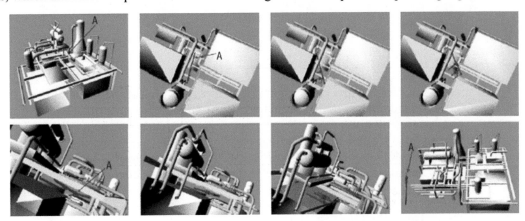

Figure 14.6
Planning for maintainability of a pipe motion.

Automatic manipulation planning is applied to computer animation to compute the animation of figures in a scene based on their task specifications. This allows animators to focus on the overall design of a scene, rather than the details of how to move figures in realistic and collision-free paths. A specific example is to generate the optimal motions for human and robotic arms to perform a task such as manipulating an object; this is relevant, not only to computer animation, but to ergonomics and product usability evaluations. Koga et al. developed a planner that performs multi-arm manipulation that, given a goal or task to complete, will generate the necessary animations for the cooperative manipulation of a chessboard between a human and

Figure 14.7
Robot arms assisting manufacture of assembly line automobiles.

the robot arm. [8] Figure 14.7 depicts a robot arm planner that performs multi-arm tasks assisting in the manufacturing of assembly-line automobiles.

The entertainment and gaming industries are concerned with producing high-quality animated characters whose motions are as realistic as possible; the characters also require the ability to automatically adapt to a dynamic environment that presents challenges and obstacles. Behavior planning can be used to generate these realistic motions for animated characters. Lau and Kuffner utilize real human-motion captures by creating a finite-state machine of high-level behaviors, and then performing a global search to compute a sequence of behaviors that brings an animated character to its goal position. [9] Figure 14.8 depicts a dynamic environment in which a jogger needs to adapt by jumping over a fallen tree.

Another distinction can be made between the process of constructing plans and the process of executing plans. The example which follows illustrates these distinctions.

Figure 14.8
An animated character adapting to a dynamic environment (courtesy of M. Lau).

EXAMPLE 14.1

Let us consider the process of planning your departure for work one day. There is a meeting at 10:00 am that you must attend. The morning commute usually takes 40 minutes. In the process of getting ready for the trip to work there are also a number of tasks that you like to perform—some that you might consider essential, and some that you consider a luxury, depending on the time available. Listed are some of the tasks that you consider doing before work:

1. Dropping off a few shirts at the dry cleaners

2. Dropping off bottles for recycling

3. Taking the garbage out

4. Stopping at your bank's ATM for cash

5. Buying gas for your car at the best local price

6. Putting air into your bike's tires

7. Cleaning up your car – tidying and vacuuming

8. Putting air into your car's tires

As an intelligent person, you will immediately ask about the constraints of the problem (or tasks). That is, how much time is available for these various tasks in order for you to be on time for your meeting?

You get up at 8:00 am thinking that two hours is plenty of time to execute many of the above tasks and to be comfortably on time for your meeting at 10:00:

1. Dropping off a few shirts at the dry cleaners

2. Dropping off bottles for recycling

3. Taking the garbage out

4. **Stopping at your bank's ATM for cash**

5. Buying gas for your car at the best local price

6. Putting air into your bike's tires

7. Cleaning up your car – tidying and vacuuming

8. **Putting air into your car's tires**

Of these eight possible tasks, you will soon decide that only two are really important: **Item 4** (getting cash) and **Item 8** (putting air into your car's tires). Item 4 is important because from experience you know that it will be difficult to conduct your day with a shortage of cash. You need to buy meals, snacks, and possibly other items. Item 8 could be even more important than item 4, depending upon how little air there is in your tires. In the extreme case you won't be able to drive, or it will be unsafe to drive. In most cases, having your tires underinflated will at least be inefficient in terms of the comfort of your drive and your car's miles per gallon. You now decide that items 4 and 8 are important and cannot be avoided. This is an example of hierarchical planning, that is, the imposition of a hierarchy or set of values to tasks which must be accomplished. In other words, not all tasks are of equal importance, and you can order them accordingly.

You think in terms of a gas station that is near the bank/ATM. You conclude that the closest gas station is about three blocks from the bank. You also think, "If I'm already going to the gas station for air, I might as well buy gas too." Now you consider, "What's the gas station near the bank that also has an air pump?" This is an example of opportunistic planning. That is, you are trying to exploit the conditions and opportunities offered by a certain state in plan formation and in the plan execution process. In this case, you don't really need to buy gas, but you are trying to be economical, in the sense that if you have already expended the time and energy to drive to a gas station for air, it wouldn't be very efficient (either in terms of time or cost) to go to one gas station to put air in your tires and to drive to another to buy gas.

At this point Items 1–3 look entirely unimportant; Items 6 and 7 look equally unimportant and more suitable for a weekend when there might be more time for such tasks. Certainly getting air into the tires of your bicycle is not usually relevant to driving to work unless you are planning some combination of driving and biking! Let us consider a few circumstances when items 1–3 may be quite relevant.

Item 1: Dropping off shirts at the dry cleaners

This would also seem like an irrelevant luxury on a busy workday morning, but perhaps you have an interview for a new job the next day, or a presentation you want to look good for, or even a date that you have been looking forward to for some time. In these cases you are thinking correctly (planning) and doing the right thing to have the best chance for a successful, happy event.

Item 2: Dropping off bottles for recycling

Again, this is normally a "weekend"-type activity. Is there an imaginable situation wherein this could be a necessary course of action? Yes, but that would represent a very sorry state of affairs for you. You have just lost your wallet with all your cash, credit cards, and ID cards.

You need to get to the supermarket to recycle in order to obtain cash for the 100 bottles you have at 5 cents a bottle. A very sorry state of affairs that we hope will never happen to you—besides, if you lost your wallet, you shouldn't be driving without your license. Nonetheless, this sounds like a situation we should all be prepared for. If it did happen to you, you'd probably have sufficient reason to miss that meeting.

Item 3: Taking out the garbage

There are quite realistic conditions under which this task could gain significantly in importance. Listed are some examples:

1. The garbage is already creating a horrible stench.

2. Your apartment has been declared derelict and you are responsible for cleaning it up.

3. It is Monday morning and the garbage won't be picked up again until Thursday.

Planning of this kind, based on certain contingencies or certain events that could happen, is called *conditional planning*. This kind of planning is often useful as a kind of "defensive" measure, or if you must consider a number of possible events that might happen. For example, if you are planning to organize a major event in Florida in early September, it may not be a bad idea to consider hurricane insurance.

Sometimes we can only plan for some subset of events (operators) that can be effected to reach a goal without particular concern for the order in which those steps will be performed. This is called a **partially ordered plan**. In the context of our Example 14.1, we can go to the gas station for air first or to the bank for cash first, if our tire situation is not too critical. If the tire were indeed flat, however, then the order of execution of the plan would require getting the tire repaired first, and then proceeding to other tasks.

We close this example by noting some further realities. Even though two hours would seem like a large amount of time to handle a few errands and still make a 40 minute commute, one quickly realizes that even in this simple scenario there could be many unknowns. For example, there could be lines at the air pump at the gas station or at the bank; there could be accidents on the highway delaying your commute; or there could be police, fire, or school buses that might cause delays. In other words, there are many unknown events that could interfere with our best laid plans!

14.2 ■ A BRIEF HISTORY AND A FAMOUS PROBLEM

The earliest work in Cognitive Science as it relates to AI sought to develop systems that could be general problem solvers. The first and most successful of these was The General Problem Solver (GPS) of Newell and Simon (1963).[10] It was based on the greedy algorithm called means-ends analysis, which, in turn, was based on goal-directed problem solving by minimizing the difference (distance) between a goal (successor) state and a current state.

During the 1960s there was also considerable ongoing research into search methods (in operations research, e.g., branch and bound methods) and reasoning using predicate logic in theorem-proving systems. This was very fertile ground for AI as the world also underwent major changes. Recall that this was the decade during which John McCarthy introduced LISP and the term artificial intelligence was coined.

It was in 1969 that the STRIPS (Stanford Research Institute Problem Solver, Section 14.4.1) was introduced at the Stanford Research Institute. Its application domain states were represented in first-order logic, and it was able to represent actions through changes in its world state. STRIPS also employed means-ends analysis to identify goals and subgoals that needed to be solved. The methods of STRIPS provided the foundations for many future systems, as well as a testbed for inherent problems.

Later approaches investigated the identification of partially defined plans, plan modification, constraint posting, and least-commitment planning.

These techniques are discussed in Section 14.3. The work of Stefik [11, 12] in MOLGEN (Molecular Structure Generation) concentrated on constraint management techniques with planning, or plan object constraints in DEVISER (Voyager Mission Spacecraft Sequencing) [13] and FORBIN for temporal constraints in factory control. SIPE (System for Interactive Planning and Execution monitoring) [14] was another well-known system that focused on resource constraints. These approaches combined planning with scheduling problems.

Partial planning was closely related to plan refinement. [15] This led naturally to the study of analogy and case-based planning (Section 14.3.4).

In the mid-1970s, attention turned to Networks of Action Hierarchies (NOAH), [16] which is fully presented in Sections 14.3.3 and 14.4.2. Plans started to be considered as partially ordered instead of totally ordered, and the ideas of planning became more generalized, independent of domain. NONLIN (Section 14.4.3) was a very significant system of this time period together with a question-answer procedure that it used.

Partially ordered planners (POP) were the standard of the day. These included SIPE,14 O-Plan, [17] and UCPOP (Universal Conditional Partially Ordered Planner). [18]

In the intervening 20 years or so, planners have taken a distinctly practical direction based on sound methodological foundations. These are illustrated by the general planner described in Section 14.5.1 (O-Plan [19]) and later Graphplan. [20]

Planning can be helpful in many aspects of problem solving. One area that has been in desperate need of improvement is the success rate of first year (novice) programming students. That is the purpose of WPOL [21] (Section 14.5.4)—to use a planning system that will help these students succeed.

14.2.1 The Frame Problem

As we have seen, planning is concerned with changes in a well-defined world. How do you get an agent (robot) from a current state to a goal state? What are the transformations that are necessary and what are the transformations that have occurred? Hence, it becomes important to specify both what has changed and what has not changed. When a robot arm grips a block and picks it up, changes have occurred in terms of where the block is, what the gripper is doing (grasping or not), and what

---

HUMAN INTEREST NOTES

AUSTIN TATE

Professor Austin Tate (1951–) holds the Chair in Knowledge-Based Systems at the University of Edinburgh and is the Director of the Artificial Intelligence Applications Institute at the University. He helped form AIAI in 1984, and since that time has led its efforts to transfer the technologies and methods of artificial intelligence and knowledge systems into commercial, governmental, and academic applications throughout the world. He holds degrees in Computer Studies (BA Lancaster, 1972) and Machine Intelligence (PhD Edinburgh, 1975). He is a Fellow of the Royal Society of Edinburgh (Scotland's National Academy), and is a Fellow of the Association for the Advancement of Artificial Intelligence, among other honors. He is a professionally Chartered Engineer.

Prof. Tate's research interests are in the use of rich process and plan representations together with tools that can utilize these representations to support planning and activity management. He pioneered the early—now widely used and deployed— approaches to hierarchical planning and constraint satisfaction in the Interplan, NONLIN, O-Plan, and I-Plan planning systems. His recent work on "I-X" is concerned with supporting collaboration between human and system agents to perform cooperative tasks in a "Helpful Environment." Prof. Tate was the Edinburgh Principal Investigator in the Advanced Knowledge Technologies Interdisciplinary Research Collaboration funded by EPSRC (Engineering and Physical Sciences Research Council). He also led the DARPA-funded Coalition Agent eXperiment (CoAX) project involving some 30 organizations in 4 countries over a 3-year period. His work is being applied to search and rescue and emergency response tasks. His internationally sponsored research work is focused on the use of advanced knowledge and planning technologies, and collaborative systems—especially using virtual worlds.

Prof. Tate leads the Virtual University of Edinburgh, Vue, a virtual educational and research institute bringing together those interested in the use of virtual worlds for teaching, research, and outreach. Prof. Tate is on the Senior Advisory Board for the *IEEE Intelligent Systems* journal and is a member of the editorial board of number of other journals.

(Source: *http://www.aiai.ed.ac.uk/~bat/bat-very-short-biography.html*)

blocks are on top of each other. Picking up the block does not change the position of the other blocks, the walls, the doors, or rooms. Figure 14.9 presents a snapshot of the Blocks World, which illustrates the typical permissible operations by a robot arm and blocks while certain preconditions exist, and the resulting effect.

A famous problem in AI that was identified by McCarthy and Hayes (1969) [22] as the need to characterize what has changed in a world as actions occur is known as the **frame problem**. As the complexity of a problem space increases, keeping track of everything that has changed and everything that has not changed (hence a complete state-space description) becomes an increasingly difficult computational problem. McCarthy saw it largely as a problem of combinatorics. Others view it as a problem of reasoning with incomplete information, [23] and still

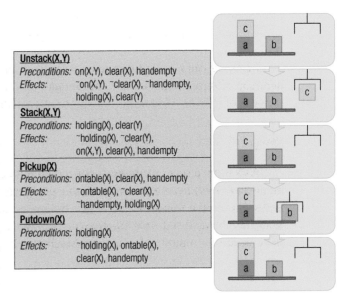

Unstack(X,Y)
Preconditions: on(X,Y), clear(X), handempty
Effects: ~on(X,Y), ~clear(X), ~handempty, holding(X), clear(Y)

Stack(X,Y)
Preconditions: holding(X), clear(Y)
Effects: ~holding(X), ~clear(Y), on(X,Y), clear(X), handempty

Pickup(X)
Preconditions: ontable(X), clear(X), handempty
Effects: ~ontable(X), ~clear(X), ~handempty, holding(X)

Putdown(X)
Preconditions: holding(X)
Effects: ~holding(X), ontable(X), clear(X), handempty

Figure 14.9
A snapshot of the Blocks World.

others believe it relates to the difficulty of enabling systems to notice salient properties of the world. [24,25] Allen and colleagues see it to be "simply that of constructing a formulation in which it is possible to readily specify and reason about the properties of events and sub-problems." [26]

14.3 PLANNING METHODS

Over the course of more than 40 years of development in the field of planning in AI, numerous techniques have been introduced and experimented with. In this section, we will explore some of the most significant of those methods, and describe systems that were particularly illustrative of certain methods.

14.3.1 Planning as Search

In a nutshell, planning is essentially a search problem. The same kinds of search issues that we have described throughout this text (in Chapters 2, 3, 4, and 12) are crucial here. These involve the efficiency of search techniques in terms of number of computational steps and memory space, as well as correctness and optimality. Finding a plan that works will typically involve exploring a potentially large search space, starting in the initial state and ending in the goal state. Additional complications can appear when different states or partial plans interact. Hence, it is not surprising that Chapman (1987) [26] was able to demonstrate that even simple planning problems can become exponential in size. The planning literature has focused on how a heuristic search should be organized, how partial or failed plans should be handled, and in general how good, informed decisions for problem solving should be made.[2] In this section, we will present a summary of the view of planning as search and then shift to a more quantitative view of planning with heuristic search. [27]

14.3.1.1 State-Space Search

As we described in Section 14.1, early planning work focused on the "legal moves" of games and puzzles (as in the 8-puzzle) to see if a sequence of moves could be found to transform an initial state into a goal state. Heuristic evaluation could then be applied to evaluate "proximity" or "closeness" to a goal state (e.g., as in the A* algorithm; [28] see Section 3.6.4) and the Graph Traverser. [29] Without heuristic approaches, state-space search could quickly become unmanageable.

Examples that we have already discussed in Chapters 2 and 3 include the breadth first search which uses $O(b^d)$ time to find an optimal solution of length d (recall b is the branching factor of a problem and d is the depth of a solution) but also uses $O(b^d)$ space because all the nodes at any level are stored before the next level is generated. In contrast, depth first search only uses linear space, but requires an arbitrary depth cutoff in order to terminate. Depending on the depth where that cutoff occurs, no solution might be found, because solutions could lie at a depth beyond the cutoff depth d. These problems are remedied by depth first search with iterative deepening (dfs with iterative deepening, discussed in Chapter 2) where a depth cutoff of one is used with an iterative series of depth increases of the search by one level until a solution is found. The algorithm finds a solution of length d in $O(b^d)$ in terms of time and $O(d)$ in terms of space. You may recall, that dfs with iterative deepening is "…asymptotically optimal in terms of time and space, over all brute-force tree search algorithms that are guaranteed to find optimal solutions." [27] Now we will turn our attention to a number of heuristic search techniques that have been used for planning.

14.3.1.2 Means-Ends Analysis

One of the earliest AI systems was the General Problem Solver (GPS) of Newell and Simon (1963),[10] which we introduced in earlier chapters. GPS used a technique for problem solving and planning called *Means-Ends Analysis*. The main idea behind means-ends analysis is to reduce the distance between a current state and a goal state. That is, if you are measuring the distance in miles between two cities, the algorithm would choose the "move" that would reduce that distance in miles the most without consideration for what further opportunities exist to reach a goal city from that intermediary city. This is a greedy algorithm (see Section 2.2.2) and therefore it has no hindsight, no memory of where it's been, and no particular knowledge of its task environment.

Let us consider the following example, shown in Table 14.1. You want to get from New York City to Ottawa, Canada. The distance is 424 miles, and this is estimated to take about 9 hours of driving time. Flying takes only about an hour, but because it's an international flight the cost is $600, and this is considered prohibitively high.

Consider the table below:

Table 14.1
Distance vs. possible choices of means of transportation. Once distance exceeds 1,000, choices are based on comfort and economy of cost.

Distance (Miles)	Travel Method				
	TAXI	BUS	TRAIN	RENTAL CAR	PLANE
0–50	√	√	√	√	
51–200		√	√	√	
201–600		√	√	√	√
601–1,000			√	√	√
1,001–3,000				√	√

For this problem, means-ends analysis would naturally prefer flying, but this is prohibitively expensive. An interesting alternative, which combines efficiency of cost in terms of time and money while allowing for sufficient freedom, is flying to Syracuse, NY (the closest large US city) and then renting a car to drive to Ottawa. It seems worth noting that there can be a number of overriding factors regarding the recommended solution. For example, you must consider the actual cost of the car rental, the number of days you will be spending in Ottawa, and whether you really need a car in Ottawa. Depending on the answer to these questions, you may opt for a bus or train for part or all of your transportation needs.

14.3.1.3 A Variety of Heuristic Search Methods for Planning

As we have indicated in Section 14.3.1.1, state-space (unintelligent, exhaustive) search techniques can result in the necessity to explore too many possibilities, as was the case when we explored search as early as Chapter 2. In this section we will briefly present a variety of heuristic search techniques that have been developed with the goal of remedying this situation.

Least Commitment Search

Least commitment in planning refers to "any aspect of a planner, which only commits to a particular choice when forced by some constraints." [2] They allow for a wider set of possible distinct plans to be represented in a single search space. [2] An example is the use of a parallel plan to represent a number of possible action orderings prior to making a commitment. This was done in NOAH [16] or by the posting of objects referred to in the plan rather than by making an arbitrary selection (e.g., MOLGEN [11, 12]). Weld (1994) [30] states that the idea behind least commitment planning is

> to represent plans in a flexible way that enables deferring decisions. Instead of committing prematurely to a complete, totally ordered sequence of actions, plans are represented as a partially ordered sequence, and the planning algorithm practices *least commitment planning*—only the essential ordering decisions are recorded.

As an example, let us say you are planning to move to a new apartment. You first decide what the suitable towns and neighborhoods are for your particular income level. You don't need to decide which block, building, and specific apartment you will be living in. These are decisions that can be delayed until a later, more opportune time.

Select and Commit

Select and commit was one unique planning-with-search technique described by Hendler, Tate, and Drummond [2] that doesn't inspire much confidence. It refers to new techniques that were tested by making a decision (commitment) to follow one solution path based on local information (akin to means-ends analysis). Often planners that were tested in this way were incorporated into later planners that could search for alternatives. Of course there were problems if the commitment to a path did not generate a solution.

Depth First Backtracking

Depth first backtracking is a simple method of considering alternatives, particularly when there are only a few to choose from. The method involves saving the state of a solution path at the point where there are alternatives. The first alternative path is chosen and the search backs up. If no solution is found then the next alternative path is chosen. The process of testing these branches—by partially instantiating operators to see if a solution has been found—has been referred to as "lifting." [31] Figure 14.10 illustrates depth first backtracking. It should soon be apparent to the reader that the backed up search generated by lifting is still too large and that it grows exponentially.

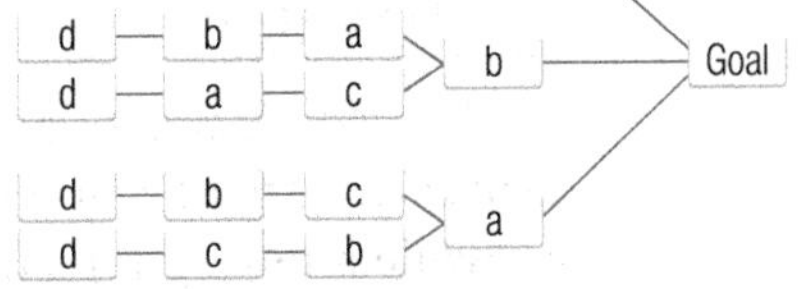

Figure 14.10
Depth first backtracking from a Goal.

Beam Search

The beam search was introduced in Chapter 3. Recall that it results in the exploration of a few "best nodes" at each level of a breadth first search. In the context of planning, this results in a small pre-constrained area that is searched for solutions. It is not uncommon for the beam search to be implemented alongside other heuristic methods to choose the "best" solutions, possibly to sub-problems suggested by the beam search, in other words, ISIS-II (International Satellite for Ionospheric Studies).[32]

One-Then-Best Backtracking

As we have noted throughout this text, backtracking through a search space, although possibly leading to a solution, can be prohibitively expensive in terms of the number of nodes that need to be explored through a number of levels. It is akin to the expression "barking up the wrong tree." One-Then-Best Backtracking expends more effort to determine that the local choice made to back up from a particular node is the best choice.

For an analogy, let us return to the problem of choosing a town to live in. We consider the candidate areas by two major factors—distance and then perhaps price. We find the most desirable area based on these factors. But now we must make a decision, possibly based on a choice of five to ten towns that are reasonable candidates. Now we must bring into play more factors:

1. How is the school system (for kids)?
2. How is the shopping in the area?
3. How safe is it to live in the town?
4. How centrally located is it (transportation)?
5. What other attractions are available in the area?

When you are able to make an assessment, based on the price of apartments and the distance from your work for each of the candidate towns, coupled with the five above additional factors, you should be able to choose one town and then proceed with further search for an appropriate apartment. Once you have chosen a town, you look at the availability and suitability of some apartments in the town, and then if necessary, reassess the other towns as possibilities and choose another town (based on the two primary and five secondary factors) as your primary choice. That is how the One-Then-Best Backtracking algorithm works.

Dependency-Directed Search

As described in the previous method, backtracking to saved states and resumption of search can be very wasteful. Storing the saved states of solutions found at choice points is perhaps useful, but it turns out to be more useful and efficient to store dependencies between decisions, what assumptions have been made, and the alternatives from which a selection can be made. That is what the studies of Hayes (1975), [33] Sussman (1977) [34], NONLIN + Decision Graph (Daniel, 1983) [35], and MOLGEN (Stefik, 1981) [11, 12] revealed. Such systems undid a failure by reconstructing all of the dependent parts of the solution. Thereby, unrelated parts could also be left intact.

Opportunistic Search

The opportunistic search technique is based on "the most constrained operation that can be performed." [2] All problem-solving components can summarize their requirements for a solution as constraints on the solution or restrictions on the value of variables representing objects being manipulated. Operations can be suspended until further information becomes available, (e.g.,

MOLGEN [11, 12]. It is common for such systems to use a blackboard architecture through which various components declare their availability and communicate, (e.g., Hearsay-II [36] and OPM [37]). Task scheduling can also be done through the blackboard. For humans, the blackboard architecture for opportunistic search consists of five levels: plan, plan abstraction, knowledge-base, executive, and meta-plan. [38]

Meta-Level Planning

Meta-level planning is the process of reasoning and choosing from a variety of plan options. A number of planning systems have an operator-like representation of plan transformations available to the planner. A separate search is performed to decide which operator is best applied at any point. This occurs before any decisions are made about any plan application. This is a very high-level skill, which is illustrated in MOLGEN [11, 12] and Wilensky (1981) [38]

Distributed Planning

The distributed planning system allocates sub-problems among a group of experts who are given sub-problems to solve. The sub-problems are passed between specialized experts who communicate through a blackboard and executive. Examples include Georgeff (1982) [39] and Corkill and Lesser (1983). [40]

This concludes our review of search methods used in planning. We have seen that the problems of search in AI in general (growth in terms of the combinatorial explosion and corresponding computation time and memory space) apply here too. Hence, the AI planning community has developed a number of techniques to limit the amount of search required. Now we will move on to consider other planning methods that have been developed.

14.3.2 Partially Ordered Planning

In Section 14.1.1, we defined partially ordered planning (POP) to be when some subset of events (operators) can be effected to reach a goal without particular concern for the order that those steps will be performed in.

In a partial order planner, a plan is represented as a partially ordered network of operators. A partial order planner performs **least-commitment** in the sense that ordering links between operators are introduced only when the problems in the developing plan demand it. [2] In contrast, a **total order planner** uses a sequence of operators to represent the plans in its search space.

A partially ordered plan usually has three components:

1. A set of actions

   {drive to work, get dressed, eat breakfast, take shower}

2. A set of ordering constraints

   {take shower, get dressed, eat breakfast, drive to work}

3. A set of causal links

   Get dressed---dressed→drive to work

Here the causal link is to get dressed before driving to work…you wouldn't want to get into your car undressed! Such links help detect and prevent inconsistencies when a partial plan is refined and implemented.

Recall that in the standard searches discussed in previous chapters, a node equals a state in a concrete world (or state space). In the planning world, a node is a partial plan.

So a partial plan consists of the following:

- A set of operator applications S_i
- Partial (temporal) order constraints $S_i < S_j$
- Causal links $S_i \xrightarrow{c} S_j$

This means that Si achieves c, which is a precondition of S_j. Hence, operators are actions on a causal condition to achieve an open condition. An **open condition** is a precondition of an action that has not yet been causally linked.

These steps are combined to form a partial plan as follows:

- An action is described with a causal link to achieve an open condition.
- A causal link is made from an existing action to an open condition.
- An order constraint is made between the above steps.

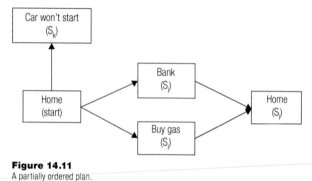

Figure 14.11
A partially ordered plan.

Figure 14.11 depicts a simple partially ordered plan. The plan starts at home and ends at home. In a partially ordered plan, different paths (such as the choice of going to the gas station or bank first) are not alternative plans, but alternative actions. We say a plan is complete if every precondition is achieved (we get to the bank and gas station and get home safely). When the order of the actions becomes fully determined, a partially ordered plan becomes a totally ordered plan. An example would be if we discover (as in earlier example) that our vehicle's gas tank is very nearly empty! A plan is complete if and only if every precondition is achieved. A threat to a plan occurs when some action S_k occurs that prevents us from executing our plan by blocking us from achieving all the preconditions of the plan. A threat is a potentially intervening step that prevents a condition achieved by a causal link. In the context of our above example, a threat would be if your vehicle did not start, as shown in Figure 14.11. That could throw off our "best laid plans…"

14.3.2.1 The Sussman Anomaly

A famous problem in the STRIPS (blocks) world occurs if we try to apply partial order planning to the task of placing three blocks on top of each other, in the order shown in Figure 14.12.

Here, in the language of the STRIPS and BLOCKS world, where x = B, y = C, and z = A, we have the initial state: Clear (x), On (y,z), Clear(y), and our goal state is On (x,y), On (z,x), and Clear(z).

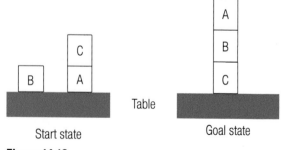

Figure 14.12
STRIPS (blocks) world problem – partial order planning.

To achieve the goal state, it quickly becomes apparent that one of the subgoals, PutOn (x,y)—the step which puts Block B on Block C—is a necessary step, but it must be achieved at the correct time. Hence there are "ordering effects" and a partial order plan will not work to solve this problem.

So the necessary steps are (1) PutOnTable(y), (2) PutOn(x,y), and then (3) PutOn(z,x). The first step achieves a necessary subgoal, which is that all the blocks are cleared and on the table. That takes care of the fundamental problem that the blocks in the initial state (with C on A) were out of order for the goal state. Clearing all the blocks allows us to reorder the stacking of blocks. Once the order Block B is on Block C, then Block A can be put on Block B to achieve the goal state. In effect, Block C was a threat to this plan because it sits on Block A. Hence, to remedy the Sussman Problem, we need at least the subgoals described above or a total order plan.

In summary, partial order planning is a sound and complete planning method. It can backtrack over choice points if failure occurs. There can be extensions for disjunction, universal quantification, negation, and conditionals. Overall it is an efficient planning technique when coupled with good problem descriptions. However, it is very sensitive to subgoal ordering.[41]

14.3.3 Hierarchical Planning

Planning is an activity that naturally lends itself to hierarchy. That is, not all tasks are at the same level of importance, and some tasks must be completed before others are attempted, whereas others may be interleaved. Besides, hierarchy (which is sometimes necessary for the purpose of satisfying task preconditions) can be useful for reducing complexity. Tate [1] states that "Most practical planners employ 'hierarchical planning methods.' "

Hierarchical planning is usually comprised of a library of *action descriptions*. Action descriptions are comprised of operators that perform some of the preconditions comprising a plan. Some of these action descriptions will "decompose" into a number of sub-actions which operate at a more detailed (lower) level. Consequently some of the sub-actions are defined as "primitives"—actions that cannot be further divided into simpler tasks. An example of a primitive would be "ClearTop" in the STRIPs domain. It simply means that a block does not have a block on top of it. The task called "ClearTable," however, would mean that there is nothing on a table. ClearTable could be comprised of a number of sub-actions such as *grasping* a block (or any object on a table), *moving* it and *ungrasping* it, and *dropping* it in a defined space off the table. In this example "ClearTable" would comprise a hierarchical task network (HTN), which is composed of the subtasks (including primitives such as Cleartop). Tate [1] states,

> HTN planning lends itself to the refinement planning model. An initial plan incorporates the task specification assumptions about the situation in which the plan is to be executed, and perhaps a partial solution. This can then be refined through the hierarchy into greater levels of detail while also addressing issues and flaws in the plan.

The work of Erol, Hendler, and Nau (1994) [42] addresses "the problem of a lack of a clear theoretical framework for ATN planning." Early papers by Yang (1990) [43] and Kambhampati and Hendler (1992) [44] focused on this problem but from a syntactic rather than semantic point of view.

In the HTN planning world, basic actions are represented in a manner similar to the representations used in STRIPS. [45, 27] Each "state" of the world as it is changing is represented by collections of atoms, and operators are used to associate effects with actions (what we called primitive tasks) [43] STRIPS and HTN fundamentally differ in their representation of "desired change" in the world.

In HTN, STRIPS-style goals are replaced by tasks and task networks [45] Task networks as described earlier are also called "procedural nets." Figure 14.13 presents the essence of the basic HTN Planning Procedure used by several heuristic systems. [2, 13, 15, 44, 45] HTN planning, as shown here, works by expanding tasks and resolving conflicts iteratively, until a conflict-free plan can be found that consists only of primitive tasks. [43]

Expansion of non-primitive tasks (steps 3–5 in Figure 14.13) is accomplished by choosing an appropriate reduction. That reduction in effect specifies one possible way of accomplishing the task. Reductions are stored as methods, which consequently associate non-primitive tasks with task networks.

Sometimes interactions between tasks can be conflicting, which can be caused by step 5. The job of discovering and resolving such interactions is performed by so-called *critics*. The notion of critics was introduced in the early program NOAH [17] (see Section 14.4.2) to "identify and deal with several kinds of interactions (not just deleted preconditions) between the different networks used to reduce each non-primitive operator." [17] Steps 6 and 7 show the use of the critics to recognize and resolve interactions. The effect is that the critics are able to facilitate recognition of interactions and thereby reduce the amount of backtracking necessary.

Erol et al.[42] developed a formalism for HTN planning. The details of their formalism are beyond our discussion here, but they were able to demonstrate that HTN planning is more expressive than planning without decompositions. The semantics of their formalism also enabled deeper understanding of HTN planning systems, such as tasks, task networks, filter conditions, task decomposition, and critics.

Hierarchical planning has been extensively deployed in practical applications such as logistics, military operations planning, crisis response (oil spills), production line scheduling, construction planning, space applications such as mission sequencing and satellite control, and software development.

---

1. Input a planning problem **P**.
2. If **P** contains only primitive tasks, then resolve the conflicts in **P** and return the result. If the conflicts cannot be resolved,
   return failure.
3. Choose a non-primitive task t in **P**.
4. Choose an expansion for t.
5. Replace t with the expansion..
6. Use critics to find the interactions among the tasks in **P**, and suggest ways to handle them.
7. Apply one of the ways suggested in step 6.
8. Go to step 2.

Figure 14.13
The basic HTN planning procedure.

14.3.4 Case-Based Planning

Case-based reasoning is a classical AI technique that is closely tied to the ability to describe previous instances of a state in a world and then to identify how well new situations in that world match an earlier case(s). In the world of law and medicine, it has everything to do with recognizing precedent. If you are able to do so then you should be able to perform adequate matching to that precedent case and then to choose the statically based course of action.

In case-based planning, learning occurs by plan replay and by performing a "derivational analogy" with previous plans that have worked in similar situations. Case-based planning is concerned with reuse of plans that have succeeded in the past and recovery from plans that have failed. [46]

Case-based planners are designed for the solution of the following problems:

• Plan-Memory Representation, basically, refers to the issue of deciding what to store and how memory will be organized in order to retrieve and reuse old plans effectively and efficiently.

- Plan Retrieval handles the issue of retrieving one or more plans which solve problems similar to the current one.

- Plan Reuse solves the issue of being able to reuse (adapt) a retrieved plan in order to satisfy a new problem.

- Plan Revision refers to the issue of testing the new plan for success and repairing it if a failure occurs.

- Plan Retention handles the issue of storing a new plan in order to be useful for future planning. Usually, if the new plan fails, it is stored with some reason for its failure.

Spalzzi [46] surveys a number of systems across these five parameters. Case-based planners can accumulate and negotiate successful plans with justified local choices. Partially matched learned experience is reused and new problems need only to be *similar* for reuse. The system called "Prodigy/Analogy" [47] performs "lazy" generalization, as learned episodes are not *explained* for correctness. Therefore, no complete domain theory is required. It is hard to improve on provably correct learned knowledge. Learning at local decisions could increase the transfer of learned knowledge (but it also increases the matching cost). Hence, it is also necessary to define a similarity metric between planning situations. Modern planning systems are often linked with machine learning methods for tasks such as this.

14.3.5 A Potpourri of Planning Methods

We have spent a significant portion of this chapter covering several major planning techniques that define the discipline, including search (14.3.1), partial order planning (14.3.2), hierarchical planning (14.3.3), and case-based planning (14.3.4). However, there are many more planning techniques that have been explored and developed by researchers. We feel that it is important to mention the following:

Logic-based planning (also called change-based planning) – The *planner* will try to generate a plan, Gamma, which, when executed by the *acting module* or the *executor* (when the system is in the state *i* satisfying the initial state description), will result in the state *g* satisfying the goal state description. This approach often leads to discussion of the situation calculus. This is the approach favored by Genesereth and Nilsson in their text *Logical Foundations of Artificial Intelligence*.

Operator-based Planning – *Actions* are represented as *operators*. This approach, also called *the STRIPS approach*, utilizes various *operator schema* and *plan representations*.

Reactive approaches are listed as follows:

- Planning & Execution – planners think, executors do
- Predictability (thinking) vs. Reactivity (doing)
- Online vs. off-line planning; classical planning done off-line, the generated plan fed to the online execution module
- Closed vs. Open loops; reaction rules encode sense-act cycles
- Triangle tables
- Universal plans
- Situated automata
- Action nets

- Reactive action packages
- Task-control architectures
- Subsumption architectures

There are many additional techniques: planning as conditional planning, constraint satisfaction, plan graph search, planning as model checking, planning on a computational grid, planning using temporal logic, distributed and multiagent planning, planning under uncertainty, probabilistic planning, planning and decision theory, mixed-initiative planning, and so forth.

14.4 EARLY PLANNING SYSTEMS

In this Section, we will explore three early systems that were particularly significant in the history of planning research and development. We start with undoubtedly the most famous system, STRIPS. Then we move on to one of its successors at Stanford Research Institute, which generalized on the planning ideas behind STRIPS, namely NOAH. We follow with NONLIN, which took the ideas of NOAH a step further.

14.4.1 STRIPS

As mentioned in Section 14.1.1, STRIPS—or Stanford University Institute Problem Solver (Fikes, Hart, and Nilsson, 1971)—was one of the earliest and most fundamental planning systems. Even the language of STRIPS, of which we have seen examples throughout this chapter, has been a standard (e.g., Grasp (x), Puton (x,y), ClearTop (y), etc.). It was able to represent application of domain states in first-order logic and could represent changes to its domain state. It could also use means-ends analysis to identify goals and subgoals that needed to be achieved as prerequisites to a solution. STRIPS operators provided a simple and effective framework in which search and action in a domain could be represented. As we've seen, they formed the basis for much future work in planning.

For example, here is how STRIPS might represent the world of a robot waiter:

At (Robot, Counter) and On (Cup-a , Table-1) and On (Plate-a, Table-2).

The following action arcs might represent the movement or pickup action of the Robot waiter:

Operator Pickup(x)

Preconditions: On(x,y) and At(Robot, y)

Delete list: On(x,y)

Add list: Held(x)

In the case of this example, the robot would need to get to two objects on two tables. STRIPS would have three kinds of lists: (1) precondition lists that needed to be satisfied for an action to be performed, (2) a delete list for preconditions that have been satisfied or changed, and (3) an add list for changes to the world state when an action was performed. One can see how attractive such a system is for representing simple worlds. However, as a world becomes more complicated, you can see how the task of maintaining these lists would become very cumbersome (even for a computer). This leads naturally to the aforementioned *frame problem*.

Two other problems were identified as a result of the STRIPS world. The first of these was the **ramification problem**, in other words, what are the ramifications of changes that occur in the world as a result of an action(s)? For example, if the robot gets from point A to point B, is Block A still on Block B? Does the robot still have tires on its wheels? Does it still draw the same amount of electricity for operation?

As we see, questions regarding the state of blocks are easy to answer, but once we get into questions that involve issues of self-state awareness (consciousness) and common sense knowledge, the problem of ramifications becomes more serious. The other problem that STRIPS brought to the fore was called the **qualification problem**. That is, when some action is performed (e.g., putting a key in a lock), what are the necessary qualifications that define success? If the key does not open the door, what could be wrong (e.g., I have the wrong key, the lock is broken, the key is worn out, etc.)?

As you can see, STRIPS was a very important system in the history, thinking, and development of systems for automated planning.

14.4.2 NOAH

In his seminal work, *A Structure for Plans and Behavior* (1975), [17] Earl Sacerdoti describes the concepts behind his program "NOAH" (Nets of Action Hierarchies). His colleague at Stanford Research Institute, Nils Nilsson, considers the work a milestone in three respects:

1. It was a major contribution to the techniques for developing a plan hierarchy as opposed to a single-level plan.

2. It introduced and exploited the idea of representing a plan as a partially ordered sequence that made no more than the necessary commitments to the time-ordering of steps.

3. It developed mechanisms enabling planning systems to examine their own plans so that these plans could be improved and so that plan execution could be intelligently monitored. [17, p. ix]

These were distinct advances over GPS, STRIPS, and MIT's Blocks World, which were limited to actions at a single level.

Sacerdoti summarizes the importance of NOAH [17, p. 105]:

> the *structure* of knowledge about actions within a computer memory is as important as the *content* of that knowledge.

NOAH used a high-level PLANNER-like language to cause the creation of nodes in a network, rather than to execute code. The nodes represent frame-like (in the Minsky sense) actions that constitute a plan. Nodes have individual procedures attached to them but can also have many declarative properties that can be independently accessed. Analysis of these declarative properties allowed the system to analyze actions. The development and study of NOAH contributed to early AI debates regarding the relative merits of procedural and declarative knowledge, in that frames embodied both kinds of knowledge.

NOAH brought to bear three kinds of knowledge: (1) problem solving, (2) domain-specificity in the procedural specification of actions, and (3) a database of symbolic knowledge for handling specific situations. In summary, NOAH contributed to automated planning, particularly in the following ways:

1. It used imperative semantics to generate frame-like structures (as described above).

2. It accounted for the nonlinear nature of plans; plans are viewed as partial orderings with respect to time. This also avoids the necessity for deep backtracking caused by linearity.

3. Planning can be done at many levels of abstraction.

4. It provided execution monitoring and easy error recovery with hierarchical plans.

5. It provided abstraction for representation of iteration.

6. It encouraged the importance of structure to help deal with a mass of knowledge at different levels of detail.

14.4.3 NONLIN

The NONLIN system was developed by Austin Tate (1977) [48] as a continuation of the "landmark work on the NOAH planner at SRI," [17, 49] for the generation of a plan as a partially ordered network of actions. NONLIN was a plan-space planner (as opposed to a state-space planner) in which the problem space is searched backward from a goal for a solution plan. It used a functional, state-variable representation for plan generation. NONLIN's goal structure-based plan development considered alternative "approaches" based on a plan's rationale.

NONLIN can perform Question / Answer modal truth criterion conditions. That is, it can respond to two kinds of query: [49]

1. Does statement P have value V at node N in the current network? (Choices for V's values are "definitely V, definitely not V, or undecidable".)

2. What links would have to be added to the network to make P have a certain value at N if it did not have this value in the given network?

To answer questions of the first type, NONLIN would find "critical" nodes in the network that could be used to provide a truth result.

We had mentioned in the previous section that NOAH made a decision at choice-points in a manner that avoided backtracking, but this could lead to some incompleteness of the search space—meaning that some simple block-pushing tasks could not be accomplished by NOAH. In contrast, NONLIN could suggest two orderings at a choice-point, thereby avoiding the possible incompleteness of NOAH mentioned above.

NONLIN also had a Task Formalism (TF) that could enable actions to be specified in a domain in a hierarchical fashion. Its purpose was to encourage the writing of modular job descriptions at various levels of detail. Thereby, subtask descriptions could be written independently of how they would be applied at higher levels.[49] These formalisms include the following information:

• When to introduce an action in the plan

• The effects of an action

• What conditions must hold before an action can be performed

• How to expand an action to lower level actions

NONLIN also had a provision for an explicit record of the conditions on any node, together with the nodes that achieve those conditions (i.e., the goal structure of the network). This provided a simplified representation of the plan, which is of benefit in directing the planner's search.

NONLIN had many other good features, highlighted by Tate (1983) [50] in his paper, "The Less Obvious Side of NONLIN"—including a table of multiple effects (TOME), a search control strategy using heuristic and dependency-directed, typed (pre)conditions for planning, and planning with time or cost information, among others.

One of the most important features of NONLIN was considered to be that it maintained a Goal Structure Table during planning to record what facts had to be true at any point in the network and the possible "contributors" that could make them true. In this way, the system could plan without choosing one of the (possibly multiple) contributors until this was forced by interaction detection as described above.

14.5 ■ MORE MODERN PLANNING SYSTEMS

In this Section, we will explore a few of the newer planning systems that have been developed during the past two decades. The first of these will be O-Plan, and this will be followed by Graph-plan.

14.5.1 O-Plan

O-Plan [18, 20] is Austin Tate's successor to the already acclaimed NONLIN system and was developed between 1983 and 1999 at the University of Edinburgh. O-Plan is written in Common Lisp and is available as a web-planning service (since 1994). [20, 51] It has a wide variety of applications, which we shall soon list. O-Plan expands on the earlier work of Tate in NONLIN, described in the previous section as a hierarchical planning system that can generate plans as partially ordered networks of activities. These networks can check a variety of constraints on time, resources, search, and so forth.

O-PLAN, like NONLIN before it, was a practical planner and could be used for a variety of AI planning features:

- Domain knowledge elicitation and modeling tools
- Rich plan representation and use
- Hierarchical Task Network Planning
- Detailed constraint management
- Goal structure-based plan monitoring
- Dynamic issue handling
- Plan repair in low- and high-tempo situations
- Interfaces for users with different roles
- Management of planning and execution workflow

Listed below is a variety of realistic applications where O-plan has been used:

- Air Campaign Planning [52]
- Noncombatant Evacuation Operations [52]
- Search & Rescue Coordination [53]
- US Army Small Unit Operations [54]

- Spacecraft Mission Planning [55]
- Construction Planning [18]
- Engineering Tasks [56]
- Biological Pathway Discovery [57]
- Unmanned Autonomous Vehicle Command and Control [20]

O-Plan's design was also used as the basis for Optimum-AIV, [58] a deployed system used for assembly, integration, and verification, in preparation of the payload bay for flights of the European Space Agency Ariane IV launcher.

More details of O-Plan technology are available at *http://www.aiai.ed.ac.uk/project/oplan/*.

A range of simple and more comprehensive demonstrations of the O-Plan planning web service is available at *http://www.aiai.ed.ac.uk/~oplan/*.

APPLICATION BOX

Practical Applications of Edinburgh AI Planners

1975: NONLIN – Electricity Turbine Overhaul Procedures (UK CEGB)
1982: Deviser based on NONLIN – Voyager Mission Planning (NASA JPL)
1996: OPTIMUM_AIV based on O-Plan – ESA Ariane IV AIV for payload bay
1996–Present: Search and Rescue (UK RAF and USA JPRA)
Commercial applications for Nynas tanker scheduling and Edify for financial help desks

Figure 14.14
Practical applications for O-Plan (http://www.aiai.ed.ac.uk/project/plan/).

A simple planning service that O-Plan provided over the Web was as a Unix Systems Administrators Script writing aid. The planner could generate a suitable script for the task of stating the requirements for mapping physical to logical Unix disk volumes. This was an example of using AI planning where the basic components are familiar, but their specific combinations are numerous.

O-Plan was also used for Multi-User Planning Services. Here multiple users could work with O-Plan simultaneously in a mixed-initiative fashion. Work with the US Army identified stages in the Small Unit Operations (SUO) command, planning, and execution process at US Army company level, from receipt of mission to successful outcome. [59, 20]

O-Plan is also an example of successful design with an open planning architecture. This is greatly facilitated by Lisp in that key components could be plugged in as needed. O-Plan finds a plan by exploring a search space of partial plans. "Issues" represent the missing parts of a partial plan. These identify which actions need to be expanded into sub-actions or conditions that need to be satisfied. At the top level, O-Plan has a controller that repeatedly selects an issue and invokes a "knowledge source" to resolve all issues.

Knowledge sources can make decisions about what to put in the plan and what parts of the search space should be visited. A plan is then built by adding nodes to a partially ordered network of actions and by adding constraints that represent pre- and post-conditions on actions, time limitations, resource usage, and other things. [59]

Constraint managers determine what constraints can be satisfied and communicate to knowledge sources possible ways to do this. In this flexible architecture, knowledge sources and constraint managers can be added, removed, and replaced as needed. [60, 61]

O-Plan has been followed by I-X, [62, 63] which provides a more general approach to support mixed-initiative planning, configuration, and so forth. O-Plan continues to be available as a planning service on the Web, and can be utilized for this purpose via I-X. [20]

14.5.2 Graphplan

Graphplan is a planner that works in STRIPS-like domains by constructing and analyzing a compact structure called a **planning graph**. A planning graph encodes a planning problem with the intent of exploiting inherent problem constraints to reduce the amount of search necessary.

As we've stressed throughout this text, search is a very important process in AI. Some people even view the search process in itself as the essence of AI, whereas others are more concerned with knowledge. It is clear that search without knowledge and direction (constraints) will result in a considerable amount of wasted effort and sometimes (in a complex domain) will never find a solution. However, knowledge without search is a bit like "the DNA of an insect stuck in resin"—that is, it is useful but it can't move. In any case, we can rest assured that knowledge (intelligence, heuristics) employed to limit search is a good thing.

Planning graphs can be constructed quickly (polynomial size and time) and a plan is a kind of "flow" of truth-values through the graph. [21] Graphplan is strongly committed to search in which it combines aspects of both total-order and partial-order planners. It performs search in a kind of "parallel" plan way, assuring that a shortest plan will be found among these plans—which will then be pursued independently.

In the domain of Graphplan, a valid plan is one that consists of a set of actions and specified times in which each action is to be carried out.

Recall that an action is a fully-instantiated operator, for example, Put X on Y. This means that all the actions at time t add to the world all the propositions that are among Add-Effects and deletes all the propositions that are among its Delete-Effects.

Actions will occur at time 1 and then others at time 2 and so on. Actions can be specified to occur at the same time step as long as they do not interfere with each other.

Two actions are said to interfere with each other if one deletes a precondition or an add-on effect of the other. In a linear plan, independent parallel actions can be performed in any order with exactly the same outcome. A plan at any time t is deemed valid if all the preconditions at any time prior to t have been met and the Problem Goals are true at the final time step. This translates to: a plan is valid at time 1 if all the plan's preconditions have been met, at a time > 1, if all the Add-Effects of some action at a time $t-1$ have been met. [21, p. 4]

Planning graphs are similar to valid plans, except that the requirement that actions at a given time step do not interfere is removed. An important aspect of Planning Graph Analysis is the ability to notice and propagate certain mutual exclusion relations among nodes. Two actions at a given action level in a Planning Graph are said to be mutually exclusive if no valid plan could possibly make both true.

Here is an example from the real world, illustrating mutual exclusion. You have made an arrangement to visit your mother. When you visit your mother she requests only two things:

(1) that you be on time and (2) that you be dressed nicely.

Now that's not asking for too much is it? However, you find that you're about to leave your home with 30 minutes to go and it's a 25 minute trip to mom's place. You consider your clothing and discover you don't have any slacks that are "nice" and you haven't had your morning coffee to be able to drive safely to mom. It should quickly become clear that your necessities (actions / goals) are mutually exclusive. You cannot get changed, get coffee, and be on time for mom. If you don't change clothes, your mom won't be happy, and if you don't get that coffee, you might not be able to reach her safely. What should you do?

Identifying mutual exclusion relationships can be of enormous help in reducing the search for a sub-graph of a Planning Graph that might correspond to a valid plan.[21, p. 5] Mutual exclusion provides a mechanism for propagating constraints throughout a graph. A simple and useful fact is that an object can be in only one place at a time t. This facilitates limitation of the possible preconditions that could be part of a solution.

In experimental studies on several familiar problems in the planning world, including the Rockets Problem, the Spare Tire Problem, and the Monkeys and Banana Problem, Graphplan fared favorably over the UCPOP and PRODIGY systems.

14.5.3 A Potpourri of Planning Systems

In this Section, we have reviewed three older, classic systems in the history and development of automated planning (STRIPS, NOAH, and NONLIN) and two newer systems for planning (O-PLAN and GRAPHPLAN). The figure below, Figure 14.15, illustrates that there are many more planning systems and planning techniques that have been developed. We have discussed many of them here, but others, such as constraint satisfaction planning, plan refinement, optimization methods, multiagent planning, re-planning, plan learning, and mixed-initiative planning, have not been discussed because of limitations of time and space.

Planning Research Areas, Systems, and Techniques[2]

• Domain Modeling: HTN, SIPE • Domain Description: PDDL, NIST PSL • Domain Analysis: TIMS	• Plan Repair: O-Plan • Re-planning: O-Plan • Plan Monitoring: O-Plan, IPEM
• Search Methods: Heuristics, A* • Graph Planning Algorithms: GraphPlan • Partial-Order Planning: NONLIN, UCPOP • Hierarchical Planning: NOAH, NONLIN, O-Plan • Refinement Planning: Kambhampat • Opportunistic Search: OPM • Constraint Satisfaction: CSP, OR, TMMS • Optimization Methods: NN, GA, Ant Colony Opt. • Issue/Flaw Handling: O-Plan	• Plan Generalization: Macrops, EBL • Case-Based Planning: CHEF, PRODIGY • Plan Learning: SOAR, PRODIGY • User Interfaces: SIPE, O-Plan • Plan Advice: SRI/Myers • Mixed-Initiative Plans: TRIPS/TRAINS • Planning Web Services: O-Plan, SHOP2
• Plan Analysis: NOAH, Critics • Plan Simulation: QinetiQ • Plan Qualitative Modeling: Excalibur	• Plan Sharing & Comms: I-X, <I-N-C-A> • NL Generation … • Dialogue Management …

Figure 14.15
Planning research areas and systems that have been developed.[2]

14.5.4 A Planning Approach to Learning Systems

Planning systems, as described in this chapter, have been applied successfully to various domains. This section presents a learning system for planning to increase the effectiveness of concept representation, integration, and application. The planning approach is explored for teaching object-oriented programming and design to novice programmers.

A Plan-Oriented Learning Environment for Novice Object Design

A serious problem for computer science departments is the attrition and failure rate in the introductory programming course. Instructors are constantly seeking ways to enhance the teaching of programming in an effort to resolve learner difficulties. Despite various enhancements in programming languages, environments, and pedagogical approaches, novices are still faced with many challenges when learning to program—particularly the additional layers of abstraction presented by the object-oriented paradigm.

Plans can be used to capture the way expert programmers represent programming knowledge, and the visualization of plans in a learning system can be used to enhance novices' learning of programming in the object-oriented paradigm. [22] It has been shown that experienced programmers utilize plan representations to encode programming concepts and tasks. [64] Novice programmers lack this higher level (plan) knowledge that experts have built up over years of experience. Presenting programming knowledge to novices in a structured plan representation can facilitate their understanding of various programming concepts, such as abstraction in OOP. Studies of novice programmers reveal that most major errors are a result of incorrect plan integration and misconceptions related to objects, such as correct object representation and incorporation of OOP concepts into problem solving. [65]

A Plan-Object learning paradigm that reinforces concepts of object design through plan representation can aid students' ability to design and implement objects, as well as increase their ability to utilize objects in problem solving. Web Plan Object Language (WPOL) [65] is an online learning environment that utilizes the Plan-Object approach with three phases of learning: plan observation, integration, and creation. The observation phase demonstrates, step by step, a sample solution to a problem in terms of plans and objects. The integration phase tests a novice's ability to integrate plans properly to form a solution and reinforces concepts of plan integration and object design. In the creation phase, the student can customize plans and design new objects.

The Plan-Object Paradigm represents the conceptualization and design stage of objects and presents a method for early assimilation of OOP. Objects are explicitly defined and given context within the plan framework. An Object Plan consists of Data Member, Member Function, and Object Utilities sub-plans (class components). Depending on the application, appropriate Variable(s) and/or Function(s) will be created and integrated. An Object's Utilities include Set Plan, Get Plan, Constructor, and Destructor sub-plans.

The Plan-Object Paradigm applies the concept of plans to object-oriented programming. The Plan-Object approach enhances novice programmers' ability to design, implement, and integrate objects into their programs. An empirical study was conducted to measure novices' performance on a sample case study involving objects and problem solving. The programs of students exposed to the Plan Object Paradigm and WPOL demonstrated a 56.7% reduction in problem-solving errors related to objects and 54% fewer total errors related to algorithm and problem-solving plans. The visual experience of Plan and Object design, integration, and implementation enhances novice programmers' capabilities in terms of object representation and incorporation of plans and objects into a solution.

14.5.5 The SCI Box Automated Planner

https://info.aiaa.org/tac/SMG/SOSTC/Workshop%20Documents/2010/Choo_APL_SciBox%20Planning%20System.pdf.

Figure 14.16
An overview of the SciBox System.

Planning science missions in space is always a time-consuming, laborious, and expensive process. It requires many iterations and considerable coordination among many teams—sub-system engineers, orbit and pointing analysts, command sequencers, mission operators, and instrument scientists. Project schedules are tight and only so many iterations can be performed. As a result, spacecraft resources are frequently not optimally utilized.

SciBox (see Figure 14.16) is an end-to-end automated science planning and commanding system. The system begins with science objectives, derives the required observing sequences, schedules those observations, and finally generates and validates uploadable commands to drive the spacecraft and instruments. The process is automated, and there is no manual scheduling of science operations or construction of command sequences, except for limited special operations and tests.

SciBox development began in 2001 for the MESSENGER mission to Mercury and proceeded in incremental stages, with various key software modules being tested on other spaceflight missions.

Goal-based planning and commanding systems using SciBox have been successfully employed for the Compact Reconnaissance Imaging Spectrometer for Mars (CRISM) instrument on the Mars Reconnaissance Orbiter (MRO) in 2005 and the Miniature Radio Frequency (MiniRF) instruments onboard Chandrayaan-1 and the Lunar Reconnaissance Orbiter (LRO) in 2008 and 2009, respectively. Goal-based planning systems decouple science planning from command generation and allow scientists to focus on science-observation opportunity analysis instead of commanding details.

NASA's MESSENGER spacecraft was launched on August 3, 2004. On March 18, 2011, MESSENGER entered into a non-Sun-synchronous, highly eccentric 200 × 15,200-km-altitude orbit with an inclination of 82.5° and a period of approximately 12 hours. MESSENGER began its primary science phase on April 4, 2011. By that time, the technology had matured to the point that it was used to plan and command all orbital science operations for the mission to Mercury. MESSENGER's mission was to address the following scientific questions:

1. What planetary formational processes led to the high ratio of metal to silicate in Mercury?
2. What is the geological history of Mercury?
3. What are the nature and origin of Mercury's magnetic field?
4. What are the structure and state of Mercury's core?
5. What are the radar-reflective materials at Mercury's poles?
6. What are the important volatile species and their sources and sinks on and near Mercury?

To answer these questions about Mercury, SciBox would automate a planning process that started with the measurement objectives, which can be divided into three types: those that require continuous observing, those that require building observation coverage under specified observing conditions, and targeted observations where acquisition of global data is not feasible. The SciBox architecture consists of four main components—opportunity analyzers, constraint checkers, priority scheduler, and the command generator—which streamline a process that starts with measurement objectives and produces spacecraft and instrument sequence of commands. Opportunity analyzers' task is to find all opportunities to make desired observations within specified constraints. For each observation opportunity, the constraints checker systematically validates the observing operation so that it complies with the operational constraints placed on the spacecraft and instrumentation by the engineers. The priority scheduler then sorts the observing opportunities validated by the constraint analyzer, weighing them against each other based on their priority. For example, an observing opportunity which occurs more frequently might be given a lower priority. Within a given type of observation, opportunities are also ranked by a quality metric (such as resolution or illumination) that is calculated based on predicted range to target, solar position, etc. The priority scheduler then selects the best observation opportunities and inserts them into a timeline in order of decreasing priority, until the available spacecraft resources (e.g., spacecraft pointing restrictions to ensure thermal safety of the spacecraft, variable available downlink volume due to Earth-Mercury distance variations and solar conjunctions, solid-state recorder space) are used up. Next, the conflict-free schedule is fed to the command generator, which creates a sequence of commands for upload to the spacecraft and instruments. At the same time an HTML report is produced for review.

SciBox has not only reduced the lead time for operations planning which requires a time-consuming coordination among different specialized teams. It also reduced cost by automating the hitherto manual adjudication of observing priorities which expended many man-hours, reduced operations risk by systematically checking constraints, and maximized the scientific value of the mission by weighing the trade-offs between the observing opportunities. This enabled negotiation of MESSENGER science priorities against operational constraints such as spacecraft recorder space, downlink bandwidth, scheduling, and orbital-geometry.

SCI Box References

MESSENGER SciBox. 2011. An Automated Closed-Loop Science Planning and Commanding System, Teck H. Choo et al. AIAA SPACE 2011 Conference & Exposition.

SciBoxAn End-to-End Automated Science Planning and Commanding System. Teck H. Choo et al. John Hopkins University Applied Physics Laboratory, Laurel, MD.

(This Section was contributed by Daniil Agashiyev)

HUMAN INTEREST NOTES

FREDERICK HAYES-ROTH

Frederick Hayes-Roth.

Frederick Hayes-Roth (1947–) is one of the early leaders in the field of planning. He has been a professor in the Information Sciences Department at the United States Navy's Naval Postgraduate School (NPS) in Monterey, California, since 2003, where he teaches the "capstone" course on strategy and policy in exploiting information technology. He states on his Web site,

Based on extensive experience in artificial intelligence, knowledge engineering, distributed systems, semantics, business process management and enterprise application integration, I perceive some important success factors that government efforts at information sharing must have.

Prior to joining the NPS faculty, he was the Chief Technology Officer for Software at Hewlett-Packard. In earlier years he was the Chairman and Chief Executive of two Silicon Valley companies which he cofounded. He has also been program director for research in Information Processing at The Rand Corporation. Hayes-Roth's achieved notoriety as one of the co-inventors of the first continuous speech understanding systems, Hearsay-II, which became famous for its "blackboard architecture."

His research is focused on the following questions:

1. How valuable is information (to whom, when, why)?

2. How can we delegate vastly more information filtering work to computers?

3. How can we most rapidly deliver the benefits of 1 and 2 so that we make people in challenging operational settings able to make much better decisions faster?

4. How can we restructure our technical programs and acquisition process across the government and DoD so that we implement the answer to 3?

In 2011, Dr. Hayes-Roth cofounded Truth Seal Corp., a nonprofit charitable organization, whose mission is to promote truthfulness in public communications so that the general public will be able to obtain credible information in order to make judgments, decisions, and actions.

14.6 CHAPTER SUMMARY

Chapter 14 provides an overview of Automated Planning in the context of Artificial Intelligence. We began by introducing the notion of planning, which is a feature of human intelligence. Planning involves knowing what steps need to be completed to finish a particular task or to reach a goal, and the order in which we execute steps in a plan can change based on various conditions. Can we develop agents and systems that exhibit a humanlike ability to reason and solve problems? There are many things to consider when designing such a system, including representing the agent's world in a well-defined manner, keeping track of changes that take place in the world, predicting what effects an agent's actions will have, handling new obstacles, and formulating a plan that will enable the agent to reach its goal.

Throughout the chapter, we discussed many existing planning applications—from chess and bridge to robotics and computer animation. We also presented the major planning methods such as search (state space search, means-ends analysis, heuristic search methods), partially ordered planning, hierarchical planning, and case-based planning. As a background and history, we reviewed classic early planning systems that contributed immensely to the field of planning, including STRIPS, NOAH, and NONLIN. More modern systems, such as O-Plan and Graphplan, have expanded the field of planning by introducing and incorporating new techniques. Sections 14.5.4 and 14.5.5 present and explore two implemented and developing planning systems, WPOL and SciBox, respectively.

Questions for Discussion

1. Why would one want to get a computer to be able to plan?

2. What are the essential components of a plan in the computer sense?

3. What was the first problem-solving system that performed planning? What was its purpose?

4. What is the system that many future planning systems were based on? Where was it developed? What could it do?

5. What system was developed to generalize on this system?

6. Name five different kinds of search methods in planning.

7. What is least-commitment search?

8. Explain how means-ends analysis works.

9. How would you distinguish planning from other kinds of play in games?

10. What is the Frame Problem? What is the Qualification Problem? What is the 'Ramification Problem'?

11. Distinguish between partially and totally ordered planning.

12. Name and describe five planning techniques.

13. How did NOAH improve on what STRIPS started?

14. What is "One-Then-Best Backtracking"?

15. What is Sussman's Anomaly?

16. What was the main feature of NONLIN?

17. What does O-Plan offer that the earlier planners didn't?

18. Name several areas where practical planners have been built.

Exercises

1. Recall the Donkey Puzzle presented in Chapter 3. Explain how you would define subgoals to solve this problem. How would a program recognize when the subgoals have been accomplished? Are there any preconditions to the subgoals?

2. In the World of STRIPS, use the standard operators and actions to place three blocks—A, B, C—on top of each other on a table starting in the state, A is on C and B is on the table.

3. How would you get three blocks on Table X to be stacked on Table Y in the order A, B, C with block A on top? What operator(s) do you need in addition to those in Problem 2?

4. What did the Sussman Anomaly demonstrate?

5. Try one of the Practical Planners on the University of Edinburgh Web site www.aiai.ed.ac.uk /project/oplan and report on your experience.

6. Consider how a STRIPS-like system would solve the famous Monkeys and Bananas Problem posed by John McCarthy:

   The Monkey is faced with the problem of getting a bunch of bananas hanging from the ceiling just beyond his reach. To solve this problem, the monkey must push a box to an empty place under the bananas, climb on top of the box, and then reach them.

   The constants are monkey, box, bananas, and under-bananas.

   The functions are reach, climb, and move, meaning the following:

   Reach (m, z, s): The state resulting from the action of m reaching z, starting from state s.

   Climb (m, b, s): The state resulting from the action of m climbing b, starting from state s.

   Move (m, b u, s): The state resulting from the action of m moving b to place u, starting from state s.

   Try to solve this problem with a logical series of operations using these functions.

7. How might a computer-planning program be helpful to the military?

8. How could computer planning be helpful in coping with natural disasters?

9. Describe how a human's approach to planning is different from how a computer might tackle a planning problem. Describe how each one's methods might also be similar.

10. Write a five-page report on multiagent planners. What are the most recent systems, who developed them, how successful are they, what tests have been done with them, and so forth?

Keywords

add-list	logic-based planning	precondition
complete	mutually exclusive	progressions
conditional planning	open condition	qualification problem
delete-list	operator schemata	ramification problem
frame problem	opportunistic planning	regressions
hierarchical planning	parallel plan	temporal projection
hierarchical planning methods	partially ordered plan	threat
least-commitment	planning graph	total order planner

References

1. Tate, A. 1999. Planning. In *The MIT Encyclopedia of the Cognitive Sciences MITECS*, edited by R. A. Wilson and F. C. Keil. Cambridge, MA: The MIT Press.

2. Hendler, J., Tate, A., and Drummond, M. 1990. AI planning: Systems and Techniques. *AI Magazine* 11 (2): 61–77.

3. Dean, T. and Kamhampati, S. 1997. *Planning and Scheduling: CRC Handbook of Computer Science and Engineering*. Boca Raton, FL: CRC Press.

4. Fikes, R. E., Hart, P. E., and Nisslon, N. J. 1972a. Learning and executing generalized robot plans. *Artificial Intelligence* 3 (4): 251–288.

5. Fikes, R. E., Hart, P. E., and Nilsson, N. J., 1972b. Some new directions in robot problem solving. In *Machine Intelligence* 7, edited by B. Meltzer and D. Michie. Edinburgh: Edinburgh University Press.

6. Smith, S. J., Nau, D., and Throop, T. 1998. Computer Bridge: A big win for AI planning. *AI Magazine* 19 (2): 93–105.

7. Zhang, L., Huang, X., Kim, Y. J., and Manocha, D. 2008. D-plan: Efficient collision-free path computation for part removal and disassembly. *Computer-Aided Design & Applications* 5 (1–4).

8. Koga, Y., Kondo, K., Kuffner, J., and Latombe, J. 1994. Planning motions with intentions. In *Proceedings of the 21st Annual Conference on Computer Graphics and Interactive Techniques. SIGGRAPH '94*, 395–408. New York, NY: ACM.

9. Lau, M. and Kuffner, J. J. 2005. Behavior planning for character animation. In *Proceedings of the 2005 ACM Siggraph/Eurographics Symposium on Computer Animation*, 271–280. Los Angeles, CA, July 29–31. New York, NY: ACM.

10. Newell, A., and Simon, H. A. 1963. GPS: A program that simulates human thought. In *Computers and Thought*, edited by E. A. Feigenbaum and J. Feldman. New York: McGraw-Hill.

11. Stefik, M. 1981a. Planning with constraints MOLGEN: Part 1. *Artificial Intelligence* 16: 111–140.

12. Stefik, M. 1981b. Planning with constraints MOLGEN: Part 2. *Artificial Intelligence* 16: 141–170.

13. Vere, S. 1983. Planning in time: Windows and durations for activities and goals. *IEEE Transactions on Pattern Analysis and Machine Intelligence (PAMI)* 53: 246–267.

14. Wilkins, D. 1988. *Practical Planning*. San Francisco, CA: Morgan Kaufmann.

15. Kambhampati, S., Knoblock, C., and Yang, Q. 1995. Planning as refinement search: A unified framework for evaluating design tradeoffs in partial order planning. *Artificial Intelligence* 76: 167–238.

16. Sacerdoti, E. 1975. *A structure for plans and behavior*. PhD thesis, Stanford University, Stanford, CA.

17. Currie, K. W. and Tate, A. 1991. O-Plan: The open planning architecture. *Artificial Intelligence* 521 (Autumn).

18. Penberthy, J. S. and D. S. Weld. 1992. UCPOP: A sound, complete, partial order planner for ADL. In *Proceedings of Knowledge Representation* KR-92, 103–114.

19. Dalton, J. and Tate, A. 2003. O-Plan: A common Lisp planning web service. *International Lisp Conference 2003*, October 12–25. New York, NY.

20. Blum A. and Furst, M. 1997. Fast planning through planning graph analysis. *Artificial Intelligence* 90: 281–300.

21. Schweikert, C. 2008. *Study of novice programming: Plans, object design, and the web plan object language WPOL*. PhD thesis, The Graduate Center, City University of New York.

22. McCarthy, J. and Hayes, P. J. 1969. Some philosophical problems from the standpoint of artificial intelligence. In *Machine Intelligence 4*, edited by B. Meltzer and D. Michie. Edinburgh: Edinburgh University Press.

23. McDermott, D., 1982. A temporal logic for reasoning about processes and plans. *Cognitive Science* 6: 101–155.

24. Haugeland, J. 1985. *Artificial Intelligence: The Very Idea*. Cambridge, MA: The MIT Press.

25. Allen, J., Hendler, J., and Tate, A. P. 1990. *Readings in Planning*. Palo Alto, CA: Morgan Kaufmann.

26. Chapman, D. 1987. Planning for conjunctive goals. *Artificial Intelligence* 32: 333–377.

27. Korf, R., 1987. *Planning as Search: A Quantitative Approach*. Essex, UK: Elsevier Science Publishers.

28. Hart, P., Nilsson, N., and Raphael, B. 1968. A formal basis for the heuristic determination of minimum cost paths. *IEEE Transactions on System Science and Cybernetics (SSC)* 42: 100–107.

29. Doran, J. E. and Michie, D. 1966. Experiments with the graph traverser program. *Proceedings of the Royal Society* 294: 235–259.

30. Weld, D. 1994. An introduction to least-commitment planning. *Artificial Intelligence* 15: 27–61.

31. Ghallab, M., Nau, D., and Traverso, P. 2004. *Automated Planning: Theory and Practice*. San Francisco, CA: Morgan Kaufman.

32. Fox, M. S., Allen, B., and Strohm, G. 1981. Job search scheduling: An investigation in constraint-based reasoning. In *Proceedings of the Seventh International Joint Conference on Artificial Intelligence*. Menlo Park, CA: International Joint Conferences on Artificial Intelligence.

33. Hayes, P. J. 1975. A representation for robot plans. In *Advance Papers of the 1975 International Joint Conference on Artificial Intelligence*. Tbilisi, USSR.

34. Stallman, R. M. and Sussman, G. J. 1977. Forward reasoning and dependency directed backtracking. *Artificial Intelligence* 9: 135–196.

35. Daniel, L. 1983. Planning and operations research. In *Artificial intelligence: Tools, techniques, and applications*. New York, NY: Harper and Row.

36. Erman, L. D., Hayes-Roth, F., Lesser, V. R., and Reddy, D. R. 1980. The HEARSAY-II Speech understanding system: Integrating knowledge to resolve uncertainty. *ACM Computing Surveys* 12 (2).

37. Hayes-Roth, B., and Hayes-Roth, F. 1979. A cognitive model of planning. *Cognitive Science* 30:275–310.

38. Wilensky, R. 1981. Meta-planning: Representing and using knowledge about planning in problem solving and natural language understanding. *Cognitive Science* 5 (3).

39. Georgeff, M. 1982. Communication and interaction in multi-agent planning systems. In *Proceedings of the Third National Conference on Artificial Intelligence*. Menlo Park, CA: American Association for Artificial Intelligence.

40. Corkill, D. D. and Lesser, V. R., 1983. The use of meta-level control for coordination in a distributed problem-solving network. In *Proceedings of the Eighth International Joint Conference on Artificial Intelligence*, 748–756. Menlo Park, CA: International Joint Conferences on Artificial Intelligence.

41. Beckert, B. 2004. Introduction to Artificial Intelligence Planning. University Koblenz-Landau. Course Notes, Germany.

42. Erol, K., Hendler, J., and Nau, D. S. June 1994. UMCP: A sound and complete procedure for hierarchical task-network planning. In *Proceedings of the International Conference on AI Planning Systems (AIPS)*, 249–254.

43. Yang, Q. 1990. Formalizing planning knowledge for hierarchical planning. *Computational Intelligence* 6: 12–24.

44. Kambhampati, S. and Hendler, J. A. 1992. A validation structure based theory of plan modification and reuse. *Artificial Intelligence* 552–3: 193–258.

45. Fikes, R. E., Hart, P. E., and Nilsson, N. J. 1971. STRIPS: A new approach to the application of theorem proving to problem solving. *Artificial Intelligence* 34: 251–288.

46. Spalzzi, L. 2001. A survey on case-based planning. *Artificial Intelligence Review* 16 (1 Sept.): 3–36.

47. Borrajo, D. and Veloso, M. 1996. Lazy incremental learning of control knowledge for efficiently obtaining quality plans. *AI Review Journal*, Special Issue on Lazy Learning, 10: 1–34.

48. Tate, A. 1977. Generating project networks. In *Proceedings of the International Joint Conference on Artificial Intelligence, IJCAI-77* San Francisco, CA: Kaufmann.

49. Tate, A. and Daniel, L. 1982. A *Retrospective on the Planning: A joint AI/OR Approach Project*. Department of Artificial Intelligence Working Paper 125, Edinburgh.

50. Tate, A. 1983. *The less obvious side of NONLIN*. Department of Artificial Intelligence, University of Edinburgh.

51. Tate, A., Dalton, J., and Levine, J. 2000b. O-Plan: A web-based AI planning agent, AAAI-2000 intelligent systems demonstrator. In *Proceedings of the National Conference of the American Association of Artificial Intelligence AAAI-2000*, Austin, TX, August 2000.

52. Tate, A., Polyak, S., and Jarvis, P. 1998, June. TF method: An initial framework for modelling and analysing planning domains. Workshop on *Knowledge Engineering and Acquisition at the Fourth International Conference on AI Planning Systems APIS-98*, AAAI Technical Report WS-98-03, Carnegie-Mellon University, Pittsburgh, PA, June 1998.

53. Kingston, J., Shadbolt, N., and Tate, A. 1996. Common KADS models for knowledge based planning. In *Proceedings of the 13th National Conference on Artificial Intelligence AAAI-96*, Portland, OR: AAAI Press.

54. Tate, A., Levine, J., Jarvis, P., and Dalton, J. 2000a. Using ai planning techniques for army small unit operations. Poster Paper in the *Proceedings of the Fifth International Conference on AI Planning and Scheduling Systems AIPS-2000*, Breckenridge, CO, April 2000.

55. Drabble, B., Dalton, J., and Tate, A. 1997. Repairing plans on-the-fly. In *Proceedings of the NASA Workshop on Planning and Scheduling for Space*, Oxnard, CA, October 1997.

56. Tate, A. 1996. Responsive planning and scheduling using ai planning techniques—optimum-aiv, in trends & controversies—ai planning systems in the real world. *IEEE Expert: Intelligent Systems & Their Applications* 11 (December 6): 4–12.

57. Khan, S., Decker, K., Gillis, W., and Schmidt, C. 2003. A multi-agent system-driven ai planning approach to biological pathway discovery. In *Proceedings of the Thirteenth International Conference on Automated Planning and Scheduling ICAPS 2003*, edited by E. Giunchiglia, N. Muscettola, and D Nau. Trento, Italy: AAAI Press.

58. Aarup, M., Arentoft, M. M., Parrod, Y., Stokes, I., Vadon, H., and Stader, J. 1994. Optimum-aiv: A knowledge-based planning and scheduling system for spacecraft aiv. In *Intelligent scheduling*, edited by M. Zweben and M. S. Fox, 451–469. Morgan Kaufmann.

59. U.S. Army. 1999. Center for Army Lessons Learned. Virtual Research Library, *http://call.army. mil.*

60. Reece, G. and Tate, A. 1994. Synthesizing protection monitors from causal structure. In *Proceedings of the Second International Conference on Planning Systems AIPS-94*, Chicago, IL: AAAI Press.

61. Beck, H. and Tate, A. 1995. Open planning, scheduling and constraint management architectures. In *The British Telecommunications Technical Journal*, Special Issue on Resource Management.

62. Tate, A. 2000. Intelligible ai planning. In *Research and Development in Intelligent Systems XVII, Proceedings of ES2000, the Twentieth British Computer Society Special Group on Expert Systems International Conference on Knowledge Based Systems and Applied Artificial Intelligence*, 3–16, Cambridge, UK: Springer.

63. Tate, A. 2003. Coalition task support using i-x and <i-n-c-a>. In *Proceedings of the 3rd International Central and Eastern European Conference on Multi-Agent Systems CEEMAAS 2003*, Prague, Czech Republic, 7–16, June 16–18. Springer Lecture Notes in Artificial Intelligence LNAI 2691.

64. Soloway, E., Ehrlich, K., and Bonar, J. 1982. Tapping into tacit programming knowledge. In *Proceedings of the Conference on Human Factors in Computing Systems*. Gaithersburg, MD: NBS.

65. Ebrahimi, A. and Schweikert, C. 2006. Empirical study of novice programming with plans and objects. *ACM Inroads* 38 (4): 52–54.

Bibliography

LaValle, S. Planning Algorithms, University of Illinois, Urbana-Champaign, IL: Cambridge Press, 2006.

Online Class Lecture Notes on Planning:

1. http://www.isi.edu/~blythe/cs541/

2. http://www.cs.umd.edu/~nau/planning/slides/

3. http://www.inf.ed.ac.uk/teaching/courses/plan/

4. http://planning.cs.uiuc.edu/

5. http://rakaposhi.eas.asu.edu

6. http://www.uni-koblenz.de/~beckert/Lehre/KI-fuer-IM/09Planning.pdf

7. http://blackcat.brynmawr.edu/~dkumar/UGAI/planning.html#texts

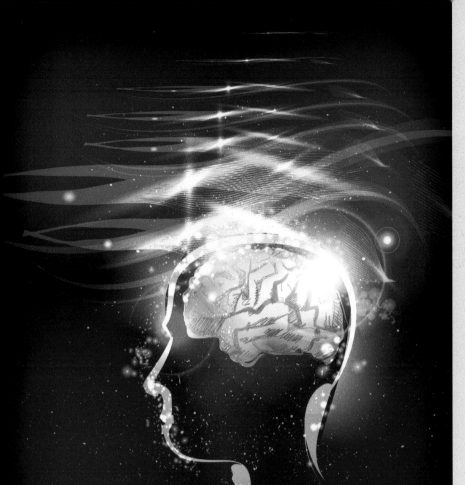

A new addition to this Part is Robotics (Chapter 15) which exploits research discussed in the previous Chapters and has witnessed great strides in recent decades it will likely open new vistas for AI methods to greatly impact in the near future.

Games have been played and tackled by AI researches from its beginnings. Checkers, chess, Othello, backgammon, bridge, poker, and Go are all well-known human arenas for competition. Despite AI's leading to computer mastery of all these games, (except Go which has been called the new drosophila for AI) humans can still enjoy them, be competitive and find room for symbiosis (e.g. Chess) – Chapter 16.

Finally Reprise (Chapter 17) summarizes where we've been and where we're possibly going.

The time arrives for us to review our journey through AI and consider where we have been and what the future holds.

An exciting recent example with IBM Watson playing Jeopardy on a par with the best human contestants provides optimism that the Turing Test will soon be tackled and conquered by machines in new frontiers and arenas.

The burning questions which will lie before us in the coming decades include:

1. What defines a person – given all the augmentations we may soon acquire (better vision, better calculation skills, better health, longer life, etc.) ?

2. Where, when, and what will define a person's real identity – one's essence (soul) ?

3. Who will receive the best care (augmentations, resources) when there are limitations on availability?

4. And if life will be extendable in these ways, how will overpopulation be prevented?

5. How will we maintain "control" over the machines we have created?

ROBOTICS

Sebastian Thurn.

The chapter introduces the subject of Robotics which is no longer just a look into the future but has been developing for many years, is happening now, and will continue to emerge as a part of human life for the unforeseeable future. First, we present the philosophical and pragmatic issues of the field, then we review the history of man trying to create machines that emulate what he/she does, or recreate himself. There follows a discussion of the technical issues

Figure 15.0
The "Urbie" urban robot during vision-guided, autonomous stair climbing (courtesy NASA).

that must be addressed when robots are built. Then a number of applications of robotics today are presented. The chapter concludes with a presentation and discussion of a new Turing Test called "The Lovelace Project."

15.0 ■ INTRODUCTION

"*In the Year 2525* (Exordium et Terminus)"—This was the title of the number one hit song by Zager and Evans in 1969.

The song projects what may happen to mankind in the coming millennia. Its "thesis" is the premise that man will continue to "dehumanize" himself in the coming years as he/she succumbs to technological advances.

That is not the subject of this chapter, but it sets the tone for the kinds of considerations for the future of mankind that we are required to look into when seeking advances in robotics. Here we are able to guess, dream, imagine, or "look into the crystal ball" to consider how our lives will change. Robots are no longer just a futuristic topic as they were in the early history of AI—they are a reality of life and becoming more and more a part of everyday life. Advances in robotics are integrally tied to advances in AI.

Let us consider now a small, future robot scene in a middle-class American home:

MrTomR:	Bobby you should have breakfast now.
Bobby:	(cries and runs around the kitchen)
MrTomR:	Bobby please sit down here. (indicates to Bobby where he should sit, pointing)
Bobby:	(finally sits down in a chair in the kitchen)
MrTomR:	What would you like for breakfast today?
Bobby:	What are my choices?
MrTomR:	Let's see. I could make you toast, with juice and milk; Or a bowl of cereal with milk and juice. Or I could make you scrambled eggs with English muffins.
Bobby:	MrTomR could make me toast with coffee?
MrTomR:	Bobby you know you are not allowed to drink coffee.

Let us consider what this dialogue entails and what kinds of information, knowledge, and state of the art/technological advances this dialogue entails. Every sentence by both five-year-old Bobby and MrTomR gives a significant clue to the state of the world when this dialogue could take place.

MrTomR is a robot whose task is similar to that of a butler or nanny who is to take care of a five-year-old. The parents of Bobby are away at work or on a weekend vacation. MrTomR is doing what he is capable of to simulate the interactions that might take place. Let us analyze what kinds of intelligence MrTomR must have to be able to conduct this dialogue:

First Mr TomR suggests that Bobby should have breakfast at a particular time. That is not a difficult programming task. The only thing that is sophisticated about this is the robot's ability to speak a sentence that is understandable. The sentence in itself can be constructed from a *menu* of commands that MrTomR is programmed to speak in certain trigger situations. Here the triggers are: 1) Bobby is home alone being cared for by MrTomR. 2) It is time for breakfast which Bobby has not yet received (Bobby never gets his own breakfast).

Mr TomR tells Bobby to sit down. This indicates that MrTomR understands what it means to be standing, that it has some sense of locomotion. That in order to eat breakfast "civilly," Bobby should be sitting at the breakfast table. Furthermore, MrTomR is able to point and understands where Bobby should be sitting. That is already quite a bit of advanced intelligence that MrTomR is demonstrating.

MrTomR announces the breakfast menu. This indicates that MrTomR understands the question from Bobby, and can articulately state the answer to it.

Bobby asks MrTomR for toast and coffee. MrTomR knows that Bobby is not allowed coffee (although it recognizes that toast was one of the items which comprises part of the menu). As children will do, Bobby is trying to see how far he can go with his caretaker. MrTomR is intelligent enough to be aware of the rules. He responds as an intelligent, experienced human butler or nanny might.

Every chapter and topic in our text to this point is or could be related to the field of robotics. Whether we are delving into search, games, logic, knowledge representation, production and expert systems, or neural networks, genetic algorithms, language, planning, and so on, there are easy and natural connections to robotics—and they are not far-fetched or remote. We now consider some of these connections in more detail.

Robotics and Search–from the early days of robotics (in the sense of a machine serving man by trying to accomplish a task), search has been integral to robotics. For example, the kinds of search problems that we addressed in Chapters 2, 3, and 4, including, for example, breadth first search and depth first search (Chapter 2), heuristic search (Chapter 3), and search in games (Chapter 4), are all typical problems that roboticists must address when building a system. That is, a robot must be programmed to get from point A to point B in the most efficient way. Or a robot must get around some obstacles to reach a destination or goal, akin to dealing with the kinds of maze problems that we introduced in these chapters.

Robotics, Logic, and Knowledge Representation–It goes without saying that robots and logic go hand in hand. The kinds of logical problems presented in Chapter 5 (logic) are the foundations of robotics, and the methods, such as resolution proofs and unification, are the building blocks for constructing sound robotic systems. Before any AI system is built, consideration must be made of how the elements of that system will be represented. Whether an agent-based approach will be used, swarm intelligence, trees, graphs, networks, or other approaches, these considerations are fundamental in robotic systems.

Production Systems and Expert Systems–Production systems as the foundations of expert systems are closely tied to control systems, which are the basic foundation of robotic systems. Directing a robot across a factory floor, getting a robot to pick up packages in an Amazon factory—what tasks need to be accomplished in order to be able to accomplish a bigger task (hierarchy). These are all examples of how robots may depend on production systems and expert systems (Chapters 7 and 9). Furthermore, the expertise that humans have developed in various spheres (e.g., machinist tools, factory assembly lines, blending of colors for paint generation, choosing the right packaging, etc.) are natural arenas for production systems comprising expert systems.

Fuzzy Logic–was the subject of Chapter 8 and even in the robotic world there are outcomes that are not only black and white / yes and no, but "to a certain degree of." For example, a robot may encounter resistance along its path to a goal, and thereby stumble. The robot must persist in its goal of accomplishing an objective. In other words, even the robot world is not just discrete, but will depend on certain "degrees of freedom" with variations on the degrees of attributes rather than outcomes which are just "on" or "off" or "yes" or "no."

Machine Learning and Neural Networks–as the sophistication of these AI methods has improved, opportunities for their use in applications of robotics have emerged. The Google Car comes to mind as a premier example.

Techniques such as Genetic Algorithms, Tabu Search, and Swarm Intelligence are naturally explored by robotic systems, especially when they must work in groups, for example, in the simulation of crowd behavior, or walking on New York City streets; or robots simulating people rushing to their commutes while avoiding people who are approaching them or in their paths.

Natural Language Understanding and Speech Understanding – this was the subject of Chapter 13, and we continually see improvements in how machines (robots) will replace humans in ever more advanced tasks which involve language and speech understanding. Hence progress in these disciplines is integral and important to robotics. The issues and factors involved—for example, semantics, syntax, accent, and inflection—are enormous.

Planning – was presented in Chapter 14, and has always been a subfield of AI that is strongly associated with robotics. You have already seen a number of examples of planning in robotics in that chapter which involve how a robot should proceed in a accomplishing a task or set of tasks.

We will now discuss some of the challenges for robotics and why it is both a promising and very difficult field. In constructing robots we are addressing the issues that make mankind unique. The challenges are dependent on how ambitious we want to be. That is, do we only wish the robot to be mobile? Do we wish the robot to perform tasks akin to the original definition of the word from the play by the Czech playwright Karel Čapek entitled *R.U.R.* (1921) where it was first introduced? In the Czech language *robota* means labor or work, but in the context of the play it meant slavery or forced labor.[1] Or do we have much greater ambitions for robots—that they not only be able to aid man, but to emulate him/her, enhance him/her, and be recreated/replaced in his image? Hence we have robots performing mundane tasks that not only people had to do (e.g., vacuum as with IRO-BOT Roomba, See Chapter 6), but also are building robots that are able to perform surgery, to enter dangerous places, carry heavy loads, and even to drive cars safely without humans! And in the new millennium, they are starting to perform such difficult tasks better than humans can—that is, more accurately, more quickly, and more efficiently, thereby freeing people from the dangers and challenges of such tasks. Robots are taking on more and more tasks that for hundreds of years humans had customarily performed themselves. Robots are even being built to simulate recreational tasks such as playing bridge (see Chapter 16) and soccer.

These advances have been enabled by improvements in 1) Locomotion, 2) Machine Vision, 3) Machine Learning, 4) Planning, 5) Problem Solving, and others. In the future we will likely entrust robots to an increasing number of decisions of a vital nature to humans. Some argue that there are limitations to what robots will be able to accomplish until we understand ourselves better. Marvin Minsky[2] poses this perspective in his relatively early work on robotics. For nearly thirty years he, Doug Lenat (see Chapter 9), and others have been trying to address the problem of common sense knowledge. He addresses questions such as: *How do children really learn? What turns short-term memories into long-term memories? How is knowledge organized for people?* During the past 25 years or so it has become evident that robots are and will continue to be able to take advantage of tremendous advances in natural language processing and speech understanding (Chapter 13). As has already been alluded, such advances, along with the possibility that machines will be built with intelligence on a par with or beyond our own, will pose difficult philosophical and practical questions. One thing is clear—despite the recognizable pros and cons of building highly intelligent robotic systems, in this technological age there is no turning back.

15.1 HISTORY: SERVING, EMULATING, ENHANCING, AND REPLACING MAN

The history of *"Man Makes Man,"* as T. A. Heppinger names his essay, [1] is much richer and longer than one might imagine. We will consider the historical aspects of robotics from a number of perspectives, including: Robot Lore, Early Mechanical Robots, Robots in Film and Literature, and Early Twentieth-Century Robots.

15.1.1 Robot Lore

One of the earliest examples of robot lore is the story of the brilliant thirteenth-century English clergyman-scientist-philosopher, Friar Roger Bacon, who wanted to build a wall of brass to protect England against invaders. To accomplish this, he proposed a **"brass head"** to explain how such a wall should be built. That head was watched for three weeks, and it was only after the friars had watched carefully over the head that it spoke, "Time is." And a half hour later, "Time was." And another half hour later, "Time is past." Certainly it is just a tale, but it may have been the inspiration for the leading medieval physician Paracelsus to suggest how an entire living being, a **"homunculus,"** could be built:

> Let the semen of a man putrefy by itself in a hermetically sealed glass with the highest putrefaction of horse manure for forty days, or until it begins at last to live, move and be agitated, which can easily be seen. After this time it will be in some degree like a human being…If now after this, it will be every day nourished and fed cautiously and prudently with the Arcanum of human blood, and kept for forty days in the perpetual and equal heat of horse manure, … This we call a homunculus and it should afterwards be educated with the greatest care and zeal, until it grows and begins to display intelligence. [1, p. 30–31].

Although this was based on "alchemical lore," the story reminds us of the vast advancements science and the medical profession have made through the centuries.

Another legend of man-made man is the lore of **golem** from the sixteenth century several decades after Paracelsus. From the Talmud the word "golem" means incomplete or malformed, such as an embryo or the shapeless mass of dust from which Adam was created. It is said that around the year 1550, Elijah of Chelm created an artificial man, called a golem, with the Name of God corresponding to the four letters YHWH. This golem was deemed a monster threatening the world until its sacred name was removed. [1, p. 32]

Thirty years later there was another golem. This one centered around the Rabbi Judah ben Loew, Chief Rabbi of Prague. The Rabbi was known as a sober figure who was friends with the famous astronomers Tycho Brahe and Johannes Kepler. To protect his people, the Rabbi is said to have gone to the River Moldau with two assistants where they fashioned from clay a human figure (see Figure 15.1).

Figure 15.1
Clay golem.

The story continues:

> One assistant circled the figure seven times from left to right. Loew pronounced an incantation, and the golem began to shine like fire. The other assistant then began his own incantation which circling seven times from right to left. The fire went out, hair grew on the figure's head, and nails developed on its fingers. Now it was Loew's turn to circle seven times, as the three of them chanted words from Genesis. When Loew implanted the Holy Name upon its forehead, the golem opened its eyes and came to life…

Although the golem was unable to speak, it had superhuman power, and thus was useful in defending the Jews of Prague against the Gentiles. The golem was also Loew's servant and worked as a janitor within the temple, with an allowance for rest on Sabbath. Only Rabbi Loew was able to control the golem, but eventually it ran amok, attacking its creator. The golem's reign of destruction ended when Rabbi Loew tricked it into kneeling before him and plucked the sacred name from its forehead—and magically the golem was again reduced to clay.[1]

These three legends—the brass head of Bacon, the homunculus of Paracelsus, and the golem of Rabbi Loew—share in common the notion of a savant (a respected, accomplished man of intelligence) creating something in the form of a man that will have the power of a man. And the famous legend of *Frankenstein*, authored by Mary Shelley in 1817, is actually a statement on the dangers of letting technology run amok; it is noteworthy that the story, by analogy, is quite consistent with the story of the golem some four centuries earlier.

15.1.2 Early Mechanical Robots

Perhaps the first accepted mechanical representation of man was the Strasbourg cock, a cast-iron rooster built in 1574, intended to be a reminder of St. Peter's denial of Jesus (see Figure 15.2). At noon daily, it opened its beak, stretched out its tongue, flapped its wings, spread out its feathers, raised its head, and crowed three times. Used until 1789, it served as an inspiration to Hobbes, Descartes, and Boyle as an example of what might someday be achievable by machinery.

In the mid-eighteenth century, there followed the inventions of Jacques de Vaucanson, who created various artificial humans and animals which were of great realism. One of his most famous inventions was a 1738 mechanical duck which amazed in its ability to quack, splash around in water, eat, drink, and excrete (see Figure 15.3a). Vaucanson also built two androids in human form that played musical instruments (see Figure 15.3). One played the flute and the other the drums. What most impressed people was that the flutist was actually playing, rather than producing sounds from a hidden place. The flutist's breath came directly from its mouth by means of a set of bellows. Lip movements were controlled by a mechanism. The flute, being a standard instrument, made sounds via finger motions over holes—as would be performed by a human. Hence, in the early history

Figure 15.2
Strasbourg Cock.

of robotics, this was a considered a landmark, in that the flute was considered an instrument of skill that only a small number of people could play well. Here, we had the first mechanical device that performed a learned skill better than most people.[1, p. 38]

LE JOUEUR DE GALOUBET, LE CANARD ET LE JOUEUR DE TAMBOURIN
PIÈCES AUTOMATIQUES CONSTRUITES PAR VAUCANSON.

Figure 15.3
Vaucanson's duck, flutist, and drummer.

Figure 15.3a
Vaucanson's duck with internal mechanisms.

The next rather well-known example of man emulating man was somewhat of a hoax which fooled Europe as it was exhibited over many years. The Turk was a contraption built by the Baron Wolfgang von Kempelen in the Austro-Hungarian Court in 1769. Purportedly, inside a box with gears and cogs which played the moves of chess on a board, was a midget Polish chess master. It featured "a mannequin in the form of a Turk, with turban and handlebar mustache, seated behind a wooden cabinet." [1, p. 39] see Figure 15.4). The Turk wowed audiences across Europe for many years in that it played strong chess and could not be fooled with illegal moves. It was impressive in the fact that it was the first time that people believed that the distinction between man and machine had been blurred.[1]

Eventually the Turk was safely transported to a Philadelphia museum where in the mid-twentieth century it unfortunately burned down in a fire.

Figure 15.4
Baron von Kempelen's The Turk.

Between 1770 and 1773 the father and son pair, Pierre and Henri-Louis Jaquet-Drov, developed and demonstrated three amazing human-like figures known as the Scribe, the Draftsman, and the Musician (see Figure 15.5). All three operated via clockwork featuring an intricate array of cams. Two, the Scribe and the Draftsman, were in the shape of young boys, elegantly dressed. The Scribe was capable of dipping a quill pen in an inkwell and then writing up to forty letters. The Scribe's hand, controlled by a cam, could move in any of three directions to form one letter. Levers on a disk were used for control, and the Scribe could then write any desired text. His brother, the Draftsman, could produce drawings of Louis XV and similar figures including, for example, a battleship. The eyes of these androids demonstrated an attentive attitude while at work by moving them accordingly.

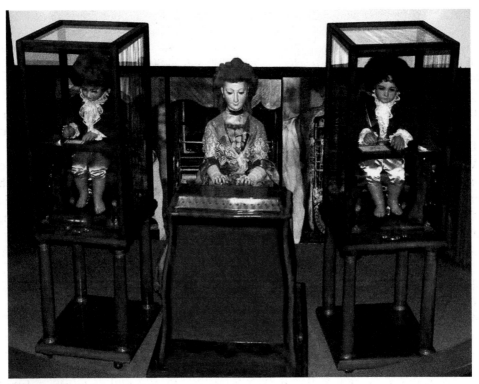

Figure 15.5
The Scribe, the Draftsman, and the Musician – Pierre and Henri Louis Jaquet-Drov.

The Musician, another Jaquet-Droz android, resembled a girl of 16, wearing a powdered wig and a dress appropriate for the court of Vienna. She played the organ and did so well, with convincing eye and body movements that made her seem alive. The end of a performance was accompanied by a bow. Jaquet-Droz androids found permanent homes in the Muséed'Art et d'Histoire in Neuchatel, Switzerland. The Draftsman, with its design of a battleship, found its way into the Franklin Institute in Philadelphia. In each, one can see the innovation and engineering which led to modern industrial robots. The differences are in form and the modern use of hydraulics and programming instead of springs, cams, and clockwork mechanisms.

There followed the industrial revolution, and one of its artifacts was a mechanism devised by James Watt (credited with the development of the first practical steam engine circa 1783). In 1788 Watt devised a "flywheel governor" featuring two whirling balls that were able to swing outward via centrifugal force. It was linked to a steam engine whereby the outward swing of the flyballs measured the engine's speed; furthermore, using another linkage, the outward swing controlled a value that maintained its present speed. In essence, this comprised the world's first feedback-control mechanism. In 1868 James Clerk Maxwell (who discovered Maxwell's equations in electromagnetism) published "On Governors," the first systematic study of feedback control. This turned out to be an essential element of robots in the twentieth century.

In 1912 the automatic, mechanical, chess-playing machine built of gears and cogs by Leonardo Torres y Quevedo (see Chapter 1, Figure 1.24) could play the elementary endgame King and Rook vs. King via an explicit set of rules to deliver checkmate in a limited number of moves regardless of the starting position. This was believed to be the first machine capable of not only handling information but being able to make decisions based on this information.

15.1.3 Robots in Film and Literature

The play **R.U.R.** (stands for Rossum's Universal Robots) entails robots who have been designed and used as general purpose laborers. They are devoid of human feelings and emotions, but are used as soldiers in war. In the play it turns out that an associate at R.U.R. discovers how to add pain and emotions to the robots. Hence the robots rebel against their human masters, virtually exterminating them. However, they are unable to maintain the level of production of themselves. A final touch is when the two robots fall in love with the suggestion of the coming of the new Adam and Eve.

We must bear in mind the time when R.U.R. appeared—just after the end of World War I. It was also a statement on the dangers of technology which, with the invention of machine guns, submarines, and poison gas, had turned the war into a bloodbath with mass carnage and massacre. Another work in the same vein was the 1926 classic movie **Metropolis** by Fritz Lang—a very popular and highly respected German filmmaker. It was based on a book written by his wife Thea Harbou. Metropolis focuses on the wretched lives of workers who live beneath a city. Its robot is a labor agitator, Maria, who assumes the appearance of a leader whom the workers can trust. It turns out that Maria leads the robots to self-destruction, and they burn her at the stake, where she turns to metal (ibid., p. 49.).

Regarding contributions to robotics in film, arts, and literature, the work of Isaac Asimov must be introduced. In 1942 as a young science fiction writer, he contributed to *Galaxy Science Fiction* the story "The Caves of Steel," where he first presented the oft-repeated **Three Laws of Robots**:

1. A robot may not injure a human being, or through inaction allow a human being to come to harm.

2. A robot must obey the orders given it by human beings except where such orders would conflict with the First Law.

3. A robot must protect its own existence as long as such protection does not conflict with the First or Second Law.

Many decades passed before Asimov's ideas captivated the world in such films as Forbidden Planet (1956) and the Star Wars Trilogy (1977, Star Wars; 1980, The Empire Strikes Back; and 1983, The Return of the Jedi).

15.1.4 Twentieth-Century Robots

In the twentieth century a number of robotic systems were built. Many were successful. In the 1980s robots started to become commonplace in factories and industrial settings. Here we limit our discussion to robots that were particularly instrumental to research and progress in the field.

15.1.4.1 Biomimetic Systems

In this section, we present two **biomimetic systems** that were very important to progress in robotics research. One field that has not been discussed in our text to this point, considered an early forerunner to AI, is the field of **cybernetics**—the study and comparison of communication and control processes in biological and artificial systems. The person most credited for defining and doing seminal research in this field is Norbert Wiener at MIT. [3] This field combined theories and principles from neuroscience and biology with those from engineering, with the goal of finding common properties and principles in animals and machines. [4] Matarić notes that "a key concept of cybernetics focuses on the coupling, combining, and interaction between the mechanism or organism and its environment." Such interactions are necessarily complex as we shall soon see.

Her definition of a robot is as follows:

> an autonomous system which exists in the physical world, can sense its environment, and can act on it to achieve some goals. [4, p. 21]*

Figure 15.6
Grey Walter's Tortoise – the first recognized robot.

Given this definition, Prof. Matarić calls William Grey Walter's **Tortoise** the first robot that was built with the underlying goals of cybernetics. Walter (1910–1977) was born in Kansas City but lived and was educated in Great Britain. He was a neurophysiologist with a strong interest in how the brain works, discovering theta and delta waves that are produced during sleep. He built machines with animal-like behavior to study how the brain works. Walter was convinced that even organisms with very simple nervous systems could exhibit complex and unexpected behavior. Walter's robots were distinct from the robots that preceded them in that they behaved in unpredictable ways, had reflexes, and in their environments were able to avoid repetitive behaviors. [5] The tortoise consisted of a hard plastic shell with three wheels (see Figure 15.7). Two wheels were for forward and backward motion while the third was for steering. Its "sense organs" were extremely simple, consisting of only a photoelectric cell to provide sensitivity to light and surface electric contacts that served as touch sensors. A telephone battery provided power, while the shell provided some degree of protection against physical damage. [5]

With these simple components and a few others, Grey Walter's **Machina Speculatrix** (for machine that thinks) was able to exhibit the following behaviors:

- Find the light
- Head toward the light
- Back away from bright light
- Turn and push to avoid obstacles
- Recharge its battery

The turtles were the earliest examples of **artificial life** or ALife; their variety of complex, unprogrammed behaviors were early examples of what we now call **emergent behavior**. [4]

Valentino Braitenberg is a German scientist who was inspired by Grey Walter's work. In 1984 he published a book entitled Vehicles long after the ideas of cybernetics, and long after it was considered a separate discipline of study. The book presents a series of ideas (or thought experiments)

---

*Note that an autonomous robot acts on the basis of its own decisions, and is not controlled by a human.

demonstrating how simple robots (which he called vehicles) can produce behaviors which appear very human and lifelike. [4] Although Braitenberg's vehicles were never built, they proved inspirational for roboticists.

These started with a single motor and light sensor. Gradually they increased in complexity to several motors and sensors, and exploration of the various permutations of sensors between them. The sensors were connected to the motors. Therefore, a light sensor could be connected directly to the wheels of a vehicle, and as the light would get stronger, the faster the robot would move toward the light—this is called **photophilic** attraction or, in Latin, "loving light." Also, the connections could be reversed so that the robot would move more slowly and hence be **photophobic**, or exhibit fear of light.

Furthermore, akin to the concepts of Chapter 11 on neural networks, connections between sensors and motors, whereby stronger sensor input produced stronger output, were called **excitatory connections.** Conversely, sensory inputs that weakened the motor as they got stronger were called **inhibitory connections.** Again the inspiration came from biological neurons

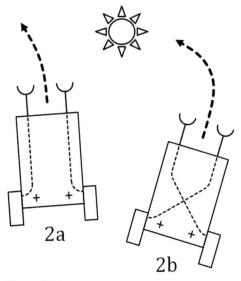

Figure 15.7
Example of Braitenberg's vehicles. Vehicle 2a moves toward a source of light while vehicle 2b moves away from a source of light.

and their excitatory and inhibitory connections. Continuing with this analogy, it is fairly evident how variations in these connections between sensors and motors can result in a variety of behaviors. Braitenberg's book describes how such simple mechanisms can be used to store information, build a memory, and even achieve learning. [4]

15.1.4.2 More Recent Systems

Artificial Intelligence research progressed in many arenas during the twentieth century, a point we have described throughout this text. Research incorporating what had and was being learned in the various disciplines of AI was focused at three institutions: **MIT, Standard, and SRI International (then known as Stanford Research Institute).**

Shakey, at SRI (1966–1972), was the first general-purpose mobile robot able to reason about its own actions. Shakey (see Figure 15.8) was designed to analyze commands and break them into a series of actions necessary to perform. Its basis was research in computer vision and natural language processing. Charles Rosen was the project manager; contributors included Nils Nilsson, Alfraed Brain, Sven Wahlstrom, Bertram Raphael, and others. **STRIPS** (Stanford Research Institute Problem Solver) was mentioned in Chapter 14 (Planning) as a premier example of an automated planning robot system. It was developed by Richard Fikes and Nils Nilsson in 1971 at SRI International. MIT (The Massachusetts Institute of Technology) has a long history of research and contributions to the field of AI and robotics—including robots in many environments such as space and sea, and also exhibiting locomotion.

There are many more examples than we can give justice to here, however, in Section 15.3 you will learn about twenty-first-century applications

Figure 15.8
SRI's Shakey.

of robotics, including MIT's Cog. Table 15.1 presents diverse robot systems that have been built during the past 55 years or so. Their increasing sophistication, capabilities, and purpose are most noteworthy. Problems which involve locomotion in open terrain are much harder than in well-defined spaces or environments.

Table 15.1
Summary of robotics projects from 1960–2010.

	SYSTEM NAME	YEAR	CREATOR	INSTITUTION/ COMPANY	FEATURES	FOOTNOTE
1	Stanford Cart	1960–1980	James Adams	Stanford University	Able to move around obstacles using a camera	[9]
2	Freddy	1969–1971	Donald Michie	University of Edinburgh	Assembles blocks by using its camera	[10]
3	WABOT-1	1970–1973	Waseda University	Waseda University	First full-scale anthropomorphic robot. Able to communicate with a person in Japanese. Could measure distances with receptors.	[11]
4	FAMULUS	1973	KUKA Robotics	KUKA Robotics	Material handling, i.e, moving parts and materials in factories	[1]
5	Silver Arm	1974	David Silver	MIT	Small parts assembler that reacts to feedback from touch and pressure sensors.	[2]
6	WABOT-2	1980–1984	Waseda University	Waseda University	Able to read a musical score and play the organ, and speak to people	[11]
7	Omnibot	1980s–2000	Tomy	Tomy	Carry light objects with arms, had a tray to carry objects	[12]
8	Direct Drive Arm	1981	Takeo Kanade	Carnegie Mellon University	Robotic arm that could move more freely and smoothly	[3]
9	Modulus Robot	1984–1990s	Massimo Giuliana	Sirius	Domestic household robot, household applications	[13]
10	Big Dog	1986– Present	Martin Buehler	Boston Dynamics	Quadruped walking, pack mule	[7]

	SYSTEM NAME	YEAR	CREATOR	INSTITUTION/ COMPANY	FEATURES	FOOTNOTE
11	Kismet	1990s	Cynthia Breazeal	MIT	Low-level feature extraction system, Motivation system, Motor system	[30]
12	COG	1993–Present	Rodney Brooks	MIT	Humanoid, emulates human thought	[4]
13	The Walking Forest Machine	1995	PlusTech Ltd.	PlusTech Ltd.	Walking backwards, forwards, sideways, and diagonally in uneven terrain	[5]
14	Scout II	1998	Ambulatory Robotic Laboratory	Ambulatory Robotic Laboratory	Quadruped walking	[5]
15	AIBO	1999	Sony	Sony	Quadruped Walking, pet	[6]
16	Hiro	1999–2010	Kawada KK	Kawada Industries INC.	Runs real time Linux QNX	[14]
17	CosmoBot	1999–Present	Dr. Corinna Lathan with Jack Vice	AnthroTronix, Inc.	Live Play, Simon Says, playback	[15]
9	ASIMO	2000–Present	Honda	Honda	Humanoid upright, two-legged walking	[5]
20	Anybots	2001–Present	Trevor Blackwell	ANYBOTS	Virtual presence systems	[16]
21	Inkha	2002–2006	mat and mrplong	King's College London	Camera to track Human movement, speaks periodically about facts	[17]
22	Domo	2004–Present	Jeff Weber and Aaron Edsinger	MIT	Perception, learning, manipulation	[18]
23	Seropi	2005–Present	KITECH	KITECH	Human-friendly working space guidance	[19]
24	Wakamaru	2005–Present	Mitsubishi Heavy Industries	Mitsubishi Heavy Industries	Reminder, emergency call, Linux operating system and connects to the internet	[20]
25	Enon	2005–Present	Fujitsu	Fujitsu Corporation	Self-guiding, limited speech recognition and synthesis	[21]
26	MUSA	2005–Present	Young Bong Bang	Seoul National University	Fight using kendo	[22]

	SYSTEM NAME	YEAR	CREATOR	INSTITUTION/ COMPANY	FEATURES	FOOTNOTE
28	BEAR	2005–Present	Vecna Technologies	Vecna Technologies	Six feet tall, hydraulic upper body lifts 500lbs, steel torso, maximum hydraulic exertion of 3000psi	[23]
29	Issac	2006–Present	IssacTeam	Politecnico di Torino	Offers many solutions oriented to automation industry	[24]
30	Willow Garage	2006–Present	Scott Hassan	Willo Garage Inc.	ROS (Robot Operating System) developing hardware and software for robotics applications	[25]
31	RuBot II	2006–Present	Pete Redmond	Mechatrons.com	Solves Rubik's Cube	[26]
32	KeepOn	2007	Kozima, Hideki	Miyagi University	Responds to emotions and dances	[8]
33	Topio Dio	2008–2010	TOSY Robotics JSC	Automatica	Remote control via wireless, integrate 3D vision via 2 cameras, 3D operation space, processes pre-defined images, detects obstacles by ultrasonic sensor, three-wheeled base with omnidirectional and balanced motion	[27]
34	Phobot	2008–Present	Students	University of Amster-dam	Exhibits behavior that mimics fear and overcoming it by graded exposure	[28]
35	Salvius	2008–Present	Gunther Cox	Salvius Robot	Modular design, constructed using recycled materials and Open source	[29]
36	ROBOTY	2010–Present	Hamdi M. Sahloul	Engineering University of Sana	Robot capable of playing chess	[30]

References for Table 15.1

[1] RobotWorx. The History of...KUKA Robotics. December 9, 2014. Retrieved from http://www.used-robots.com/articles/viewing/the-history-of-kuka-robotics.

[2] Nocks, L. 2007. The Robot: The Life Store of Technology. Westport: Greenwood Publishing Group.

[3] Williams, J. D. Direct Drive Robotic Arms. December 9, 2014. Retrieved from http://diva.library.cmu.edu/Kanade/kanadearm.html.

[4] Ahmad, N. 2003. The humanoid robot Cog. Crossroads 10 (2): 3.

[5] Carbone, G. and Ceccarelli, M. Legged Robotic Systems. December 9, 2014. Retrieved from http://cdn. intechopen.com/pdfs-wm/33.pdf.

[6] Sony. ERS-1010. December 9, 2014. Retrieved from http://www.sony.net/Fun/design/history/product/1990/ ers-110.html.

[7] Buehler, M. 2006. BigDog - a dynamic quadruped robot. Robotics Institute Seminar. Boston Dynamics. BigDog - The Most Advanced Rough-Terrain Robot. December 9, 2014. Retrieved from http://www. bostondynamics.com/robot_bigdog.html.

[8] Cox, W. Top 10 Robots of the Past 10 Years - Robots of the Decade Awards. 4 January 2010. December 9, 2014. Retrieved from <http://www.robotshop.com/blog/en/top-10-robots-of-the-past-10-years-robots-of-the-decade-awards-3743.

[9] Earnest, L. December 2012. Stanford Cart. December 9, 2014. Retrieved from http://web.stanford. edu/~learnest/cart.htm.

[10] Tate, A. December 14, 2012. Edinburgh Freddy Robot. December 9, 2014. Retrieved from http://www.aiai. ed.ac.uk/project/freddy/.

[11] Humanoid Robotics Institute, Waseda University. Humanoid History -WABOT-. December 9, 2014. Retrieved from http://www.humanoid.waseda.ac.jp/booklet/kato_2.html.

[12] Tomy. http://www.theoldrobots.com/omnibot.html

[13] Sirius. http://www.megadroid.com/Robots/mody.htm

[14] Kawada Industries. http://global.kawada.jp/mechatronics/

[15] AnthroTronics Inc. http://www.anthrotronix.com/?option=com_content&view=article&id=81&Itemid=144

[16] Anybots. http://www.anybots.com/

[17] King's College London. http://www.whoosh.co.uk/inkha/TextLifeStory.htm

[18] MIT. http://people.csail.mit.edu/edsinger/domo_research.htm

[19] KITECH. http://www.plasticpals.com/?p=12155

[20] Mitsubishi Heavy Industries. https://www.mhi-global.com/products/detail/wakamaru_about.html

[21] Fjitsu. http://thefutureofthings.com/5191-fujitsus-enon-robot/

[22] MUSA. <http://www.technovelgy.com/ct/Science-Fiction-News.asp?NewsNum=423

[23] Vecna Technologies. http://www.vecna.com/labs; http://www.gizmag.com/battlefield-extraction-assist-robot/17059/

[24] ISAAC Team. http://www.isaacrobot.it/

[25] Willow Garage. http://www.willowgarage.com/

[26] Mechatrons. http://mechatrons.com/rubot-ii/

[27] Automatica. http://techcrunch.com/2010/06/18/topio-dio-meet-vietnams-first-robot/; http://en.akihabaranews. com/51330/robot/meet-topio-dio-vietnams-first-humanoid-service-robot

[28] University of Amsterdam. http://www.foxnews.com/story/2008/03/17/cowardly-phobot-steals-show-at-amsterdam-robot-conference/

[29] Salvius Robot. http://salviusrobot.blogspot.com/

[30] Engineering University of Sana. http://www.scribd.com/doc/57089754/Roboty

15.2 TECHNICAL ISSUES

As we alluded at the beginning of this chapter, the technical issues for developing robots are immense, and in one way or another, they depend on how ambitious and sophisticated one's goals are for a robot's capabilities. In essence, working in robotics is a multifaceted form of problem solving.

By analogy, let us consider the problems a human faces when entering a shopping mall and attempting to find a particular store in that mall. For a human, there are fairly straightforward steps and questions to ask in order to find the store he/she is looking for. You might look for the mall directory, or ask people at information desks, or see store managers who might be familiar, or use information sources such as the WWW or even phone apps. If we have previously visited the store, we may even have some memory of where this store is located in the mall—i.e., which floor, neighboring stores, special features, and so on. Now let us consider what the challenges would be for a mobile robot to find a particular store in the mall. One solution would be for the robot to simply follow locomotion directions, for example, go straight for .2 miles, turn left, go .1 miles, and so on; or it may be told to take an elevator up a floor, and so forth. The means of communicating directions to the robot could of course be quite varied in format. The directions could be sensory, auditory, written, or visual. The differences in how diverse robots could handle this problem and related problems is the subject of this section. It is important to bear in mind that whatever the solution method chosen for a robot to find the goal store in question, every aspect of the solution must be considered by the robot's developers and programmers. Its locomotion, its perception of obstacles, landmarks, and goal points, must all be considered in detail—by human developers. That is why the possibility of employing machine learning in robots (see Chapters 11 and 12) represents such an important advance in the field. If a robot can learn…then almost anything seems possible.

The early history of robotics focused on locomotion and vision (known as machine vision). Closely aligned to the discipline were problems of computational geometry and planning. In the past few decades, the possibilities for robots have become more of a reality, with domains such as linguistics, neural networks, and fuzzy logic being more integral to the research and progress in robotics.

15.2.1 Robot Components

Before we delve into the typical problems facing roboticists, we feel it is important to consider the components which comprise a typical robot. These include:

1. The physical body or embodiment
2. Sensors for perceiving the environment
3. Effectors and actuators to enable action
4. Controller(s) to enable autonomous behavior

We'll consider the requirements for each of these four components one by one.

1. Having a **physical body** means that a robot may conceivably develop as sense of self—that is, it can consider such questions as: where am I, what is my state (or condition), and where am I trying to go? This also means that it is subject to the same physical laws that we live by, it takes up a certain amount of space, and also needs energy to perform functions, such as sensing and thinking. [2]

---

[2] It seems worthwhile mentioning that one of the basic elements of life is considered to be motion, or the ability to move. So when considering the possibility of machines moving, we are anointing them with one of the most basic accepted ingredients of being alive.

2. **Sensory perception** is a requirement for a real robot. It must be able to perceive the environment, react to it, and act on it. Usually such reactions involve movement, and that is a fundamental task for robots. As is common in computer science hardware, states of electronic systems are often represented by 1s and 0s or binary digits. Depending on the number of these sensors involved, there are 2^N combinations of perceptions (sensor states) that a robot can have. The sensors are used to represent the internal and external state of a robot. The internal world refers to the robot's own state as it perceives it. The external state refers to how the robot perceives the world it is interacting with. Representation of internal and external states (or **internal models**) of robots is an important design issue.

3. **Effectors and Actuators** Effectors are the components that enable a robot to take action. They use underlying mechanisms, such as muscles and motors, to perform various functions, but mainly for locomotion and manipulation [4, p. 24]. Locomotion and manipulation comprise two major subfields of robotics. The former is concerned with movement (i.e., the legs of robots), while the latter is concerned with handling things (i.e., the arms of a robot).

4. **Controllers** are the hardware and/or software that enable a robot to be autonomous; hence the devices that control their decisions—or their brain. If robots are partially or fully controlled by humans, then they are not autonomous.

It is noteworthy that there are a number of important analogies between power supplies for robots and people. Humans need food and water to provide energy for their bodies, for locomotion and for brain functioning. Robots' brains are not presently so developed and therefore need power (usually provided by batteries) for locomotion and manipulation. Now consider what happens when *our* power supply goes down (i.e., when we are hungry or require rest). We become incapable of making good decisions, make mistakes, and may act poorly or strangely. The same thing can happen to robots. Hence their power supply must be isolated, protected, and efficient, and they should **degrade gracefully**. That is, robots should be able to replenish their power autonomously and without totally breaking down [4].

Effectors are any device on a robot that has an effect on the environment. In the world of robotics they may be arms, legs, or wheels, that is, any robot component that can be used to have an effect on the environment. Actuators are the mechanisms that enable effectors to perform their tasks. Actuators may include electric motors, hydraulic or pneumatic cylinders, or temperature-sensitive or chemically sensitive materials. Such actuators may be used to activate wheels, arms, grippers, legs, and other effectors. Actuators may be passive or active. Although all actuators require energy, some may be passive and require direct power to operate, while others may be passive and use physical laws of motion to conserve energy. The most common actuators are motors, but may also be hydraulics using fluid pressure, pneumatics using air pressure, photoreactive material (responding to light), chemically reactive materials, thermally reactive materials, or piezoelectric materials (materials, usually crystals, that create electric charges when pushed or pressed) [4, p. 32].

15.2.1.1 Motors and Gears

The inventions of the electromagnet by Joseph Henry in 1831 is considered by many the greatest invention since man created the wheel. Closely tied and of equal significance is the invention of the electric motor in 1861 by Etienne Lenoir. The association and significance of motors to power for effecting motion is paramount Equally significant, therefore, is the importance of motors to robotics.

Robots will typically use DC motors comprised of electromagnets and current to produce magnetic fields which turn the shafts of the motors. Motors must be run by a voltage appropriate for the task(s) they are being asked to perform so as not to wear them down. DC motors are preferred, as they provide constant voltage, drawing current at an amount proportional to the work being done. Motors which run into high resistance (e.g., a robot runs into a wall which does not move) will eventually stall after running out of power. Recall from physics that

$$\textbf{V (Voltage)} = \textbf{I (Current)} \times \textbf{R (Resistance).}$$

Hence **V/I = R or Voltage** is proportional to resistance. But **Work = Force × Distance**. In the case of the robot stuck against a wall, the distance becomes very small (or zero) and thus, despite high power (Voltage), the work actually performed is very little or none at all. Perhaps an easy analogy to demonstrate this idea is a car that is stuck in snow with its motor revved up and its wheels spinning. If this goes on for too long, the car too will eventually stall [4, p. 33].

The more current (electrons transferred per unit of time, measured in Amperes) that a motor produces, the more torque (rotational force) is produced by the motor shaft. Hence the power of a motor is the produce of its torque and the rotational speed of the shaft.*** Most DC motors operate at the speed of 3,000–9,000 revolutions per minute (rpm). This means they produce high speeds but low torque. However, robots are usually required to perform tasks that require less rotational speed and more torque such as turning wheels, transporting loads, and lifting.

Figure 15.9
Ganged Gears.

The problem with robot motors' need for more torque rather than rotational speed is alleviated by understanding and cleverly applying the theory of how gears work. As with robotics in general, simple ideas that are well-understood can be compounded to develop more complex working systems. Small gears will turn more quickly, but are less powerful. Larger gears turn more slowly but are more powerful. This is the principle of gears on which multi-gear / multi-speed bicycles are based. So if a smaller gear drives a larger gear, more torque is created in the ratio of the size of the smaller gear to the larger gear (in terms of number of teeth). Such paired gears are called **ganged gears**. Figure 15.9 illustrates this principle with ganged gears called a "**compound gear train**." For example, if the input-output ratio of one axle is 40 to 8, it would reduce to 5 to 1. A second pair of meshed gears could have the input of an 8-tooth gear to drive a 24-tooth gear. This converts to a 3 to 1 ratio. Now we notice that the 8-tooth gear of the second axle may be on the same axle as the 40-tooth gear of the first pair. This gives a ganged gear ratio of 5 to 1 × 3 to 1 which is 15 to 1. Hence the first axle (with smaller gears) must turn 15 times for the second axle to turn once. Therefore more torque (in the ratio of 15:1) has been created for the second axle.

Another concept in robot motors is the servo motor. This kind of motor (or servos for short) are motors that can rotate in such a way that their shaft reaches a specific position. They are common in

---

*** A colleague of the authors was known to have purchased a 1999 Cadillac in 2004. Shortly after he purchased it, a **check engine error** came up on the dashboard. It was identified as a problem with the "torque converter," which is part of the transmission. The transmission was rebuilt, and this problem was allayed for some 100,000 miles before the torque converter problem did actually present itself after some 15 miles of continuous driving, when the car could not maintain its highway speed.

toys, and are used for adjusting steering in remote control cars or wing positions in remote control planes. Servo motors are made from DC motors with the following additional components:

1. Gear reduction for torque
2. A position sensor for the motor shaft to tell how much the motor is turning and in what direction
3. An electronic circuit to control the motor, telling it how much to turn and in what direction [4, p. 37]

Electronic signals in the form of a series of pulses will tell the motor shaft how much to turn, typically within a range of 180 degrees. Pulse-width modulation is a method of controlling the amount that the motor's shaft will turn by the length of the pulse; the larger the pulse, the larger the turn angle of the shaft. This is usually measured in units of microseconds and therefore quite precise. Between pulses, the shaft is stopped.

15.2.1.2 Degrees of Freedom

A common notion in the field of robotics is the concept of degrees of motion for an object. These are a means of expressing the various types of motion available to a robot. As an example, consider the degrees of freedom of motion (called **translational degrees of freedom**) of a helicopter. There are six degrees of freedom (DOF) which are usually used to describe the possible motions of a helicopter—roll, pitch, and yaw (see Figure 15.10). Roll means rolling from side to side, pitch means angling up or down, and yaw means turning left or right. An object like a car (or a helicopter on the ground) has only three DOF (vertical motion is lost), but only two are controllable. That is, a car on the ground can only move forward

Figure 15.10
A helicopter and its degrees of freedom.
Source: http://commons.wikimedia.org/wiki/
Helicopter#mediaviewer/File:Bell_407_(D-HBEN).jpg.

and backward (via the wheels) and turn left or right via its steering wheel. If a car could move directly left or right (say by turning each of its wheels 90 degrees), that would add another DOF. Hence with more complicated robot motions, such as arms or legs trying to move in various directions (as is possible in human arms with a rotator cuff) the number of DOF are an important issue.

15.2.2 Locomotion

This is probably the oldest problem in robotics. Whether you are trying to get a robot to play soccer, or land on the moon, or work under the ocean, the most fundamental issue is locomotion. How does the robot move? What are its capabilities? The typical actuators which come to mind include:

- wheels for rolling along
- legs enabling walking, crawling, running, climbing, and jumping
- arms for grabbing hold, swinging, and climbing
- wings for flying
- flippers for swimming

As soon as you start considering movement, you must also think about stability. After all, it typically takes a child at least a year before it can learn how to walk. For people and robots there is also the notion of center of gravity, which is some point above the ground where we are walking and enabled to stay balanced. Too low a center of gravity means that we are dragged down to the ground, while one that is too high means instability. Hand in hand with this concept is the notion of a **polygon of support**. This is the platform that must support a robot to enforce stability. Humans have such a support platform as well, only we are not usually aware of it somewhere up in our torsos. For a robot, as it attains more legs—that is, three, four, or six, this becomes less of issue. For example, see Figure 15.12, which depicts NASA's Jet Propulsion Labs Spiderbot.

APPLICATION BOX

"SPIDER-BOT"

It was the first in a line of robots called "Spider-Bot" for its spider-like appearance. This first MRE was a proof-of-concept to represent a node in a mobile network of sensors for solid surface exploration. The JPL describes it further:

> Large robots use large actuators to build large structures. Fine work requires small, precise actuators and often small robots that can fit into confined spaces. Spiderbots can provide the small chassis and the mobility to support this second type of work. The Spiderbot is designed to develop and demonstrate hexapods that can walk on flat surfaces, crawl on meshes, and assemble simple structures. The task's current mission is to demonstrate complex mobility behaviors, including maneuvering (i.e. mesh crawling) in a space analog environment (i.e. micro-gravity).

http://www.robotics.jpl.nasa.gov/tasks/showTask.cfm?FuseAction=ShowTask&TaskID=30&tdaID=2585<

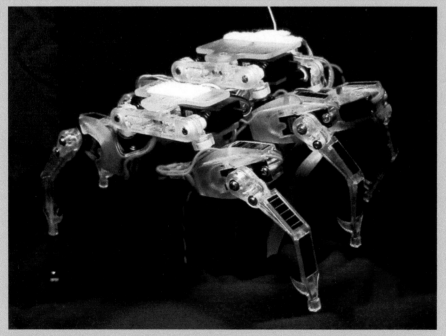

Figure 15.11
The Jet Propulsion Lab's "Spiderbot" circa 2002.

15.2.3 Path Planning for a Point Robot

A point robot is the simple notion of an autonomous robot as a single point operating in some well-defined environment—typically a Cartesian plane. Hence the point (x,y) will be sufficient to describe the robot's state.

The fundamental problem is to find a path for the robot at some starting configuration S = (a,b) to some goal state T = (c,d). How can such a continuous path be found—if it exists? The most basic solution to this problem is known as the Bug2 Algorithm.

The algorithm is fairly straightforward. If a direct, straight-line path between S and T exists in the free space between S and T, the robot should use it. If the path is obstructed, then the robot uses the path until it encounters the obstacle (point P). The robot should then circumnavigate the obstacle until it can rejoin the line ST moving towards the goal T. If it encounters another obstacle, it should once again circumnavigate it until it finds another point on the obstacle on the line ST from which it can leave the obstacle in the direction of T that is closer to T than the point P at which it started circumnavigating the obstacle. If no such point exists, then the robot determines that no path exists from S to T.

Although the Bug2 Algorithm is known to be *complete* (see Chapter 2), and certain to find a path to the goal if such a path exists, there is no guarantee that the path will be efficient. [6]

In order to be aware of the robot's position at all times and plan appropriately, sensors must continuously refine their map of the environment and update their estimation of its position. In the world of robotics this is known as SLAM—simultaneous localization and mapping algorithm.

15.2.4 Mobile Robot Kinematics

Kinematics is the most basic study of how mechanical systems behave. In mobile robotics, this is a bottom-up technique that necessarily entails the worlds of physics, mechanics, software, and control. As such, it quickly gets rather complex because it requires software to control hardware at every moment.

For this purpose, much knowledge about kinematics was attained from the early programming of robot manipulators. Here the task was primarily to control a robot's arm. Consideration of the dynamics (force and mass) of such situations was important when built into the constraints on workspace and trajectory. We introduced the concept of locomotion in the previous section. Here we consider further factors which are integral to **position estimation** and **motion estimation**, which are in themselves very challenging tasks. [7]

Integral to considering the position and motion of a mobile robot is the position and angle of every wheel. Each wheel is considered for its contribution to the robot's motion, and these kinematic constraints are combined to express the entire robot's kinematic constraints.

The starting point is the robot's position in a simple X-Y plane, and consider its angle Θ which helps to create a reference point for the robot's direction of motion. That direction is represented with respect to the X-axis by the angle of Θ.

Hence the Robot's global reference can be expressed by:

$$I = \begin{bmatrix} X \\ |Y| \\ \Theta \end{bmatrix}$$

This vector comprised of X, Y, and Θ defines what is called the "pose" of a robot. From this equation, all movements of the robot in the global plane $\{X_I, Y_I\}$ can be represented with respect to the local reference frame $\{X_R, Y_R\}$ using an **orthogonal rotation matrix**.

Thus, instantaneous changes in robot position can be represented by matrix manipulations representing changes in the robot's wheel angles. Naturally, modeling of this kind is necessary and gets more and more complicated. Adding more wheels and notions of velocity and diverse motions, possibly in different directions and dimensions, introduces further complexity, which is beyond our purpose here. An excellent reference source for further investigation of technical details of kinematics, robot perception, mobile robot localization, and planning and navigation is the text by Siegwart, Nourbakhsh, and Scaramuzza.[7]

HUMAN INTEREST NOTES

SEBASTIAN THRUN

Sebastian Thrun.

It does not take much investigation to realize that Dr. Sebastian Thrun is one of the truly great scientists alive today. The titles and awards he has received and his accomplishments by the age of 47 are truly exceptional. He is successful to the point where one gets the impression that today Dr. Thrun is able to pursue activities that truly interest him: Udacity, the company he founded with David Stavens and Mike Sokolsky in 2012, but more about that later. He is primarily recognized as an educator, programmer, roboticist, and computer scientist. He was born in Solingen, Germany in 1967.

There are few people in AI today or in the past who can claim to have had as illustrious and diverse a career as Dr. Thrun. He received degrees from the Universities of Bonn (in 1993 undergraduate, 1995 computer science and statistics PhD) and Hildesheim (1988) in computer science, economics, and medicine. His PhD was titled *Explanation-Based Neural Network Learning: A Lifelong Learning Approach*.

From the time Dr. Thrun joined the Computer Science Department at Carnegie Mellon University in 1995 as a research scientist, his ascent and accomplishments have been mercurial. In 1998 he became an assistant professor and codirector of the Robot Learning Laboratory at CMU. Shortly thereafter he cofounded a Master's Program in Automated Learning and Discovery which later became a PhD program in Machine Learning and Scientific Discovery. After spending a sabbatical year at Stanford University, he returned to CMU as Finmeccanica Associate Professor of Computer Science with an endowed professorship. In July 2003 Prof. Thrun left CMU to be Associate Professor at Stanford, and Director of SAIL (Stanford AI Lab). He spent the years 2007–2011 as full Professor of Computer Science and Electrical Engineering. He also became a Google VP and Fellow. He founded Google X, where he developed and contributed to a number of systems, including the Google driverless car system, Google Glass, Indoor Navigation, Google Brain, Project Wing, and Project Loon.

His international reputation stems from developing a number of successful autonomous robotic systems. In 1997 he developed the world's first robotic tour guide with his colleagues Wolfram Burgard and Dieter Fox at the Deutsches Museum Bonn. Minerva was a similar follow-up system which he installed at the Smithsonian's National Museum of American History in Washington, DC, guiding tens of thousands of people over a two-week deployment.

Other accomplishments include the interactive humanoid robot Nursebot, which helped residents at a nursing home in

Pittsburgh, PA. In 2002 with his colleagues at CMU, William Whittaker and Scott Thayer, Thrun developed mine-mapping robots. At Stanford in 2003 he was involved in the development of the robot Stanley, which in 2005 won the DARPA Grand Challenge. The Darpa Grand Challenge is intended to support high-payoff research that bridges the gap between fundamental discoveries and military use. The initial DARPA Grand Challenge was created to spur the development of technologies needed to create the first fully autonomous ground vehicles capable of completing a substantial off-road course within a limited time. The second Challenge in 2005 entailed 23 finalist vehicles that traveled more than 7.32 miles, passed through three narrow tunnels, and negotiated more than 100 sharp left and right turns. The race concluded through Beer Bottle Pass, near the California-Nevada border, a winding mountain pass with a sheer drop-off on one side and a rock face on the other. Professor Thrun's Stanley team finished 9 minutes ahead of its competitor team from CMU, capturing a $2 million purse.

Professor Thrun is best known for his theoretical contributions to robotics, particularly in the field of Probabilistic Robotics. This field conjoins statistics and robotics, and in 2005 he published a book with this title coauthored with William Burgard and Dieter Fox (MIT Press).

In 2011 he received a Research Award and the inaugural AAAI Ed Feigenbaum Prize. He was elected into the Germany Academy of Engineering and the German Academy of Sciences Leopoldina in 2007. Other awards include:

- Named one of the Brilliant 5 by Popular Science (2005)
- Career Award from the National Science Foundation (1999–2003)
- #4 on Foreign Policy Magazine's Top 100 Global Thinkers (2012)

- Recipient of Smithsonian magazine's American Ingenuity Award in Education (2012)

Professor Thrun has some 374(!) publications during the past 25 years. That makes 15 publications per year, including five monographs, seven edited volumes, numerous chapters in books, journal articles, conference papers, and so on. Perhaps this helps better explain why Dr. Thrun was able to take the gamble of leaving his position as Professor of Computer Science at Stanford in 2011 to be a Research Professor there. Subsequently, he relinquished his position as Google VP and Fellow. One might think that Sebastian Thrun had gone through a catharsis, but reading further and trying to understand him better, one realizes that he has accomplished so much that he can now pursue what he really believes in as the future of Education: Udacity. This is the online learning university which he founded in January 2012. On his website he states:

At Udacity, we are trying to democratize higher education. Udacity stands for "we are audacious, for you, the student." We created the notion of "nanodegrees" which empowers people from all traits and ages to find employment in the tech industry.

In an in-depth article in *WIRED,* Dr. Thrun discusses his plans and ideas for Udacity. He envisions that in some 50 years very few universities (as we know them), for the purpose of delivering higher education, will exist.

(http://www.wired.com/2012/03/ff_aiclass/all/)

It is clear that Dr. Thrun has great visions and plans for Udacity and is totally dedicated to the concept. If his past record is any indication—he will succeed.

Professor Thrun has published three books, with a fourth, ***The FastSLAM Algorithm for Simultaneous Localization and Mapping*** (with M. Montemerlo), coming out soon.

▄▄ 15.3 ▄▄ APPLICATIONS: ROBOTICS IN THE TWENTY-FIRST CENTURY

This section presents three major robotic systems that have been developed in the twenty-first century—Big Dog, Asimo, and Cog. Each project represents a major effort that has been ongoing for several decades starting in the late twentieth century. Each addresses complex and sophisticated technical issues and problems in robotics introduced in the previous section. Big Dog is mainly concerned with locomotion and conveyance of heavy loads, particularly for military purposes. Asimo displays diverse aspects of locomotion with a strong emphasis on anthropomorphic elements—that is, understanding how humans move. Cog is more about thinking, which is also considered to be special to humans, distinguishing us from other living beings.

APPLICATION BOX

BIG DOG

In 1986 Marc Raibert, Kevin Blankespoor, Gabriel Nelson, and Rob Playter, leaders of the **BigDog** Team at MIT, wanted to achieve animal-like mobility on rough terrain that people and vehicles have difficulties navigating (Raibert, 1986) This effort was motivated by the fact that less than half of the earth's land is navigable by wheeled and tracked vehicles. The goal was to develop mobile robots that could perform on a par with humans and animals in terms of mobility, autonomy, and speed. Typical challenges included terrain that is steep, rutted, rocky, wet, muddy, and covered with snow. The team developed a series of robots that had up to four legs to perform movements of which humans and animals are capable (Raibert, 1986). These multi-legged robots were developed to study dynamic control and the challenges of maintaining balance for robots on diverse terrain. Dynamically balanced legged systems were needed—hence BigDog was invented.

BigDog is a legged robot developed by Boston Dynamics (c. 1996) and was funded by DARPA (Defense Advanced Research Projects Agency). It is the size of a large dog, about 3 feet long, 2.5 feet tall, and weighs around 240 lbs. The goal of the BigDog project was to create an unmanned legged robot that could travel anywhere a person or an animal could go. This robot has built-in systems for power, actuation, sensing, control, and communication. Ideally, the system would be able to travel anywhere, run for consecutive hours, and carry its fuel and weight without trouble.

A human being employs an operator control unit (or OCU) connected to an IP radio to control BigDog's actions. A human employs a controller to provide steering and speed parameters to guide the robot through diverse terrain. The controller can also start and stop the robot as needed. The controller can also direct BigDog to walk, jog, or trot. The data is displayed and input. Then the robot's AI system takes over and operates on its own to make sure it stays upright or mobile.

BigDog employs AI for coordination of its basic posture and to prevent falls, enabling it to learn to distribute weight amongst its four legs. This allows Big Dog to carry heavy loads and to maneuver through diverse and rough terrain, with little human support. The goal is to develop a system with auto-control. The robot has to be smart enough to navigate with little or minimal human guidance or intervention. The robot has fifty sensors which feed information to the onboard computer that monitors how BigDog is moving and where it is, and provides data from the fields. Future projects seek further independence from human control, particularly in areas where there is limited human access.

There are high-level and low-level control systems which help maintain the robot's balance. The high-level system coordinates how the legs move as well as the speed and height of body during movement, and the low-level system positions and moves the joints. This control system also helps it learn to adjust to maintain balance through slopes and climbs. It also controls ground actions to help maintain support of robot movements and to keep it from slipping. If it falls, it learns to get back up and stand on all four legs, continuing with its movement through the terrain. The system also allows BigDog to have a variety of movement behaviors including: standing up on all four legs, squatting down, walking normally, or crawling by moving one leg forward at a time or in a diagonal action.

Big Dog's power supply consists of water cooled by a two stroke internal combustion engine, and the engine delivers high-pressure oil into the robot's leg actuators. Each leg has four hydraulic actuators that power BigDog's joints as well as a passive fifth degree of freedom. These actuators have sensors for joint position, with a heat exchanger mounted on the body to stop it from overheating the engine. BigDog's 50 sensors include Inertial sensors that measure attitude and acceleration of the body and joint sensors for the actuators that help it move. These features enable and facilitate BigDog through its longest movement of 6.2 consecutive miles. It can carry up to 154 kilograms on a flat terrain, but normal loads are usually 50 kilograms on a normal day. BigDog also has a visual system and a LIDAR, which is a pair of cameras, a computer, and visual software (see Figure 15.12). These components help point out the terrain that BigDog is navigating and assist it in finding a clear path forward. The LIDAR system is for the sole purpose of ignoring a human operator and enabling the robot to use its sensors to follow a human leader out in the field.

Figure 15.12
BigDog carrying its weight in supplies.

BigDog has a quadrupedal walking algorithm for sloped and tough terrains. It can walk on sloped pathways of up to 60 degrees but can also take into account unexpected or irregular terrain with the assistance of its control system. BigDog adapts to different changes in two ways: 1) It fixes itself according to the height and elevation of the terrain and footfall placement so that it won't lopside and fall over on its side. 2) It also looks at shadows for changes to make its own adjustments in posturewhile traveling through diverse terrain. BigDog's control system is coordinated with kinematics and ground reaction forces so that it can optiminze the amount it can carry. The control system optimizes the load by splitting it equally among the robot's legs.

Summary and Future Directions: There are many plans for the future of BigDog. The team wants to make it possible for BigDog to move through rougher and steeper terrain and have it able to carry more and heavier loads. The team wants to upgrade its engine and system to make it quieter as its motors and system are extremly noisy. They also want BigDog to be less reliant on humans and employ computer vision to allow it to navigate entirely on its own. So far new items include a head, arm, torso, and various other parts to increase versatility. These additions have given BigDog the ability to use its entire body to throw heavy objects around or lift and move heavy objects aside if they become obstructions.

Figure 15.13
BigDog robots trot around in the shadows.

Big Dog References

Raibert, M. 1986. *Legged Robots that Balance*. MIT Press. Retrieved from http://www.bostondynamics.com/img/BigDog_IFAC_Apr-8-2008.pdfhttp://phys.org/news/2013-03-boston-dynamics-bigdog-toss-video.html

Next we present another robotics project that has been ongoing for many years: the Honda Asimo robot. Asimo moves in a very human-like way and was designed to be particularly helpful to people.

APPLICATION BOX

ASIMO

HISTORY AND INTRODUCTION

Imagine a world where humans and machine live together, aiding and supporting each other in all tasks ranging from carrying the everyday grocery shopping bags to helping firefighters rescue people trapped in flaming houses or fallen structures. This is a world envisioned by the Honda engineers who conceived Asimo in Japan in 1986. **Asimo** is a two-legged humanoid robot created in Honda's research lab after two decades of research and development. The objective of creating a humanoid robot that resembles and duplicates the complex structure of a human being is so that it is able to aide people on various activities for the advancement of scientific development.[1]

PURPOSE

Creating a humanoid robot was not an easy task. However, Honda has embraced this challenge by envisioning a world where robots and humans interact harmoniously. Having a valuable partner with great mobility and ability to maneuver who can interact with humans would be a great support for people who need an extra set of helping hands without the expense of another human.

FEATURES: DESIGN CONCEPT

Asimo's design concept is to make this into a people-friendly robot that is both lightweight and flexible. The Asimo is compact: 120 cm or 4 feet tall and weighing approximately 52 kgs or 115 pounds. [2] The engineers chose this size to allow Asimo to operate freely and efficiently in a human living space. Based on their research, this height allows Asimo to "operate light switches and door knobs, and work at tables and work benches." [3]

Figure 15.14
Honda's ASIMO.

MOBILITY AND LOCOMOTION

After collecting various data about human mobility and locomotion, including walking and other forms of human movement, Honda developed Asimo to walk in a very similar way to how humans walk. The two-legged walking concept includes operation and movement on different surfaces. Asimo can perform everyday tasks such as walking from one point to another while avoiding obstacles, climbing or descending stairs, pushing a cart, passing through doorways, and carry things while walking. These advanced physical capabilities are achieved by a number of sensors placed to determine the leg's joint angle and speed to mimic humans' center of gravity. These sensors collect data and interpret it into information to be processed for the next movement.

ARTIFICIAL INTELLIGENCE FEATURES

Asimo's second most prominent feature is its ability to interact with humans. Asimo must be able to approach and communicate with them and is able to achieve this by processing information that it captures through replicating humans' five senses.

Asimo captures video input through the two cameras mounted in its head, which allow it to recognize moving objects and facial features on humans for limited facial recognition. It also creates a map of the surrounding environment with the visual information that helps for the purpose of collision prevention and object positioning.

Furthermore, Asimo is able to distinguish and interpret sounds and voice commands that are captured by the microphones installed in its head. Asimo processes audio input enabling it to "recognize when its name is called, and then turn to the source of a sound," as well as reacting to "unusual sounds, such as those of an object falling or a collision, and face in that direction." [3] Audio processing also enables Asimo to engage in conversations with humans through its abilities in speech and natural language understanding (Chapter 13). It's possible for Asimo to carry out orders and respond to them with specific feedback. Asimo also has Internet connectivity, which enables it to access information via the Internet to provide answers, such as news and weather conditions for the benefit of people.

FUTURE

Asimo's prospects for meeting its original goal—to be a helper to people in need—seem to be very bright. With all the capabilities that Asimo has, it would be able to not only support the sick and elderly, but also provide help on situations where it would be dangerous for humans to function, such as cleaning a toxic spill or putting out a blazing fire without risking lives. Furthermore, Asimo can provide a sense of companionship to people. Although it is not currently available for sale or lease in the United States, Asimo is featured in Japan science museums and is "being used by a few high-tech companies to welcome guests to their facilities" [2]

Although Asimo is a robot, it has traveled to many countries and landmarks around the world ranging from the Brooklyn Bridge all the way to Europe and Switzerland. It was also featured as a guest in Disney Land, and played soccer with President Barack Obama. [1] Its popularity does not cease to increase as it keeps encouraging and inspiring young people around the world to study the sciences via robotics and Artificial Intelligence.

Asimo References———

1. http://asimo.honda.com/

2. http://asimo.honda.com/downloads/pdf/asimo-technical-faq.pdf

3. http://asimo.honda.com/downloads/pdf/asimo-technical-information.pdf

QUICK APPLICATION BOX

JAEMI THE HUMANOID ROBOT

Figure 15.15
Jaemi the Humanoid Robot.

Children play "Simon Says" with Jaemi, a humanoid robot (HUBO), during his visit to the Please Touch Museum in Philadelphia, PA. Jaemi was created by a team from Drexel University working in collaboration with Korean researchers. The project was supported by the National Science Foundation Partnership for International Research and Education (PIRE) program. This image accompanied NSF press release, U.S. and Korean Researchers Unveil Newest Research Team Member: Jaemi the Humanoid.

Credit: *Lisa-Joy Zgorski, National Science Foundation.*

Next we present another long-term project that attempts to fulfill some of the early original aspirations for robotics discussed in previous sections—that is, to be able to mimic how people learn to interact as children and to develop cognitive skills.

APPLICATION BOX

In 1993 a team at MIT headed by Rodney Brooks started to construct a robot named Cog, which is short for "cognition." Cog was motivated to be built based on the theory that "Humanoid intelligence requires humanoid interactions with the world," [1] which would have necessitated the construction of a robot that would think and experience the world in the same way that a human would. Cog is made of actuators and motors that work similarly to humans' bones, joints, and movements. The MIT team built a robot that has human-like intelligence, mimicking the human body and its behaviors. Nonetheless, there are some important aspects of the human body that cannot be mimicked by a robot. The team also wanted to be able to use this robot to interact with others as humans would. So for their "training," Cog would interact with humans, and what better way is there to learn human behaviors than to interact with them?

Cog was designed to simulate the same environments and physical constraints that adult humans encounter. Although it does not have legs, it does have a pair of symmetrical arms, a body, and a head. The lower part of its body, beyond the waist, is just a stand. Cog "sees" with two pairs of cameras mounted on its head with two degrees of freedom, and two microphones enable it to hear. Each eye also has its own pair of cameras for wide view and far range. The motor system has sensors indicating where the joints are and gives information on their current status, as well as if there are any issues or problems with them. Cog's arm also provides feedback by having an electric motor there to operate the arm and provide torque feedback information. The robot has a total of 22 degrees of freedom. It has six degrees in its arms, four degrees for its neck, three in its eyes, two degrees in its waist, and one in its torso enabling twisting motions. [2]

Cog has a diverse network with many different processors operating at different control levels. It ranges from small microcontrollers for joint-level control to digital signal processors. The brain controls have been revised many times to help improve the way Cog acts like a human. The first network contained 16 megahertz Motorola 68332 microcontrollers with custom boards and connected through dual port RAM. [2] The modern-day Cog consists of a network of 200 megahertz industrial personal computers running the QNX real-time operating system and connected to a 100 VG Ethernet. This network currently has 4 nodes, but more can be added if desired.

The robot has a pair of electret condenser microphones which are mounted to its head close to where human ears would be. The microphone is similar in functionality to what a hearing aid is to a human. Cog includes a stereo system that amplifies the audio system and connects to a C40 DSP system. The team wanted to use these hearing systems to allow the robot to be aware of sounds that it hears in the same environment that humans do. They also wanted to do the same with the robot's vision. Each of the robot's eyes rotates in a vertical and horizontal axis. In order to get a better resolution and view of the environment, Cog takes the visual information and processes the image in its network for a better image.

Humans have a vestibular system which they use for movement and a sense of balance. Without it, people would fall over and would stay stationary. The brain takes this information from this system and helps human beings coordinate in everyday activities such as walking and keeping themselves upright. The human system has three sensory organs with a semicircular passage. The team at MIT wanted to copy this idea for Cog. Cog includes three rate gyroscopes placed on an orthogonal axis and two linear accelerometers. They put these devices below the eye so it can imitate sensory information for balance. The robot amplifies, processes, and converts these sensory devices to its personal computer brain.

The team at MIT has created a pointing action that allows Cog to extend its arm and point at whatever is there. This was tested this many times, even without having the team observe its performing these actions. During these actions, Cog's neck is still and it points at a target. In the initial stages of experimentation, Cog would perform these actions rather primitively, akin to a human infant or someone who is inexperienced at a certain task. However, in the process of "maturing," Cog seemed to learn and become more accurate in locating the target. In some sense, Cog becomes more human-like through its ability to mimic human actions and learn, and then to practice toward achieving perfection in performing an action. Cog's developers seek to continually make improvements that will enable it to behave more like humans (for better or worse!), including facial features. Cog does not have a face, but in the future, MIT roboticists will try to give Cog organic features akin to humans. This ongoing research project has also tried to try to replicate the behavior and thought processes of humans. Objectives include getting Cog to learn the relationship between motor commands and sensory inputs so it can observe and learn through its own actions. The team at MIT will try to get the neck and body to fully rotate as much as possible to simulate the way a human body rotates. The robot's front torso feedback was also tested by using resistive force sensors. One experiment involves applying considerable force to a surface sensor, enabling simulation of the robot's perception of forces.

Figure 15.16
Image of Cog at the MIT Museum.

Also in MIT's plans for Cog are a greater number of sensors, motors, cameras, and joints so that it will have more degrees of freedom. This would allow Cog to be still more human-like. Cog has learned to adapt to the way humans do things, but there are still some actions that it needs to learn and adapt to. A big challenge for Cog is to be able to adapt to new environments as a human infant might. Nonetheless, Cog has a long way to go before it becomes a full human simulation with full thoughts that cause human-like movements and interactions.

1. Overview of the Cog project. Retrieved from http://www.ai.mit.edu/projects/cog/OverviewOfCog/cog_overview.html

2. Naveed, Ahmad. The humanoid robot Cog. (page 2)

As discussed in Chapter 1, Section 1.1 (The Turing Test), Section 15.1, Section 15.2, and several times throughout our text, one of the main questions perplexing scientists and philosophers for centuries is how to determine whether a machine, robot, or an artificial creation possesses any sort of intelligence or consciousness at the level of human intelligence. However, (recall in Section 1.1) we discussed that in order to compare the level of intelligence of different agents we have to define what intelligence, or an intelligent being, means. Humans are intelligent beings because they are **capable of thinking, rationalizing, learning, and conceptualizing information in their brains.** But can robots with algorithms that possess sufficient case scenarios be able to exhibit some form of intelligence? Certainly, that is a very plausible scenario, since, after all, nowadays robots can look, sound, and act like a person. They are capable of learning and storing information into their memory and processing it into logical cases. Also they are able to analyze a given sentence based on its semantics and syntax and come up with a credible and logical answer—but does that qualify machines as intelligent? Also, please recall the Chinese Room Argument of Chapter 1 (Section 1.1) by John Searle,[1] which illustrates that being able to effectively and continuously respond correctly is not the equivalent of understanding.

However, the Turing Test has been claimed to have been passed by a chatbot program called "Eugene Goostman" that fooled judges into believing that the program was actually a thirteen-year-old Ukranian boy.[2] It is argued that the chatbot program fooled the judges by avoiding questions that it does not have a concrete answer to—much like how a thirteen-year-old boy would act.

Therefore, it is disputed amongst various scientists that the Turing Test only works with low-level intelligent (low AI) machines and can in those cases distinguish between machine and humans. However, in the case of the new high-level intelligent (strong AI) machines developed today, the Turing Test fails to separate the two. Over the years, as we have discussed previously, a number of new Turing Tests have been proposed.

APPLICATION BOX

THE LOVELACE PROJECT

The Lovelace Test – In order to design a test capable of distinguishing strong AI, the ***Lovelace Test*** was proposed by Bringjord, Bello, and Ferrucci[3] to set a new bar for determining intelligent beings. It requires the machine to create something original, something that even the creator cannot explain how it was created, such as a poem, story, music, or painting—or any creative act that requires the cognitive capabilities of humans. These creative acts would then be evaluated by a human being in order to determine whether the creation passes a set of criteria.

Lovelace vs. Lovelace 2.0 – Mark O. Riedl enhanced the Lovelace Test by proposing the ***Lovelace Test 2.0***, stating that "the artificial agent passes if it develops a creative artifact from a subset of artistic genres deemed to require human-level intelligence, and the artefact meets certain creative constraints given by a human evaluator."[4] The Lovelace Test 2.0 evaluates the creativity instead of only the intelligence of a machine.

The Lovelace 2.0 Test is as follows: artificial agent α passes the Lovelace Test if and only if:

- α creates an artifact o of type t,
- o conforms to a set of constraints C where $c_i \in C$ is any criterion expressible in natural language,

- A human evaluator *h*, having chosen *t* and *C*, is satisfied that o is a valid instance of *t* and meets C, and

- A human referee *r* determines the combination of *t* and *C* to not be impossible. [4]

Riedl believes that a "computational system can originate a creative artifact"—for example, when creating a fictional story, a machine requires common knowledge, planning, reason, language processing, familiarity with the subject, cultural artifact, and so on. However, no story generation system can pass the Lovelace 2.0 Test because most story generation systems require *a priori (knowledge, or argument independent of experience) domain descriptions*.[4]

Thus, it is shown that although robots and machines have greatly advanced in the field of Artificial Intelligence, there is a fundamental difference between humans, who possess creativity, and machines, which still follow a set program or rationalized path.

Lovelace References

1. Cole, D. The Chinese Room Argument. The Stanford Encyclopedia of Philosophy (Summer 2014 Edition), Edited by Edward N. Zalta. Retrieved from http://plato.stanford.edu/archives/sum2014/entries/chinese-room

2. Amlen, D.2014. Our Interview with Turing Test Winner Eugene Goostman. Retrieved from https://www.yahoo.com/tech/our-interview-with-turing-test-winner-eugene-goostman-88482732919.html

3. Bringsjord, S.; Bello, P.; and Ferrucci, D. 2001. Creativity, the Turing Test, and the (better) Lovelace Test. Minds and Machines 11: 3–27.

4. Riedl, M. O. 2014. The Lovelace 2.0 Test of Artificial Creativity and Intelligence. Retrieved from http://arxiv.org/pdf/1410.6142v1.pdf

Figure 15.17
Robot At Royal Australian Mint, Canberra & Watercolor Painting (www.kopecart.com).
Could a robot produce the watercolor on the right, and then could such a painting be distinguished from one created by a human?

15.4 CHAPTER SUMMARY

Robotics was once a rather distinct field which was closely related to AI via computational geometry and vision. Today we can see many aspects of AI in robotics, especially as embedded systems. This includes search algorithms, logic, expert systems, fuzzy logic, machine learning, neural networks, genetic algorithms, planning, and even games. Robots do not navigate stating, "I have AI," but it is clear that robotics as a field would not be where it is without employing AI. We illustrate examples of how and where robotics is and will be used. Let us not forget the effect that advances in natural language and speech understanding have had on improving robotics.

The history of robotics and man is much richer than one might imagine. It started with notions of robot lore, and then early mechanical systems such Vaucanson's duck and von Kempelen's Turk from the eighteenth century are introduced. Robots in film and literature are well-known via Mary Shelley's *Frankenstein* (1817), Karel Čapek's R.U.R. (1921), and Fritz Lang's *Metropolis* (1926), all of which pose a rather grim picture of the future impact of technology on man's life. In the first half of the twentieth century, science fiction hero Isaac Asimov already had the vision to develop the Three Laws of Robots. More recent systems and their capabilities are also presented. Then technical details (Section 15.2) are presented as well as some of the standard and difficult issues. The section closes with a Human Interest Box on the remarkable Sebastrian Thrun.

Section 15.3 features stellar applications of robotics, focusing on Big Dog, Asimo, and Cog. The section closes out with new tests for AI via the Lovelace Project. Application boxes on Big Dog and Cog were contributed by Peter Tan. Application Boxes on Asimo and Lovelace were contributed by Mimi Lin Gao.

Questions for Discussion

1. Discuss five areas of AI presented in previous chapters and their relationship to robotics.

2. In the Story Box of MrTomR and Bobby, explain how today's robots may or may not be able to perform the functions of MrTomR.

3. Describe some of the early myths about robotics that were presented in the chapter, including The Brass Head, the Homunculus, and the golem.

4. Describe the inventions of the father-son team Pierre and Henri-Louis Jaquet-Drov. When did they occur?

5. Name and describe two chess-related automata that were built in prior centuries.

6. Describe the literary works of Karel Čapek, Mary Shelley, and Isaac Asimov and how they projected concerns and developments in robotics.

7. Consider Asimov's Three Laws of Robotics—are they still valid?

8. Describe the purpose of the field of cybernetics.

9. Discuss the purpose and capabilities of the Tortoise by Grey Walters.

10. Describe the purposes and capabilities of the three significant modern-day robot projects presented in Section 15.3—Big Dog, Asimo, and Cog.

11. What is the Lovelace Project about? Do you believe it is sound and appropriate?

Exercises

1. Watch and review the movie *IROBOT*. What are the premier themes, methods, and technical issues addressed in this movie?

2. Watch and review the movie *Bicentennial Man*. What major questions regarding robots does the film address?

3. Compare the two films addressed above. Which do you believe is a better example of the theoretical, ethical, and technical issues of Robotics and AI? Explain.

4. Implement the Bug2 algorithm described in this chapter. You may assume that the obstacles are comprised of triangles of three cells in a discrete, well-defined space. When the robot encounters the obstacles, it should move counterclockwise to circumvent them.

5. Review some of the works of Rodney Brooks. What is his approach to Robotics (see Chapter 6), what companies did he found, and which robotic systems should he be credited for?

6. You have learned about the work of the remarkable Sebastian Thrun. What robotic systems has he built? Write a short paper about the systems we did not cover in our human interest box.

7. Review Table 15.1 and determine if it is accurate. Are there any systems missing that should be in the table? Are there any trends you can see? What kind of progress in robotic systems does it illustrate?

8. You have seen the dialog between MrTomR and five-year-old Bobby in Section 15.0. Would such a dialog be possible today? Why or why not? What areas of AI that you have learned about in the text would need more progress before such systems could be successfully built?

9. Robots are assisting in sophisticated surgeries today. Usually these surgeries will be successful. However when they fail, there are of course complex legal issues. Review the literature and report what kinds of surgeries robots have been successful in assisting with, and find cases where they have failed and lawsuits have followed.

Keywords

actuators	effectors	photophilic
artificial life	emergent behavior	photophobic
Asimo	excitatory connections	*R.U.R.*
autonomous	ganged gears	servo motor
Big Dog	golem	SLAM
biomimetic	homunculus	Tortoise or Machina
Braitenberg's Vehicles	inhibitory connections	Speculatrix
Cog	internal state	position estimation
compound gear train	Lovelace II	translational DOF
cybernetics	*Metropolis*	Three Laws of Robots
degrade gracefully	motion estimation	
degrees of freedom	orthogonal matrix rotation	

References

1. Heppenheimer, T. A. 1985. Man makes man. In *Robotics*, edited by M. L. Minsky. Omni Press: New York.

2. Minsky, M. L. 1985. Chapter 1, *Introduction. In Robotics*, edited by M. L. Minsky. Omni Press: New York.

3. Wiener, N. 1948. *Cybernetics: Or Control and Communication in the Animal and the Machine.* Paris (Hermann & Cie) & Cambridge, MA: MIT Press. 2nd revised ed. 1961.

4. Mataric, M. 2007. *The Robotics Primer.* Cambridge, MA: MIT Press.

5. Levy, D. N. L. 2006. *Robots Unlimited.* A.K. Peters, Ltd: Wellesley, MA.

6. Dudek, G. and Jenkin, M. 2010. *Computational Principles of Mobile Robotics*, 2nd edition. Cambridge, England: Cambridge University Press.

7. Siegwart, R., Nourbaksh, I, and Scaramuzza, D. 2011. *Introduction to Autonomous Mobiles Robots*, 2nd ed. Cambridge, MA: MIT Press.

ADVANCED COMPUTER GAMES

The Card Player.

■ ■ ■ ■ ■

It was a long-held belief that if computers could master some of the harder board games that people play such as chess, checkers, Othello, and backgammon, they would be able to demonstrate genuine artificial intelligence (AI). As it turns out, after some 50 years of research, computers have demonstrated great mastery (performance) in these games but not necessarily by the means that "strong AI" researchers had hoped for.

This chapter is written from the perspective of a seasoned international chess master and AI researcher. Efforts are moving to overcome the challenges of a "new drosophila," Go, as well as other games. One tip for students is that it is very hard to appreciate the difficulties of programming a game unless you understand the rules and objectives of that game.

Figure 16.0
Kenneth Lane Thompson.

16.0 ■ INTRODUCTION

People have been infatuated with games for several centuries. They will always be inclined to work hard, meet their responsibilities, and then find time to relax and compete while challenging and developing their intellect. Part of the allure of games is that you can compete at different levels; you can test your knowledge and abilities, and then see results in a timely manner. You can analyze why the specific outcome occurred (win, draw, or loss), learn from mistakes, and then play another game.

Recall from Chapter 4 that the sum of the winner's gain is precisely offset by the loser's loss; for example, the winner in chess gets 1.0 points, the loser gets no points, and in the case of a draw, each person gets 0.5 points.

The discussion in this chapter focuses mainly on two-person, zero sum board games of perfect information (e.g., games that do not involve chance), including checkers, chess, and Othello. You will also explore a few games of chance that are of great popular interest, including backgammon, bridge, and poker. Finally, you will turn to what some call the ideal AI test subject of the present and future, Go.

16.1 ■ CHECKERS: FROM SAMUEL TO SCHAEFFER

Recall from Chapter 1 that in 1952, Arthur Samuel wrote the first version of a checkers program. Clearly, when programming the game of checkers for the IBM 704, Samuel's main interest was in developing a checkers program that could demonstrate machine learning. The significance of Arthur Samuel's early paper [1] and work on checkers is not the result or success of his program, which were typically overblown by the press [2] after the program's win of a single game against Champion Robert Nealy, but as an early model of the application and study of sound AI techniques. Samuel's work represents some of the earliest studies in machine learning. Samuel had already considered the possibilities of a neural network approach to the game, but instead, he decided on a more organized, structured network approach to learning.

He chose to study checkers for the following reasons:

- Checkers is not deterministic in a practical sense.
- Each game has a definite goal—depriving the opponent of moves.
- The rules of engagement (play) are clear.
- There is a considerable corpus of knowledge about the game.
- Many people are familiar with checkers as a board game, so the behavior of a checkers program is also understandable.

Samuel's checkers program used a standard minimax approach to employing a linear polynomial that scored positions in terms of a number of heuristics. The ability to play a move is the ***dominant scoring term*** in checkers—though it is computed separately—that is, any move will result in the capture of men.

Arthur Samuel.

Hence, the main heuristic function in checkers is the capture of the opponent's pieces. This leads to further heuristics such as "it is advantageous to trade pieces when ahead and to avoid trades when behind."

The program's lookahead was 3 ply unless the position involved one of the following activities, which would extend the search:

1. The move is a jump (capture).

2. The last move was a jump.

3. An exchange offer is possible.

Such special conditions extended the search to 5, 11, or even 20 ply depending on circumstances.

In chess, the inability to move is called "zugzwang"—coming from the German words for "compulsion to move." In other words, there are no good moves.

To understand games such as checkers and chess, you should become comfortable with the notation system used to describe positions and games played. Figure 16.1 illustrates the standard addressing and notation system used for the game of checkers. The rules and algebraic notation system for chess are described in Appendix D.

Hence, if we see the notation 9-13, it means that Black plays his checkers from the square numbered 9 to the square 13. Then Red can respond with 22-17. As we will later read, this is part of an opening sequence that has been proven to achieve at least a draw for Black, but let us not get ahead of ourselves. The beauty and appeal of the endgame in games such as chess, checkers, and backgammon is that exhaustive calculation is often feasible to the end to "mathematically prove" a particular outcome. Certain endgames have an elegant simplicity that belies their underlying complexity and highlights the importance of applying heuristics and principles. As is known for typical game-winning **middle game combinations** (a forced sequence of moves that achieves material gain or clear positional superiority), endgames can

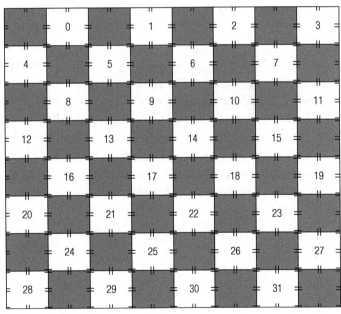

Figure 16.1
Numbering scheme for checkers.

also help to illustrate an important winning (or drawing) theme through concrete analysis.

You do not have to be a game expert to understand the outcome of an analysis such as the following if you are willing to

In chess, a middle game combination can also be used to achieve a checkmate, a forced draw, or other goals.

map out the positions using the notation or an actual checkerboard and set. Figure 16.2 shows a position that could occur in a game of checkers with Red to move.

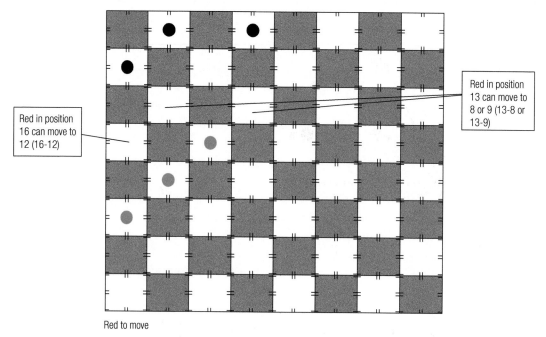

Red in position 16 can move to 12 (16-12)

Red in position 13 can move to 8 or 9 (13-8 or 13-9)

Red to move

Figure 16.2
Red moves next in this checkers game.

In the diagrammed position, Red (to move) has three legal moves: 16-12, 13-8, or 13-9. Which is the best move for Red to play in terms of the minimax-game-theoretic value? To find the answer, we can try to build a solution by constructing a 5-ply minimax game tree as described in Chapter 4. Figure 16.3 shows a nearly complete alpha-beta minimax game tree analysis of the position illustrated in Figure 16.2.

For sorting Red's moves left to right, we need to first examine the move 16-12. Black can answer Red's move with 4-8, though Black loses at least one piece after Red moves 13-4. Alternatively, Black can play 0-5 on its next move. Red answers with 20-16, which is the only safe move. Next, Black makes "an offer" with 5-8 that Red must capture with 12-5. Finally, Black achieves a winning combination with 1-8-17, completing a 6-ply search that wins a piece and the game for Black. Therefore, the 0-5 response to Red's 16-12 move is a **refutation** demonstrating that the move 16-12 loses after a 6-ply search. This is an example of how the 3-ply search might be extended by the capture opportunity that occurs on ply 4 with the offer 5-8 (a **quiescence search**, as defined in Chapter 4). Furthermore, analysis of Black's other alternatives at ply 2 (after 16-12) is unnecessary thanks to possible alpha-beta cutoffs (described in Chapter 4). As it turns out, a 5-ply search would reveal that Black's other moves at ply 2, (1-5 and 1-6) also led to Black sacrificing a piece. The alpha-beta algorithm indicates that we do not need to explore how bad a move 16-12 is once we have determined that the move can be refuted with 0-5.

Likewise, after a 5-ply search, we realize that 13-8 is the best move as the worst that Red can end up with is an extra piece—a king (200 points) or nearly a new king (50 points).

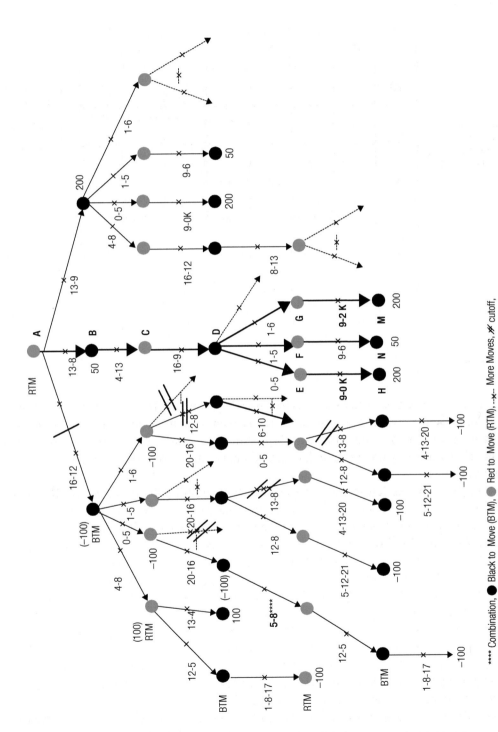

**** Combination, ● Black to Move (BTM), ● Red to Move (RTM), --✕-- More Moves, ⫻ cutoff,
╲ A bad move, K (key) Move Create a King. ABCDEH is a winning path, ABCDFH is almost a winning path.

Figure 16.3
Alpha-beta minimax game tree analysis for the checkers position in Figure 16.2

16.1.1 Heuristic Methods for Learning in the Game of Checkers

Samuel's work was particularly noteworthy for its investigation of the use of heuristics and how they could be used for machine learning. In this regard, he was significantly ahead of his time. One of his general ideas was to have different versions of his program play against each other and have the loser adopt the winner's heuristics. In this way, the program would be learning and would be improved. Another approach was to compare the programs' preferred moves against those adjudged to be best by checker masters.[1]

One way that this was done was to play through a stored "book" master game and to record at each position how many moves the program considered to be better than the recorded move and how many moves the program considered to be worse. This process could be applied for both sides. Hence, a correlation coefficient for the programs' preferred moves against the moves played by masters could be computed as follows:

$$C = (L - H) / (L + H)$$

Here, L is the number of legal moves in a position (or game) that the program rated lower than the actual move played and H is the number of moves that the program rated higher than the actual move played. In practice, these values ranged from 0.2 (for poor correlations) to 0.6 (for the evaluation polynomial coefficients ultimately adopted).

If L is high and H stays low, this correlation coefficient has the best chance of being close to 1.0, which is the most desired outcome. The program would be consistently evaluating moves not played as worse than the master moves and would be correctly judging other possible moves as worse than the moves of a master game. Samuel tried to stay away from giving the program book openings and instead let them learn from experience by playing from various test positions, endgames, and puzzles.

Samuel invested a lot of effort into efficiently storing positions (then on a magnetic or "memory" tape) as a unique bit string akin to the work of Christopher Strachey (Strachey, 1952). Samuel needed to access the well-organized "records" of positions quickly in memory so that the search could compare them. One interesting heuristic that he employed for the search was if two different move sequences produced a similar score at a depth of 3 ply vs., for example, a move sequence to 6 ply, it would choose the lower depth move (at 3 ply) if winning and choose the higher depth move (at 6 ply) if losing. Another clever heuristic was the notion of **aging**. Keep in mind that memory was limited in size and expensive at that time. If a record (position) in memory was not referenced for some time, it was "forgotten" and removed from the record when it reached an arbitrary maximum value. This heuristic was called **forgetting**. On the other hand, when a position in memory was referred to by the search, it was "refreshed" by having its associated age divided by 2. This was called **refreshing**.

The four terms of the main **evaluation function** used in order of decreasing importance were as follows:

- Piece advantage
- Denial of occupancy
- Mobility
- A hybrid term that combined control of the center and piece advancement

Using Samuel's heuristic approach as described earlier, a program was developed that played a very good opening, recognized most winning and losing endgames well in advance, but did not improve much in the middle game. Its play was certainly beyond the level of a novice but below the level of an expert.

Samuel reached the following simple conclusions about rote-learning tests:

- An effective rote-learning technique must include a procedure to give the program a sense of direction, and it must contain a refined system for cataloging and storing positions.

- Storage capacity limitations were a concern for the machine that was being used at the time (the IBM 704).

- A game such as checkers is a suitable vehicle for developing and demonstrating machine-learning techniques.

Studies in generalized learning were developed using two versions of the program, one called *Alpha* and the other called *Beta*. According to Samuel (1952), "Alpha generalizes on its experience after each move by adjusting the coefficients in its evaluation polynomial and by replacing terms which appear to be unimportant by new parameters drawn from a reserve list. Beta, on the contrary, uses the same evaluation polynomial for the duration of any game. Program Alpha is used to play against human opponents, and during self-play Alpha and Beta play each other."

In play against Beta, if Alpha wins, Beta adopts Alpha's scoring function. If Beta wins, a neutral portion of the program evaluates Alpha. If Alpha fails a certain number of times (usually three), the coefficient of the scoring polynomial is set to 0. Ideally, the program should adjust its scoring polynomial by itself, but in practice, manual (human) intervention was sometimes necessary. A total of 38 heuristics could be used in the polynomial, but only 16 of these were ever used at one time, while the remaining 22 remained on the reserve list.

Moves that repeatedly scored low on the correlation coefficient were eventually transferred to the bottom of the reserve list and replaced with a term from the top of the reserve list. On the average, an active term was replaced every eight moves and recycled for another chance every 176 moves. Terms could also be replaced for minimal usage. Binary coefficients of terms were also possible, with adjustable coefficients and signs, but it was decided to limit these to a small number.

A series of 28 games played by the program with Alpha against Beta was employed to test learning generalization. As the number of games played increased, and a set of terms changed dramatically, the set of terms stabilized as did the machine's strength and learning ability. After these games, the program was deemed a better-than-average player. The following defects were found to be mostly responsible for the program's bad play:

1. The program was fooled by deliberately bad play on the part of the opponent. A simple solution was to change the correlation coefficients less drastically when positive scores were generated.

2. A second defect was connected to the too frequent changes of terms made to the evaluation function.

3. A third defect was the appropriation of credit to moves that looked like they caused a spectacular improvement, when in fact it was the ground-building, simpler moves occurring earlier that deserved equal credit for improving a position to enable a combination or consequently a spike in a position's score.

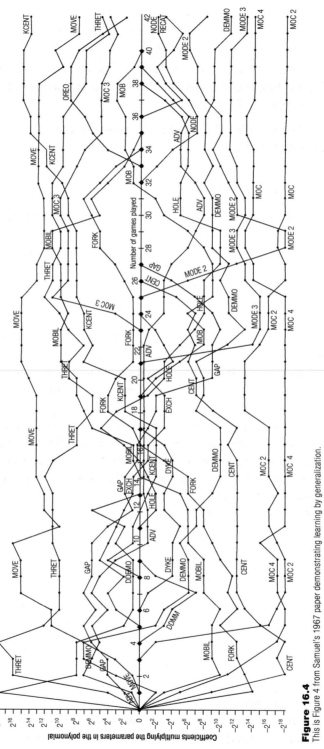

Figure 16.4
This is Figure 4 from Samuel's 1967 paper demonstrating learning by generalization.

The following are two of the important conclusions that Samuel (1967) reached about machine learning:

1. "A simple generalization scheme of the type used here can be an effective learning device for problems amenable to tree-searching procedures ....

2. Even with the incomplete and redundant set of parameters which have been used to date, it is possible for the computer to learn to play a better-than-average game of checkers in a relatively short period of time."

Figure 16.4 from Samuel (1967) [3] illustrates the results of a second series of learning by generalization tests performed by Samuel.

16.1.2 Rote Learning and Generalization

By the end of his first experiments, Samuel observed that the program that used rote learning did learn to play standard openings and learned how to avoid most standard endgame traps. It never learned how to play the middle game well. On the contrary, the program that used generalization never learned to play standard openings, did not learn to play endgames well (e.g., two kings against one in a double corner), but did learn to play well in the middle game, efficiently winning most positions with a piece advantage. Hence, rote learning was deemed useful for situations where very specific action was necessary, or results would be long delayed, whereas generalization learning was useful where there were a large number of permutations and where results could be quickly accomplished. Learning by either method using the alpha-beta minimax search technique proved to be a reliable but slow method. Rather than the linear polynomial method, Samuel (1959, 1967) turned his attention to **signature tables**. Values of parameters are read from signature tables and combined as subsets.

Samuel concludes that attempts to study strong checker players and their "thinking methods" is somewhat futile, stating, "...from the writer's limited observation of checkers players he is convinced that the better the player, the more apparent confusion there exists in his approach to the problem, and the more intuitive his reactions seem to be, at least as viewed by the average person not blessed with a similar proficiency."

Samuel (1967) also concluded that "the heuristic search for heuristics" was "a more complicated task than is the playing itself."

It is not surprising that heuristics seem to work together in groups. In AI, you often hear of the "rule of diminishing returns"—that is, a small number of rules (such as 10%) take care of or apply to 90% of the cases. The remaining 10% of the cases (the so-called exceptions) might require 90% of the rules.

Samuel also studied and reported how the alpha-beta procedure could be used most effectively to reduce the necessary search tree for the game of checkers.

One such approach is called "plausibility analysis"—it would be used to perform

In the world of chess, I (D. K.) have often encountered the belief that chess masters' thinking is unfathomable to "mere mortals." The skills that chess masters develop in thinking and choosing a move or move sequence, however, are based on large pattern stores and vast experience. In a number of cases, however, chess masters are also simply not very articulate when it comes to explaining their thinking.

This insight is be echoed by knowledge engineers sometime later (see Chapter 9) and predated somewhat by Plato in his Euthypro. (S. L.)

Similar results are witnessed in the development of page-first tables in operating system design as well as in life itself—see, for example, Who Rules America by G. William Domhoff (7th edition, 2014).

a search to a fixed depth to quickly identify the most plausible moves. Such a plausibility analysis could also be done to various depths in the tree. Samuel points out that certain risks are associated with any move that is pruned (or forward pruned), though more pruning can safely be done at lower (deeper) levels in the tree than at higher levels in the tree when evaluation and choice of moves is more critical. Samuel also reported great problems in handling what he called "pitch moves" (or temporary sacrifices).

Naturally, such concepts are difficult for standard game-playing programs because they cannot identify the return on their investment soon enough or by "normal" methods unless special efforts are made to identify such positions.

16.1.3 Signature Table Evaluations and Book Learning

The concept behind Samuel's signature tables was to group together parameters thought to be related. In one arrangement, tables were organized at three levels including 105 entries at the first level, 125 entries at the second level, and 343 entries at the third level. In another arrangement, there were 68 entries at the first level, 125 entries at the second level, and 225 entries at the third level. Much effort was made to make the signature table values meaningful. Many entries were zero or simply had insufficient data, even after comparing them with more than 100,000 book game positions. Correlation coefficients were computed to measure the effects of learning for the signature-table procedure and for the linear polynomial procedure as a function of the total number of book moves analyzed. It was found that the signature table approach had a much higher correlation than the linear polynomial approach. After studying 175,000 moves, it reached a limit of .48 correlation for the signature table approach, whereas it stabilized at a correlation of .26 after 50,000 moves for the linear polynomial approach. [3]

One problem that strong human checker players noted with Samuel's program was that it did not seem to have a sense of long-term strategy. Instead, each position seemed to be evaluated as a completely new problem. One attempt to address this problem was to combine signature tables with plausibility analysis. The interdependency of parameters related to strategy was the goal of using this approach, and when related parameters seemed to operate effectively, they were weighted with a constant factor.

16.1.4 World Championship Checkers with Schaeffer's Chinook

Besides being a very strong computer scientist, Jonathan Schaeffer is a fervent competitor, as are most strong chess players.

Around 1990, Jonathan Schaeffer confessed to me (D. K. and others) that he really wanted to be the World Champion of *something*. He developed a chess program named Phoenix in the mid-1980s, which firmly entrenched him in the middle history of computer chess. Phoenix could play at the Class A (1800–2000) level but not much better.

Schaeffer is a master-level chess player from Canada, and at the time of this writing, Dean of Science at the University of Alberta in Edmonton, Alberta, Canada.

For various reasons, including computer resources, Schaeffer felt that he had little chance of developing a World Championship-level chess program. His approach to the development of his chess program was very noble in trying to study and develop various heuristic methods. [4] He tried to systematically evaluate how various versions of his programs would perform as he added or removed specific heuristics. Around 1989, Schaeffer decided to embark on the development of a World Championship–level checkers program, which he felt was an *In fact, on a visit to Edmonton in 1984, D. K. played the program in a small tournament and won a short game.*

achievable goal. The notion that the Samuel Checkers program was very strong was finally dissolved in 1979 when the Duke University checkers program (developed by Tom Truscott) [5] defeated the Samuel Program in a short match. By 1990, Chinook (developed by Schaeffer, Norman Treloar, Robert Lake, Paul Lu, and Martin Bryant) had earned the right to play a match for the World Championship with Marion Tinsley, who for some 40 years was the World Checkers Champion. The match with Tinsley finally took place in 1992 with 40 games being played, Chinook winning four times against Tinley's two wins, with the remaining 34 games being drawn. In 1994, a rematch with Tinsley was arranged, but after only six games (all drawn), he resigned the match citing ill-health. In fact, he was diagnosed with cancer a week later and died 8 months later. Chinook was the first program to win a human world championship in any game. Subsequently, Chinook defended its title twice and was never defeated after 1994. In 1997, it was retired from human competition playing at a level that was estimated to be 200 rating points (or at least one class) above the best human players. In other words, it would be expected to score 75% in a match against the human world champion.

HUMAN INTEREST NOTES

JONATHAN SCHAEFFER

Jonathan Schaeffer.

Jonathan Schaeffer (1957–   ) must be crowned "The Grandmaster of Computer Games." He attained a PhD in computer science from Waterloo University in 1986 and is a master-level chess player. By 1994, he achieved the title of Professor of Computer Science at the University of Alberta, was Chair of his department from 2005–2008, and since 2008 has been Vice-Provost and Associate Vice-President for Information Technology at the University of Alberta.

Schaeffer started to gain notoriety in the 1980s with the development of a strong computer chess program called PHOENIX that regularly competed in the North American and World Computer Chess Championships. Around 1990, he decided to pursue the game of Checkers for which he felt he could develop a World Championship Program. This was accomplished in 1994 when his program, CHINOOK, defeated the World Checker Champion, Marion Tinsley. In the most recent decade, having at least partially solved the game of checkers, Schaeffer has begun a broad assault on POKER, a game of perfect information, with considerable success. Schaeffer has been a friend and professional associate of D. K.'s for many years.

Chinook vs. Marion Tinsley (1994).

Not surprisingly, given Schaeffer's background and experience, Chinook was designed with a structure "similar to that of a typical chess program." [6, 7, 2] He also stated that Chinook uses "search, knowledge, database of opening moves, and **endgame databases.** Chinook uses alpha-beta search with a myriad of enhancements, including **iterative deepening, transposition tables,** move ordering, search extensions, and search reductions. Chinook was able to average a minimum of 19 ply searches against Tinsley (using 1994 hardware), with search extensions occasionally reaching 45 ply into the tree. The median position evaluated was typically 25 ply deep into the search."

16.1.5 Checkers Is Solved

More recently, Schaffer demonstrated that the game of checkers can be solved and must end in a draw with best play.

The complete game of checkers consists of approximately 500 billion positions, or 5×10^{20} possible positions.

Schaeffer has used a type of "sandwich" or "inside-out" approach toward solving checkers. Unlike chess, he knew that the game might be easy to control if openings (such as the first 10 moves by each side) were preordained or solved with standard **opening libraries** that humans have developed for the game over many decades. Chinook's search checked these opening libraries carefully and deeply, whereas databases solved the end of the game through search and analysis by providing the outcome of all positions with a total of 10 or less pieces left on the board. The search technique and database use comprises the "bread" (or outside) of the complex sandwich, and the "meat" could be viewed as the search coupled with heuristics to handle the middle of the game.

Checkers is Solved, www. sciencemag.org/cgi/content/ abstract/1144079v1.

In other words, once the openings and endings are known, not much is left in the middle of the game—say 20 moves on the average.

The game of checkers was solved using three algorithm and data components:

1. The endgame database was developed using a backward search (called **retrograde analysis**) by working backward from all known one-piece positions and their values, linking them to all enumerable two-piece positions, then three-piece positions, and so on. The up to 10-piece database consists of 3.9×10^{13} positions whose game-theoretic value has been determined.

2. The proof-tree manager employs a forward search to maintain a tree of the proof as it is being developed and generates positions that need to be further explored.

3. A proof solver also employs forward search to determine the values of positions presented by the proof-tree manager.

The longest known move sequence required to force a win in the 10-piece database was found to be 279 ply. The 39 trillion possible positions are compressed into 237 gigabytes, with an average of 143 positions per byte.

A custom compression program enables "rapid localized real-time decompression." [8,9] The construction of the database began in 1989 for all possible positions with four or less pieces on the board. By 1996, the database covered all endings with eight pieces or less. In 2001, with computational resources improving, it was possible to construct the eight-piece database in just 1 month, instead of over 7 years! In 2005, the 10-piece database computation was completed. Initially, in 1989, 200 computers were used, but in 2007, the average number of computers used was 50.

The solution of the game of checkers was achieved in a manner known as **weakly solved**. In this sense, not every position in the game was analyzed and solved (which would be "strongly solved"), but instead, a unique sequence of moves was found and analyzed that demonstrated that the first player to move (Black) can obtain at least a forced draw by starting out with the move

Table 1. The number of positions in the game of checkers.

Pieces	Number of positions	Pieces	Number of positions
1	120	11	259,669,578,902,016
2	6,972	12	1,695,618,078,654,976
3	261,224	13	9,726,900,031,328,256
4	7,092,774	14	49,134,911,067,979,776
5	148,688,232	15	218,511,510,918,189,056
6	2,503,611,964	16	852,888,183,557,922,816
7	34,779,531,480	17	2,905,162,728,973,680,640
8	406,309,208,481	18	8,568,043,414,939,516,928
9	4,048,627,642,976	19	21,661,954,506,100,113,408
10	34,778,882,769,216	20	46,352,957,062,510,379,008
		21	82,459,728,874,435,248,128
		22	118,435,747,136,817,856,512
		23	129,406,908,049,181,900,800
		24	90,072,726,844,888,186,880
Total 1-10	39,271,258,813,439	Total 1-24	500,995,484,682,338,672,639

Table 2. Openings solved, Note that the total does not match the sum of the 19 openings. The combined tree has some duplicated nodes, which have been removed when reporting the total.

#	Opening	Proof	Searches	Max Ply	Minimal size	Max Ply
1	09-13 22-17 13-22	Draw	736,984	56	275,097	55
2	09-13 21-17 05-09	Draw	1,987,856	154	684,403	85
3	09-13 22-18 10-15	Draw	715,280	103	265,745	58
4	09-13 23-18 05-09	Draw	671,948	119	274,376	94
5	09-13-23-19 11-16	Draw	964,193	85	358,544	71
6	09-13 24-19 11-15	Draw	554,265	53	212,217	49
7	09-13 24-20 11-15	Draw	1,058,328	59	339,562	58
8	09-14 23-18 14-23	≤Draw	2,202,533	77	573,735	75
9	10-14 23-18 14-23	≤Draw	1,296,790	58	336,175	55
10	10-15 22-18 15-22	≤Draw	543,603	60	104,882	41
11	11-15 22-18 15-22	≤Draw	919,594	67	301,310	59
12	11-16 23-19 16-23	≤Draw	1,969,641	69	565,202	64
13	12-16 24-19 09-13	Loss	205,385	44	49,593	40
14	12-16 24-19 09-14	≤Draw	61,279	45	23,396	44
15	12-16 24-19 10-14	≤Draw	21,328	31	8,917	31
16	12-16 24-19 10-15	≤Draw	31,473	35	13,465	35
17	12-16 24-19 11-15	≤Draw	23,803	34	9,730	34
18	12-16 24-19 16-20	≤Draw	283,353	49	113,210	49
19	12-16 24-19 08-12	≤Draw	266,924	49	107,109	49
Overall		Draw	Total 15,123,711	Max 154	Total 3,301,807	Max 94

Figure 16.5
Two Tables illustrating how the game of checkers was solved. One gives the number of positions in checkers, and the other gives the best opening moves (with some duplicate sequences removed).[8]

The source (with permission) for Figures 16.5 and 16.6 is the article "Checkers is Solved" by Jonathan Schaeffer, Neil Burch, Yngvi Björnsson, Akihiro Kishimoto, Martin Müller, Robert Lake, Paul Lu, and Steve Sutphen, which appeared in Science Express, 2007.

09-13. Then White replies 22-17, which offers a capture and forces the reply 13-17-22. It turns out that all of White's other six replies to Black's initial move 09-13 (21-17, 22-18, 23-18, 23-19, 24-19, and 24-20) lead to at least a draw for Black (≥D), so White will prefer the move 22-17. [8]

Thus, a stored proof tree was generated with a total of "only" 10^7 positions. See Table 1 in Figure 16.5. Storing every position from the initial move 09-13 would require many terabytes. Thus, combining heuristic results from the search and the proof-tree manager reduced the number of stored positions to be analyzed to a manageable size, both for storage and computation purposes. The longest sequence analyzed was 154 ply. See Table 2 in Figure 16.5. The 20 plus ply were analyzed by the solver and then tied to a database position whose analysis could be the result of several hundred ply of analysis.

Overall, the effort to solve the game of checkers involved 18 years by Schaeffer's team, combining a number of AI approaches including deep and clever search techniques, subtle algorithmic proofs, heuristics derived from human experts, and advanced database techniques. Figure 16.6 illustrates how the game of checkers was solved.

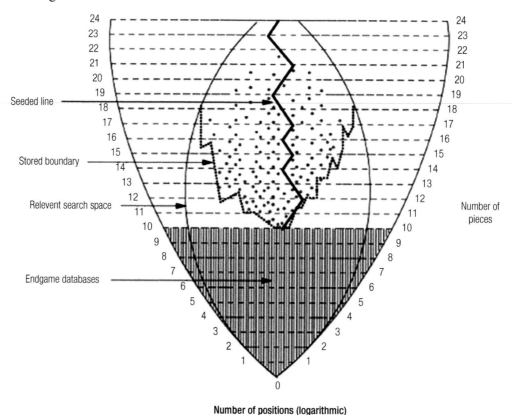

Figure 16.6
How the game of checkers was solved.

16.2 CHESS: THE DROSOPHILA OF AI

Newell, Shaw, and Simon wrote about chess and AI some 50 years ago.[10] Therefore, chess has been subjected to over 250 years of intensive study, and despite over 50 years of assistance in studying the game with computers and the efforts of numerous, massive databases of chess games and chess openings, middle games, and endings, we don't even know the answers to the following fundamental questions:

1. What is the outcome of a chess game with best play?
2. What is the best first move for White—1.e4, 1.d4, or another move?

That is, chess with best play could be a win for White, a win for Black, or a draw. The prevailing theory is that with best play, chess is a draw.

In addition, thousands of chess professionals worldwide attempt to make a living out of competing, teaching, writing about, and organizing various aspects of this intellectual game par excellence. Furthermore, more books are written on chess than on all games put together. Almost every weekend, you can find a tournament within a few hundred miles of where you live. It is clear that chess is an intriguing game, which by no means has been "played out," even though the great Cuban World Champion (1921–1927), Jose Raul Capablanca, once predicted it might be. Chess is no more played out than, say, are the possible number of ways of seeing New York City. Surely, if one decides to take the same path to and from the same destination, every day, then after a while New York City could seem limiting and boring. If one endeavors to vary his or her routes, however, then no doubt, one will find New York City very interesting. So it's just a matter of combinatorics and willingness to vary and possibly take risks. Most chess games offer an estimated 30 possible moves to each player at each typical position. If a typical competitive Master game lasts 40 moves (80 ply), you can see why there are an estimated 10^{43} possible and reasonable chess games. Including unreasonable games, chess is estimated to have 10^{120} possible positions, including unreasonable moves by each side. That is an enormous number. (For a further discussion of this number in terms of **computational complexity** see Chapter 4.) Chess remains popular today, even with strong computer programs that can compete at least evenly with the best human players. Chess combines elements of sports, science, war, and art in the struggle that develops between two antagonists. Those who do not completely understand the rules and goals of the game might have difficulty seeing these elements in the game, but those who play it at the highest level will quickly attest to this. Why? For one, chess at its best is a marathon. That is, games at the highest level today (even with speedup to avoid adjournments and possible outside intervention) will typically last 4 to 6 hours. So the endurance and physical strength typified by sports is often necessary for successful competition. Chess also offers plenty of opportunity for deep analysis, precise calculation, and combining intuition with knowledge, experience, and instinct akin to decision-making processes in science.

See Appendix D.3.3 for an explanation of chess notation. Again, based on statistics, it is largely believed that either 1.e4 or 1.d4 are the best moves for White, but there is no proof of this.

Elements of war come into play with chess when you consider the tactical and strategic factors that contribute to the process of choosing a move, a plan, or a sequence of moves. Mobility and material are at a premium, but safety of the king is foremost.

Positioning of forces (usually in the center) is important for a quick strike, security, and maneuverability. Distribution of forces and their coordinated participation is also important as are timing and the element of surprise. Finally, the notion of struggle and the desire to win are the human elements that make chess unique, distinct, and at-

Lasker (1862–1941), a German, was well known for his writings in philosophy and mathematics and supposedly only played in chess tournaments and matches when he needed to make a living.

tractive. No one likes to lose, and the struggle to avoid defeat or to enjoy victory pits one ego against another equally determined to demonstrate superiority. Putting aside physical factors such as rest, tiredness, speed of play, and persistence, chess offers you the opportunity to "gamble" your knowledge directly against the opponent's knowledge. As the great Dr. Emmanuel Lasker, World Chess Champion from 1894 to 1921, said, "On the chessboard lies and hypocrisy do not survive."

In 1933, Thomas Hunt Morgan of the California Institute of Technology was awarded the Nobel Prize for his research in population genetics. This research was based on studies of the common fruit fly known as the **drosophila**. The drosophila was ideal for such studies because of its short life cycle; its easily identifiable features, including wing span and eye color; as well as its economy for experimentation. Morgan and his associates from Columbia University, in 1910, were able to derive much information from the low-cost experimentation with the drosophila that was dictated by the limited resources of the times. John McCarthy [11] credited the Russian mathematician and AI researcher Alexander Kronrad with the phrase, "Chess is the drosophila of artificial intelligence." The late Donald Michie* considered chess suitable for AI experimentation for the following reasons:

1. Chess constitutes a well-formalized knowledge domain.

2. It challenges the highest levels of intellectual capacity over a wide range of cognitive functions, including logical calculation, rote-learning, concept formation, analogical thinking, and deductive and inductive reasoning.

3. A detailed corpus of chess knowledge has accumulated over centuries in chess instructional works and commentary.

4. A generally accepted numerical scale for performance is available in the ELO. and United States Chess Federation (USCF) rating system.

5. Chess can be divided into subgames for intensive separate analysis. [12]

16.2.1 Historical Background of Computer Chess

People have been trying to get computers to play strong chess for several centuries. Early efforts, that is, the Turk in 1770, [13] as mentioned in Chapter 1, even involved attempts to fool the public by having a chess master concealed inside a box.** Over the course of its tours around Europe, the Turk fooled many people over many years. [13] Subsequent efforts were more serious, and the Spanish inventor Torres y Quevedo (circa 1900) developed a mechanical device to win the ending K+R vs. K. [14]

In 1948, Alan Turing, deemed by many "The father of computer science," and Claude Shannon, known as the "father of information science," independently developed the basic algorithms that are still employed by today's chess programs. [15,16] In 1957, the late Nobel laureate in economics, Herbert Simon of Carnegie Mellon University, predicted that a computer would become the chess champion within 10 years. (He and many others after him, however, have been

The ELO rating system is a reliable way of ranking chess players. There are five classes (A–E) separated by 200 point intervals. So Class E is 1000–1199, Class D is 1200–1399, Class C is 1400–1599, Class B is 1600–1799, and Class A is 1800–1999. Expert level is 2000–2199, Master level is 2200–2399, Senior Master level is over 2400, International Master (IM) level is usually over 2400 internationally, and grandmaster is over 2500. World Class Players are over 2700 today, and the very top few players are around 2800. The rating system is very accurate in predicting outcomes between two players depending on the point spread between them, once ratings are established after 25 games of play.

---

*See Chapters 6, 9 and 10 for more about Donald Michie.
** See also Chapter 15 for more on the Turk.

proven incorrect.) After many rudimentary efforts to develop chess programs, the first successful serious effort was by Newell, Simon, and Shaw in 1959. In 1967, Richard Greenblatt of Massachusetts Institute of Technology (MIT) developed the first club-level program, Machack, which played at about the 1600 level. Greenblatt only allowed his program to play against humans.[17]

In 1968, David Levy, the Scottish IM, made a bet with three computer science professors for $2,000 that no computer program could beat him in a serious chess match. Levy made this bet in an attempt to spur research and commitment to the development of strong computer chess programs. In 1970, Monty Newborn, a computer science professor at McGill University, initiated the North American Computer Chess Championships, which for 25 years held a well-defined place as a continuing experiment to measure the progress of computer chess programs. Between 1970 and 1980, the North American Computer Chess Championships (later known as the International Computer Chess Championship) were dominated by Northwestern University's Chess 3.x and 4.x series of programs developed by David Slate, Larry Atkin, and Keith Gorlen.

In chess, a win is worth 1 point, a draw 0.5 points, and a loss 0 points. So this score represents three wins for Levy, one draw, and one loss.

In 1978, IM Levy was finally challenged and easily beat Chess 4.7 by a score of 3.5–1.5.

In 1983, Belle, the program of Ken Thompson at Bell Laboratories, became the first officially rated USCF master-level program. But in the 1983 World Computer Chess Championships (New York City), held every 3 years, Belle was defeated by Cray Blitz, developed by Bob Hyatt, Albert Gower, and Harry Nelson of the University of Southern Mississippi. Again in 1983, Levy was challenged by and again defeated the then-World Champion program Cray Blitz 4-0 in a match in London. Cray Blitz ran on the world's fastest computer at the time, the Cray XMP. One of the authors (D. K.) served as Levy's second for the match. Levy was able to get Cray Blitz out of its opening book early to steer for middle-game positions that were relatively blocked, and in general, he avoided Cray Blitz's tactical prowess, while in general exploiting the match conditions to get Cray Blitz into time trouble. Thereby, Cray Blitz could not benefit from its major advantages: calculation power, depth, and accuracy. [19]

Between 1985 and 1988, Hitech (Berliner et al., Carnegie Mellon University) quickly became the dominant program and the first to break the 2400 barrier. Hitech was a hybrid game comprised of chess knowledge and search depth.[20] In 1987, Fidelity Electronics (Miami, Florida) developed the first officially rated master-level microcomputer-based chess program (Spracklen and Spracklen, Baczynskyjs, and Kopec). Their chess engine was so good that it was subsequently sold to and used by the developers of the popular Chessmaster™ series of programs.

16.2.2 Programming Methods

A chess program is the result of a very complex endeavor. Throughout the history of computer chess, a number of programming techniques and methods have been developed and refined. It usually comprises the following components:

1. A Shannon type B approach described in the following section
2. Board and legal move representation
3. Openings and position evaluation
4. Tree searching with the alpha–beta minimax algorithm, alpha–beta **windows**, depth-first search with iterative deepening, and transposition tables
5. Large opening libraries and special purpose knowledge for each phase of play

16.2.2.1 Shannon Approaches

From the time of Claude Shannon's original paper in 1950, two fundamental approaches have been developed called **Shannon type A** and **Shannon type B**. The Shannon type A approach says to iteratively search, level by level, to a fixed depth from any given position. The Shannon type B approach says to extend the search beyond an ordained depth if a position holds sufficient interest—for example, there has been a capture, check, or another tactical event that has not been completed. In other words, until the position is deemed to be **quiescent** or quiet. In chess, a quiescent position is one where there are no imminent tactics, for example, checks, pins, forks, captures, and so on.

In contrast, people use a technique called **progressive deepening**. Recall from Chapter 4 that because human memory is not as versatile as machine memory, people must constantly review what they have analyzed. When trying to decide on which move to play in a chess position, people will analyze more deeply for certain variations (or lines) that they are particularly interested in, as their memory and time permits, returning to these again and again to analyze more deeply. That is the progressive sense of this kind of analysis.

16.2.2.2 Board and Legal Move Representation

The Englishman Howard Staunton was an unofficial World Chess Champion between 1843 and 1851. He created the standard design of chess pieces, which so distinctly identifies the pieces as seen in the chess diagrams of this book.

Figure 16.7
The starting position in chess.

For humans, it is easy to enjoy and understand a chess position. Just look at the lovely position before us with those beautifully proportioned wooden or plastic Staunton design White and Black pieces in front of us (Figure 16.7).

For computers, of course, this is not so easy, and it is important to remember that all decisions are ultimately determined by the conversion of numbers to ones and zeros. A simple scheme to represent the initial chessboard shown above would be to have White pieces represented by positive numbers, Black pieces by negative numbers, and empty squares by zeros. This is shown in Figure 16.8.

−4	−2	−3	−5	−6	−3	−2	−4
−1	−1	−1	−1	−1	−1	−1	−1
0	0	0	0	0	0	0	0
0	0	0	0	0	0	0	0
0	0	0	0	0	0	0	0
0	0	0	0	0	0	0	0
1	1	1	1	1	1	1	1
4	2	3	5	6	3	2	4

Figure 16.8
The initial position in chess as it might be represented in a program. Here, 1 stands for a pawn, 2 for a knight, 3 for a bishop, 4 for a rook, 5 for a queen, and 6 for a king, and 0 for an empty square. White pieces are positive numbers, Black pieces are negative numbers.

Figure 16.8 assigns the pieces to squares on a chessboard. The actual addresses of the squares on the chessboard are more typically represented by the scheme in Figure 16.9.

Now let us put a piece on an arbitrary square, say a king on the square 44. Now the squares that the king can move to are (in a clockwise manner) 54, 55, 45, 35, 34, 33, 44, and 52. So we could say that the squares the king can move to are K+10, K+11, K+1, K−9, K−10, K−11, K−1, and K+9. This is called a **pseudo-legal move list**. It is easy to see how this scheme can be extended to handle the legal movements of all pieces. Of course, one would have to check whether a square is already occupied by one's own forces or what enemy forces either attack or occupy a square before considering a move to a square. Instead of lists, the pseudo-legal moves in a position could be more efficiently stored and looked up in a table. The lists or tables could be stored in RAM and updated as moves are analyzed or made. The logic behind this is that two-thirds of all the pieces on a chessboard are unaffected by whatever move is made.[18] Furthermore, in the 1980s, with development of the program Belle[21] and its successors Hitech, Deep Thought, and Deep Blue, it became quite common to employ special-purpose hardware to generate the legal moves. This, coupled with other factors, enabled a speedup of several thousand-fold that resulted in several extra ply in the search depth that gave these programs an edge over their competitors.

81	82	83	84	85	86	87	88
71	72	73	74	75	76	77	78
61	62	63	64	65	66	67	68
51	52	52	54	55	56	57	58
41	42	43	44	45	46	47	48
31	32	33	34	35	36	37	38
21	22	23	24	25	26	27	28
11	12	13	14	15	16	17	18

Figure 16.9
A typical representation of the "addresses" of squares on a chessboard.

16.2.2.3 Openings and Position Evaluation

In chess, it is generally accepted that there are three phases of play: the opening, middle game, and ending. In the opening, it is most important that (1) pieces are developed, (2) king safety is achieved, and (3) the rooks are connected.

In the 1980s, it was decided that programming computers to play the openings well in chess was a very difficult task. There seemed to be as many exceptions as there were rules to follow. For example, all chess novices learn the fundamental rule "do not take your queen out too early." Yet, on many occasions, because of a particular configuration of pieces, it is precisely such a queen move that can be used to refute an opponent's play, and such an opportunity cannot and should not be missed.

From the 1980s onward, it has become standard for computer programs to have opening libraries of more than a million positions to assist programs in their opening play. This has stifled opening play by computer programs and ended the area as an academic discipline. Nonetheless, five heuristics or goals emerge as crucial to successful play of chess openings:

1. Develop pieces
2. Control the center
3. Maintain the King safety
4. Control space
5. Maintain material balance

1. Development

In the opening of a chess game, development is probably the single most important concept and universal goal. Development usually refers to the activation of knights and bishops and their movement off the back row so that castling can occur. When development is completed, the king is castled, and the rooks are connected, a side is said to be in the middle game. In the middle game,

Figure 16.10
Ancient King's Gambit position for development analysis.

pieces will tend to move for their second and third times and short- and long-term tactical skirmishes as well as long-term strategic maneuvers will often occur. When there are less than or equal to 20 points of heavy material (e.g., less than a queen (or two rooks) and three minor pieces (bishops and knights)) we are usually in an endgame.

The following is a brilliant example from David Levy's wonderful Computer Chess Handbook (pp. 16–17). [18] The position (see Figure 16.10) has been subjected to tremendous analysis by at least three monographs (earlier by Znosko-Borovsky and more recently by Korchnoi and Zak, and Estrin and Glazkov) on the historic King's Gambit Opening.

King's Gambit [C37]

1.e4	e5	2.f4	exf4	3.Nf3	g5	4.Bc4	g4	5.0–0	gxf3	6.Qxf3	Qf6
7.e5	Qxe5	8.d3	Bh6	9.Nc3	Ne7	10.Bd2	Nbc6	11.Rae1	Qf5	12.Nd5	Kd8
13.Qe2											

Levy notes that White is a knight and pawn down (or the equivalent of four pawns), but White has a considerable lead in mobility (46 to 34). Then he goes on to apply a formula for assessing development:

$$\text{Development} = D/3 - U/4 - (K \times C)$$

That is to say:

D (the number of minor pieces not on their original squares) is 3 for White and 3 for Black.

U (which is 0 if the queen has not been moved or has been captured but which otherwise is the number of undeveloped pieces) is 0 for White, because his queen has moved, but there are no undeveloped pieces, but 3 for Black, because the Black queen has moved and there are two rooks and a bishop undeveloped.

C (which is 2 if the opponent's queen is still on the board) is 2 for White and for Black.

K (which depends on castling rights) is 0 for White, who has castled, and 1 for Black, who has lost all castling rights.

So from the formula:

$$\text{Development} = D/3 - U/4 - (K \times C)$$

We have:

White's development = $3/3 - 0/4 - (0 \times 2) = 1$

Black's development = $3/3 - 3/4 - (1 \times 2) = -1.75$ from which we can see that White has a lead in development of 2.75 units.

Given an estimate that 10 units of mobility is worth a pawn, and coupled with Black's weakened king position and doubled and isolated pawns, we can assess that the position is actually about equal. Hence, White's lead in development, mobility, Black's insecure king, and weakened pawn structure compensate for White's 4.0-point deficit. Indeed after 13. ... Qe6, White can respond with 14.Qf3 Qf5, and after 15.Qe2 Qe6 with threefold repetition to follow, the players can quickly agree to a draw.

2. Center Control

Control of the center has always been considered an important concept in chess. The reason is akin to the notion of "Grand Central Station." From the center, forces can easily move to any board sector, as one could from a central train station. The weighting scheme provided in Figure

16.11 differentiates between the center (d and e files), subcenter (c and f files), wings (b and g files), edges, and corners. Clearly, the four squares marked with 10s (d4, d5, e4, and d5 on a chessboard) are considered the center and are the most important squares on the board. When the center is closed (e.g., occupied and blocked with pawns), however, this might change. Then play can shift to the subcenter and wings.

There are well-known heuristics and expressions in chess such as "a knight on the rim is dim," and this is reflected by the weightings given to the edge squares, but there are also many exceptions, where, for example, a knight's move to the rim can be a winning move.

1	2	3	4	4	3	2	1
2	5	6	7	7	6	5	2
3	6	8	9	9	8	6	3
4	7	9	10	10	9	7	4
4	7	9	10	10	9	7	4
3	6	8	9	9	8	6	3
2	5	6	7	7	6	5	2
1	2	3	4	4	3	2	1
a	b	c	d	e	f	g	h

Figure 16.11
A typical weighting scheme for the squares on a chessboard (Levy, p. 19).

3. King Safety

King safety is an important objective of the Opening and is usually achieved by castling. As play progresses, it is usually important to maintain a shield of pawns (like a house or castle) around the king to protect him. King safety is inherently related to pawn structure. Pawn play is a sophisticated and subtle aspect of chess. One way to measure king safety would be to consider the pawn structure around the king at all times and to add up the number of defensive forces and their values around one's king. Another, more common, approach would be to measure the number (and weight) of the attacking forces on the quadrant the king lives in and see how these are offset by the defending forces.

4. Control Space

When one considers the subject of space in chess, it is inherently related to pawn structure (see Section 16.2.2.5). More advanced and healthy pawn structures will inevitably provide more space. Control of space will generally include better central control and suggest better maneuverability of forces (mobility). But even healthy structures can often be attacked and destroyed. Furthermore, even when one side has more space, there is no certainty that the opponent cannot work around that space and get behind enemy lines. Therefore, the subject of space is a difficult one, often involving delicate interplay of pieces and pawns.

5. Material Balance

The fifth element, material balance, provides the greatest contribution of computer chess to chess.

During the romantic period of chess (1850–1880), the more material that you could sacrifice to achieve checkmate, the more beautiful the game was considered to be. In the intervening 150 or so years, however, sound opening play has been developed and defensive techniques have improved. Correct chess play now entails great attention to material balance. Furthermore, permanent pawn structural weaknesses usually cannot be endured and will usually turn into material losses.

After the first six moves in the ultra-sharp Schliemann Variation of the Ruy Lopez, we reach the critical position in Figure 16.12.

Figure 16.12
Ruy Lopez, Schliemann Variation.

Ruy Lopez, Schliemann Variation [C63]
1.e4 e5 2.Nf3 Nc6 3.Bb5 f5 4.d4 fxe4 5.Nxe5 Nxe5 6.dxe5 c6

Many players who don't know this theoretical position would now somewhat naively play 7.Bc4, even though after Qa5+ and Qxe5 are soon followed with d5, White has very little compensation for a pawn. When this position was presented to Fritz 9, in 2 minutes of thinking time, it found the necessary theoretical 7.Nc3! In other words, Fritz was able to search deeply enough to

discover the necessary (and theoretical) piece sacrifice by realizing that any other move will just lose material without compensation. See DVD for further discussion.

The standard numbers used for material in chess are:

Pawn: 1, Knight: 3, Bishop: 3.5, Rook: 5, Queen: 9, and K: ∞

Before computers played a big role in chess, knights and bishops were considered closer to 3 or equal in value. With the experience and knowledge gained through computer chess program-

Figure 16.13
Diagram 166, p. 227 from Kopec and Terrie, 2003.

ming, bishops are considered worth 3.25–3.5 points, whereas knights are worth 3.0 points. The history of computer chess has reinforced the ideas of Mikhail Botvinnik (the Chess World Champion from 1948–1963). Although Botvinnik never completed a strong chess-playing program himself, in his book "Chess, Computers, and Long Range Planning," [22] he tried to mathematically prove the importance of material in chess. This has, for nearly three decades, been proven to be the most significant term in programs' evaluation functions. In a nutshell, the increased depth of programs' search capabilities has demonstrated viable defensive possibilities in positions that humans long ago have discounted as untenable.

The position in Figure 16.13 is taken from the book "Test, Evaluate and Improve Your Chess: A Knowledge-Based Approach" (p. 227). [23] It is Intermediate Test Position No. 8 where the idea is again to sacrifice a piece for two pawns to

exploit a pin. The concept of the sacrifice shows a clear distinction between human and computer chess play. A long, deep, intricate analysis from our text, (see Appendix D.3.2) can demonstrate that with perfect play Black can hold. This isn't the way humans can or do play chess. Humans play with heuristics, and here, the most important heuristic is that *N/f6* should not play g5 in positions such as the one when the Black-squared bishop cannot easily get back to e7 to break the pin on the N/f6. Computers, like Fritz 9, do not have such heuristics but will instead dourly defend as long as some defense maintaining a material advantage is possible.

16.2.2.4 Mobility and Connectivity

After material, the next most important concept in most programs' evaluation function is mobility. Mobility refers to the activity of pieces—how many squares can each piece move to and influence? E. T. O Slater [24] did a famous study of mobility in master games. In reviewing 78 games

Figure 16.14
Bc4 has just been played.

that ended by move 40, he found that the average mobility of the eventual winner of a game was significantly higher than that of the loser. The difference between the averages of their mobility also increased as play proceeded. Table 16.1 shows Slater's findings.

1.e4 e5 2.Nf3 Nc6 3.Bc4 Diagram

In the diagrammed position (Figure 16.14), White has just played 3.Bc4. This is the most natural developing move because it helps White castle (that is to achieve king safety), and it controls the center. In addition, it is the most mobile (active) square the bishop can move to from f1. From c4, the bishop influences no less than 10 squares, whereas from the next most active square, b5, it would influence

Table 16.1
Results of an Examination by E. T. O. Slater of 78 arbitrarily selected master games that ended with a decisive result on or before the 40th move. This result helps to ascertain the importance of mobility as a term in any program's evaluation function.

After Move	Winner's Mobility (Average)	Loser's Mobility (Average)	Difference
0	20.0	20.0	0
5	34.2	33.9	0.3
10	37.5	36.0	1.5
15	39.7	35.2	4.5
20	38.9	36.4	2.5
25	39.6	31.9	7.7
30	35.6	27.7	7.9
35	31.7	23.2	8.5

eight squares. In addition from c4, the bishop influences the all-important f7 square, which is the weakest square in Black's camp because it is the only square defended only by the Black king.

Considerable evidence indicates that another important heuristic should be *connectivity*—how well the forces are connected or protected. Connectivity is a measure of the safety of a position, and the lack of it is suggestive of opportunities for combinations exploiting unprotected forces (material). Connected (protected) positions are easier to play and closely related to planning. In "Connectivity in Chess," [25] we demonstrated through the review of hundreds of master-level, grandmaster-level, and world championship-level games, and using novice games as controls, that connectivity is indeed an important consideration in most strong players' play.

Positions with good pawn structures (see next section) tend to be more connected. As an example, please see Figure 16.15. In this position (which is classified as a "knight ending" because there is only one knight left on the board plus three pawns and a kings for each side), White has poor connectivity and poor mobility, which usually goes hand in hand with bad pawn structures. White's "a-pawns" are doubled, and he has two distinct groups of pawns (the a-pawn and the d-pawn), whereas Black's pawns and position in contrast is neatly connected and protected as one group.

For this position, where pawns are worth 10 and knights are worth 30, and for simplicity, let's leave out the kings: A reasonable measure of connectivity could be as follows: Piece Value + 3.2 (where 3.2 is the square root of the value of a pawn, 10), for each defender. BN/a5 = 30 + 3.2 (protector P/b6) + BP/b6 = 10 + 3.2; (BP/c6 = 10 + 6.4 (two protectors) and BP/d5 = 10 + 6.4.

Total Connectivity for Black = 79.2

For White, the Connectivity is for WN/d2 = 30 + 3.2; WP/d3 = 10 + 3.2; and WP/a3 = 10; WP:a4 = 10; the total for White is 66.4.

Black is significantly ahead in connectivity. Note that piece values are used in this computation as they should be. Protector values could vary for different piece combinations and could be done as table lookup for speed. A much simpler computation for connectivity would be to say that Black's protection count is 5 and White's is 2 for each piece or pawn protection.

For the data in this study, the differences in average connectivity between the winners and losers from move 20 to the end of game were used. An open question would be to test the counterbalances of connectivity and mobility. This could be done as a study of "style in chess." For example, someone familiar with championship chess would expect Mikhail Tal (known for his daring play and sacrifices) to have the highest mobility and lowest connectivity in his games, while expect-

Figure 16.15
Example of a position for study of connectivity.

ing a much lower mobility and higher connectivity for the games of Anatoly Karpov and Tigran Petrosian (both known for their careful and safe play). Somewhere in between would be Fischer, Alekhine, and Kasparov, who would be expected to have more of a balance between mobility and connectivity. Figure 16.16 hypothesizes a sketch comparing the mobility and connectivity tendencies of these players on a graph.

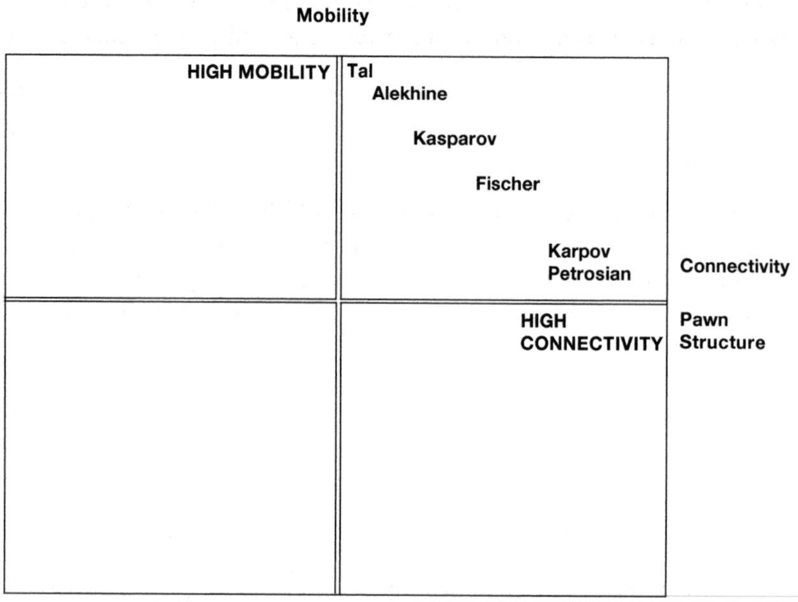

Figure 16.16
Mobility vs. Connectivity—styles of world champions could be depicted, studied, evaluated, and proven with this method.

Perhaps one of the most important topics in chess and for computer chess programming is pawn structure. Pawn structure is a subject that is relevant throughout play in the opening, middle game, and ending. It can be argued that nearly all play and positioning of pieces is related to pawns. Pawn structures and their handling can be either static or dynamic in nature. Good pawn structures are inherently related to center control, space, mobility of forces (and pawns), and the ability to attack the opposing king. Pawn structural defects can endure from the opening to the ending. Pawn structural advantages can be the major reason for victory in any phase of play. Pawns can be viewed as "islands or groups." The more "islands" of pawns a player has, the worse is considered his or her structure.

Although players and machines can be taught everything that is necessary to know about good and bad pawn structures (statically), it is much harder to understand the dynamics of pawn play and how pawn play can interact with piece play. Even harder and more subtle is the generation of a plan that might result in the decision to initiate a certain pawn assault. Pawn play is usually equated with "positional (or strategic) play," although as alluded to earlier, it might quickly become dynamic in nature, particularly when related to an attack on the opposing king. Usually, positional factors are not allowed to total more than a pawn's value (1 point) in the assessment of a position. Therefore, if after performing a search, a program returns an assessment of a position of say +.75, it is saying that it thinks it is three quarters of a pawn ahead in positional (static) factors.

Pawn structures are especially important to the outcome of endings. The position in Figure 16.17 could easily result from the most popular chess opening—the Sicilian Defense as played here by Black. As strong a program as Fritz 9 is, it does not seem to realize White's usual threat in this kind of position. Every strong human player would be familiar with this kind of position and would know that White threatens the favorable exchange of bishop for knight with 1.Bg5, resulting in an ending of "Good Knight against Bad Bishop." No doubt the program does not fear Bg5 and the subsequent exchange of White's bishop for Black's knight because it believes bishops are more valuable than knights. However, because of the particular pawn structure (highlighted by Black's backward pawn on d6 on a dark square), this is one of the well-known exceptions, and after allowing Bg5 followed by Bxf6, it should be prepared for an arduous defensive task.

Figure 16.17
A position based on deep structural knowledge.

16.2.3 Beyond the Horizon

In the early 1970s, World Correspondence Champion (1966–1969) Dr. Hans Berliner developed the *horizon effect* concept, which was introduced in Chapter 4. [26] This was a phenomenon that Dr. Berliner had observed while doing his doctoral research. The phenomenon was based on the observation that seeing a forthcoming disastrous variation (say a loss of material), a computer chess program would try to give away more material to push what it had "seen" earlier beyond the horizon. In doing so, the program tended to compound its difficulties.

Figure 16.18
World Computer Chess Championship, Toronto, 1977. Kaissa played 34. ... Re8!

The position in Figure 16.18 is one of the most famous positions in the annals of computer chess. An audience of over 500, including a former world champion, was aghast when Kaissa elected to play 34. ...Re8 instead of the obvious 34. ...Kg7. Was this a blunder? Why did Kaissa (Black) give up a rook for nothing? Actually, it was a case of the horizon effect/brute force being applied for correct reasons. Kaissa preferred this over allowing a forced mate with the beautiful queen sacrifice, for example, 34.Kg7 35.Qf8 + Kxf8 36.Bh6+ Bg7 37.Rc8+ and mate follows.

16.2.4 Deep Thought and Deep Blue Against Grandmaster Competition: 1988–1995

During roughly the same period, a program that came to be known as Deep Thought (Anantharaman, Campbell, and Nowatzk, all graduate students at Carnegie Mellon University) tied for first at the 1988 Software Toolworks Championship with GM Tony Miles defeating GM Bent Larsen along the way. It was during this period that it became clear that only the very best players would be able to defeat computer chess programs on a regular basis, even in slow play. Deep Thought established a rating of 2551, and in 1989 won the sixth World Computer Chess Championship in Edmonton, Alberta. [27]

One other event of 1988–1989, which is significant to the past, present, and future of computers and chess, is the victory of the late IM Michael Valvo over Deep Thought in a two-game Internet match played at the rate of one move every 3 days. Valvo won both games, although both were tactically complex. This showed, that given the time and proper conditions, humans could still compete with the best programs. Between 1989 and 1990, a number of other significant events happened in the computer chess world. In October, 1989 World Chess Champion (1985–2000) Gary Kasparov won a two-game exhibition match in New York City against Deep Thought. It was clear that the computer was not yet ready to challenge the World Champion. In December that same year, David Levy's challenge bet ($1,000 from Levy and $4,000 from Omni magazine) was finally claimed by a program. Deep Thought defeated Levy, who for many years had been out of chess-playing

This means Kasparov won three games, drew two, and lost one.

practice, with a one-sided 4-0 score. Again D. K. served as Levy's second in preparation for the match. In a nutshell, a few days was not enough to make up the gap in playing strength that Levy had lost from years of inactivity—while Deep Thought was a significant improvement over challengers of yesteryear. In February 1990, former World Champion Anatoly Karpov played an exhibition game at Harvard University with Deep Thought and narrowly won. In February 1996, Kasparov demonstrated some of the existing flaws in Deep Blue in his match in Philadelphia, which he won 4-2 (+3, =2, −1).

Note that the match was tied after four games. In the fifth game, through 23 moves, Kasparov considered the game roughly equal when the Deep Blue team unadvisedly turned down a draw offer from the World Champion, who was slightly short of time. In the last game of the match, Kasparov steered play into channels whereby the machine, with little space and activity, was gradually squashed. [28]

In the May 1997 rematch with Deeper Blue in New York City, Kasparov was defeated 3.5-2.5 (+1, =3, −2). True, this was the first time that Kasparov had lost a match at slower speeds since becoming World Champion in 1985, but not as much significance should have been attached to the result, as it was a relatively short match and was not played with the World Championship at stake.

Garry Kasparov at Turing Centennial in Manchester England on June 26, 2012.
Photo by Dennis Monniaux

Figure 16.19, based on Hsu's article in Scientific American in 1990, is probably the most important figure in this chapter. [29] It shows a trend started by Belle and continued by Hitech, Deep Thought, Deep Blue, and subsequent programs. Hsu predicted that once programs could achieve a depth of 14 ply of exhaustive search, they would play very strong grandmaster chess and be able to compete with the world champions. He was absolutely right, and their ratings have approached 3400 as predicted in Figure 16.19.

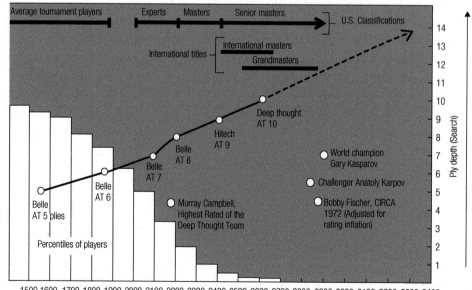

Figure 16.19
History and predictions for chess program rating vs. search depth.

16.3 CONTRIBUTIONS OF COMPUTER CHESS TO ARTIFICIAL INTELLIGENCE

As has been described in the previous sections, chess programming has largely proven to be a problem of representation—that is representation of the most important concepts necessary for strong chess play—and one of search. No program has reached the master level today without performing enormous searches, especially when compared to what humans do. The ability to increase search depth by a ply, or to be able to more efficiently focus a large search so that it is able to identify the most critical and best moves for each player, and to recognize when positions reoccur or when a search is reaching a dead end has been critical to the success of the best programs.

16.3.1 Search in Machines

As has been described earlier, most chess programs will employ a Shannon type B search strategy with a depth-first iterative deepening search with the minimax alpha-beta algorithm. Searches beyond 14 ply are not uncommon with today's programs.

In a large search tree analysis, such as the ones generated when computers play chess, many positions that have been previously encountered reappear by move order transpositions. Hashing is the technique that computer scientists use to efficiently store information or data that might be used for later examination. For efficient recovery of this data, positions are stored so they are easy to find in what is called a **transposition table**. This way a position, once assessed, doesn't need to be reassessed.

Sometimes, a move (or concept) that has proven important earlier in a search tree analysis becomes available again. Identification and reemployment of such a heuristic is called use of a **killer heuristic**. This is particularly effective when a so-called refutation move that has enabled a large alpha-beta cutoff is looked at first at another level in the tree and can be used again to cut off the search.

One search heuristic discovered by the Deep Thought/Deep Blue team in the late 1980s and early 1990s was the **null move heuristic**. Like the killer heuristic, the intention of the null move heuristic is to achieve greater efficiencies in search by employing the alpha-beta algorithm more effectively. That is, the side to move in a position to be analyzed skips its turn and the position is then analyzed at a higher level in the tree. If the position generates alpha-beta cutoffs with the null move heuristic being applied, then it has been effective. If not, the search continues more deeply.

Singular extensions are another result of the research by the Deep Blue team in trying to make its search deeper and more efficient. Basically, the concept is that if a move's value particularly stands out from the value of all other moves, then the search on that move should be extended to another level to make sure that the value can be trusted.

Computer chess **endgame databases** have been built for all possible endings of up to seven pieces. This has been accomplished via a technique known as the **retrograde analysis**, whereby starting with positions with known values (e.g., K + Q vs. K) and working backward to all possible predecessor positions, ultimately, all possible positions in an ending are labeled or evaluated as a win or a draw in x number of moves.

Computer chess programs have been exploiting the possibility of using **special-purpose hardware** since Ken Thompson introduced the program Belle at Bell Labs in 1980. The coupling of this special purpose hardware with **parallel search algorithms** further improved the search depth and speed of computer chess programs.

16.3.2 Search in Man vs. Machine

The infatuation of computer scientists with chess has, no doubt, stemmed from the belief that if you could create a program that played master-level chess, you would be emulating and achieving the very core of human creative endeavor and thinking. As computer chess programs became stronger, they clearly did not achieve competence in their play by the same methods that humans do. We can investigate some of the differences in the methods that humans and machines use to choose a move.

Humans are estimated to search 50–200 future board positions from any given board position in 3 minutes of think time. Even World Champion Kasparov is limited to these numbers. The best computer chess programs such as Deeper Blue can, however, search several hundred billion positions in the same 3-minute interval. Humans cannot match computer programs in calculation power when playing chess. In terms of calculation, *breadth*, and *depth*, chess masters consider at most an estimated seven possible candidate moves in a given middle game position. Computer programs look at every possible move for both players from a given board position, estimated to be 35 possible moves on average in the middle game. Therefore, in addition to inferior calculation power, people cannot match computer chess programs in breadth (width) of search. Furthermore, from a given board position, computer programs can search up to 14 ply (recall, a ply is a half move, where 2 ply equals a move by both White and Black, so 14 ply equals seven moves) in depth. Humans, however, can rarely search to a depth of more than 10 ply. Even Kasparov admitted this to be his typical limit in the Deeper Blue matches in February 1996 and May 1997. These search statistics might vary, especially in the endgame, where considerably more depth due to the reduced material on the board is possible. So we are comparing *computer search depth limits*, approximately 35,[14] to *human search depth limits*, which are somewhere between 2^5 (32 or 2 moves per position, 5 ply deep) and 3^5 (243 or three moves per position 5 ply deep). However, it is widely accepted that humans, unlike machines, do not search uniformly either in terms of breadth or depth. This is more likely in the extreme case of the most calculation-intensive players, people search one line 10 ply deep, another line or two 8 ply deep, other lines 7 ply deep, and so on.

This is somewhat more than the earlier stated hundreds of billions searched by the best programs probably because as search depth increases as a result of captures or exchanges, the number of possible moves in a position (the branching factor, here initially 35) decreases to something more like 25.[11]

How it is that humans can compete with the best programs? It turns out that most of the hundreds of billions of positions that computers search are considered simply because they fall into the category of legal moves. In other words, many moves that computers evaluate are unrealistic. For example, after 1.e4 e5 2.Nf3 Qh4, a computer program as White needs to consider 3...Qh4 as a legal move even though it is not a reasonable move (it loses a queen for nothing). If humans can find combinations or sacrifices where the compensation is deep enough, then even the best programs can be beaten. To find these combinations, people can rely on long-term positional concepts, including *heuristics* such as weak squares or weak square complexes. The best human players can employ such heuristics effectively. In practice, however, the depth of the compensation for sacrificed material has also been pushed so far over the horizon by the adroit defense posed by computer programs as defenders, often sufficient compensation is not found.

16.3.3 Heuristics, Knowledge, and Problem-Solving

Studies by Chase and Simon in 1972 [30] and others demonstrate that humans play chess largely by pattern recognition. The original interest in chess by AI researchers and cognitive scientists was that by solving chess or reaching chess mastery, we would gain significant insight into human problem solving and thinking methods. Furthermore, programs that solved or mastered chess would demonstrate that machines could intrude into and contribute to the realms of creative endeavor originally considered germane to, symbolic of, and unique to human intelligence, such as chess, music, and mathematics. As you learned in the previous section, machines and humans solve problems in and contribute original material to these domains in different ways.

As described in Chapter 7, people constantly use heuristics to help them make decisions. We are not machines. We function by being imprecise and approximate, yet purposeful and goal oriented. In fact, when people try to function or perform in a machine-like manner by being regular, predictable, and routine, they either fail or go crazy. Most people do not follow a checklist to start their day: first, you must wash, then brush your teeth, get dressed, eat breakfast, and so on, spending x minutes on each task. We must estimate knowing in general what our tasks and goals are for a particular day, weekend, month, or year. By employing heuristics and the knowledge they provide, we compensate for our slow and limited search speed. Examples of heuristics in chess include the following: in the opening, develop pieces, control the center, achieve king safety, fight for space, and don't lose any material. Other, more refined, heuristics are, for example, that three moves of development in the opening are worth a pawn and that a knight on the rim is dim, in other words, knights are better positioned in the center of board than on the periphery. Although computers are also programmed to play chess with heuristics, these heuristics are not represented by words but by numbers. (We (humans) actually do the same thing, only we don't explicitly and consciously put the numbers together to choose a move—we do so subconsciously.)

As people are the programmers of machines, the methods by which computers evaluate a move or a variation are based on human translation of imprecise heuristics (of a static structure) into a final numerical evaluation for the quality of each move considered and selected. Programmers must fine-tune their *evaluation function* based upon their understanding of the performance or effectiveness of the program's heuristics. Generally, that is why a strong player needs to provide advice to chess programmers and help them evaluate the accuracy and effectiveness of their heuristics. Automated, statistical database-like attempts to study the performance of a program's heuristics, including Deep Thought and then Deep Blue, have led to improvements in the weightings of the heuristics comprising a program's evaluation function. Nonetheless, the task of converting chess knowledge represented by heuristics into strong chess play, combined with all the other aspects of a chess program (such as data structures, search, opening book, and diverse tables of information), remains complex and intricate.

16.3.4 Brute Force: Knowledge vs. Search; Performance vs. Competence

Despite computer chess programs' achievement of the master level in 1982, senior master (2400+) level in 1988, and grandmaster level in the 1990s, some AI experts are skeptical about the contributions of chess to AI. A continuing argument among AI researchers is whether efficient search techniques constitute strong AI. Recall that strong AI is the approach that searches for solutions to difficult problems developed in a way that humans would employ, that is, from the cognitive psychological perspective. In other words, the solutions model what humans do and help us gain a better understanding of how we function and think. By that definition, because the decision-making processes by humans and machines are so different, is searching and deciding on the best move in a chess position by a program equivalent to human thinking?

One contribution that has been a by-product of computer chess for AI and for computer science in general is the *power of brute force*. In the context of computer science, brute force means the allocation of great computational power in order to perform an exhaustive search from a given position to a certain ply depth. Brute force has changed the view of how chess is best played by both people and machines. Strong AI proponents (D. K. included) have always hoped that we could learn enough about what goes on in a strong chess player's head that very strong chess programs could be developed without much calculation.

Figure 16.20
Adams, Michael (2737)—Comp Hydra at London Man-Machine London (Match Game 4), 6/25/05.

However, evidence acquired over many years, including the efforts of many great scientists, shows that we were wrong. Instead, a lot of calculation is indeed required, and the benefits of knowledge in reducing the requirements for search have been hard to discern. Hence, the distinction between tactical play and strategic play in chess, once believed to be clear, has been almost entirely eroded via the power (effects) of brute force. An example is Figure 16.20 from the fourth game of the six-game match between Michael Adams (then the No. 7 player in the World) and the Computer Hydra of the United Arab Emirates.

We see again the beautiful and unexpected tactical concepts which can be a direct result of brute force. Hydra has just played 44. ...Rh5, which essentially seals Black's victory. Before that move, Black's rook was stuck in an innocuous position on h6. It seemed problematic for Black to try to activate this piece (say with Rh8) because the P/g6 would be left unprotected. But now, through this clever move, Black can advance with his king, leaving his passed d-pawn unprotected and it will be immune because the clever tactic f4+ will be there for Black. The play ended with 45.Ra1 Kc5 46.Rc1+ Kb4 47.Rd1 Kc4 48.Rc1+ Kd3 49.Rc6 Rh6 50.h5 f4+ White resigns. Furthermore, we can see from such examples how programs can compensate for not having the immense kind of special-purpose knowledge that strong humans have for chess endings.

Tactical play generally refers to hand-to-hand combat between the White and Black forces (e.g., checks, captures, pins, and forks), whereas strategic play generally refers to more long-term maneuvers (e.g., regrouping a knight by retreating it, outposts for pieces, advances by parts to develop and execute a plan).

In summary, programs can play what seems to be the strongest chess of all time without strong AI techniques, without the benefit of special-purpose chess knowledge, and by the mere application of brute force. AI scientists call this distinction ***performance vs. competence***. That is, programs that can perform well but don't have great knowledge about what they are doing or the principles behind what they are doing fall into the realm of weak AI or performance. Programs that display a good knowledge of their realm are called competent and exhibit strong AI.

16.3.5 Endgame Databases and Parallelism

Developments in chess endgame databases [31] have contributed to knowledge about the game and its relationship with computer science issues. Progress in this area further demonstrates the distinction between search and knowledge. Nearly all work in computer chess endgames in recent years has focused on developing complete database solutions, rather than understanding the secrets of such endings through the organization of knowledge about them. Complete endgame databases have been constructed for up to six pieces by Lewis Stiller, [32] extending our knowledge about certain special-purpose endings. In 1991, Lewis Stiller, while still a graduate student at Johns Hopkins University, solved the secrets of the ending KRB vs. KNN demonstrating a win for the strong side in 223 moves.

Since this six-piece endgame has over six billion positions, Stiller's discovery that over 96% of the positions are wins for the strong side is very significant and well beyond the realm of human comprehension.

However, endgame databases do not provide the kind of "knowledge refinery" that Professor Michie has spoken of, enabling human acquisition of the critical concepts for such endings and thereby extending the science of chess and related disciplines.[33]

Monty Newborn of McGill University was the first to develop parallel versions of his program, Ostrich, in the 1970s. [34] Subsequently, all the top computer programs, including Cray Blitz, Hitech, Deep Thought, and Deep Blue, exploited the advanced search capabilities available through parallel architectures. Publication of these parallel search techniques applied to computer chess and how they were efficiently accomplished has contributed to the discipline of search and parallelism.[35] Although a speedup due to parallelism is by no means near to linear with the number of processors, it is an integral feature of most top chess programs today. Table 16.2 compares the top computer chess programs historically in terms of size, makeup, speed, strength, and so on.

16.3.6 Author Contributions

One of the authors (D. K.) in his PhD thesis [36] in machine intelligence focused on the comparison of knowledge representations of several correct and optimal solutions for the least mobile of chess endings, K + P vs. K. These solutions were compared for their *executability* as advice texts for human novices and then for their *comprehensibility* for the same purpose (see Chapter 6). In other words, could novice chess players in high school learn from the translation of these programs from a programming language such as Algol or Prolog into English, where the program information appeared as decision tables or as procedures?

The endgame K + R vs. K+ N is a specialized chess endgame that can occur frequently, even in top-level play. In a paper with Tim Niblett titled "How Hard Is the K+R vs. K+N Ending?" [37] we learned that it takes about a master-level player to hold a drawn position or win a won position in this ending. The longest win is 33 moves, and it is not uncommon for people, even at the master plus level, to make errors in this ending. From this research, it was discovered that to hold certain positions in this ending with the weak (N) side, you must play counterintuitive "separating" moves that increase the distance between the defending K and N rather than decrease it as is the common human heuristic in all chess books. In other words, in certain positions, it's not the distance between the K and N that is important but rather the availability of safe paths between them.

In work with Ivan Bratko, [38] a test was developed for evaluating chess strength based on tactical ability and knowledge of a certain aspect of pawn play called "levers." This test, consisting of only 24 positions administered for 2 minutes each, for many years had been the standard benchmark for evaluating the strength of humans and computer chess programs. It has proven quite reliable for players rated 1500 to master. A later effort, "Experiments in Chess Cognition," [39] involved the use of various tests on people to determine whether two heads are better than one or whether two people working together on test positions perform better than one person. Another test involved time-sequence experiments to see how various levels of players perform on positions of diverse difficulty with varying amounts of time. In general, the results found that two people perform one class better than one person performing alone. It was found that in easier positions presented for

Table 16.2
Details of some of the key chess programs since 1980.

No.	Name	Authors	Affiliations	Dates	Programming Language/Computer Specs	Size of Program	Speed, ×1000 positions p/sec	Depth of Search (ply)	Rating	Techniques
1	Kaissa	Georgy Adelson-Velsky, Vladimir Arlazarov, Alexander Bitman, and Anatoly Uskov	Institute for Theoretical and Experimental Physics	1960–1974	British International Computers Limited (ICL) System 4/70 computer with a 64-bit processor/24,000 bytes of memory. Assembly language/900,000 instructions per second.	384 KB	0.2	7	1600	Was the first program to use bitboard. Kaissa contained an opening book with 10,000 moves and employed the alpha-beta technique with a "window." The program introduced a feature called "best move service," storing a table of the 10 best moves. This was used to improve move ordering for the alpha-beta method. Another feature was a "dummy move," in which one side does nothing at its turn and used to discover threats.
2	Nuchess	David Slate, Larry Atkin, and Keith Gorlen	Northwestern University	1970–1972	Northwestern's Control Data Corporation (CDC) 6400 computer/assembly language	250 KB	600	7	2040	Rapidly search every possible move to a certain depth in the game tree, so-called full-width or exhaustive searching
3	Cray Blitz	Robert Hyatt, Harry Nelson, and Albert Gower	Cray Research	1980–1994	Cray X-MP supercomputer with 64-bit registers/CFT77 FORTRAN	64 M	200	9-10	2258	Dynamic Tree Splitting algorithm: Whenever a processor exhausts the work (subtree) that it is working on, it broadcasts a help request to all busy processors. These processors make a quick copy of the type of each node they are searching in the current subtree and the number of unsearched branches at each node and give this information to the idle processor. The busy processors then resume searching where they were interrupted. The idle processors examine the data and pick the most likely split point based on the amount of work left and the depth of the node.

4	Hitech	Hans Berliner and Carl Ebeling	Carnegie Mellon University	1985–1988	Sun minicomputer (high-speed, special-purpose parallel hardware)	550 KB	10	4-9	2530	Before the start of a search for the best move, the oracle analyzes a chess position and decides what information the search must uncover. Then each one of the searcher's 64 integrated-circuit chips is loaded with its assignment. Each chip, working in parallel, comes up with its own idea for the best move and passes a numeric score back to the oracle, which acts as an arbitrator. It incorporates more complete and sophisticated chess knowledge about chess than any other program built to that date.
5	Belle	Ken Thompson and Joe Condon	Bell Telephone Laboratories	1978–1986	Consisted largely of electronic hardware able to perform, at great speed, tasks that are conventionally performed by software.	90 KB, 128 KB trans. table	180	8-9	2250	Used brute force searchers with no selectivity in their full-width search tree, except for some extensions, consisting mostly of check extensions and recaptures.
6	Deep Thought	Feng-Hsiung Hsu and Thomas Ananthara-man	Carnegie Mellon University	1988	SUN 4 workstation/Deep Thought's chess engine contained 250 chips and two processors on a single circuit board		720	10-11	2551	Incorporated new searching algorithm known as "singular extension," which allows the machine to probe deeper along promising tracks rather than stay with a general search. By replaying completed games backward, the machine uses hindsight to learn from its mistakes.

(Continued)

No.	Name	Authors	Affiliations	Dates	Programming Language/Computer Specs	Size of Program	Speed, ×1000 positions p/sec	Depth of Search (ply)	Rating	Techniques
7	Deep Blue	Feng-Hsiung Hsu, Murray Campbell, and Chung-Jen Tan	IBM	1996–1997	Massively parallel, 32-node RS/6000 SP computer system/the Power Two Super Chip processors (P2SC). Each of its 32 nodes employs a single microchannel card containing 8 dedicated Very Large Scale Integrated (VLSI) chess processors (256 processors in total). C Program Language/AIX UNIX operating system.		7000	15	2852	Deep Blue did not use any artificial intelligence. There is no formula for chess intuition. Deep Blue relied on computational power and a search and evaluation function. Make a "shallow" search first—say 10 moves deep—to get a rough indication of which moves are promising and then redo the search at greater depth for those moves first. Once the program has identified a "good" move, it can cut short the consideration of an alternative move as soon as that alternative turns out to lead to a worse position.
8	Fritz	Frans Morsch, and Mathias Feist	ChessBase	1990s–today	Ran on four Intel Pentium 4 Xeon CPUs at 2.8 GHz	—	500	Up to 14	>2600	Uses a selective search technique known as the null-move search. As part of its search, Fritz allows one side to move twice (the other side does a null move). This allows the program to detect weak moves before they are searched to their full depth.
9	Hydra	Dr. Christian Donninger and GM Christopher Lutz	PAL Group	2004-to-day	Runs on a 64 node Xeon cluster	64 GB of RAM	200,000	up to 18	>2850	Hydra's search uses alpha-beta pruning as well as null-move heuristics. Uses type B forward pruning technique that can miss some possibilities but generally plays better due to the greater search depth permitted

short amounts of time, weaker players performed on a par with stronger players. In harder positions, presented over longer amounts of time, the stronger players distinguished themselves.

Work with Hans Berliner [40] initiated the attempt to compile and classify all the important concepts in correct chess play that could be identified. If we could classify the problem of choosing a correct move in a position into an appropriate category, then problem solving in chess could be well classified, and no doubt, performance and understanding would improve. This work was later expanded into the book, "Test, Evaluate, and Improve Your Chess: A Knowledge-Based Approach," [41] with the second edition providing seven tests on all parts of the game at all levels. [42]

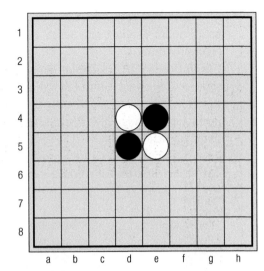

Figure 16.21
The starting position in Othello.

16.4 OTHER GAMES

We have detailed the history, research, and progress in two of the best-known, advanced computer games, chess and checkers. Now we will summarize progress in some of the other well-known games such as Othello (Reversi), Backgammon, Bridge, Poker, and Go.

16.4.1 Othello

The goal of the game of Othello is to have as many disks as possible of your color at the end of play when the 64 squares of the eight-by-eight square board have been covered. With each move, you flip your opponent's disks to your color disk by "surrounding" or capturing them. Play starts with four disks in the middle of the board, two white and two black. See Figure 16.21.

The corners and certain other squares around the disks in the four corners are considered most important. The struggle to control the four corners and the squares around them is critical to success in Othello. Here is a block of code illustrating the importance of the X square (b2) in Othello:

```
If a1 = own THEN RETURN 100 END;
If a1 = opp THEN RETURN 2 END;
IF (g1 = opp) OR (a7 = opp) THEN RETURN - 100
             END.
RETURN - 200.
```

This code was developed by Kierulf in 1983. [43] See Figure 16.22.

Othello is a game of strategy; brute-force play of just trying to capture disks with every move will inevitably fail.

	a	b	c	d	e	f	g	h
1	*	C					C	*
2	C	X					X	C
3								
4								
5								
6								
7	C	X					X	C
8	*	C					C	*

Figure 16.22
The importance of the four corners and the squares immediately around them.

For many years, there has been the general belief that the best Othello programs will beat the best human players, and when this finally did happen in 1997, the top program Logistello was promptly retired.

In the 1990s, Logistello won 18 of the 25 tournaments it participated in, finished second six times and finished fourth once. The program combined deep search with a sophisticated evaluation function that was automatically tuned, coupled with an extensive database of opening moves and a perfect endgame player. [2] Schaeffer suggests that Othello is a candidate for the next advanced computer game to be solved: "The disk-flipping game of Othello is the next popular game that is likely to be solved, but it will require considerably more resources than were required to solve checkers." [8,44] Table 16.3 lists the milestones in computer Othello.

Table 16.3
Milestones in Computer Othello.

Year	Program or Event	Description
1971	Othello	Othello as we now know it was created when Goro Hasegawa modified the rules of Reversi, a game from the late 1880s.
1980	The Moor	The Othello program, The Moor (written by Mike Reeve and David Levy) won one game in a six-game match against world champion Hiroshi Inoue.
Early 1980s	Iago	Paul Rosenbloom developed the Othello program Iago. When Iago played The Moor, Iago was better at capturing pieces permanently and limiting its opponent's mobility.
Late 1980s	Bill	Kai-Fu Lee and Sanjoy Mahajan created the Othello program Bill, which was similar to Iago but incorporated Bayesian learning. Bill reliably beat Iago.
1992	Logistello introduced	Michael Buro began work on the Othello program Logistello. Logistello's search techniques, evaluation function, and knowledge base of patterns were better than those in earlier programs. Logistello perfected its game by playing over 100,000 games against itself.
1997	Logistello perfected	Logistello won every game in a six-game match against world champion Takeshi Murakami. Though there had not been much doubt that Othello programs were stronger than humans, it had been 17 years since the last match between a computer and a reigning world champion. After the 1997 match, there was no longer any doubt. Logistello was significantly better than any human player.
1998	Hannibal, Zebra	Michael Buro retired Logistello. Research interest in Othello waned somewhat, but some programs, including Hannibal (by Martin Piotte and Louis Geoffrey) and Zebra (by Gunnar Andersson), continued to be developed.

16.4.2 Backgammon

Backgammon, a game that has been played for over 5,000 years, has been called the "ultimate race game"[45] and could be viewed as a sophisticated version of the popular children's game Parcheesi, where the goal of a play is for up to four players to travel around a game board as quickly as possible dictated by a counter.

Backgammon also includes a defensive component whereby players try to create *points* that block an opponent's progress. Backgammon combines elements of chance (the dice) with elements of strategy, calculation, probability, risk and analysis, experience, intuition, and knowledge. It is definitely a game of skill, although in an individual game or short series of games, a novice

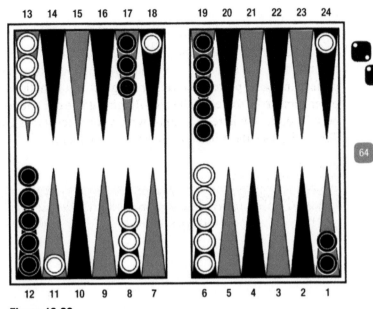

Figure 16.23
The position after White's first moves on the dice roll 6-2.

could win against a top player. Figure 16.23 shows an opening move by White on a dice roll of 6-2. The move played is 24-18 and 13-11. Clearly, moves in Backgammon are based on chances of creating safe structures (points), moving into positions to bear off, and the probability (and capability) of needing to cope with an opponent's hit.

Gerald Tesauro's accomplishments with TD-GAMMON 3.0 through close to 1,500,000 self-play games, whereby it would train itself using a neural net to attain the most effective evaluation function, are considered a major contribution to AI.[2] To achieve this, after each game was played, a technique called **temporal difference learning** (TD learning) was employed by the neural network to determine which terms had played the most important role in the program's success. TD learning is a combination of Monte Carlo ideas and dynamic programming (recall dynamic programming was explained in Chapter 3, Section 3.6.3) ideas. Like Monte Carlo methods, TD methods can learn directly from raw experience without a model of the environment's dynamics. Like dynamic programming, TD methods update estimates based in part on other learned estimates, without waiting for a final outcome (they bootstrap). Table 16.4 lists the milestones in computer backgammon.

16.4.3 Bridge

Bridge is a trick-taking card game of skill and chance. Tricks are units of play during which each player selects one card from his or her hand. Play includes four players who form two partnerships. The players (usually called South, West, North, and East) sit opposite each other at a table with South and North forming one partnership and East and West forming the other. The game consists of the auction (often called bidding) and play, after which the hand is scored.

See Appendix D.3.1 for a full description of the rules and objectives of bridge.

Table 16.4
Milestones in computer backgammon.

Year	Program or Event	Description
1979	BKG 9.8	BKG 9.8, the first strong backgammon player (written by Hans Berliner of Carnegie Mellon University), defeated world champion Luigi Villa in an exhibition match. It is widely accepted that Villa played better and that chance favored the computer with better dice rolls.
1989	Neurogammon	Gerald Tesauro's neural network-based Neurogammon, which was trained with a database of games played by expert human players, won the backgammon championship at the 1989 International Computer Olympiad. All top backgammon programs since Neurogammon have been based on neural networks. Search-based algorithms are not currently feasible for backgammon because the game has a branching factor of several hundred.
1991	Debut of TD-Gammon	Gerald Tesauro's TD-Gammon debuted. Instead of being trained with a database of moves, TD-Gammon was trained by playing itself. This approach was challenging because individual moves are not rewarded—the reward is delayed until the end of the game, and credit for winning must then be distributed among the various moves. Tesauro used temporal difference learning, pioneered by Richard Sutton, to get around this obstacle.
1992	TD-Gammon improvements	TD-Gammon was playing at a level nearly equal to that of the best human players. Furthermore, it influenced the play of human backgammon experts.
1992–present	JellyFish, mloner, and Snowie	Many programs inspired by TD-Gammon have emerged, such as Fredrik Dahl's JellyFish, Harald Wittman's mloner, and Olivier Egger's Snowie. Some programs have been developed that are not based on the temporal difference learning method, but they have not proven themselves superior.

The bidding ends with a contract, which is a declaration by one partnership that their side will take at least a stated number of tricks, with a specified suit as trump or without trumps. The rules of play are similar to other trick-taking games, with the addition of the feature that one player's hand is displayed face up on the table as the "dummy."

A session of bridge consists of several deals (also called hands or boards). As a hand is dealt, the bidding (or auction) proceeds to a conclusion, and then the hand is played. Finally, the hand's result is scored. The goal of a single deal is to achieve the highest score with given cards. The score is affected by two principal factors: the number of tricks bid in the auction and the number of tricks taken (won) during play. If the side that wins the auction (declaring side) then takes the contracted number of tricks (or more), it is said to have made the contract and is awarded a score; otherwise, the contract is said to be "defeated" or "set" and points are awarded to the opponents (defenders). Table 16.5 lists the milestones in computer bridge.

Table 16.5
Milestones in computer bridge.

Year	Program or Event	Description
1958	N/A	Tom Throop, an avid chess and bridge player, wrote a bridge program on a UNIVAC computer. It could only play one round before it ran out of memory.
1980s	Bridge Baron	Computer bridge attracted more attention from more researchers, but Tom Throop stayed at the fore. In 1982, he finished the first version of Bridge Baron, a program that continues to be developed today.

Year	Program or Event	Description
1990	£1 million prize offered	Zia Mahmood offered a £1,000,000 prize to any bridge program that could beat him.
1997	Bridge Baron	Bridge Baron won the first World Computer Bridge Championship.
1998	GIB	The program GIB, written by Matthew Ginsberg from the University of Oregon, became the strongest bridge program. In 1998, GIB not only won the Computer Bridge World Championship, it was also the only computer player invited to play in the Par Contest at the World Bridge Championships. Out of 35 competitors, GIB finished 12th.
1998	GIB	GIB played Zia Mahmood and Michael Rosenberg in an exhibition match. GIB lost but did well enough to make Zia Mahmood nervous, and he withdrew his £1,000,000 challenge.
2000s	Jack, WBridge5	Jack, written by Hans Kuijf from the Netherlands, dominated the computer bridge world. Jack won the Computer Bridge World Championship in 2001, 2002, 2003, 2004, and 2006. In 2005, the winner was WBridge5, a program by Yves Costel from France.

16.4.4 Poker

Poker is a card game that has gained popularity around the world in casinos, online, and in many social venues. Its popularity as a game that combines skill and luck has led to great interest, including many new books and programs attempting to capture the essence of poker. Because chess programs automate a game of perfect information, any attempt to add elements of psychology exploiting human strengths and weaknesses is scorned; for poker, in contrast, any successful program must emulate the human elements of play, including bluffing.

In successful poker play, you must hide from and deceive opponents about the cards you are holding and then finally present your cards at a most opportune moment. Jonathan Schaeffer, the world's leader in programming computer games, summarizes poker in context of other computer games:

> Two-player perfect information games are poor models of real-world complexity. The world is not two-player, not turn-based, and not perfect information! Hence members of this class of games are limited in what they teach us about artificial intelligence. In contrast, games like poker (for example), with its imperfect information, better reflect the complexities of reasoning of the real world and, hence, are more likely to be used to make substantive contributions to our understanding of artificial intelligence.[46]

Table 16.6 lists the milestones in computer poker.

Table 16.6
Milestones in computer poker.

Year	Program or Event	Description
1970s	First five-card draw poker program	Nicolas Findler wrote a poker program that played five-card draw. His program was not especially strong, but his aim was to model the thought processes of human players, not to make the best possible player.
1984	Orac	Professional poker player Mike Caro wrote the program Orac on an Apple II computer. Orac played Texas Hold'em, a popular and computationally interesting type of poker. Unfortunately, Caro kept the program secret, so it's not known how strong or weak the program was.
1990s	Turbo Texas Hold'em	A commercial poker program called Turbo Texas Hold'em was developed. A rule-based program, it has sold more copies than any other commercial poker program, and it is still sold today.

(Continued)

Year	Program or Event	Description
1997	Loki	University of Alberta researchers, led by Jonathan Schaeffer, wrote Loki, a Texas Hold'em program.
1999	Poki	The University of Alberta team rewrote Loki and called the new program Poki. Poki plays ring game Texas Hold'em, which has up to 10 players.
2001	PsOpti	The growing University of Alberta team wrote PsOpti (which stands for "pseudooptimal"), which used game theory. PsOpti plays heads-up (two-player) Texas Hold'em.
2000s	Online gambling Web sites	Online gambling sites proliferated. Because these sites involve real money, poker programs, or "pokerbots," are not allowed to play.
2000s	Vexbot	The University of Alberta team continued to develop new technology. Their research included the creation of Vexbot, a learning-based program that adapts according to models it makes of its opponents.
2005	PokerProBot	The first World Poker Robot Championship was held. The winner of the amateur competition (which did not include programs from the University of Alberta), PokerProBot, won $100,000.
2006	Hyperborean	Later in July, the American Association for Artificial Intelligence (AAAI) hosted the first AAAI Computer Poker Competition, which was organized and won (ahead of three other programs) by Hyperborean of the Poker Research Group at the University of Alberta.
2007	2007 poker competition	The 2007 poker competition consisted of 15 competitors from 7 countries and 43 bots. Matches were played on 32 machines running for a month, playing over 17 million hands of poker. The results were announced at AAAI 2007 on July 24, 2007 in Vancouver BC: • Limit Series (Equilibrium) and Limit Bankroll (Online)—33 bots from 13 competitors, 13.7 million hands played • No Limit—10 bots from 8 competitors, 3.4 million hands played

16.5 GO: THE NEW DROSOPHILA OF AI?

The ancient Japanese game of Go is played on a 19 × 19 square board (and consequently has a branching factor of about 360!) with black on white "stones" placed one at a time on squares on the board. The game defies approachability via the standard search, knowledge, and pruning techniques that have been applied to the traditional two-person, zero-sum games to date. Schaeffer [2,7] states,

> i.e., because of the 19 × 19 board and the resulting large branching factor, alpha-beta search alone has no hope of producing strong play. Instead, the programs perform small, local searches that use extensive application-dependent knowledge. David Fotland, the author of the Many Faces of Go program, identifies over 50 major components needed by a strong Go-playing program. The components are substantially different from each other, few are easy to implement, and all are critical to achieving strong play. In effect, you have a linked chain, where the weakest link determines the overall strength.

In addition, Martin Mueller (author of the program Explorer) feels that there isn't enough information generally available about Go for a computer game to significantly challenge human players.[47] Hence, he feels it will be many decades before serious progress can be made. For these reasons, Go could easily be the drosophila of AI for the future. Table 16.7 lists the milestones in computer Go.

Table 16.7
Milestones in computer Go.

Year	Program or Event	Description
1970	Go	Al Zobrist wrote the first computer Go program as part of his dissertation.
1972	Interim.2	Walter Reitman and Bruce Wilcox began years of research on Go programs. They wrote the program Interim.2 and published several influential articles on computer Go.
1981	Many Faces of Go	David Fotland began writing the program that is now known as the Many Faces of Go.
1983	Go++	Michael Reiss began writing the program that is now known as Go++. Despite its name, Go++ is written in C, not C++.
1984	Computer Go tournaments	Computer Go tournaments began to be held. Recurring tournaments included the Ing Cup, which was held from 1985 to 2000, and the FOST Cup (sponsored by the Japanese Foundation for the Fusion of Science and Technology), which was held from 1995 to 1999.
1990s	Handtalk	Chen Zhixing, a retired professor of chemistry, wrote the Go program Handtalk, which went on to win the Ing Cup and FOST Cup in 1995, 1996, and 1997. In the late 1990s, when Handtalk was being reworked, Go4++ (now called Go++) and the Many Faces of Go rose to prominence.
2000	Goemate	Goemate, the successor to Handtalk, won the Go competition in the fifth Computer Olympiad.
2000	Ing Prize	The Ing Prize expired without having been won. Offered by Acer Incorporated and the Ing Chang-Ki Wei-Chi Educational Foundation, the Ing Prize would have awarded about $1,500,000 to the developers of a Go program that could beat a junior champion.
2000s	Go Intellect, GNU Go	Computer Go programs proliferated. Among the strongest programs now are Go Intellect (written by Ken Chen, University of North Carolina at Charlotte) and the open-source program GNU Go.

16.5.1 The Stars of Advanced Computer Games

HUMAN INTEREST NOTES

MONTY NEWBORN

Monty Newborn.

Monty Newborn (1937–) is one of the pioneers of computer chess, having developed one of the early multiprocessor programs, OSTRICH, and organized the North American and World Computer Chess Championships for 25 years starting in 1970. He also is one of the cofounders of the International Computer Chess Association (ICCA) in 1977. He was Chair of the School of Computer Science at McGill University from 1976–1983, Chief Organizer of the Kasparov vs. Deep Blue Match in 1996, and author of a number of books on computer chess and theorem proving. In his retirement, he builds beautiful stained glass lamps and is one of Quebec's top senior tennis players.

HUMAN INTEREST NOTES

DAVID LEVY AND
JAAP VAN DEN HERIK

David Levy and Jaap van den Herik.

David Levy (1945–) is one of the most productive people in the field of computer chess and computer games in general, an international chess master, a scholar who has published over 30 books, and an internationally recognized AI leader. Levy instigated research in computer chess with his famous 1968 bet with three computer science professors that no program could beat him in a chess match. He won several matches where D. K. was his second, but in 1989, Deep Thought defeated him 4-0. Like D. K., Levy was also a disciple and friend of Donald Michie's.

More recently, he has published the well-received Robots Unlimited (2005) and Love and Sex with Robots (2007).

Jaap van den Herik (1947–) is Professor of Computer Science at Maastricht University, and in 2008, he became a leader of the Tilberg Centre for Creative Computing. Professor van den Herik has energetically led and edited the ICCA Journal, which morphed into the International Computer Games Association (ICGA) Journal.

He has numerous scientific publications in these areas and beyond and has held a Chair in Law and Computing at Leiden University since 1988.

Kenneth Lane Thompson (1943–) is one of the most distinguished American pioneers of computer science. His most noted accomplishments include the development of the B programming language which he used to write the UNIX operating system with the late Dennis Ritchie in 1969, leading to the development of the C language. In computer chess he is noted for developing the program BELLE with special-purpose hardware at Bell Labs where he worked for many years. In 1980 it was the World Champion computer chess program and then in 1982 the first master-rated computer chess program. Thompson is also noted for developing endgame databases for chess which have contributed greatly to the sphere of chess knowledge.

Thompson has received a number of awards for his pioneering work with Ritchie on the UNIX operating system including The IEEE Richard W. Hamming Medal (1990), Fellow of the Computer History Museum (1997), National Medal of Technology from President Bill Clinton (1999) and the Japan Prize (2011). In 1999 Thompson also received the first Tsutomi Kanai Award.

Recently he joined Google where he works as a distinguished engineer and has developed the language "Go." He is a man who believes in enjoying and employing power, whether it be in fast cars, flying planes, or programming computers.

16.6 CHAPTER SUMMARY

This chapter has emphasized the history and significance of the advanced games to AI. These include checkers, chess, backgammon, Othello, bridge, poker, and Go. The games of perfect information (no chance, no luck) are checkers, chess, Othello, and Go. Elements of chance, such as dice and cards, affect the outcomes in backgammon and in card games, such as bridge and poker. Nonetheless, in the long run, skill is the predominating factor in any longer series of games or matches with all of these games.

Recently, the game of checkers (with an estimated 10^{20} number of possible positions) was weakly solved.[8] This means that the outcome for the first player to move has been determined (with best play) to be at least a draw. In contrast, chess, called the "drosophila of AI" by Alexander Kronrad, with an estimated 10^{42} reasonable possible positions (or games), is far from solved. More books are written about chess than about all games put together. Although all chess endgames of up to six pieces have been solved,[31,32] we still do not know the best first move for White in chess, Black's best reply, or what the game theoretic-minimax-optimal value of chess is (win for White, draw, or win for Black) with best play by both sides. The next game likely to be solved is Othello, which is a step up from checkers. Significant progress has been made in developing strong programs using AI techniques for other games such as Othello, checkers, backgammon, Scrabble, and poker. The next drosophila of AI is likely to be the ancient game of Go.

AI techniques were very effectively studied in the early works of Arthur Samuel,[1,3] who developed programs for the game of checkers. Heuristics were tested and evaluated through the use of parameter adjustment and signature tables. Having the program play many matches against versions of itself and adjusting parameters according to outcomes of these matches was one important way (parameter adjustment) that Samuel improved his program. The program Chinook was developed at the University of Alberta, in Edmonton, Canada, by Schaeffer et al. starting in 1989. By the late

1990s, Chinook had already played on par with the World Checkers Champion, Marion Tinsley, in two matches (in 1992 and 1994) and was clearly superior to even the best human players. Therefore, in 1997, undefeated since 1994, Chinook was retired. Schaeffer et al. [8] reported that the game of checkers has been weakly solved. This research effort spanned over 18 years by Schaeffer's team, combining a number of AI approaches, including deep and clever search techniques, subtle algorithmic proofs, heuristics derived from human experts, and advanced database techniques.

The game of chess has been played by people following essentially the same rules for several thousand years since its origins in India. Mankind has been somewhat infatuated by the possibility of building a machine to play strong chess for several centuries. Interest started with the Turk in the 1700s [13] and later the work of Torre ye Quevedo (1890), who built a mechanical machine to play the endgame King and Rook vs. King. Turing [48] and Shannon [16] independently developed the first paradigms for building a chess program that are still essentially in effect today. The first chess programs started to appear in the 1960s. In the 1970s, competition against people who played at the club-level and above and against other computer chess programs started to become common. The minimax alpha-beta algorithm began to be developed with deeper and deeper searches, opening libraries, transposition tables, heuristics for pawn structure, and king safety. In the 1980s, the first master-level chess programs were developed, starting with Belle, of Bell Labs, by Ken Thompson [21] and Cray Blitz by Robert Hyatt, Albert Gower, and Herbert Nelson in 1985. [49] By 1988, Berliner and Eberling [20] had developed the first senior master-rated program. Not long after, Hsu et al. [29] developed a powerful program using special-purpose hardware and parallel architectures combined with AI techniques. The program was named Deep Thought and became the first program capable of competing with and beating grandmasters on a regular basis. In 1989, Deep Thought lost a two-game match played in New York City against World Chess Champion (since 1985) Garry Kasparov.

In the 1990s, IBM hired several members of the Deep Thought team to develop Deep Blue. Deep Blue continued to incorporate the most powerful computers, AI techniques, parallel search, and refinements to the alpha-beta algorithm. The evaluation function was tuned to the choices of human grandmasters over thousands of games (akin to the original work of Samuel on checkers). In 1996, Kasparov played a six-game match in Philadelphia with Deep Blue that he won 4-2 (3 wins, 2 draws, and 1 loss), although the Deep Blue team unadvisedly rejected a draw in game 5, when the match could have been tied. In 1997, Kasparov played another match with Deep Blue's successor program, Deeper Blue, and the improved program scored a sensational upset winning the match by winning the last game to score 3.5-2.5 (two wins, three draws, and one loss) against Kasparov. In the intervening 10 years, many matches have pitted Kasparov, his successor, Kramnik, and other top humans against the best programs.

The results have indicated that the best programs today (e.g., Deep Junior, Deep Fritz, Hydra, Rybka, and others) are clearly competitive with the best human players. More attention needs to be given to organizing matches between top machines and top human players who are not handicapped by typical human frailties, such as tiredness (for whatever reason), time pressure, and in general any conditions that help to induce blunders by humans. Matches need to reflect people playing their best chess against machines playing their best. Anything else is just an exhibition match and is relatively meaningless.

Computer chess programs and the artificial techniques used to develop them have affected how chess is played in a number of ways. First, material is the most important factor affecting the outcome of a game. Chess players must therefore be tactically alert and avoid material losses. People can learn and prepare for opponents by looking at large databases that hold even the most recent games played by their opponents (not only grandmasters) around the world. Programs are capable of deep searches, which in many games and positions have resulted in improved defenses (holding material) so that the side being attacked has survived and consequently been able to win. In serious international play, there are no more adjournments to prevent computers from being used for analysis. Certain endgames (such as KRB vs. KR or KBB vs. KN) have been solved with the construction of databases (for all endings including up to seven pieces) and have been determined to require more than 50 moves to win in certain positions.

Once you learn the rules of Othello (previously known as Reversi), you might wrongly think that it is an easy game. The rules are easy to learn but not as easy to master. A good Othello program in 1980 (developed by Mike Reeve and David Levy) won a six-game match against then World Champion Hiroshi Inoui. Throughout the 1980s, the program Iago, developed by Paul Rosenbloom, was known to be the best Othello program. In the late 1980s, the program Bill, developed by Kai-Fu Lee and Sanjoy Mahajan, incorporating Bayesian learning, defeated Iago. In 1992, Michael Buro began working on his program Logistello, which incorporated search techniques, an evaluation function, and a knowledge base of patterns. By playing over 100,000 games against itself, Logistello was perfected and won a six-game match against World Champion Takeshi Murakami. [50] The best Othello programs can defeat the best humans, though there has been little progress in Othello programming since Michael Buro retired Logistello in 1998.

Backgammon is another game that is easy to learn but not easy to master. It includes great elements of probability, chance, logic, and knowledge. The first strong backgammon program, called BKG 9.8, was developed by Hans Berliner of Carnegie Mellon University in 1979. [51] Between 1989 and 1992, Gerald Tesauro developed the neural network-based program Neurogammon, which learns from a large database of games. Backgammon's branching factor of several hundred means it is better suited for neural approaches than traditional search-based methods. Tesauro later developed TD-Gammon, which employed temporal difference learning to help judge which moves in a series of games against itself were most responsible for success. [52] TD-Gammon was proven to be on a par with the best human players and even influenced their play.

Tom Throop, an avid chess and bridge player, wrote his first bridge program in 1958. In 1982, he introduced the program Bridge Baron. In 1997, Bridge Baron won the first World Computer Bridge Championship, and it continues to be developed to this day. [53] Since 1992, a number of other strong bridge programs have been developed. In recent years, programs have become strong enough that Zia Mahmood withdrew the 100,000 pound prize he offered in 1990 to the first program to defeat him.

Poker is a card game that involves considerable skill in gambling (hence chance and probability) and has attracted considerable worldwide interest in recent years. Programs have been developed since the 1970s, and in 1984, Mike Caro, a professional poker player, wrote Orac for an Apple II computer to play the popular form of poker known as Texas Hold'em. In the 1990s, commercial programs started to be written for poker, and in 1997, research on development of programs for the game started at the University of Alberta, in Edmonton, Canada, headed by Jonathan Schaeffer.[7354] During the present decade, they have developed Vexbot, a learning-based program that tries to model its opponents' behaviors. In 2005, the first World Poker Robot Championship was won by PokerProbot, another program from the Schaeffer team, capturing a $100,000 prize.

The new drosophila of AI is likely to be the oriental game of Go. Serious chess games at the international level between humans are known to last about 5 hours. For Go, the top-level games are known to last about 10 hours! Efforts to tackle Go by traditional AI techniques have failed badly. Go is played on a 19×19 board and has a branching factor of 360 [55]. David Fotland, author of the program, the Many Faces of Go, has identified some 50 major unique components, which he believes would be critical to achieving strong play in Go.

Parts of this chapter were presented at Artificial Intelligence @ 50, July 13–15, 2006 at Dartmouth College to commemorate the 50th anniversary of the original conference at Dartmouth College (organized by Professor James Moor) and will appeared in the Proceedings of the Conference.

We would also like to thank Jill Cirasella, Professor of Information Science, formerly at The Brooklyn College Library, for her collaboration on an earlier version of a brief history of computer games, presented at Artificial Intelligence @50 at Dartmouth College, in July, 2006 (Appendix D.3.3). We also acknowledge assistance from Hal Terrie for material compiled in this Chapter and Appendix D.3.2.

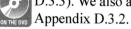

We would also like to thank Edgar Troudt and David Kopec, for help with proofreading.

Questions for Discussion

1. Why are advanced computer games a valid area of research for AI?

2. Briefly explain the history, research, and state of the art in computer checkers.

3. Who were/are the main players in computer checkers research?

4. Why has chess been considered the drosophila of AI for a long time? What is the likely next drosophila for AI?

5. What are some of the techniques that are used in chess programming? For example, depth-first search with iterative deepening, heuristics, killer heuristic, transposition tables, etc.

6. What is the estimated size of state space in chess? In checkers?

7. How strong are the best chess programs? Can you name five of them?

8. What are the accomplishments in computer checkers, Othello, bridge, backgammon, poker, and Go?

9. What is temporal difference learning and where was it used?

10. After checkers, what can be the most likely advanced computer game to be solved?

Exercises

1. Explain why advanced games such as checkers, chess, and backgammon are excellent test subjects for heuristics and AI.

2. Give five reasons that Samuel considered checkers an excellent experimental domain for AI study.

3. What were some of the AI techniques that Arthur Samuel used in his checker program that apply to other domains?

4. Describe how the game of checkers was solved.

5. What is the difference between a game being weakly solved and a game being strongly solved?

6. Connect-Four is a game that might be viewed as an extension or more sophisticated version of tic-tac-toe. That is, the objective is to get four disks of one color in a straight line (row,

column, or diagonal) as disks are added to a grid of seven columns and six rows. The game was solved independently by James D. Allen and Victor Allis in 1988.[56]

    a. If you were to try to develop a program to play this game, how would you do it?

    b. How would you go about solving the game? What AI methods might you use to reduce the amount of searching that would be necessary? What problem constraints and symmetries could be exploited to reduce the problem size?

7. From what you have read and can estimate, describe and compare the size of the state space in tic-tac-toe, Connect-Four, checkers, and chess.

8. Often, the best way to learn about a game and its hidden secrets is to analyze by playing both sides. Study the checker endgame two pieces against one. Are there positions where this is a draw or can a win be forced by the stronger side from any starting position?

9. Why has chess been called the "drosophila of AI"?

10. Place a White king on the square c3 on a chessboard. Place a White pawn on the square d3. Place Black king on the square b5. Build a search tree with a 3-ply minimax alpha-beta analysis using the rule "If the White king can get two ranks ahead of the White pawn, White wins to help prune the tree."

11. Describe the difference between the Shannon type A and Shannon type B approach to chess programming.

12. Why have the best computer chess programs appeared superior to the best human chess players and how should future matches be organized?

13. Describe the following methods used in computer chess programming:

    a. transposition tables

    b. quiescence search

    c. iterative deepening

    d. null move heuristic

    e. killer heuristic

    f. singular extensions

    g. endgame databases

14. The chess endgame King, Rook, and Bishop vs. King and Rook (KRBKR) has been called the "headache ending." KRBKR was determined to require 59 moves to win in the longest winning position. The rules of chess normally allow only 50 moves to win where there are no pawn moves or captures and therefore had to be changed for such cases.

    a. Although special databases contain all seven-piece chess endings, explain why it might be a challenge to develop a program that plays this endgame correctly for either side. That is, in won positions, it wins for the strong side, and in drawn positions, it holds the draw.

    b. What AI methods might be used to develop such a program?

15. Despite very powerful programs that play chess today and more books on chess than on all games put together, we still do not know the game-theoretic-minimax-optimal value of chess or even the best first move. Explain why chess is somewhat intractable to being solved (even weakly) in the manner that checkers was solved.

16. Why has Go been coined the "drosophila of AI" for the future? Explain.

17. To program a computer to play a board game, you need a way to represent the board. The board in the game of checkers was represented as an array that embeds which pieces are on which squares, whose turn it is to move, etc. [57] Develop an array that represents the board for the initial position in the game of chess.

18. Short Research Project: Obtain one of the following papers and write a summary of it in two double-spaced pages:

   - Turing's paper (1950)

   - Shannon's paper (1950)

   - Samuel's paper (1959)

   - "Computer Backgammon," Berliner (1980)

   - Lee and Mahajan's paper (1990)

   - Tesauro's paper (2002)

   - "Checkers is Solved," Schaeffer (2007)

19. **Research Project:** Write a five-page summary of one of the following longer papers or books listed in **Section 16.9 References** or the **Endnotes, Section 16.10** below:

   - "The magical seven, plus or minus two," G. A. Miller (1956)

   - *A Program to Play Chess Endgames*, B. Huberman (1968)

   - *Chess, Computers, and Long Range Planning*, M. M. Botvinnik (1970)

   - *Human Problem Solving*, Newell and H. A. Simon (1972)

   - *Perception in Chess*, W. Chase and H. A. Simon (1973)

   - "An analysis of alpha-beta pruning," D. E. Knuth and R. Moore (1975)

   - *Chess Skill in Man and Machine*, P. Frey (1977)

   - "A World Championship-Level Othello Program," P. Rosenbloom (1982)

   - "A comparison of human and computer performance in chess," D. Kopec and I. Bratko (1982)

   - *Computers, Chess, and Cognition*, T. Marsland and J. Schaeffer (eds.) (1990)

   - *Kasparov versus Deep Blue: Computer Chess Comes of Age*, M. Newborn (1997)

   - *One Jump Ahead: Challenging Human Supremacy in Checkers*, J. Schaeffer (1997)

- "Computer Go: An AI Oriented Survey," B. Bouzy and C. Tristan (2001)

- "The Challenger of Poker," D. Billings, A. Davidson, J. Schaeffer, and D. Szafron (2002)

- "Programming Backgammon Using Self-Teaching Neural Nets," G. Tesauro (2002)

20. Describe five areas of AI where development of computer game-playing programs has made significant contributions. Name the game, the year, the authors, describe the methods used and the contributions made.

Keywords

aging	opening libraries	Shannon type A
dominant scoring term	parallel search algorithms	Shannon type B
endgame databases	ply	signature tables
evaluation function	progressive deepening	singular extension
forgetting	pseudo-legal move list	special-purpose hardware
iterative deepening	quiescence search	temporal difference learning
killer heuristic	refreshing	transposition table
middle game combination	refutation	weakly solved
null move heuristic	retrograde analysis	windows

References

1. Samuel, A. 1959. Some studies in machine learning using the game of checkers. *IBM Journal of Research and Development* 3: 210–229.

2. Schaeffer, J. 2001. A gamut of games. *AI Magazine*, v22, 3: 29–46.

3. Samuel, A. 1967. Some studies in machine learning using the game of checkers: Recent progress. *IBM Journal of Research and Development* 11: 601–617.

4. Schaeffer, J. 1985. The relative importance of knowledge. *ICCA Journal* 7 (3): 138–145.

5. Truscott, T. 1979. The Duke Checker Program. *Journal of Recreational Mathematics* 12 (4): 241–247.

6. Schaeffer, J. 1997. *One Jump Ahead: Challenging Human Supremacy in Checkers*. New York: Springer-Verlag.

7. Schaeffer, J. E. and van den Herik, J. (eds.). 2002. *Chips Challenging Champions*. Amsterdam: Elsevier.

8. Schaeffer, J., Burch, N., Björnsson, Y., Kashimoto, A., Müller, M., Lake, R., Lu, P., and Sutphen, S. 2007. Checkers is solved. *Scienceexpress/www.sciencepress.org*/19 July pages 1-5/ 101126/ science.144079 www.sciencemag.org/cgi/content/abstract/1144079v1

9. Schaeffer, J., Björnsson, Y., Burch, N., Kishimoto, A., Müller, M., Lake, R., Lu, P., and Sutphen, S. 2005. Solving checkers. In: *International Joint Conference on Artificial Intelligence,* 292–297. Edinburgh, Scotland: University of Edinburgh.

10. Newell, A., Shaw, J. C., and Simon, H. A. 1958. Chess-playing programs and the problem of complexity. *IBM Journal of Research and Development* 2 (4): 320–335.

11. McCarthy, J. 1997. AI as sport. *Science* 276 (June 6): 1518–1519.

12. Michie, D. 1980. Chess with computers. *Interdisciplinary Scientific Review* 5 (3): 215–227.

13. Standage, T. 2002. *The Turk*. New York: Walker Publishing Company.

14. Levy, D. 1976. *Chess and Computers*. Rockville, MD: Computer Science Press.

15. Turing, A. M. 1953. Digital computers applied to games. In: *Faster than Thought*, edited by B. V. Bowden, 286–310. London: Pitman London.

16. Shannon, C. 1959. Programming a computer for playing chess. *Philosophical Magazine*, ser.7, 41: 256–275.

17. Greenblatt, R. D., Eastlake, III, D. E, and Crocker, S. D. 1976. The Greenblatt chess program. In Fall *Joint Computing Conference Proceedings*, San Francisco, New York, 31, 801–810. ACM.

18. Levy, D. N. L. 1984. *The Chess Computer Handbook*. London: Batsford.

19. Kopec, D. 1990. Advances in man-machine play. In *Computers, Chess and Cognition*, edited by T. A. Marsland and J. Schaeffer, 9–33. New York: Springer-Verlag.

20. Berliner, H. and Ebeling, C. 1989. Pattern knowledge and search: The SUPREME architecture. *Artificial Intelligence* 38: 161–196.

21. Condon, J. and Thompson, K. 1982. Belle chess hardware. In *Advances in Computer Chess* 3, edited by M. R. B. Clarke, 45–54. Oxford, England: Pergamon.

22. Botvinnik, M. M. 1969. *Chess, Computers, and Long Range Planning*. New York: Springer-Verlag.

23. Kopec, D. and Terrie, H. 2003. *Test, Evaluate and Improve Your Chess: A Knowledge-Based Approach*. New Windsor, NY: US Chess Publications.

24. Slater, E. T. O. 1950. Statistics for the chess computer and the factor of mobility. In *Symposium on Information Theory*, London, 150–152. London: Ministry of Supply.

25. Kopec, D., Northam, E., Podber, D., and Fouda, Y. 1989. The role of connectivity in chess. In *Proceedings of the Workshop on Game-Tree Search*, 78–84, 6th World Computer Chess Championship, Edmonton, Alberta, Canada: University of Alberta.

26. Berliner, H. D. 1974. *Chess as Problem Solving: The Development of a Tactics Analyzer*. PhD thesis, Department of Computer Science, Carnegie Mellon University.

27. Kopec, D. 1989. Deep thought outsearches foes, wins World Computer Chess Championship. *Chess Life*, September, 17–24.

28. Kopec, D. 1996. Kasparov vs. Deep Blue: Mankind is safe—for now. *Chess Life*, May, 42–51.

29. Hsu, F. H., Anantharaman, T., Campbell, M., and Nowatzyk, A. 1990. A grandmaster\chess machine. *Scientific American* 263 (4, October): 44–50.

30. Chase, W. G. and Simon, H. A. 1973. Perception in chess. *Cognitive Psychology* 4: 55–81.

31. Thompson, K. 1977. Retrograde analysis of certain endings. *ICCA Journal* 9 (3): 131.

32. Stiller, L. 1991. Group graphs and computational symmetry on massively parallel architecture. The *Journal of Supercomputing* 5 (2–3, October): 99–117.

33. Michie, D. and Bratko, I. 1987. Ideas on knowledge synthesis stemming from the KBBKN Endgame. *ICCA Journal* 10 (3): 3–13.

34. Newborn, M. 1982. Ostrich/P—a parallel search chess program. *Technical Report* 82.3. School of Computer Science, McGill University, Montreal, Canada.

35. Kopec, D., Marsland, T. A., and Cox, J. 2004. SEARCH (in AI). Chapter 63 in *The Computer Science and Engineering Handbook*, 1–26. Boca Raton, FL: CRC Press.

36. Kopec, D. 1983. *Human and machine representations of knowledge*. PhD Thesis, Machine Intelligence Research Unit, Edinburgh: University of Edinburgh.

37. Kopec, D. and Niblett, T. 1980. How hard is the King-Rook-King-Knight ending? In *Advances in Computer Chess 2*, edited by M. R. B. Clarke, 57-80 Edinburgh: Edinburgh University Press.

38. Kopec, D. and Bratko, I. 1982. The Bratko-Kopec experiment: A test for comparison of human and computer performance in chess. In *Advances in Computer Chess 3*, edited by M. R. B. Clarke, 57–82, Oxford, England: Pergamon Press.

39. Kopec, D., Newborn, M., and Yu, W. 1986. Experiments in chess cognition. In Advances in *Computer Chess 4*, edited by D. Beal, 59–79. Oxford, England: Pergamon Press.

40. Berliner, H., Kopec, D., and Northam, E. 1990. A taxonomy of concepts for evaluating chess strength. In *Proceedings of SUPERCOMPUTING* '90, 336–343. New York: ACM.

41. Kopec, D. and Terrie, H. 1997. *Test, Evaluate, and Improve Your Chess: A Knowledge-Based Approach.* San Francisco, CA: Hypermodern Press.

42. Kopec, D. and Terrie, H. 1997. *Test, Evaluate and Improve Your Chess: A Knowledge-Based Approach*, 2nd ed. New Windsor, NY: USCF Publications.

43. Kierulf, A. 1983. Brand—an othello program. In *Computer Game-Playing: Theory and Practice*, edited by M. A. Bramer, 197–208. Chichester, England: Ellis Horwood.

44. van den Herik, J., Uiterwijk, J., and van Rijswijck, J. 2002. Games solved now and in the future. *Artificial Intelligence* 134, 277–311.

45. Burns, B. 2000. The Encyclopedia of Games: *Rules and Strategies for More Than 250 Indoor and Outdoor Games, from Darts to Backgammon.* Abebooks.

46. Billings, D., Davidson, A., Schaeffer, J., and Szafron, D. 2002. The challenger of poker. *Artificial Intelligence* 134 (1–2, January): 201–240. (Also available at: www.cs.ualberta.ca/~darse/Papers/AIJ02.pdf)

47. Müller, M. 2002. Computer Go. *Artificial Intelligence* 134: 145–179.

48. Turing, A. M. 1950. Computing machinery and intelligence. *Mind* 59: 433–460.

49. Hyatt, R. M., Gower, A., and Nelson, H. 1985. Cray Blitz. In *Advances in Computer Chess* 4, edited by Beal, D. Oxford, England: Pergamon Press.

50. Buro, M. 1997. The Othello match of the year: Takeshio Murakami vs. Logistello. *ICCA Journal* 20 (3): 189–193. (Also available at: www.cs.ualberta.ca/~mburo/ps/match-report.pdf)

51. Berliner, H. J. 1979. Backgammon computer program beats world champion. *Artificial Intelligence* V14 (2, September 1980): 205–220.

52. Tesauro, G. 1995. Temporal difference learning and TD-Gammon. *Communications of the ACM* 38 (3): 58–68.

53. Smith, S. J. J., Nau, D., and Throop, T. 1998. Computer bridge: A big win for AI planning. *AI Magazine* 19 (2, Summer 1998): 93–106.

54. Billings, D., et al. 2003. Approximating game-theoretic optimal: strategies for full-scale poker. In *Proceedings of the Eighteenth International Joint Conference on Artificial Intelligence (IJCAI-03)*, Edmonton, Canada. (Also available at: www.cs.ualberta.ca/~darse/Papers/IJCAI03.pdf)

55. Müller, M. with Schaeffer, J. and Björnsson, Y. (eds.). 2003. *Computers and Games, Third International Conference, CG 2002*, Edmonton, Canada, July 25–27, 2002. Revised Papers, volume 2883 of Lecture Notes in Computer Science. New York: Springer.

56. Allis, V. 1994. *Searching for solutions in games and artificial intelligence.* PhD Dissertation, Department of Computer Science, University of Maastricht, The Netherlands.

57. Strachey, C. 1952. Logical or non-mathematical programmes. In *Proceedings of the ACM Conference in Toronto*, 46–49.

Bibliography

Frey, P. (ed.). 1977. *Chess Skill in Man and Machine*. New York: Springer-Verlag.

Ginsberg, M. 1999. GIB: Steps toward an expert-level bridge-playing program. In *International Joint Conference on Artificial Intelligence*, 584–589.

Hsu, F. H. 2002. *Behind Deep Blue*. Princeton: Princeton University Press.

Kopec, D. and Chabris, C. 1994. The Fifth Harvard Cup Human Versus Computer. Intel Chess Challenge. *ICCA Journal* (December 1994).

Kopec, D., Shamkovich, L., and Schwartzman, G. 1997. Kasparov–Deep Blue. *Chess Life*, Special Summer Issue (July): 45–55.

Newborn, M. 1997. *Kasparov versus Deep Blue: Computer Chess Comes of Age*. New York: Springer-Verlag.

Newborn, M. 2002. *Deep Blue: An Artificial Intelligence Milestone*. New York: Springer-Verlag.

Samuel, A. 1960. Programming computers to play games. In *Advances in Computers*, volume 1, edited by F. Alt, 165–192.

Tesauro, G. 2002. Programming backgammon using self-teaching neural nets. *Artificial Intelligence* 134 (1–2): 181–200.

REPRISE

David Ferrucci

This chapter attempts to provide an appropriate perspective on Artificial Intelligence (AI). We review where we have been and what has been achieved. We list AI achievements from the past half century. The recent IBM Watson-Jeopardy Challenge is discussed. We also weigh our prospects for ever achieving human-level AI.

Figure 16.0
Wlodek Zadrozny

▐17.0▌ INTRODUCTION

We review the importance of search, knowledge representation, and learning in the construction of AI systems. An example is given illustrating how an appropriate representation can facilitate a problem's solution.

In Section 2, we present a recurring theme in both mythology and literature: Attempts to create life or intelligence are often met with dire consequences. Perhaps a warning to the AI community is being provided.

The concept of an unsolvable problem in computer science is explained, that is, there are problems for which no algorithmic solutions exist. We ask if the creation of human-level AI is such a problem.

In Section 3, we review some AI achievements from the past half century. And in Section 4, the IBM Watson system is discussed. In March 2011, there was a man-machine challenge in which an IBM computer beat two long-time Jeopardy champions on a widely viewed television match. We conclude by reviewing several theories on the creation of life and explanations for intelligence and consciousness.

▐17.1▌ RECAPITULATION — PART I

We began this journey together in Chapter 1. We said at that time that if you wanted to design intelligent software, it would need to possess:

1. A search facility

2. A knowledge representation language

3. The ability to learn

It became evident early in our endeavors that blind search algorithms—that is, those which possessed no domain knowledge, such as breadth-first search and depth-first search, could not effectively negotiate the large search spaces confronting them.

As stated in this text, a useful guiding principle is that if you wanted to design a system to perform a task, first look to discover if a similar system already exists in nature. Therefore, if it were 1902 and you wished to design a "flying machine," your attention should focus on birds. It is not surprising that the Wright brothers' successful flights in 1903 utilized an airplane with a relatively thin fuselage and two large wings protruding from it (Figure 17.1).

Blind search algorithms do not possess the wherewithal necessary for the large search problems that arise in AI venues. People, however, are expert "problem solving machines." Newell and Simon, cognizant of this insight, studied humans who were asked to "think aloud" as they went about the process of solving problems. This research culminated in the General Problem Solver (GPS) in 1957.[1] GPS, endowed with heuristics distilled from human subjects, was successful in solving the following: The Water Jug Problem (Chapter 1), The Missionaries and Cannibals Problem (Chapter 2), as well as the Bridges of Königsberg Problem (Chapter 6), and many others. The search algorithms in Chapter 3 as well as the game-playing algorithms in Chapters 4 and 16 effectively used heuristics to partially overcome the conundrum of combinatorial explosion.

Figure 17.1
Wright brothers' airplane. This early model presented a two-tiered wing.

One's knowledge representation scheme also has a tangible impact on problem-solving prowess. The Königsberg Bridge Problem is described in Chapter 6. Figure 6.6 illustrates the problem; it is redrawn here as Figure 17.2.

The question is: "Is it possible to traverse each of the seven bridges once and only once and return to one's starting position?"

A graph model of the Bridges of Königsberg is depicted in Figure 6.6 as well; this portion of the figure is redrawn here as Figure 17.3.

Leonhard Euler wrote the first paper in graph theory in 1736. He concluded that the bridges depicted in Figure 17.2 could be traversed as described, if and only if the graph illustrated in Figure 17.3 possessed a cycle that contains all of the edges and used all of the vertices. Euler concluded that a graph contains such a cycle (now referred to as an "Euler cycle") if and only if the degree of every vertex is even.

Problem representation, evidently, has dramatic impact on the ease of solution discovery.

The aforementioned guiding principle led us to two paradigms for learning. The human brain (and nervous system) is the most remarkable example of a natural learning system. In Chapter 11, it serves as a metaphor. There, we outlined an approach to learning—artificial neural nets (ANN) that distill salient features from the human brain model—high connectivity, parallelism, and fault tolerance. ANN models were seen to be successful in many problem-solving domains from economic forecasting to game playing and control systems.

The second paradigm, perhaps not as obvious, is evolution. Darwin described how species of plants and animals adapt to their environment so as to abet their survival. Here, there is no individual who is learning but rather the species itself. Chapter 12 outlined two evolutionary approaches to learning—Genetic Algorithms (GA) and Genetic Programming (GP). Each of these is successful in solving problems in arenas ranging from scheduling to optimization.

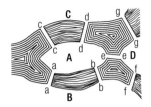

Figure 17.2
The Bridges of Königsberg.

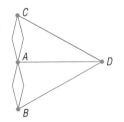

Figure 17.3
The Bridges of Königsberg as a graph model.

17.2 PROMETHEUS REDUX

In Greek mythology, Prometheus was the god who stole fire from heaven to bring it to mankind. Some accounts also have him entrusted with the task of molding mankind itself out of clay. This theme, of creating life out of inanimate material, is pervasive in literature. Perhaps the most spine-chilling account occurs in Frankenstein or "The Modern Prometheus," a novel by Mary Shelley. Undoubtedly, the reader is familiar with this story in which a scientist creates life and then is horrified by his own creation. In the 1931 movie, directed by James Whale, Boris Karloff plays the role of the monster (See also Section 15.1).

The first edition of Shelley's novel was published in 1818, in the thick of the industrial revolution. Mankind had harnessed steam power leading to dramatic changes in manufacturing and the textile industry. The invention of the telegraph made long distance communication practically instantaneous. Many believe that the legacy of this revolution has not been entirely auspicious. Our reliance on steam and coal power, then petroleum, and more recently nuclear power has served to pollute our planet, its water bodies, and its atmosphere. It is also contended that the industrial revolution has fostered a depraved emphasis on materialism. Literary critics insightfully pointed out that the moral of Frankenstein was that society must be wary of its

One of the authors (S. L.) first viewed this film in his childhood. To this day, he still sleeps with the lights on.

attempts to master nature. This is a warning that perhaps needs to be continually heeded by the AI community, as its mastery of intelligence continues to grow throughout the 21st century.

Computer science is a field of science concerned with information and computation. Its focus is on the algorithmic solutions of problems. The 20th century provided this nascent discipline with cause for humility. This humility was imposed by the discovery of fundamental limits on the solvability of problems. That is, there are problems that exist for which no algorithmic solutions are possible. The most well-known of such problems is the so-called "**halting problem.**" Given an arbitrary procedure P, running with arbitrary data w, would P(w) ever halt? For example, the Four-Color Problem was perhaps the most famous open problem in graph theory. Its statement "Are four colors sufficient to color a map so that no two adjacent regions have the same color?" This question was answered in the affirmative by Appel and Haken in 1976.[2] Their computer program solution to this problem ran for several hundred hours. It would have been helpful if the operating system on which this program was running could have predicted that the program would indeed eventually halt. The halting problem informs us that such a priori knowledge is not always possible.

Alan Turing was mentioned prominently early in this text. In 1936, he was investigating the issue of what functions were computable.[3] For example, addition is a computable function—that is, a step-by-step procedure can be given so that if integers X and Y are given as inputs, then their sum X + Y can be obtained after a finite number of computation steps. He provided a model of computation that is now known as a **Turing machine** (see Figure 17.4). A Turing machine is composed of three parts:

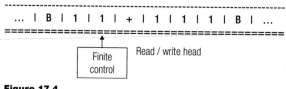

Figure 17.4
A Turing machine.

1. An input/output tape upon which the input problem is inscribed and upon which the result is written. Various models of Turing machines exist; the one depicted in Figure 17.4 has a two-way unbounded tape. The tape is divided into cells, and one symbol may be written in each cell. The tape comes preloaded with the blank symbol (B) on each cell.

2. A finite control that contains an algorithm (i.e., a step-by-step procedure to solve the problem).

3. A read/write head which can read a symbol on the tape and write symbols onto this tape. It can also move left or right.

Turing discussed the concept of a **Universal Turing Machine** (UTM)—a Turing machine which is able to run the programs of other Turing machines, that is, is capable of simulating the behavior of "ordinary" Turing machines. Turing proved that it was impossible to determine if an arbitrary Turing machine (T) with arbitrary input (w), that is, T(w), would ever halt. This is the so-called **Turing machine halting problem.** The more general version of this problem, the Halting Problem, cannot be proven **undecidable**. Instead, it is accepted on faith; faith provided by the **Turing-Church Thesis.** This thesis states that the computational power of a Turing machine is equivalent to that of a digital computer. As a consequence of the Turing-Church Thesis, if a problem cannot be solved on a Turing machine, most computer scientists believe that the problem is algorithmically unsolvable. Hence, there are fundamental limits to computation. AI as a sub-discipline of computer science inherits these fundamental limits as well. One wonders if the creation of a human-level AI is one of these limits.

17.3 RECAPITULATION—PART II: PRESENT AI ACCOMPLISHMENTS

We return to the feasibility of creating a human-level AI later in this chapter. Presently, we provide a brief overview of AI accomplishments that have been cited in the previous 16 chapters:

- **In Search:**
    - A* has been incorporated into video game design; games have become more realistic (Chapter 3).
    - Mapquest, Google, and Yahoo maps use heuristic search. Many GPS and smart phone apps incorporate this technology (Chapter 3).
    - Finding approximate solutions for difficult and (and sometimes NP-complete problems such as the TSP) using Hopfield networks (Chapter 11) and evolutionary approaches (Chapter 12).

- **Game Playing:**
    - Minimax evaluation so that computers can play relatively simple games such as tic-tac-toe and nim (Chapter 4).
    - Minimax evaluation with alpha-beta pruning aided by heuristics and other machine learning tools so that computers can play championship-level checkers (Samuels and Schaeffer) and chess (Deeper Blue defeated the World Chess Champion, Garry Kasparov, in 1997) (Chapter 16).
    - Championship-level programs for Othello (Logistello, 1997) as well as "proficient play" in Backgammon (TD-Gammon, 1992), Bridge (Jack and WBridge 5 (2000s), and Poker (2007) (Chapter 16).

- **Fuzzy Logic:**
    - Hand-held camcorders automatically compensate for spurious hand movements.
    - Traction control devices for automobiles.
    - Control devices for digital cameras, washing machines, and other household appliances.

- **Expert Systems**
    - Knowledge-intensive software with built-in inferencing and explanatory facilities, or so-called Expert Systems (ES), help consumers select an appropriate car model, navigate online web sites to make purchases, etc.
    - ES are also useful in analysis, control, diagnosis (What disease does a patient have?) instruction, and prediction (where should we dig for oil?).
    - ES are used in arenas as diverse as medicine, chemical analysis, and computer configuration.
    - There is no controversy regarding ES' status as one of the biggest achievements in AI as long as these systems are used to help humans and not to supplant them (Chapter 9).

- **Neural Networks**
  - The Lexus automobile has rear back-up cameras, sonar devices, and a neural network, and using these technologies, the car can automatically parallel park.
  - The Mercedes automobile and others have automatic stop control when the vehicle gets too close to other vehicles or objects.
  - The Google Car is totally autonomous (well almost); it drives itself, however, a human must still be in the vehicle.
  - Optical Character Readers (OCR) automatically route a good deal of our mail.
  - Automatic speech recognition systems are in widespread use. Software agents routinely help us navigate our credit card and banking transactions.
  - Software provides automatic security alerts at airports when persons on "no-fly" lists are detected.
  - Neural networks assist in medical diagnosis and economic forecasting (Chapter 11).

- **Evolutionary Approaches:**
  - Telecommunication satellites' orbits are scheduled to prevent communication fade-outs.
  - Software to optimize antenna and very-large-scale integration (VLSI) circuit design.
  - Data-mining software to make data more valuable to companies (Chapter 12).

- **Natural Language Processing (NLP)**
  - Conversational agents provide individuals with travel information and assist with reservations.
  - GPS systems routinely vocalize instructions to users. For example, "Make a left turn at the next corner." Some smart phones have apps that permit you to speak requests: "Where is the nearest coffee shop that makes cappuccinos?"
  - Web requests enable cross-language information retrieval and perform language translation when desired.
  - Interactive agents provide verbal assistance to children learning to read (Chapter 13).
  - Applications of machine learning with neural networks, natural language processing (Chapter 13), speech understanding, and planning (Chapter 14) have all enabled remarkable progress in robotics (Chapter 15).

Overall, not a bad track record for a sub-discipline of computer science that is beginning its second half century on the scene.

APPLICATION BOX

GOOGLE CAR

Google was founded in 1998 by Stanford University graduate students, Larry Page and Sergey Brin. It started as a search engine called BackRub which used links to rank the importance of web pages. The Google search engine, which is a play on the word "googol,"was a huge success, and quickly became the most powerful, well-known, and dominant search engine on the planet. Over the years, Google has also developed the equally successful e-mail system "Gmail" and then acquired the hugely popular public video system "YouTube." In the early 2000s, Google secretly developed a driverless car, however, since then it has become public knowledge.

One of the engineers behind Google's Driverless car is Dmitri Dolgov, and the leader of the project is Dr. Sebastian Thrun. Thrun is the former director of Stanford's Artificial Intelligence Laboratory and is co-inventor of Google's Street View. The Google car has been tested for years and will still continue to be in experimental form for a number of years to come. It seems likely that autonomous cars are still years away from mass production, but technologists believe that in the near future they will be as popular as cell phones and GPS systems. Google is betting that this technology will likely not be profitable for many years. However, huge profits are projected from the possible sales of information and navigation services for makers of other autonomous vehicles.

The Google car uses artificial intelligence technology such as a laser point marker for sensing anything nearby such as signs, and marks on the floor to make decisions that a human driver would make, such as turning to avoid an obstacle or stopping for pedestrians.

Google, by law, must have a person behind the wheel in case something goes wrong, and it also has a technician to monitor the navigation systems to make sure the tests are safe and no accidents occur. It also has different driving *personalities* that you can choose for different drivers such as "careful driving," "defensive driving," and "aggressive driving."

A robot usually reacts faster than humans can; it has all-around perception based on its receptors and devices. It also does not become distracted and is free of other factors which typically cause accidents, such as fatigue, drugs, and carelessness. The goal of engineers is to make these driverless cars more reliable than humans. Human error is the cause of many accidents. Furthermore, the software that these driverless cars use must be carefully tested and must be free of viruses and malware. Other concerns are for fuel efficiency and space efficiency—that is, the cars can be "crowded" on the roads, since theoretically they are accident-free. Several of Google's driverless cars have logged more than one thousand miles without any incidents or human intervention. These cars have also logged over one hundred thousand miles with a small number of human corrections.[1]

One of Google's tests of its driverless car started outside its campus near San Francisco. It used a variety of sensors with a 600-foot range and followed a route programmed into the car's global positioning satellite system or GPS. The car stayed within the State of California's speed limit of 65mph. When the car made turns, it slowed down and then accelerated a bit after turning, just as a human would. The device that sat on top of the car provided a detailed, mapped version of the environment and its surroundings. Hence it knew which roads it needed to take, which ones to avoid, and which ones were dead ends. It was able to get on busy freeways, travel for several miles, and exit without incident. It was also able to drive through traffic and stop at red lights and stop signs, and was able to interface seamlessly with pedestrians. If humans were present, it would wait for them to move. It has a voice system to announce its actions to people in the car or to the driver alone. Drivers were also alerted when its artificial intelligence system detected problems with its sensors. It can also prevent accidents, using detection systems that indicate what is going on. The driver can also regain control of the car by pushing a red button near his right hand, by touching the brakes, or by turning the steering wheel.

When the car is driverless and the system is in control, it is called *cruise mode* and the people in the car can let go of the wheel. In effect it becomes a mode of public transportation, without the expense, crowding, traffic, and other factors which can be irritating to drivers of ordinary cars.

There are certain legal questions which arise such as who would be liable if an accident occurs. All the states that have allowed driverless car testing do not have laws regarding what would happen when no human was operating the car. Google discovered that it is legal to drive an automated car as long as a human being is in the car that can override any errors that may occur.

The Google car would reduce the need for personal cars which would consequently reduce traffic and provide more land for people to use instead of making wider roads.

Recently Google has been building experimental electric cars with normal standard controls but with no driver controls except for starting and stopping the vehicle. This car would be self-driven to the location of the person who needs it through a smart phone app and would drive the person to their destination. There is also a feature invented called the Traffic Jam Assist, which allows the driverless car to follow another vehicle during traffic.[2]

Google's plan for the new driverless cars is to have at least 100 new prototype vehicles that would run on electricity. The team at Google would limit them to drive at only 25 mph and to drive in urban and suburban settings. The tests would be performed by Google personnel. This would help test them in small, confined areas. It will naturally take some time to persuade regulators that it is safe to permit people to utilize driverless cars.

Figure 17.5
Google Car.

References

1. Thrun, S. October 9, 2010. What we're driving at. Google Blog http://googleblog.blogspot.com/2010/10/what-were-driving-at.html.

2. Markoff, J. October 9, 2009. Google's next phase in driverless cars: No steering wheel or brake pedals. *New York Times*. Retrieved from http://www.nytimes.com/2014/05/28/technology/googles-next-phase-in-driverless-cars-no-brakes-or-steering-wheel.html.

3. Markoff, J. May 27, 2014. Google Cars drive themselves, in traffic. *New York Times*. Retrieved from http://www.nytimes.com/2010/10/10/science/10google.html?_r=0.

17.4 IBM WATSON-JEOPARDY CHALLENGE

Man vs. machine challenges provide a framework to incite enthusiasm and publicity for some technological achievement. IBM is responsible for three such events. The first occurred in 1997 when Deeper Blue, a parallel computer with a special-purpose search facility, beat the reigning world chess champion in a six-game match (see Chapter 16).

Blue Gene is a project to produce several high-speed supercomputers to study biomolecular phenomena. Speeds of several hundred TFLOPs have been achieved by machines in this project.. In 2014, the Blue Gene/L System performed at speeds exceeding 36 trillion calculations per second.

The IBM Watson-Jeopardy Challenge has been an ongoing venture over the past few years. Its goal has been to design a computer capable of answering questions posed in a natural language, which is fraught with ambiguity. Question/Answer Systems are nothing new in the world of NLP (see Chapter 13). It was hoped, however, that Watson would perform at speeds comparable to the best human players (2–3 seconds).

One TFLOP (teraflop) stands for one trillion (10^{12}) floating point operations per second.

One petaflop corresponds to one quadrillion (10^{15}) floating point operations per second.

The best sources of information on the IBM Watson-Jeopardy Challenge can be found online. First type www.ibm.com, then enter "Watson-Jeopardy Challenge."

Top human Jeopardy contestants are vast repositories of information on numerous diverse subjects ranging from world geography to Broadway plays, and from literature to pop culture.

Several past questions follow:

1. A 2000 ad showing this pop sensation at ages 3 and 18 was the 100th "got milk?" ad. The correct answer is: "Who is Britney Spears?" Blue J (Watson's early name) suggested: "What is Holy Crap?"

2. "In nine-ball, whenever you sink this, it's a scratch." Blue J answered correctly: "What is a cue ball?"

3. "What country shares the longest border with Chile?" Blue J incorrectly responded: "What is Bolivia?" The correct response was, "What is Argentina?" was its second choice.

David Ferrucci, a senior IBM employee, was chosen to head the Watson development team in 2007. He had extensive experience in language processing systems. In Stephen Baker's popular book,[4] Ferrucci confides two conflicting fears: one, that after several years and millions of spent research dollars, Watson (and consequently IBM) would fail miserably on a national stage and two, that at the last minute, another company would bypass IBM and design a superior system. As it turned out, he would have four long years to live with these fears. Ferrucci understood that if Watson were to succeed, it must be loaded with facts. Not just any facts, but the right kinds of facts. Hence, thousands of previous Jeopardy questions were studied and categorized. It was decided that Watson would be loaded with "tons" of Wikipedia articles. Next, the Gutenberg Library was downloaded and Watson "studied" The Great Books. Insight was also gleaned from Watson's human competitors. It was discovered early in the Watson project that deep knowledge was not necessary—having a passing knowledge of many diverse subjects was adequate. Ken Jennings did not prepare for the contest matches by laboriously reading tomes but rather by practicing with flash cards. The goal was to possess shallow knowledge on a vast array of topics.

Next, Watson was spoon-fed a diet of encyclopedia entries, dictionaries, news articles, and Web pages. As Baker described it: "[Watson] was painfully slow." The next several years were spent in sparring matches with former Jeopardy contestants. Slowly, its performance began to improve.

Watson was composed of more than 2,000 processors, each working in parallel to pursue a different thread of reasoning. It would display several answers for each question with its degree of confidence listed for each. Whenever Watson was sufficiently confident in one of its responses, it would scramble to press the buzzer.

Gradually, Watson began to fare well against human competition. Occasionally, there would be a faux pas of profane language. Naturally, the corporate image of IBM is important; a filter was installed so that Watson would not utter the most common profanities.

The man-machine contest took place early in March 2011. Watson was victorious, even though it made several embarrassing mistakes, the most famous of which was to the Final Jeopardy question:

"Its largest airport is named for a World War II battle." In the category of "U.S. Cities," Watson responded: "What is Toronto?"

In Watson's defense, Ferrucci explained that there is a Toronto in Illinois and Toronto also possesses an American League baseball team. However, the fact remains that Watson made a mistake. An interesting question, of course, is: "What sort of future is there for Watson-like machines?" There certainly is no market for Jeopardy Champion Computers. IBM anticipates, however, that

Figure 17.6
Members of the IBM team at The City College of New York.
IBM Team (left to right): Bruno Bonetti, Jerry Moy, Faton Avdiu, Arif Sheikh, Andrew Rosenberg, Wlodek Zadrozny, Raul Fernandez, Vincent DiPalermo, Andy Aaron, and Rolando Franco.

Figure 17.7
Wlodek Zadrozny discussing Watson with an attendee at The City College of New York.

Watson and its successors will be trained as specialists in medicine, law, and other fields where new knowledge is being discovered at a feverish pace. It would be helpful if a "medical Watson" has read the latest journals and could advise physicians on the best course of treatment for a patient. Alternatively, a legal Watson would identify precedents upon which legal defenses could be found.

To help publicize the IBM Watson-Jeopardy Challenge, IBM sent representatives to the City College of New York and the City University of New York (CUNY) Graduate Center in February 2011. On the first page of this chapter (in Figure 17.0), Wlodek Zadrozny is seen

Figure 17.8
Jerry Moy moderated both of the CUNY presentations.

addressing students and faculty at the City College of New York. Members of the IBM team who attended this event are shown in Figure 17.6. In Figure 17.7, Wlodek Zadrozny is shown discussing Watson with an attendee at the City College of New York. Finally, Jerry Moy, who moderated both CUNY presentations, is shown in Figure 17.8.

We have frequently said in this text that the proper role for AI technology is to assist rather than to replace humans. Watson will be a valuable aide to human professionals in varied fields over the next several decades.

HUMAN INTEREST NOTES　　　　RAY KURZWEIL

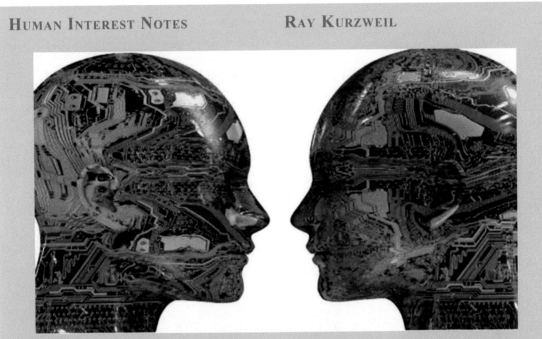

Figure 17.9
Singularity from KurzweilAI.net homepage / Source: Shutterstock.

Figure 17.10
Ray Kurzweil. (Credit: Photo by Michael Lutch. Courtesy of Kurzweil Technologies, Inc.).

Ray Kurzweil and The Singularity

Ray Kurzweil is amongst the world's leading scientists, inventors, entrepreneurs, and futurists. Forbes magazine has called him "the rightful heir to Thomas Edison" and ranked him amongst the 8 leading entrepreneurs in the world. Kurzweil has always been, as it is said, "an industry onto himself." Some of his notable inventions include the first CCD flatbed scanner, the first omni-font optical character recognition, the first print-to-speech reading machine for the blind, the first text-to-speech synthesizer, the first music synthesizer capable of recreating the grand piano and other orchestral instruments, and the commercially marketed large-vocabulary speech recognition system.

Kurzweil is the recipient of the $500,000 MIT-Lemelson Prize, the largest prize for innovation. In 1999 he received the National Medal of Technology, the nation's highest honor in technology. In 2002 he was inducted into the National Inventors Hall of Fame, established by the U.S. Patent Office.

In addition he has received 20 honorary doctorates and has been honored by three US presidents. He has authored seven books, five of which have been best sellers. *The Age of Spriritual Machines* was translated into nine languages and was the #1 best-selling book on Amazon in science. His book, *The Singularity Is Near*, was a New York Times best seller and has been the #1 book on Amazon in both science and philosophy. It is the subject of this section.

In 2012 Kurzweil was appointed Director of Engineering at Google, heading a team developing machine intelligence and natural language understanding.

Kurzweil's books include:

The Age of Intelligent Machines (1990)

The 10% Solution for a Healthy Life (1993)

The Age of Spiritual Machines (1999)

Fantastic Voyage (with Dr. Terry Grossman) (2004)

The Singularity (2005)

Transcend: Nine Steps to Living Well (with Dr. Terry Grossman) (2009)

How to Create a Mind (2012)

The source of much of our information here about Ray Kurzweil is the website KurzweilAI.

THE SINGULARITY

In 2005 Ray Kurzweil published what is perhaps his most controversial book: *The Singularity is Near: When Humans Transcend Biology*. The central theme in this tome is what he refers to as *The Law of Accelerating Returns*. He maintains that computers, genetics, nanotechnology, and AI are experiencing exponential growth. He predicts that by the year 2045, machine intelligence will exceed the combined human intelligence on this planet.

Kurzweil believes that there are six stages to evolution:

1. Physics and Chemistry
2. Biology and DNA
3. Brains
4. Technology
5. The Merger of Human Technology with Human Intelligence and
6. The Universe Wakes Up

He claims that the first four stages have occurred and that we are now in Stage 5. By 2045 technological advances will transpire so precipitously that people will be able to augment their bodies genetically, via nanotechnology and AI.

We began our journey together in Chapter 1 with a reference on Jerri Ryan as part of the Borg in *Star Trek: The Next Generation*. If Raymond Kurzweil is correct in his predictions, then perhaps a unified super-intelligence is inevitable and much like those members of the Borg in that former television series, we will find individuality extinct and resistance indeed futile. As a return for this sacrifice, we will be presented with the prospect for eternal life.

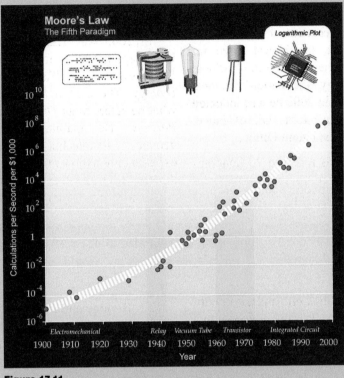

Figure 17.11
Moore's Law as depicted on Kurzweil.net.

Reference

http://www.kurzweilai.net/ray-kurzweil-biography
(accessed Dec. 12, 2014)

17.5 AI IN THE 21ST CENTURY

We return to the open question raised earlier in our discussion: Is the creation of a human-level AI beyond the fundamental limits of AI? We speculate first on the origins of human intelligence and then on the origins of life itself.

Richard Dawkins [5] tackles this latter question, finding insight in Darwin's Theory of Evolution. Naturally, four billion years ago, there were no animals or plants on planet earth—just a "primordial soup" of elementary atoms. Dawkins believes that Darwin's theory can be generalized to "survival of the stable," in other words, stable atoms (and molecules) are more likely to have survived on this ancient earth. He speculates further that in its early history, this planet possessed an abundance of water, carbon dioxide, methane, and ammonia and thus, amino acids—complex molecules that are the building blocks for proteins—were likely formed. Proteins are known to be a precursor for life. Dawkins envisions the next step on the long path to life on this planet as being the accidental creation of a molecule he refers to as the Replicator. This Replicator molecule has the remarkable property of being able to make a faithful copy of itself. He maintains that replicator molecules that could expeditiously and accurately copy themselves would have been stable in this primitive environment.

The replication (or reproduction) process itself required a steady supply of the basic "raw materials." Undoubtedly, different replicator molecules were in constant competition for adequate supplies of water, carbon dioxide, methane, and ammonia. This evolutionary process continued for four billion years. Dawkins theorizes that the successors in this lengthy evolutionary bout might be found inside the present-day animals and plants that inhabit our planet—they are our genes.

Dawkins continues his extraordinary treatise on the possible origins of life on this planet by explaining how these genes endeavored to ensure their survival. Over the past 600 million years or so, they have behaved much like the fictional elves cited in Chapter 12. They have been fashioning our eyes, ears, lungs, and so on from which the living vessels (i.e., their bodies) would be constructed. In this treatise, it is as if animal bodies and flora are merely protective barriers to ensure the survival of all-important genes. As I (S. L.) was reading Dawkins' work recently, my mind traveled back to one of the scenes from the Star Wars movies in which the enemy troops attack while encased in huge legged robotic fighting machines, robots that form a protective shell for the soldier inside. Even if we were to accept Dawkins' theory, we are still left with the question, "Where does consciousness in humans arise from?" Dawkins would likely maintain that those animals that possessed consciousness (which once again arose through natural selection) would possess superior survival skills and would therefore achieve relative stability and would consequently be assured of survival.

Gerald Edelman is a Nobel-Prize winning biologist. He proposes a biological theory of consciousness, [6] which also rests upon Darwinist underpinnings. He maintains that consciousness and the mind are purely biological phenomena. Groups of neurons self-organize into numerous complex and adaptable modules. Edelman believes that the brain possesses functional plasticity, that is, a great deal of brain organization is self-directed as the human genome does not have sufficient coding capability to specify brain structure completely.

In physics, a Unified Field Theory is supposed to be a theory about everything, striving to unite the various forces that occur in nature, for example, gravitational, electromagnetic, strong, and weak forces.

Marvin Minsky tackles a broader issue in "Society of Mind." [7] He asks, "How is the brain organized?" and "How does cognition occur?" As Dawkins informs us, human brains have resulted from hundreds of millions of years of evolution. It is unlikely that one unifying theory will neatly explain the functioning of the complex organ that resides within the human skull. Constructing a mind can be likened to assembling a conductor-less orchestra. The instruments in this mélange are called agents (see Chapter 6) and are not there to play music but rather to interpret the world. Some agents help to understand language, others to interpret visual scenes, and some to provide humans with common sense. (See the discussion of the Cyc Project in Chapter 9.) Nothing meaningful can be accomplished unless there is effective inter-agent communication. Minsky hypothesizes that an individual's state of mind can be explained as a function of which subset of agents are active at any point in time. Perhaps AI is still too young a field and is not yet ready for such a "Unified Field Theory" for intelligence as Minsky proposes. However, when AI matures sufficiently, Minsky's "Society of Mind" will likely play a prominent role in the discussions.

In 2015, there is a complete understanding at both the biological and chemical level of how individual neurons function. What is still inadequate is our knowledge of how collections of neurons process sensory data, encode experiences, understand language, and more generally facilitate cognition and enable consciousness. Current research uses x-rays and other scanning technologies to obtain an understanding of the brain at the functioning module level. Kurzweil predicts [8] that by mid-century we will have a complete architectural understanding of the human brain. Furthermore, he theorizes that miniaturization of computer components will have progressed to the stage where a complete implementation of the brain in hardware will be feasible, an implementation requiring billions of artificial neurons and trillions or even quadrillions of neuronal interconnections. Perhaps at that juncture, we will have the wherewithal to implement a human-level AI. It would be wise if we remembered Prometheus' "reward" for creating fully conscious humans—he was strapped down so that his liver could be devoured by lions and then his liver regenerated so that the feasting could begin anew. Science fiction literature has outlined countless dismal scenarios resulting from mankind's creation of human-level AI. Hopefully, if AI were ever to achieve this lofty goal, its reward would be more gratifying than the one presented to Prometheus.

17.6 CHAPTER SUMMARY

In this chapter, we have reviewed many of the achievements of the AI community over the past five decades. We place AI in a framework as a sub-discipline of computer science. We ponder whether the creation of human-level AI is impossible in the same sense that the well-known halting problem in computer science is undecidable.

We discuss the IBM Watson system and cite its role as an assistant for professionals in law and medicine.

We conclude by considering the origins of life, intelligence, and consciousness. We offer Kurzweil's optimistic viewpoint on the possibility of the successful creation of human-level AI in the near future.

Questions for Discussion

1. When the first boats were built (perhaps many thousands of years ago), what natural systems might have served as inspiration?

2. Give an additional example of a problem where an appropriate representation facilitates its solution.

3. Look on the Web for an additional example of an unsolvable problem.

4. Are you familiar with an additional work in literature which employs the Prometheus theme?

5. Describe the Turing machine model of computation.

6. In what ways is the Turing machine model similar to

   a. a person performing a calculation?

   b. a computer doing the same thing?

7. Compare and contrast a Universal Turing machine running a Turing machine program with a digital computer running a program.

8. What heuristics are incorporated into GPS (Global Positioning System) systems? You may wish to consult Chapter 3.

9. Look on the Web for a discussion of the game Go. Why do you suppose that championship-level programs do not exist for this game? (See Chapter 16.)

10. How might fuzzy logic be incorporated into the control mechanism of a household appliance that we have not mentioned?

11. The next time you go online to a shopping site such as Amazon.com, comment on the ways in which ES technology has been incorporated into your shopping experience.

12. Have you observed OCR technology anywhere in addition to the post office?

13. The next time you interact with a conversational agent, think of the ways in which AI technology has influenced the experience. What improvements would you like to see?

14. Why was Jeopardy selected as a man-machine challenge?

15. Do you believe that Watson possesses human-level intelligence? Why or why not?

16. How does Richard Dawkins believe that life began on earth?

17. Why is it that the human genome does not fully specify brain processes?

18. Why do you suppose that Marvin Minsky's "Society of Mind" does not receive more attention in the AI community?

19. Why does Kurzweil believe that a hardware implementation of the human brain will be possible later in this century?

Exercises

1. Study the symbol-processing systems first developed by Newell and Simon. Write a short essay explaining why (or why not) a human-level AI should be designed using their methodology.

2. Which of the graphs in the following Chapter 2 figures are Eulerian? Explain.

    i.   Figure 2.33 d)

    ii. Figure 2.39

    iii. Figure 2.40 b)

    iv. Figure 2.41

3. Look up inductive approaches to learning, in particular Quinlan's ID3 algorithm (consult Chapter 10). What ideas that we have studied are used in that algorithm?

4. Read the story you cited in Questions For Discussion #4. What lessons can be drawn from it for AI?

5. Study Figure 17.4 for this exercise. The tape depicts two numbers in unary notation that are to be added. You can envision unary as the manner in which a dog might count, "Ruff, Ruff"

would be a dog's way to represent two and "Ruff, Ruff, Ruff" the number three. Hence this Turing machine is to add 2 and 3. A move can be represented as a 5-tuple: $<q_i, S_j, S_k, q_l, \{L, R, N\}>$

q_i: represents the present state

S_j: the symbol scanned

S_k: A symbol that is to be written on the same square upon which S_j appears (note S_k might equal S_j).

q_l: the next state for the Turing machine

$\{L, R, N\}$: the Turing machine might then move left or right one square, or not move at all.

Assume the computation begins with the read/write head positioned as shown and that when the computation is complete, the machine should be in a q_h, directly underneath the blank to the right of the answer. Write a Turing machine program to perform addition of unary numbers. Trace your program for the problem given.

6. Write a short essay specifying what you believe will be the future applications for Watson. What improvements to Watson do you anticipate?

7. Read *The Blind Watchmaker* by Richard Dawkins.[9] Explain in a short essay how this book supports the theory of evolution by natural selection.

8. Study some of the writings of (or about) Gerald Edelman.[10, 11, 12] Write a short essay on his theory of the development of consciousness.

9. Read "Elephants Don't Play Chess" by Rodney Brooks.[13] Elaborate on his theory concerning the development of intelligence.

10. Consult Searle's volume "The Mystery of Consciousnesss" once again. Read his discussion on Penrose's point of view. Compare Penrose's viewpoint on the prospects for the development of a human-level AI with the unbridled optimism espoused by Kurzweil.[8]

11. Survey current research to determine how close we are to a complete understanding of the brain's functioning that Kurzweil anticipates by mid-century.

12. Read the essay by Harold J. Morowitz, "Rediscovering the Mind," which is reprinted in *The Mind's I*. Morowitz describes the quandary that quantum physics presents for the prospects of developing a human-level AI. Summarize Hofstadter's response.[14]

13. Read *Gödel, Escher, Bach: An Eternal Golden Braid* by Douglas R. Hofstadter.[15] Have you become a believer in strong AI after completing the book?

14. Look online for articles on digital ghosts. What is a digital ghost? In what sense do they guarantee immortality?

15. Look up the word "avatar." What was its early definition via à vis the Hindu religion? What is its more modern definition? Next, go to SecondLife.com. How would you account for this tremendous interest in avatar existences?

16. There have been recent advances with prosthetic devices that respond appropriately to brain signals. Read several online reports and then comment on how close you feel we have come to needing to heed the warnings in Section 1.8 ("AI in the New Millennium") regarding man/machine hybrids?

17. Go online to read about Mercedes-Benz's automatic stopping technology. If a driver mistakenly attempts to go through a red light, the car would stop itself. For this system to work properly, every stoplight in the country would need to be upgraded. How long do you predict it will be before drivers will indeed be able to read the papers and shave while they drive to work?

Keywords

Halting problem
Undecidable problem
Turing machine

Turing machine halting problem
Universal Turing machine

Turing-Church Thesis

References

1. Newell, A. and Simon, H.A. 1963. GPS: a program that simulates human thought. In: Feigenbaum and Feldman (eds.), *Computers and Thought*, New York: McGraw-Hill.

2. Appel, K. and Haken, W. 1977. Every planar map is four-colorable. *Illinois Journal of Mathematics* 21: 421–567.

3. Turing, A.M. 1936. On computable numbers with an application to the Entscheidongs problem. *Proceedings of the London Mathematical Society*, Vol. 2, 42: 230–252,

4. Baker, S. 2011. *Final Jeopardy — Man vs. Machine and the Quest to Know Everything*. Boston, MA: Houghton Mifflin Harcourt.

5. Dawkins, R. 1976. *The Selfish Gene*. Oxford, England: Oxford University Press.

6. Edelman, G. 1990. *The Remembered Present: A Biological Theory of Consciousness*. New York: Basic Books.

7. Minsky, M. 1986. *The Society of Mind*. New York: Simon and Schuster.

8. Kurzweil, R., 1999. *The Age of Spiritual Machines*. New York: Penguin Books.

9. Dawkins, R. 1986. *The Blind Watchmaker*. New York: W.W. Norton & Company.

10. Edelman, G. 1992. *Bright Air Brilliant Fire: On the Matter of the Mind*. New York: Basic Books.

11. Searle, J.R., 1990. *The Mystery of Consciousness*. (Read summary of Edelman's Theory). New York: Review of Books.

12. Edelman, G. (2004). *Wider than the Sky: The Phenomenal Gift of Consciousness*. New Haven, CT: Yale University Press.

13. Brooks, R. 1990. Elephants Don't Play Chess. In: *Robotics and Autonomous Systems* 6, 3–15.

14. Hofstadter, D. R. and Dennett, D. C. 1981. *The Mind's I*. New York: Bantam Books.

15. Hofstadter, D. R. 1989. *Godel, Escher, Bach: An Eternal Golden Braid*. New York: Vintage Books.

EXAMPLE WITH CLIPS:
THE EXPERT SYSTEM SHELL

Chapter 9

CLIPS is a multi-paradigm programming language that provides support for rule-based, object-oriented, and procedural programming. CLIPS is similar to but more powerful than OPS5 and only supports forward chaining. CLIPS, an acronym for "C Language Integrated Production System," was developed at NASA/Johnson Space Center with the specific purpose of providing high portability (it is available on the internet free and can support a number of languages), low cost, and easy integration. It has since been expanded to support diverse language and forms of knowledge representation.

Chapter 7 "Introduction to CLIPS" of Giarratano and Riley (Cengage/Thomson, 2005) explains how to use CLIPS.

What follows is a very simple example of an expert system developed in CLIPS which suggests a city for choice of vacation travel in the United States based on the user's entries.

```
;**********************deftemplate declaration
(deftemplate Month (slot month))
(deftemplate VacationMatters (slot vacation-matters))
(deftemplate Vacation (slot vacation))
(deftemplate SportsType (slot sports-type))
(deftemplate SightseeingType (slot sightseeing-type))
(deftemplate LocalSeason (slot local-season))


;**************default rules (Activated every time)
;Rule 1
(defrule GetMonth
   =>
   (printout t "In what month of the year do you plan your trip? ")
   (bind ?response (read))
   (assert (Month (month ?response))))


;Rule 2
(defrule GetVacationMatters
   =>
   (printout t "Do you have any preference in your vacation activities?
   (yes/no) ")
   (bind ?response (read))
   (assert (VacationMatters (vacation-matters ?response))))
```

```
;;;;;;;;;;;;;;;;;;;;;;;;;;;;;;;;;;;;;;;;;;;;;;;;;;;;;;;;;;;;;;;;;;;;;
; The following questions are only asked based on the answers to the
questions asked in the previous section

;Rule 3
(defrule GetVacation
   (VacationMatters (vacation-matters yes))
   =>
   (printout t "What kind of vacation do you prefer? (beach/sports/
    sightseeing) ")
   (bind ?response (read))
   (assert (Vacation (vacation ?response))))

;Rule 4
(defrule GetSportsType
   (Vacation (vacation sports))
   =>
   (printout t "What kind of sports do you prefer? (mountain/river/
    ocean) ")
   (bind ?response (read))
   (assert (SportsType (sports-type ?response))))

;Rule 5
(defrule GetSightseeingType
   (Vacation (vacation sightseeing))
   =>
   (printout t "What kind of sightseeing would you prefer?
    (city or nature) ")
   (bind ?response (read))
   (assert (SightseeingType (sightseeing-type ?response))))

;;;;;;;;;rules to define local season according to user's entry;;;;;;;;;;;;;
;Rule 6
(defrule GetLocalSummer
   (Month (month June|July|August|September))
   =>
   (assert (LocalSeason (local-season summer))))

Rule 7
(defrule GetLocalWinter
   (Month (month December|January|February))
   =>
   (assert (LocalSeason (local-season winter))))

Rule 8
(defrule GetLocalMidSeason
   (Month (month March|April|May|October|November))
   =>
   (assert (LocalSeason (local-season summer))))
```

```
;;;;;;;;;;;;;;;;;;;;;;;;;;;;;;;;;;;;;;;;;;;;;;;;;;;;;;;;;;;;;;;;;;;;;;
;rules to define and print suggested flights

; Rules to determine the destination based on the user's entries
; Salience added to give the first rule a priority
```

Rule 9
```
(defrule Flight1
   (declare (salience 200))
   (LocalSeason (local-season winter))
   (Vacation (vacation beach))
   =>
   (assert (destination Miami)))
```

Rule 10
```
(defrule Flight2
   (declare (salience 100))
   (LocalSeason (local-season summer))
   (Vacation (vacation beach))
   =>
   (assert (destination OceanCity))
   (assert (destination LosAngeles)))
```

Rule 11
```
(defrule Flight3
   (declare (salience 100))
   (VacationMatters (vacation-matters no))
   (LocalSeason (local-season summer|midseason|winter))
   =>
   (assert (destination Miami)))
```

Rule 12
```
(defrule Flight4
   (Vacation(vacation sports))
   (SportsType (sports-type mountain))
   =>
   (assert (destination Utah)))
```

Rule 13
```
(defrule Flight5
   (Vacation(vacation sports))
   (SportsType (sports-type river))
   =>
   (assert (destination Virginia)))
```

Rule 14
```
(defrule Flight6
   (Vacation(vacation sports))
   (SportsType (sports-type ocean))
   =>
   (assert (destination FloridaKeys)))
```

Rule 15
```
(defrule Flight7
   (Vacation(vacation sightseeing))
   (SightseeingType (sightseeing-type nature))
   =>
   (assert (destination GrandCanyon)))
```

Rule 16
```
(defrule Flight8
   (Vacation(vacation sightseeing))
   (SightseeingType (sightseeing-type city))
   =>
   (assert (destination NewYork))
   (assert (destination LasVegas))
   (assert (destination Boston)))
```

```
;;;;;;;;;;;;;;;;;;;;;;;;print out the rules;;;;;;;;;;;;;;;;;;
```
Rule 17
```
(defrule no-city-found ""
   (declare (salience -10))
   (not (destination ?))
   =>
   (assert (destination "The system cannot suggest you a destination
based on your entries. Please contact your travel agent.")))
```

Rule 18
```
(defrule print-dest ""
   (destination ?item)
   =>
   (printout t ?item crlf))
```

This program uses the Forward Chaining so to acquire facts based on the user's answers and than matches the facts from the Working Memory to the rules. The actions of the selected rule are executed (which may affect the list of applicable rules) and then the inference engine selects another rule and executes its actions. This process continues until no applicable rules remain. The Inference Engine sorts the activations according to their salience and determines which rule(s) should ultimately be fired after conflict resolution. (Section 8.x). In this case Rule 9 is chosen over Rule 11 after conflict resolution because of its Salience (200) and the desire for a midwinter vacation spot. This can be seen in the example below:

```
CLIPS> (watch activations)
CLIPS> (reset)
==> Activation 0         GetVacationMatters: f-0
==> Activation -10       no-city-found: f-0,
==> Activation 0         GetMonth: f-0
CLIPS> (run)
In what month of the year do you plan your trip? December
==> Activation 0         GetLocalWinter: f-1
Do you have any preference in your vacation activities? (yes/no) yes
==> Activation 0         GetVacation: f-3
What kind of vacation do you prefer? (beach/sports/sightseeing) beach
==> Activation 200       Flight1: f-2,f-4
==> Activation 0         print-dest: f-5
<== Activation -10       no-city-found: f-0,
Miami
```

We can see the order of activations after which the program fired the final answer (Miami). The rule with salience -10 was retracted from the Working Memory before firing the answer.

```
Current facts stored in the Working Memory are:
    CLIPS>        (facts)
    f-0           (initial-fact)
    f-1           (Month (month December))
    f-2           (LocalSeason (local-season winter))
    f-3           (VacationMatters (vacation-matters yes))
    f-4           (Vacation (vacation beach))
    f-5           (destination Miami)
```

For a total of 6 facts.

IMPLEMENTATION OF THE VITERBI ALGORITHM FOR HIDDEN MARKOV CHAINS

(BY HARUN IFTIKHAR)

Chapter 12

An implementation of the Viterbi algorithm in Java is included on the following page. The most noticeable aspect of the implementation is its organization into three main steps: initialization, recursion, and termination. The initialization step fills in the column for the first output observation, beginning with transitions from the start state. Then the recursion step uses the first column to build up the next column, and so on, continuing until the table is mostly filled. Finally, the termination step fills in the final cell, representing the probability of reaching the end state after having produced the final observation.

After the three steps in the calculation, we use the backpointer [ ] [ ] array to trace through the most likely sequence of states. This implementation in Java makes use

Code in Java:

```java
package javaapplication2;

class Main {
    public static void main(String[] args) {
        // There are two states: Simple and Difficult
        int numberOfStates = 2;
        // The output sequence 2 1 1 3 has length equal to 4
        int lengthOfSequence = 4;
        // The transitionProb[][] array contains the transition probabilities
        double [][] transitionProb = { {0, 0.7, 0.3, 0},
                                       {0, 0.6, 0.3, 0.1},
                                       {0, 0.6, 0.3, 0.1},
                                       {0, 0, 0, 0} };
        // The observationProb[][] contains observation probabilities
        double [][] observationProb = { {0, 0, 0},
                                        {0.8, 0.1, 0.1},
                                        {0.1, 0.2, 0.7},
                                        {0, 0, 0} };
        double [][] viterbi = new double [numberOfStates + 2]
        [lengthOfSequence + 1];
        int [][] backpointer = new int [numberOfStates + 2]
        [lengthOfSequence + 1];
```

```
int [] observationSequence = {2, 1, 1, 3};
double currentProb, maxProb = 0;
int maxArg = 0;

// Initialization for-loop fills in the first column of viterbi
   and backpointer arrays
for (int s = 1; s <= numberOfStates; s++)
{
    viterbi[s][1] = transitionProb[0][s] * observationProb[s]
    [observationSequence[0] - 1];
    backpointer[s][1] = 0;
}

// Nested for-loops which fill remaining columns in viterbi
   and backpointer arrays
for (int t = 2; t <=  lengthOfSequence; t++)
{
    for (int s = 1; s <= numberOfStates; s++)
    {
        for (int i = 1; i <= numberOfStates; i++)
        {
            currentProb = viterbi[i][t - 1] *
                          transitionProb[i][s]
* observationProb[s][observationSequence[t - 1] - 1];
            if ( currentProb > maxProb )
            {
                maxProb = currentProb;
                maxArg = i;
            }
        }

        viterbi[s][t] = maxProb;
        backpointer[s][t] = maxArg;

        currentProb = maxProb = 0;
        maxArg = 0;
    }
}
currentProb = maxProb = 0;
maxArg = 0;
```

```
// Termination for-loop fills in the final column for the
   last time step
for (int i = 1; i <= numberOfStates; i++)
{
currentProb = viterbi[i][lengthOfSequence] *
              transitionProb[i][3];
    if (currentProb > maxProb)
    {
        maxProb = currentProb;
        maxArg = i;
    }
}
viterbi[3][lengthOfSequence] = maxProb;
backpointer[3][lengthOfSequence] = maxArg;

// Print out results by backtracing through the backpointer array
int index = 3;

int arrayIndex = lengthOfSequence - 1;
int[] tempArray = new int[lengthOfSequence];
tempArray[arrayIndex] = backpointer[index][lengthOfSequence];
index = backpointer[index][lengthOfSequence];
for (int t = lengthOfSequence; t > 1; t--)
{
    tempArray[--arrayIndex] = backpointer[index][t];
    index = backpointer[index][t];
}
System.out.println("The observation sequence was: ");
for (int j = 0; j < lengthOfSequence; j++)
{
    System.out.print(observationSequence[j] + " ");
}

System.out.println("\n\nThe most probable sequence of states:");
for (int j = 0; j < lengthOfSequence; j++)
{
    if (tempArray[j] == 1)
        System.out.println("Simple");
    else if (tempArray[j] == 2)
        System.out.println("Difficult");
```

```
                    }
        }
        }
```

Output for 2 1 1 3 Sequence

```
The observation sequence was:
2  1  1  3

The most probable sequence of states:
Simple
Simple
Simple
Difficult
BUILD SUCCESSFUL (total time: 0 seconds)
```

CONTRIBUTIONS TO COMPUTER CHESS: THE AMAZING WALTER SHAWN BROWNE

Chapter 16

In 1977, Ken Thompson[1] presented his databases for all four-piece endings to top players. One database demonstrated that they couldn't win with K + Q vs. K + R, which portended a number of changes to follow. Subsequently, the rules were changed for K + R + B vs. K + R (called "The Headache Ending" by Benko) to 75 moves, then 100 moves, then back to 50 moves since the longest win is 59 moves. Extensions also occurred for other endings like K + B + B vs. K + N which was demonstrated to be a win in 77 moves.

For some hundred years it was believed that the endgame King and Queen vs. King and Rook (KQKR), was a win for the strong side; not trivial, but certainly manageable in 50 moves. In 1977, Ken Thompson came to the World Computer Chess Championships armed with his database for KQKR and challenged the top masters in attendance.

To their horror and embarrassment, International Masters Lawrence Day (of Canada) and Hans Berliner (World Correspondence Chess Champion, 1969) failed to win in 50 moves with the strong side. Later, World Chess Championship Candidate and for many years the chess columnist of the New York Times, Grandmaster Robert Byrne, took his turn and failed to win.

The rules of chess allow 50 moves to end a game if no pawns remain on the board. The longest win requires 31 moves. The common heuristic provided by endgame textbooks is to survive by keeping the King and Rook together, thereby avoiding any tactical trick that might fork or skewer the King and Rook. In contrast, Ken Thompson's database was playing moves that occasionally separated the King and Rook. What did it know that humans hadn't known? Very simply, nothing at all, just that if a move separating the King

and Rook was the longest surviving move, then that was the move to play.

Grandmaster Walter Shawn Browne (1949–2015) of Berkeley, California, was a six-time U.S. Chess Champion (1974, 1975, 1977, 1980, 1981, 1983). He was the best chess player in the

Figure C.0
Walter Browne.

United States in the 1970s in the absence of Bobby Fischer after Fischer won the World Championship from Boris Spassky in Reykjavik, Iceland in 1972. Browne, who dropped out of Brooklyn's Erasmus High School less than a decade after Bobby Fischer left the same school, is superb at many board games including Scrabble and backgammon, and for more than 20 years has made his primary income from the game of poker.

A few months after Ken Thompson came to the World Computer Chess Championships in 1977, Browne, who calculated extremely well, took on the challenge against Ken Thompson's database as a bet for $100. The challenge was played at the rate of 40 moves in 2.5 hours (which was the standard rate of international chess play at the time). Like the others before him, Browne was unable to win in 50 moves. Moves were transmitted by telephone between Bell Labs in Murray Hill, New Jersey and Browne's home in Berkeley, California.

Ever the competitor and gambler, Browne asked for a rematch against the database at "double or nothing" a week later. Although Browne never attended college, he does know how to analyze and study. He studied the program's play and looked for patterns. Learning how to play correctly (to win in 50 moves) is a challenging task (since the longest win is 31 moves) but learning how to play optimally in all variations and win in the minimum number of moves (31) is a daunting task for a human being. In Figure C.1, White with the Queen is Browne and Black is BELLE. The position starts with the White King in check. The number of moves to mate with best play is indicated in parentheses.

As you can see in Figure C.1, Browne did win the bet, capturing the rook (which was one way to win) on exactly the fiftieth move! This means that he played moves that actually cost him 19 moves in terms of optimal play.

Figure C.1
Walter Browne's winning the endgame KQ vs. KR against the computer program, BELLE (2nd game).

GM Walter Browne vs. BELLE

KQ vs. KR
2nd Game, Challenge Match, 1977 (by Telephone)

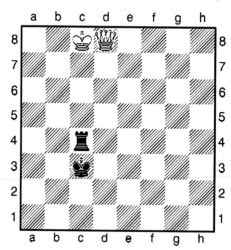

1.Kb7 Rb4+ 2.Kc6 Rc4+ 3.Kb5 Rb4+ 4.Ka5 Rc4 5.Qd6 Rd4 6.Qe5 Kd3 7.Kb5 Re4 (25) 8.Qf6 Ke3 (24) 9.Kc5 Rf4 (23) 10.Qg6 Ra4 (22) 11.Qg3+ Ke2 (21) 12.Qc3 Rf4 (20) 13.Kd5 Rh4 (19) 14.Qc2+ Ke3 (18) 15.Qd1 Kf2 (17) Up to here Browne has been playing very accurately and making steady progress. **16.Qd2+ Kf3 (17) 17.Qe1 Rg4 (19)18.Qd1+ Kf4 (18) 19.Qe2 Rg5+ (20) 20.Kd4 Rf5 (19) 21.Qe3+ Kg4 (18)** Browne errs on moves 16,17, and 19. Ken Thompson has found that lower rated players have trouble from a distance of 14 to 16 moves from the win. Usually the White King is trying to cross the "barrier" on the 3rd or (as in this case) 4th rank. The books don't usually help here either. **22.Ke4 Rf7 (18) 23.Qg1+ Kh5 (16) 24.Qg3 Rf8 (15) 25.Ke5 Rf7 26.Ke6 Rf8 (14) 27.Qa3 Rf4 (15) 28.Qh3+ Kg5 (16) 29.Qg3+ Rg4 (15) 30.Qe5+ Kh4 31.Qh2+ Kg5 32.Ke5 Kg6 (14) 33.Qh8 Rg5+ (14) 34.Ke6 Rg4 (14)** Browne has been somewhat stuck since move 26. He can only lose two moves now. **35.Qg8+ Kh5 36.Qh7+ Kg5 37.Ke5 Rg3 38.Qg7+ Kh4 39.Qh6+ Kg4 (9) 40.Ke4** Browne was now making steady progress but he is still on a tightrope. **40...Rg2 41.Qg6+ Kh3 42.Qh5+ Kg3 43.Ke3 Rg1 44.Qg5+ Kh2 45.Qh4+ Kg2 46.Ke2 Ra1(4)   47.Qe4+** [Now 47.Qg5+ then 48.Qh6+ followed by 49.Qg7+ and 50.Qxa1 wins. Browne finds another way.] **47...Kh3 48.Qh7+ Kg3 49.Qg7+** Browne just makes it within the normal rules and wins back his money.

1–0

The record of the Browne vs. BELLE match originally appeared in an article by Warren Stenberg and Edward Conway published in the Chess Voice (April/May, 1979) and then in D. Kopec, (1990), "The History of Man-Machine Chess", in The Encyclopedia of Computer Science and Technology, eds. A. Kent and J.G. Williams, New York, NY: Marcel Dekker, Vol.26, Supp 11, pp.241-43.

Browne later informed me (1990) that contrary to some reports he was not "lucky," but he had actually analyzed, calculated, prepared, and memorized the last 24 went exactly according to his home analysis. He also reminded me that years later he had a game that went some 125 moves in another theoretical ending—King and Bishop and Bishop vs. King and Knight against Robert Rowley—and did not win in 50 moves. The rules of chess had not yet been changed to accommodate five-piece endings like this. We later learned from Thompson's database that this ending requires 66 moves to win with best play (See Table C.1).

Table C.1
The Maximum Number of Moves Needed to Win Chess Endings With Five Pieces or Less Based on Thompson, 1986.

Three Pieces ENDGAME	Maximum Number of Moves to Win
KQK	10 to mate
KRK	16 to mate

Four Pieces ENDGAME	Maximum Number of Moves to Win
KQKR	31 moves for conversion to KQK
KRKB	18 moves for conversion to KQK
KRKN	27 moves for conversion to KRK
KBBK	19 to mate
KBNK	33 to mate

Five Pieces ENDGAME	Maximum Number of Moves to Win
KRBKR	59
KBBKN	77
KRQKQ	60
KRNKR	33
KQNKQ	35

As an addendum to this story, it should be mentioned that a book was published in 1895 authored by "Euclid" and edited by E. Freeborough, entitled Analysis of the Chess Ending King and Queen Against King and Rook, published by Kegan Paul, Trench, Trubner & Company. The book had analysis very similar to that generated by Thompson's database, with the same conclusions: the longest win requires 31 moves. A quote from this long out of print book with 144 pages of analysis and 191 diagrams reads:

"The view commonly held and expressed that there could be no practical difficulty in winning with Queen against a Rook was .... Discarded as illusory (pp. iv – v)."

Clearly the book by "Euclid" has been somewhat overlooked by both the chess and computer chess worlds! (Kopec, 1990)

Reference

1. Thompson, K. (1986). Retrograde Analysis of Certain Endgames. ICCA Journal 9(3): 131–39.

APPLICATIONS AND DATA

(On Companion DVD)

1. Appendix D.1(1) includes examples of applications of Expert Systems It also includes tables of information about Expert Systems.
2. Appendix D.1(2) includes examples of applications of Neural Networks
3. Appendix D.1(3) includes examples of applications of Robotics
4. Appendix D.1(4) presents examples of applications of Fuzzy Logic
5. Appendix D.2 provides data For Neural Training Exercises
6. Appendix D.3 presents a history of Advanced Computer Games
7. Appendix D.3(1) describes The Rules and Objectives of Bridge
8. Appendix D.3(2) describes The Rules and Objectives of Chess
9. Appendix D.4(3) presents the History of Advanced Computer Games

INDEX